MOON

P9-DEI-401

HANDBOOKS

NORTHERN CALIFORNIA

LIZ HAMILL SCOTT

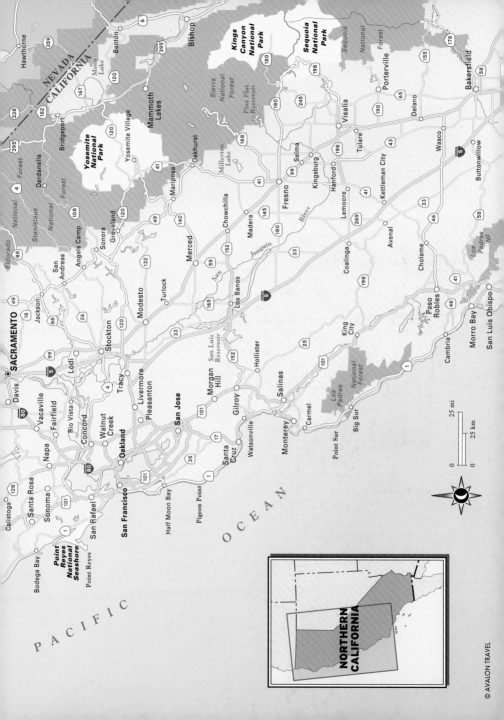

Contents

Discover
Northern California

From its geographic wonders to its urban pulse, diversity
defines Northern California. Majestic mountain peaks,
craggy coastal cliffs, verdant vineyards, and towering
redwoods shape the land, while cutting-edge cuisine,
winsome wines, and hip urban sprawl shape the people.

San Francisco sits perched on a narrow peninsula
between the ocean and the bay, its population packed in like (local, sustainable) sardines. Yet this 49-mile spit of land is the urban center of
Northern California, home to an embarrassment of riches: modern museums, culinary geniuses, and a famously liberal, creative, and multicultural
community. The surrounding Bay Area extends north in a rich display of
parks and reserves, east in an equally rich display of radical politics, and
south to the gateway of the wild Central Coast.

North of San Francisco, a bucolic countryside produces world-class
wines from endless acres of vineyards in the Napa and Sonoma Valleys –
the center of Northern California's Wine Country. Oenophiles come from
around the world to taste the California wines made here, while numerous small towns in the surrounding country provide the charm.

Heading further up the coast, you leave the studied chic of the popular and populous regions behind. Forests filled with preternaturally tall
trees preside over chill, windswept beaches and small logging towns. This

wild beauty stretches east toward the remote volcanic peaks of Mounts Shasta and Lassen and culminates at Lake Tahoe, where both ski resorts and boulder-strewn beaches await.

Sacramento is the capital of California, with gardens, museums, and attractions galore. Beyond the capital city, numerous boomtowns of the famed Gold Rush-era maintain their rough appeal. Amid the saloons and gold mines lie vineyards, apple orchards, and insight into the Golden State's historic appeal.

But the true "gold" discovered here lay further south in Yosemite National Park. Gushing waterfalls, jagged peaks, epic vistas – Yosemite offers a wealth of experiences from the sedate to the extreme. Down at less-traveled Sequoia and Kings Canyon National Parks, the tallest mountain in the contiguous United States and the biggest tree on the planet reach for the sky.

Whatever your pleasure – from the city to the country, from mountains to the coast, from the ultimate urban getaway to silence and solitude – your Northern California adventure will be as diverse as you are.

Planning Your Trip

▶ WHERE TO GO

San Francisco and the Bay Area

The weather, the politics, the technology, the food—San Francisco and the surrounding Bay Area are world famous. Come to San Francisco to dine on cutting-edge cuisine, tour avant-garde museums, bike through Golden Gate Park, and stroll the waterfront at Fisherman's Wharf. Venture out to explore the unspoiled wilderness of the North Bay, the radical yet cultural East Bay, Coastside's iconic elephant seals, and the latest technology in Silicon Valley.

Wine Country

The heart and soul of California's statewide collection of vineyards are the Napa and Sonoma Valleys. Locals and travelers alike crowd onto Highway 29 and the Silverado Trail every weekend to swirl and sip top Napa vintages. Sonoma is more spread out—tasters take their time journeying from southern Carneros north to the Russian River Valley appellations, then west to the up-and-coming Sonoma Coast.

North Coast

While tourists flock to Southern California beaches, many California residents turn north to spend weekends meditating on the wild waters of the far North Coast. Mendocino welcomes both locals and visitors, with a plethora of bed-and-breakfasts, fine-art galleries, small wineries, and rugged rocky beaches. Further north, the surprisingly cosmopolitan town of Eureka celebrates Northern California history while offering all the conveniences of the modern age. In between, Redwood National and State Parks create a unique landscape that visitors travel the world to see.

Lake Tahoe and the Northern Sierra

Mountains dot Northern California, but three draw outdoor sporting enthusiasts the world over. Lake Tahoe offers fabulous skiing and snowboarding, while the lake itself beckons wakeboarders in summer. Mount Shasta challenges mountaineers, and surrounding

---

IF YOU HAVE...

- **A WEEKEND:** Visit San Francisco.
- **ONE WEEK:** Add the Wine Country.
- **TWO WEEKS:** Add the North Coast or Yosemite.
- **A MONTH:** Add Lake Tahoe and the Northern Sierra or Sacramento and Gold Country.

rugged Sonoma County coastline

Shasta Lake offers beautiful wilderness. Mount Lassen is one of only two active volcanoes on the continent, and the main road tours past the devastation caused by a 20th-century eruption.

Sacramento and Gold Country

California's capital, Sacramento is the river town that served as a transport and communications center for the sprawling gold fields of the Sierra foothills. View the Capitol Building and enjoy the history of the state through Sutter's Fort. Gold Country's tiny towns—once booming mining communities—keep the Gold Rush history alive through restored mines and cavern tours, while the Central Valley shelters a thriving agricultural community.

Golden Gate Bridge at night, San Francisco

McWay Falls at Julia Pfeiffer Burns State Park, Big Sur

Yosemite

The work of Ansel Adams and John Muir have helped make Yosemite National Park a worldwide icon. Thousands crowd into Yosemite Valley to view the much-photographed Half Dome, Yosemite Falls, and El Capitan. On the other side of the Sierras, Mono Lake, Mammoth Lakes, and the Sequoia and Kings Canyon National Parks provide a wealth of recreation and wilderness to explore.

Central Coast

Some of the most beautiful coast in all of California sits right in the middle of the state. Ogle gray whales and sea lions off the rugged Monterey bay. Camp and hike the unspoiled wilderness of Big Sur. Check out the views from Hearst Castle, San Simeon's grandiose mansion, or go wine tasting in the rolling hills of nearby Paso Robles. Further south, Santa Barbara beaches await.

▶ WHEN TO GO

Northern California is a year-round destination. Winter sports enthusiasts come for excellent skiing at Lake Tahoe and Mammoth Lakes, or just to enjoy the beauty of a snow-frosted Yosemite. Winter is also a great time for a Wine Country weekend—and avoiding high-season crowds.

Spring shows itself off with minimal fog, mild temperatures, and fewer crowds. Visit San Francisco, the Central Coast, and the North Coast—just be aware that many mountain passes remain closed well into May.

Summer is high season, but not necessarily the best time to hit the beaches or *the* City: Everything you've heard about the chill and fog of a San Francisco summer is true. However, Sacramento, Yosemite, and Lake Tahoe experience intense summer heat and are popular outdoor getaways.

Unsung fall may be the best season of all. Fog clears up along the coast and snow has yet to deluge the mountains. Markets brim with fresh produce, while the Wine Country enjoys a frenetic, high-season harvest.

▶ BEFORE YOU GO

The easiest place to fly into Northern California is San Francisco, though surrounding suburban airports offer a minimum of hassle.

If San Francisco is your sole destination, skip the rental car and use public transit. If planning to leave the urban confines of the City, get a car. Really. Otherwise you risk missing anything outside of the urban reaches of the state—which would be a shame, because the wilderness, beaches, and parks are more than worth your time.

Coming to Northern California from abroad? You'll need your passport and possibly a visa.

Bring layered clothing, including a parka or raincoat—even in summer. Coastal fog socks in many of the beaches and seaside cities during summer, making the air damp and chilly. Bring (and use!) sunscreen; that cold fog doesn't stop the rays.

Make reservations and buy tickets in advance, especially if visiting during high season or on a holiday weekend. It's also a good idea to make early reservations at popular hotels and inns.

fall harvest in Sonoma County

Explore Northern California

▶ DRIVING THE COAST

This 10-day tour winds through the best views and beaches, wineries and redwoods, bed-and-breakfasts and culinary treats of the Northern California coast. Get in the car and drive!

Day 1

San Francisco is a great place to start your trip. Explore the natural attractions of the City with a walk through Golden Gate Park. Browse the exhibits at the de Young Museum, stopping for lunch in the museum café or for a cup of green tea at the peaceful Japanese Tea Garden. Zip up your coat for a sandy stroll along (usually) chilly Ocean Beach and walk up to Sutro's at the historic Cliff House for a hot cup of cocoa (or something stronger). Spend the evening in the Marina District, window-shopping the chi-chi stores and indulging in upscale cuisine.

Day 2

From the Marina, it's a quick hop across the Golden Gate Bridge north into verdant Marin County. U.S. 101 meets coastal Highway 1, leading to Point Reyes National Seashore. Climb the 300 stairs to the Historic Lighthouse and its original Fresnel lens, then take a less strenuous walk down to McClures Beach. Stop in Point Reyes Station to pick up picnic supplies from Marin Sun Farms and Cowgirl Creamery, then head

Japanese Tea Garden in Golden Gate Park, San Francisco

A ROMANTIC GETAWAY

sunset on the Mendocino Coast

Whether you and your sweetie prefer to comb windswept beaches, stroll in secluded woods, or snuggle beside a wood-burning fireplace, you'll find the perfect spot for romance in Northern California.

For the best in urban luxury, stay in **San Francisco.** Check into a boutique hotel near Union Square, then splurge on a shopping spree. For a stylish night out, make reservations for a play, the symphony, or an opera, or arrange table service for the evening at a chic nightclub.

Coastside, **Half Moon Bay** beckons lovers with its windy beaches, downtown bed-and-breakfasts, and charming restaurants. Rent a kayak for a sunset paddle, then end the day with a relaxing massage.

To take your beloved out for the ultimate wining and dining experience, finagle – or fight – for a reservation at **French Laundry.** Stay in downtown **Yountville** so you can walk back from the restaurant, thus indulging in their amazing wine list.

Art, wine, beaches, and snuggling are the order of the day on the **Mendocino Coast.** After a chilly day of beachcombing, indulge in a hot tub, massage, and plush room at one of several local spa resorts.

Perhaps the best – and most surprising – romantic destination is **Eureka.** This historic logging port remains rich in Victorian inns, and has attracted top chefs and chic boutiques to its renewed downtown.

When locals plan a weekend retreat à deux, they look to the lavish resorts of **Big Sur.** The ultra-upscale Ventana and Post Ranch cater to couples looking for perfect pampering, while the redwoods and beaches call to nature lovers seeking solitude amid the woods, stones, and sand.

South of Big Sur, the funky decadence of **Cambria** attracts hopeful romantics. After touring Hearst Castle, stroll down Moonstone Beach, searching for the perfect treasure to present to your sweetheart.

recreation on the Russian River

north on Highway 1 to Marshall for a picnic lunch at Hog Island Oyster Co. Follow Highway 1 north into Guerneville to spend the night.

Day 3

Spend the day exploring the wineries along the Russian River Valley. Sip bubbly at Korbel and J Winery, or savor the Cabs at A. Rafanelli. Spend the afternoon tubing along the Russian River, then enjoy tiny Guerneville's relatively large nightlife.

Day 4

Skip inland a bit, taking U.S. 101 north to Highway 128 and the Anderson Valley, the heart of the Mendocino wine region. After an afternoon of sipping vintages (and brews!), follow Highway 128 to return to the coast and the artsy town of Mendocino. Spend the night at one of the many quaint bed-and-breakfasts.

Day 5

Spend the afternoon touring the Mendocino County Botanical Gardens, strolling along Glass Beach, or window-shopping past Mendocino's many art galleries and upscale boutiques.

Day 6

Continuing north, you'll share the road with fewer cars. Highway 1 turns inland at Leggett and terminates at U.S. 101, leaving the coast for the redwoods. U.S. 101 from Garberville to Fortuna is known as the Avenue of the Giants, a famous stretch of redwoods. Stop the car and get out for a short hike to see these giants up close. The highway also skirts the remote and beautiful wilderness area known as the Lost Coast. To view this rugged area without actually backpacking the Lost Coast Trail, take slow and twisting Mattole Road to the Victorian town of Ferndale and stay at a bed-and-breakfast.

Day 7

Take U.S. 101, now called the Redwood Highway, north to slow down and spend some

coast redwood in Redwood National Park

time in the fabulous Redwood National and State Parks. Patrick's Point State Park boasts a re-created Native American village, while farther north Prairie Creek Redwoods State Park offers lovely, shady day hikes through the trees and down to the beaches.

Day 8

The return drive down U.S. 101 gives you an opportunity to visit or revisit any sights you missed. Turn east onto Highway 128 at Healdsburg for a detour into Napa Valley. Spend the night in Calistoga, pampering yourself with spa treatments.

Day 9

Follow Highway 29 as it winds south through Napa Valley. The road is dotted with numerous wineries and restaurants serving top-notch California cuisine. Spend the day indulging (not too much!) before returning to San Francisco.

Day 10

Spend your last day in San Francisco shopping in Union Square, grazing at the sumptuous Ferry Building, and relishing the cosmopolitan nightlife after your rural, coastal road trip.

▶ WILD WEST ROAD TRIP

Some of the most interesting destinations in Northern California lie east of its popular coast. California's Gold Rush–era boomtowns, abandoned mines, and historic sights will thrill history buffs, while the region's rugged mountains, rivers, and forests appeal to adventure seekers or anyone yearning for a breath of fresh air.

Day 1

Spend the day in San Francisco, exploring the City that owes much of its existence to the easy transit it provided during California's Gold Rush. Visit the Presidio for a peek at San Francisco's military beginnings, take the ferry to Alcatraz for some penitentiary pondering, and stop at the Wells Fargo Bank History Museum to view original artifacts from the Gold Rush era. Spend the evening taking in a show at one of Union Square's many theaters, all of which are convenient to numerous hotels and restaurants.

Day 2

Hop on I-80 north to the state capital, Sacramento. Take a walking tour of the Capitol Building and its extensive grounds, then head down to Old Sacramento where cobblestone streets and wooden sidewalks resurrect the area's Gold Rush beginnings. Spend the night in a stateroom aboard the *Delta King*.

Day 3

Enjoy a leisurely breakfast in town (and avoid the commute traffic) before heading north on I-80 to Highway 49 and Grass Valley, where the Empire Mine State Historic Park awaits. This living-history museum and park offers an excellent introduction to California's hard-rock-mining past. Stop for lunch at the Golden Gate Saloon, the oldest continually operating saloon in the state, and stroll through the historic Victorian sections of this quaint Gold Rush town. Spend the night in Placerville, where plenty of spooky ghosts inhabit creaky old hotels and dive-bar saloons.

Day 4

From Placerville, head east on Highway 50, stopping in Apple Hill, where apple orchards

Old Sacramento

BIG TREES

Redwood trees stand tall as some of Northern California's most prominent icons. These towering giants can reach more than 300 feet in height and grow only in areas of California and China. California is home to two distinct types of redwoods: coast redwoods (*Sequoia sempervirens*) cluster along the North Coast in a series of parks; giant sequoias (*Sequoiadendron giganteum*) prefer the climate of the Eastern Sierras.

The best places to view coast redwoods are in the **Redwood National and State Parks.** This interlocking series of parks runs from Garberville near the Lost Coast to Crescent City at the tip of the state. Highway road signs announce each park; pick up a multi-park map at any visitors center for a list of hiking trails and campgrounds.

Humboldt Redwoods State Park is most famous for the Avenue of the Giants, where sky-high redwoods line the road. The Founder's Grove nature loop brings these giants up close.

On the Eastern Sierra, **Sequoia and Kings Canyon National Parks** are dedicated to educating visitors about the life and ecology of their prized giant sequoias. The parks are home to the four largest trees in the world (by volume), including the biggest of them all: the immense General Sherman tree.

Yosemite National Park has its own grove of giant sequoias in Mariposa Grove (one of three groves throughout the park). Take the free shuttle from Wawona or Yosemite Valley to minimize traffic and maximize your enjoyment.

a "Cathedral Tree," Prairie Creek Redwoods State Park

cluster the Sierra foothills. Spend some time wine tasting and gorging at delicious orchard-based eateries before continuing east to Lake Tahoe. (Check road conditions in winter.) The El Dorado National Forest presses in along the road, making for a sparse and scenic drive. In South Lake Tahoe, choose from any of the ski resorts, cabins, bed-and-breakfasts, and budget motels that carpet the area.

Day 5

Take a day off from driving to enjoy the fabulous recreation opportunities and attractions of Lake Tahoe. In winter, skiing and snowboarding take top billing; in summer it's hiking and boating. Sneak in some history with a walk through Tallac Historic Site and spend the evening at one of the Stateline casinos.

Day 6

Backtrack to Highway 49 and explore the southern Gold Country. Highway 49 is known as the Gold Rush Road, and you'll pass through the Gold Country towns of Plymouth (stop for wine tasting in Shenandoah Valley), Sutter Creek, Jackson, Jamestown, and Sonora. In Murphys, take a tour of Mercer Cavern, then stop in Columbia at Columbia State Historic Park and learn about the history of one of California's earliest mining towns.

Day 7

Head the car east on Highway 120 for a bucolic cruise into Yosemite National Park. Stay in Yosemite Valley and splurge on a room at the soaring Ahwahnee Hotel or pitch a tent at one of the valley campgrounds (make reservations in advance for either).

Day 8

Spend the day exploring Yosemite. Hop aboard the convenient valley shuttle and hike

snowboarder at Lake Tahoe

the Mist Trail to Nevada Fall, or take a sedate stroll along the flat Valley Floor Loop. (In summer, expect crowds on both the roads and the hiking trails.) Re-fuel at the Curry Pavilion or luxuriate at the Ahwahnee Dining Room.

Day 9

Exit Yosemite through its south entrance to reach Sequoia and Kings Canyon National Parks four hours away. Highway 180 drops you at the General Grant Grove, where you can ogle the third-largest tree on earth. Reserve a camping spot at Azalea or book one of the cabins at Grant Grove Village.

Summer alternative: Highway 120 opens through Tuolumne Meadows in Yosemite's high country. Stop for a hike to Tenaya Lake or Olmstead Point before continuing to

Mono Lake Tufa Preserve

Highway 395 and Mono Lake. Take a self-guided tour of Bodie State Historic Park, ogle the strange calcite formations at Mono Lake Tufa Preserve, then head south on Highway 395 to explore Devils Postpile National Monument.

Day 10

Squeeze in a short hike in General Grant Grove or drive down the Generals Highway to check out the General Sherman Tree before heading back to San Francisco, a six-hour drive away.

▶ TRAIL MIX

Outdoors enthusiasts make it a point to visit Northern California at least once in a lifetime. Travel just a few miles anywhere in this region and you're sure to stumble across at least one hiking trail—even in urban San Francisco. Fans of roughing it in all its permutations—whether car campers or minimalist backpackers—will find their bliss here.

Coastside

The wild and little-populated coast south of San Francisco has campgrounds and hiking trails galore. Do some upscale camping in Pescadero at Costanoa Lodge and Campground, which also functions as a trailhead for coastal and forest trails.

In winter, take a guided tour at Año Nuevo State Reserve to watch the breeding elephant seals wallowing on the beach. The reserve stays open in summer for hikers and beachcombers.

Redwood State and National Parks

A day spent camping and hiking under towering redwoods is the epitome of the Northern California outdoors experience, and a plethora of Redwood State and National Parks stand ready to provide the experience.

Lush Fern Canyon in Prairie Creek Redwoods is rightly famous as the setting for *Return of the Jedi*. Humboldt Redwoods State Park provides closer access to its namesake giants with three popular campgrounds,

WINTER WONDERLAND

cross-country skiing on the Lake Tahoe shore

Imagine visiting California and you'll usually picture sun-drenched beaches, not icy mountaintops. Unless, of course, you're serious about winter sports. For you, the snow-carpeted playgrounds of Tahoe, Shasta, Mammoth, and Yosemite may be high on your list of dream destinations, where endless opportunities to ski, snowboard, snowshoe, sled, and more await.

TAHOE

Lake Tahoe is the undisputed king of California winter sports. More than a dozen downhill ski resorts divide the North and South Shores, offering breathtaking views and breakneck slopes. Lift lines run longest at the biggest and most popular resorts – **Squaw Valley** (home of the 1960 Winter Olympic Games), **Alpine Meadows,** and **Heavenly.** The runs don't pack quite as much thrill at smaller spots like **Boreal, Sierra-at-Tahoe,** and **Donner,** but beginners and intermediates will find shorter lines and friendlier slopes. Most resorts have freestyle areas to welcome extreme skiers and boarders.

Tahoe's winter attractions include winding acres of cross-country ski areas, snowmobile parks, sledding hills, ice-skating rinks, après-ski hot tubs, and cozy fireplaces with hot cocoa on tap nearby.

SHASTA

The stunning snow-clad peak of Mount Shasta glistens in the cold winter sun, beckoning skiers and snowboarders who head to **Mount Shasta Ski Park** for downhill adventures. Cross-country trekkers aim for **Mt. Shasta Nordic Center** with miles of trails for beginners and hard-cores alike.

MAMMOTH

Mammoth Lakes exists for winter sports, and nowhere is this more apparent that at the ski mecca of **Mammoth Mountain,** home to 3,500 snowy acres. **June Mountain,** further south, caters to beginners and intermediates, while **Sierra Meadows** welcomes cross-country beginners. Or explore the ungroomed forest of the **Blue Diamond Trails.**

YOSEMITE

Though Tioga Pass may be closed during winter, **Badger Pass** is emphatically open, with plenty of outdoor activities. Learn to downhill and cross-country ski, snowshoe, snowboard, and spot winter stars with the experts at this family friendly ski area. Or sign up for a cross-country ski tour with Yosemite's **Cross Country Ski School.**

the impressive Founder's Grove Nature Loop Trail, and plenty of hard-core hiking.

Tahoe

Are you serious about your outdoor pursuits? Head for Lake Tahoe, Northern California's top outdoor destination. The region has much to offer in summer: campgrounds, hiking trails, biking trails, and of course, an immense lake.

Camp Richardson Resort offers rustic cabins or a place to pitch a tent. Serious hikers head for the North and South Rim Trails, which encircle the lake. Casual day hikers can content themselves with scenic strolls along the shore or in the Tallac Historic Site.

mountain biking on the north shore of Lake Tahoe

Shasta and Lassen

Only serious climbers should attempt the one or two-day ascent to the summit of Mount Shasta. But the lower mountain, and the many regional parks surrounding the volcanic peak, offer gentler trails suitable for casual day hikers. The sparsely populated backcountry satisfies the desires of wilderness backpackers.

Lassen Volcanic National Park lies east of Mount Shasta and Redding. It's a long drive just to get to the entrance of Lassen, and you need to acclimate to the high altitude before hitting the trails. Happily, charming campgrounds like Manzanita Lake and Butte Lake help visitors spend the night getting used to the thinner air while enjoying some of the most beautiful and unspoiled wilderness areas in all of California. In the morning, take the easy day hike to Kings Creek Falls or hop on a stretch of the more strenuous Pacific Crest Trail.

Kings Creek Trail, Lassen Volcanic National Park

Yosemite

The day hikes at Yosemite National Park are understandably famous around the world. Climb to the top of Upper Yosemite Fall, scale Half Dome, or enjoy the sedate Valley Floor Loop. Camping is in designated areas only and reservations are required *far* in advance. The ever-popular lottery for a shot at the plush High Sierra Camps in Yosemite's backcountry happens each February.

Sequoia and Kings Canyon

For a wilder and less-crowded Sierra experience, head to the big trees at Sequoia and Kings Canyon National Parks. For an easy stroll, take the short North Grove Loop or the Hazelwood Nature Trail. Hardy hikers can climb the Sunset Trail or to the granite top of Little Baldy. The Lodgepole, Azalea, and Potwisha campgrounds are open year-round, or you can get a backcountry permit and leave the crowds behind.

Big Sur

The Central Coast is dotted with parks and campgrounds from Santa Cruz to Santa Barbara. Hikers from around the world trek to the wild, unspoiled parks of Big Sur. Discerning campers pitch their tents at Pfeiffer Big Sur State Park, then hit the many surrounding trails that stretch from the woods to the sea. Admire waterfalls on the Pfeiffer Falls Trail or take a short drive to Julie Pfeiffer Burns for stunning McWay Falls.

▶ WINE, WINE EVERYWHERE

Thousands of people come to Northern California specifically to drink glass after glass of fermented grape juice. California wines have grown up and now compete with the *vins fins* of France for the (completely subjective) title of "Best in the World." You can go wine tasting in almost any region—practically every foot of bare dirt has a vine planted in it—but your experience depends on the wine region you visit.

Napa

If you're new to wine (or California wine specifically) or just looking for tours and tastings

spring in Napa Valley

CULINARY CULTURE

Alongside Northern California's world-class wine industry has grown a world-class culinary culture. Renowned chefs such as Alice Waters, Thomas Keller, Wolfgang Puck, Gary Danko, Michael Mina, and Traci des Jardins make their homes here and the region is widely recognized as the place where new culinary trends are set. Whatever's coming up in the foodie world, you'll taste it here first.

Famous, fabulous restaurants crowd the streets of San Francisco, ever vying for the top locations and reputations. With so many famous names gracing the eateries of the City, the problem is picking just one or two a day. How *do* you choose when your options include **Fifth Floor, Gary Danko, Jardinière, The Slanted Door**...and so many, many more?

Serious culinary travelers cross the bay to Berkeley to pay homage to the grandmother of the sustainable food movement, the amazing Alice Waters. While the main dining room at her **Chez Panisse** restaurant can be tough to get into, the upstairs café offers equally great yet more casual dishes at much more reasonable prices.

So where does Ms. Waters go to find the grass-fed meat, artisan cheeses, and organic produce she insists on? She often buys from the farmers and growers in Point Reyes. **Marin Sun Farms** sells excellent grass-fed beef butchered out of their own shop. **Cowgirl Creamery**'s star cheeses grace the cheese boards of Northern California's top restaurants. And **Hog Island Oyster Co.** grows and serves sustainable seafood right along the shores of Tomales Bay.

But if there's a place richer in food choices than San Francisco, it's got to be Wine Country. Even if you can't get a reservation at the vaunted **French Laundry,** you can still get the Keller experience from **Bouchon** or its namesake bakery. More amazing meals can be had at **Étoile** and **The FARM,** or create your own at local markets like **Oakville Grocery** and **St. Helena Olive Oil Company.**

If heading further afield from San Francisco or Wine Country, don't think you're leaving the fabulous cuisine of Northern California behind. Some of the best restaurants in the state don't sit within its major urban areas. Heading to the redwoods? The tasting menus and award-winning wine list at **Restaurant 301** in Eureka could easily compete with Bay Area palates. On the way to Tahoe? Stop at **Moody's** in Truckee, where fresh ingredients meet vivid imagination. Houseboating on Shasta Lake? The down-to-earth **Black Bear Diner** in Redding can fill you up with classic dishes that folks drive out of their way for. Wherever you go, there you eat.

the French Laundry

in the *grands chateaux* of California, the place to taste is Napa Valley. The granddaddy of California winemaking regions, Napa is home to some of the best Cabernet Sauvignons in the world. Wine-tasting along the ever-gridlocked Highway 29 has become *the* weekend activity for many California residents, who flock into the valley on Friday (or even Thursday) afternoons. Expect lavish tasting rooms packed with tour-bus passengers, high tasting prices ($20 and up is common), and little personal attention unless you come to Napa during off-season.

Visit: Corison, Flora Springs, Grgich Hills, Hill Family Estate, and Rutherford Hill.

Sonoma

Sonoma County has long labored under its reputation as Napa's little sister. In reality, the Russian River Valley, Sonoma Valley, Carneros, and the Sonoma Coast have more diverse climate, more vineyard acreage, and more wineries. You can take your pick of tasting styles. Dry Creek, near the Russian River, offers famous wineries, fancy tasting rooms, and plenty of souvenirs. On the other hand,

Russian River winery

the Sonoma Coast isn't over-discovered yet and small family wineries still provide informal and inexpensive tastings of vintages you won't find elsewhere.

Visit: A. Rafanelli, Dutton Estate, Ferrari-Carano, and Russian River Vineyards.

Mendocino

Cool-weather lovers who enjoy rugged coastal views should head into artsy Mendocino for a romantic weekend among the trees. Dungeness crab season draws a surprising number of winter visitors to this chilly yet beautiful region, but it's the wineries in Hopland and Anderson Valley that keep folks coming back year after year.

Visit: Brutocao Cellars, Navarro, and Roederer Estate.

Gold Country

The once gold-filled rivers of the Sierra foothills now run deep with a red "gold." Vineyards full of Syrah and Zinfandel, planted years before Prohibition, have been found and rehabilitated. The small wineries that cluster in Sacramento's nearby Gold Country remind veteran tasters of Napa 40 years ago—here tiny tasting rooms still offer free sips of unique wines, often poured by the winemakers themselves.

Visit: Boeger Winery, Ironstone Vineyards, and Story Winery.

Central Coast

Serious oenophiles often skip Napa and head straight for the Central Coast to taste serious wines without the serious crowds or traffic jams. Sippers in the know prefer Paso Robles, but adventurous cork dorks also journey to Carmel Valley and Santa Barbara.

Visit: Chateau Julien, Hunt Cellars, Meridian, and Zaca Mesa Winery.

SAN FRANCISCO AND THE BAY AREA

Famed for its ethnic diversity, liberal politics, and chilling dense fog, the San Francisco Bay Area manages somehow to both embody and defy the stereotypes heaped upon it. Street-corner protests and leather stores are certainly part of the landscape, but family farms and friendly communities also abound. English blends with languages from around the world in an occasionally frustrating, often joyful cacophony. Those who've chosen to live here often refuse to live anyplace else, despite the infamous cost of housing and the occasional violent earthquake.

San Francisco perches restlessly on an uneven spit of land overlooking the Bay on one side and the Pacific Ocean on the other. Refer to the City as "San Fran," or worse, "Frisco," and you'll be pegged as a tourist immediately. To locals, the City is the City, and that's that. Urban travelers can enjoy San Francisco's great art, world-class music, unique theater and comedy, and a laidback club scene. Many visitors come to the City solely for the food; San Francisco functions as a culinary trendsetter that competes with the likes of Paris for innovation and prestige.

The Golden Gate Bridge leads into the North Bay, with its reputation for fertile farmland, intense material wealth, windswept coasts, and towering redwoods. An adventure here can be urban and touristy or rural and outdoorsy. The far more locally used Bay Bridge leads to the East Bay, with an emphasis on ex-military and pro sports culture, especially in Oakland and in more residential Alameda, formerly occupied by the Navy. But it's also home to erudite, progressive (and sometimes aggravating) Berkeley—the birthplace of many liberal political movements

© LANCE SCOTT

HIGHLIGHTS

◖ **Ferry Building:** The 1898 Ferry Building has been renovated and reimagined as the foodie mecca of San Francisco. The Tuesday and Saturday farmers market is not to be missed (page 35).

◖ **Alcatraz:** Spend the day in prison...at the historically famous former maximum security penitentiary in the middle of the bay. Audio tours bring to life the the cells that Al Capone, George "Machine Gun" Kelly, and Robert "Birdman of Alcatraz" Stroud called home (page 40).

◖ **Exploratorium:** Kids and adults alike love to explore the Exploratorium, San Francisco's innovative and interactice science museum. The exhibits here are meant to be touched, heard, and felt (page 45)!

◖ **The Presidio:** The original 1776 El Presidio del San Francisco is now a dormant military installation and national park. Tour the historic buidlines that formerly housed a military hospital, barracks, and fort – all amid a peaceful and verdant setting (page 47).

◖ **Golden Gate Bridge:** Nothing beats the view from one of the most famous – and fascinating – bridges in the country. Pick a fogless days for a stroll or bike ride across 1.7-mile span (page 48).

◖ **de Young Museum:** The revamped de Young has become the showpiece of Golden Gate Park. A mixed collection of media and regions is highlighted by the 360° view from the museum's tower (page 49).

◖ **Point Reyes National Seashore:** Point Reyes provides acres of hiking, biking, and bird-watching at the tip of the Marin coast. Brave the 300 steps to check out the 1870 lighthouse with its orignal Fresnel lens (page 112).

◖ **USS *Hornet*:** This retired military aircraft carrier housed in Alameda now plays host to swing dancers, military historians and afficiandos, and even, gulp, ghosts (page 125)!

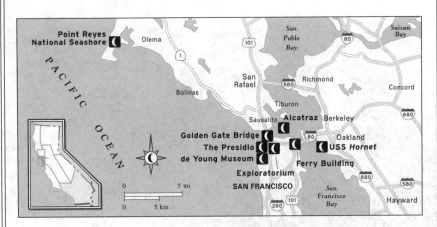

LOOK FOR ◖ TO FIND RECOMMENDED SIGHTS, ACTIVITIES, DINING, AND LODGING.

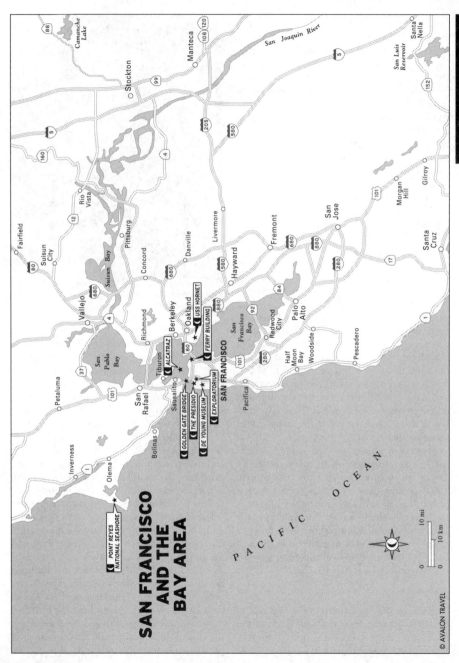

SAN FRANCISCO AND THE BAY AREA

© AVALON TRAVEL

from the 1960s all the way up to today. The original University of California sits in Berkeley, offering protest groups for liberals and top-flight technical educations to multitudinous engineers.

South of the City, Silicon Valley is all about the technology. With the likes of Hewlett-Packard, Apple Computer, Google, and eBay headquartered here, it's no surprise that even the museums run to technology and the residents all seem to own the latest iPod. Visitors gravitate toward the rarified landscape of Stanford University and the multicultural wonderland of San Jose.

For a more relaxed, outdoorsy experience, the Coastside region has a small-town feel with big-time extreme ocean sports. Locals know that this is not Southern California, and pack sweatshirts and parkas as well as swimsuits and sunhats for a day at the beach in Half Moon Bay or Pescadero.

PLANNING YOUR TIME

San Francisco's rich, diverse culture and immense range of activities and entertainment make it a destination worth a day, a week, or a month. For new visitors to the region, plan to spend the bulk of your time in the City, exploring its neighborhoods and museums, taking a few walking tours and maybe catching a cable car, and eating at its restaurants whenever possible. If you have only two or three hours to spend in the City, consider spending them in a restaurant.

For return visitors, as well as more adventurous first-timers, consider taking at least a day or two (or more) out of the City proper. The Bay Area grew up as rich as the city that gave it life. Spend a day visiting the high-tech world of the Silicon Valley, stopping to try the affordable and delicious ethnic food. Enjoy a stellar meal and a view of activism in the East Bay. Or spend a whole weekend on the beautiful, welcoming Coastside beaches.

HISTORY

Amazingly, the San Francisco Bay was one of the last major features of the California coast to be discovered by Spanish and other European explorers. Because the Golden Gate is so narrow

© ROBERT HOLMES / CALTOUR

The Golden Gate Bridge links San Francisco to the North Bay.

and often shrouded in thick fog, explorers in their ships simply missed its existence. And so the Ohlone native people who inhabited the area were able to continue their lives in peace into the latter half of the 18th century. It wasn't until 1776 that the Spanish military arrived, bringing with them the diseases and prejudices that changed the Ohlone way of life forever.

The modern history of San Francisco began with the Gold Rush. With the Bay's safe harbor, and the Sacramento River sitting right there and providing easy transit out to the gold fields, San Francisco made the perfect port of entry for gold seekers sailing in from all over the world. It was this mass immigration that started San Francisco on its journey of ethnic diversity and tolerance. (Granted, this tolerance didn't come easy, and minorities fight for equality to this very day.) The funding of the Transcontinental Railroad came from San Francisco tycoons eager to create a direct link from the big cities back east to their lucrative western enterprises. The 19th century saw incredible growth and development in the City of San Francisco and the beginnings of population in the surrounding Bay Area.

The Bay Bridge connects San Francisco to the East Bay.

was its rise as a great place to live gay. Unlike much of the rest of the country, San Francisco's citizens have allowed and even encouraged the gay culture in their town, inviting queer folk by the thousands to live in a place that acccepted them. Sadly, the large concentration of gay men in San Francisco led to the City becoming an early epicenter of the AIDS epidemic. AIDS activism followed soon afterward, and today the gay community spearheads organizations that educate and inform the public about HIV/AIDS.

Down south, Stanford University and its associated research organizations spent the 1960s and 1970s quietly working on a crazy new idea. They had the bizarre notion that if they used telephone lines and special equipment, they could get one computer to talk to another computer all the way across the country at MIT. And so the Internet was born. The 1980s in the formerly pastoral Santa Clara Valley saw the rise of Apple and the personal computer and the coining of the nickname "Silicon Valley." The 1990s hosted the dot-com boom, with money being thrown around like confetti and jobs for everyone who wanted them. In the 21st century, the dot-com bust leveled out an industry that had gone completely out of its mind. Despite the bust, the whole of the Bay Area was changed forever, and technology remains an integral part of a region that's almost always the first to adopt the latest new high-tech gadgets.

Today, technology, tolerance, and innovation continue to inform the unique culture that permeates the San Francisco Bay Area.

San Francisco had a strong identity as a military town in the middle of the 20th century. Tens of thousands of troops shipped out of the Presidio and Angel Island to the Pacific theater in World War II. It was only in the 1980s and 1990s that the military presence at Alameda and the Presidio declined and eventually ceased altogether.

In the late 1960s, San Francisco became a haven for flower children, anti-war activists, and civil rights leaders working to usher a new era of peace and tolerance to the United States. One lasting result of the City's tolerance of the hippies

Sights

UNION SQUARE AND NOB HILL

Wealth and style mark these areas near the center of San Francisco. Known for their lavish shopping areas, cable cars, and mansions, Union Square and Nob Hill draw both local and visiting crowds all year long. Sadly, the stunning 19th-century mansions built by

the robber barons on Nob Hill are almost all gone—shaken then burned in the 1906 earthquake and fire. But the area still exudes a certain elegance; restaurants are particularly good on Nob Hill.

If you shop in only one part of San Francisco, make it Union Square. Even if you don't like chain stores, you can just climb up to the top

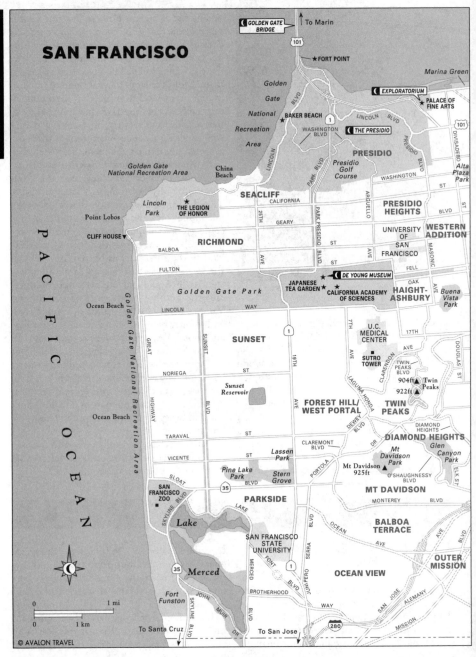

SAN FRANCISCO

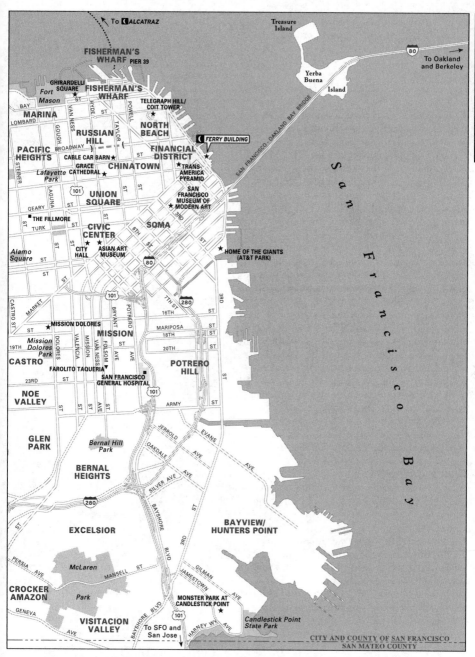

of the Square itself, grab a bench, and enjoy the views and the live entertainment on the small informal stage.

Cable Cars

Perhaps the most recognizable symbol of San Francisco are the cable cars (www.sfcablecar .com), originally conceived by Andrew Hallidie as a safer alternative for traveling the steep, often slick hills of San Francisco. The cable cars ran as regular mass transit from 1873 into the 1940s, when buses and electric streetcars began to dominate the landscape. Dedicated citizens, especially "Cable Car Lady" Friedel Klussmann, saved the cable car system from extinction, and today the cable cars are a rolling national landmark.

Today, you can ride the cable cars from one tourist destination to another throughout the City. A full day "passport" ticket (which also grants access to streetcars and buses) costs about $9. Cable car routes can take you up Nob Hill, through Union Square, down Powell Street, out to Fisherman's Wharf, and through Chinatown. Take a seat, or grab one of the exterior poles and hang on! Just be aware that cable cars have open-air seating only, making a ride chilly on foggy days.

For aficionados, a ride on the cars can take you to **The Barn** (1201 Mason St., 415/474-1887, daily 10 A.M.–6 P.M., until 5 P.M. Oct.–Mar., free), a museum depicting the life and times of the San Francisco cable cars.

Grace Cathedral

A local icon, Grace Cathedral (1100 California St., 415/749-6300, www.gracecathedral.org, Mon.–Fri. 7 A.M.–6 P.M., Sat. 7 A.M.–7 P.M.) is many things to many people. The French-Gothic-style edifice, completed in 1964, attracts architecture and beaux-arts lovers by the thousands with its facade, stained glass, and furnishings. The labyrinths—replicas of the Chartres Cathedral labyrinth in France—appeal to meditative walkers seeking spiritual solace. Concerts featuring world music, sacred music, and modern classical ensembles draw audiences from around the Bay and farther afield.

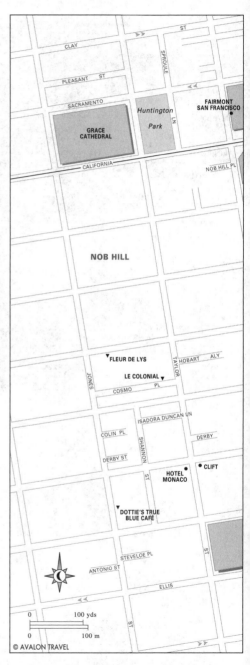

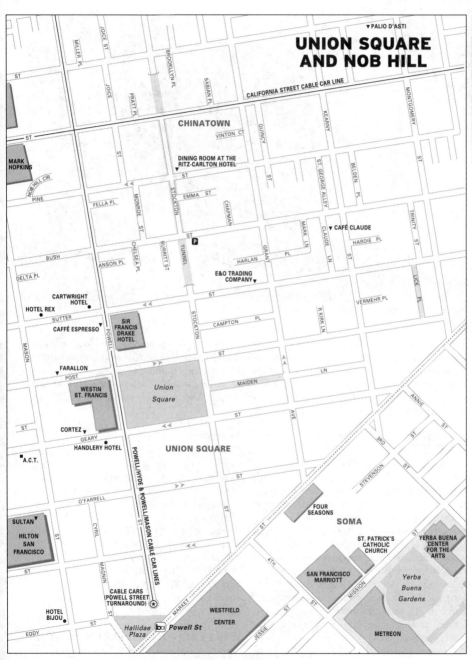

UNION SQUARE AND NOB HILL

▼ PALIO D'ASTI

CALIFORNIA STREET CABLE CAR LINE

MILLER PL

JOICE ST

BROOKLYN PL

SABAN PL

MONTGOMERY

CHINATOWN

VINTON CT

QUINCY

KEARNY

ST. GEORGE ALLEY

BELDEN PL

MARK HOPKINS

NOB HILL CIR

PINE

FELLA PL

MONROE ST

STOCKTON ST

EMMA ST

CHAPMAN

MARK LN

CLAUDE LN

HARDIE PL

TRINITY ST

DINING ROOM AT THE RITZ-CARLTON HOTEL ▼

▼ CAFÉ CLAUDE

BUSH

ANSON PL

CHELSEA PL

BURRITT ST

TUNNEL

HARLAN

GRANT

PL

LICK PL

DELTA PL

E&O TRADING COMPANY ▼

VERMEHR PL

CARTWRIGHT HOTEL

HOTEL REX

SUTTER

CAFFÉ ESPRESSO

POWELL

STOCKTON

CAMPTON PL

R R KIRK LN

SIR FRANCIS DRAKE HOTEL

MASON

FARALLON

POST

Union Square

MAIDEN

LN

ANNIE

WESTIN ST. FRANCIS

ST

AVE

3RD ST

ST

CORTEZ ▼

GEARY

HANDLERY HOTEL

UNION SQUARE

STEVENSON

A.C.T.

POWELL/HYDE & POWELL/MASON CABLE CAR LINES

O'FARRELL

CYRIL

ST

FOUR SEASONS

SOMA

ST. PATRICK'S CATHOLIC CHURCH

YERBA BUENA CENTER FOR THE ARTS

SULTAN ▼

HILTON SAN FRANCISCO

MAGNIN

MISSION

4TH ST

SAN FRANCISCO MARRIOTT

Yerba Buena Gardens

CABLE CARS (POWELL STREET TURNAROUND) ✪

MARKET

HOTEL BIJOU

EDDY

WESTFIELD CENTER

JESSIE

METREON

Hallidae Plaza Powell St

© ROBERT HOLMES / CALTOUR

San Francisco's cable cars are a rolling landmark.

But most of all, Grace Cathedral opens its doors to the community as a vibrant, active Episcopal church. The doctrine of exploration and tolerance matches well with the San Francisco community of which the church remains an important part.

FINANCIAL DISTRICT AND SOMA

The skyscrapers of the Financial District create most of the San Francisco skyline, which extends out to the waterfront, locally called the Embarcadero. It's here that the major players of the San Francisco business world make and spend their money. The Stock Exchange sits in the midst of the action, making San Francisco not just rich but important in the international financial scene. But even businesspeople have to eat, and they certainly like to drink, so the Financial District offers a wealth of restaurants and bars. Hotels tend towards expensive tall towers, and the shopping here caters to folks with plenty of green.

SoMa (local shorthand for the South of Market area) was once a run-down post-industrial mess that rented warehouses to artists. Urban renewal and the ballpark have turned it into *the* neighborhood of the 21st century, complete with upscale restaurants and chi-chi wine bars.

Transamerica Pyramid

The single most recognizable landmark on the San Francisco skyline, the Transamerica Pyramid (600 Montgomery St.) was originally designed to look a little like a tree, and to be taller and prouder than the nearby Bank of America building. Designed by William Pereira, the pyramid has four distinctive wings, plus the 212-foot aluminum-plated spire, which is lit up for major holidays. Visitors can no longer ride up to the 27th-floor observation deck (a post-9/11 precaution), but a "virtual observation deck" can be viewed via cameras in the lobby.

Wells Fargo Bank History Museum

One of a number of Wells Fargo museums

© LANCE SCOTT

the Transamerica Pyramid

in California and the West, the Wells Fargo Bank History Museum (420 Montgomery St., 415/396-2619, www.wellsfargohistory.com, Mon.–Fri. 9 A.M.–5 P.M., free) in San Francisco boasts the distinction of sitting on the land of the original Wells Fargo office, opened in 1852. Here you'll see an 1860s Concord stagecoach, gold dust and ore from the Gold Rush era, and an exhibit called "Wells Fargo C.S.I. Officers in Pursuit." Enjoy the history of the stagecoach line that became one of the country's most powerful banks.

◖ Ferry Building

In 1898, the City of San Francisco created a wonderful new Ferry Building to facilitate commuting from the East Bay. But the rise of the automobile after World War II rendered the gorgeous construction obsolete, and its aesthetic ornamentation was covered over and filled in. But then the roads jammed up and ferry service began again, and the 1989 earthquake led to the removal of the Embarcadero Eyesore (an elevated freeway). Restored to

QUAKING AND SHAKING

The single most famous event ever to occur in San Francisco happened at 5:12 A.M. on Wednesday, April 18, 1906, when the ground beneath the City jolted violently as the result of a magnitude 7.8 earthquake. Buildings shook and tumbled and a great crack opened along the San Andreas Fault. Gas and water mains ruptured all over the City, and even as the trembling earth settled down, fires broke out. It was the fires that caused the widespread devastation of San Francisco – with the water mains broken, firemen couldn't adequately fight the conflagrations that engulfed whole neighborhoods. Neither rich nor poor residents were spared as the mansions on Nob Hill and the slums of Chinatown felt equal destruction and desolation.

Despite $235-400 million in damage (well over $5 billion in today's dollars), the City persevered. Rebuilding quickly (and with a shocking lack of concern for earthquake safety in construction), San Francisco was back on its feet by the time the 1915 World Exposition rolled around.

Then, in 1989, right in the middle of a San Francisco-Oakland World Series game, another major earthquake struck the Bay Area. Known as the Loma Prieta Quake (the epicenter was down by Loma Prieta near Santa Cruz), this quake registered 6.9 on the Richter scale and was not nearly as destructive as the 1906 monster. Still, a section of the arterial Bay Bridge collapsed, as did part of an Oakland freeway. The disused Embarcadero freeway was badly damaged (and later torn down). Much of downtown Santa Cruz was destroyed, and the quake affected the lives of almost all Bay Area residents – but again rebuilding started almost before the ground stopped quivering.

Today, it's hard to find evidence of the Loma Prieta quake anywhere in the Bay Area. Meanwhile, earthquakes continue to remake the land, reminding us that the only constant here is change.

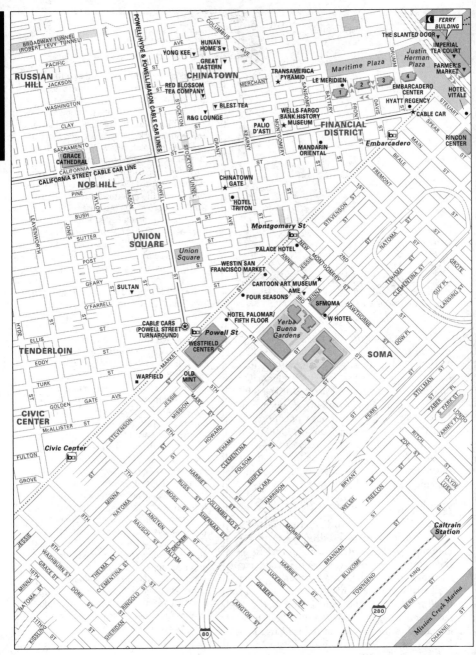

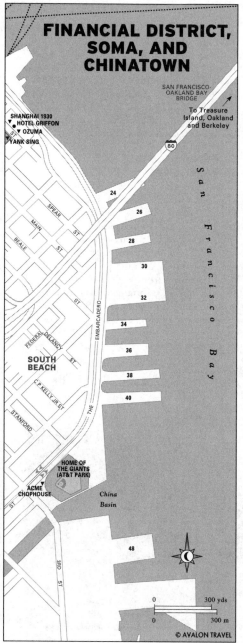

FINANCIAL DISTRICT, SOMA, AND CHINATOWN

SAN FRANCISCO-OAKLAND BAY BRIDGE

To Treasure Island, Oakland and Berkeley

SHANGHAI 1930
HOTEL GRIFFON
OZUMA
YANK SING

San Francisco Bay

80

24
26
28
30
32
34
36
38
40

SPEAR ST
MAIN ST
BEALE ST
EMBARCADERO
FEDERAL DELANCY ST

SOUTH BEACH

C.P. KELLY JR ST
STANFORD

HOME OF THE GIANTS (AT&T PARK)
ACME CHOPHOUSE

China Basin

THE EMBARCADERO

48

3RD ST

0   300 yds
0   300 m

© AVALON TRAVEL

the Ferry Building clock tower

© LANCE SCOTT

glory in the 1990s, the San Francisco Ferry Building (1 Ferry Bldg, 415/693-0966, www.ferrybuildingmarketplace.com, Mon.–Fri. 10 A.M.–6 P.M., Sat. 9 A.M.–6 P.M., Sun. 11 A.M.–5 P.M., check with businesses for individual hours) stands at the end of the Financial District at the edge of the water. You can get a brief lesson in the history of the edifice just inside the main lobby, where photos and interpretive plaques describe the life of the Ferry Building.

Inside the handsome structure, it's all about the food. The famous **Farmers Market** draws crowds each Tuesday and Saturday. Accompanying the fresh produce, the permanent shops provide top-tier artisan food and drink, from wine to cheese to high-end kitchenware. Local favorites Cowgirl Creamery and Acme Bread Company maintain storefronts here. For immediate gratification, a few incongruous quick-and-easy restaurants offer reasonable eats.

Perhaps surprisingly, out on the water side of the Ferry Building, you can actually catch a ferry. Boats come in from Larkspur, Sausalito, Tiburon, Vallejo, and Alameda each day. Check with the Blue and Gold Fleet (www.blueandgoldfleet.com), Golden Gate Ferry (www.goldengateferry.org), and Bay Link Ferries (www.baylinkferry.com) for information about service, times, and fares.

AT&T Park

The name changes every few years, but the place remains the same. AT&T Park (24 Willie Mays Plaza, 415/972-2000, http://sfgiants.com) is home to the San Francisco Giants, endless special events, several great restaurants, and arguably California's best garlic fries. From the ballpark, you can look right out onto the Bay. During baseball games, a motley collection of boats float beside the stadium, hoping that an out-of-the-park fly ball will come sailing their way.

Cartoon Art Museum

The Cartoon Art Museum (655 Mission St., 415/227-8666, www.cartoonart.org, Tues.–Sun. 11 A.M.–5 P.M., adults $6, seniors and students $4, children $2) offers a fun and funny outing for the whole family. The 20-year-old museum displays both permanent and traveling exhibits of original cartoon art, from international newspaper cartoons to high-quality comics to Pixar Studios' big-screen animated wonders. Even young children are captivated by the beauty and creativity found here.

San Francisco Museum of Modern Art

SFMOMA (151 3rd St, 415/357-4000, www.sfmoma.org, Fri.–Tues 11 A.M.–5:45 P.M., Thurs 11 A.M.–8:45 P.M., adults $12.50, students $7), as it's fondly called, is a local favorite. Even if modern art isn't your favorite, MOMA has a wonderful array of pieces to suit every taste. Amazing permanent collections include works by Ansel Adams, Henri Matisse, and Shiro Kuramata. Enjoy the paintings and sculptures in the fine arts collections, the wonderful photography, the funky modern

© ROBERT HOLMES / CALTOUR

San Francisco Museum of Modern Art (SFMOMA)

furniture, and some truly bizarre installation art. MOMA brings in a number of special exhibitions each year, featuring the works of the hottest current artists and retrospectives of post-1900 legendary figures.

CHINATOWN

The massive Chinese migration to California began almost as soon as the news of easy gold in the mountain streams made it to East Asia. And despite rampant prejudice and increasingly desperate attempts on the part of "good" Americans to rid their pristine country of these immigrants, the Chinese not only stayed, they persevered and eventually prospered. Many never made it to the gold fields, preferring instead to remain in bustling San Francisco to open shops and begin the business of commerce in their new home. They were basically segregated to a small area beneath Nob Hill, where they created a motley collection of wooden shacks that served as homes, restaurants, shops, and more. This neighborhood quickly became known as Chinatown. Chinatown, along with much of San Francisco, was destroyed in the 1906 earthquake and fire. Despite xenophobic attempts to relocate Chinatown as far away from downtown San Francisco as possible (back to China was a suggestion), the Chinese prevailed and the neighborhood was rebuilt where it originally stood.

Today, visitors see the post-1906 tourist-friendly Chinatown that was built after the quake. Beautiful Asian architecture mixes with the more pedestrian blocky city buildings to create a unique skyscape. Small alleyways wend between the broad touristy avenues, creating an atmosphere that speaks of the secrecy and much closed culture of the Chinese in San Francisco.

Chinatown Gate

Visible from the streets leading into Union Square, the Chinatown Gate (Grant Ave. at Bush St.) perches at the southern "entrance" to the famous Chinatown neighborhood. The gate, built in 1970, is a relatively recent

carved dogs guard the Chinatown Gate

© LANCE SCOTT

addition to this history-filled neighborhood. The design features Chinese dragons, pagodas, and other charming details. The inscription reads "All under heaven is for the good of the people," originally said by Dr. Sun Yat-sen. Its gaudy colorful splendor draws droves of tourists with cameras each day. On weekends it can be tough to find a quick moment to get your own picture taken at the gate!

Chinatown truly is a sight in and of itself. Visitors stroll the streets, exploring the tiny alleys and peeking into the temples, admiring the wonderful Asian architecture on occasionally unlikely buildings. Among the best known of these is the **Bank of America Building** (555 California St.)—an impressive edifice with a Chinese tiled roof and 60 dragon medallions decorating the facade. The **Bank of Canton** (743 Washington St.) is even more traditional in its look. The ultra-Chinese style of this small beautiful building that acted as the Chinatown Telephone Exchange came to be just after the 1906, when the Great Earthquake demolished the original structure. The Bank purchased the bereft building in 1960 and rehabilitated it. The **Sing Chong Building** (Grant Ave. at California St.) was another 1906 quick-rebuild, the reconstruction beginning shortly after the ground stopped shuddering and the smoke cleared.

The **Golden Gate Fortune Cookie Company** (56 Ross Alley, 415/781-3956, daily 8 A.M.–8 P.M.) makes for a great stop, especially if you've brought the kids along. Heck, even if you're alone, the delicious aromas wafting from the building as you pass the alley on Jackson Street may draw you inside. Expect to have a tray of sample cookies pressed upon you as soon as you enter. Inside the factory, you'll see the cookies being folded into their traditional shapes by workers, but the best part of coming to the factory is checking out all the different types of fortune cookies therein. Yes, there are lots of kinds you'll never see on the tablecloth at a restaurant: chocolate and strawberry flavors, funky shapes, various sizes, and who can leave out the cookies with the X-rated fortunes.

Asian architecture mixes with city buildings to create a unique skyscape.

©LANCE SCOTT

Perfect to bring home and share with friends! Bags of cookies cost only $3–4, making them attractive souvenirs to pick up, though with their lovely scent, they might not make it all the way home with you!

NORTH BEACH AND FISHERMAN'S WHARF

The Fisherman's Wharf and North Beach areas are an odd amalgam of old-school residential neighborhood and total tourist mecca. North Beach has long served as the Italian district of San Francisco and the restaurants in the area bear this out. Fisherman's Wharf was the spot where 19th-century Italians came to work; they were a big part of the fishing fleet that provided San Francisco with its legendary supply of fresh seafood.

Today, Fisherman's Wharf is *the* spot where tourists to San Francisco come to visit and snap photos. If you're not into crowds, avoid the area in the summertime. For visitors who can hack a ton of other people, some of the best views of the air show during Fleet Week and the fireworks on the Fourth of July can be found down on the Wharf.

(Alcatraz

Going to Alcatraz (www.nps.gov/alcatraz), one of the most famous landmarks in the City, feels a bit like going to purgatory; this military fortress turned maximum-security prison, nicknamed "The Rock," has little of warmth or welcome on its craggy forbidding shores. The fortress became a prison in the 19th century while it still belonged to the military, which used it to house Civil War prisoners. The isolation of the island in the Bay, the frigid waters, and the nasty currents surrounding Alcatraz made it a perfect spot to keep prisoners contained with little hope of escape and near-certain death if the attempt was ever made. In 1934, after the military closed down their prison and handed over the island to the Department of Justice, construction began to turn Alcatraz into a new style of prison ready to house a new style of prisoner: Depression-era gangsters. A few of the honored guests of

© ROBERT HOLMES / CALTOUR

Alcatraz, also known as "The Rock"

this maximum-security penitentiary were Al Capone, George "Machine Gun" Kelly, and Robert Stroud ("the Birdman of Alcatraz"). The prison closed in 1963, and in both 1964 and 1969, occupations were staged by Indians of All Tribes, an exercise that led to the privilege of self-determination for North America's original inhabitants.

Today, Alcatraz acts primarily as a tourist attraction for visitors to San Francisco. **Alcatraz Cruises** (415/981-7625, www.alcatrazcruises .com, 9 A.M.–3:55 P.M., 6:15 and 6:50 P.M., adults $24.50–31.50, children $15.25–18.75) offers ferry rides out to Alcatraz and tours of the island and the prison. Tours depart daily from Pier 33. It's a good idea to buy tickets at least a week in advance, especially if you'll be in town in the summertime and want to visit Alcatraz on a weekend. Tours often sell out, especially evening tours. Be carefully after dark; the prison and the island are both said to be haunted!

Fisherman's Wharf

Welcome to the tourist mecca of San Francisco! Just don't go looking for an actual wharf or single pier when you come to visit Fisherman's Wharf. In fact, the Fisherman's Wharf (Beach St. from Powell St. to Van Ness, backs onto

Bay St., reachable by Muni F line, www.fisher manswharf.org) area sprawls along the waterfront and inland several blocks, creating a large tourist neighborhood. The Wharf—as it's called by locals, who avoid the area at all costs—features all crowds, all the time. Be prepared to push through a sea of humanity to see sights, buy souvenirs, and eat seafood. Fisherman's Wharf includes many of the sights that tourists come to San Francisco to see: Pier 39, Ghirardelli Square, and of course **The Wax Museum of Fisherman's Wharf** (145 Jefferson St., 800/653-9592, www.waxmuseum.com, adults $12.95, juniors $9.95, children $6.95), the presence of which tells most serious travelers all they need to know about the Wharf.

Pier 39

One of the most-visited spots in San Francisco, Pier 39 hosts a wealth of restaurants and shops. If you've come down to the pier to see the sea life, start with the unusual **Aquarium of the Bay** (888/732-3483, www.aquariumofthe bay.com, 9 A.M.–8 P.M. daily in summer, call for winter hours, $13.95 adults, $7 seniors, $7 children). This 300-foot clear-walled tunnel lets visitors see thousands of species native to the San Francisco Bay, including sharks, rays, and plenty of fish. For a special treat, take the

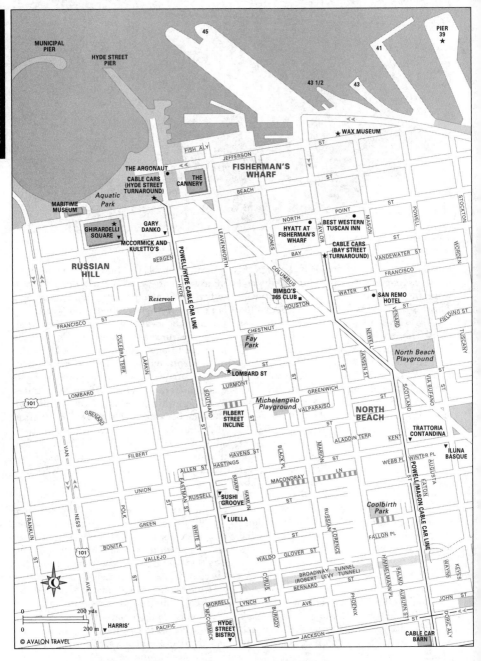

PIER 39 ★

45

41

43 1/2   43

★ WAX MUSEUM

ST

FISH ALY

JEFFERSON

FISHERMAN'S WHARF

ST

MUNICIPAL PIER

HYDE STREET PIER

THE ARGONAUT

CABLE CARS (HYDE STREET TURNAROUND)

THE CANNERY

BEACH

Aquatic Park

MARITIME MUSEUM

GHIRARDELLI SQUARE

GARY DANKO

MCCORMICK AND KULETTO'S

BERGEN

RUSSIAN HILL

Reservoir

FRANCISCO

ST

CULEBRA TERR

LARKIN

LOMBARD

101

GRENARD

VAN

NESS

FRANKLIN

ST

BONITA

VALLEJO

ST

101

0   200 yds

0   200 m

HARRIS'

PACIFIC

© AVALON TRAVEL

POINT

ST

NORTH

HYATT AT FISHERMAN'S WHARF

BEST WESTERN TUSCAN INN

MASON

POWELL

STOCKTON

JONES

TAYLOR

CABLE CARS (BAY STREET TURNAROUND)

BAY

VANDEWATER ST

FRANCISCO

LEAVENWORTH

COLUMBUS

BIMBO'S 365 CLUB

HOUSTON

WATER ST

SAN REMO HOTEL

VENARD

FIELDING ST

WORDEN

CHESTNUT

Fay Park

HYDE

ST

POWELL/HYDE CABLE CAR LINE

SOUTHARD

★ LOMBARD ST

LURMONT

FILBERT STREET INCLINE

Michelangelo Playground

GREENWICH

VALPARAISO

NEWELL

JANSEN ST

North Beach Playground

SCOTLAND

VIA BUFANO

TUSCANY

ST

NORTH BEACH

ALADDIN TERR

KENT

TRATTORIA CONTANDINA

FILBERT

HAVENS ST

HASTINGS

ALLEN ST

EASTMAN ST

RUSSELL

SHARP

BLACK PL

MACONDRAY

HAMLIN

ST

LN

MARION

ST

WEBB PL

WINTER PL

POWELL/MASON CABLE CAR LINE

EATON

AUGUSTA

ILUNA BASQUE

SUSHI GROOVE

LUELLA

UNION

POLK

WHITE ST

GREEN

Coolbirth Park

RUSSIAN

FLORENCE

FALLON PL

WAYNE

KEYES

WALDO

GLOVER ST

CYRUS

BROADWAY TUNNEL (ROBERT LEVY TUNNEL)

BERNARD

AVE

PHOENIX

HIMMELMANN PL

SALMO

AUBURN ST

JOHN   ST

MORRELL

LYNCH ST

BURGOY

MCCORMICK

HYDE STREET BISTRO

JACKSON

CABLE CAR BARN

DORIC ALY

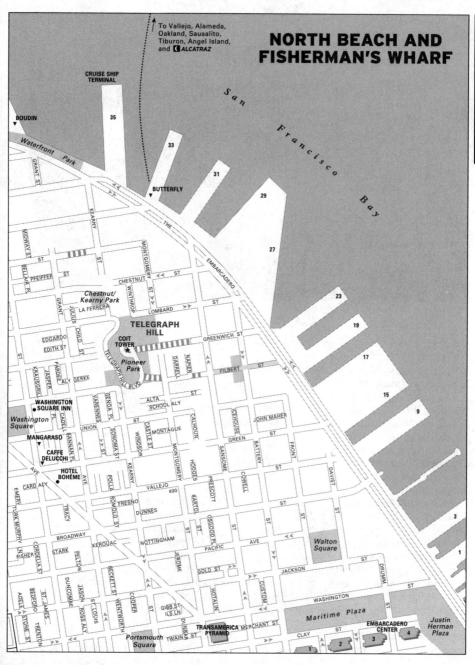

To Vallejo, Alameda,
Oakland, Sausalito,
Tiburon, Angel Island,
and (ALCATRAZ

NORTH BEACH AND
FISHERMAN'S WHARF

San

Francisco

Bay

CRUISE SHIP
TERMINAL

BOUDIN

35

33

Waterfront Park

31

BUTTERFLY

29

27

23

19

17

15

9

Chestnut/
Kearny Park

TELEGRAPH
HILL

COIT
TOWER
★

Pioneer
Park

Washington
Square

WASHINGTON
SQUARE INN

MANGARASO

CAFFE
DELUCCHI

HOTEL
BOHÈME

Walton
Square

3

1

BROADWAY

KEROUAC

Maritime Plaza

Justin
Herman
Plaza

Portsmouth
Square

TRANSAMERICA
PYRAMID

EMBARCADERO
CENTER

1   2   3   4

© LANCE SCOTT

Pier 39

Behind the Scenes Tour or sign up for a Sleeps with the Sharks family sleepover. Farther down the pier, get personal (but not *too* close) to the local colony of **sea lions.** These big, loud mammals tend to congregate at K-Dock in the West Marina. The best time to see the sea lions is wintertime, when the population grows into the hundreds. To learn more about the sea lions, head for the interpretive center on Level 2 of the **Marine Mammal Center** (415/289-7325, www.marinemammalcenter.org).

A perennial family favorite, the **San Francisco Carousel** ($3/ride) is painted with beautiful scenes of San Francisco. Riders on the moving horses, carriages, and seats can look at the paintings or out onto the Pier. Kids also love the daily shows by local street performers. Depending on when you're on the Pier, you might see jugglers, magicians, or stand-up comedians out on the **Alpine Spring Water Center Stage.** Shows are free, and show times vary.

Ghirardelli Square
Jammed in with Fisherman's Wharf and Pier

39, Ghirardelli Square (900 North Point St., www.ghirardellisq.com, pronounced "geer-ah-del-ee") has recently reinvented itself as an upscale shopping, dining, and living area. Its namesake, the famous **Ghirardelli Chocolate Factory** (415/474-3938, www.ghirardelli .com, Sun.–Thurs. 9 A.M.–11 P.M., Fri. and Sat. 9 A.M.–midnight) sits at the corner of the square. Here you can take a tour of the factory, getting a mouth-watering view of how chocolate is made. Afterward, you can browse the rambling shop and pick up truffles, wafers, candies, and sauces for all your friends back home. Finally, get in line at the ice cream counter to order a hot-fudge sundae. These don't travel well, so you'll have to enjoy it all yourself. Once you've finished gorging on chocolate, you can wander out into the square to enjoy more shopping (there's even a cupcake shop if your teeth haven't dissolved yet) and the sight of an unbelievably swank condo complex overlooking the Bay.

Lombard Street
You've no doubt seen it in movies, on TV,

and on postcards: Lombard Street, otherwise known as "the crookedest street in the world." The truth is, Lombard Street is a major artery running through San Francisco. So, why bother braving the bumper-to-bumper cars navigating its zigzag turns? For one, you can't beat the view from the top. With its 27-percent grade, Lombard Street offers unobstructed vistas of San Francisco Bay, Alcatraz Island, Fisherman's Wharf, Coit Tower, and the city.

The part that visitors flock to spans only a block, from Hyde Street at the top to Leavenworth Street at the bottom. Lombard was originally created to keep people from rolling uncontrolled down the treacherously steep grade. Brave travelers can walk up and down the sides of the brick-paved street, enjoying the hydrangeas and Victorian mansions that line the roadway. For convenience during the peak summer months, take a cable car directly to the top of Lombard Street and walk down the non-curvy stairs on either side.

Coit Tower

It's big, it's phallic, and it may or may not have been designed to look like a fire hose nozzle or a power station. But since 1933, Coit Tower (1 Telegraph Hill Blvd., 415/362-0808, daily 10 A.M.–7 P.M., call for tour times) has beautified the City just as benefactor Lillie Hitchcock Coit intended when she willed San Francisco one-third of her monumental estate. Inside, murals depicting city life and works of the 1930s cover the walls. From the top of the tower on a clear day, you can see the whole of the City and the Bay. Part of what makes Coit Tower special is the walks up to it. Rather than contributing to acute congestion in the area, consider taking public transit to the area and walking up the Filbert Steps to the tower. It's steep, but there's no other way to see the lovely little cottages and gardens that mark the path up from the streets to the top of Telegraph Hill.

MARINA AND PACIFIC HEIGHTS

The Marina and Pacific Heights shelter some of the amazing amount of money that flows in the City by the Bay. The Marina is one of the San Francisco neighborhoods constructed on landfill (sand dredged up from the bottom of the ocean and piled in what was once a marsh). It was badly damaged in the 1989 Loma Prieta earthquake, but you won't see any of that damage today. Instead, you'll find a wealthy neighborhood, a couple of yacht harbors, and lots of good museums, dining, and shopping.

Palace of Fine Arts

The Palace of Fine Arts (Bay and Lyon Sts., 415/567-6642, www.nps.gov) was originally meant to be nothing but a temporary structure—part of the Panama Pacific Exposition in 1915. But the lovely structure won the hearts of San Franciscans, and a fund was started to preserve the Palace beyond the Exposition. Through the first half of the 20th century efforts could not keep it from crumbling, but in the 1960s and '70s, serious rebuilding work took place, and today the Palace of Fine Arts stands proud and strong and beautiful. It houses the Palace of Fine Arts Theater, which hosts events nearly every day, from beauty pageants to conferences on the future of artificial intelligence. It also houses the Exploratorium.

◖ Exploratorium

Kids around the Bay Area have loved the Exploratorium (3601 Lyon St., www .exploratorium.edu, Tues.–Sun. 10 A.M.–5 P.M. plus some Mon. holidays, adults $14, youth and students $11, children $9) for decades. This innovative museum makes science the funnest thing ever for kids of all ages—though adults are welcome to join in on the interactive exhibits too! Here you can learn about everything from frogs to the physics of baseball, sound to seismology; the Exploratorium seeks to be true to its name and encourage exploration into all aspects of science. For an utterly unusual experience, pay an extra $3 and walk bravely (and blindly) into the Tactile Dome, a lightless space where you can "see" your way only by reaching out and touching the environment around you.

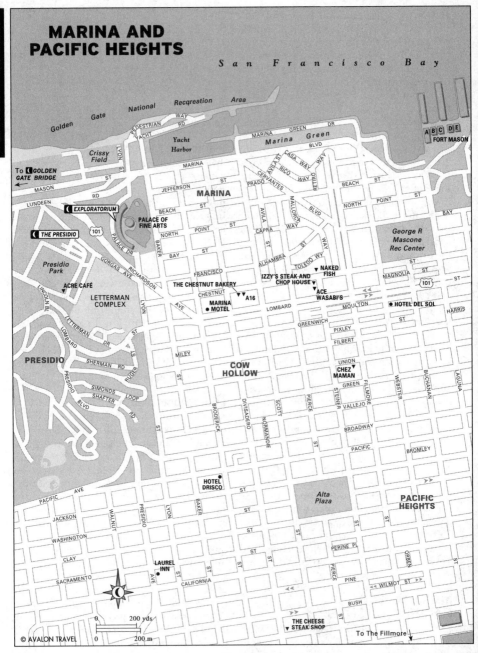

MARINA AND PACIFIC HEIGHTS

San Francisco Bay

© AVALON TRAVEL

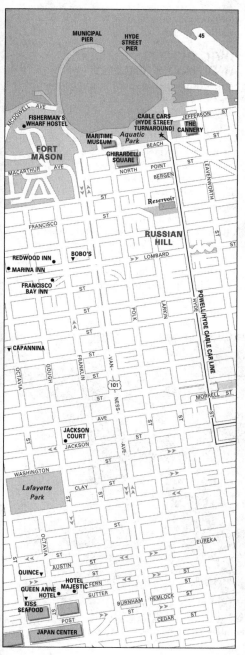

Fort Mason

Once the Port of Embarkation from which the United States waged World War II in the Pacific, Fort Mason Center (Buchanan St. and Marina Blvd., www.fortmason.org) now acts as home to numerous nonprofit, multicultural, and artistic organizations. Where soldiers and guns departed to fight the Japanese, now visitors find dance performances, independent theatrical productions, art galleries, and the annual **San Francisco Blues Festival** (www.sfblues.com). At any time of year, a number of great shows go on in the renovated historic white and red buildings of the complex; check the online calendar to see what's coming up during your visit.

◖ The Presidio

It seems strange to think of progressive, peace-loving San Francisco as a town with tremendous military history. Yet the City's warlike past is nowhere more evident than at the Presidio (foot of Lombard St., www.nps.gov/prsf). This sweeping stretch of land running along the San Francisco Headlands down to the Golden Gate has been a military installation since 1776, when the Spanish created their El Presidio del San Francisco fort on the site. In 1846, the United States army took the site (peacefully) and in 1848 the American Presidio military installation formally opened for business. It was finally abandoned by the military and became a national park in 1994. The Presidio had a role in every Pacific-touching war from the Civil War through Desert Storm.

To orient yourself among the more than 800 buildings that make up the Presidio, start at the **visitors center** at the Officers' Club, Building 50 (Moraga Ave. near Arguello Blvd., 415/561-4323, daily 9 A.M.–5 P.M.). As you explore the huge park, you can visit pioneering aviation area **Crissy Field,** Civil War–era fortifications at **Fort Point,** and the **Letterman Digital Arts Center** (Chesnut and Lyon Sts., www.onelettermandrive.com) built on the site of the Letterman Army Hospital, which served as a top-notch care facility for returning wounded and ailing soldiers over more than a century's worth of wars.

(Golden Gate Bridge

People come from the world over to see and walk the Golden Gate Bridge (Hwy. 101/Hwy.1 at Lincoln Blvd., http://goldengatebridge.org, $6 toll for cars). A marvel of human engineering constructed in 1936 and 1937, the suspension bridge spans the narrow "gate" from which the Pacific Ocean enters the San Francisco Bay. On a clear day, walkers can see the whole Bay from the east sidewalk, then turn around to see the Pacific Ocean spreading out on the other. The bridge itself is not golden, but a rich orange color called "international orange" that shines like gold when the sun sets behind it on a clear evening. But newcomers to the City beware—not all days and precious few evenings at the bridge are clear. One of the most beautiful sights in San Francisco is the fog blowing in over the Golden Gate late in the afternoon. Unfortunately, once the fog stops blowing and settles in, the bridge is cold, damp, and viewless. So plan to come early in the morning, or pick the springtime or the fall for your best chance of a clear sight of this most famous and beautiful of manmade structures.

CIVIC CENTER AND HAYES VALLEY

Some of the most interesting neighborhoods in the City cluster toward its center. The Civic Center functions as the heart of San Francisco; the beautiful building actually houses the mayor's office and much of San Francisco's government. Visitors who last visited San Francisco a decade or more ago will notice that the Civic Center has been cleaned up quite a lot in the last few years. It's now safe to walk here—at least in the daytime.

As the Civic Center melts towards Hayes Valley, the high culture of San Francisco appears. Near the border you'll find Davies Symphony Hall, home of the world-famous San Francisco Symphony, and the War Memorial Opera House. And servicing these, you'll find fabulous Hayes Valley hotels and restaurants.

The beautiful row of "painted ladies" is representative of the colorful array of traditional Victorian houses in San Francisco.

City Hall

Look at San Francisco's City Hall (1 Dr. Carleton B. Goodlett Pl., www.sfgov.org, Mon.–Fri. 8 A.M.–8 P.M.) and you'll think you've somehow been transported to Europe. The stately building with the gilded dome is the pride of the City, and houses much of its government. Enjoy walking through the park-like square in front of City Hall (though this area can get a bit sketchy after dark). The inside has been extensively renovated after being damaged in the Loma Prieta earthquake in 1989. You'll find a combination of historical grandeur and modern accessibility and convenience as you tour the Arthur Brown Jr.–designed edifice.

Alamo Square

Possibly the most photographed neighborhood in San Francisco, Alamo Square (Hayes and Steiner Sts.) is home to the "painted ladies" on "postcard row." These are a row of stately Victorian mansions, all immaculately maintained, that appear in images of the City. Stroll in Alamo Square's green park and enjoy the serenity of this charming residential neighborhood.

MISSION AND CASTRO

Perhaps the most famous, or infamous, neighborhoods in the City are the Mission district and the Castro district. The Castro is the heart of Gay San Francisco, complete with leather shops, bars, and all sorts of fun festivals. It's become pretty touristy, but you can still find the occasional jewel here. Just don't expect the Halloween party you've heard about—the City law has cracked down and Halloween has become sedate in this party-happy neighborhood.

With its mix of Latino immigrants, working artists, and SUV-driving professionals, the Mission is a neighborhood bursting at the seams with idiosyncratic energy. Changing from block to block, the zone manages to be blue-collar, edgy, and gentrified all at once. The heart of the neighborhood is still very much Latin American, with delicious burritos and *pupusas* around every corner. It's a

haven for ethnic restaurants and real bargains in thrift shops, as well as the hippest (and most self-conscious) clubs in the City.

Mission Dolores

Mission Dolores (3321 16th St., 415/621-8203, www.missiondolores.org, daily May–Oct. 9 A.M.–4:30 P.M., Nov.–Apr. 9 A.M.–4 P.M.), formally named Mission San Francisco des Asis, was founded in 1776. Today, the Mission is the oldest intact building in the City, survivor of the 1906 earthquake and fire, the 1989 Loma Prieta quake, and more than 200 years of use. You can attend Catholic services here each Sunday. Or you can visit the Old Mission Museum and the Basilica, which houses artifacts from the Native Americans and Spanish of the 18th century. The beauty and grandeur of the Mission recall the heyday of the Spanish empire in California, so important to the history of the state as it is today.

GOLDEN GATE PARK AND THE HAIGHT

Perhaps the most spectacular "sight" in Golden Gate Park is, well, Golden Gate Park (main entrance at Stanyan St. at Fell St., McLaren Lodge Visitor Center at JFK Dr., 415/831-2700, www.golden-gate-park.com). Acres of land roll from forest to desert to formal garden to museum to buffalo pasture. Enjoy a free concert in the summertime, or a walk under the trademark fog in the summertime.

Haight-Ashbury (locally known as "the Haight") is best known for the wave of counterculture energy that broke here in the 1960s. The area became a magnet for drifters, dropouts, and visionaries who preached (and practiced) a heady blend of peace, love, and psychedelic drugs. If the door to the promised new consciousness never swung fully open, it nevertheless remains ajar here today, where head shops and tie-dye emporiums hold their own amid an influx of upscale boutiques.

◖ de Young Museum

Haven't been to the City in a while? Then take some time out to visit the completely rebuilt de Young Museum (50 Hagiwara Tea Garden

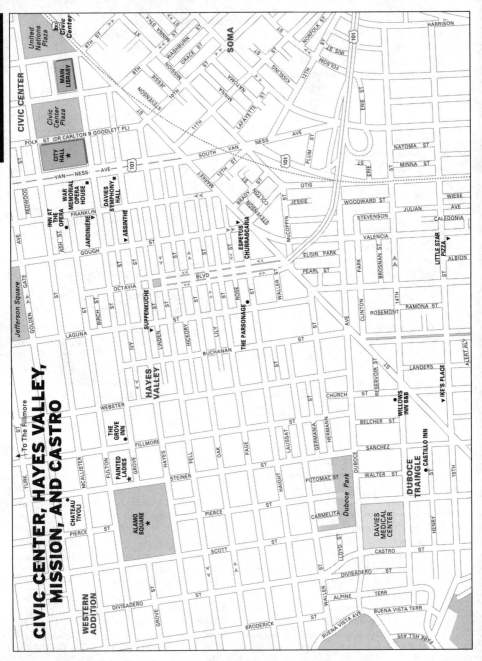

CIVIC CENTER, HAYES VALLEY, MISSION, AND CASTRO

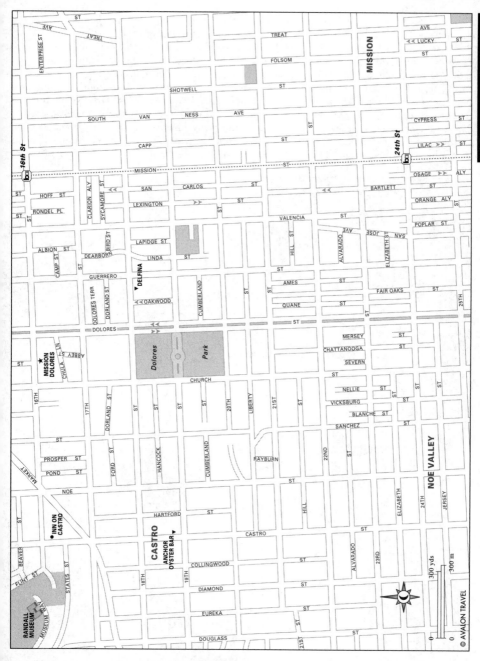

Dr., 415/750-3600, www.famsf.org/deyoung, Tues.–Sun. 9:30 A.M.–5:15 P.M., Fri. until 8:45 P.M., adults $10, children $6) in Golden Gate Park. Everything from the striking exterior, to the art collections and exhibitions, to the 360-degree panoramic view of San Francisco from the top of the tower have been renewed, reborn, replaced, or newly re-created. The reason for the recent renewal was the 1989 earthquake, which damaged the original de Young beyond simple repair. The renovation

took more than 10 years, and the results are a smashing success. For a special treat, brave the lines and grab a meal at the museum's café.

The collections at the de Young include works of varying media: painting, sculpture, textiles, ceramics, and more modern graphic designs and "contemporary crafts." Some collections focus on artists from the United States, while many others contain art from around the world. The exhibitions that come through the de Young range from the William Morris Art

Nouveau art from Britain to the exquisite glass of the Chihuly collection. There's something for just about everyone here—even classic art purists who eschew SFMOMA will find a gallery to love inside the de Young.

Japanese Tea Garden

The Japanese Tea Garden (Golden Gate Park, summer daily 8:30 A.M.–6 P.M., winter daily 8:30 A.M.–5 P.M.) is a haven of peace and tranquility that's a local favorite within the park.

The planting and design of the garden began in 1894 for the California Exposition. Today the flourishing garden displays a wealth of beautiful flora, including stunning examples of rare Chinese and Japanese plants, some quite old. As you stroll along the paths, you'll come upon sculpture, bridges, ponds, and even traditional *tsukubai* (a tea ceremony sink). If that's your taste, you can visit the tea house, the brilliant pagoda and temple, and the gift shop as well.

GREENING THE CITY

Encompassing more than 1,000 acres of meadows, lakes, forests, and exotic gardens, Golden Gate Park provides plenty of refreshing green space and amusements for the urban dwellers and visitors it serves. Extending from Haight-Ashbury for more than three miles to the Pacific Ocean, the park makes a great spot for a long walk or bike ride; plenty of marked trails and paved pathways link the park's highlights. On weekends especially, the entire place is a hub of recreational pursuits, with softball teams and Frisbee tossers sharing grassy stretches with picnicking families.

Incredibly, this lushly landscaped haven, set aside by the city in 1870, was coaxed out of barren, wind-swept sand dunes. While the park's founder, William Hammond Hall, was the first to bring the dunes under control using innovative sand-reclamation techniques, it was his handpicked successor, John McLaren, who devoted most of his life to the landscaping and development of the park. Thanks to his foresight, winding pathways discourage speeding traffic, rich foliage attracts birds and wildlife, and more than a million trees shelter visitors from harsh winds.

Some of the park's most popular attractions - the **Japanese Tea Garden,** the **Music Concourse,** and the **Bison Paddock** - were part of the 1894 Midwinter International Exposition, Golden Gate Park's official opening extravaganza. A century later, the park became famous for its "Summer of Love" spectacles, including the 1967 Human Be-In, and a few decades later, Jerry Garcia's memorial. The popular **Conservatory of Flowers** (JFK and Conservatory Drs., 415/666-7001, www.conservatoryofflowers.org) reopened in 2003 after an eight-year renovation. The treasured Victorian landmark houses hundreds of exotic plants and flowers. A highlight is the Aquatic Plants exhibit, where beautiful pools of water feature floating flowers and giant lily pads.

The Legion of Honor

A beautiful museum in a town filled with beauty, The Legion of Honor (near 34th Ave. and Clement St., 415/750-3600, www.famsf.org/legion, Tues.–Sun. 9:30 A.M.–5:15 P.M., adults $10, seniors $7, youth $6) sits on its lonely promontory in Lincoln Park, overlooking the Golden Gate. A gift to the City from philanthropist Alma Spreckels in 1924, this French beaux arts–style building was built to honor the memory of California soldiers who died in World War I. From the first, the Legion of Honor was a museum dedicated to bringing European art to the population of San Francisco. Today, visitors can view gorgeous collections of European paintings, sculpture, and decorative arts, ancient artifacts from around the Mediterranean, thousands of paper drawings by great artists, and much more. Special exhibitions come from the Legion's own collections and museums of the world. If you love the living arts and music, visit the Florence Gould Theater or come to the museum on a Sunday for a free organ concert on the immense Skinner Organ, which is integral to the Legion structure.

California Academy of Sciences

A triumph of the sustainable, scientific principles it exhibits, the California Academy of Sciences (55 Music Concourse Dr., 415/379-8000, www.calacademy.org, Mon.–Sat. 9:30 A.M.–5 P.M., Sun. 11 A.M.–5 P.M., adult $24.95, children under 11 $14.95, youth/student/senior $19.95) drips with ecological perfection. Inside the grass-topped building, visitors will encounter an undersea aquarium, a bubble-encased rainforest, and a digital glimpse of outer space courtesy of the planetarium. Nature-lovers could spend days exploring the Natural History Museum, which includes favorite exhibits like an 87-foot blue whale skeleton. Though it might appear an adult destination, the Academy is kid-friendly, with interactive exhibits, thousands of live animals, and endless opportunities for learning.

Entertainment and Events

NIGHTLIFE
Bars
UNION SQUARE AND NOB HILL

These ritzy areas are better known for their shopping than their nightlife, but a few bars hang in there, plying weary shoppers with good drinks. Most tend toward the upscale. Some inhabit upper floors of the major hotels, like the **Tonga Room and Hurricane Bar** (950 Mason St., 415/772-5278, www.fairmont.com, Sun.–Thurs. 5 P.M.–11:45 P.M., Fri.–Sat. 5 P.M.–12:45 A.M.), where an over-the-top tiki theme adds a whimsical touch to the stately Fairmont Hotel on Nob Hill. Enjoy the tropical atmosphere with a fruity rum drink topped with a classic paper umbrella.

Just outside the Union Square area in the sketchy Tenderloin neighborhood, lucky brave souls find a gem. **Café Royale** (800 Post St., 415/441-4099, www.caferoyale-sf.com, Sun.–Thurs. 4 P.M.–midnight, Fri.–Sat. 4 P.M.–2 A.M.) isn't a typical watering hole by any city's standards, but its intense focus on art fits in perfectly with the endlessly eclectic ethos of San Francisco. Local artists exhibit their work in the Café Royale on a monthly basis, and plenty of live performers grace the space. Live music tends toward the folksy and indie unplugged. In amongst the artwork some liquor lurks—think trendy sake and soju cocktails, good glasses of wine, and imported beers. The menu includes French sandwiches, gourmet salads, and small plates.

Part live music venue, part elegant bar, **Top of the Mark** (InterContinental Mark Hopkins, 999 California St., 415/616-6916, www.topofthemark.com, Sun.–Thurs. 5 P.M.–midnight, Fri.–Sat 4 P.M.–1 A.M.) has something for every discerning taste in nighttime entertainment. Since World War II, the views and drinks in this wonderful lounge at the top of the InterContinental Mark Hopkins hotel have drawn visitors from around the world. The lounge doubles as a restaurant that serves breakfast and lunch, but the best time for cocktails is of course at night. That's when live bands play almost every night of the week. Dress code is business casual or better, and is enforced, so leave the jeans in your room. Have a top-shelf martini and let your toes tap along!

A classic American bar and restaurant, **Lefty O'Doul's** (333 Geary St., 415/982-8900, www.leftyodouls.biz, daily 7 A.M.–2 A.M.) offers one of the biggest selections of liquor in the Union Square area, along with plenty of on-tap beers and inexpensive Woodbridge wines. Stop in and enjoy a pint, and maybe a good American meal while you're at it.

Do you love the color red? Then the best place in the City to grab a drink is no doubt **The Red Room** (827 Sutter St., 415/346-7666, Mon.–Sat 5 P.M.–2 A.M., Sun. 7 P.M.–2 A.M.). The decor can best be described as *red,* right down to the speaker system. The crowd tends toward the young and single, and they type to enjoy a mellower vibe than what's found in some of the louder local clubs. The small room fills up quickly, so come early if you want to grab a seat and stay a while.

FINANCIAL DISTRICT AND SOMA

All those high-powered, business suit–clad executive types working in the Financial District need places to drink too. One of these is the **Royal Exchange** (301 Sacramento St., 415/956-1710, www.royalexchange.com, Mon.–Fri. 11 A.M.–11 P.M.). This classic pub-style bar has a green-painted exterior, big windows overlooking the street, and a long narrow barroom. The Royal Exchange serves a full lunch and dinner menu, a small wine list, and a full complement of top-shelf spirits. But most of all, the Exchange serves beer. With 73 taps pouring out 32 different types of beer, the hardest problem will be choosing one. This businessman's watering hole is open to the public on weekdays only—on weekends they host private parties only.

Looking for something a bit more chic in an upscale downtown bar? Order your favorite top-shelf vodka at **Voda** (56 Belden Pl., 415/677-9242, www.vodasf.com, Mon.–Fri. 4:30 P.M.–2 A.M., Sat.–Sun. 7 P.M.–2 A.M.). Tucked away in one of the City's many little alleys, Voda brings a taste of the luxury vodka lounge to the Financial District. Inside, the decor runs to stark white walls and bright red banquettes and settees, lit with blue to complete the ultra-modern streamlined effect. Any vodka lover will be amazed by the fabulous list of popular and arcane vodkas from around the world—and a few from right nearby. (Hangar One comes from Alameda across the Bay, and Skyy originates right here in San Francisco.) A true drinking establishment, Voda doesn't offer a dinner menu—just a few light snacks. Voda attracts two distinct crowds: the after-work crowd in the early evening and young urban partiers later at night. DJs start spinning late, and a dance floor offers space to sweat out the vodka to make room for more.

The Cosmopolitan Café (121 Spear St., Ste. B8, 415/543-4001, www.thecosmopolitancafe.com, Mon.–Sat. 6 P.M.–2 A.M.) offers the best of both worlds: a bar and piano lounge serving top-shelf liquors and reasonably priced well drinks, and a large dining room serving an ever-changing California cuisine menu. You're more than welcome to enjoy drinks only at the bar, or make a reservation for a complete upscale dinner in the restaurant. If you're lucky, you might even get some live entertainment from a local musician plying the lounge piano.

In recently urban-renewed South of Market (SoMa to the locals), upscale wine bars are all the rage. Among the trendiest you'll find **District** (216 Townsend, 415/896-2120, www.districtsf.com, Mon.–Sat. 5 P.M.–2 A.M.). A perfect example of its kind, District features bare-brick walls, simple wooden furniture, and a big U-shaped bar at the center of the room with wine glasses hanging above it. While you can get a cocktail or even a beer here, the point of coming to District is to sip the finest wines from California, Europe, and beyond. With more than 30 wines available by the glass each night, it's easy to find a favorite, or enjoy a "flight" of three similar wines to compare. While you can't quite get a full dinner at District, you will find a lovely lounge menu filled with small portions of delicacies to enhance your tasting experience (and perhaps soak up some of the alcohol).

CHINATOWN

Nightlife in Chinatown runs to dark, quiet dive bars filled with locals. Perhaps the perfect Chinatown dive, **Li Po Lounge** (916 Grant Ave., 415/982-0072, daily 2 P.M.–2 A.M., cash only) has an appropriately dark and slightly spooky atmosphere that recalls the opium dens of another century. Cheap drinks and Chinese dice games attract locals, and it's definitely helpful to speak Cantonese. But even an English-speaking out-of-town visitor can get a good cheap (and strong!) mai-tai or a beer here. The hanging lantern and Buddha statue behind the bar complete the picture.

Red's Place (672 Jackson St., 415/956-4490, cash only) is the oldest bar in Chinatown. It's a classic dive filled with hard-drinking, hard-smoking, hard-gambling locals, but visitors can come for an inexpensive, quiet drink and a taste of the "real" Chinatown most tourists never see. Another great local hangout worth checking out is the **Buddha Cocktail Lounge** (901 Grant Ave., 415/362-1792, daily 1 P.M.–2 A.M.).

NORTH BEACH
AND FISHERMAN'S WHARF

For a good time down on the Wharf, you can choose from a number of popular bars. **Rosewood** (732 Broadway, 415/951-4886, www.rosewoodbar.com, Mon.–Sat. 5 P.M.–2 A.M.) glows with namesake wood paneling and soft lighting. Join the young, hip, urban crowd and sip a specialty cocktail, or quaff a draft beer inside the bar or out on the bamboo-strewn patio. A popular hangout, Rosewood can get crowded (and service can get spotty) on weekends.

One of the oldest and most celebrated bars in the City, **Tosca** (242 Columbus Ave.,

415/986-9651, Tues.–Sat. 5 P.M.–2 A.M., Sun. 5 P.M.–midnight) loves its unpretentious yet glam 1940s style. Hunter S. Thompson once tended bar here when the owner was out at the dentist. The jukebox plays grand opera to the patrons clustered in the big red booths. Locals love the lack of trendiness, the classic cocktails, and the occasional star sightings.

Dress up a little for a night out at **15 Romolo** (15 Romolo Pl., 415/398-1359, daily 5:30 P.M.–2 A.M.). You'll have to hike up the steep little alley (Fresno Street crosses Romolo, which can be a little hard to find) to this hotel bar, but once you're there you'll love the fab cosmos, edgy jukebox music, and often-mellow crowd. The bar is smallish and can get crowded on the weekends, so come on a weeknight if you prefer a quiet drink.

If you prefer pool and a plasma big-screen showing sports, head for **Gino & Carlo** (548 Green St., 415/421-0896, daily 6 A.M.–2 A.M.), an Italian sports bar in the heart of North Beach. Buy a huge beer or moderate cocktail, yell at the football and baseball games, and enjoy being part of the local crowd.

MARINA AND PACIFIC HEIGHTS

Marina and Pacific Heights denizens enjoy a good glass of vino, and the wine bars in the area cater to local tastes. The **Bacchus Wine Bar** (1954 Hyde St., 415/928-2633, nightly 5:30 P.M.–2 A.M.) is a tiny local watering hole that offers an array of wines, sake cocktails, and even delivered-to-your-table sushi from nearby Sushi Groove. DJs sometimes spin on Thursday and Friday nights. For a high-end wine experience, visit **Nectar Wine Lounge** (3330 Steiner St., 415/345-1377, www.nectarwinelounge .com, Mon.–Thurs. 5 P.M.–10:30 P.M., Fri.–Sat. 5 P.M.–midnight, Sun. 3 P.M.–10 P.M.). Choose from an ever-changing menu of 50 wines by the glass, or order one of the 800-plus bottles on the list. An intricate menu of small plates complements the day's featured wine selections.

If you love Old World style and New World wines, stop in for a glass at **Ottimista Enoteca** (1838 Union St., 415/674-8400, www.ottimista sf.com, Tues.–Thurs. 2 P.M.–11 P.M., Fri.

noon–2 A.M., Sat. 11 A.M.–2 A.M., Sun. 11 A.M.–10 P.M.). This Italian wine bar showcases its heritage with a list of the best wines in Italy (including artisan Tuscan wines) mixed with great vintages from elsewhere in Europe, California, and the New World. Don't be shy—this wine bar seeks to take the pretension out of wine, creating a welcoming atmosphere for anyone who wants to sip. Small plates made with fresh local ingredients complement the wine selection

Another favorite bar is the **City Tavern** (3200 Fillmore St., 415/567-0918, Mon.–Fri. 3 P.M.–2 A.M., Sat.–Sun. 10 A.M.–2 A.M.). Here you'll get a mix of sports, drinks, and good company. Good solid American food comes at reasonable prices. Weekend brunch features an array of tasty classics as well as some health-conscious fare. The full bar pours an array of beers, wines, liquors, and cocktails.

All that's really left of the original Matrix is the ground you stand on, but the **MatrixFillmore** (3138 Fillmore St., 415/563-4180, Mon.–Thurs. 8 P.M.–2 A.M., Fri.–Sun. 6 P.M.–2 A.M.) does claim huge mid-20th-century musical fame. The Matrix, then a live music venue, was opened by Marty Balin so his freshly named band, Jefferson Airplane, would have a place to play. Subsequent acts included The Grateful Dead, Janis Joplin, and The Doors. Today, the MatrixFillmore's Lincoln-log fireplace and top-shelf cocktails appeal to the quiet drinking crowd on weeknights and the bridge-and-tunnel–heavy singles scene on the weekends. DJs spin techno most nights, though you can catch an occasional live act here too. There's valet parking at the Balboa Café down the street.

CIVIC CENTER AND HAYES VALLEY

Hayes Valley bleeds into Lower Haight (Haight St. btw. Dividadero and Octavia) and supplies most of the neighborhood bars. For proof that the independent spirit of the Haight lives on in spite of encroaching commercialism, stop in and have a drink at the **Noc Noc** (557 Haight St., 415/861-5811, www.nocnocs.com, nightly 5 P.M.–2 A.M.). The whole small bar is alive with modern art, and there's no mass-produced American beer on the menu. Enjoy imported and microbrews on tap, California wine, and even premium sake. DJs spin every night of the week. Do take care when you walk from public transit to the bar—the Lower Haight area can be sketchy at night, especially if you're a woman walking alone.

Mad Dog in the Fog (530 Haight St., 415/626-7279, nightly 5 P.M.–2 A.M.) feels as much like an English (or Irish, depending on whom you talk to) pub as you can find on the left coast of America. You'll meet rowdy expat Londoners and authentic Haight weirdos here when you in come for a pint of Guinness. You can watch a game of *real* football on the televisions, or enjoy the DJs on weekends.

In this part of the City, you can find just about any style of bar you want. If the young punk scene is what you crave, go to **Molotov's** (582 Haight St., 415/558-8019, Mon.–Fri. 4 P.M.–2 A.M., Sat.–Sun. noon–2 A.M.). Cement and stainless steel provide the perfect backdrop for the tattooed and pierced clientele. The jukebox is hand-stocked with classic and unusual punk music. Strong drinks served in the big bar room please the crowd, which can get rowdy on weekends.

The bar scene heads upscale with **Cav** (1666 Market St., 415/437-1770, www.cavwinebar .com, Mon.–Thurs. 5:30 P.M.–11 P.M., Fri.–Sat 5:30 P.M.–midnight). This wine bar offers a wide array of still, sparkling, and dessert wines by the glass and by the bottle as well as in tasting flights for those who prefer variety. The small plates menu pairs perfectly with the wines.

A classy Hayes Valley lounge, **Jade** (650 Gough St., 415/869-1900, www.jadebar.com, Tues.–Sat. 5 P.M.–2 A.M., Sun. 8 P.M.–2 A.M.) specializes in signature cocktails and top-quality wines and beers.

If what you really want is a dive bar, **Place Pigalle** (520 Hayes St., 415/552-2671) is the place for you. This hidden gem in Hayes Valley offers beer and wine only, a pool table, lots of sofas for lounging, and an uncrowded genuinely laid-back vibe on weeknights and even sometimes on weekends. The too-cool-for-school hipster vibe somehow missed this place, which manages to maintain its friendly neighborhood feel.

MISSION AND CASTRO

These neighborhoods seem to hold a whole city's worth of bars. The Mission, despite a recent upswing in its economy, still has plenty of no-frills bars, many with a Latino theme. And of course, men seeking men flock to the Castro's endless array of gay bars. (But if you're a lesbian, the Mission might be a better bet.)

For folks who believe that "bar" means "live music," there's **Blondie's Bar and No Grill** (540 Valencia St., 415/864-2419, www.blondies bar.com, Mon.–Thurs. 4 P.M.–2 A.M., Fri.–Sun. 2 P.M.–2 A.M.). Specializing in Latin, jazz, and funk, Blondie's has all sorts of acts playing throughout the week. A dance floor complements the bar's musical nature, but it's the martinis that make Blondie's special. A second bar operates in the lounge on weekend evenings. Blondie's is known to locals as something of a tourist trap and haven for the bridge-and-tunnel crowd, but that doesn't stop it from being lots of fun.

Dalva (3121 16th St., 415/252-7740, daily 4 P.M.–2 A.M.) is a small but sophisticated oasis in an ocean of overcrowded Mission hipster hangouts. You'll find dramatic high ceilings, modern paintings, and a jukebox stuffed with indie rock and electronica.

You'll have no trouble finding a gay bar in the Castro. One of the best is called simply **The Bar on Church** (198 Church St., 415/861-7499, www.thebarsf.com, Mon.–Fri. 4 P.M.–2 A.M., San.–Sun. 2 P.M.–2 A.M.). Just look for the red neon Bar sign set in steel out front. Inside, expect to find the fabulous red decor known as "retro-glam," delicious top-shelf cocktails, and thrumming beats spun by popular DJs almost every night of the week. Check the website for a list of weekly events and pick your favorite night to show up and party. Believe it or not, the Bar even has a ladies' night! Unlike many Castro establishments, the Bar caters to pretty much everybody: gay men, gay women, and gay-friendly straight folks. You'll find a coat check and adequate restroom facilities here, and the strength of the drinks will make you want to take off your jacket and stay awhile.

GOLDEN GATE PARK AND THE HAIGHT

Haight Street crowds head out in droves to the **Alembic** (1725 Haight St., 415/666-0822, www.alembicbar.com, Mon.–Thurs. 5 P.M.–2 A.M., Fri.–Sun. noon–2 A.M.) for artisan cocktails laced with American spirits. On par with the whiskey and bourbon menu is the cuisine: Wash down truffle mac-and-cheese with a Sazerac.

The restored **Beach Chalet Brewery** (1000 Great Hwy., 415/386-8439, Sun.–Thurs. 9 A.M.–10 P.M., Fri.–Sat. until 11 P.M.) is now an attractive brewpub and restaurant. Directly across from Ocean Beach, you can sip a pale ale while watching the sunset. Check out the historic murals downstairs.

In the neighboring Sunset district, bars profligate along 9th and Irving, a quick jaunt from the park. The **Blackthorne Tavern** (834 Irving St., 415/564-6627, www.blackthornsf .com, Mon.–Thurs. 4 P.M.–2 A.M., Fri.–Sat 3 P.M.–midnight, Sun. 12:30 P.M.–2 A.M.) is an honest-to-goodness Irish tavern owned by genuine Irish immigrants. You can get a pint of Guinness here, play a game of pool or darts, and get to know a mostly local crowd. This neighborhood tavern has a small, funkily shaped bar and a big open seating area that invites folks in and makes them feel at home. Lots of evening activities find their way to the Blackthorne—you might stop in and find trivia night, a live football game, a karaoke setup, or a live band. Join in the fun with the usually manageable crowds to get the best laidback local-style experience.

Another Inner Sunset watering hole, the **Mucky Duck** (1315 9th Ave., 415/661-4340, www.muckyduckpub.com, daily 11 A.M.–2 A.M.) offers fun, beer, and a really silly name. This low-key bar, often described as a dive, serves Pabst Blue Ribbon *and* Guinness on tap. It also serves up decorative bras on the ceiling and a "boobie memory" game along the back wall (not kidding). A mixed, mainly local crowd includes kids in their twenties and folks in their forties.

Clubs

Some folks are surprised at the smallish list of San Francisco clubs. The truth is, San Francisco just isn't a see-and-be-seen, hip-new-club-every-week kind of town. In the City, you'll find gay clubs, vintage dance clubs, goth clubs, and the occasional underground Burner rave mixed in with the more standard dance floor and DJ fare.

If you're up for a full night of club-hopping and don't want to deal with transit headaches, several bus services can ferry your party from club to club. Many of these offer VIP entrance to clubs, and will stop wherever you want to go. **Think Escape** (800/823-7249, www.think escape.com, $30/person minimum) has buses and limos with drivers and guides to get you to the hottest spots with ease.

UNION SQUARE AND NOB HILL

Defying San Francisco expectation, **Ruby Skye** (420 Mason St., 415/693-0777, www.rubyskye.com, Thurs.–Sat. 9 P.M.–4 A.M., cover $15–20) books top DJs and occasional live acts into a big, crowded dance club. The building, built in 1890, was originally once the Stage Door Theatre, but it's been redone to create dance floors, bars, DJ booths, and VIP spaces. Crowds can get big on the weekends, and the patrons tend to be young and pretty and looking for action. The sound system rocks (so conversation isn't happening) and the drinks tend towards pricey vodka and Red Bull.

For a chic, New York–style club experience, check out **Vessel** (85 Campton Place, 414/433-8585, www.vesselsf.com, Wed.–Thurs. 5 P.M.–midnight, Fri. 5 P.M.–2 A.M., Sat. 9 P.M.–2 A.M., cover up to $20). With old-school bottle service at some tables (and they'll save your bottle for you if you don't finish it), Vessel caters to a wealthier crowd that likes postmodern decor, top-shelf liquors, and a bit of dancing to round out the evening. Dress up if you plan to get in.

Down the brightly lit staircase in the aptly-named **The Cellar** (685 Sutter St., 415/441-5678, www.cellarsf.com, Mon.–Fri. 9 P.M.–2 A.M., Sat. 9 P.M.–2 A.M., cover varies), you'll find a combo bar-and-club. Two dance floors share the space with pool tables favored by the after-work happy hour crowd. (Beers are $1 during weekday happy hour.) With regular themes like '80s night, this red-and-blue plush velvet club often attracts a slightly older crowd, and there's often no cover before 10 or 11 P.M. An online guest list, reserved tables, and bottle and cocktail service are available through the website. The Cellar's a favorite with many local urbanites.

Harry Denton's Starlight Room (450 Powell St., 21st Floor, 415/395-8595, www .harrydenton.com, opens nightly at 6 P.M., cover up to $15) brings the flamboyant side of San Francisco downtown. Enjoy a cocktail

---

FESTIVALS AND EVENTS

No town does a festival, holiday, or parade like San Francisco. If you're in town for a big event, prepare to check your inhibitions at the airport. Nudity, sex displays, and oddity abound. Even the "tame" festivals include things like fireworks and skeletons.

GAY PRIDE

Pride parades and events celebrating queer life have sprung up all over the country, spreading joy and love across the land. But the granddaddy of all Pride events still reigns in San Francisco. San Francisco Lesbian Gay Bisexual Pride (Market St., 415/864-3733, www.sfpride.org) officially lasts for a weekend – the last weekend of June of each year. But in truth, the fun and festivities surrounding Pride go on for weeks. The rainbow flags go up all over the City at the beginning of June, and the excitement slowly builds, culminating in the fabulous parade and festival. Everyone is welcome to join the wall-to-wall crowds out in the streets to stroll the vendor booths and pack in to see the Dykes on Bikes and cadres of magnificent drag queens.

BAY TO BREAKERS

Are those naked people you see trotting through the fog? Yes! But why? It must be Bay to Breakers (www.ingbaytobreakers.com)! On the third Sunday of May every year since 1912, San Franciscans have gotten up early to get to the starting line of the legendary 12K race. But Bay to Breakers is like no other race in the world. Sure, there are plenty of serious runners who enter the race to win it or to challenge themselves and their abilities. And then there are the other racers...San Franciscans and visitors who turn out by the thousands wearing astonishing outfits, pulling carts and wagons, and stripping down to the buff as they make their way along the course without any care for their pace. A huge audience packs the racecourse, eager to see costumes and conveyances that may well be recycled for Pride the following month. If you want to participate in B2B, check the website for all the details you'll need. Specatators can also scope out the course location and best spots to find a place to watch.

CHINESE NEW YEAR

When Chinese immigrants began pouring into San Francisco in the 19th century, they brought their culture with them. One of the most important (and most fun) traditions the Chinese gave us is the Southwest Chinese New Year Festival and Parade (www.chineseparade.com, $30 parade bleacher seating). Cast off the weariness and bad luck of the old year, and come party with the dragons to celebrate the new! Chinese New Year is a major cultural event in San Francisco – schoolchildren of all races are taught the significance of the dancing dragons and the little red envelopes. The parade, with its costumed fan dancers and stunning handmade multicolored dragon's heads, is one of the most beautiful in the world. It's got more history than almost any other California celebration; the parades and festival events began in the 1860s, helping to bring a few days of joy to a Chinese population feeling the hardships of a life thousands of miles from home. Today, crowds in the tens of thousands join to help bring in the new year towards the end of January or the beginning of February each annum (on the Western calendar).

in the early evening or a nightcap and a bite of dessert after the theater later on in this true old-school nightclub. Dress in your best to match with the glitzy red-and-gold decor and mirrors. On Sundays, come during the afternoon to whoop it up at Sunday's a Drag shows (noon and 2:30 P.M. every Sun.). Management recommends making reservations.

Small, crowded, and hip, the **Element Lounge** (1028 Geary St., 415/440-1125, www.elementlounge.com, Wed.–Thurs. 9 P.M.–2 A.M., Sat.–Sun. 9 P.M.–3 A.M., cover $10) is a favorite for birthday and bachelorette parties. Put your name on the online guest list for a lower cover charge, and stick by the fans on the dance floor to stay cool.

SAN FRANCISCO CONVENTION & VISITORS BUREAU PHOTO BY GARRETT CULHANE

Chinatown dragon parade

DIA DE LOS MUERTOS

On the other end of the thematic spectrum, the Hispanic community turns out into the so-often marched upon San Francisco streets each autumn to celebrate their ancestors. The dead ones, that is. The Dia de los Muertos and Festival of Altars procession takes place as close as possible to All Saint's Day (also Halloween, Samhain, and other cultures' harvest festivals) in the Mission District. Walkers are encouraged to bring flowers, candles, and special items to create altars in honor of their deceased loved ones, and artists create beautiful murals and signs to celebrate those who have come and gone. You'll note a distinct theme to the artwork: skulls and bones, mostly, though roses also tend to twine through the scenes. Unlike a funeral, Dia de los Muertos truly is a celebration, so expect music and dancing and a genuine sense of joy in the lives of the dead, rather than somber mourning.

FOLSOM STREET FAIR

Celebrating the uninhibited side of San Francisco each year, the Folsom Street Fair (www .folsomstreetfair.com) brings sex out of the bedroom and into the street. Literally. This fair pays homage to the best perversions and fetishes of consenting adults. You can watch a live BDSM show, shop for sex toys, get something pierced, or just listen to the top alternative bands rocking out on the main stage. The fair takes place at the end of September each year on Folsom Street between 7th and 12th Streets. To say too much more about this major leather event would do damage to the rating of this book; check the fair's website, or better still, head on down to find out what's really going on.

FINANCIAL DISTRICT AND SOMA

111 Minna Street Gallery (111 Minna St., 415/974-1719, www.111minnagallery.com, Tues. noon–10 P.M., Wed. noon–11 P.M., Thurs.–Fri. noon–2 A.M., Sat. 5 P.M.–2 A.M., cover $5) really is an art gallery. But it's also one of the hottest dance clubs in SoMa. Artophiles who come to 111 Minna to enjoy the changing exhibitions of new art in peace and quiet do so during the daytime (up until 5 P.M.). After 5 P.M., gallery transforms into a nightclub, opening up the full bar and bringing in DJs who spin late into the weekend nights. While it sounds pretentious, really the mix of modern art and lots of liquor feels just right. Check the website for special events, including '80s dance parties and art show openings.

On the other end of the spectrum, you've got **House of Shields** (39 New Montgomery St, 415/975-8651, www.houseofshields.com, Mon.–Fri. 2 P.M.–2 A.M., Sat. 7 P.M.–2 A.M.). This club has a 100 -year history in the City. The original incarnation opened in 1908, the bar became an illegal speakeasy during Prohibition (it's even got an under-street tunnel to the neighboring Sheraton hotel), the whole thing closed down for years, and now it has reopened as a live jazz and underground party venue. During happy hour, expect a huge crowd of local working stiffs, which thins out after about 8 P.M. or so. Check the website for dance parties and live music during your stay. And when you visit, take a moment to look up at the ceiling.

It's dark, it's dank, and it's very, very goth. Okay, so the **Cat Club** (1190 Folsom St., 415/703-8964, www.catclubsf.com, Tues. and Thurs.–Sat. 9 P.M.–3 A.M., cover varies) does get pretty energetic on '80s dance party and "hot pants" (lesbian) nights. But it's still a great place to go after you've donned your best down-rent black attire and painted your face deathly pale, especially on goth/industrial/electronica nights. In fact, there's no dress code at the Cat Club (unlike many local night spots), which makes it great for travelers who live in their jeans. You'll find a friendly crowd, decent bartenders, mediocre cocktails, and easy access to smoking areas. Each of the two rooms here has its own DJ, which somehow works perfectly even though they're only a wall apart from each other. Check the website to find the right party night for you, and expect the crowd to heat up after 11 P.M.

And of course, there's the **DNA Lounge** (375 11th St., 415/626-1409, www.dnalounge .com, Thurs. 9:30 P.M.–3 A.M., Fri.–Sat. 9:30 P.M.–4 A.M.). Looking for *the* DJs and dance parties? You'll find them here. With Bootie twice a month, '80s parties, lots of sex-themed (both gay and straight) parties and shows, and even live music, the DNA Lounge has been one of the City's perpetual hot night spots for decades. (It's even got its own entry in Wikipedia.) It's also one of the few clubs that's open till 4 A.M. on weekends.

NORTH BEACH AND FISHERMAN'S WHARF

The North Beach neighborhood has long been San Francisco's best-known red-light district. To this day, Broadway Avenue is lined with the neon signs of strip clubs and adult stores, all promising grown-up good times. Do be aware that cover charges at most of the strip clubs tend to be on the high side, and lone women should approach this area with extreme caution after dark.

If you're just looking for a good time at a PG-rated (okay, maybe R-rated if you get lucky) dance club, check out the **Bamboo Hut** (479 Broadway, 415/989-8555, www.maximum productions.com, Mon.–Fri. 5 P.M.–2 A.M., Sat.–Sun. 7 P.M.–2 A.M.). It's part tacky tiki bar, part impromptu dance club, with a cheerful vibe and friendly scene that can be hard to come by in this part of town. You'll see the tiki god, the bamboo decor, and the fun umbrella-clad fruity rum drinks. The house specialty is the Flaming Volcano Bowl—yes, it's really on fire, and it's probably a good idea to share one with a friend. DJs spin on weekends at the Bamboo Hut; they might not be the hippest in town, but regulars have a great time dancing anyhow.

The reality is that the clubs people come to

North Beach to visit are the strip clubs. One of these is **Broadway Showgirls** (412 Broadway, 415/391-2800, www.showgirlssf.com, nightly 6 P.M.–2 A.M., cover $20). This club aspires to elegance, and actually manages to pull it off better than many. After paying your cover (check the website for no-cover days and hours), you'll be ushered into a plush red main room, rife with smaller VIP rooms and of course the multi-level main stage at one end of the room. Upstairs, you'll find the Sizzle Lounge (a small dance club-like space with more VIP rooms and its own full-service restaurant). Lots of solo straight women and couples frequent Showgirls, and are made welcome (though most must pay the cover). Because Showgirls has a full bar, the dancers don't get completely nude (in California it's one or the other, but not both, by law).

MARINA AND PACIFIC HEIGHTS

Clubs in the Marina are all about the trendy and the spendy. Among these, you can check out **Gravity** (3251 Scott St., 415/776-1928, www.gravityroomsf.com). Sure it's crowded, parking is awful, it's sometimes tough to get in, and the drinks can sometimes be weak. But DJs do spin decent hip-hop and pop, and plenty of young singles crowd in every weekend.

The **Hi-Fi Lounge** (2125 Lombard St., 415/345-8663, www.maximumproductions .com, Wed.–Sat. 8 P.M.–2 A.M., Fri. 5 P.M.–2 A.M.) personifies the fun that can be had in smaller San Francisco venues. This one-floor wonder with a tiny dance floor gets incredibly crowded. Yet even the locals have a good time when they come out to the Hi-Fi. The decor is funky and fun, and the patrons are young and affluent. Most visitors find the staff friendly and the bartenders attentive. It being the Marina, come early to get decent parking and to avoid the cover charge.

CIVIC CENTER AND HAYES VALLEY

Not your slick, shiny nightclub, the **Rickshaw Stop** (155 Fell St., 415/861-2011, www.rick shawstop.com, Wed.–Thurs. 5 P.M.–midnight, Fri.–Sat. 5 P.M.–2 A.M.) in the Hayes Valley neighborhood next door to the Civic Center welcomes one and all with a cavernous lower bar/room/stage area/dance floor, and a quirky balcony area complete with comfy old sofas. Up-and-coming live acts play here, DJs spin, and special events and parties add to the action most every week. Have a drink, enjoy the music, grab a small bite if you're hungry, and get comfortable! You'll feel almost as though you're in a friendly neighborhood coffee shop (albeit a really big one) than some fancy nightspot.

True adult entertainment lovers know that the most famous gentlemen's club in the City is **Mitchell Brothers O'Farrell Theatre** (895 O'Farrell St., 415/776-6686, www.ofarrell.com, Mon.–Thurs. 11:30 A.M.–1:30 A.M., Fri.–Sat. 11:30 A.M.–2:30 A.M., Sun. 5:30 P.M.–1:30 A.M., cover $20 before 6 P.M., $40 after 6 P.M.). The O'Farrell started out as a adult movie house in 1969, featuring its own productions on the silver screen. Live shows began in 1976, though films still run in the CineStage room to this day. Today, patrons can choose between five different show rooms, plus VIP booths. Unlike many City strip clubs, Mitchell Brothersoffers full nudity and features live shows. Many of the performers and dancers are major adult film stars who perform limited engagements at the O'Farrell. The catch? No liquor. Of course that means that 18–20 year old patrons are welcome to join in the fun....

The **Crazy Horse Gentlemen's Club** (980 Market St., 415/771-6259, Mon.–Wed. noon–2 A.M., Thurs.–Sat. noon–3 A.M., Sun. 6 P.M.–2 A.M., 18 and older) is another favorite. Much smaller than the O'Farrell, with one main movie-theater-style room containing a single stage, the Crazy Horse offers a more (ahem) intimate adult experience. There's also the semi-private "couch room" and of course a few private VIP spaces. A few adult film stars do guest shows at this all-nude, liquor-free club. Expect to see more true pole dancing than at the O'Farrell.

MISSION AND CASTRO

The Mission and the Castro are *the* clubbing

districts in San Francisco, and as the urban renewal continues, SoMa is making its own play to create a hot nightlife rep. Naturally the biggest concentration of gay clubs sits in the Castro.

Looking for something a little different in the Mission? Check out **Levende Lounge** (1710 Mission St., 415/864-5585, www .levendesf.com, Wed.–Fri. 5 P.M.–2 A.M., Sat. 6 P.M.–2 A.M., Sun. 11 A.M.–4 P.M.). This new-school establishment fuses two of the coolest things in San Francisco; a high-end restaurant and top-shelf cocktail bar come together to bring you in early and keep you in late. The short but luscious world cuisine–inspired menu is served until 11 P.M. most nights, while the cocktail and wine bar stays open late. Margaritas are the house specialty, but don't overlook the other mixed drinks and the wine selection. Or if you're hung over on a Sunday morning and in need of replenishment, Levende can hook you up with some hearty made-to-order brunch fare.

Fans of the hipster lounge scene flock to the **Fluid Ultra Lounge** (662 Mission St., 415/615-6888, www.fluidsf.com, Thurs.–Sat. 9 P.M.–2 A.M., cover varies). The second you walk in, you'll probably feel you're not chic enough for this David Oldroyd–designed postmodern wonderland. Gleaming metal meets fascinating floral-esque accessories in a series of rooms that boast really uncomfortable white chairs. If you're not up for lots of young and *ultra* cool clubsters, you may find the decor the best part of Fluid. You can definitely dance on an interestingly lit floor, though it can be tough to pry a drink out of the bartenders at times. Come early or get your name on the guest list (you can sign up online) to avoid the hefty cover charge.

Looking for a stylin' gay bar-turned-club, Castro style? Head for **Badlands** (4121 18th St., 415/626-9320, www.sfbadlands.com, daily 2 P.M.–2 A.M.). This Castro icon was once an old-school bar with pool tables on the floor and license plates on the walls. Now you'll find an always-crowded dance floor, au courant peppy pop music, ever-changing video screens, and

plenty of gay men out for a good time. Are you a straight woman who loves the energy and lack of sleaze at gay clubs? You're welcome to get your groove on at Badlands! Any number of local straight ladies count themselves among the regulars at this friendly establishment, which attracts a youngish but mixed-age crowd. Do be aware that Badlands gets incredibly crowded, complete with a hot and packed dance floor, especially on weekend nights. There's a coat check on the bottom level.

GOLDEN GATE PARK AND THE HAIGHT
In the infamous Haight, the club scene is actually an eclectic mix of everything from trendy to retro. **Milk** (1840 Haight St., 415/387-6455, www.milksf.com, nightly 7 P.M.–2 A.M., cover varies) counts itself among the trendy. It's tiny. It's often empty on weekdays and packed solid on weekends. The music ranges from reggae to hip hop to '80s tunes depending on the night and the DJ. Don't expect much of a tourist crowd here; Milk attracts more locals than out-of-towners, but if that's what you're looking for in your visit to the City, a night of Milk might be just what the doctor ordered.

Live Music
ROCK AND POP
Opened in the late 1960s, **The Fillmore** (1805 Geary Blvd., 415/346-6000, www.thefillmore .com) ignited the careers of legendary bands such as Santana and The Grateful Dead. This popular venue now hosts everything from concerts to theme parties.

Started by rock veteran Boz Scaggs in 1988, **Slim's** (333 11th St., 415/255-0333, www .slims-sf.com) showcases everything from the Subhumans to Billy Bob Thornton. Dinner tickets are the only way to score an actual seat.

The **Warfield** (982 Market St., 415/567-2060) is one of the older rock venues in the City. It started out as a vaudeville palace in the early 1900s, booking major jazz acts as well as variety shows. The Warfield's configuration is that of a traditional theater, with a raised stage, an open orchestra section below it, and two balconies rising up and facing the stage. There's limited table seating on the lowest level (mostly by reservation), reserved seats in the balconies, and open standing in the orchestra below the stage. The Warfield books all sorts of acts, from Bill Maher to alternative rock; the likes of Evanescence, Weezer, and Death Cab for Cutie have played the Warfield. The downsides of hitting the shows at the Warfield include the somewhat shabby details of the interior, which is minor. The bigger problem is the total lack of parking—you'll need to hunt for a spot at one of the local public parking structures, and you'll pay for the privilege.

Given the dense crowd of tourists in the Fisherman's Wharf area, it's no surprise that a few bars and clubs offer live music to entertain the masses and keep them buying drinks late into the evening. Despite its locale, **Bimbo's 365 Club** (1025 Columbus Ave., 415/474-0365, www.bimbos365club.com, tickets $15–35, cash-only bar) retains its reputation as a favorite venue for locals. Opened in 1931 by an Italian immigrant looking to create a fun and fabulous club to help San Francisco residents take their minds off the gloom of the Depression. The club moved to the Columbus Avenue location in 1951, and became a favorite of San Francisco legend Herb Caen as well as many other local socialites. Today, major accessible acts such as Chris Isaak and the Brian Setzer Orchestra play Bimbo's. You might even luck out and catch Robin Williams working up new stand-up material here. The club itself, with its shabby chic interior and atmosphere, remains a beloved elder statesman with a heavy local following.

The **Gold Dust Lounge** (247 Powell St., 415/397-1695, daily 7 A.M.–2 A.M.) hosts country, pop, and R&B bands most every night of the week. You can also get a decent drink, and enjoy the slightly bizarre red and gold decor of this San Francisco landmark.

BLUES AND JAZZ

The neighborhood surrounding Union Square is one of the most fertile areas in San Francisco for live music. Whether you're into blues or rock, or even country, you'll find a spot to have a drink and listen to some wonderful live tunes.

Biscuits and Blues (401 Mason St., 415/292-2583, www.biscuitsandblues.com, Tues.–Thurs., Sun. 6 P.M.–midnight, Fri.–Sat 3:30 P.M.–12:30 A.M.) is a local musicians' favorite. Just around the corner from the big live drama theaters, this house dedicates itself to jazz and blues. Headliners at Biscuits and Blues can range from Joe Louis Walker to Jimmy Thackery to Jim Kimo. One of the best things about this club is that you can in fact get biscuits as well as blues. Dinner is served nightly, and features a surprisingly varied and upscale menu combining California cuisine with the mystical flavors of New Orleans. Yum! So when you plan for your night of blues, consider showing up early to enjoy a jam session and a meal, then stay on for the main acts and headliners (and of course cocktails).

At the **Boom Boom Room** (1601 Fillmore St., 415/673-8000, www.boomboomblues.com, Tues.–Sat. 4 P.M.–2 A.M., Sun. 2 P.M.–1 A.M.), you'll find the latest in a legacy of live blues, boogie, groove, soul, and funk music.

The Saloon (1232 Grant Ave., 415/989-7666) fills the role of the live-music dive in North Beach. Don't expect much in the way of decor or chic amenities, and do expect the clientele to more closely resemble the denizens of Mos Eisley Space Port than the hip clubs of the Mission or the wine bars of SoMa. So what kind of music goes up at a low-rent live-music bar in North Beach? The blues, of course. So grab a pint of beer and sit back to enjoy the show (half of which is put on by the patrons).

Comedy

San Francisco's oldest comedy club, the **Punch Line** (444 Battery St., 415/397-7573, www.punchlinecomedyclub.com) is an elegant and intimate venue that earned its topnotch reputation with stellar headliners such as Robin Williams, Ellen DeGeneres, and Dave Chappelle. An on-site bar keeps the audience primed.

Cobb's Comedy Club (915 Columbus Ave.,

415/928-4320, www.cobbscomedy.com) has played host to star comedians such as Jerry Seinfeld, Sarah Silverman, and Margaret Cho since 1982. The 425-seat venue offers a full dinner menu and a bar to slake your thirst.

THE ARTS
Theater
UNION SQUARE AND NOB HILL

Just up from Union Square, on Geary Street, the traditional San Francisco theater district continues to entertain crowds almost every day of the week. The old Geary Theater is now the permanent home of **A.C.T.** (415 Geary St., 415/749-2228, www.act-sf.org, shows Tues.– Sun., $17–82). A.C.T. puts on a season filled with big-name, big-budget productions. Each season sees an array of high-production-value musicals such as *Urinetown,* American classics by the likes of Sam Shepard and Somerset Maugham, and intriguing new works; you might even get to see a world premiere here. Don't expect to find street parking on Geary. Discount parking is available at the Mason-O'Farrell garage around the corner with a ticket stub from A.C.T. Tickets can be reasonably priced, especially on weeknights, but do be aware that the 2nd Balcony seats are truly high altitude—expect to look nearly straight down to the stage, and take care if you're prone to vertigo.

The **Curran Theater** (445 Geary St., 415/551-2000, www.curran-theater.com, $105–250), right next door to the A.C.T., has a state-of-the-art stage on which to put up classic, high-budget musicals. Audiences have watched *Les Miserables, Phantom of the Opera,* and *High School Musical* from the plush red velvet seats. Expect to pay a premium for tickets to these musicals, which can sometimes run at the Curran for months or even years. Check the schedule for current shows, and please leave children under five years old at home—they won't be permitted in the Curran.

NORTH BEACH AND FISHERMAN'S WHARF

There's one live show that's always different, yet it's been running continuously for three and a half decades. This musical revue is crazy and wacky and offbeat and pretty much defines live theater in San Francisco. It's **Beach Blanket Babylon** (678 Green St., 415/421-4222, www.beachblanket babylon.com, shows Wed.–Sun., $25–78). Even if you saw *Beach Blanket Babylon* 10 years ago, you should come see it again; because it mocks current pop culture, the show evolves almost continually to take advantage of tabloid treasures. While minors are welcome at the Sunday matinees, evening shows can get pretty racy (and liquor is involved) so these are restricted to attendees 21 and over.

The hats. Oh, the hats. You'll never forget the hats.

MARINA AND PACIFIC HEIGHTS

Beyond the bright lights of Geary and Market Streets lie any number of tiny up-and-coming (or down-and-going, depending) theaters, many of which produce new plays by local playwrights. One of the best known of the "small" theaters, the **Magic Theatre** (Fort Mason Center, Bldg. D, 415/441-8822, www .magictheatre.org, $25–75) produced Sam Shepard's new works back before he was anyone special. They're still committed to new works, so when you go to a show at the Magic you're taking a chance or having an adventure, depending on how you look at it. For some of the cheapest seats in the City, show up at the box office on a Wednesday for same-day, cash-only, sliding scale $5–25 tickets to the current show.

At the **Palace of Fine Arts Theatre** (3301 Lyon St., 415/567-6642, www.palaceoffinearts .org, $25–100) you'll find accessible avant-garde performing arts pieces, live music performance, dance recitals, and the occasional children's musical recital or black-and-white film.

CIVIC CENTER AND HAYES VALLEY

Down on Market Street, the **Orpheum Theater** (1192 Market St., 415/551-2000, www.shnsf.com, $91–214) runs touring productions of popular Broadway musicals.

MISSION AND CASTRO

Take care getting to **Theatre Rhinoceros** (2926 16th St., 415/552-4140, www.therhino .org, $15–25), as it's in a less-than-ritzy part of town. But it's worth it. The Rhino puts on a wonderfully entertaining set of gay and lesbian plays, and has recently been branching out to explore the whole spectrum of human sexuality, especially as it's expressed in anything-goes (even conservative Republicans!) San Francisco.

Focusing on short works by new writers, **Three Wise Monkeys** (415/776-7427, www .threewisemonkeys.org, $19–22) productions usually run at the **Eureka Theater** (215 Jackson St.). Each year TWM hosts the Bay One Acts (BOAs) as well as the Short Leaps Festival, where all plays read are 10 minutes or less. Another favorite is the **EXIT Theatre** (156 Eddy St., 415/931-1094, www.sffringe .org), where you'll see plenty of unusual experimental plays, many by local playwrights.

The EXIT also participates in the annual San Francisco Fringe Festival.

Classical Music and Opera

Right around the Civic Center, music takes a turn for the upscale. This is the neighborhood where the ultra-rich (and not so much) classics lovers come to enjoy a night out. Acoustically renovated in 1992, **Davies Symphony Hall** (201 Van Ness Ave., 415/864-6000, www.sfsymphony.org) is home to Michael Tilson Thomas' San Francisco Symphony. Loyal patrons flock for performances that range from the classic to the avant-garde.

The **War Memorial Opera House** (301 Van Ness Ave., 415/621-6600, www.sfwmpac.org), a beaux arts–style building designed by Coit Tower and City Hall architect Arthur Brown, Jr., houses the San Francisco Opera and San Francisco Ballet. Tours are available Mondays 10 A.M.–2 P.M.

Shopping

UNION SQUARE AND NOB HILL

For the biggest variety of chain and department stores, plus a few select designer boutiques, locals and tourists alike flock to Union Square (btwn. Geary St., Stockton St., Post St., and Powell St.). The shopping area includes more than just the square proper. More designer and brand-name stores cluster for several blocks in all directions.

Clothing

The wealthy and stylish of San Francisco shop Union Square for the premier designers who maintain shops here. If you feel you can afford to breathe the rarified air, go in to **Dior** (216 Stockton St., 415/544-0394, Mon.–Sat. 10 A.M.–6 P.M., Sun. noon–5 P.M.) and the others of his ilk who sell their multi-thousand dollar blouses and dresses here. On the other end of the style spectrum, and far more accessible

to the masses, you'll find **Niketown** (278 Post St., 415/392-6453, Mon.–Sat. 10 A.M.–8 P.M., Sun. 11 A.M.–7 P.M.). Got shoes?

Department Stores

Several big, high-end department stores call Union Square home. **Macy's** (170 O'Farrell St., 415/397-3333, Mon.–Wed. 10 A.M.–8 P.M., Thurs.–Sat. 10 A.M.–9 P.M., Sun. 11 A.M.–7 P.M.) has two immense locations, one for women's clothing and another for the men's store and housewares. **Neiman Marcus** (150 Stockton St., 415/362-3900, www.neimanmarcus.com, Mon.–Wed. and Fri.–Sat 10 A.M.–7 P.M., Thurs. 10 A.M.–8 P.M., Sun. noon–6 P.M.) is a favorite among high-budget shoppers and PETA fur protesters, while **Saks Fifth Avenue** (384 Post St., 415/986-4758, Mon.–Wed. and Fri.–Sat. 10 A.M.–7 P.M., Thurs 10 A.M.–8 P.M., Sun. 11 A.M.–6 P.M.) adds a touch of New York style to funky-but-wealthy San Francisco.

© LANCE SCOTT

shopping in Union Square

Health and Beauty

Another thing the elite of the City do down at Union Square is attend to their hair, faces, nails, and general beauty. One of the most rarified salons in Union Square is the **Elizabeth Arden Red Door** (126 Post St., #4, 415/989-4888, Mon.–Wed. and Sat. 9 A.M.–7 P.M., Thurs.–Fri. 9 A.M.–8 P.M., Sun. 10 A.M.–6 P.M.). You'll definitely need an appointment to get a trim or a color touch-up here.

FINANCIAL DISTRICT AND SOMA

Is there anyplace in San Francisco where you *can't* shop? Even the Financial District has plenty of retail opportunities. Antique, art, and design lovers come down to **Jackson Square** (Jackson and Montgomery Sts., 415/398-8115) for the plethora of high-end shops and galleries. Don't expect to find much in the way of cheap tchotchkes here—the objets d'art and interior accessories here find places in the exquisite homes of the wealthy buyers who can

afford such luxuries. But as always, it's free to look, to imagine, and to dream.

Art and Design

Kathleen Taylor - The Lotus Collection
(445 Jackson St., 415/398-8115, www.ktaylor-lotus.com, Mon.–Fri. 10 A.M.–5 P.M., Sat. 11 A.M.–4 P.M.) specializes in antique textiles from around the world. Whether you fancy a medieval tapestry for your wall or an ancient Asian table runner, this is the place to find it. A more classic but intensely high-end and well-known gallery sells works of fine art to the cream of West Coast society. The **Montgomery Gallery** (406 Jackson St., 415/788-8300, www.montgomerygallery.com, Tues.–Fri. 10 A.M.–5:30 P.M., Sat. 11 A.M.–5 P.M.) seems like a museum, displaying works of the Old Masters as well as the top tier of more modern artists.

The modern design shops, while still catering to the high end, offer more items within the reach of normal folks. **Area** (540 Jackson St., 415/989-2732, www.areasanfrancisco.com, Tues.–Fri. 11 A.M.–6 P.M., Sat. 10 A.M.–6 P.M.) is one of these, offering both indoor and outdoor decorative items of the very latest styles. While much of their stock is pricey, some of the smaller items such as planters and knick-knacks, cost under $100.

NORTH BEACH AND CHINATOWN

Shopping in Chinatown isn't really about seeking out a specific store. Instead, visitors stroll Grant Street, browsing in the dozens of similar souvenir shops, marveling at the strange herbal medicines in the windows of the apothecaries, and contemplating cups of tea from the scattered tea shops. For a sense (and a scent) of the more authentic side of Chinatown, head off the main drag to Stockton Street and seek out the local food markets.

Books and Music

The North Beach district is filled with fun, beauty, and great Italian restaurants and cafés. The Italian district also boasts some of the hippest shops in all the City, so it's a great place for shoppers who eschew chains to seek out thrift shops and funky independents. One of the most famous independent bookshops in a city famous for its literary bent is **City Lights** (261 Columbus Ave., 415/362-8193, www.citylights.com, daily 10 A.M.–midnight). It opened in 1953 as an all-paperback bookstore with a decidedly Beat aesthetic, focused on selling modern literary fiction and progressive political tomes. As the Beats flocked to San Francisco and to City Lights, the shop put on another hat—that of publisher. Allen Ginsberg's *Howl* was published by the erstwhile independent, which never looked back. Today they're still selling and publishing the best of cutting-edge fiction and non-fiction. The store still sits in its original location on the point of Columbus Avenue, though it's expanded somewhat since the '50s. Expect to find your favorite genre paperbacks along with the latest intriguing new works. The nonfiction selections can really make you take a step back and think about your world in a new way, which is just what the founders of City Lights wanted.

Finally, to top of the ultimate hip North Beach shopping trip, stop in at **101 Music** (1414 Grant Ave., 415/382-6369). This independent shop is short on copies of the latest pop CDs and long on vintage vinyl and secondhand instruments and musical equipment. Expect to see turntables, keyboards, and all sorts of fun arcane stuff as soon as you walk in the door. The vinyl collection hides downstairs. The organization of the records and CDs could be better, but isn't browsing for treasure in the bins part of the fun at such a shop? Customer service, much of it provided by the owner, keeps locals coming back.

Clothing

For hip dressers who prefer classic style to the latest stuff fresh out of the sweatshops, **Old Vogue** (1412 Grant Ave., 415/392-1522, Mon.–Tues. and Thurs. 11 A.M.–6 P.M., Wed. 11 A.M.–8 P.M., Fri.–Sat. 11 A.M.–10 P.M., Sun. noon–6 P.M.) is the perfect North Beach destination. Stop in at the funky little storefront and plan to spend a little while browsing through the racks of vintage apparel: one floor dedicated to comfy old jeans and pants, the other to coats, blouses, dresses, and accessories. Old Vogue can provide you with just the perfect hat to top off your favorite clubbing outfit.

MARINA AND PACIFIC HEIGHTS

Pacific Heights and its neighbor Presidio Heights, two quiet residential areas, are connected by Sacramento Street. Sacramento is home to interior design and clothing boutiques that display high-end wares that appeal to the well-heeled residents of this area. With 12 blocks' worth of shops, galleries, salons, and eateries, the main trouble folks have is getting through all of it in one shopping session.

Clothing

You'll have plenty of high-end boutiques to choose from. For the latest outfits, try **Bettina** (3615 Sacramento St., 415/563-8002, www .bettinasf.com, Mon.–Fri. 11 A.M.–7 P.M., Sat. 11 A.M.–6:30 P.M., Sun. noon–5 P.M.). If you prefer fashions from earlier decades, browse through **GoodByes Consignment Shop** (3483 Sacramento St., 415/674-0151, www .goodbyessf.com, Mon.–Wed. and Fri.–Sat. 10 A.M.–6 P.M., Thurs. 10 A.M.–8 P.M., Sun. 11 A.M.–5 P.M.). GoodByes also has a men's store just across the street at 3464 Sacramento.

Unique

It takes a ritzy San Francisco neighborhood to support a six-day-a-week orchid store. **Beautiful Orchids** (3319 Sacramento St., 415/567-2443, www.beautifulorchids.com, Mon.–Fri. 10 A.M.–9 P.M., Sat. 10 A.M.–5 P.M.) specializes in rarified live orchid plants. Every color of the rainbow, amazing shapes, and waterfall figures spill from elegant planters. Expect to pay a premium for these rare handtended flowers, and to spend even more to ship them home. You can also find elegant home accessories here, most picked to complement the orchids rather than the other way around.

CIVIC CENTER AND HAYES VALLEY

In the Hayes Valley neighborhood adjacent to the Civic Center, shopping goes uptown, but the unique scent of counterculture creativity makes it in somehow. This is a fun neighborhood to get your stroll on, checking out the art galleries and peeking in to the boutiques for clothing and upscale housewares, then stopping at one of the lovely cafés for a restorative bite to eat.

Art

The **Tinhorn Press/Gallery** (511 Laguna St., 415/621-1292) is at once a gallery and an artists' workshop. All the works you'll see are rendered on that most common of media: paper. The owners and resident artists can often be found working on their stone lithography and intaglio works. They display their own creations as well as works on paper by select other artists.

Clothing

Ver Unica (437-B Hayes St., 415/431-0688, www.ver-unica.com)is a vintage boutique that attracts locals and celebrities alike with high-quality men's and women's clothing and accessories dating from the 1920s to the 1980s, as well as a small selection of new apparel by up-and-coming designers.

Italian for hip, fresh, and attractive, **Bulo** (418 Hayes St., 415/225-4939, www.bulo shoes.com) caters to the fashion- and quality-conscious foot fetishist. The men's store is at 437-A Hayes St.

MISSION AND CASTRO

In the 21st century, the closest you can come to the old-school Haight Street shopping experience is in the Mission. The big shopping street with the coolest stuff is definitely Valencia Street, which has all the best thrift shops and funky stuff.

On Castro Street, shopping is sexy. Whether you want toys or leather, fetish or lace, or just a pair of fabulous spike-heeled boots, you can find it in one of the racy shops found in the City's notoriously "everything goes" district.

Books

There's a **Books Inc.** (2275 Market St., 415/864-6777, www.booksinc.net, daily 10 A.M.–11 P.M.) in the Castro. This small independent Bay Area bookseller's chain hosts numerous author events and stocks plenty of local authors. You can also find your favorite paperbacks here. At this location, the managers stock lots of great gay literature (fiction and nonfiction) in keeping with the neighborhood. You're welcome to stay as long as you like, browsing through the books here. (I love the Books Inc. chain and wrote much of this guidebook in the café at the Mountain View location.)

Clothing

One of the local favorite vintage/secondhand clothing stores in the Mission is **Schauplatz** (791 Valencia St., 415/864-5665, daily 1–6 P.M., closed Tues.). It might be a bit more expensive than your average Goodwill, but you'll be wowed by the fabulous and unusual apparel at this unique vintage shop. Surf the racks for everything from 1940s dresses to vintage sunglasses.

Need shoes? One of the few honest-to-goodness local, family-owned shoe stores, **De La Sole** (4126 18th St., 415/255-3140, www .delasole.com, daily 11 A.M.–7 P.M.) in the Castro proffers both men's and women's foot fashions. You'll find the shop friendly to all shoppers, even those who come in often if you know what I mean. The shoes shine with the latest fashions, from sneakers to formals. Even the shop's interior carries on the theme of fun, fashinable modernity, making visitors feel hip just by walking in the door.

Unique

Five and Diamond (510 Valencia St., 415/255-9747, www.fiveanddiamond.com) can bring you every aspect of the stereotypical San Francisco experience all in one storefront. Inside this unique space, you'll find off-the-wall art, unusual clothing, and downright scary jewelry. Those who make an appointment in advance can also get a tattoo here, or purchase some keen body jewelry. A trip inside

Five and Diamond can be an exciting adventure for the bold, but might be a bit much for the faint of heart. Decide for yourself whether you dare to take the plunge.

Rock Hard (518 Castro St., 415/437-2430) is one of the neighborhood's favorite "adult stores." This store sells large selection of large, uhm, products at prices lower than many similar shops in the City. Expect to find dildos, vibrators, lubricants, S&M toys, porn DVDs, and much, much more. Though it's in the Castro and it's primarily known as a gay men's shop, women are welcome and can certainly find their share of fun. Call for store hours, or just drop by since Rock Hard is likely to be open late.

GOLDEN GATE PARK AND THE HAIGHT

The Haight-Ashbury shopping district isn't what it used to be, but if you're willing to poke around a bit, you can still find a few bargains in the remaining thrift shops.

Books and Music

Music has always been a part of the Haight. To this very day, you'll find ill-bathed folks pounding out rhythms on *doumbeks* and congas on the sidewalks. The ever-changing face of commerce has made the old favorite all-local, all-handmade **Sol Drums** (3275 San Bruno Ave., 415/468-4700, www.soldrums.com) part of the megalithic Drum Workshop. But the legendary **Haight-Ashbury Music Center** (1540 Haight St., 415/863-7327, www.haight-ashbury-music.com, call for hours) remains. Come in and check out one of the best collections of musical instruments and gear anywhere on the West Coast.

Located in an old bowling alley, **Amoeba** (1855 Haight St., 415/831-1200, www.amoeba.com, Mon.–Sat. 10:30 A.M.–10 P.M., Sun. 11 A.M.–9 P.M.) is a larger-than-life record store that promotes every type of music imaginable. Amoeba's staff, many of whom are musicians themselves, are among the most knowledgeable in the business.

The award-winning **Booksmith** (1644 Haight St., 415/863-8688, www.booksmith.com, Mon.–Sat. 10 A.M.–10 P.M., Sun. 10 A.M.–8 P.M.) bookstore boasts a helpful and informed staff, a fabulous magazine collection, and Northern California's preeminent calendar of readings by internationally renowned authors.

Clothing

If it's used clothing you're after, try the legendary **Aardvark's Odd Ark** (1501 Haight St., 415/621-3141, Mon.–Fri. 11 A.M.–7 P.M., Sat.–Sun. 11 A.M.–8 P.M.), known to its friends as Aardvark. Join the countless bargain shoppers who prowl the racks for fabulous forgotten garments. Just don't expect to pay $0.25 for that great 1930s bias-cut dress or $0.50 for a cast-off Dior blouse; the merchants in the Haight are experienced used clothiers who know what the good stuff is worth.

Unique

Get yourself a new tattoo, a split tongue, or a Prince Albert down at **Mom's Body Shop**

Unique shops line Haight Street.

(1408 Haight St., 415/864-6667, www.moms bodyshop.com, opens daily at noon).

One relic of the 1960s counterculture still thrives on the Haight: smoke shops. All pipes, water pipes, and other paraphernalia are *strictly for use in smoking legal tobacco,* you understand. Be sure not to mention anything else inside these shops, for legal reasons. Shops like **Ashbury Tobacco Center** (1524 Haight St., 415/552-5556) also sell clothing and accessories made from the much-maligned hemp plant, stickers and T-shirts bearing pretty green leafy designs, cigarette lighters, and other such trinkets. You know why you're in the Haight, so go on in and look at all the pretty swirling colors!

Sports and Recreation

PARKS

Crissy Field (603 Mason St. at Halleck St., 415/561-7690, www.crissyfield.org, daily 9 A.M.–5 P.M.), in the Golden Gate National Recreation Area, is a park with a mission. In partnership with the National Park Service, ecology programs are the centerpiece of the Center. Check the website for a list of classes, seminars, and fun hands-on activities for kids of all ages. Many of these include walks out into the marsh beyond the center and the landscape of the Presidio and beyond.

Many people who like to hike, like to do it in some semblance of solitude. That can be tough to come by in the ever-crowded Golden Gate Park and Presidio. **McLaren Park** (Persia Ave. at Naples St., 415/239-7735, www .jennalex.com/projects/fomp/homepage/ index.html) is something of a hidden gem in the busy City—an uncrowded park with miles of hiking trails, dozens of picnic tables, athletic fields, an indoor pool, and even a nine-hole golf course. You can enjoy a set of tennis, swim some laps, or play a quick round. But most of all, you can walk. Seven miles' worth of trails are asphalt paved, and plenty of undeveloped trails wend off into the brush and trees all around. If you've got the stamina, you can circle the whole park just by following its trails. Feel free to bring your canine companion with you to this dog-friendly park. On the other hand, take care walking here if you're a woman alone. McLaren Park is generally quite safe in the daylight hours. But at night it becomes much less safe, so plan to finish up your hiking, picnicking, and playing by sunset.

BEACHES

San Francisco boasts of being a city that has everything, and it certainly comes close. This massive urban wonderland even claims several genuine sand beaches within its city limits. No doubt the biggest and most famous of these is **Ocean Beach** (The Great Highway, parking at Sloat, Golden Gate Park, and the Cliff House). This five-mile stretch of sand forms the breakwater for the Pacific Ocean along the whole west side of the City. Because it's so large, you're likely to find a spot sit down and maybe even a parking place somewhere on Ocean Beach, except perhaps on that rarest of occasions in San Francisco: a sunny, warm day. Locals love Ocean Beach, but there's plenty of room for visitors too. Just please, we're begging you, *don't* go out for a nice ocean swim at Ocean Beach. Extremely dangerous rip currents kill at least one person every single year.

The **Aquatic Park** (Beach St. and Hyde St.) beach sits right in the middle of Touristville, San Francisco (Fisherman's Wharf, that is). Of course this makes Aquatic Park incredibly convenient for visitors who want to grab a picnic on the Wharf to enjoy down on the beach. To be honest, the coolest part of Aquatic Park is its history rather than its current presence. The park was built in the late 1930s as a bathhouse catering to wealthy San Franciscans, and today one of the main attractions of Aquatic Park remains swimming: triathletes and hard-core swimmers brave the frigid waters to swim for miles in the protected cove. More sedate visitors prefer to find a seat and enjoy a cup of coffee, a newspaper, and some people-watching.

Baker Beach (Golden Gate Point and the Presidio) is best known for its scenery. And that doesn't just mean the lovely views of the Golden Gate Bridge from a new angle (from the west and below). Baker is San Francisco's own clothing-optional (that is, nude) beach. But don't worry, plenty of the denizens of Baker Beach wear clothes while flying kites, playing volleyball and Frisbee, and even just strolling the beach. Baker Beach was the original home of the Burning Man festival, before it moved out to the Black Rock Desert of Nevada. Because Baker is much smaller than Ocean Beach, it gets crowded in the summertime. Whether you choose to sunbathe nude or not, don't try to swim here. So close to the gate, the currents at Baker get seriously strong and dangerous. Stay safe by staying on land.

HIKING

Yes, you can go for a hike inside the city of San Francisco. Most of the parks in the City offer hiking trails to suit various tastes and ability levels. The City also boasts some longer and more interesting trails that present serious hikers with a real challenge.

For an easy nature walk in the Presidio, try the **Lobos Creek Trail** (Lincoln St. at Bowley St., daily dawn–dusk, 0.6 mi, easy). Less than a mile long, this flat boardwalk trail is wheelchair-accessible and shows off the beginning successes of the ecological restoration of the Presidio. You'll get to see restored sand dunes and native vegetation, which has attracted butterflies and other insects, which in turn bring the birds to the trail area. While it's still in the City, this trail gives walkers a glimpse of what the Presidio might have been like 500 years ago, before the encroachment of the European military.

The closest thing to a true serene backwoods hike in San Francisco can probably be found at **Mount Davidson** (Dalewood St., West Portal, daily 6 A.M.–10 P.M., 0.5 mi, easy). Park in the adjacent West Portal residential area and wander through the gate and into the woods, or something like them. Take the main fire road straight up the gentle slope to the top of the mountain, then find the smaller track off to the left that leads to the famous "cross at the top of the mountain." To extend your stay in this pleasant place, either walk down the other side of the mountain, or head back to find the smaller branch trails that lead off into the trees.

For a stouter and better-known walk, take the trail at **Glen Canyon** (Bosworth St., 1 mi, moderate). Feel free to bring your canine companion on this trail through a lovely little unlikely urban canyon. It only takes about a half an hour to explore Islais Creek, the non-native eucalyptus and blackberry, and the attractive if non-spectacular views. Take care to avoid the prolific poison oak that spreads throughout the canyon.

The **California Coastal Trail** (Golden Gate National Recreation Area, 10.5 miles, difficult) runs right through the city of San Francisco on its way down the state. Originating beneath the Golden Gate Bridge, the Coastal Trail meanders all the way down the west side of the City. It passes by many major monuments and parks, so you can take a break from hiking to visit Fort Point, the Palace of the Legion of Honor, and the site of the Sutro Baths. You'll get to walk right along the famous beaches of San Francisco as well, from Baker Beach to China Beach and on down to Ocean Beach, which comprises five miles of the Coastal Trail. You can keep on walking all the way down to Fort Funston, and the San Francisco portion of the trail terminates at Philip Burton Memorial State Beach. You can enter the trail from just about any place, and exit wherever feels convenient. Just be sure you've got a current trail map to be sure you're aware of any partial trail closures.

BIKING

In other places, bicycling is a sport or a mode of transportation. In San Francisco, bicycling is a religion. (The concept of mountain biking

TWIN PEAKS

Twin Peaks rises up from the center of San Francisco, and is the second-highest point in the City. Twin Peaks divides the City between north and south, catching the fog bank that rolls in from the Golden Gate and providing a habitat for lots of wild birds and insects, including the endangered Mission Blue Butterfly.

While you barely need to get out of your car to enjoy the stunning 360-degree views of the City from the peaks, the best way to enjoy the view is to take a hike. If you want to scale the less traveled South Peak, start at the pullout on the road below the parking lot. You'll climb a steep set of stairs up to the top of the South Peak in less than 0.2 mile. Stop and marvel at man's industry: the communications tower that's the massive eyesore just over the peak. Carefully cross the road to access the red-rock stairway up to the North Peak. It's only a 0.25 mile, but as with the South Peak,

those stairs seem to go straight up! It's worth it when you look out across the Golden Gate to Mount Tamalpais in the north and Mount Diablo in the east.

If it's the view you're seeking rather than the wildlife and exercise, head to Twin Peaks only on a sunny day. If the fog is in, as so often happens in the summertime, you'll have trouble seeing five feet in front of you. Oh, and don't expect a verdant paradise up there – the grass doesn't stay green long in the spring, so most visitors get to see the dried-out brush that characterizes much of the Bay Area in the summertime and fall.

To get there, drive west up Market Street (eventually turning into Portola Dr.), and turn right onto Twin Peaks Boulevard and past the parade of tour buses to the parking lot past the north peak. Parking is free and Twin Peaks is open year-round.

---

originated in the City.) As a newcomer to biking in the City, it's wise to start off gently, perhaps with a guided tour that avoids the dangerous traffic areas. The fabulously named **Blazing Saddles** (2715 Hyde St., 415/202-8888, www.blazingsaddles.com) rents bikes and offers guided bicycling tours all over the Bay Area. If you prefer the safety of a group, take the daily guided tour (10 A.M., 3 hours, reservations required) through San Francisco and across the Golden Gate Bridge into Marin. You'll return to the City by ferry. Blazing Saddles can also supply intrepid cyclists with bike maps of the City and the greater Bay Area. For a sedate introductory ride, you can take the popular self-guided tour of the waterfront. With five Blazing Saddles locations, most set into the touristy Fisherman's Wharf area, it's easy to find yourself a cruiser and head out for a spin.

Not a serious cyclist? Or are you a serious cyclist who's new to the City? Take the easy and flat nine-mile ride across the **Golden Gate Bridge** and back. This is a great way to see the Bridge and the Bay for the first time,

and it takes only an hour or two to complete. Another option is to ride across the Bridge and into the town of Sausalito (8 miles) or **Tiburon** (16 miles), enjoy an afternoon and dinner in Marin, then ride the ferry back into the City. (Bikes are allowed onboard.)

If you've got a bit more time and leg strength, consider a scenic ride on the paved paths of **Golden Gate Park and the Presidio** (20 miles, 2–4 hours without stops). A bike makes a perfect mode of transportation from which to explore the various museums and attractions of these two large parks, and you can spend all day and never have to worry about finding parking spaces.

Looking for some great urban mountain biking? Miles of unpaved roads and trails right inside the city limits are open to bikers, and provide technically challenging rides for adventurous bikers willing to get away from the tourist realms and take a risk or two. Check out the website for **San Francisco Mountain Biking** (www.sfmtb.com) for information about trails, roads, routes, and regulations.

GOLF

A number of golf courses hide in the parks of San Francisco. The premier golf course in the City, the **Presidio Golf Course** (Arguello St., 50 yards from Arguello Gates, 415/561-4653, www.presidiogolf.com) was once reserved for the exclusive use of military officers, government officials, and visiting dignitaries. Since 1995, its 18-hole, par 72 course, driving range, practice putting greens, and clubhouse have been available to the public. Reserve your tee time by phone or online. Lessons are available, offered by the Arnold Palmer Golf Academy (the Arnold Palmer Management Company operates the course).

Lincoln Park Golf Course (34th Ave. and Clement St., 415/750-4653) is an 80-year-old, public 18-hole, par 68 course in the Outer Richmond district. It hosts the annual San Francisco City Golf Championships. Another 18-hole municipal golf courses is the **Harding Park Golf Course** (Skyline Blvd. at Harding Rd., 415/664-4690).

Nine-hole courses with challenging golf and great views include the **Golden Gate Park Golf Course** (47th Ave. at Fulton St., www.goldengateparkgolf.com) and the **Gleneagles Golf Course** (2100 Sunnydale Ave., www.gleneaglesgolfsf.com).

For tee times at any municipal course, call 415/750-4653.

KAYAKING

For the adventurous, kayaking on San Francisco Bay is a great way to experience the famous waterway on a personal level. **City Kayak** (415/357-1010, www.citykayak.com) has locations at both South Beach Harbor (Pier 40, Embarcadero at Townsend St.) and Fisherman's Wharf (Pier 39, slip A21). Beginners can take guided paddles along the shoreline, getting a new view on familiar sights. More advanced kayakers can take trips out to the Golden Gate and around Alcatraz Island. Rental equipment is available daily 10 A.M.–7 P.M. at the South Beach Harbor location.

SAN FRANCISCO CONVENTION & VISITORS BUREAU PHOTO BY MAMI MIYATA

Lincoln Park Golf Course, the first public golf course in San Francisco

TRAMPOLINE

Frequent Flyers (Fisherman's Wharf, Pier 39, 415/981.6300, $10/session) offers a high-flying view of Pier 39, the marina, and the Bay. This bungee-cord secured trampoline experience lets bouncers safely jump 20 feet into the air, and try a few gymnastic tricks while they're up there. Kids must be at least 30 pounds to jump.

SPECTATOR SPORTS

Big-league lovers will find fun in San Francisco and around the Bay Area. The City plays home to the NFL's **San Francisco 49ers** (www .sf49ers.com). The 49ers play at **Monster Park** (490 Jamestown Ave.) way out away from the center of the City on Candlestick Point. This doesn't seem to matter to "the Faithful," the loyal fans who've seen the team through their dismal beginnings, rejoiced in their domination of the NFL through the 1980s and 90s, and continued to cheer as the team "rebuilds" (that is, loses a lot) in the 21st century. Check the website for current single-ticket prices. And be sure to bring a coat to the games—the fog rolls in off the Bay and makes the park chilly and windy.

The MLB's **San Francisco Giants** (http:// sanfrancisco.giants.mlb.com) play out the long summer baseball season at **AT&T Park** (24 Willie Mays Plaza, 3rd and King Sts.). Come out to enjoy the game, the food, and the views at San Francisco's still-shiny and new ballpark. Giants games take place on weekdays and weekends, both day and night. It's not hard to snag last-minute tickets to a regular season game. Oh, and be sure to check out the gourmet restaurants that ring the stadium; it wouldn't be San Francisco without top-tier cuisine to complement a midsummer ball game.

Accommodations

San Francisco has plenty of accommodations to suit every taste and budget. The most expensive places tend to be in Union Square and SoMa. You'll find the most character in the smaller "boutique" hotels, but plenty of big chain hotels have at least one site here, if you prefer a known quantity.

Be aware that many hotels in San Francisco are entirely non-smoking. If you need a smoking room, you may have to hunt for one.

Parking is not included free with your hotel room, and can be excruciatingly expensive in the overnight garages. Check with your hotel to see if they have a "parking package" that takes care of this expense (and possibly offers valet service as well). Otherwise, if you don't plan to leave the City, consider saving a bundle by using public transit.

UNION SQUARE AND NOB HILL

In and around Union Square and Nob Hill, you'll find about a zillion different hotels. As a rule, those closest to the top of the Hill or to Union Square proper are the most expensive. For a one- or two-block walk, you get more personality and genuine San Francisco experience for less money and less prestige. There's little cheap in these areas; hostels run down in the direction of the Tenderloin, where safety becomes an issue after dark.

Under $150

While the best bargains aren't in these neighborhoods, you can still find one or two budget-conscious lodgings in the Union Square and Nob Hill regions. The **Hotel Bijou** (111 Mason St., 800/771-1022, www.jdv hotels.com/bijou, $100–150) might be the most fun of the inexpensive lot. Whimsical decor mimics an old-fashioned movie theater, and in fact a tiny "movie house" downstairs runs free-to-patrons double features every night—with all movies shot in San Francisco. Guest rooms are small, clean, and nicely appointed.

$150-250

C Hotel Rex (562 Sutter St., 800/433-4434, www.jdvhotels.com/rex, $235–275) has a classic feel, evoking a hotel in San Francisco early in the 1900s. Guest rooms are comfortable and spacious, decorated with the work of local artists and artisans. The dimly lit lobby bar is famous in the City for its literary bent—you may find yourself embroiled in a fascinating conversation as you enjoy your evening glass of wine. Amenities include a small elevator (not all boutique hotels in SF have them), access to a nearby gym, and valet parking packages for an additional fee. The attached Café Andre serves dinner each night; ask at the desk about reservations.

It might look small compared to the mammoth hotels on Union Square, but **The Cartwright Hotel** (524 Sutter St., 415/421-2865, www.cartwrighthotel.com, $175–285) has plenty of room for budget-minded guests. Guest rooms are freshly redecorated with antiques, and the small lobby has a light, airy feel. Enjoy a complimentary continental breakfast, a wine reception each evening, and free Wi-Fi access. Only about two blocks from Union Square and half a block from the Powell cable car line, this boutique hotel is perfectly located for both business and pleasure travelers.

Just off Union Square, the **Handlery Hotel** (351 Geary St., 800/995-4874, www.handlery .com, $175–330) offers a wide variety of rooms for all different price ranges. Value rooms in the historical section of the hotel tend to be small, and the appointments a bit sterile, but the amenities are as good as those in the newer, pricier Club section of the complex. For a serious splurge, rent the Rooftop Garden Suite, complete with an outdoor patio overlooking the City. A heated outdoor pool is available to all, and the Daily Grill restaurant serves up large portions of standard California cuisine all day long.

Only half a block down from the square, the **Sir Francis Drake** (450 Powell St., 800/795-7129, www.sirfrancisdrake.com, $190–250) has its own history beginning in the late 1920s. Here at the Drake you'll find a bit less opulence in the lobby (compared to the St. Francis) and a bit more in the guest rooms. The Beefeater doorman (almost always available for a photo), the unique door overhang, and the red and gold interior all add to the character of this locals' and tourists' favorite.

Over $250

The **C Hotel Monaco** (501 Geary St., 415/292-0100, www.monaco-sf.com, $310–600) shows the vibrant side of San Francisco. Big guest rooms are whimsically decorated with bright colors, while baths are luxurious and feature cushy animal-print bathrobes. Friendly service comes from purple-velour coated staff, who know the hotel and the City and will cheerfully tell you all about both. Chair massage complements the free wine and cheese in the large, open guest lounge. Be sure to check out the Grand Café and the dining room as well. Because the Hotel Monaco is located a couple of blocks off the Union Square, you get more, and more fun, for your money.

A San Francisco legend, the **Clift** (495 Geary St., 415/775-4700, www.clifthotel .com, $350) has a lobby worth walking into, whether you're a guest of the hotel or not. The high-ceilinged, industrial gray space is devoted entirely to modern art. Yes, you really are supposed to sit on the antler sofa and the metal chairs, though most folks avoid the *seriously* oversized vintage seat. By contrast, the big Philippe Starke–designed guest rooms are almost Spartan in their simplicity, with colors meant to mimic the City skyline. Stop in for a drink at the Redwood Room, done in brown leather and popular with a younger crowd. For dinner, a branch of Jeffrey Chodorow's Asia de Cuba restaurant is located inside the hotel. The Clift is perfectly located for theatergoers, and the Square is an easy walk away.

The opulence of the lobby at the **Westin St. Francis** (335 Powell St., 415/397-7000, www .westinstfrancis.com, $390–490) matches its elegant address. With more than a century of history as San Francisco's great gathering spot, the St. Francis still garners great prestige.

Rooms are attractive but small. The price of admission pays mainly for the decadent fixtures of the common areas, the four eateries (including Michael Mina, the executive chef's signature restaurant), the state-of-the-art gym, top-quality meeting and banquet spaces, and the address on Union Square.

Certain names just mean luxury in the hotel world. The **Fairmont San Francisco** (950 Mason St., 415/772-5000, www.fairmont.com, $460) is among the best of these. With a rich history, above-and-beyond service, and spectacular views, the Fairmont makes any stay in the City memorable. Check online for package specials or to book a tee time or spa treatment, and note that some of the rooms in this rarified hostelry actually allow smoking.

Another Nob Hill contender with a top name, the **Ritz-Carlton** (600 Stockton St., 415/296-7465, www.ritzcarlton.com, $490) provides patrons with ultimate pampering. From the high-thread-count sheets to the five-star dining room to the full-service spa, guests at the Ritz all but drown in sumptuous amenities. Even the "standard" rooms are exceptional, but if you've got the bread, spring for the Club Floors, where they'll give you an iPod, a personal concierge, and possibly the kitchen sink if you ask for it.

FINANCIAL DISTRICT AND SOMA

Top business execs make it their, well . . . business to stay near the towering offices of the Financial District, down by the water on the Embarcadero, or in SoMa. Thus, most of the lodgings in these areas cater to the expense account set.

$150-250

An unlikely hotel in the midst of the stuffy suit-clad Financial District, the (**Hotel Triton** (342 Grant Ave., 800/800-1299, www .hoteltriton.com, $170–400) welcomes guests with whimsical decor and an ecological theme. Jerry Garcia and Carlos Santana both decorated guest rooms here, and the environmentally friendly practices developed at the Triton

are being adopted by sister hotels all over the world. You'll find the rooms tiny but comfortable, and well stocked with eco-friendly amenities and bath products. The flat-panel televisions offer a 24-hour yoga channel, and complimentary yoga props can be delivered to your room upon request. For the most eco-zany experience at the Triton, book a Celebrity Eco-Suite. Or if you're traveling alone, consider reserving a Zen Den—specially designed for solo travelers and offering the finest Buddhist-inspired amenities. And don't forget to adopt a rubber ducky for the duration of your stay!

For something posh but not overwhelmingly huge, check out **Hotel Griffon** (155 Steuart St., 800/321-2201, www.hotelgriffon.com, $185–450). A boutique business hotel with a prime vacation locale, the Griffon offers business and leisure packages to suit all travelers' needs. They're a bit pricier, but the best guest rooms overlook the Bay, with views of the Bay Bridge and Treasure Island.

It may be part of a chain, but at the **Westin San Francisco Market** (50 Third St., 415/974-6400, www.westinsf.com, $182–600) you'll find plenty of San Francisco charm at your doorstep. Guests stay in pleasant rooms with pretty cityscapes at this large hotel (formerly known as The Argent). Amenities mimic the more expensive SoMa hotels, and seasonal special rates dip down into the genuinely affordable. The attached Ducca restaurant serves three meals each day, and the lounge is open until midnight for nightcaps.

Over $250

Le Meridien San Francisco (333 Battery St., 415/296-2900, $350) stands tall in the Embarcadero Center, convenient to shopping, dining, and the streetcar and cable car lines to all the favorite downtown destinations. This expensive luxury hotel pampers guests with Frette sheets, plush robes, marble bathrooms, and stellar views. Expect nightly turndown service, free newspapers, and 24-hour room service.

The perennial business favorite, sitting right in the midst of the Embarcadero

Center, the **Hyatt Regency San Francisco** (5 Embarcadero Center, 415/788-1234, www .sanfranciscoregency.hyatt.com, $270–355) has it all. A great location across the street from the Ferry Building, more than 800 rooms for easy bookings anytime, fabulous views, and every amenity the business (or pleasure) traveler needs. Guests enjoy the comforts provided with the Hyatt name, a café and bar in-house, and convenient access to Muni, BART, and cable car lines.

Hotel Vitale (8 Mission St., 888/890-8688, www.hotelvitale.com, $300–800) professes to restore guests' vitality with its lovely guest rooms and exclusive spa, complete with rooftop hot soaking tubs and yoga studio. Many of the good-sized guest rooms also have private deep soaking tubs. If you happen to reside in the greater Bay Area (or you know someone who does), check out the deeply discounted "Sunday Locals Only" package.

The only problem with staying at the **(Mandarin Oriental San Francisco** (222 Sansome St., 415/276-9888, www.mandarin oriental.com, $690) is that you may never leave your room. Redefining decadence, the Mandarin Oriental includes raised beds in all rooms so guests can enjoy the panoramic city and bay views while snuggling under the covers. In the swank corner rooms and suites, raised bathtubs let bathers enjoy stunning sights (such as the Transamerica Pyramid, Alcatraz, and the Golden Gate Bridge) from the warmth of the bubbly water. All rooms boast top amenities and Asian-inspired decor, and families are welcome. You can find the best room rates on the hotel's website (the prices will make a budget-minded traveler's eyes bleed), as well as various stay-and-play packages with an emphasis on golf and spa treatments.

The tall, proud **Four Seasons Hotel San Francisco** (757 Market St., 415/633-3000, www.fourseasons.com, $450) sits right on Market Street, convenient to SoMa, Union Square, and all of downtown San Francisco. Unlike many of the City's other luxury hotels, the Four Seasons interiors sparkle with ultramodern art and decor. Spacious guest rooms feature tasteful appointments, and many have picture windows with city and bay views. A large lobby, bar, and dining room provide guests with services day and night.

With specials occasionally ranging under the $250 mark, The **W San Francisco** (181 3rd St., 415/777-5300, www.starwoodhotels .com, $310) brings City luxury to an almost reasonable level. In the heart of SoMa, W guests can walk to the Yerba Buena Gardens or the SFMOMA. Inside the hotel, you'll enjoy spa pampering, fine dining, and rooms with a view. Check out the Internet packages, which cater to everyone from businesspeople to Pride-goers.

For a unique San Francisco hotel experience, book at room at the famous **Hotel Palomar** (12 Fourth St., 866/373-4941, www.hotel palomar-sf.com, $260–575). You'll find every amenity imaginable, from extra-long beds for taller guests to in-room spa services to temporary pet goldfish. The overall decorative motif evokes M. C. Escher, and whimsical colorful touches accent each room. Be sure to book reservations for dinner at the award-winning Fifth Floor restaurant during your stay. Check the website for special deals, some quite reasonably priced, that focus on shopping and spa-style relaxation. You can even book a spa package with your dog!

The **Palace Hotel** (2 New Montgomery St., 415/512-1111, www.sfpalace.com, $300–575) enjoys its reputation as the grande dame of all San Francisco hotels. The original Palace was the dream of William Ralston, who bankrupted himself creating the immense hotel. The rich history of the Palace began when its doors opened in 1875. It was gutted by fires following the 1906 earthquake, rebuilt and reopened in 1909, and refurbished for the new millennium over the years 1989–1991. In 1919, President Woodrow Wilson negotiated terms of the Treaty of Versailles over lunch at the Garden Court. Today, guests take pleasure in beautiful bedrooms, exercise and relax in the full-service spa and fitness center, and dine in the Palace's three restaurants. If you're staying at the Palace, having a meal in the exquisite Garden Court dining room is a must, though you may forget to eat as you gaze upward at the stained-glass domed ceiling.

NORTH BEACH AND FISHERMAN'S WHARF

Perhaps it's odd, but the tourist mecca of San Francisco is not its land of a zillion hotels. Most of the major hostelries sit down nearer to Union Square. But you can stay near the Wharf or in North Beach if you choose; you'll find plenty of chain motels here, plus a few select boutique hotels in all price ranges.

Under $100

The **San Remo Hotel** (2237 Mason St., 415/776-8688, www.sanremohotel.com, $85–105) is one of the best bargains in the City. The old yellow blocky building has been around since just after the 1906 earthquake, offering inexpensive rooms to budget-minded travelers. One of the reasons for the rock-bottom pricing is the bathrooms—you don't get your own. Four shared baths with shower facilities located in the hallways are available to guests day and night. The rooms boast the simplest of furnishings and decorations, as well as clean white painted walls and ceiling. Some rooms have their own sinks, all have either double beds or two twin beds, and none have telephones or televisions—so this might not be the best choice of lodgings for large, media-addicted families. Couples on a romantic vacation can rent the Penthouse, a lovely room for two people with lots of windows and a rooftop terrace boasting views of North Beach and the Bay.

$150-250

Hotel Bohème (444 Columbus Ave., 415/433-9111, www.hotelboheme.com, $200–225) offers comfort, history, and culture at a pleasantly low price for San Francisco. At the Bohème, a long history in the City meets a recent renovation to create an intriguing, comfortable lodging. Rooms are small but comfortable, Wi-Ri is free, and the spirit of the 1950s bohemian Beats lives on. Smallish, warmly, colored and gently lit rooms are particularly welcoming to solo travelers and couples, with

their retro brass beds covered by postmodern geometric spreads. All rooms include private bathrooms, and the double-queen rooms can sleep up to four people for an additional charge.

The **Washington Square Inn** (1660 Stockton St., 415/981-4220, www.wsisf.com, $195–350) doesn't look like a typical California B&B. With its city-practical architecture and canopy out on the sidewalk, it's more of a small, elegant hotel. The Inn offers 16 rooms with queen or king beds, private bathrooms, elegant appointments, and fine linens. Some rooms have spa bathtubs, and others have views of Coit Tower and Grace Cathedral. Only the larger rooms and junior suites are spacious; the standard rooms are "cozy" in the European urban style. A few of the amenities include a generous continental breakfast brought to your room daily, afternoon tea, a flat-screen TV (all rooms), and free Wi-Fi. To stay at the Washington Square Inn is to get a true sense of the beauty and style of San Francisco.

Over $250

For an ultra-luxurious stay in the City, save up for a room at **The Argonaut** (495 Jefferson St., 866/415-0704, www.argonauthotel.com, $350). With stunning bay views from its prime Fisherman's Wharf location, in-room spa services, and a yoga channel, The Argonaut is all San Francisco, all the time. Bold patterns in blues, golds, and black and white dominate guest room decor. Rooms range from cozy standards up to posh suites with separate bedrooms and whirlpool tubs. The hotel is located steps from the Maritime Museum and Ghirardelli Square.

It may be part of a chain, but the **Hyatt at Fisherman's Wharf** (555 North Point St., 415/563-1234, www.fishermanswharf.hyatt .com, $300) still merits a visit. The unusual-for-San Francisco brick facade hides an ultra-modern lobby and matching guest rooms. Though not too big, rooms are elegantly appointed with lots of decadent white linens. Many packages aim at both business travelers and visiting families. Perhaps the best of these is the "Summer

Parking Package," which includes overnight valet parking with the room rate.

Another great upscale hotel in the heart of San Francisco's visitors' district is the **Best Western Tuscan Inn** (425 North Point St., 415/561-1100, www.tuscaninn.com, $275–725). This luxurious Italian-inspired hotel offers great amenities and prime access to Fisherman's Wharf, Pier 39, Alcatraz, and all local shopping and dining. The attractive and very modern exterior gives way to earth tones and country-style charm in the common areas. The guest rooms boast bright colors and up-to-date furnishings—much fancier than you might be accustomed to from a Best Western. All rooms have private baths. They've also got Internet access, cable TV, and limo service to the Financial District three times daily. Check online for discount rates if you're coming during the middle of the week or booking more than two weeks in advance.

MARINA AND PACIFIC HEIGHTS

These areas are close enough to Fisherman's Wharf to walk there for dinner, and the lodgings are far more affordable than downtown digs.

Under $100

For an unexpected, bucolic park hostel within walking and biking distance to frenetic downtown San Francisco, stop for a night at the **Fisherman's Wharf Hostel** (Fort Mason Bldg. 240, 415/771-7277, www.sfhostels.com/fishermans-wharf, bed $26–30, private room $75–125). The hostel sits on Golden Gate National Recreation Area land, pleasantly far from the problems that plague other SF hostels. The best amenities (aside from the free linens, breakfast, and no curfews or chores) are the views of the Bay and Alcatraz, and the sweeping lawns and mature trees all around the hostel.

Few frills clutter the clean comfortable guest rooms at the **Redwood Inn** (1530 Lombard St., 800/221-6621, www.sfredwoodinn.com, $105–120). But if you need a reasonably priced motel room in ever-expensive San Francisco, this is a great place to grab one. From the

location on Lombard, you can get to points of interest throughout the City.

$100-150

The **Marina Inn** (3110 Octavia St., 800/274-1420, www.marinainn.com, $110–120), built in 1924, exudes old-fashioned San Francisco charm but boasts pleasant modern amenities. This small family-friendly hotel offers a continental breakfast, concierge services, and free Wi-Fi. The Inn is within walking distance of major City attractions, including Fisherman's Wharf, Ghirardelli Square, and the cable cars. And if you're feeling a bit scruffy and want to freshen up before your big night on the town, visit the Inn's attached barbershop or salon.

The rooms at the **Marina Motel** (2576 Lombard St., 800/346-6118, www.marinamotel.com, $147–200) may be small, but the motel is big on charm and character. At this friendly little motel, decorated in French-country style, you're welcome whether you smoke, have kids, or bring your dog. Just ask for the room type that best suits your needs when you make your reservations. Rooms are pleasantly priced for budget travelers, and several vacation packages offer deep discounts on tours, spa treatments, and outdoor adventures.

The stately **Queen Anne Hotel** (1590 Sutter St., 800/227-3970, www.queenanne.com, $109–259) brings the elegance of downtown San Francisco out to Pacific Heights. Sumptuous fabrics and rich colors spread through the guest rooms and common areas add to the feelings of decadence and luxury in this boutique hotel. Small, moderate rooms offer attractive accommodations on a budget, while superior rooms and suites take guests up the scale. Continental breakfast is included with each room, as are a number of high-end services such as courtesy car service and afternoon tea and sherry.

$150-250

The **Francisco Bay Inn** (1501 Lombard St., 800/410-7007, www.franciscobayinn.com, $172–210) offers good motel lodgings at reasonable-for–San Francisco rates. The stellar location provides easy access to the Golden Gate Bridge, famously crooked Lombard Street, and Fisherman's Wharf. Best of all, the Francisco Bay offers free parking—a City rarity worth upwards of $50 per day.

Pack the car and bring the kids to the **Hotel del Sol** (3100 Webster St., 415/921-5520, www.thehoteldelsol.com, $230–275). This unique hotel-motel embraces its origins as a 1950s motor lodge, decorating the guest rooms in bright bold colors with whimsical accents, maintaining the heated courtyard pool, and offering the ever-popular free parking with rooms. Family suites and larger rooms have kitchenettes. The Marina locale offers trendy cafés, restaurants, bars, and shopping within walking distance, as well as access to major tourist attractions.

A cute small inn only a short walk from the Presidio, the **Laurel Inn** (444 Presidio Ave., 800/552-8735, www.jdvhotels.com/laurel_inn, $230–265) provides the perfect place for people with pets, or for travelers who want to stay a bit longer in the City. Many of the rooms have kitchenettes, and all are comfortable and modern. The G Bar lounge next door offers a nice place to stop and have a cocktail, and the exclusive boutiques of Pacific Heights beckon visitors looking for a way to part with their cash.

The exterior and interior amenities of the **Hotel Majestic** (1500 Sutter St., 415/441-1100, www.thehotelmajestic.org, $185–295) evoke the grandeur of early 20th-century San Francisco. The Edwardian-styled 1902 building now boasts antique furnishings and decorative items from England and France. Cozy guest rooms, junior suites, and one-bedroom suites are available. If you're in the City on business or just want to go shopping, take advantage of free car service to Union Square and the Financial District on weekday mornings. The Café Majestic serves breakfast and dinner, with a focus on local, healthful ingredients.

Another Pacific Heights jewel, the **Jackson Court** (2198 Jackson St., 415/929-7670, www.jacksoncourt.com, $210) presents a lovely brick facade out into the exclusive neighborhood.

The 10-room inn offers comfortable, uniquely decorated queen-bed rooms and a luscious continental breakfast each morning.

Over $250

Tucked in with the money-laden mansions of Pacific Heights, **Hotel Drisco** (2901 Pacific Ave., 800/634-7277, www.jdvhotels.com/drisco, $300–700) offers elegance to discerning visitors. Away from the frenzied pace and noise of downtown, at the Drisco you get quiet, comfy rooms with overstuffed furniture, breakfast with a latte (if you want it), and a glass of wine in the evening. Economy rooms have detached baths, and lavish suites have stellar views.

CIVIC CENTER AND HAYES VALLEY

You'll find a few reasonably priced accommodations and classic inns in the Civic Center and Hayes Valley areas.

$100-150

The Grove Inn (890 Grove St., 415/929-0780, www.grovinn.com, $138) offers simple, quiet rooms with double-paned windows and fluffy feather beds. Rooms are equipped with televisions and phones, and a continental breakfast is served every morning. You can walk from the Inn to "postcard row" (ask the innkeepers for directions), take a longer stroll down to the Civic Center, or take public transit or a cab to any of the City's attractions.

$150-250

Located in Hayes Valley a few blocks from the Opera House, the **Inn at the Opera** (333 Fulton St., 800/325-2708, www.shellhospitality.com/hotels/inn_at_the_opera, $205) promises to have guests ready for a swanky night of San Francisco culture. In fact, overnight shoeshine and clothes-pressing services count among the inn's many amenities. French interior styling in the rooms and suites once impressed visiting opera stars and now welcomes guests from all over the world.

Take a step back into an older San Francisco

at the **Chateau Tivoli** (1057 Steiner St., 800/228-1647, www.chateautivoli.com, $150–340). The over-the-top colorful exterior matches perfectly with the American Renaissance interior decor. Each unique room and suite showcases an exquisite style evocative of the Victorian era. Most rooms have private baths, though the two least expensive share a bath. With a reasonable price tag even on the most opulent suites, this B&B is perfect for families (though there are no TVs in any room) and for longer stays. Try to get a room for a weekend so you can partake of the gourmet champagne brunch.

It might seem strange to stay at an inn called **The Parsonage** (198 Haight St., 888/763-7722, www.theparsonage.com, $180). But this classy Victorian bed-and-breakfast exemplifies the bygone elegance of the City in one of its most colorful neighborhoods. Rooms are decorated with antiques, and each bathroom has a stunning marble shower. Enjoy pampering, multi-course breakfasts, and brandy and chocolates when you come "home" each night.

MISSION AND CASTRO

Accommodations in these neighborhoods are few and tend to run toward modest B&Bs.

Under $100

For a sweet, affordable little Castro inn experience, try the **Castillo Inn** (48 Henry St., 800/865-5112, $95). With only four rooms and shared baths, you'll imagine you've found a family pension in Tuscany transported to San Francisco. In the midst of the Castro, you've got all sorts of queer-life entertainment options only a short stroll way.

$100-150

For a romantic visit to the Castro with your partner, stay at the **Willows Inn Bed & Breakfast** (710 14th St., 800/431-0277, www.willowssf.com, $125–180). The Willows has European-style shared baths and comfortable guest rooms with private sinks and bent willow furnishings, and serves a yummy continental breakfast each morning. Catering to the queer community, the innkeepers at the Willows can help you with nightclubs, restaurants, and festivals in the City and local to the Castro. One of the best amenities is the friendship and camaraderie you'll find with the other guests and staff at this great Edwardian B&B.

At the **Inn on Castro** (321 Castro St., 415/861-0321, www.innoncastro.com, $120–220), you've got all kinds of choices. You can pick an economy room with a shared bath, a posh private suite, or a self-service apartment. Once ensconced, you can chill out on the cute patio, or go out into the Castro to take in the legendary entertainment and nightlife. The self-catering apartments can sleep up to four and have fully furnished and appointed kitchens and dining rooms. Amenities include cable LCD televisions, DVD players, and colorful modern art.

GOLDEN GATE PARK AND THE HAIGHT

Accommodations around Golden Gate Park are surprisingly reasonable. Leaning towards Victorian and Edwardian inns, most lodgings sit in the mid-tier price range for well-above-average rooms and services. However, getting downtown from the quiet residential spots can be a trek; ask at your inn about car services, cabs, and the nearest bus lines.

$100-150

The Summer of Love seems endless to guests at the **Red Victorian Bed, Breakfast, and Art** (1665 Haight St., 415/864-1978, www.redvic.com, $105–270). The Red Vic serves up peace, love, and literature along with breakfast, while community and color (but absolutely no TVs) decorate the guest rooms. Part of the economy of this B&B includes shared, named bathrooms for some rooms, though many rooms do have their own private baths. Enjoy the intellectual, peaceful conversations over breakfast, browse the Peace Arts Gift Shop, and if you can, get in a chat with owner Sami Sunchild.

A charming Victorian, the **Inn 1890** (1890 Page St., 415/386-0436, www.inn1890.com,

$115–195) embodies truth in advertising. The Queen Anne Victorian mansion was built in 1890, at 1890 Page Street. Budget travelers enjoy the smaller rooms with private baths and memory-foam mattresses, while those with a bit more money pick the larger rooms with the original wood fireplaces. Enjoy a continental breakfast each morning, and feel free to use the guest kitchen 24 hours a day.

Down in the residential Richmond district, the **Ocean Beach Bed & Breakfast** (611 42nd Ave., 415/668-0193, www.ocean beachbb.com, $140–175) sits three blocks from the all-day attractions of Golden Gate Park. Book early, since this B&B has only two rooms: a queen room and a suite both decorated with country-style antiques and traditional quilts. With its family-style continental breakfast each morning and cookies and milk

in the afternoons, this inn may be as close as you can come to living in San Francisco by the sea. To round out your stay, peruse the collection of movies set in San Francisco, books on local history, and menus for local restaurants.

$150-250

The **Stanyan Park Hotel** (750 Stanyan St., 415/751-1000, www.stanyanpark.com, $170–400) graces the Upper Haight area across the street from Golden Gate Park. This renovated 1904–1905 building, listed on the National Register of Historic Places, shows off its Victorian heritage both inside and out. Rooms can be small, but are elegantly decorated, and a number of multi-room suites are available. For a special treat, ask for a room overlooking the park.

Food

One of the main reasons people come from near and far to San Francisco is to eat. Some of the greatest culinary innovation in the world comes out of the kitchens in the City. The only real problem is how to choose which restaurant to eat dinner at tonight!

UNION SQUARE AND NOB HILL
American

Looking for a good old-fashioned American breakfast? Walk on down to **Dottie's True Blue Café** (522 Jones St., 415/885-2767, Wed.–Mon. 7:30 A.M.–3 P.M., $6–12). The menu is simple: classic egg dishes, light fruit plates, and an honest-to-goodness blue-plate special for breakfast, and salads, burgers, and sandwiches for lunch. The service is friendly and the portions are huge. So what's the catch? Everyone in San Francisco knows that there's a great breakfast to be had at Dottie's. Expect lines up to an hour long for a table at this locals' mecca, especially at breakfast on weekend mornings.

Asian Fusion

It seemed unlikely that anything worthy could possibly replace Trader Vic's, but **Le Colonial** (20 Cosmo Pl., 415/931-3600, www.le colonialsf.com, Sun.–Wed. 5:30 P.M.–10 P.M., Thurs.–Sat. 5:30–11 P.M., $25–40) does it. This Vietnamese-fusion hot spot takes pride in its tiki lounge, which features local DJs spinning Thursday–Saturday 4:30 P.M.–2 A.M. Cocktails are big and tropical, and pay proper homage to the building's illustrious former occupant. But don't skip the food; the lush French-Vietnamese fare comes family-style and blends flavors in a way that seems just perfect for San Francisco.

You'll find all of Southeast Asia in the food at **E&O Trading Company** (314 Sutter St., 415/693-0303, www.eotrading.com, lunch Mon.–Sat 11:30 A.M.–5 P.M., dinner Mon.–Thurs. 5–10 P.M., Fri.–Sat. 5–11 P.M., Sun. 5–9:30 P.M.). This fusion grill serves up Indian flatbreads with Vietnamese small plates mixed in with big grilled dishes. Enjoy the wine list and full bar, or consider ordering takeout. Reservations are recommended.

California

A San Francisco legend, make reservations in advance if you want to dine at **Farallon** (450 Post St., 415/956-6969, www.farallonrestaurant .com, Mon.–Thurs. 5:30–10 P.M., Fri.–Sat. 5:30–11 P.M., Sun. 5–10 P.M., $30–55). Dark, cavelike rooms are decorated in an undersea theme—complete with the unique Jellyfish Bar. The cuisine, on the other hand, is out of this world. Chef Mark Franz has made Farallon a 10-year fad that just keeps gaining ground. The major culinary theme, seafood, dominates the pricey-but-worth-it menu. Desserts by award-winning pastry chef Emily Luchetti round out what many consider to be the perfect California meal.

A minimalist decor lets the unbridled creativity of **Michael Mina**'s (Westin St. Francis, 335 Powell St., 415/397-9222, www.michael mina.net, Tues.–Thurs. 5:30–9 P.M., Fri.–Sat. 5:30–9:30 P.M., $50) shine at the star chef's well-known and well-respected restaurant. Choose from a prix-fixe three-course dinner or sample the seasonal tasting menu. The excellent and innovative cuisine is complemented by delicious desert offerings and a selection of over 3,000 wines.

Even with high name-brand and San Francisco–level expectations, the **Dining Room at the Ritz-Carlton** (600 Stockton St., 415/773-6168, www.ritzcarlton.com, Tues.–Thurs. 6 P.M.–9 P.M., Fri.–Sat. 5:30–9:30 P.M.) measures up. Consistently named a top national restaurant by major ratings organizations, the Dining Room serves up mouth-watering French-inspired California cuisine, including plenty of meat, seafood, and creative vegetarian options. You don't need to be a hotel guest to get a reservation here or to take advantage of the convenient valet parking.

Chinese

It may not be in Chinatown, but the dim sum at **Yank Sing** (101 Spear St., 415/957-9300, www.yanksing.com, Mon.–Fri. 11 A.M.–3 P.M., Sat.–Sun. 10 A.M.–4 P.M.) is second to none. The family owns and operates both this restaurant and its sister on Stevenson Street, and now

the third generation is training to take over. In addition to the traditional steamed pork buns, shrimp dumplings, egg custard tarts and such, the "Creative Collection" offers unique bites you won't find elsewhere in the City. Lunch only!

French

The famed **Fleur de Lys** (777 Sutter St., 415/673-7779, www.fleurdelyssf.com, daily 5:30–10:30 P.M., prix fixe $70–92, reservations strongly recommended) is open again. The San Francisco institution burned nearly to the ground in 2001, and the rebuilding took over a year to complete. But now one of the longest running and finest dining establishments has had the time to re-establish itself, and chef Hubert Keller (Keller may be *the* best name in Bay Area dining, ever) continues to create delectable and inventive dishes. The dining room is magnificent, with its elaborate tented ceiling, lushly upholstered chairs, and perfect glass accent pieces. But the reason people flock to Fleur de Lys is and has always been the food. The absolutely cream-of-the-crop menu isn't really à la carte-instead, you're encouraged to peruse the items and create your own three-, four-, or five-course feast. Vegetarians aren't left out here, since Keller creates fish-only and vegetable-only with the same love he dedicates to his meats. You'll probably want wine with your meal, which means it's going to cost a bundle. But it's worth your money to save up and splurge at this world-famous spot.

Tucked away in a tiny alley that looks like it might have been transported from St. Michel in Paris, **Café Claude** (7 Claude Ln., 415/392-3505, www.cafeclaude.com, Mon.–Sat. 11:30 A.M.–10:30 P.M., Sun. 5:30–10:30 P.M., bar Mon.–Sat. until 2 A.M., $10–25) serves classic brasserie cuisine to French expatriates and Americans alike. Much French is spoken here, but the simple food tastes fantastic in any language. Café Claude is open from lunch all the way through dinner, serving an attractive post-lunch menu for weary shoppers looking for sustenance at 3 or 4 P.M. In the evening it can get crowded, but reservations aren't strictly necessary if you're willing to order a classic French cocktail or a glass of wine and enjoy the bustling atmosphere and live music (on weekends) for a few minutes.

Mediterranean

◖ **Cortez** (550 Geary Blvd., 415/292-6360, www.cortezrestaurant.com, nightly 5:30– 10:30 P.M., $10–15/small plate) exemplifies what happens when nouveau cuisine goes *right*. The Mediterranean-inspired food is utterly delectable. Friendly servers know the menu and the wine list, and are happy to make recommendations. It's best to order two or three small plates per person, and it's also the most fun. The more people you bring, the more dishes you get to try! The desserts, created by a master pastry chef, are worth saving room for. The sugar and spice beignets (with a chocolate fondue for dipping) are a house favorite, but must be ordered in advance. Rservations are a good idea on weekend evenings, especially for theatergoers.

Coffee

The best latte I have ever tasted came from ◖ **Caffé Espresso** (462 Powell St., 415/395-8585, www.caffeespresso.com, breakfast, lunch, and dinner daily). On the ground floor of the Sir Francis Drake Hotel, this coffee bar with its soft yellow walls and vintage Parisian framed prints feels like it belongs in Europe. Alcoholic coffee drinks are served at the bar, and off to one side you can get a sandwich, salad, or panini from the little deli counter. This is the perfect place to sit and rest your weary feet after a long day of shopping or sightseeing, and watch the cable cars roll past the window on Powell Street.

FINANCIAL DISTRICT AND SOMA
California

A locals' favorite, especially for weekend brunch, **Butterfly** (Pier 33, 415/864-8999, www.butterflysf.com, Mon.–Fri. 11:30 A.M.–3 P.M., 3:30–11 P.M., Sat.–Sun. 11 A.M.–3 P.M., 3:30– 10 P.M., $16–30) attracts a young, hip crowd with its ultra-modern decor and cocktails for both lunch and dinner. You can sit at a window table enjoying the Asian-inspired California cuisine and watching the city-sized cruise ships dock next door. The brunch menu offers fun breakfast-type dishes. Butterfly can draw a crowd, so make reservations to get a seat at your favorite time. The bar is open until 2 A.M. nightly.

Chinese

Shanghai 1930 (133 Steuart St., 415/896-5600, www.shanghai1930.com, Mon.–Thurs. 11:30 A.M.–2 P.M., 5:30–10 P.M., Fri.–Sat. 11:30 A.M.–2 P.M., 5:30–11 P.M., $16–35) evokes the bygone elegance of Shanghai in the early 1900s. Classic American-Chinese restaurant styling meets San Francisco elegance in a dining room decorated with Asian antiques and Oriental rugs. Even if you're new to serious Chinese food, you'll enjoy the choice of dim sum baskets, upscale entrées, and tasty hot appetizers. The American twist comes in the evening, when local jazz combos play live music for diners six nights a week.

French

There's no question that the **Fifth Floor** (12 Fourth St., 415/348-1555, www.fifthfloor restaurant.com, Mon.–Sat. 5:30–10 P.M., $30–40) is one of the top French restaurants in San Francisco. Which is saying something. The restaurant sits on the fifth floor of the Hotel Palomar. It's got both a casual café and a full-scale formal dining room to serve as many diners as possible. The cuisine exemplifies the best of southern France—the chef specializes in Gascon food and loves to create dishes that show off his early life and training. An ultra-expensive dinner up on the Fifth Floor is the perfect excuse to dress to the nines. Don't worry, the dining room decor can take it.

For the lower end of the French cuisine spectrum, check out **Crepes A Go Go** (350 11th St, 415/503-1294, daily 11 A.M.–10 P.M., $3.50–6) in SoMa. Believe it or not, the tiny but clean premises, single guy working the crepes, and late-night hours (call to check what the *real* closing hours are) are all quite reminiscent of

Paris. Crepes A Go Go can make you up some quick and hearty nighttime sustenance or perhaps a fruity dessert. The house special is the turkey, egg, and cheese—a great way to fuel a full night of drinking and clubbing.

Italian

Palio d'Asti (640 Sacramento St., 415/395-9800, www.paliodasti.com, lunch Mon.–Fri. 11:30 A.M.–2:30 P.M., dinner Mon.–Fri. 5:30–9 P.M., $15–33) is one of the City's elder statesmen. The restaurant has been around since just after the 1906 earthquake, and the decor in the dining areas recreates an era further gone in the Old Country. Try either lunch or dinner, and enjoy the classical Italian menu, which includes wood-fired handmade pizzas as well as homemade pastas and classic Italian entrées. If you're in the City in fall, be sure to stop in and sample the luscious, expensive, and exceedingly rare Piedmont white truffles.

Japanese

In these neighborhoods, you'll find plenty of sushi restaurants to choose from, from the most ultra-casual walk-up lunch places to the fanciest fusion joints. **Ame** (689 Mission St., St. Regis Hotel, 415/284-4040, www.ame restaurant.com, daily 5:30–10 P.M., $34–42) is one of the latter. Appropriately situated in stylish SoMa, this upscale eatery serves a California-Japanese fusion style of seafood. Raw fish fanciers can start out with (or make a meal of) the offerings from the sashimi bar, while folks who prefer their food cooked will find a wealth of options in the appetizers and main courses. The attractively colored blocky dining room has a modern flair that's in keeping with the up-to-date cuisine coming out of the kitchen. You can either start out or round off your meal with a cocktail from the shiny black bar.

Forget your notions of the plain-Jane sushi bar; **Ozumo** (161 Steuart St., 415/882-1333, www .ozumo.com, lunch Mon.–Fri. 11:30 A.M.–2 P.M., dinner Sun.–Wed. 5:30–10 P.M., Thurs.–Sat. 5:30–11 P.M.) takes Japanese cuisine upscale, San Francisco style. Order some classic nigiri, a small-plate Izakaya pub dish, or a big chunk of meat off the traditional robata grill. The high-quality sake lines the shelves above the bar and along the walls. For non-imbibers, choose from a selection of premium teas. If you're a night owl, enjoy a late dinner on weekends and drinks in the lounge nightly.

Steak

An old-school chop house seems like an unlikely venture for sustainable food junkie Traci Des Jardins. But the **Acme Chophouse** (24 Willie Mays Plaza, 415/644-0240, www.acmechop house.com, lunch Tues.–Fri. 11 A.M.–2:30 P.M., dinner Tues.–Sat. 5:30–10 P.M., $23–47) proves that great food truly comes in all styles. The perfect place to enjoy an upscale meal before a ballgame, Acme serves locally ranched steaks, delicious fries, stylish salads, and yummy desserts. If you spring for the grass-fed beef, you're in for a special treat. Though the sauces that come with each steak are delicious in their own right, the grass-fed steaks are so juicy and flavorful you'll forget all about the sauce. With a big sweeping dining room and an open kitchen, Acme succeeds in creating a casual atmosphere apropos of the ballpark and welcoming to diners in jeans. Sure, you'll spend a pretty penny on your meal, but at least you'll feel comfy while you're eating it.

Vietnamese

Probably the single most famous Asian restaurant in a city filled with eateries of all types is **The Slanted Door** (1 Ferry Plaza, #3, 415/861-8032, lunch daily 11 A.M.–2:30 P.M., tea daily 2:30–5:30 P.M., dinner Sun.–Thurs. 5:30–10 P.M., Fri.–Sat. 5:30–10:30 P.M.). If all you know of Vietnamese cuisine is rubbery summer rolls and tripe-and-tendon *pho,* you are in for some seriously tasty re-education. Owner Charles Phan, along with more than 20 family members and the rest of his staff, pride themselves on welcoming service and top-quality food. Organic, local ingredients get used in both traditional and innovative Vietnamese cuisine, creating a unique dining experience. Even experienced local foodies often remark that they've never had green papaya salad, glass noodles, or shaking beef like this before. The light afternoon tea menu can be the perfect pick-me-up for weary travelers who need some sustenance to get them through the long afternoon until dinner. (Vietnamese coffee: the ultimate Southeast Asian caffeine experience!)

Bakeries and Delis

One of the Ferry Building mainstays, the **Acme Bread Company** (1 Ferry Plaza, #15, 415/288-2978, Mon.–Wed. and Fri. 6:20 A.M.–7:30 P.M., Thurs. 6:20 A.M.–8 P.M., Sat.–Sun. 8 A.M.–7 P.M.) remains true to its name. You can buy bread here, but not sandwiches, croissants, or frou-frou pastries. But the bread you'll get tastes better than just about anything west of Paris. The original bakery was the brainchild of Steve Sullivan, who began his baking career while working as a busboy at (where else?) Chez Panisse in Berkeley. To this day, all the bread that Acme sells is made with fresh organic ingredients in traditional style. Beware: The baguettes are traditionally French, so they start to go stale after only 4–6 hours. Eat fast!

Coffee and Tea

For their daily caffeine, local workers rely on the usual Starbucks and Peet's shoved into every convenient small storefront. If it's tea you favor, try the **Imperial Tea Court** (1 Ferry Plaza, #27, 415/544-9830, www.imperialtea.com, Tues.–Fri. 10 A.M.–6 P.M., Sat. 8 A.M.–6 P.M., Sun. 11 A.M.–5 P.M.) at the Ferry Building. This intensely Chinese tea shop sells black teas in bulk, beautiful Asian tea ware, and of course serves hot tea at its six Chinese rosewood tables. If you want to get *into* the tea experience, consider signing up for a class with owner Ray Fong, who is a published author and tea consultant. You'll learn about the traditions of tea, from plant to cup, including the Chinese ceremonial modes of serving.

Farmers Markets

While farmers markets litter the landscape in just about every California town, the **Ferry Plaza Farmer's Market** (1 Ferry Plaza, 415/291-3276, www.ferrybuildingmarket place.com, Tues. 10 A.M.–2 P.M., Sat. 8 A.M.–2 P.M.) is special. At the granddaddy of Bay Area farmers markets, you'll find a wonderful array of produce, cooked foods, and even locally raised meats and locally caught seafood. Expect to see the freshest fruits and veggies from local growers, grass-fed beef from Marin, and seasonal seafood pulled from the Pacific beyond the Golden Gate. Granted, you'll pay for the privilege of purchasing from this market—if you're seeking bargain produce, you'll be better served at one of the weekly suburban farmers markets. But even locals flock downtown to the Ferry Building on Saturday mornings, especially in the summertime when the variety of California's agricultural bounty become staggering.

CHINATOWN
Chinese Banquets

The "banquet" style of Chinese restaurant may be a bit more familiar to American travelers. Banquet restaurants offer tasty meat, seafood, and veggie dishes, and rice, soups, and appetizers, all served family-style. Tables are often round, with a lazy Susan in the middle to facilitate the passing of communal serving bowls around the table. In the City, most banquet Chinese restaurants have at least a few dishes that will feel familiar to the American palate, and menus often have English translations.

The **R&G Lounge** (631 Kearny St., 415/982-7877, www.rnglounge.com, daily 11 A.M.–9:30 P.M., $12–40, reservations suggested) takes traditional Chinese-American cuisine to the next level. The menu is divided by colors that represent the five elements, according to Chinese tradition and folklore. In addition to old favorites like mu shu, chow mein, and lemon chicken, you'll find spicy Szechuan and Mongolian dishes and an array of house specialties. Salt-and-pepper Dungeness crab (served whole on a plate) acts as the R&G signature dish, though many of the other seafood dishes are just as special. Expect your seafood to be fresh, since it comes right out of the tank in the dining room. California cuisine mores have made their way into the R&G Lounge, in the form of some innovative dishes and haute cuisine presentations. This is a great place to enjoy Chinatown cuisine in an American-friendly setting.

Another great banquet house is the **Hunan Home's Restaurant** (622 Jackson St., 415/982-2844, http://hunan home.ypguides.net, Mon.–Thurs. and Sun. 11:30 A.M.–9:30 P.M., Fri.–Sat. 11:30 A.M.–10 P.M., $20). This one's a bit more on the casual side, and it's even got another location in suburban Los Altos. You'll find classic items on the menu such as broccoli beef and kung pao chicken, but do take care if something you plan to order has a "spicy" notation next to it. At Hunan Home's (and in fact at most Bay Area Chinese restaurants), they mean *really* spicy.

Dim Sum

The Chinese culinary tradition of dim sum is literally translated as "touch the heart" or "order to your heart's content" in Cantonese. In practical terms, it's a light meal—a lunch or an afternoon tea—composed of small bites of a wide range of dishes. Americans tend to eat dim sum at lunchtime, though it can just as easily be dinner or even Sunday brunch. In a proper dim sum restaurant, you do not order anything or see a menu. Instead, you sip your oolong and sit back as servers push loaded steam trays out of the kitchen, one after the other. Servers and trays make their way around the tables; you pick out what you'd like to try as it passes and enough of that dish for everyone at your table is placed before you.

One of the many great dim sum places in Chinatown is the **Great Eastern Restaurant** (649 Jackson St., 415/986-2500, daily 10 A.M.–midnight, $15–25). Ironically it's *not* a standard dim sum place—instead of the steam carts, you'll get a menu and a list. You must write down everything you want on your list and hand it to your waiter, and your choices will be brought out to you. (Family-style is undoubtedly the way to go here.) Reservations are strongly recommended for diners who don't want to wait 30–60 minutes or more for a table

at Great Eastern. This restaurant jams up fast, right from the moment it opens, especially on weekends. The good news is that most of the folks crowding into Great Eastern are locals. You know what that means.

Another well-known dim sum spot, **Yong Kee** (732 Jackson St., 415/986-3759, Tues.–Sun. 7 A.M.–6 P.M., $10, cash only) offers a completely different dim sum experience. This Cantonese-only hole in the wall caters primarily to locals, but if you've ever had dim sum or even just Chinese steamed buns before, you'll want to try them here. They're famous for their enormous fresh-made chicken buns *(gai bow)*, though you can also get a great pork bun here if that's your preference. (The Chinese women lined up at the take-out counter have come for the buns.) The rest of their dim sum nibbles are right tasty too. No reservations are necessary (or taken) here. Do be aware that Yong Kee isn't a good beginner's dim sum place unless you've got a Cantonese-speaking friend to guide you. But if you're a fan of the cuisine already, you'll love Yong Kee even if you can't understand the menu or the staff.

Tea Shops

Official or not, there's no doubt that the world believes that tea is the national drink of China. While black tea (often oolong) is the staple in California Chinese restaurants, you'll find an astonishing variety of teas if you step into one of Chinatown's small tea shops. You can enjoy a hot cup of tea in these, and buy yourself a pound of loose-leaf to take home with you. Most tea shops also sell lovely imported teapots and other implements of proper tea-making.

At the **Red Blossom Tea Company** (831 Grant Ave., 415/395-0868, www.redblossom tea.com, Mon.–Sat. 10 A.M.–6:30 P.M., Sun. 10 A.M.–6 P.M., $10–20) you'll find top-quality teas of every type you can think of and probably some you've never heard of before. Red Blossom has been in business for more than 25 years importing the best teas available from all over Asia. For the tea-adventurous, the blossoming teas, specific varieties of oolong, and *pu-erh* teas make great souvenirs to bring home and share with friends. And if you fall in love, never fear; Red Blossom takes advantage of Bay Area technology to offer all their loose teas on the Internet. (Sadly, their website isn't scratch-and-sniff, or they'd probably run out.)

Another option is **Blest Tea** (752 Grant Ave., 415/951-8516, http://hk.myblog.yahoo.com/blesttea, tasting $3). This shop boasts of the healthful qualities of their many varieties of tea. You're welcome to taste what's available for a nominal fee, to be sure you're purchasing something you'll really enjoy. If you're lucky enough to visit when the owner is minding her store, ask lots of questions—she'll tell you everything you ever needed to know about tea. Be aware that the Blest website isn't particularly English-friendly.

NORTH BEACH AND FISHERMAN'S WHARF
California
San Francisco culinary celebrity Gary Danko has a number of restaurants around town, but perhaps the finest is the one that bears his name. **Gary Danko** (800 North Point St., 415/749-2060, www.garydanko.com, nightly 5:30–10 P.M., prix fixe $65–96) offers the best of Danko's California cuisine, from the signature horseradish-crusted salmon medallions to the array of delectable fowl dishes. The herbs and veggies come from Danko's own farm in Napa. Make reservations in advance to get a table, and consider dressing up a little for your sojourn in the elegant white-tablecloth dining room.

European
Basque cuisine is all the rage these days, and you can experience it in San Francisco at **Iluna Basque** (701 Union St., 415/402-0011, www.ilunabasque.com, Sun.–Thurs. 5:30–11 P.M., Fri.–Sat. 5:30 P.M.–midnight, $9–15). Start your meal with tapas (which come from this region) so you can linger over drinks before indulging in a flavorful main course, and finishing up with a fruity Mediterranean dessert. In Basque country, dinner traditionally starts late and goes on for hours; to mimic this charm-ing custom in the New World, Iluna Basque is open late, even on weeknights.

With a culinary style perhaps best described as European fusion, **Luella** (1896 Hyde St., 415/674-4343, www.luellasf.com, Mon.–Sat. 5:30–10 P.M., Sun. 5–9 P.M., $17–28) brings the flavors of Italy, France, and Spain to the City. The tasty original dishes, most with a distinctive splash of California style that com-plements the European roots, are best enjoyed with a glass of wine from the extensive wine bar. If you're out late or on the run, dinner is served at the wine bar, and a bar menu offers tasty treats after the dining room closes.

French
The **Hyde Street Bistro** (1521 Hyde St., 415/292-4415, Wed.–Mon. 5:30–10:30 P.M., $20) definitely belongs in San Francisco, what with the cable car clanging by outside the front door and the fog blowing past overhead. But in romance and cuisine, it's all Parisian splen-dor. A prix-fixe menu offers economy, while the à la carte menu provides a variety of tradi-tional French bistro fare, including snails, foie gras, and coq au vin. Perhaps best of all, the prices at the Hyde Street Bistro are affordable by the masses. This is a perfect place to bring a date for romantic night out, or to celebrate an anniversary.

Italian
Some of the best Italian food in the City hides in family-owned North Beach restaurants. Poke around and find your favorite hole in the wall, or try a bigger, more upscale spot.

At busy **Caffe Delucchi** (500 Columbus Ave., 415/393-4515, www.caffedelucchi.com, Mon.–Wed, 11 A.M.–10 P.M., Thurs, 11 A.M.–11 P.M., Fri.–Sat, 8 A.M.–11 P.M., Sun. 8 A.M.–10 P.M., $12–20), down-home Italian cooking meets fresh San Francisco produce to create affordable, excellent cuisine. You can get hand-tossed pizzas, salads, and entrées for lunch and dinner, plus tasty traditional American breakfast fare with an Italian twist on the weekends. Drinks run to soju cocktails and artisan Italian and California wines.

Trattoria Contadina (1800 Mason St., 415/982-5728, Sun.–Thurs. 5:30–9:30 P.M., Fri.–Sat. 5:30–10:30 P.M., $15–23) presents mouthwatering Italian fare in a fun, eclectic dining room. Dozens of framed photos line the walls and fresh ingredients stock the kitchen in this San Francisco take on the classic Italian trattoria. Kids are welcome, and vegetarians will find good meatless choices on the menu.

Japanese

Even in a town with hundreds of sushi bars, **Sushi Groove** (1916 Hyde St., 415/440-1905, www.sushigroove.com, Sun.–Thurs. 5:30–10 P.M., Fri.–Sat. 5:30–10:30 P.M., $15–23) stands out. With an immense sushi bar, friendly chefs, and innovative sushi that blends traditional Japanese fish with unusual California touches, the Groove finds favorites with locals and visitors alike. For a special treat, order one of the chef's choice specials.

Seafood

Don't be shocked, but the major ingredient in the cuisine of an area called Fisherman's Wharf is…fish! It's tough to walk down the streets of the Wharf without tripping over at least three big shiny seafood restaurants. You can pick just about any of the big ones and come up with a decent (if touristy) meal. A good way to choose is to stroll past the front doors and take a look at the menus.

It's got the look of a big tourist trap, but at ◖ **McCormick and Kuleto's** (900 North Point St., 415/929-1730, www.mccormickand schmicks.com, Sun.–Thurs. 11:30 A.M.–10 P.M., Fri.–Sat. 11:30 A.M.–11 P.M., $18–25), the chefs know how to cook seafood to satisfy even the pickiest local foodie. In the grand dining room with slightly scary light fixtures and the stellar views out to the Bay, you'll find an array of fresh fish and a list of innovative preparations. For fresh fish beginners, McCormick does offer some classic fries and grills as well. Be aware that this is a seafood restaurant, so land-based entrées are minimal here. Enjoy the fine wine list, and save room for in-season dessert.

South American

If you're looking for something different and special for dinner in North Beach, seek out **Mangarosa** (1548 Stockton St., 415/956-3211, www.mangarosasf.com, Tues.–Thurs. 6–11 P.M., Fri. 6 P.M.–midnight, Sat. 5 P.M.–midnight Sun. 5 P.M.–10 P.M., $16–30). The "pink mango" offers a scrumptious taste of sunny Brazil under the chill San Francisco fog. The Italian neighborhood influence touches the South American cuisine here, and the dining room is open late for visitors who prefer to eat like Europeans.

Steak

A New York stage actress wanted a classic steakhouse in San Francisco, and so **Harris'** (2100 Van Ness Ave., 415/673-1888, www.harris restaurant.com, Mon.–Thurs. 5:30–9:30 P.M., Fri. 5:30–10:30 P.M., Sat.–Sun. 5–10 P.M., $25–40) came to be. The fare runs to traditional steaks and prime rib, with a bit of upscale with a Kobe rib-eye steak and a surf-and-turf featuring a whole Maine lobster. Music lovers can catch live jazz in the lounge on weekends.

Bakeries and Delis

Serving some of the most famous sourdough in the City, the **Boudin** (Pier 39, Space 5-Q, 415/421-0185, www.boudinbakery.com, $6–8) is a Pier 39 institution. Grab a loaf of bread to take with you, or order in one of the Boudin classics. Nothing draws tourists like the fragrant clam chowder in a bread bowl, but if you prefer you can try another soup, a signature sandwich, or even a fresh salad. For a more upscale dining experience with the same great breads, try **Bistro Boudin** (160 Jefferson St., 415/351-5561, Mon.–Fri. 11:30 A.M.–9:30 P.M., Sat.–Sun. 11 A.M.–9:30 P.M. $19–39).

MARINA AND PACIFIC HEIGHTS
French

Classic **Chez Maman** (2223 Union St., 415/771-7771, www.chezmamansf.com, daily 11:30 A.M.–11 P.M., $9–18) has not succumbed to modern food fancification. A host of simple lunch and dinner dishes add a distinct California flair to the classic French bistro fare. You can get a crepe or a quesadilla, a burger or a croque monsieur. Enjoy the tasty, inexpensive dishes in the soft pastel dining room that evokes the south of France. And if you're looking for good food outside the Marina, Chez Maman has another location in Potrero Hill.

For the finest European cuisine, make a reservation at **Quince** (1701 Octavia St., 415/775-8500, www.quincerestaurant.com, Mon.–Wed. and Sun. 5:30–10 P.M. Fri.–Sat. 5:30–10:30 P.M., $27–39) in Pacific Heights. Chef/owner Michael Tusk blends French and Italian culinary aesthetics to create his own unique style of cuisine. It's best to arrive at Quince hungry; the menu is divided into four different courses, or you can try the six-course tasting menu. And once you've gotten a look at the dishes, almost all made with the finest local and sustainable ingredients, you'll want to try at least one from every course!

Italian

The name **A 16** (2355 Chestnut St., 415/771-2216, www.a16sf.com, lunch Wed.–Fri. 11:30 A.M.–2:30 P.M., dinner Sun.–Thurs. 5–10 P.M., Fri.–Sat. 5–11 P.M., $8–20) refers to the major road cutting through the Campania region of southern Italy. But at A 16 in San Francisco, you'll find fabulous southern Italian food rather than traffic. Handmade artisan pizzas, pastas, and entrées tempt the palate with a wealth of hearty flavors. Pasta dishes come in two sizes—a great thing for those with smaller appetites. Also in the proper Old Country tradition, a wonderful wine list has been built to complement the food.

For a southern Italian meal with a soft touch, **Capannina** (1809 Union St., 415/409-8001, Mon.–Thurs. 4:30–10:30 P.M., Fri.–Sun. 4:30–11 P.M., $17–23) is the place to dine. Soft green walls with marble and glass accents provide a sense of peace. The menu features classic Italian styling with an emphasis on the fruits of the sea. Many of the ingredients are imported

directly from Italy, enhancing the authenticity of each dish.

Japanese

For a super-hip San Francisco sushi experience, strut on down to **Ace Wasabi's** (3339 Steiner St., 415/567-4903, www.acewasabisushi.com, Mon.–Thurs. 5:30–10:30 P.M., Fri.–Sat. 5:30–11 P.M., Sun. 5–10 P.M., $6–13 per item). Advertising "rock 'n' roll sushi" and created with the atmosphere of an Izakaya (a sort of Japanese bar and grill), Ace Wasabi's appeals to a young, fun crowd. Be aware that the party can get loud on weekends.

On the other hand, the ◖ **Naked Fish** (2084 Chestnut St., 415/771-1168, www.nakedfishsf.com, Mon.–Thurs. 5:30–10 P.M., Fri.–Sat. 5:30–11 P.M., Sun. 5:30–9:30 P.M., $5–12 per item) proffers an upscale Japanese dining experience. In a fine dining room, taste the sushi, robata grill skewers, Hawaiian-style tapas, and spicy appetizers. Don't skip the sake—Naked Fish has a stellar menu of premium sakes, including unfiltered and high-quality bottles rarely found outside of Japan. Consider taking a date here for dinner to start an elegant night on the town.

If you're in Pacific Heights, give **Kiss Seafood** (1700 Laguna St., 415/474-2866, Tues.–Sat. 5:30–9:30 P.M., $30–50) a try. This tiny restaurant (12 seats total) boasts some of the freshest fish in town—no mean feat in San Francisco. The single chef prepares all the fish himself, possibly due to the tiny size of the place. Obviously, reservations are a good idea. When it comes to the menu, anything seafood is recommended, but if you're up for sashimi you'll be in raw-fish heaven. Round off your meal with a glass of chilled premium sake.

Steak

The Marina is a great place to find a big thick steak. One famed San Francisco steakhouse, **Bobo's** (1450 Lombard St., 415/441-8880, www.boboquivaris.com, nightly 5–11 P.M., $25–40) prides itself on its dry-aged beef and fresh seafood. In season, enjoy whole Dungeness crab. But most of all, enjoy "The

Steak," thickly cut and simply prepared to enhance the flavor of the beef.

Another great house of beef is **Izzy's Steak and Chop House** (3345 Steiner St., 415/563-0487, www.izzyssteaksandchops .com, Mon.–Thurs. 5:30–10 P.M., Fri.–Sat. 5:30–10:30 P.M., Sun. 5–10 P.M., $17–26). Here you'll find an array of tasty steak preparations, seafood, and select non-steak entrées. Be sure to save room for one of Izzy's classic desserts! Izzy's has two out-of-the-City locations, in Corte Madera and San Carlos (convenient to the airport).

Bakeries and Delis

Just looking for a quick snack to tide you over? Drop in at **The Chestnut Bakery** (2359 Chestnut St., 415/567-6777, www.chestnut bakery.com, Mon. 7 A.M.–noon, Tues.–Sat. 7 A.M.–6 P.M., Sun. 8 A.M.–5 P.M.). This small-ish, family-owned storefront opened in 2002 and quickly drew a devoted local following. Only a block and a half from Lombard Street, it's also a perfect spot for weary tourists to take the weight off their feet and enjoy a cookie, pastry, or one of the bakery's famous cupcakes. If you come in the morning, you'll find scones, croissants, and other favorite breakfast pastries. Do be aware that this is a favorite spot for locals, which means that some items sell out during each day. Come early or call ahead if you've got a specific goodie in mind that you just can't live without.

CIVIC CENTER AND HAYES VALLEY
Brazilian

Some diners prefer a little South American flare with their steak dinner. **Espetus Churrascaria** (1686 Market St., 415/552-8792, www.espetus .com, lunch Mon.–Thurs. 11 A.M.–3 P.M., Fri. 11:30 A.M.–3 P.M., and Sat.–Sun. noon–3 P.M., dinner Mon.–Thurs. 5–10 P.M., Fri.–Sat. 5–11 P.M., Sun. 4–9 P.M., $30–80) can give you all the fire you want and more. Most of all, Espetus will give you meat. Lots of meat, both in quantity and variety. As much meat as you can handle, and more, until you wave a little flag of surrender to get the servers to stop bringing around the hot carts of meat carved to order. You'll pay handsomely for the delectable privilege of stuffing yourself at Espetus, but if you love meat, it will be worth every penny.

French

◀ **Jardinière** (300 Grove St., 415/861-5555, www.jardiniere.com, nightly 5–10:30 P.M., later on performance nights, $20–60) was the first restaurant opened by local celebrity chef Traci Des Jardins. The bar and dining room blend into one another, and feature stunning art deco decor (the light fixtures are particularly fabulous if you're into that sort of thing). The ever-changing menu is a masterpiece of French-California cuisine. Des Jardins has long supported the sustainable restauranting movement, and she creates her enticing dishes with a wealth of local, organic ingredients. And her staff, even the bussers and dishwashers, are paid above industry standard wages and are given English classes that help them to move into higher-paying positions. Eating at Jardinière is not only a treat for your senses, it is a way to support the best of trends in San Francisco restaurants.

Be sure to make reservations if you're trying to catch dinner before a show. If you're dining before a performance, be sure to let your server know, and prompt service will be forthcoming. Or if you can wait until after the symphony or opera for dinner, Jardinière takes late-night diners on a first-come, first-served basis, so hit the exits at a run to get a good table.

Absinthe (398 Hayes St., 415/551-1590, www .absinthe.com, Tues.–Fri. 11:30 A.M.–12 A.M., Sat. 11 A.M.–12 A.M., Sun. 11 A.M.–10 P.M., $23–28) takes its name from the notorious "green fairy" drink made of liquor and wormwood. The U.S. ban on absinthe was lifted in 2007 and Absinthe indeed does now serve absinthe—including St. George Spirits Absinthe Verte, the first domestically produced absinthe since Prohibition, made locally in Alameda by St. George Spirits.

It also serves upscale French bistro fare, including what may be the best French fries in the

City. The French theme carries on into the decor as well—expect the look of a Parisian brasserie or perhaps a café in Nice, with retro-modern furniture and classic prints on the walls. The bar is open until 2 P.M., so if you want drinks or dessert after your show at the Opera or Davies Hall, just walk around the corner.

German
In a city full of ethnic food, it can be tough to find German food. **Suppenkuche** (525 Laguna St., 415/252-9289, www.suppenkuche.com, nightly 5–10 P.M., Sun. 10 A.M.–2:30 P.M., $8–18.50) brings a taste of Bavaria to the Bay Area. The beer list makes a great place to start, since you can enjoy a wealth of classic German brews on tap and in bottles, plus a few Belgians thrown in for variety. On the dinner menu, expect to find German classics from various regions of the Old Country, with a focus on Bavarian cuisine. Spätzle, pork, sausage…you name it, they've got it, and it will harden your arteries right on up. Eat and enjoy!

Indian
You can find amazing East Indian cuisine within the city limits, including at **Sultan** (340 O'Farrell St., 415/775-1709, daily 11:30 A.M.–2:30 P.M., 5–10 P.M., $15–20). The simplicity of the red-walled dining room makes it all the easier to concentrate on the cuisine. The chicken masala and garlic naan are local favorites, and the lunch buffet costs about $12.95 for all-you-can-eat delicious food. Just be aware that if you're not familiar with spicy cuisines, you'll want to ask for "not spicy" versions of most dishes. On the other hand, if you're into the high spice, you'll find Sultan perfect.

MISSION AND CASTRO
Mexican
Much of the rich heritage of the Mission district is Hispanic, thus leading to the Mission's being *the place* to find a good taco or burrito. The **Farolito Taqueria** (2950 24th St., 415/641-0758, Sun.–Thurs. 10 A.M.–12:45 A.M., Fri.–Sat. 10 A.M.–2:45 A.M., $10) has found favor with the ultra-picky locals who have dozens of taqueria options within a few blocks. It seems that every regular has a different favorite: the burritos, the enchiladas, the quesadillas…whatever your pleasure, you'll find a tasty version of it at Farolito. A totally casual spot, you'll order at the counter and sit at picnic-style tables to chow down on the properly greasy Mexican fare. Do be aware that if you come late at night, you'll encounter some of the less savory residents of the Mission. (Don't confuse this Farolito with the taqueria by the same name on Mission St.)

Italian
Sometimes, even the most dedicated culinary explorer needs a break from the endless fancy food of San Francisco. When the time is right for a plain ol' pizza, head for **Little Star Pizza** (400 Valencia St., 415/551-7827, www.littlestarpizza.com, Tues.–Thurs., Sun. 5–10 P.M. Fri.–Sat. 5–11 P.M., $10–15). A jewel of the Mission district, this pizzeria specializes in Chicago-style deep-dish pies, but also serves thin-crust pizzas for devotees of the New York style. Once you've found the all-black building and taken a seat inside the casual eatery, grab a beer or a cocktail from the bar if you have to wait for a table. Pick one of Little Star's specialty pizzas, or create your own variation from the toppings they offer. Can't get enough of Little Star? They've got a second restaurant in the Western Addition at 846 Divisadero Street (415/441-1118).

On the other end of the Italian spectrum, you'll find **Delfina** (3621 18th St., 415/552-4055, www.delfinasf.com, Mon.–Thurs. and Sun. 5:30–10 P.M., Fri.–Sat, 5:30–11 P.M., $18–26). Delfina takes Italian cuisine and gives it a hearty California twist. From the antipasti to the entrées, all the dishes speak of local farms and ranches, fresh seasonal produce, and the best Italian-American taste that money can buy. With both a charming warm indoor dining room and an outdoor garden patio, there's plenty of seating at this lovely restaurant. As for the service? The wait staff at Delfina have actually won awards.

Seafood

For great seafood in a lower-key atmosphere, locals eschew the tourist traps on the Wharf and head for the **Anchor Oyster Bar** (579 Castro St., 415/431-3990, Mon.–Fri. 11:30 A.M.– 10 P.M., Sat. noon–10 P.M., Sun. 4–9:30 P.M., $15–30) in the Castro. Yes, it's got a raw bar that features oysters—enough different varieties, but not so many as to be overwhelming or pretentious. The dining room serves all sorts of seafood, including local favorite Dungeness crab. Service is friendly as befits a neighborhood spot, and the odd overlooking of the place by the restaurant-hungry media means that it sees fewer ridiculous crowds than other places. This doesn't diminish its quality, and it makes for a great spot to get a delicious meal before heading out to the local clubs for a late night out.

Bakeries and Delis

Need to grab a quick sandwich before heading off on another San Francisco adventure? Get it at **Ike's Place** (3506 16th St., 415/553-6888, Mon. noon–4:30 P.M., Tues.–Thurs., Sat.–Sun. 11 A.M.–4:30 P.M., Fri. 11 A.M.–8 P.M., $10). An independent deli, Ike's serves big hearty homemade sandwiches that will fuel up even the most energetic travelers. The place really is owned by a man named Ike, who operates the deli with his mother. So if you prefer to patronize local family-owned businesses, Ike's is the perfect place to buy your daily carry-away lunch.

GOLDEN GATE PARK AND THE HAIGHT
American

Sometimes even the most dedicated of healthy eaters find themselves craving pizza, TV dinners, even (oh, the horror) hot dogs. If you happen to find yourself suffering with such a craving while touring the Sunset, **Underdog** (1634 Irving St., 415/665-8881, www.myspace .com/underdogorganic, daily 11:30 A.M.–9 P.M., $4) can hook you up. This genuine hot-dog stand sells organic sausages, from full-fledged brats to grass-fed beef dogs to vegetarian and even vegan sausages. Everything else is organic too-the rolls, the condiments, the side salads, and the sodas. Even the packaging and disposable items are made with recycled and biodegradable materials. So grab yourself a dog—guilt free! Be prepared to carry it with you or eat standing up, since seating at this tiny eatery is severely limited.

For visitors from parts east who long for a taste of home, **The Cheese Steak Shop** (1716 Divisadero St., 415/346-3712, www.cheesesteak shop.com, Mon. and Sat. 10 A.M.–9 P.M., Tues.– Thurs. 9 A.M.–9 P.M., Fri. 9 A.M.–10 P.M., Sun. 11 A.M.–8 P.M., $10) provides a welcome respite from the endless California cuisine. Heck, even locals can't live on bean sprouts all the time. This smallish franchise serves up hearty cheesesteak sandwiches, Philadelphia style, to order. You can even get a Tastykake, a goodie you won't find many other places in California.

Cafés

The Sunset lends itself to a proliferation of cafes. Among the best of these is the 🅲 **de Young Museum Café** (50 Hagiwara Tea Garden Dr., 415/750-2614, Tues.–Thurs. and Sat.–Sun. 9:30 A.M.–4 P.M., Fri. 9:30 A.M.–8:30 P.M., $10–20). Situated inside the museum on the ground floor, with a generous dining room plus outdoor terrace seating, the Café was created with the same care that went into the de Young's galleries. From the day it opened, the focus has been on local, sustainable food that's often organic but always affordable. Service is cafeteria-style, but the salads and sandwiches in the boxes are made fresh several times each day on the premises. Perhaps most surprising of all is the cheeseburger—you wouldn't think that one of the best cheeseburgers in the City is made at a museum café, but it is. Just be sure to get lunch early, or pick an off hour to eat; the lines at lunchtime can extend for what feels like miles.

Visitors to the Presidio can enjoy a quick bite or a leisurely lunch at the **Acre Café** (1013 Torney Ave., 415/561-2273, Mon.–Fri. 7:30 A.M.–3 P.M., $10). This simple café serves up fresh food for almost (but not quite) reasonable prices. Open for both breakfast and lunch, it's also a good spot to grab a cup of coffee to enjoy with a morning walk along the paths of the Presidio. Just keep in mind that this is a walk-up style café, so don't expect much by way of customer service.

California

One of the most famous restaurant locations on the San Francisco coast is the Cliff House. It's been through a number of different restaurants over the decades. Currently, the high-end eatery inhabiting the famed facade is **Sutro's** (1090 Point Lobos, 415/386-3330, www.cliffhouse .com, daily lunch 11:30 A.M.–3:30 P.M., dinner 5–9:30 P.M., $18–36). The appetizers and entrées here run to seafood in somewhat snooty preparations. Though the cuisine is expensive and fancy, in all honesty it's not the best in the City. What *is* amazing are the views from the floor-to-ceiling windows of Sutro's out over the vast expanse of the Pacific Ocean. These views make Sutro's a perfect spot to enjoy a romantic dinner while watching the sun set into the sea.

Japanese

Sushi restaurants are immensely popular in these residential neighborhoods. **Koo** (408 Irving St., 415/731-7077, www.sushikoo. com, Tues.–Thurs. 5:30–10:30 P.M., Fri.–Sat. 5:30–11 P.M., Sun. 5–10 P.M., $30–50) is a favorite in the Sunset. While sushi purists are happy with the selection of nigiri and sashimi, lovers of fusion and experimentation love the small plates and unusual rolls the chef/owner creates to delight his diners. Complementing the Japanese cuisine is a small but scrumptious list of premium sakes. Only the cheap stuff is served hot, as high-quality sake is always chilled.

Thai

Dining in the Haight? If the touristy cafés don't appeal to you, check out the flavorful dishes at **Siam Lotus Thai Cuisine** (1705 Haight St., 415/933-8031, daily 11 A.M.–10 P.M., $7–13). You'll find a rainbow of curries, pad thai, and all sorts of meat, poultry, and vegetarian dishes in the Thai style. Look to the lunch specials for bargains, and to the Thai iced tea for a lunchtime pick-me-up. Locals enjoy the casually romantic ambiance at Siam Lotus, and visitors will make special trips down to the Haight just to dine here.

Coffee and Tea

One of the prettiest spots in Golden Gate Park is the Japanese Tea Garden. And within the garden, you'll find the famous **Tea House** (Tea Garden Dr. and Martin Luther King Jr. Dr, 415/752-1171, daily 10 A.M. to 4:30 P.M., $10–20), where you can purchase a cup of hot tea to take with you on a soothing walk through the beautiful and inspiring garden.

Information and Services

INFORMATION
Tourist Information

The main San Francisco **Visitor Information Center** (900 Market St., 415/3911-2000, www .onlyinsanfrancisco.com, Mon.–Fri. 9 A.M.– 5 P.M., Sat.–Sun. 9 A.M.–3 P.M., closed Sun. Nov.–Apr.) can help you even before you arrive. See the website for information about attractions and hotels, and to order a visitors' kit. Once you're in town, you can get a "San Francisco Book" at the Market Street location, as well as the usual brochures and a few useful coupons.

English not your first language? You'll find materials at the Visitor Information Center in 12 different languages, as well as multilingual staff.

Media and Communications

The major daily newspaper in San Francisco is the *San Francisco Chronicle* (www.sfgate .com). With an appropriately liberal slant on the national political news, a free website, and separate food and wine sections, it's the right paper for its city.

San Francisco also has about a zillion alternative

papers, free at newsstands all over town. The *San Francisco Bay Guardian* (www.sfbg.com) is one of the best known and best reputed of these. The alternative rags often have the best up-to-date entertainment information available, so if you're looking for nighttime fun, be sure to pick one up while you're out and about.

Need the **Internet?** You got it! This is San Francisco, after all. Most hotels have Internet access of some kind, the jillion Starbucks locations (sometimes two in the same block) often have Wi-Fi for a fee, and plenty of other restaurants and cafés also make it easy to get online. You can even try war-hacking if you're brave enough.

SERVICES
Banks and Post Offices
Just about every **bank** on earth seems to have a branch in San Francisco. **ATMs** abound, especially in well-traveled areas like Fisherman's Wharf and Union Square. Ask at your hotel or restaurant for the location of the nearest branch or ATM.

Post offices and mailing centers are common in San Francisco; again, ask your concierge or desk clerk for the facility nearest to your hotel. The **main post office** (1300 Evans Ave., 415/550-5501) boasts of its short lines and friendly(!) employees.

Luggage and Laundry
If your hotel doesn't have valet service, you can take your dirty linen down to a coin laundry. As with most cities, take care—especially if you're a woman alone. Don't go after dark if you can help it, and bring a buddy if possible. My favorite laundry sits in Hayes Valley. It's the **Don't Call It Frisco Laundromat** (609 Hayes St., 415/626-1835, daily until 9 P.M.). It's clean and it's in a good, centrally located neighborhood, and the name says it all.

If you want to store your bags for a short time to make exploring easier, you can do so through the **Airport Travel Agency** (650/877-0422, daily 7 A.M.–11 P.M., no reservations necessary) on the Departures/Ticketing Level of the International Terminal at SFO, near Gates G91–G102. Fees vary by size of object stored, from $3 for a purse to $6–10 for a suitcase, up to $15 for surfboards or bicycles. All rates are for 24 hours storage.

Medical Services
The **San Francisco Police Department** (766 Vallejo St., 415/315-2400) is headquartered in Chinatown, on Vallejo Street between Powell and Stockton.

San Francisco boasts a large number of full-service hospitals. The **UCSF Medical Center** (1600 Divisadero, 415/567-6600) is world renowned for its research and advances in cancer treatments and other important medical breakthroughs. People come from all over the world to be treated here. The main hospital sits at the corner of Divisadero and Geary, a mile or three west of Union Square. Right downtown, **St. Francis Memorial Hospital** (900 Hyde St., 415/353-6000, www.saintfrancismemorial.org) at the corner of Hyde and Bush has an emergency department.

Getting There and Around

GETTING THERE
Air
The **San Francisco International Airport** (800/435-9736, www.flysfo.com) doesn't sit within the City of San Francisco. SFO is actually about 13 miles south in the town of Milbrae, right on the Bay. You can easily get a taxi or other ground transportation into the heart of the City from the airport. Both CalTrain and BART are accessible from SFO, and Some San Francisco hotels offer complimentary shuttles from the airport as well. You can also rent a car here.

As one of the 30 busiest airports in the world, SFO has long check-in and security lines much of the time, and dreadful overcrowding

WALKING TOURS

The best way to see San Francisco is to get out and take a walk. You can find dozens of companies offering walking tours of different parts of the City. Here are a few of the best and most interesting:

One of the most popular walking tour companies in the city is **Foot** (800/979-3370, www.foottours.com, $30-45/person). Foot was founded by stand up comedian Robert Mac, and hires comics to act as guides for their many different tours around San Francisco. If you're a brand-new visitor to the City, pick the two-hour *San Francisco in a Nutshell* tour for a funny look at the basics of San Francisco landmarks and history, or the three-hour *Whole Shebang*, a comprehensive if speedy look at Chinatown, Nob Hill, and North Beach. For visitors who are back for the second or third time, check out the more in-depth neighborhood tours that take in Chinatown, the Castro, or the Haight. You can even hit *Nude, Lewd, and Crude*, a look at the rise of 18-and-up entertainment in North Beach. Tour departure points vary, so check the website for more information about your specific tour and about packages of more than one tour in a day or two.

San Francisco is famous for its incredibly steep hills. Logic suggests that residents would build stairways to make getting to their homes and businesses easier. And so it went. Today, some of the best and most beautiful walks in the City run up and down these stairways. A great guide to these walks is *Stairway Walks in San Francisco* (http://wilderness-press.com/book148.htm); with this book, you can plan routes through beautiful residential neighborhoods filled with lush gardens and attractive vintage homes. At the tops of the hills you'll be rewarded for your efforts with amazing views out over the City – one of the big reasons residents are willing to deal with all those steps and slopes. Just be aware that you'll need to be in reasonably good shape to tackle the stair walks.

For an inside look at the culinary delights of Chinatown, sign up for a spot on **I Can't Believe I Ate My Way Through Chinatown** (212/209-3370, www.wokwiz.com, $80/person). This three-hour bonanza will take you first

on major travel holidays. On a normal day, plan to arrive at the airport about two hours before your domestic flight, or three hours before an international flight.

Train

Amtrak does not run directly into San Francisco. You can ride into San Jose, Oakland, or Emeryville, then take a connecting bus into the City. See the *San Jose* section of this chapter for more information about Amtrak service into the Bay Area.

Bus

Greyhound (www.greyhound.com) offers bus service to San Francisco from all over the country. Buses usually come in to the **Transbay Terminal** (435 Mission St., 415/495-1569, station open 5:30 A.M.–1 A.M., ticket window open 5:30 A.M.–midnight).

Car

Certainly you can drive into San Francisco. All major highways funnel onto the City. The Bay Bridge links I-80 from the east and the Golden Gate connects Highway 1 from the north. From the south, U.S. 101 and I-280 snake up the Peninsula and into the City. Be sure to get a detailed map and good directions to drive into San Francisco—the freeway interchanges, especially surrounding the east side of the Bay Bridge, can be confusing.

GETTING AROUND
Car

A car of your own is not necessarily a boon in San Francisco. The hills are daunting, traffic is excruciating, and parking prices are absurd. If you plan to spend all of your time in the City, consider dispensing with a car and using cabs and public transit options.

for a classic Chinese breakfast, then out into the streets of Chinatown for a narrated tour around Chinatown's food markets, apothecaries, and tea shops. You'll finish up with lunch at one of Chef Shirley's favorite hole-in-the-wall dim sum places. For folks who just want the tour and lunch, or the tour alone, check out the standard Wok Wiz Daily Tour ($40/person with lunch, $30/person tour only).

To check out another side of Chinatown, take the **Chinatown Ghost Tour** (877/887-3373, www.sfchinatownghosttours.com, Fri.-Sat. 7:30 P.M., adults $24, children $16, tour lasts 1.5 hours). It's hard to find a neighborhood with a richer history rife with ghost stories than San Francisco's Chinatown. The whole thing burned down more than a century ago, and it was rebuilt in exactly the same spot, complete with countless narrow alleyways. This tour will take you into these alleys after the sun sets, when the spirits are said to appear on the streets. You'll start out at Kan's Restaurant (708 Grant Ave.) and follow your loquacious guide along the avenues and side streets of Chinatown. As you stroll, your guide will tell you the sto-

ries of the neighborhood spirits, spooks, and ancestors. The curious get to learn about the deities worshipped by devout Chinese to this day, along with the folklore that permeates what was until recently a closed and secretive culture. This information delights all walkers, whether or not they actually get to see one of the legendary spirits.

Can't get enough of the spooky side of San Francisco? Check out a walking tour that's a favorite even with the locals: the **San Francisco Vampire Tour** (866/424-8836, www .sfvampiretour.com, Fri.-Sat. 8 P.M., adults $20, children $15). You'll take a two-hour walk around some of the City sites rich with history, and learn both about that history and some charming stories about the vampires' role in the creation and culture of the City. Guide Mina Harker is something of a vamp herself – at least she dresses the part. In fact, goth dress is encouraged for participants in the tour, so break out your black lace, your top hat, and your white makeup and become part of the show! This walking tour sticks mostly to the sights and famous hotels of Nob Hill.

Driving in San Francisco can be even more confusing. Like most major metropolitan centers, one-way streets, alleys, streetcars, taxis, bicycles, and pedestrians all provide impediments to navigation. Touring around the City to see the sights means traffic jams filled with workers on weekdays and tourists on weekends. It means negotiating the legendary steep hills without crashing into the cars behind and in front of you. And after all that, you come to the worst part....

To call parking in San Francisco a nightmare is to insult nightmares. Every available scrap of land that can be built on has been built on, with little left over to create parking for the zillions of cars that pass through on a daily basis. Parking a car in San Francisco can easily cost $50 per day or more. Street parking spots are as rare as unicorns, and often require permits (which visitors as a rule cannot obtain,

Scooters are popular with City residents.

unless they're friends of Danielle Steel). Lots and garages fill up quickly, especially during special events.

If you can avoid it, don't bring a car into the City. Start your journey here and rent a car when you're ready to leave San Francisco, or turn your rental in early if the City is your last stop.

But if you absolutely must have your car with you, try to get a room at a hotel with a parking lot and either free parking or a parking package for the length of your stay.

All the major car rental agencies have a presence at SFO. In addition, if you're staying at a big hotel, check at the desk to see if they offer a car rental service. Rates tend to run $90–160 per day (including most taxes and fees), with discounts for full-week and longer rentals.

Muni

The local opinion of the Muni (www.sfmta.com, adults $1.50 basic, $7 special event) light rail system isn't printable in guidebooks. The truth is, Muni can get you where you want to go in San Francisco, so long as time isn't a concern. A variety of lines snake through the City—those that go down to Fisherman's Wharf use vintage streetcars to heighten the fun for the tourists. See the website for a route map, ticket information, and (ha, ha, ha) schedules.

To buy tickets, use one of the vending machines that sit near some stops. Muni ticket machines sit outside of the CalTrain station. See the website for more information about purchasing tickets.

Muni also runs the bus lines, which require the same fares and can be slightly more reliable than the trains and go all over the City. Muni's website can get you to information about bus routes, schedules, and fares.

BART

Bay Area Rapid Transit, or BART (www.bart.gov, fares vary $3–10/one-way) to locals, is the Bay Area's late-coming answer to major metropolitan underground railways like Chicago's L-train and New York's subway system. Sadly, there's only one arterial line

The N Judah Muni line runs from Ocean Beach to downtown San Francisco.

through the City. However, service directly from San Francisco International Airport into the City now runs daily, as does service to Oakland International Airport, the cities of Oakland and Berkeley, plus many other East Bay destinations. BART connects to the CalTrain system and SFO in Milbrae. See the website for route maps, schedules (BART usually runs on time), and fare information.

To buy tickets, use the vending machines found in every BART station. If you plan to ride more than once, you can "add money" to a single ticket. Then keep that ticket and reuse it for each ride.

CalTrain

This traditional commuter rail line runs along the Peninsula into Silicon Valley, from San Francisco to San Jose with limited continuing service to Gilroy. CalTrain (www.caltrain .com, fares vary $2.25–11/one-way) "Baby Bullet" trains can get you from San Jose to San Francisco in under an hour during commuter hours. Extra trains are often added for San Francisco Giants, San Francisco 49ers, and San Jose Sharks games.

You must purchase a ticket in advance at the vending machines in all stations, or get your 10-ride card stamped before you board a train. The San Francisco main CalTrain station sits at the corner of 4th Street and King Street, within walking distance of AT&T Park and Moscone Center.

Taxis

You'll find plenty of taxis scooting around all the major tourist areas of the City. Feel free to wave one down or ask your hotel to call you a cab. If you need to call a cab yourself, try **City Wide Dispatch** (415/920-0700).

North Bay

MARIN HEADLANDS

Over the Golden Gate Bridge and through the Rainbow Tunnels, to Marin County we go! The Marin Headlands begins at the north side of the Golden Gate and encompass a wide swath of virgin wilderness, former military land, and an historic lighthouse.

Visitors Center

A great place to start your exploration of the Marin Headlands is at the visitors center (Field Rd. and Bunker Rd., 415/331-1540, daily 9:30 A.M.–4:30 P.M.), located in the old chapel on Fort Barry. The rangers here can give you the current lowdown on the best trails, beaches, and campgrounds in the Headlands.

Point Bonita Lighthouse (415/331-1540, www.nps.gov/goga/pobo.htm, Sat.–Mon. 12:30 P.M.–3:30 P.M.) has been protecting the Headlands for over 150 years. It remains an active light station to this day. You need some dedication to visit Point Bonita, since it's only open a few days each week and there's no direct access by car. A half-mile trail with steep sections leads from the trailhead on Field Road. Along the way, you'll pass through a handmade tunnel chiseled from the hard rock by the original builders of the lighthouse, then over the bridge that leads to the building proper. Point Bonita was the third lighthouse built on the West Coast and is now the last manned lighthouse in California. Today, the squat hexagonal building shelters automatic lights, horns, and signals. For a special treat, call the lighthouse to book a spot on a romantic full-moon tour.

Muir Beach

Few coves on the California coast can boast as much beauty as Muir Beach (just south of the town of Muir Beach, www.nps.gov/goga, daily sunrise–sunset). From the overlook above Highway 1 to the edge of the ocean beyond the dunes, Muir Beach is a haven for both wildlife and beachcombers. In the wintertime, beachgoers bundle up against the chill and walk the

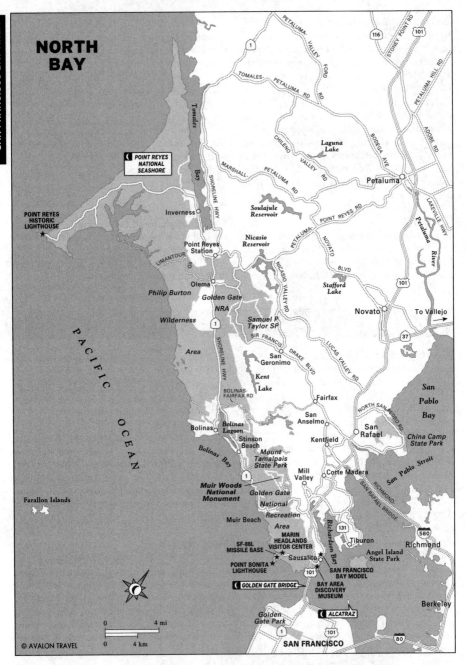

NORTH BAY

POINT REYES
NATIONAL
SEASHORE

POINT REYES
HISTORIC
LIGHTHOUSE

Inverness

Point Reyes
Station

Olema

Philip Burton

Golden Gate
NRA

Wilderness

Samuel P.
Taylor SP

Area

San
Geronimo

Kent
Lake

BOLINAS-
FAIRFAX RD

Fairfax

Bolinas

Bolinas
Lagoon

San
Anselmo

Stinson
Beach

Kentfield

Mount
Tamalpais
State Park

Muir Woods
National
Monument

Golden Gate
National

Muir Beach

Recreation

Area

MARIN
HEADLANDS
VISITOR CENTER

SF-88L
MISSILE BASE

Sausalito

POINT BONITA
LIGHTHOUSE

SAN FRANCISCO
BAY MODEL

GOLDEN GATE BRIDGE

BAY AREA
DISCOVERY
MUSEUM

Golden
Gate Park

ALCATRAZ

SAN FRANCISCO

PACIFIC

OCEAN

Farallon Islands

Tomales
Bay

SHORELINE HWY

LIMANTOUR RD

SHORELINE HWY

SIR FRANCIS DRAKE BLVD

Bolinas Bay

Mill
Valley

Corte Madera

Richardson Bay

Tiburon

Angel Island
State Park

131

Laguna
Lake

CHILENO VALLEY RD

MARSHALL PETALUMA RD

PETALUMA RD

TOMALES PETALUMA FORD RD

PETALUMA VALLEY FORD RD

Soulajule
Reservoir

Nicasio
Reservoir

POINT REYES RD

PETALUMA RD

NOVATO BLVD

NICASIO VALLEY RD

Stafford
Lake

LUCAS VALLEY RD

NORTH SAN PEDRO RD

San
Rafael

China Camp
State Park

San Pablo Strait

RICHMOND-SAN RAFAEL BRIDGE

Petaluma

Novato

To Vallejo

San
Pablo
Bay

Richmond

Berkeley

116

101

STONEY POINT RD

PETALUMA HILL RD

ADOBE RD

BODEGA AVE

LAKEVILLE HWY

Petaluma
River

101

37

580

80

© AVALON TRAVEL

0   4 mi

0   4 km

sands of the cove or along the many trails that spread out from the beach. If you're lucky, you might find a Monterey pine tree filled with sleepy monarch butterflies, here to overwinter before making their long migration back north in the spring. Springtime brings rare rays of sunshine to Muir Cove, and as the air grows (a little bit) warmer in summer, the north end of the cove attracts another breed of beach life: nudists. If the clothing-optional California lifestyle makes you uncomfortable, stick to the south side, the brackish Redwood Creek lagoon, and the wind-swept picnic grounds.

SF-88L Missile Base

Military history buffs jump at the chance to tour a restored Cold War-era Nike missile base. The lyrically named SF-88L (Field Rd. past the Headlands visitors center, 415/331-1453, www .nps.gov/goga/nike-missile-site.htm, Wed.–Fri. 12:30 P.M.–3:30 P.M. and 1st Sat. each month, fees) is the only such restored Nike base in the United States. Volunteers continue the restoration and lead tours every half-hour at the base, which is overseen by the Golden Gate National Recreation Area. On the tour, you'll get to see the fueling area, the testing and assembly building, and even take a ride on the missile elevator down into the pits that once stored missiles created to defend the United States from the Soviet Union. Because restoration work continues endlessly, the tour changes as new areas become available to visitors.

Hiking

Folks come from all over the world to hike the trails that thread through the Marin Headlands. The landscape is some of the most beautiful in the state. One of the most popular (and crowded, especially on summer weekends) places to start is the **Tennessee Valley Trailhead** (end of Tennessee Valley Rd., portable toilets, no water). A wealth of trails spring from this major trailhead. A quicker hike from the trailhead can take you out to the **Haypress Campground** (about 1.5 mi, moderate), which has picnic tables and pretty views. For a nice long hike, take the **Old Springs Trail** (2 mi)

down to the **Wolf Ridge Trail** (0.7 mi) heading west, then across to the **Valley Trail** (2 mi) back north to the trailhead.

The **Rodeo Beach Trailhead** (end of Bunker Rd., running water, flush toilets, paved parking lot) offers access to Point Bonita, loop and one-way trails, and of course Rodeo Beach. An easy spot to get to, Rodeo Beach draws many tourists on summer weekends—expect not to be alone on the beach or the trails, or even in the water. Locals come out to surf at Rodeo when the break is going, while beachcombers watch from the shore. An easy walk from this trailhead is the **Lagoon Trail** (0.5 mi, easy), which gives bird-watchers an eagle's-eye view of the egrets, pelicans, and other seabirds that call the shelter of the Rodeo lagoon home. For a longer hike, you can take the **Miwok Trail** (1.8 mi) north, catch the **Wolf Ridge Trail** (2.3 mi) heading west, then pick up the **California Coastal Trail** (approx. 2 mi) heading back south past the Marine Mammal Center toward the road and the parking lots.

Naturally, hardcore hikers doing a serious

© LANCE SCOTT

the Marin coastline

survey of the **California Coastal Trail** can get in a good chunk of it here at the Headlands. Head north from Rodeo Beach and meander through the hills, then down closer to the beach past Tennessee Valley at Pirate's Cove. This chunk of the trail terminates at Muir Beach.

For more information about hiking and biking trails, visit the Golden Gate National Recreation Area online at www.nps.gov/goga.

Biking

If you prefer two wheels to two feet, you'll find the road and trail biking in the Marin Headlands both plentiful and spectacular. From the Tennessee Valley Trailhead, you'll find plenty of multi-use trails designated for bikers as well as hikers. The **Valley Trail** (4 mi round-trip) takes you down the Tennessee Valley and all the way out to Tennessee Beach. A longer ride runs up the **Miwok Trail** (2 mi) northward. Turn southwest onto the **Coyote Ridge Trail** (0.9 mi), then catch the **Coastal Fire Road** (2 mi) the rest of the way west to Muir Beach. Another fun ride leads from just off U.S. 101 at the Rodeo Avenue exit. Park your car on the side of Rodeo Avenue, then bike down the **Bobcat Trail** (2.5 mi) straight through the Headlands to the **Miwok Trail** for just 0.5 mile, and you'll find yourself out at Rodeo Beach.

Need to rent a bike for your travels? In San Francisco, **Bike and Roll** (899 Columbus Ave., 415/771-8735, www.bikerental.com, daily 8 A.M.–10 P.M. in summer, until 6 P.M. in winter) offers off-road biking tours of the Marin Headlands, plus bike rentals that let you go wherever the spirit moves you.

Accommodations

Lodging options are fairly limited in the Marin Headlands. Options run toward hostels and campgrounds, along with one lonely posh inn. Many luxury-minded travelers choose to stay in Tiburon or Sausalito, while budget-motel seekers head for San Rafael. While camping might sound appealing, it requires some planning. It can be foggy, cold, and windy in July and August (or any other month) in Marin. So bring your warm camping gear if you plan to seek out one of the precious few campsites in the Marin Headlands.

The most popular and biggest campground in the region is **Kirby Cove** (877/444-6777, www.recreation.gov, reservations required). Secluded and shaded campsites provide a beautiful respite from the busy world. Do make your reservations well in advance for summer weekends, since this popular campground fills up fast.

The **Bicentennial Campground** (Battery Wallace parking lot, 415/331-1540) boasts a whopping three campsites, each easily accessible from the parking lot. Each site can accommodate two people maximum, and there's no water or fires allowed on-site. A nearby picnic area has barbecue grills that campers can use to cook themselves a nice hot dinner. On the opposite end of the accessibility spectrum, you'll find the **Hawk Campground** (415/331-1540). The three-site (four people per) campground sits a two-mile hike up from the Tennessee Valley trailhead. Your reward for the work of packing in all your gear and water is a near-solitary camping experience that lets you kick back and get to know the wilderness surrounding you. Amenities include chemical toilets, but no water or fires.

Travelers who want budget accommodations indoors often choose the **Marin Headlands Hostel** (Fort Barry Bldg. 941, 415/331-2777, www.norcalhostels.org/marin, $22 dorm bed, $60 private room). You'll find full kitchen facilities, Internet access, laundry rooms, and a rec room—all the amenities you'd expect from a high-end U.S. hotel. Surprisingly cozy and romantic, the hostel is sheltered in the turn of the (last) century buildings of Fort Barry, creating a unique atmosphere. And of course, with the Headlands right outside your door and 24-hour access to all registered guests, no visitor lacks in activities or exploration opportunities here.

One fine Marin lodging rests inside **The Pelican Inn** (10 Pacific Way, Muir Beach, 415/383-6000, www.pelicaninn.com, $215). Inside the Tudor structure, the guest room decor continues the historic ambiance, with big beam construction, canopy beds, and historic portrait prints. The seven mostly small rooms each come with private bathrooms and a full English-style breakfast, but no televisions or telephones. The Pelican Inn is a perfect spot to unplug, disconnect, and truly get away from it all.

Food

Few restaurants grace the wilderness and abandoned forts of the Marin Headlands. Never fear: The fine dining and fast food of Sausalito and Tiburon are a short drive away. You can also pick up supplies for camping or hostel cooking in either of these towns.

In addition to quaint bedchambers, you can get hearty food at **The Pelican Inn** (daily lunch 11:30 A.M.–3 P.M., dinner 5:30–9 P.M., $15–30). Dark wood and a long trestle table give the proper Old English feeling to the dimly lit dining room. The cuisine brings home the flavors of Merry Old England, with dishes like beef wellington and shepherd's pie,

and sherry trifle and bread pudding for dessert. Though breakfast is served only to overnight guests, lunch and dinner are open to anyone who passes by. True fans of the Isles will round off their meal with a pint of stout.

SAUSALITO AND TIBURON

Once a plain-Jane fishing town, Tiburon now supports some of the most expensive waterfront real estate in the world. The small downtown area that backs onto the marina is popular with the young and affluent crowd as well as the longtime yacht owners.

The affluent town of Sausalito wraps around the north end of the San Francisco Bay. The main drag runs along the shore, and the concrete boardwalk is perfect for strolling and biking. A former industrial fishing town, Sausalito still has a few old cannery buildings and plenty of docks, most now lined with pleasure boats.

Angel Island State Park

Angel Island has a long history, beginning with regular visits (though no permanent

© LANCE SCOTT

downtown Tiburon

settlements) by the Coastal Miwok tribe. The Northern U.S. army created a fort on the island in anticipation of Confederate sea attacks from the Pacific. Though those attacks never came, the army maintained a base. Today, many 19th-century army buildings remain. You can see them on the tram tour ($13.50, 1 hour), walking, or on a docent-led segway tour ($65 per person). Later, the Army built a Nike missile base on the island to protect strategically important San Francisco from possible Soviet attacks. The missile base is not open to the public, but can be seen from roads and trails.

Not all the history of Angel Island brings pride to the state of California. The West Coast's answer to Ellis Island in the early 20th century, Angel Island served as an immigration station for incoming ships, and a concentration camp for the flood of Chinese attempting to escape the collapse of their homeland. While Europeans were waved through with little more than a head-lice check, the Chinese were herded into barracks while government officials scrutinized their papers. After months and

sometimes years of waiting, many were shipped back to China. Today, poetry lines the walls of the barracks, expressing the despair of the immigrants who had hoped for a better life and found little more than prison. Docent-led tours show this poetry and the buildings of the camps.

Angel Island is a major destination for hikers both casual and serious. The island-wide park offers kayaking, swimming, hiking, and road and mountain biking. Trails of varying difficulty levels crisscross the island, creating fun for hikers and bikers alike. Adventurous trekkers can scale Mount Livermore via either the **North Ridge Trail** or the **Sunset Trail.** Each runs about 4.5 miles round-trip for a moderate, reasonably steep hike. But stopping at the top for a rest and some of the gorgeous Bay views hardly feels like a chore or a defeat. For the best experience, make a loop of your trip, taking one trail up and the other one back down the mountain. If you're up for a long paved-road hike, take the **Perimeter Road** (5 mi, moderate) all the way around the island.

© LANCE SCOTT

barracks at Angel Island State Park

Angel Island is located in the middle of San Franicsco Bay. To get there, you must either boat yourself in or take one of the ferries that services the island. The harbor at Tiburon is the easiest place from which to access Angel Island State Park (415/435-1915, www.parks.ca.gov, daily 8 A.M.–sunset, prices vary by ferry company). The private **Angel Island-Tiburon Ferry** (21 Main St., Tiburon, 415/435-2131, www.angelislandferry.com, $13.50 adults, $11.50 children, $1 bikes, no advance ticket sales) can get you out to the island in about 10 minutes and runs several times a day. You can also explore the **Blue and Gold Fleet** (415/703-8200, www.blueandgoldfleet.com), which runs out to Angel Island from Oakland/Alameda and San Francisco.

Ferries have plenty of room for you to bring your own bike, or you can rent one at the main visitors' area for $10 per hour or $35 per day. Grab a map from the gift shop. Not all trails are open to bikes, but those that are include the easy five-mile, paved Perimeter Road around the island, which is perfect for newcomers.

Bay Area Discovery Museum

The Bay Area Discovery Museum (557 McReynolds Rd., Sausalito, 415/339-3900, www.baykidsmuseum.org, Tues.–Fri. 9 A.M.–4 P.M., Sat.–Sun. 10 A.M.–5 P.M., $10 adults, $8 children) offers kids of all ages a chance to explore the world they live in. The focus definitely rests on the younger set here; most of the permanent exhibits are geared toward small children, with lots of interactive components and places to play. Kids can check out easy-to-understand displays that describe the natural world, plus lots of Bay Area–specific exhibits. The Discovery Museum also boasts a theater and a café.

San Francisco Bay Model

One of the odder attractions you'll find in the North Bay is the an Francisco Bay Model (2100 Bridgeway, Sausalito, 415/332-3871, www.spn.usace.army.mil/bmvc, summer Tues.–Fri. 9 A.M.–4 P.M., Sat.–Sun. 10 P.M.–5 P.M., call for hours in fall, winter, and spring). Here you can see a scale model of the way the Bay works, complete with currents and tides. Why would you want to see this? Scientist and engineering types love to see how the waters of the bay really move and work. For the rest of us...aw heck, why not?

Accommodations

Sausalito and Tiburon together make up some of the swankest, most expensive real estate in the United States. If you're staying as a guest, you'll absorb a little bit of that expense, but a few bargains hide here and there.

SAUSALITO

The **The Gables Inn** (62 Princess St., Sausalito, 415/289-1100, www.gablesinnsausalito.com, $200) inn was opened in 1869 and is the oldest B&B in the area. Each of the nine rooms is appointed in tasteful earth tones, with white linens and bountiful bathrooms. Though this inn honors its long history, it has also kept up with the times, adding cable televisions and Internet access. Genial innkeepers serve a buffet breakfast (available for a couple of hours) each morning and host a wine and cheese soiree each evening.

With a checkered history dating back to 1915, the **Hotel Sausalito** (16 El Portal, Sausalito, 888/442-0700, www.hotelsausalito.com, $178–325) may once have been a speakeasy, a bordello, and a home for the writers and artists of the beat generation. Today, this tiny boutique hotel, with its yellow walls and locally built furnishings, evokes the Mediterranean coast. Sink into your cozy room after a day spent walking or biking along the water and a scrumptious dinner out.

Then there's the **Casa Madrona Hotel and Spa** (801 Bridgeway, Sausalito, 800/288-0502, www.casamadrona.com, $325–575). This sprawling collection of structures, built up the side of Sausalito's hill over the course of 100 years, houses contemporary luxury hotel rooms and suites that satisfy even the pickiest celebrity guest. Poggio, the on-site restaurant, serves award-winning Italian food, and the full service spa pampers guests with a full menu of body and salon treatments. If you're treating yourself to a room at Casa Madrona, be sure to ask for one with a view overlooking the Bay or the harbor!

For a taste of the life of the richest residents of the area, stay at Sausalito's **Inn Above Tide** (30 El Portal, Sausalito, 800/893-8433, www.innabovetide.com, $350). Billed as the only hotel in the Bay Area that's actually *on* the Bay, the inn sits over the edge of the water looking out over the San Francisco skyline. Most rooms have private decks that let guests take advantage of the sublime views (well, except when it's foggy). Inside the rooms, the appointments look like something you'd find in an upscale home rather than a hotel. Guests love the rooms with oversized bathtubs set by windows to take advantage of the Bay views. From the hotel, you can walk downtown to enjoy the shops, spas, and restaurants of Sausalito.

TIBURON

The lovely **Waters Edge Hotel** (25 Main St., Tiburon, 415/789-5999, www.marinhotels.com, $310–350) is a boutique lodging that lives up to its name, backing on to the marina and docks. You can stumble right out of your room, onto the dock, and over to the Angel Island ferry. Inside, you'll love the featherbeds, cushy robes, and breakfast delivered to your room each morning. Also wonderfully close to the water and attractions of downtown Tiburon, the **Lodge at Tiburon** (1651 Tiburon Blvd., Tiburon, 415/435-3133, www.thelodgeattiburon.com, $285–500) offers the comforts and conveniences of a larger hotel while providing the personal attention and atmosphere of a boutique inn. All the guest rooms are soothing and pretty, but for a special treat book a Spa Room with a huge raised whirlpool tub set in an alcove overlooking the water. Have dinner or a drink at the attached Three Degrees Restaurant and Bar in the evening, or take a walk downtown to look into the shops.

Food
SAUSALITO

If you're jonesing for some Chinese food,

go to **Tommy's Wok Chinese Cuisine** (3001 Bridgeway, Sausalito, 415/332-5818, http://tommyswok.com, Mon.–Thurs. 11:30 A.M.–9:30, Fri.–Sat. 11:30 A.M.–10 P.M., Sun. 4–9:30 P.M., $10–20). Unlike a typical Chinese restaurant, Tommy's has gotten into the swing of California cuisine fashions. This includes organic free-range chicken, organic tofu, and a heavy emphasis on fresh vegetables—even in the meat dishes. Don't expect to find too many of your sweet syrupy favorites here. Instead, take a chance on some tasty broccoli or asparagus.

It's hard to get away from the sea when you're visiting Sausalito. So it's logical that many visitors find themselves wanting a seafood meal to accompany their experience. **Fish** (350 Harbor Dr., Sausalito, 415/331-3474, www.331fish.com, daily 11:30 A.M.–4:30 P.M., 5:30–8:30 P.M., $10–25) can hook you up with some of the best sustainable seafood in the North Bay. No farmed salmon, overfished swordfish, or other more-harm-than-good seafood makes its way into the kitchen. Fresh wild fish prepared perfectly using a California-style mix of ethnic cooking techniques results in amazing dishes you can't find anywhere else, not even in the Bay Area.

TIBURON

With its marina ferrying folks to Angel Island and the City, expect many tourist-friendly restaurants in downtown Tiburon. For a surprisingly good Italian meal, head for **Servino** (9 Main St., Tiburon, 415/435-2676, www.bestservino.com, $13–25) on the waterfront. A huge outdoor patio offers diners stunning views of the Bay, Angel Island, and the San Francisco cityscape. It can get chilly in the evening, though, so if you hate the cold, get a table inside instead. Service is as warm and friendly as the classic Italian cuisine. A full bar caters to locals and visitors alike. The menu runs to hearty, somewhat Americanized Italian dishes. You can eat yourself senseless by trying all the courses, or choose just an entrée or a "primi" to keep your meal a bit lighter. The full bar makes a great place to sit should you need to

© LANCE SCOTT

The outdoor patio at Servino offers diners stunning views.

wait for a table, and Servino's hosts live music on Thursday and Friday nights.

Rooney's (38 Main St., Tiburon, 415/435-1911, lunch Mon.–Thurs. 11:30 A.M.–3:30 P.M., Fri.–Sun. 11:30 A.M.–4 P.M., dinner Wed.–Thurs. and Sun. 5:30–9 P.M., Fri.–Sat. 5:30–9:30 P.M.) is a local favorite, serving French bistro fare in a semi-casual, semi-subterranean dining room. While the food is universally admired at Rooney's, unfortunately it seems that good service is a privilege reserved exclusively for locals. Don't expect much in the way of promptness or friendliness here. Though the overgrown outdoor patio is pretty, it can attract flies and other unwelcome visitors to your table. Reservations are recommended, especially for weekend dinners.

Practicalities

Sausalito lies just over the Golden Gate Bridge from San Francisco and is easily accessible on side roads on a bicycle or on U.S. 101 in a car. Once you're in town, navigating in a car can be a challenge, as the narrow oceanfront main road gets super-crowded on weekends. If you can, park your car and walk around town, both for your own comfort and to do your part to minimize traffic congestion. Street parking is mostly by meter.

Tiburon lies a few exits farther up U.S. 101. It's a bit easier to drive around and find parking here. To park your car still costs a pretty penny, but it's worth it to explore Main Street on foot.

Internet access is widely available in both Sausalito and Tiburon. Your hotel may have wireless, and if you ask locally you'll be able to locate the nearest Internet café. The Sausalito post office sits at 150 Harbor Drive. In Tiburon, you'll find one at 6 Beach Road. Looking for a newspaper? For something even more local than the *Chronicle,* pick up a copy of the *Marin Independent Journal* (www.marinij.com).

MUIR WOODS

The **Muir Woods National Monument** (Panoramic Hwy. off Hwy. 1, 415/388-2596, www.visitmuirwoods.com, www.nps.gov/goga, daily 8 A.M.–sunset, $5) comprises acres of staggeringly beautiful redwood forest nestled in Marin. If you're visiting on a holiday or a summer weekend, get to the Muir Woods parking areas early—they fill up and afternoon hopefuls often cannot find a spot. Lit signs on U.S. 101 will alert you to parking status at the main parking lot. To avoid all the traffic hassle, check the NPS website for information about the Muir Woods Shuttle.

Visitors Center

The Muir Woods Visitors Center (1 Muir Woods Rd., follow the signs from the Stinson Beach exit off Hwy. 1) abut the main parking area and marked the entrance to Muir Woods. In addition to the ranger station, where you can get maps, information, and advice about hiking, you'll also find a few amenities. The visitors center includes a bookstore and a café where you can purchase souvenirs and sustenance. If you're new to Muir Woods, the visitors center is a great place to begin your exploration.

Hiking

The first hike you should take if you're a first-time visitor is the **Main Trail Loop** (1 mi, easy). Leading right from the visitors center on an easy and flat walk through the beautiful Muir Woods, this trail has its own leaflet (pick one up at the visitors center) and numbers along the trail to help describe the forest-dwellers that visitors can see. You'll cross from one side to the other of the Redwood Creek on cute pedestrian bridges. This trail is wheelchair- and stroller-accessible.

The **Fern Creek Trail** (3 mi, moderate) follows—you guessed it—Fern Creek down into the depths of the redwood forest. Along the way you'll see the much-lauded Kent Tree, a 220-foot Douglas fir. (William Kent donated the whole of Muir Woods to the government for a park, and all he got was this lousy fir tree.) At the Alice Eastwood Camp, you can get a nice drink of water, use the restrooms, and even have a picnic in this developed area. You'll follow the old railroad grade back to your starting place.

The **Ocean View Trail** (5.2 mi, difficult) is a bit of a misnomer—you can't see too much of

the ocean from this trail anymore. Once upon a time, a big fire cleared the view to the Pacific from this path, but the trees have since grown back and blocked the view again. But if you take Ocean View out to the Redwood Trail, you'll get one or two quick peaks of the ocean before you reach the Tourist Club for a rest and some pretty views. At the Tourist Club, ignore the sign pointing back to Muir Woods and instead take the much safer Sun Trail back to catch the Dipsea Trail which leads you into central Muir Woods.

Muir Woods boasts many lovely trails that crisscross the gorgeous redwood forests. Check the websites for more trails and loop hikes.

MOUNT TAMALPAIS

If you want to see the whole Bay Area in a single day, go to **Mount Tamalpais State Park** (801 Panoramic Hwy., Mill Valley, www.parks.ca.gov). Always called Mount Tam by locals, this park boasts views of all nine counties of the greater San Francisco Bay Area—from Mount. St. Helena in Napa down to San Jose and across to Mount Diablo and the East Bay. The Pacific Ocean peeks from around the corner of the western Peninsula, and on a clear day you can just make out the foothills of the Sierra Nevada mountains to the east. Ample parking, interpretive walks, and friendly rangers make a visit to Mount Tam a hit even for less outdoorsy travelers.

Once upon a time, well-heeled visitors could take a scenic train ride up to and across Mount Tam. Today, you'll probably want to drive up to one of the parking lots from which you can explore the trails. Take Highway 1 to the Stinson Beach exit, then follow the (fairly good) signs up the mountain.

Hiking

Up on Mount Tam, you can try anything from a leisurely 30-minute interpretive stroll up to a strenuous hike up and down one of the many deep ravines. Mount Tam's hiking areas divide into three major sections: the East Peak, the Pantoll area, and the Rock Springs area. Each of these regions offers a number of beautiful trails, so you'll want to grab a map from the visitors center or online to get a sense of the mountain and its hikes.

At the top of the paved road up to the East Peak, you'll find a small visitors center that's open on weekends. The clearing also shelters a small refreshment stand that's open on weekends in the winter and daily in the summer. The charming interpretive **Verna Dunshee Trail** offers a short, mostly flat walk along a wheelchair-accessible trail. The views are fabulous, and you can get a leaflet at the visitors center that describes many of the things you'll see along the trail. For something with a little more vertical challenge to it, head for the Pantoll Station and take the **Old Stage Road.** For a shorter loop (about 2 mi, moderate), turn off onto **Easy Grade,** and then take the **Old Mine Trail** back. If you're looking for a longer hike, start out the same, but instead of cutting back quickly, take Easy Grade to **Rock Springs Trail,** then on to **Nora,** and finally return on **Matt Davis** for a total of five miles. This way you also get to take a peak at the Rock Spring part of the mountain.

Looking for a guided hike to help you to better understand the landscape you're seeing? The Mount Tamalpais Interpretive Association (www.mttam.net) offers a full schedule of guided hikes. Choose anything from a sedate, flat nature walk to a strenuous steep trek, all with an experienced guide who'll enrich your experience tremendously. Check the website for a schedule of upcoming guided hikes.

Biking

To bike up to the peak of Mount Tam is a watermark of local bicyclists' strength and endurance. Rather than driving up to the East Peak or the Mountain Home Inn, sturdy cyclists pedal up the paved road to the East Peak. It's a long, hard ride, but for an experienced cyclist the challenge and the views make it more than worthwhile. And then comes the fun part—whizzing back down the twisting roads at (safe) high speeds! Just take care, since this road is open to cars, many of which may not realize that bikers frequent the area.

On the other hand, mountain bikers carry their machines up the mountain on racks, then take them up and down Mount Tam's extensive network of fire roads (open to hikers, bikers, and horseback riders). Check the park map to find a great loop!

STINSON BEACH

The primary attraction at Stinson Beach is the tiny town's namesake: a broad, sandy stretch of coastline that's unusually (for Northern California) congenial to visitors. Though it's as plagued by fog as anywhere else in the Bay Area, on rare clear days Stinson Beach is the favorite destination for San Franciscans seeking some surf and sunshine.

Beachcombers can tread the sands of the beach while sunbathers plant themselves and their towels and beach chairs and catch the all-too-rare rays. Out in the water, surfers brave the chill of the Pacific to surf and kayak-surf the waves that roll in to pound the beaches. A plethora of local surf shops can hook you up with rental equipment if you didn't bring your own.

Accommodations

Given its status as a beach resort town, you will find a few inns and motels in which you can stay the night. The **Sandpiper Inn** (1 Marine Way, 415/868-1632, www.sandpiperstinson beach.com, $120–170) is one such spot. With six rooms and four cabins, you can choose between motel-style accommodations with comfortable queen beds, private bathrooms, and gas fireplaces. The four individual redwood cabins offer additional privacy, bed space for families, and full kitchens.

Another nice spot is the **Stinson Beach Motel** (3416 Shoreline Hwy. 1, 415/868-1712, www.stinsonbeachmotel.com, $150). It features eight "vintage" beach bungalow-style rooms sleeping two to four guests apiece. Some rooms have substantial kitchenettes; all have private baths, garden views, televisions, and blue decor. The motel is a great spot to bring the family for a (possibly chilly) beach vacation.

Food

A few smallish restaurants dot the town of

Stinson Beach, most of which serve seafood. Among the best is the **Sand Dollar Restaurant** (3458 Hwy. 1, 415/868-0434, www.stinsonbeachrestaurant.com, daily lunch and dinner, $15–30). This so-called fish joint actually serves more land-based dishes than seafood, but perhaps the fact that the dining room is constructed out of three old barges makes up the differences. In addition to lunch and dinner, the Sand Dollar serves a popular Sunday brunch.

Practicalities

So what's the catch to this idyllic recreation spot? As with so many other things in and near metropolitan California areas, it's the traffic. You'll learn quickly what the problem is if you try to drive into Stinson Beach on a sunny summer weekend day. With only one lane each way, and a couple of intersections with stop signs, backups that stretch for miles are all too common. Your best bet is to drive in on a weekday, or in the evening when everyone else is leaving the beach.

The nearest major medical services lie 20 miles south in San Francisco.

Out on Stinson Beach, if you possibly can, turn off your cell phone and put away your laptop. But if you can't possibly manage to disconnect, you will find limited Internet service around town. Cell phones will probably function here, though you might lose signal on Highway 1 in the more rural coastal reaches.

◖ POINT REYES NATIONAL SEASHORE

A haven for hippies and a mecca for wilderness buffs, the Point Reyes area boasts acres of unspoiled forest and beach country in the grandest Northern California tradition. Expect cool weather even in the summer, but enjoy the lustrous green foliage and spectacular scenery that result. Point Reyes National Seashore (Bear Valley Rd., 415/464-5100, www.nps.gov/pore, open daily dawn–midnight), the gem of the North Bay, stretches for miles between Tomales Bay and the Pacific, north from Stinson Beach to the tip of the land at the end of the bay. Dedicated hikers can trek from the bay to the ocean, or the beach to land's end. The protected lands shelter a range of wildlife. In the marshes and lagoons, a wide variety of birds—including three different species of pelican—make their nests. The pine forests shade shy deer and bigger elk. The land not protected often shelters and feeds some of the luckiest livestock in the country: the grass-fed cows and sheep of the local sustainable ranches.

The Point Reyes area includes the tiny towns of Olema, Point Reyes Station, and Inverness.

Visitors Centers

The **Bear Valley Visitors Center** (Bear Valley Rd., 415/464-5100, Mon.–Fri. 9 A.M.–5 P.M., Sat.–Sun. 8 A.M.–5 P.M.) acts as the central visitors center for Point Reyes National Seashore. In addition to the maps, fliers, and interpretive exhibits, you can watch a short video introducing you to the Point Reyes region. You can also talk to the rangers, either just to ask advice or to obtain beach fire permits and boat-in backcountry camping permits.

Two other visitors centers sit at different spots in the vast acreage of Point Reyes. The **Ken Patrick Visitor Center** (Drake's Beach, 415/669-1250, Sat.–Sun. 10 A.M.–5 P.M.) sits right on the beach in a decidedly appropriate structure. Its small museum focuses on the maritime history of the region, and it acts as the hosting area for the annual Sand Sculpture event held on the beach. The **Drake Beach Café** (hours and days of operation vary by season, call 415/669-1297) serves delicious food with an appropriate focus on the local, organic, and sustainable.

Finally, the **Historic Lighthouse and Visitors Center** (415/669-1534, Thurs.–Mon. 10 A.M.–4:30 P.M.) is the most difficult of the three to access. You must walk about a half a mile up a steep hill from the parking lot to get to this visitors center. On the other hand, you'll find the bonus of the lighthouse right at your feet once you arrive.

Point Reyes Historic Lighthouse

The jagged rocky shores of Point Reyes make

GRAZING POINT REYES

The Point Reyes food obsession encompasses far more than just restaurants. Local producers take enormous pride in their work, and offer it for sale retail to local cooks and visitors alike. Stopping at one or two local food markets or shops is essential to complete a true Point Reyes experience.

Several oyster farms make their home in Tomales Bay, providing their wares to fine restaurants locally and across the state. The **Hog Island Oyster Co.** (20215 Hwy. 1, 415/663-9218, www.hogislandoysters.com, daily 9 A.M.-5 P.M.) is open rain or shine and offers a picnic ground with barbecue grills. (Reservations are required for picnic tables on weekends in summer.) Far from a chi-chi tourist trap, Hog Island doesn't pretend to be anything other than a working oyster farm. You can buy the goods from a walk-up shack in the midst of warehouses, working buildings, and oyster tanks. If you prefer them raw and completely fresh, a shucker in orange hip-waders stands ready to pry open your jewels then and there. Lemon wedges and a bottle of hot sauce sit carelessly on a folding table that serves as the oyster bar. To take your oysters home, request them packed in ice for a small additional charge.

If you prefer land mammals to shellfish, Point Reyes is like a dream. Both beef and dairy cattle are grazed all over the place — even on legacy leased parkland. At the **Marin Sun Farms Butcher Shop** (10905 Hwy. 1, Point Reyes Station, 415/663-8997, www.marinsunfarms.com) you can pick up possibly the best cut of beef you'll ever eat. All Marin Sun Farms cattle are 100 percent grass-fed and humanely (even lovingly) treated. The result is beef that melts like butter and barely requires a knife to cut. Marin Sun also cuts and sells pork, lamb, goat, chicken, and eggs in season; the butcher will be happy to explain meat seasons to you, as well as give you a life history of the meat you're purchasing.

Point Reyes cheeses have become a national phenomenon in top-tier restaurants. To get some of the world's best cheese right from the source, visit the **Cowgirl Creamery** (80 Fourth St., Point Reyes Station, 415/663-9335, www.cowgirlcreamery.com, Wed.-Sun. 10 A.M.-6 P.M.) in Point Reyes Station. It's taken only a little over 10 years for this woman-owned farmhouse cheese factory to become a heavyweight in the artisan cheese world. Though Cowgirl distributes over 200 artisan cheeses from around the world, they deliberately keep their in-house production small — only seven kinds of cheese come from their factory in Point Reyes. They purchase their milk and cream locally, from the nearby Straus Family Creamery. Want to go behind the scenes of this unusual cheesemaking haven? Make a reservation for the weekly tour on Friday at 11:30 A.M.

Finally, for the best fruits and veggies the region has to offer, hit one of the weekly local farmers markets. Point Reyes Station holds its market at **Toby's** (11250 Hwy. 1, 415/663-1223, www.tobysfeedbarn.com) on Saturdays 9 A.M.-1 P.M. You can also pick up botanical bath products, locally grown and spun wool, and handmade jewelry and crafts.

© LANCE SCOTT

Hog Island Oyster Co., Point Reyes

great sightseeing but incredibly dangerous marine navigation. In 1870, the first lighthouse was constructed on the Headlands. Its first-order Fresnel lens threw out light far enough for ships to see and avoid the treacherous granite cliffs. Yet the danger remained, and soon after a life-saving station was constructed alongside the light station. It wasn't until the 20th century, when a ship-to-shore radio station and newer life-saving station were put in place, that the Point Reyes shore became truly safer for ships.

The Historic Lighthouse (415/669-1534, www.nps.gov/pore, Thurs.–Mon. 10 A.M.–4:30 P.M., light room Thurs.–Mon. 2:30–4 P.M.) still stands today. It sits down on the point past the visitors center—specifically, down 300 sometimes-treacherous, cold, and windblown stairs. (The stairs often close to visitors during bad weather for safety reasons.) But the reward can be worth it. The Fresnel lens and original workings all remain in place, and the adjacent equipment building contains foghorns, air compressors, and other implements of safety from decades gone by. Check the website for information about twice-monthly special events during which the light is lit.

Hiking and Biking

One of the main reasons people make the trip out to Point Reyes is to explore its beautiful scenery up close. Hikers fan out on the trails winding through the national seashore and surrounding state parks. Bicyclists, sometimes in big packs, ply the many small roads.

Many hiking trails, biking trails, and smallish roads run around the northern reaches of Point Reyes. To see the famed Tule elk, take the **Tomales Point Trail** (foot of Pierce Point Rd., 6 miles round-trip, difficult) right through the midst of the Tule Elk Reserve. For hikers who feel still feel energetic, 1.7 miles of additional unmaintained trail run all the way out to the tip of Tomales Point.

For a much quicker little walk from the same trailhead, stroll down to **McClures Beach** (0.8 miles round-trip, easy).

If you're staying at the local hostel, you can roll out of your bunk and onto the **Coastal Trail** (5-mile loop, moderate). This biking/hiking path takes you right to Limantour Beach. Bring a picnic or some toys and take a break on the sands. For a nice walk back along a different route, walk the Fire Lane for a mile, then take the Laguna Trail back to the hostel. (The Fire Lane and the Laguna Trail are *not* bike-accessible.)

Down in the south reaches of the park, the hikes get much longer. From the Bear Valley Visitors Center trailhead, you can hike the aptly named **Rift Zone Trail** (8.5 miles round-trip, difficult). For beach lovers, the Palomarin trailhead at the foot of Mesa Road opens onto the **Coastal Trail,** which can be as short or as long as you please. This is a great multi-day hike for backpackers, since both Wildcat Camp and Coastal Camp offer respite for weary travelers. Day hikers with good legs and lungs can stick with a 10-mile round-trip out past Bass Lake, Pelican Lake, and Crystal Lake, winding up at Alamere Falls.

For a stout mountain bike ride, take the **Bolinas Ridge Trail** (11 miles one-way, moderate), which is open to both bikers and hikers and offers stunning views down toward Tomales Bay. Trailheads sit on Sir Francis Drake Road at the north end and at the foot of Bolinas-Fairfax Road on the south side. An easier trail, more suitable for families, runs west down to **Marshall Beach** on Tomales Bay.

As for road biking, most all the paved roads in Point Reyes are open to both bicycles and cars. Ask for information about this year's hot biking spots and any trail closures at one of the local bike shops. **Cycle Analysis Point Reyes** (Hwy. 1 next to the Bovine Bakery, 415/663-9164, www.cyclepointreyes.com, Fri.–Sun. 10 A.M.–5 P.M. or by appointment) rents mountain bikes, tandem road bikes, and child trailers.

Accommodations

Unless you're camping, budget-friendly accommodations are thin in the Point Reyes area, with its local reputation as a playground for Bay Area rich folks. Prepare to spend a bundle

© LANCE SCOTT

Biking trails lead down to Tomales Bay.

on that quaint B&B, so choose carefully to make sure you find the perfect inn for your tastes. If you prefer indoor accommodations to the camping options in the national seashore and state parks, exclusive inns and boutique hotels proliferate in the small towns that dot the Point Reyes region.

OLEMA

The **Point Reyes Seashore Lodge** (10021 Hwy. 1, Olema, 415/663-9000, www.point reyesseashorelodge.com, $150–330) offers both budget and luxury in its 23 rooms. Attractive florals mix with clean white walls and attractive wooden accents. All rooms have private baths, some have whirlpool tubs, and a couple of special suites sit away from the main lodge for extra privacy and special amenities. Outside, guests can enjoy the attractive gardens with winding brick pathways that roll out to Olema Creek. The Farm House Restaurant, Bar, and Deli adjoin the hotel, providing plenty of food and drink options for all visitors of the tiny town of Olema.

POINT REYES STATION

In Point Reyes Station, you can find a room and tasty board for a reasonable price in **One Mesa Bed & Breakfast** (1 Mesa Rd., Pt. Reyes Station, 415/663-8866, www.onemesa .com, $132–210). All three rooms have private baths, down comforters and featherbeds, and free all-day and all-night coffee service. Each is decorated with a different style—most have fireplaces, some have soaking tubs, and all have televisions and VCRs. Guests can make use of the inn's hot tub and enjoy a self-service breakfast on weekdays and a basket of goodies delivered right to your door on weekends.

INVERNESS

For the flush, Point Reyes boasts an array of accommodations in the over-$250-plus range. One of the most original, the **Ⅽ Blackthorne Inn** (266 Vallejo Ave., Inverness, 415/663-8621, www.blackthorneinn.com, $215–360) perches on a hillside to the west of Tomales Bay in Inverness Park. This fascinating treehouse–meets–medieval castle was designed by its owner, who was not an architect by trade. Each guest room takes one floor of the central tower. All are spacious and pretty, with cute electric fireplaces that work as well as the heaters to warm the often-chilly rooms. A hot tub welcomes all guests until 10 P.M., when it becomes private to the top floor. While all baths are private, not all connect directly to the bedrooms. The tempting breakfast buffet changes daily, and provides hearty enough fare to sustain hikers bound for the wilds of the many parks.

Food

Dining in Point Reyes tends toward down-home country-style fare or upscale California cuisine. Few chain restaurants clutter the area. Most food comes from local, sustainable sources, a huge source of pride to the whole area.

OLEMA

If you're seeking rarified organic California cuisine, head for the tiny town of Olema and get a meal in the dining room at the **◖ Olema Inn** (10,000 Sir Francis Drake Blvd., 415/663-9559, www.theolemainn.com, lunch Sat.–Sun., dinner Wed.–Mon., closed Tues., $30–34). Here you'll find cuisine after Alice Waters' own heart—the freshest of local, organic fare presented with elegance and grace. Most shellfish comes from Tomales Bay, the beef from local ranches, and the produce from local farms. Relaxed, formal-yet-friendly service complements the fabulous food and local-heavy wine list. Be sure to save room for dessert!

POINT REYES STATION

Much of the expensive organic meat and produce that's raised in Point Reyes goes down to San Francisco for consumption in $200-a-plate restaurants. By comparison, **Rosie's Cowboy Cookhouse** (11285 Hwy. 1, Pt. Reyes Station, 415/663-8868, Wed.–Mon. 11:30 A.M.–8 P.M., $10–20) serves fairly plain Mexican and Tex-Mex food. You can get tacos, quesadillas, and tamales or ribs and mac 'n' cheese as you prefer. Right on the main drag and definitely catering to the tourist trade, Rosie's has a colorful family-friendly dining room and a fun ambiance. Most folks prefer Rosie's for lunch, though it's open for dinner as well.

Need a drink? Right off Highway 1 along Tomales Bay sits the unassuming **Point Reyes Vineyard** (12700 Hwy. 1, Pt. Reyes Station, 415/663-1011, www.ptreyesvineyardinn.com/winery.htm, Sat.–Sun. 11 A.M.–5 P.M. and by appointment). Hinting at the glory of the California wine country without the crowds and pretensions, this small winery pours some surprisingly tasty vintages. Staff can tell you about the wines as well as direct you to their favorite local restaurants and recreation spots.

INVERNESS

Of all the strange things, **Vladimir's Czechoslovakian Restaurant** (12785 Sir Francis Drake Blvd., Inverness, 415/669-1021, Tues.–Sun. 11 A.M.–2 P.M. and 5–10 P.M., $30–50) is a favorite of both locals and visitors. Enter the cool old dining room, complete with stuffed deer heads on the walls, and take a seat. The Vladimir who owns the restaurant can be rude one minute, and then hand you the best pint of beer you ever drank the next. Vlad's wife runs the kitchen, and you'll get to choose from an array of serious Czech food: borscht, rabbit, duck, and all manner of things that might seem heavy or strange to the American palate. But they're delicious.

One caution: Vladimir's is *very* serious about its no-children policy. If you bring your baby, toddler, or small child, you will be turned away at the door. The bright side? Vladimir's thus makes a perfect retreat for romantic couples looking for an escape the kids for a short time.

A great, convenient coffee stop is the **Busy Bee Bakery** (12301 Sir Francis Drake Blvd., Inverness, 415/663-9496, Mon. and Thurs.–Fri. 7:30 A.M.–4 P.M., Sat.–Sun. 8 A.M.–5 P.M.). This owner-run shop offers good espresso drinks, delectable homemade (right there in the back of the shop) pastries, and some lovely photo prints done by the owner. It's worth the time to take a table and sample a slice of whatever fresh baked goodie is on the counter!

Practicalities

Getting to Point Reyes can be quite a drive for newcomers. Though it's only an hour or so north of San Francisco, Highway 1 isn't exactly a superhighway through the wilds of Marin. Expect twists, turns, and generally slow going as you approach Point Reyes.

Once you're in the Point Reyes region, Sir Francis Drake Highway and all the other paved roads are open to bicyclists, and motorcyclists ply the fabulous twisties, so keep an eye out when you're driving from place to place. The good news is that parking is almost always free and easy in the towns and parks of Point Reyes.

As for services, there's not much out in the wilderness of Point Reyes. You can get gas in Point Reyes Station and at the Olema Ranch Campground only (no gas in Inverness), so plan carefully. You'll find mini-marts with the gas stations, but no big-box supermarkets or department stores anywhere in the region. If you need to stock up, Petaluma is the nearest major town.

Cell phones *do not work* across the majority of the Point Reyes National Seashore and adjoining parklands. Check with your inn or hotel for information about Internet access. You'll find a **post office** (11260 Hwy. 1, Point Reyes Station, 415/663-1305) in the town of Point Reyes Station.

The closest hospital to Point Reyes is **Novato Community Hospital** (180 Rowland Way, Novato, 415/209-1300, www.novatocommunity .sutterhealth.org).

East Bay

BERKELEY

There's no place on earth quite like Berkeley (except maybe Santa Cruz). While the Haight in San Francisco nurtured the creative side of the 1960s flower children, Berkeley brought out their fire. The town has long been known for its radical, liberal, progressive activism. No matter what you're doing, someone, somewhere in Berkeley is probably protesting against it right now. The youthful urban culture tends to revolve around the University of California. Yet well-heeled foodies also flock to town to sample some of the finest cuisine on earth, served only a block or two from the homeless people panhandling at the BART station.

University of California Berkeley

Berkeley is a college town, and fittingly the University of California (www.berkeley .edu) offers the most interesting places to go and things to see. If your visit to the area includes your teenagers, think about taking a free guided campus tour (510/642-3175, www .berkeley.edu/visitors/free_tours.html, Mon.– Sat. 10 A.M., Sun. 1 P.M.) to acquaint them (and yourself) with the UC and all it has to offer. To get a great view of the campus from above, take an elevator ride up the **Campanile** (Mon.–Fri. 10 A.M.–4 P.M., Sat. 10 A.M.–5 P.M., Sun. 10 A.M.–1:30 P.M., 3–5 P.M., adults $2, seniors $1), formally called Sather Tower. If you prefer to wander around campus on your own, discovering the halls where students live and learn, the stadium (perhaps you'll even see a protester up a tree!), and architectural details such as Sather Gate. Or stop in at the **Lawrence Hall of Science** (Centennial Drive, 510/642-5132, www.lawrencehallofscience. org, daily 10 A.M.–5 P.M., adults $10, seniors/ students $8, children $5.50) for a look at the latest exhibits and interactive displays.

Also on campus you'll find the **University of California Botanical Garden** (foot of Centennial Dr., 510/643-2755, http://botanical garden.berkeley.edu, adults $7, seniors $5, children $2, daily 9 A.M.–5 P.M.), an immense space with an astounding array of wild plants from around the world. Botany buffs love to spend hours in this place, studying and examining plants outdoors, in the greenhouses, and in the "arid house" (a habitat for plants requiring extremely dry, hot conditions). Others just come to

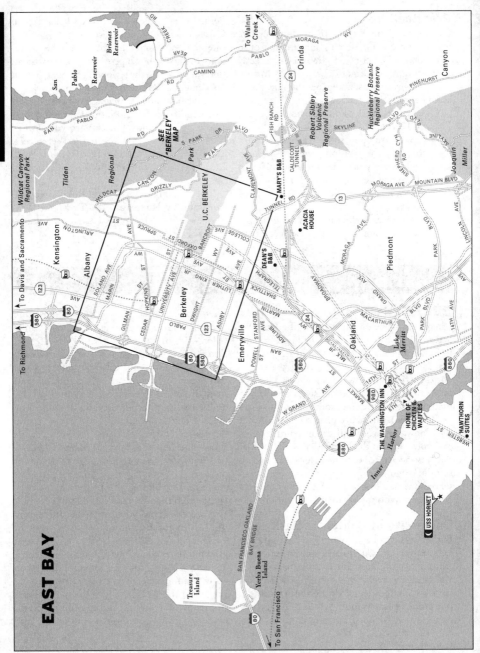

EAST BAY

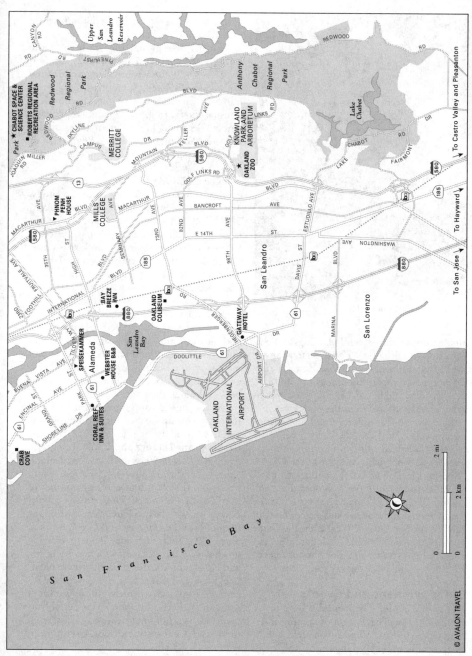

UC Berkeley's Golden Bear

amble through the peaceful plantings and perhaps stop to sniff a flower or two. You can see over 1,000 different kinds of sunflower, nearly 2,500 types of cactus, thousands of California native plants, and hundreds of rare and endangered plants collected from the world over.

Like most major universities, UC Berkeley (always called "Cal" or "the Golden Bears" by its sports fans) maintains a wide range of sports teams, many of which compete at the NCAA Division 1 level. The Cal football team's quality varies from year to year, as does the men's basketball team. Cal's main rival sits across the Bay at Stanford; the one serious college football game in the Bay Area each year is the Big Game between the two schools. Check out http://cal-bears.cstv.com for information about games of all kinds taking place during your visit.

Entertainment and Events

Not surprising for a happenin' college town, there's a reasonable selection of evening entertainment to be had. Whether you prefer a show (theatrical or musical), a dance, a drink, or all

of the above, you'll probably find it somewhere in Berkeley.

The major regional theater here is the **Berkeley Repertory Theatre** (2025 Addison St., 510/647-2949, www.berkeleyrep.org, shows Tues.–Sun., $27–69). Appropriate to the town it lives in, the Berkeley Rep puts up a bunch of unusual shows, from world premieres of edgy new works to totally different takes on old favorites. You might see a new adaptation of *Figaro* or a performance of the hit one-woman show *No Child*.

Some of the best entertainment in Berkeley echoes out from the live music venues. The **Starry Plough** (3101 Shattuck Ave., 510/841-0282, www.starryploughpub.com) is an Irish pub with a smallish stage setup. Fabulous Celtic rock groups, folk musicians, and indie bands play here almost every day of the week. Despite the lack of a formal dance floor, dedicated fans find ways to create an impromptu space to move to their favorite bands. Each Wednesday night, instead of music you'll find the famed Berkeley Poetry Slam—there's nothing like it anywhere in California. Hungry music and spoken word lovers can order a full meal from the kitchen, while the thirsty can quaff a pint or two of Guinness while they sit back and watch the stage.

Do your tastes run more toward rock and roll? Are you up for hearing struggling new bands who might one day become famous? **Blake's on Telegraph** (2367 Telegraph Ave., 510/848-0886, www.blakesontelegraph .com, Mon.–Fri. 11:30 A.M.–2 A.M., Sat.–Sun. noon–2 A.M.) plays home to any number of such bands. From the 1960s to the 1990s, Blake's was a dedicated blues club, hosting the likes of John Lee Hooker and Gregg Allman. Since 1993, Blake's has gone modern, offering up shows by top-tier bands such as Metallica and No Doubt. It's also given chances to bands like Train and Cake, who didn't yet have recording contracts when they took the small stage in Berkeley. The three-floor establishment boasts a full kitchen serving classic pub food, and a bar on each floor serving beer, wine, and cocktails.

In Berkeley, the big name acts come to the **Greek Theater** (Gayley Rd., 510/642-9988, www.ticketmaster.com/venue/229421). This outdoor amphitheater constructed in the classic Greek style sits on the UC Berkeley campus. Expect to see top-tier performers playing the Greek; you can check out artists like Steely Dan, R.E.M., and Death Cab for Cutie here. See the Ticketmaster website for a list of shows coming to the Greek

For a slightly less formal night out, Berkeley has any number of bars and clubs that offer DJs, dancing, or just a quiet drink. **The Shattuck Down Low Lounge** (2284 Shattuck Ave., 510/548-1159, www.shattuckdownlow.com, Tues.–Sat. 8 P.M.–2 A.M., Sun. 9 P.M.–2 A.M.) is a big dance club that often has live musical acts playing to get the audience up and moving. The bar serves up cocktails and wine and beer, and there's plenty of room to sit when you're tired and have a drink or two.

The Albatross Pub (1822 San Pablo Ave., 510/843-2473, www.albatrosspub .com, Sun.–Tues. 6 P.M.–2 A.M., Wed.–Sat. 4:30 P.M.–2 A.M.) might be Berkeley's favorite down-home drinking establishment. With six dart lanes, board games, Chicago deep-dish feta and spinach pizza for snacks, and a full bar, the

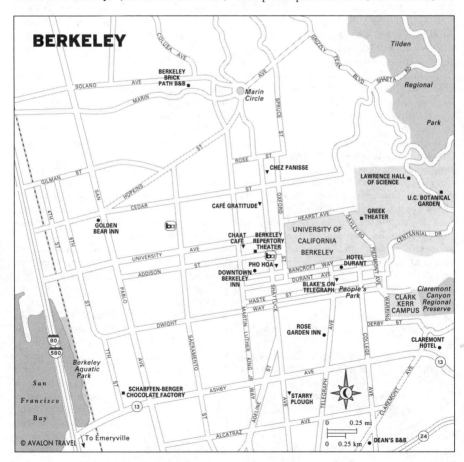

BERKELEY

Albatross has all you need for a totally laid-back night out. If you're not a lover of Guinness, you can order a fabulous hot Irish coffee—*the perfect* drink for those foggy Bay Area nights. Perhaps best of all, the relaxed crowd at the Albatross makes it easy to make new friends and really get into the local scene.

Shopping

Berkeley's citizens grow fierce at the very thought of big chain stores invading their precious downtown area. A few have succeeded, but you'll still find a variety of funky independent shops on **Telegraph Avenue** (btwn. the 2300 and 2600 blocks).

One of the best bookstores in the area is **Shakespeare & Co.** (2499 Telegraph Ave., 510/841-8916, Mon.–Thurs. 10 A.M.–8 P.M., Fri.–Sat. 10 A.M.–9 P.M., Sun. 11 A.M.–8 P.M.). This new-and-used store definitely has an old-school vibe, complete with the dust and the semi-organized shelves and the musty smell. True bibliophiles can spend hours browsing for treasures.

A shopping experience in Berkeley just wouldn't be complete without a quick browse inside of a head shop. (Don't know what a head shop is? Go ahead and skip it.) Whatever your pleasure in the semi-legal realm, **Hi Times** (2374 Telegraph Ave., 510/486-0988, Mon.–Sat. 11 A.M.–8 P.M., Sun. 11 A.M.–7 P.M.) can hook you up. Employees tend to be friendly and attentive, so feel free to ask for whatever you need. **Annapurna** (2416 Telegraph Ave., 510/841-6187, Sun.–Thurs. 10 A.M.–10 P.M., Fri.–Sat. 10 A.M.–11 P.M.) is the oldest head shop in Berkeley, offering an array of different items including adult toys, posters and t-shirts, vaporizers and grinders, and Bettie Page pinup postcards.

Clothing stores run to funky foreign stuff, like the apparel sold in **Kathmandu Imports** (2515 Telegraph Ave., 510/665-8970, Mon.–Sat. 11 A.M.–6 P.M., Sun. noon–6:30 P.M.), which specializes in Tibetan arts and crafts. Secondhand stores such as **Mars Mercantile** (2398 Telegraph Ave., 510/843-6711, daily 11 A.M.–7 P.M.) are another option. While it

bills itself as a "vintage store," the selection actually feels more like a downscale thrift shop. The provocative window displays lure shoppers inside, where a few solid basic items can be had for a reasonable price.

Accommodations

When you look for a place to stay in Berkeley, check both the hotel and the neighborhood. Plenty of unique B&Bs offer rooms in Berkeley, and adequate motel rooms make it easy for family and friends to visit students.

$100-150

Offering great value for a surprisingly small nightly fee, the **Golden Bear Inn** (1620 San Pablo Ave., 510/525-6770, www.golden bearinn.com, $99–121) has myriad small unique touches that make it special among budget motels. A family-friendly place, parents can rent an inexpensive room with two twin beds in a separate bedroom, providing privacy and relaxation for everyone. Cute rooms are nicely decorated and have televisions and wireless Internet access. Restaurants and attractions cluster comfortably nearby.

The **Downtown Berkeley Inn** (2001 Bancroft Way, 510/843-4043, www.downtownberkeley inn.com, $145) brings the inn concept into the city. The location, exterior, and room design all mimic the urban style that defines downtown Berkeley. Guest rooms boast top amenities, such as high-end beds and 42-inch plasma televisions. If you're out till the wee hours, pull the blackout drapes and sleep in!

$150-250

Mary's Bed and Breakfast (47 Alvarado Rd., 510/848-1431, $165, 2-day minimum on weekends) feels a bit like a tropical resort, with its rattan furnishing and light, airy decor. Mary's offers three bedrooms, all of which come with a full breakfast each morning in the dining room. An apartment is also available for rent by the week or the month. In the Claremont district of south Berkeley, Mary's is walking distance to the Claremont Hotel's spa and restaurant.

The **Rose Garden Inn** (2740 Telegraph Ave., 510/549-2145, www.rosegardeninn .com, $170–260, 2-night minimum over Sat. nights) is a large rambling structure with 40 guest rooms and gorgeous rose bushes (don't worry—the bushes are not in the rooms). If you come in the spring, take the time to stroll in the lush gardens and smell the pungent jasmine. Rooms are decorated in floral themes, many with light wood, white wicker, and other cute garden cottage-style touches. All rooms have private baths and televisions, and a hearty buffet breakfast is included.

Book a room at the **Berkeley Brick Path Bed & Breakfast** (1805 Marin Ave., 510/524-4277, www.thebrickpath.com, $170–210). The garden is the pride of this inn, and you can stroll down the namesake brick path among the lush greenery and gorgeous flowers, take a seat out on the patio to enjoy your breakfast, or sip an afternoon glass of wine in the gazebo. (For a complete list of the plants in the garden, complete with identifying photos and descriptions, see the inn's website.) Each of the three guest rooms has a unique style: one with a brick fireplace, one with a huge whirlpool tub, and the East-West cottage with a full kitchen and private entrance.

The **Hotel Durant** (2600 Durant St., 510/845-8981, www.hoteldurant.com, $176–215) has it all: location, location, views, and location. If you can, get a room on the upper floors to take in a view of Oakland, San Francisco, or the Bay. From the lobby, you can walk to the University, Telegraph Avenue, and the Elmwood shopping district.

Got plenty of budget for your Berkeley lodgings? Then stay at the famous **Claremont Resort and Spa** (41 Tunnel Rd., 510/843-3000, www.claremontresort.com, $210–350). Since 1915, the Claremont has catered to rich and famous East Bay visitors. No two of the 279 elegantly furnished rooms look quite the same, so you'll get a unique accommodation experience even in this large resort hotel. The rooms may be plush, but the real focus at the Claremont is fitness and pampering. A full-fledged health club, complete with yoga, Pilates, and spinning classes takes up part of the huge complex. And the full-service spa, which offers all the current popular body treatments plus aesthetic services, finds favor with visitors and locals alike.

Food

Even if you can't stomach the politics of Berkeley, try the food. Berkeley is home to Alice Waters, grandmother of the organic and sustainable restaurant movement, and amazing restaurants fall thick on the ground here.

CASUAL DINING

Only in Berkeley could any traveler expect to find a multitude of all-organic, all-raw food restaurants. Of them all, **Café Gratitude** (1730 Shattuck Ave., 415/824-4652, www.cafe gratitude.com, $7–12) might be the hippiest eatery in all of hippiedom. Not only is all the food as natural as it's possible to get, each dish is named as an affirmation. Instead of ordering a kale, beet, and celery juice, you'll ask for an "I am Worthy," or instead of a pesto pizza, order an "I am Sensational." Really. All dishes are 100 percent vegetarian, many are vegan, and most are a bit strange even for the expanded palates of the average Bay Area diner. But the chefs do work good and hard to spin the fresh ingredients into tasty dishes. So if you're willing to brave the kale, tofu, and sprouted everything, give it a shot! (Maybe even a wheatgrass shot.) You might like it.

Sometimes, a weary traveler just needs a bowl of soup on the cheap. In Berkeley (and at any number of other towns around the Bay Area), your best choice is **C Pho Hoa** (2272 Shattuck Ave., 510/540-9228, www.phohoa .com). Yes, it's a chain—there's even a location in Saigon. But for the classic Vietnamese rice noodle soup called *pho,* Pho Hoa provides some of the best big bowls of soup around. The dining rooms are clean if a bit sterile and cafeteria-like. Newcomers to the world of *pho* can choose a bowl of chicken, steak, or seafood soup, while the more adventurous (and familiar with Southeast Asian cuisine) might choose some fatty flank, tendon, or even tripe. If you've got

A TASTE OF THE EAST BAY

Food and drink rule Berkeley. For the best of the food, visit the **Scharffen Berger** (914 Heinz Ave., 510/981-4066, www.artisanconfection.com, Mon.-Sat. 10 A.M.-6 P.M., Sun. 10 A.M.-5 P.M., tours free) chocolate factory. Scharffen Berger prides itself on a wonderful array of artisanal chocolate products. Daily tours take visitors through the factory and provide a history of both chocolate itself and the chocolate-making company.

Grab a glass of a different kind of wine at **Taraka Sake USA** (708 Addison Ave., 510/540-8250, daily noon-6 P.M.). Here you can take a tour of an authentic sake factory, which ends with a complimentary sake sampling in the tasting room. Sakes made here tend toward the inexpensive types served warm here in America; the factory also produces mirin and plum wine. For true sake connoisseurs, you can buy premium sakes imported from Japan at the factory.

If your idea of a good time is a good stiff drink, you'll love a visit to one of the local area alcohol producers. Have a sip (or more) of fine California wine at either **Lost Canyon Winery** (2102 Dennison, Ste. A, Oakland, 510/534-9314, www.lostcanyonwinery.com, Fri.-Sun. 1-6 P.M., complimentary tastings) or **Rosenblum Cellars** (2900 Main St., Ste. 1100, Alameda, 510/865-7007, www.rosenblumcellars.com, daily 11 A.M.-6 P.M.). Lost Canyon specializes in Pinot Noir and Syrah, while you'll find a wide array of reds, whites, and dessert wines at Rosenblum.

For the stronger stuff, head down to **Hangar One Vodka** (2601 Monarch St., Alameda Point, 800/782-8145, www.hangarone.com, Wed.-Sat. noon-7 P.M., Sun. noon-6 P.M.) tasting room. Look out over the view of the San Francisco Bay as you sip the vodkas named for the building in which they are created.

a huge appetite, go for a large bowl; a big appetite, go for a small bowl; a normal appetite, split a large with a friend! Top it off with an iced milk coffee for the ultimate pick-me-up. All for well under $10 per person.

Another downscale but well worth the time ethnic enclave, the **Chaat Café** (1902 University Ave., 510/845-1431, www.chaatcafes.com) offers spicy Indian cuisine for the right prices. This Bay Area local chain serves chaat (small plates and appetizers), of course. You can also get a meaty curry, a tandoori dish, stuffed naan, and more. (Though you'll find a few vegetarian specialties on the menu, this particular Indian place sticks more to the northern meat-eating tradition.)

FINE DINING

The very, very best of these, and Alice Waters' baby, is ◖ **Chez Panisse** (1517 Shattuck Ave., restaurant 510/548-5525, café 510/548-5049, www.chezpanisse.com, restaurant prix fixe $55–85, café $19–24). If you plan to dine in the restaurant at Chez Panisse, you need to make your reservations early and possibly plan your entire trip to Berkeley around the date on which you get a table. You can make a dinner reservation up to one month in advance. (No, we're not kidding. You should try to get a reservation at French Laundry if you think this is ridiculous.) The desk takes phone calls 9 A.M.–9:30 P.M. Monday–Saturday. You'll get the chance to enjoy some of the best cuisine that's ever graced a plate in Berkeley or anywhere else on earth. Waters and her successors create French-California dishes at the bleeding edge of current trends—Waters sets trends, she doesn't follow them.

Upstairs, the café offers food that's a bit more casual but just as good as the rarified dining room downstairs. It's much easier to get a reservation in the bustling, energetic café than it is the restaurant, and the casual atmosphere is less intimidating for diners who are new to all this California haute cuisine excess.

Information and Services

Newcomers to Berkeley can start at the

Visitor Information Center (2015 Center St., 510/549-7040, www.berkeleycvb.com, Mon.–Fri. 9 A.M.–5 P.M.). If you prefer to read about your destination in its local rags, you'll certainly be able to find some free newspapers on the street corners of Berkeley. The **Berkeley Daily News** is published (surprise!) every day. The **Berkeley Daily Planet** comes out twice a week. Check the *Daily Planet* for live entertainment listings and reviews.

As a major metropolitan city, you'll find most all the services you need in Berkeley. ATMs for most major banks appear on Shattuck and Telegraph Avenues, and close by all the major tourist areas. Just take care using them, especially after dark. You can find **post offices** at 1521 Shattuck Avenue and 2111 San Pablo Avenue.

For medical assistance, the **Alta Bates Summit Medical Center** (2001 Dwight Way, 510/204-4444) has a 24-hour emergency room.

Getting There and Around

The closest airport to Berkeley is Oakland International (see the *Oakland and Alameda* section). From the Oakland airport, rent a car, catch a cab, or take BART to the Colesium/Airport stop and then catch the AirBART shuttle to the terminals. If you're flying into San Francisco, you can take BART across the Bay to Berkeley.

As a matter of fact, **BART** (www.bart.gov) is a major form of transit in and around Berkeley. The Downtown Berkeley station underneath Shattuck Avenue is a major structure, with six exits that can create confusion for unfamiliar riders. Other stops include North Berkeley, Ashby, and Rockridge. See BART's website for schedules and tickets.

Berkeley sits to the north of Oakland and Alameda along the east side of the San Francisco Bay. If you're driving into Berkeley, take the Bay Bridge from San Francisco, then turn north onto Highway 580/80. Major roads in town include San Pablo, Ashby, Shattuck, Telegraph, and University.

Parking in Berkeley can be a bona fide nightmare. The town can be actively hostile to the notion of new parking lots and structures. Expect to pay for the privilege of parking here, and to walk a few blocks to your destination. If you're visiting Berkeley for the day or in for an evening show, consider taking BART in and out of the town to avoid the parking hassle.

OAKLAND AND ALAMEDA

The view across the Bay from San Francisco includes both Oakland and Alameda. Oakland is the biggest city in the East Bay. Though Oakland's reputation hasn't always been perfect (and visitors should probably stay in the popular tourist areas), today a great deal of downtown urban renewal has made it a visitor-friendly place with plenty of attractions, accommodations, and good food.

Long ago, Alameda grew up around its Naval base, providing a residential community for sailors, their families, and support businesses. The base closed in the 1990s, but the quiet, pleasant community remains.

◖ USS *Hornet*

Military historians, ghost hunters, and swing dancers meet aboard the USS *Hornet* museum (Ferry Point, Alameda, 510/521-8448, www.uss-hornet.org, daily 10 A.M.–4 P.M., adults $14, students/seniors/military $12, children $6) moored at the former naval base in Alameda. Small by comparison to modern aircraft carriers, the *Hornet* doesn't seem so small when you stand on the hangar deck staring at the half-dozen planes and helicopters displayed as part of the museum. Several open decks reveal to curious crawlers what cramped, steel-clad life was like aboard the Constitution-class carriers. (Bring a map; it's easy to get lost in the maze-like lower decks.) Claustrophobic visitors can spend their time up on the flight deck or touring "the island," imagining what it must have been like to experience the stress and action of one plane launching off the carrier every 45 seconds, all day long.

The *Hornet* is reputed to be one of the most haunted structures in the Bay Area, with the ghosts of sailors who lost their lives on duty floating through their favorite spots onboard ship. Most ghost activity seems to occur at night, and overnight visits and flashlight tours are available (check the website for dates and times). Finally, the *Hornet* acts as a local dance hall and event center for Alameda, hosting swing dance soirees and holiday parties on a regular basis.

Chabot Space and Science Center

One of the most spectacular sights in the East Bay, Chabot Space and Science Center (10000 Skyline Blvd., Oakland, 510/336-7300, www .chabotspace.org, Wed.–Thurs. 10 A.M.–5 P.M., Fri.–Sat. 10 A.M.–10 P.M., Sun. 11 A.M.–5 P.M., adults $13, seniors/students $10, youth $9) makes science and space super cool. Set up in the Oakland Hills, the Chabot complex includes observatories, the planetarium, the museum, and the Megadome theater, all available to the public. (Most Bay Area observatory telescopes are private.) Unlike the other area science museums that focus most on life on earth, Chabot focuses on the life *of* earth and of the universe. You and your family can create your own solar system in an interactive exhibit, "ride" a space shuttle in the Megadome, and check out Saturn's rings through the telescopes. If your visit runs long, grab a bite to eat and a cup of coffee at the on-site Celestial Café.

Oakland Zoo and Crab Cove

Do you love animals? You can visit all different kinds in the East Bay. For a day with creatures of the land, go to the Oakland Zoo (9777 Golf Links Rd., Oakland, 510/632-9525, www.oak landzoo.org, daily 10 A.M.–4 P.M., adults $9.50, seniors/youth $6). Here you'll discover an array of amphibians, mammals, reptiles, and birds, plus children's rides. Or if you prefer sea life, head for the Crab Cove Visitor's Center (1252 McKay Ave., Alameda, 510/521-6887, www .ebparks.org, Wed.–Sun. 10 A.M.–4:30 P.M., parking $5) in Alameda. Find out what the Bay looks like from the fish's perspective, say hello to the world under the sea, or take a peek at the exhibit on local Alameda history.

Entertainment and Events

Ballroom dancers from all around the Bay gather in Oakland on a regular basis to attend the famous **Ye Gaskell Occasional Dance Society** ball (1547 Lakeside Dr., www.gaskell ball.com). This fabulous fancy-dress event encourages everybody to dress in their finest (from whatever era from 1800 through today, but Victorian is encouraged) to create a picture of beauty swirling around the dance floor. You don't need to be an accomplished dancer to enjoy Gaskell's. Dance classes are offered during the afternoon before the ball, and a quick brush-up takes place before the official opening dance—always the Viennese waltz. Oakland's Scottish Rite Temple provides the perfect backdrop for the silk dresses, swirling hoopskirts, and handsome tuxedos of the dancers. Even if you don't dance much, come to admire the beautiful costumes and skillful regulars.

If you prefer a more modern beat to dance to, you can find some good live music and dancing in Oakland. Perhaps the best-known venue is, of all things, a sushi bar called **Yoshi's** (510 Embarcadero Way, Oakland, 510/238-9200, www.yoshis.com, lunch Tues.–Fri. 11:30 A.M.–2 P.M., dinner Mon.–Wed. 5:30–9 P.M., Thurs. 5:30–10 P.M., Fri.–Sat. 5:30–10:30 P.M., Sun. 5–9 P.M., shows 8 P.M. and 10 P.M.). With the restaurant in one room and the legendary jazz club right next door at Yoshi's on Jack London Square, it's possible to enjoy the sushi without attending the concert, or vice versa. The restaurant has recently been revitalized; a new chef brought in to create an up-to-date menu of raw and cooked Japanese cuisine with just enough California flair to make it different. If you're a dinner patron, it's a *very* good idea to make reservations for the show and get your seat tag on a chair before you sit down for your meal. You might see Otis Taylor or Kurt Elling in the club at Yoshi's. Any jazz fan who's come to the Bay Area owes it to herself to check the calendar on the website and see who's playing while she's in town.

Or perhaps you'd prefer DJs and cocktails. **Luka's Taproom & Lounge** (2221 Broadway,

510/451-4667, www.lukasoakland.com, Mon.–Wed 11:30 A.M.–midnight, Thurs.–Fri. 11:30 A.M.–2 A.M., Sat. 5:30 P.M.–2 A.M., Sun. 11 A.M.–midnight) can give you all that, and a Sunday hangover brunch as a bonus. What spends the day and early evening as a restaurant becomes a lounge and dance club with full bar after the sun sets. With a separate room for the DJs and dancing, and another space that serves as a full-on pool room with 45-playing jukebox, plus the Taproom with its brasserie-style food and 16 beers on tap, almost everyone can find something to enjoy at Luka's.

Shopping

Jack London Square (www.jacklondon square.com) is a great place to go if you're new to shopping in Oakland. Down on Oakland's surprisingly pretty waterfront, the Square is a bustling crowd of tourists and locals come to eat, shop, or catch a movie. The shops here tend toward the big chains.

For more local, specialized shops with a neighborhood feel, head to **Rockridge** (bwtn. Alcatraz Ave. and 51st St.) or **Piedmont.** In Rockridge, foodies will want to explore epicurian Market Hall (5655 College Ave.), while bookworms get their fix at well-regarded and independent Diesel Bookstore (5433 College Ave., 510/653-9965). At the foot of the Oakland Hills, the Piedmont district's main draw is the delightfully retro Fenton's Creamery (4226 Piedmont Ave., 510/658-7000) which has been serving scoops since 1894. A local theater, antique shops, and several restaurants line the easily walkable neighborhood.

Sports and Recreation

The jewel of Oakland's renewed downtown culture is **Lake Merritt and Lakeside Park** (650 Bellevue Ave., 510/238-7275). Here you can take a walk around the lake, play a few holes of golf, rent a kayak for a peaceful paddle, or even get in a set of tennis. For families, Children's Fairyland provides hours of entertainment and diversion.

Recreation buffs can peruse **California Canoe and Kayak** (409 Water St.,

510/893-7833, www.calkayak.com, daily 10 A.M.–6 P.M.). CCK carries not only kayaks and equipment, but a wide selection of outdoor fashions for both men and women.

If you'd rather watch than play, Oakland is home to several professional sports teams of varying reputations and records. The best consistent players are the MLB **Oakland A's** (510/762-2277, http://oakland.athletics.mlb. com). Part of the American League, the A's have seen their ups and downs, but they almost always put on a good show for their fans. The NBA's **Golden State Warriors** (510/625-8497, www.nba.com/warriors) court action can be fun to watch, particularly if you're rooting for the away team.

The most notorious team in pro football, the **Oakland Raiders** (510/625-8497, www.raiders .com) call the East Bay home again after a stint in Los Angeles. The fact that they haven't been getting their game on too well in recent years has not lessened the devotion of Bay Area fans to their beloved Raiders. If you get tickets to a game, be aware that the gangster reputation is not for nothing—the home side of the stadium can get rowdy and rough.

All three teams play at the **Oracle Arena and McAfee Coliseum** (7000 Coliseum Way, Oakland, 510/569-2121, www.coliseum.com), a complex with both a covered basketball arena and an open-air stadium that hosts both the A's and the Raiders. Though the vast majority of event and game-goers are perfectly safe, the Coliseum isn't in the best neighborhood, so pay attention as you walk out to your car.

Accommodations

In addition to the many chain motels in Oakland and Alameda, a number of independent inns and hotels offer a more unique East Bay experience.

$100-150

In Oakland, try the **Bay Breeze Inn** (4919 Coliseum Way, Oakland, 510/536-5972, www.baybreezeinnoakland.com, $95–150). With all the amenities of a higher-priced chain motel, the Bay Breeze offers both comfort and convenience. Located just down the street from the Coliseum and only a few miles from the Oakland Airport, this is the perfect place to stay if you're into football, baseball, basketball, concerts, or other live events. Do be aware that the Coliseum area can be sketchy after dark, so take care if you're walking alone. Or across the street from the Oakland Airport, stay at the **Gateway Hotel** (10 Hegenberger Rd., Oakland, 510/635-1892, www.gatewayhotel resort.com, $77–99). In addition to the usual motel amenities, enjoy the ultra-comfy Sleep Number bed and the on-site restaurant and bar, or take a dip in the pool.

At the **Acacia House** (Acacia Ave., Oakland, 510/601-9837, www.acaciahousebb.com, $140–195, 2-night minimum), you'll find a lovely three-room suite with soaring windows overlooking the Oakland Hills, native trees, and the upscale Rockridge neighborhood. A stay at the Acacia House feels more like visiting a friend's home than checking into an anonymous motel. Walk to the Rockridge BART station to explore the area, or sit in the garden, sipping a drink from the wet bar and relaxing. But book early during high season! Another unique lodging, **Dean's Bed & Breakfast** (480 Pedestrian Way, Oakland, 510/652-5024, $140) is also in the heart of charming Rockridge. It's actually a cottage stocked with fresh food and coffee, making each guest's stay completely private. You'll enjoy the heated pool and Japanese garden in summertime, as well as the sights and attractions of Oakland and nearby Berkeley.

Stay right on the waters of Alameda at the **Coral Reef Inn & Suites** (400 Park St., Alameda, 800/533-2330, www.coralreefinn .com, $95–115). This down-to-earth motel has large rooms, all with kitchenettes and small dining tables—perfect for a longer stay in the area.

If you've got a bigger budget, grab a nice room at an upscale inn. The oldest home in Alameda is **Webster House B&B** (1238 Versailles Ave., 510/523-9697, http://webster-house2.home.comcast.net/~websterhouse2/, $105–195). Set back from the street in an older residential neighborhood, trees shade the whole Gothic Revival house (one grows right

up through the deck). Guests lounge on the deck sipping tea each afternoon. Breakfast is made to order. Each of the four guest rooms is uniquely decorated, and one has a view of the waterfall in the yard.

$150-250

The Washington Inn (495 10th St., Oakland, 510/452-1776, www.thewashingtoninn.com, $165–190) brings a hint of European elegance to Oakland. Guest rooms are done in clean lines, simple furnishings, and bright whites linens with touches of brilliant color. This inn prides itself on pampering its guests, so be sure to take advantage of the extras. And make a dinner reservation at TWIST, the hotel's wonderful white-tablecloth California-Italian restaurant. The inn's location in the heart of downtown makes it perfect for business and pleasure travelers alike.

If you prefer to stay in Alameda, the **Hawthorn Suites** (1628 Webster St., Alameda, 510/522-1000, www.oaklandhs.com, $132–165) has all the appointments and amenities of a good motel, plus big, extra-nicely decorated guest rooms. Sure, it's a chain, but it's one of the nicer ones and it's conveniently located in downtown Alameda, only a short drive from the USS *Hornet* museum.

Food
CASUAL DINING

The **Home of Chicken and Waffles** (444 Embarcadero West, 510/836-4446, www.hcw chickenandwaffles.com, Sun.–Thurs. 8 A.M.–midnight, Fri.–Sat. 8 A.M.–4 A.M., $7–14) serves up good ol' Southern comfort food late into the night. Specialties of the house include the gooey mac 'n' cheese, true Southern sides (lots of grits), and of course chicken and waffles—served together, if you please. This definitely isn't the best spot for low-carb dieters to slake their appetites! But if you don't count calories and you need some late-night grub (or breakfast, or lunch, or dinner), HCW can hook you up. Note that after 11:30 P.M., you must prepay for your meal.

Some travelers take the opportunity to try

just about every type of world cuisine that's available in the Bay Area. At **Phnom Penh House** (3912 MacArthur Blvd., 510/482-8989, Mon.–Thurs. 11 A.M.–9:15 P.M., Fri.–Sat. 11 A.M.–9:45 P.M., $7–14), you can give Cambodian food a whirl. You'll find the dishes similar to Thai cooking, with some different spice combinations. At Phnom Penh, the fish, the soup, and the green papaya salad all draw rave reviews from frequent diners. Rumor has it that the curries are worth trying as well.

If you're out on the island of Alameda and you're looking for a tasty meal, consider sampling the German food at **Speisekammer** (2424 Lincoln Ave., 510/522-1300, www .speisekammer.com, lunch Fri.–Sun. noon–3 P.M., dinner Tues.–Wed. 5–9 P.M., Thurs.–Sat. 5–10 P.M., Sun. 4–9 P.M., $15–24). This Old World eatery specializes in sausages, marinated meat, red cabbage, and sauerkraut. And, of course, beer. Check the website for information about the beer drinking contests. Just to make your dining experience that much more fun, Speisekammer hosts live entertainment every Thursday, Friday, and Saturday night—mostly jazz combos, but you might find a country band or even a local musicians showcase to enjoy with your wiener schnitzel.

FINE DINING

For a delicious upscale meal on Jack London Square, try **Soizic** (300 Broadway, 510/251-8100, www.soizicbistro.com, lunch Tues.–Fri. 11:30 A.M.–2 P.M., dinner Tues.–Thurs. 5:30–9 P.M., Fri.–Sat. 5:30–10 P.M., $16–24). You'll need to round the corner onto Third Street to find the front door. This charming spot offers French-Californian cuisine served on sparkling white tablecloths and attractive modern dinnerware. The elegant dining room with its classic tables and banquets has seen the patronage of California governors and other local celebrities. On the menu, you'll find fish, vegetarian fare, and tender meats prepared with an eye to French traditional cuisine and current California sensibilities.

Information and Services

Its proximity to San Francisco can make it easy to forget that Oakland is a major city in its own right. You can start at the **Oakland Convention and Visitors Bureau** (463 11th St., Oakland, 510/839-9000, www.oakland cvb.com) to get good advice, maps, restaurant recommendations, and traffic tips.

You'll find plenty of banks and ATM machines scattered around Oakland; it's a good idea to stick to the ATM machines in well-lit, touristy areas rather than picking a random spot off the freeway at midnight. The same goes for gas stations and mini-marts.

Oakland boasts many **post offices.** One near Lake Merritt sits at 1955 Broadway. Internet access should be little trouble in a city filled with Starbucks outlets and connected hotels.

For medical attention, you can head out to the **Alameda Hospital** (2070 Clinton Ave., 510/522-3700, www.alamedahospital.org), which has a 24-hour emergency room. In Oakland, **Alta Bates** has a summit campus (350 Hawthorne Ave., 510/655-4000).

Getting There and Around

The truth is, if you can fly into and out of the **Oakland International Airport** (www.fly oakland.com) rather than SFO, you should do so. As one of the satellite airports, it sees less traffic than San Francisco, and it's easier to get into and out of with shorter security lines.

Bay Area Rapid Transit, or **BART** (www .bart.gov) is a good means of public transportation for visitors to Oakland. It can take you up to Berkeley, across the Bay into San Francisco or down onto the Peninsula, and all over the East Bay. BART can be a little bit intimidating for lone females after dark, but it's reasonably safe these days.

Bus service in Oakland and Alameda is run by **AC Transit** (www.actransit.org, adults $1.75, children/seniors $0.85, Transbay adults $3.50, children/seniors $1.70). Check the website for route maps and schedules for local East Bay bus service.

The major freeways surrounding Oakland and Alameda are, to put it politely, a mess. Try to avoid driving I-880, I-580, or I-680 during either the morning or evening rush hour periods (8 A.M.–10 A.M. and 4–7 P.M.). And if you should find yourself on the interchange referred to on local traffic reports as the MacArthur Maze…er, good luck. Don't feel bad if you get lost and need to get off a freeway and circle back; it happens. No lane instructions are listed here for the Maze because they'd probably be wrong by the time this book is published.

Getting out to Alameda can be a bit less than straightforward, as it's not totally obvious that the city of Alameda sits out on an island in the Bay. You'll need to take one of the bridges or the "tube" accessible from I-880 to get onto the island. Find a good map or get directions in advance to avoid getting lost in what can be a confusing area for newcomers.

Parking in Oakland and Alameda is easier than in San Francisco, most of the time. Street parking can be extremely difficult to come by; it's best to follow the signs to the parking garages surrounding Jack London Square and other major attractions and areas.

Silicon Valley

Here began the Information Age, and here much of the new technology that still astounds the world gets developed every day. What was once a fertile valley filled with orchards is now an endless procession of cities that shelter the major players of the high-tech world. No less than Apple Computer, Hewlett-Packard, and Intel, among many others, maintain their headquarters here.

Because of the huge number of good tech jobs here, people of all ethnicities and from countries around the world call the Silicon Valley home. The cultural diversity makes it a fascinating place to live and visit, with food and entertainment from all around the planet represented.

SAN JOSE

Sprawled across the south end of Silicon Valley, San Jose proudly claims the honor of "biggest city in the Bay Area." It is the beating heart of the Valley's high-tech industry, and eBay, Intel, Adobe, IBM, and many more call San Jose home. Long considered a cultural wasteland, San Jose has worked in the last decade to change its image, supporting local art and attracting high-end restaurants. If you want to get a sense of how Silicon Valley residents really live, spend a few days in San Jose.

Tech Museum of Innovation

The appropriately situated Tech Museum of Innovation (201 S. Market St., 408/294-8324, www.thetech.org, Mon.–Wed. 9 A.M.–5 P.M., Thurs.–Sun. 9 A.M.–8 P.M., $8) brings technology of all kinds to kids, families, and science lovers. The interactive displays at The Tech invite touching, letting children explore and learn about medical technology, computers, biology, chemistry, physics, and more using all their senses. The IMAX theater shows films dedicated to science, learning, technology, and adventure. The standard museum ticket price includes an IMAX show, and the long daily hours allow both early birds and night owls to get their learning on at The Tech.

Winchester Mystery House

For good old-fashioned, cheesy haunted house fun, stop in at the Winchester Mystery House (525 S. Winchester Blvd., 408/247-2101, www.winchestermysteryhouse.com, daily 9 A.M.–5 P.M., adults $26, children $20). A San Jose attraction that pre-dates the rise of Silicon Valley, the huge bizarre mansion was built by famous wacko Sarah Winchester. Kids love the doors that open onto brick walls, stairwells that go nowhere, and oddly shaped rooms, while adults enjoy the story of Sarah and the antiques displayed in many of the rooms. Sarah married into the gun-making Winchesters, and became disturbed later in life by the destruction and death wrought

Winchester Mystery House

textiles. In addition, the complex includes a planetarium (shows Mon.–Fri. 2 P.M., Sat.–Sun. 2 and 3:30 P.M.). Planetarium shows are free with admission to the museum.

Entertainment and Events

San Jose is definitely blessed with all sorts of entertainment. Cultural travelers can get seats to **Ballet San Jose** (408/288-2800, www.balletsanjose.org, $25–82) at the Center for the Performing Arts (255 S. Almaden Blvd.) or to **Opera San Jose** (408/437-4950, www.operasj.org) at the California Theatre (345 S. First St.).

Live theater options also abound in downtown San Jose. The big pro company is the **San Jose Repertory Theatre** (101 Paseo de San Antonio, 408/367-7255, www.sjrep.com, $30–60), locally known as the Rep. They've rebuilt their theater space and made over their company in an attempt to lure in a younger audience with edgy new works. It's only been partly successful—the audience still leans toward their canes, and the shows sometimes get so close to the edge that they fall off into the abyss of bad theater. Still, it can be fun to see the action in the gorgeous newer space. On the other hand, **City Lights Theatre** (529 S. Second St., 408/295-4200, www.cltc.org, $25–40) just down the block from the Rep, has a tiny, black-box-style theater and little money to spend on fancy lobby light fixtures. But the shows, mostly acted by up-and-coming local performers, never fail to entertain. Their take on everything from *Lysistrata* to *The Waiting Room* is fresh and original, providing a perfect local theater experience with a definite Silicon Valley flavor.

The clubs in San Jose certainly are suburban, but the lack of self-conscious hipness can make a night out at **Agenda Lounge** (399 S. First St., 408/287-3991, www.agendalounge.com, Wed.–Sat. 5:30 P.M.–2 A.M., Sun. 9 P.M.–2 A.M.) or the **Voodoo Lounge** (14 S. Second St., 408/286-8636, www.voodooloungesj.com) more relaxed than a trek up to the City.

Live comedy is another popular Silicon

by her husband's products. She designed the house to both facilitate communication with the spirits of the dead, and to confound them and keep herself safe. Whether or not ghosts still haunt the mansion is a matter of debate and of faith—visit and make up your own mind. For an extra-spooky experience, take a Friday the 13th or Halloween flashlight tour (book early, as these tours fill up fast).

Rosicrucian Egyptian Museum

Perhaps more genuinely creepy than the Winchester Mystery House, the Rosicrucian Egyptian Museum (1342 Naglee Ave., 408/947-3636, Mon.–Fri. 10 A.M.–5 P.M., Sat.–Sun. 11 A.M.–6 P.M., adults $9, seniors/students $7, children $5) has been a part of San Jose culture for almost a century. First opened by the Rosicrucian Order AMORC in 1928, the museum has a wonderful collection of ancient Egyptian artifacts, including several mummies—partly unwrapped, a rarity today. Local children and adults love the Rosicrucian's jewels, tomb artifacts, tools, and

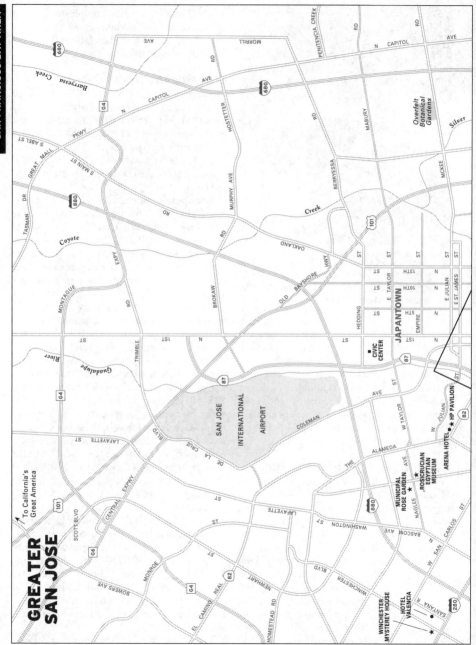

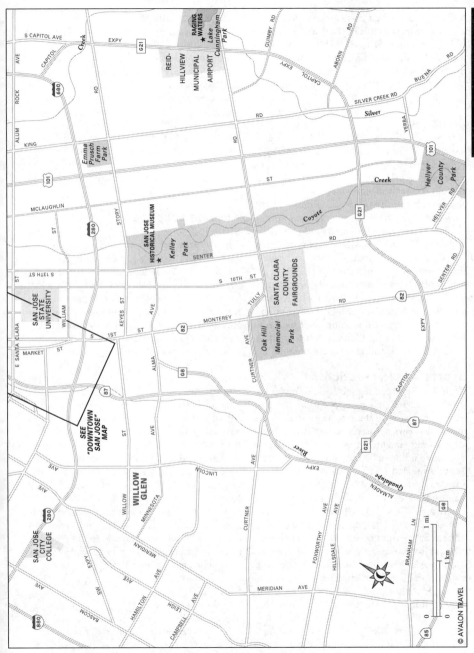

© AVALON TRAVEL

Valley option—even software engineers need a giggle sometimes! The **San Jose Improv** (62 S. Second St., 408/280-7475, www .improv2.com) often hosts major-league headliners like Bob Saget and Jamie Kennedy, while also granting stage time to local talent in showcases and contests.

Shopping

A variety of big shopping malls and an endless series of mini-malls fan out over San Jose's miles of terrain. But everyone knows that when it's time to get down to business, the top place to shop is **Santana Row** (Stevens Creek Blvd. and Winchester Blvd., www.santanarow.com). This almost frighteningly upscale outdoor center dazzles the eye with its array of chic chain and one-off boutiques, shops, and restaurants. The designers of Santana Row created the ultimate shopping experience of the 21st century—a live-in mall that rents high-end condos overlooking the courtyards full of shoppers, a high-class hotel, and a high-brow day spa. You can buy everything your heart desires at shops such as Bang & Olufsen, Anthropologie, Brooks Brothers, and many, many more.

Sports and Recreation

With all the space in the south of Silicon Valley, it's no surprise that San Jose's got the best amusement parks in the area. For a straight-up, thrill-ride-heavy amusement park that's perfect for older kids and grownups who want to spend a day pretending to be kids, go to **California's Great America** (4701 Great America Pkwy., Santa Clara, 408/988-1776 x8858, www .cagreatamerica.com, daily June–Aug., Sun.– Fri. 10 A.M.–8 P.M., Sat. 10 A.M.–10 P.M., hours sometimes vary, $54/day, parking $10). With roller coasters from classic to legs-dangling, a vertical drop, water rides and a full-fledged water park, a slime-filled kid's zone, and much more, Great America makes for an energetic, often hot, all-day romp. To cool down, head to **Raging Waters** (2333 S. White Rd., 408/238-9900, www.rwsplash.com, June– Aug., Mon.–Fri. 10:30 A.M.–6 P.M., Sat.–Sun. 10:30 A.M.–7 P.M., see website for exact dates

and times, adults $30, children $22). This sprawling water park features up-to-date slides and rides, plus plenty of serene pools for relaxing on a hot, sunny summer San Jose day.

San Jose may be mocked by its cousins in the City and the East Bay, but we've got some great and *different* professional sports worth seeing. The big dog in the area is the **San Jose Sharks** (http://sharks.nhl.com) NHL hockey team. They don't have a Cup yet, but everyone gets into the games at the downtown HP Pavilion (525 W. Santa Clara St.), making San Jose one of the loudest and liveliest places to watch a game in the league.

Accommodations

$100-150

The **Arena Hotel** (817 The Alameda, 408/294-6500, www.pacifichotels.com/ arena, $100–150) sits conveniently near the HP Pavilion, making it perfect for hockey fans and concert-goers. It's more motel than hotel, since guest rooms tend toward the small and the decor toward chain-motel floral tickytacky. You do get the standard TV, mini-fridge, coffee maker, and a surprise whirlpool tub.

Promoted as San Jose's first luxury hotel when it opened in 1911, the **Hotel Montgomery** (211 S. First St., 408/282-8800, www.jdvhotels.com/hotels/montgomery, $145) still prides itself on its old-school elegance and hospitality. But never fear, they've kept up with the times, complete with weird modern art in the lobby and uncomfortable-looking squaredoff couches in the bar. Guest rooms echo the elegance and add a touch of comfort, with Egyptian cotton linens and cushy comforters on the beds. Local original art and a standardissue red leather chair round out the room decor. Posh amenities include an on-site gym, restaurant and bar, room service, and Wi-Fi in the public areas of the hotel.

$150-250

The **Sainte Claire Hotel** (302 S. Market St., 408/295-2000, www.thesainteclaire.com, $155) offers big-city-style accommodations, starting with the elegant block you approach on

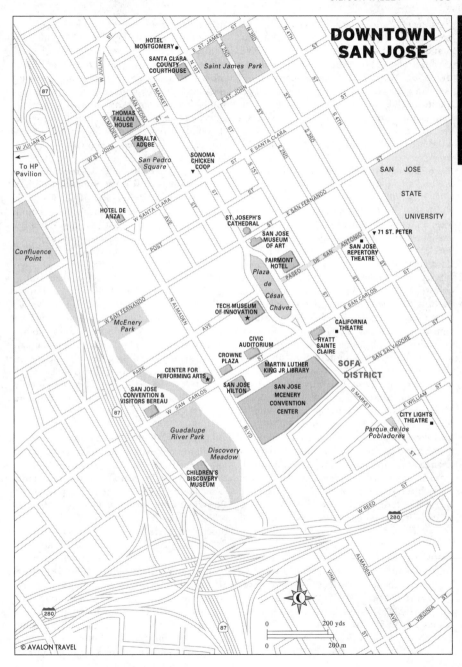

DOWNTOWN SAN JOSE

HOTEL MONTGOMERY
SANTA CLARA COUNTY COURTHOUSE
Saint James Park
THOMAS FALLON HOUSE
PERALTA ADOBE
San Pedro Square
SONOMA CHICKEN COOP
SAN JOSE STATE UNIVERSITY
HOTEL DE ANZA
ST. JOSEPH'S CATHEDRAL
SAN JOSE MUSEUM OF ART
71 ST. PETER
SAN JOSE REPERTORY THEATRE
Confluence Point
FAIRMONT HOTEL
Plaza de César Chávez
TECH MUSEUM OF INNOVATION ★
McEnery Park
CALIFORNIA THEATRE
CIVIC AUDITORIUM
HYATT SAINTE CLAIRE
SOFA DISTRICT
CROWNE PLAZA
MARTIN LUTHER KING JR LIBRARY
CENTER FOR PERFORMING ARTS ★
SAN JOSE HILTON
SAN JOSE MCENERY CONVENTION CENTER
SAN JOSE CONVENTION & VISITORS BEREAU
Guadalupe River Park
CITY LIGHTS THEATRE
Parque de los Pobladores
Discovery Meadow
CHILDREN'S DISCOVERY MUSEUM
W REED

To HP Pavilion

0   200 yds
0   200 m

© AVALON TRAVEL

the street. Inside, luxury fabrics and upscale appointments follow you up to your room. Standard guest rooms are small but attractive, with carved wood furniture and rich linens and draperies. The suites are more luxurious—if you can afford to rent the top floor, you'll get a suite much larger than the homes most locals can afford. Amenities in all rooms include a flat-screen television with DVD player, a CD/MP3 player, free Wi-Fi, plush robes, and turn-down service.

For a taste of true Silicon Valley luxury, stay at **The Fairmont San Jose** (170 S. Market St., 408/998-1900, www.fairmont.com/sanjose, $150–180). With a day spa and a limousine service, it's no surprise that the 731 guest rooms at the Fairmont, though plentiful, are something special to behold (and sleep in). Even the standard guest rooms have plenty of space, elegant fabrics and appointments, and a marble-clad private bathroom with a separate shower and bathtub. Of the two towers that comprise the Fairmont, the South Tower has the more luxurious rooms (not that it matters much).

Consumer culture takes a turn for the absurd at the **Hotel Valencia Santana Row** (355 Santana Row, 408/551-0010, www.hotel valencia.com, $225). This top-tier hotel sits right in the midst of the prestigious shopping mall incongruously named for a local musical legend. Walk into a guest room at the Valencia and you'll wonder if you've somehow been teleported into Los Angeles. Ultra-modern elegance and convenience includes everything from Internet-enabled phones on the desks to fuzzy black throw blankets on the beds. The lavish bathrooms with upscale toiletries help to make the hotel experience pleasing to all the senses.

Food

A remarkable array of restaurants tempt visitors and locals alike in San Jose. **71 Saint Peter** (71 N. San Pedro St., 408/971-8523, www.71saintpeter.com, Mon.–Fri. 11:30 A.M.–2 P.M., 5–9 P.M., Sat. 5–9 P.M., $15–28) is just one of these. Billed as a Mediterranean grill, the cuisine takes

inspiration from Europe and blends it with the flavors and fresh ingredients of California. While the à la carte menus are fine, the real treat in this charming indoor-outdoor dining room is the seasonal tasting menu. Featuring the best available produce of the current season, this four-course dinner is not only delicious, it is a bargain. Be sure to tell your server if you are a vegetarian or have other dietary concerns so that the kitchen can work with you to create a wonderful meal.

For folks who want tasty food without the white tablecloths, the **Sonoma Chicken Coop** (31 N. Market St., 408/287-4098, www.sonomachickencoop.com, Sun.–Thurs. 11 A.M.–9 P.M., Fri.–Sat. 11 A.M.–10 P.M., $7–12) offers a fun alternative to fancy California cuisine. At the Coop, you walk up to the counter to order, then find your own table either inside the always-packed dining room or out on the back terrace. Your order number will be called and you must grab your own tray of food. Choose from roast chicken (of course), fondue appetizers, duck, homemade pizzas, and other items, which you can pair with tasty side dishes. Plenty of interesting salads make a (somewhat) lighter meal. And don't forget dessert—the Chocolate Hockey Puck makes a perfect finish to a meal before a Sharks game.

Information and Services

Before you come to San Jose, visit www.sanjose .org to get all the information you need about the Silicon Valley region and its attractions. Once you're in town, you can stop in at the **San Jose Convention and Visitors Bureau** (408 Almaden Blvd., 408/295-9600) for maps, brochures, guidebooks, and local advice.

San Jose has its own major daily newspaper that competes for business with its more famous northern neighbor. The **San Jose Mercury News** (www.mercurynews.com) covers all the national news and wire service stories, plus plenty of local events and happenings. The entertainment section can provide some local entertainment info. But when it comes to nightlife, most locals pick up a copy of **The**

Wave (www.thewavemag.com), a free rag that proclaims itself the hippest of the Silicon Valley entertainment publications.

San Jose has plenty of **post offices** available for your use; downtown, you can find one at 200 South Third Street.

Here in the heart of Silicon Valley, it's tough to find a patch of air that doesn't have some Wi-Fi flowing through it. Do expect to pay for Internet access at Starbucks and some of the luxury hotels. If that's not to your taste, war-hacking is practically an art form here. (But you didn't hear that from us!)

For medical attention, **Good Samaritan Hospital** (2425 Samaritan Dr., 408/559-2552, www.goodsamsj.org) has 24-hour emergency services.

Getting There and Around

Travelers heading straight for the Silicon Valley should skip SFO and fly into **Mineta San Jose International Airport** (1667–2077 Airport Blvd., 408/501-0979, www.sjc.org) if at all possible. This suburban commercial airport has shorter lines, less parking and traffic congestion, and is convenient to downtown San Jose.

Amtrak (www.amtrak.com) trains come into San Jose, and you can catch either the Coast Starlight or the Capitol Express at the **San Jose-Diridon Station** (65 Cahill St.). See the Amtrak website for information about scheduling and fares.

The San Jose-Diridon station is also a hub for **CalTrain** (www.caltrain.com, fares $3–11), a commuter train that runs from Gilroy up to San Francisco. If you'd like to spend a day or even two up in the City but base yourself in Silicon Valley, taking CalTrain is an excellent way to go.

At Diridon, you can even catch the **VTA Light Rail** (www.vta.org, fares $2–4), a streetcar network that services San Jose and some of Silicon Valley up as far as Mountain View.

The VTA also operates Silicon Valley **buses** (same fares as light rail), which can get you almost anywhere you need to go if you're willing to be patient enough.

As with most of the Bay Area, it's best to avoid all of San Jose's major freeways 7–9:30 A.M., and again at 7:30 P.M. Arterial U.S. 101 is a dank, dirty stretch of road that's convenient to much of the Peninsula. I-280 is much prettier and less convenient, and definitely the easiest (but not the shortest) car route up to San Francisco. Highway 17 is the fast, treacherous route over the hill to the coast and Santa Cruz; it turns into I-880 in the midst of San Jose and runs past the foot of the Bay and then up the east side of the water all the way to Oakland. Highway 87, sometimes called the Guadalupe Parkway, can provide convenient access to downtown San Jose and the airport.

Parking in San Jose isn't anywhere near as bad as in San Francisco, but you should still be prepared to pay a premium for event parking and closed lots at the fancier hotels.

PALO ALTO

In a region filled with commuter towns and ever-evolving industry, the city of Palo Alto sits like an elder statesman among adolescents. This older town owes much of its prosperity to neighboring Stanford University, which was founded by Leland and Jane Stanford in memory of their deceased son.

Stanford University

The major sight in Palo Alto is of course Stanford University (at the end of University Ave., Stanford, 650/723-2560, www.stanford .edu). Stanford is one of the top universities in the world, and less than a tenth of the high school students who apply each year are accepted. The visitors center sits inside **Memorial Hall** (Memorial Auditorium, across the street from Hoover Tower, www.stanford.edu/dept/ visitorinfo, Mon.–Fri. 8 A.M.–5 P.M., Sat.–Sun. 9 A.M.–5 P.M.) and can help you with campus maps and tours. Definitely download or procure a map of campus before getting started on your explorations, as Stanford is infamously hard for newcomers to navigate.

For a taste of the beauty that surrounds students on a daily basis, begin your tour with **The Quad** (Oval at University Ave.) and

Memorial Church (Main Quad, you can't miss it). Located at the center of campus, these architectural gems are still in active use. Classes are held in the quad every day, and services take place in the church each Sunday.

Almost next door to the Quad lies **Cantor Art Center** (Lomita Dr. and Museum Way, 650/723-4177, www.museum.stanford.edu, Wed.–Sun. 11 A.M.–5 P.M., Thurs. until 8 P.M.). This free art museum features both permanent collections of classic paintings and sculpture donated by the Cantors and other philanthropists, as well as traveling exhibitions. On the other side of the Quad, down Palm Drive towards town, the **Rodin Sculpture Garden** (Lomita Dr. and Museum Way, daily 24 hours) finds favor with students who visit at night. The sculptures in the garden were cast in France from Rodin's originals and include the surprisingly petit-in-person *Thinker* and the *Gates of Hell.*

Perhaps the single most visited spot on the Stanford Campus is **Hoover Tower** (daily 10 A.M.–4:30 P.M.), the tall tower that's visible from as much as 30 miles away and from incoming airplanes. For great views of the Bay Area, head on up to the observation platform and take a look around.

Farther toward the edges of campus lurk two more treasures. **The Dish** (http://dish.stanford.edu) perches high on the Stanford hills, visible from Palm Drive and many other spots on the Peninsula. Along Junipero Serra Drive/Campus Drive East, several trails run up the hillside to the Dish. Once up the hill, you can hike back down-the observatory and radio telescope are not open to visitors. Built by the Stanford Research Institute in 1966 to study Earth's atmosphere and later used to communicate with spacecraft and satellites, the Dish rarely sees any action these days. But "hiking the Dish" along the many pedestrian trails is a time-honored Stanford tradition.

The second monument to science stretches for a full mile across Stanford land into the hills, though the building stays level. **Stanford Linear Accelerator Center** (2575 Sand Hill Rd,, Menlo Park, 650/926-2204, www.slac .stanford.edu), or SLAC to its friends, is one of only a few research facilities of its kind in the world. Here atoms are launched at one end of the building and reach high speeds before smashing into a barrier at the other end. Stanford researchers study the smashed pieces, increasing the body of knowledge about the subatomic world.

Due to a massive construction project and shift in research focus, tours were suspended at the time this book was written. Call SLAC for current information about public tour hours and prices.

Entertainment and Events

Palo Alto, with Stanford's help, enjoys a vibrant entertainment scene. **Stanford Lively Arts** (650/725-2787, http://livelyarts.stanford.edu, prices and locations vary by show) puts on an array of concerts and live staged entertainments each season. Expect to see several jazz ensembles each year, some world music, definitely a world premiere or two, and perhaps an unusual dance piece.

In town, the small **Dragon Theatre** (535 Alma St., 650/493-2006, www.dragon productions.net) puts up both well-known plays and premieres by local playwrights. You might see *Rough Crossing* by Tom Stoppard or *The Underpants* by Steve Martin go up at the Dragon. The acting pool is deep, since nearby Foothill College has an award-winning theater conservatory program that turns out excellent actors, directors, and stagehands.

Many students and long-time residents of Palo Alto enjoy seeing classic black-and-white movies back up on the big screen where they belong. Old-school movie house **The Stanford Theatre** (221 University Ave., 650/324-3700, www.stanfordtheatre.org) has red plush velvet seats, beautifully painted walls and ceiling, and a year-round schedule of fabulous old films. You might see a beloved Audrey Hepburn film or a run of Bogey's classics, since the Stanford Theatre often hosts festivals to highlight a specific star or genre.

Shopping

For a downtown boutique shopping experience in Palo Alto, head for **University Avenue** and its surrounding neighborhood. Here you'll find restaurants, salons, and both chain and independent shops and boutiques. The best art supply store in the whole of the Silicon Valley is **University Arts** (267 Hamilton St., 650/328-5000, www.universityart.com, Mon.–Sat. 9:30 A.M.–5:30 P.M., Thurs. until 7 P.M., Sun. noon–4 P.M.). Even out-of-town artists make it a point to come down to check out the vast shelves filled with the finest brushes, colors, and raw materials. Sadly, the once-fabulous, aging, and elegant Varsity Theater now houses a **Borders** (456 University Ave., 650/326-3670, www.bordersstores.com, Mon.–Thurs. 9 A.M.–11 P.M., Fri.–Sat. 9 A.M.–noon, Sun. 9 A.M.–10 P.M.). It's got everything most Borders bookstores have, plus a decent collection of Palo Alto and California local literature.

An independent jeweler with three locations in the Bay Area (and that's all), **Gleim the Jeweler** (322 University Ave., 650/323-1331, www.gleimjewelers.com) offers a wonderful range of upscale jewelry targeting the many wealthy residents of Palo Alto and the surrounding towns. Specialties of the house include diamonds, designers, and estate jewels. At Gleim, you'll find shiny baubles that don't exist anywhere else.

Gleim also has a storefront in the major area mall: the stunningly landscaped, open-air **Stanford Shopping Center** (Sand Hill Rd. and El Camino Real, www.stanfordshop.com, Mon.–Fri. 10 A.M.–9 P.M., Sat. 10 A.M.–7 P.M., Sun. 11 A.M.–6 P.M.). Here you'll find the up-scale boutiques and top-tier department stores befitting the affluence of the area. Big stores include Bloomingdales, Nordstrom, Macy's, and Neiman Marcus. Smaller shops range from designer boutiques such as Ann Taylor and to more affordable chain retailers like Banana Republic. A few truly special specialty stores, such as L'Occitane and Smith & Hawken, also cluster in the large complex.

Sports and Recreation

Stanford enjoys a reputation for athletics almost as great as its rep for academics, which makes it a great spot to enjoy some spectator sports. While the high-profile men's football and basketball teams tend to toil, the so-called lesser sports and women's teams excel. The women's basketball program is legendary, as is the men's baseball team. The golf team boasts Tiger Woods as an alumnus, and more than a few Olympians have swum in the pools and run on the tracks. For a good match, meet, or game, check the year's schedule at www.stanford.edu/home/athletics.

After a long day of exploring the Stanford campus, hiking the Dish, and touring SLAC, an hour or two in a gorgeous tiled hot tub followed by a luxurious spa treatment makes the perfect end to the day. **Watercourse Way** (165 Channing Ave., 650/462-2000, www.watercourseway.com, Sun.–Thurs. 8 A.M.–11:30 P.M., Fri.–Sat. 8 A.M.–12:30 A.M., tubs $18–28/person/hour) enjoys the title of the Silicon Valley's premier day spa. Former 49er (and Raider) Jerry Rice has been seen there on occasion. Even without the celebrity endorsement, this spa stands out in its amazing tiled tub rooms, range of treatments, and array of top-tier products. Each rentable hot tub room boasts unique and serene decor. The spa treatments are reasonably priced (relatively), and the pampering is second to none.

Accommodations

Lodgings near Palo Alto on the cheap can be had in the serene farm setting of **Hidden Villa Hostel** (26870 Moody Rd., Lost Altos Hills, 650/949-8648, www.hiddenvilla.org/hostel.php, Sept.–May only, members $21, non-members $24). A sustainably constructed main hostel building and a private cabin that's perfect for families and romantic honeymooners, the Hidden Villa hostel also has access to beautiful wilderness hiking trails, the surrounding organic farm, and the small wealthy town of Los Altos Hills. Hidden Villa is the oldest operating youth hostel in the United States, and it's incredibly popular. The newer buildings are more unique and attractive than those of most hostels, and were created to showcase features such as the radiant floor heating and bale wall construction. Reservations are required on weekends, and are a good idea even on weekdays.

Down on El Camino, south of Stanford but near enough to visit, **Dinah's Garden Hotel** (4261 El Camino Real, 800/227-8220, www .dinahshotel.com, $140–825) doesn't quite feel like a chain, despite its location and basic shape. The cute koi ponds and gardens mix with the bright floral interior decor to create a working, if kitschy, tropical paradise theme. The basic rooms tend toward the size and shape of an average motel, but the high-priced suites are something to behold. Attached to the hotel you'll find both a casual poolside grill and an upscale restaurant, a branch of the legendary **Trader Vic's.** If you're staying at Dinah's, you can enjoy as many mai tais and scorpion bowls as you please—you've only got to stumble a few yards to your room.

The **Creekside Inn** (3400 El Camino Real, 650/493-2411, www.creekside-inn.com, $145–260) provides garden accommodations set back a bit from the noisy road. The guest rooms have a touch more class than many motels in the same price range, with stylish fabrics and up-to-date amenities. This larger boutique hotel has more than 100 rooms, an outdoor heated pool, and an exercise room. All rooms have free Wi-Fi, fully stocked private bathrooms, refrigerators, coffee makers, in-room safes, and comfy bathrobes. You can get a package deal that includes breakfast with your room.

Much closer to the Stanford campus, the **Stanford Terrace Inn** (531 Stanford Ave., 650/857-0333, www.stanfordterraceinn.com, $220–360) provides appropriate luxury to parents who are spending a sweet mint to send their kids to a top private university. With all the correct pretensions of a Bay Area business, the Terrace rents "green" rooms with all hypoallergenic and sustainable furnishings, linens, and toiletries, plus filtered water and air. All the rooms, even the standards, are huge and come with attractive furnishings and luxury amenities. If you know what a T-1 line is, you'll be thrilled to know you've got access to one inside your room. The lovely indoor-outdoor restaurant is popular with the locals on holiday weekends.

Food

The denizens of Palo Alto, especially those who live near the university and downtown (sometimes called the Faculty Ghetto by locals who can't afford the area), like their food. They like it ethnic sometimes, expensive sometimes, but always delicious.

An historic favorite often associated with Stanford is **Sundance the Steakhouse** (1921 El Camino Real, 650/321-6798, http://sundancethesteakhouse.com, lunch Mon.–Fri. 11:30 A.M.–2 P.M., dinner Mon.–Thurs. 5–10 P.M., Fri.–Sat. 5–10:30 P.M., Sun. 5–9 P.M., $19–36). This place reeks of "old boys' club" from the moment you walk in the door. Dimly lit even for a restaurant, Sundance's interior features dark wood, dark booths, black-and-white prints, and antique sporting equipment. The food tends toward—you guessed it—steak. You can order a big cut of beef complete with traditional sides, or opt for a more interesting California-style seafood preparation. The salads and starters are tempting, but if you want to save room for dessert you might need to split an entrée with a dinner companion.

For something a little bit different and a whole lot more reasonably priced, pack in with the locals at **Zao Noodles** (261 University Ave., 650/328-1988, www.zaonoodle.com, $10–15). This pan-Asian noodle house shows off its popularity with bright colors and close-packed tables. Zao serves spicy, reasonably healthy noodle and rice bowls containing all manner of ingredients, plus curries, pad Thai, summer rolls, and more. You can choose from vegetarian, seafood, or meat dishes here. Be sure to pay attention to the little chile pepper markers—when Zao claims a dish is spicy, they mean it! Despite the number of folks who come to Zao, especially on weekend nights, the service is consistently fast and the servers do an amazing job of navigating the warren of tables.

Though it's not as near to the sea as some other parts of the Bay Area, Palo Alto is home to one of the most venerable seafood institutions: **Scott's Seafood Grill & Bar** (855 El Camino Real, #1, 650/323-1555, www

.scottsseafood.com, Mon. 7 A.M.–9 P.M., Tues.–Fri. 7 A.M.–9:30 P.M., Sat. 9 A.M.–9:30 P.M., Sun. 9 A.M.–9 P.M., $18–30). Scott's sits right across the street from Stanford Stadium in one of the last surviving "Town and Country Villages" in the Silicon Valley. This elegant white-tablecloth restaurant has a large window-lined dining room, and a bar on the other side. While you can wear casual clothes to Scott's, a dinner here is also a great excuse to dress up a bit. At breakfast and lunch, Scott's caters to the business set—many power lunches take place over salmon and sole here. The seafood at Scott's runs to a good variety of fish done up in fine preparations, often with exotic sauces. The wine list is worth perusing, with its fine California vintages and European wines.

Even the ultra-multicultural and sometimes snooty town of Palo Alto has its local favorite down-home diner. The **Palo Alto Creamery** (566 Emerson St., 650/323-3131, www.palo altocreamery.com, Mon.–Fri. noon–9 P.M., Sat. 9 A.M.–midnight, Sun. 8 A.M.–10 P.M., $8–15) has all the old kitschy decor to make diners believe that they've really entered some sort of time warp and a genuine 1950s soda shop. Red vinyl, shiny chrome, a black-and-white checked floor, a long counter, and funky booths help complete the total picture. The food runs to burgers, sandwiches, and American classic entrées. But what you really come to the creamery for is the house-made ice cream. Whether you order an extra-thick shake with your burger or wait for a sundae for dessert, don't skip this all-important Creamery staple. Just be aware that the Creamery gets crowded, especially on weekends. Locals know it's open pretty late and can often fill the place to the brim for an after-show meal.

Practicalities

Palo Alto is equidistant between the **Mineta San Jose International Airport** (1667–2077 Airport Blvd., 408/501-0979, www.sjc.org) and the **San Francisco International Airport** (800/435-9736, www.flysfo.com). **CalTrain** (www.caltrain.com, fares $3–11) can get you there as well. The commuter train runs from Gilroy to San Francisco, with a hub in San Jose. That same hub serves access to the **VTA Light Rail** (www.vta.org, fares $2–4), servicing San Jose up to Mountain View.

Palo Alto is easily accessed via U.S. 101 and I-280.

Coastside

The region known to locals as Coastside encompasses the San Mateo Coast area from Pacifica down to Año Nuevo State Reserve and on towards Santa Cruz. Many Bay Area locals escape to Coastside for weekend vacations, enjoying the small-town atmosphere in Half Moon Bay and Pescadero along with the unspoiled beauty of the dozens of miles of undeveloped coastline. Peak seasons for major attractions on Coastside are October (pumpkin season) and winter (elephant seals return to Año Nuevo).

HALF MOON BAY

To this day, the coastal city of Half Moon Bay retains its character as an ag town. The locals all know each other, and a spirit of community and cooperation pervades. Locally grown crops include pumpkins, strawberries, artichokes, and stinky-at-harvest-time brussels sprouts. Small family farms grow many other vegetables and fruits as well. Half Moon Bay enjoys a beautiful natural setting, and earns significant income from tourism, especially during the world-famous Pumpkin Festival each October.

Beaches

The beaches of Half Moon Bay draw visitors from over the hill and farther afield all year long. As with most of the northern Pacific, summer can be a chilly, foggy time on the beaches here. For the best beach weather, plan your Half Moon Bay trip for September or October. **Half Moon Bay State Beach** (www .parks.ca.gov) actually encompasses three discrete beaches stretching four miles down the coast, each with its own access point and parking lot. **Francis Beach** (95 Kelly Ave.) has the most developed amenities, including a good-sized campground with grassy areas to pitch tents and enjoy picnics, a visitors center, and indoor hot showers. **Venice Beach** (Venice Blvd. off Hwy. 1) offers outdoor showers and flush toilets. **Dunes Beach** (Young Ave. off Hwy. 1) is the southernmost major beach in the chain, and the least developed. The whole beach complex has wireless Internet access, but use care bringing sensitive electronic devices onto a sandy, salty, windy beach!

Perhaps the most famous beach in the area is **Mavericks** (Pillar Point Marsh parking lot, past Pillar Point Harbor). Named for the unpredictable immense waves that pile up to crash into this beach, Mavericks holds a legendary place in the California surfing world. Each winter during storm season, the Mavericks Surf Contest (http://mavericks-surf.com) happens here. *Novice surfers beware!* Mavericks is not a beginner's break, especially in winter. The giant breakers can be deadly. If you aren't positive you're up to the challenge, don't paddle out.

Just north of Half Moon Bay, **Montara State Beach** (2nd St,. Montara, www.parks .ca.gov) appeals to tidepoolers and surf fishermen as much as to picnickers and beachcombers. Bring your dogs for a wonderful walk on this windy, sandy, life-filled beach.

Entertainment and Events

The biggest annual event in this small agricultural town is the **Half Moon Bay Art & Pumpkin Festival** (www.miramarevents.com/pumpkinfest). Every October, nearly a quarter of a million people trek to Half Moon Bay to pay homage to the big orange squash. The festival includes live music, food, artists' booths, contests, kids' activities, an adults lounge area, and a parade. Perhaps the best-publicized event is the pumpkin weigh-off, which takes place

before the festivities begin. Farmers bring their tremendous squash in on flatbed trucks from all over the country to determine which is the biggest of all. The winner gets paid per pound, a significant prize when the biggest pumpkins weigh over 1,000 pounds!

Sports and Recreation

For a sedate ocean adventure, take a winter whale-watching cruise or a shallow-water fishing trip on board the **Queen of Hearts** (Pillar Point Harbor, 510/581-2628, www.fishing boat.com, adults $69, children $50, tackle rental $8–12, 1-day license $13, reservations highly recommended). Whale watching trips run January through April and cost a bit less than fishing trips on the *Queen of Hearts.* Deep-sea fishing makes for a more energetic day out on the Pacific, though Dramamine is often recommended.

You can fish for albacore tuna, rockfish, or salmon (if the season isn't cancelled) with **Huck Finn Sportfishing** (Pillar Point Harbor, 650/726-7133, www.huckfinnsportfishing .com, tackle $5–14, 1-day license $12). This major outfitter offers eight boats for a wide variety of trips. Call for trip rates.

One of the coolest ways to see the coast is from the deck of a sea kayak. It's good to be healthy and fit, but Many kayak tours with the **Half Moon Bay Kayaking Company** (2 Johnson Pier, 650/773-6101, www.hmbkayak .com) require no previous kayaking experience. For an easy first paddle, try the Pillar Point tour, the full-moon tour, or the sunset paddle. If you're looking for a wilder ride, sign up for a kayak surfing class—you'll learn how to catch waves safely in specially designed kayaks. Or if you're serious about learning to sea kayak, HMB Kayak also offers beginner through advanced classes in closed-deck kayaks.

Some visitors see the wide cool beaches of Half Moon Bay and dream of watching the sun go down over the ocean from the back of a horse. **Sea Horse and Friendly Acres Ranches** (1828 N. Hwy. 1, 650/726-9903, www.horserentals.com/seahorse.html, daily from 8 A.M., $40/hour) offers one-hour,

90-minute, and two-hour guided tours that take you along the cliffs and down onto the sands at Half Moon Bay's state beaches. Children over the age of five are welcome, as are riders of all ability levels. The horses here are sedate rental nags who know the routes in their sleep, allowing their riders to sit back and enjoy the stunning views and the company of their fellow riders. Don't expect much from the guides; they generally speak little English and simply ride along to be sure you stay safely on the horse trails.

After a long day paddling a sea kayak or reeling up rock cod, a nice massage or facial might sound just perfect. The **Primrose Day Spa** (630 Purissima St., 650/726-1244, http://primrosespa.com, daily by appointment) nods to its locale by offering pumpkin enzyme facials and body wrap treatments. You can choose any style of massage, classic facials and spa treatments, or an aesthetic treatment at Primrose.

Accommodations

Half Moon Bay offers several lovely bed-and-breakfasts and one luxury resort hotel. That resort is the **Ritz-Carlton Half Moon Bay** (1 Miramontes Point Rd., 650/712-7000, www.ritzcarlton.com, $550). Looming large over the Pacific, the hotel resembles a cliff-side medieval castle. Inside, guests enjoy the finest of modern amenities. The Ritz-Carlton has a top-tier restaurant (Navio), a world-class day spa, and posh guest rooms that really are worth the price. If you can, get a room facing the ocean. While you're there, enjoy free access to the spa's bathing rooms, an outdoor hot tub overlooking the ocean, tennis courts, and basketball court. The golfing at the Ritz is second to none in the Bay Area. And of course, the service will make you feel like royalty.

For a more personal lodging experience, try one of the local inns. The **((Old Thyme Inn** (779 Main St., 650/726-1616, www.oldthymeinn.com, $195–375) is located right downtown, next door to the Cetrella Bistro. Playing on the inn's name, each uniquely decorated room has its own garden theme. Rooms are comfortable, with luxurious amenities. Downstairs, guests can enjoy the

common sitting rooms and the gorgeous garden (yes, they do grow thyme). Each morning the owners serve up a sumptuous breakfast using fresh ingredients.

In the neighboring community of Montara, the **Goose and Turrets** (835 George St., Montara, 650/728-5451, http://goose.montara.com, $160–210) is a locals' getaway favorite. The rambling old building that houses the inn has had an exciting life—ask the friendly and knowledgeable owners about its story. Decor here runs to the eclectic, and folks who find the usual flowery B&Bs a bit cloying will love the Goose and Turrets. The Clipper Room is perfect for aviation buffs, and guests who like their space will love the sweeping expanse of hardwood floor in the Hummingbird Room. The food and accommodations here keep an eye towards ecologically friendly choices, and the owners are active in local park and community environmental organizations.

Food

The quality of food in Half Moon Bay is superb. Chefs are drawn to the array of produce fresh from the local fields, and to the idyllic Coastside setting. **((Cetrella** (845 Main St., 650/726-4090, www.cetrella.com, Sun. and Tues.–Thurs. 5:30–9:30 P.M., Fri.–Sat. 5:30–10 P.M., $18–35) bills itself as a Mediterranean bistro. In truth, the menu includes a range of Mediterranean-themed California cuisine, and the big-beam construction looks like something out of the redwood forests up north. The chef uses local, often organic ingredients to create stunning fare that varies by season. Look for Dungeness crab in wintertime and artichokes in the spring.

Pasta Moon (315 Main St., 650/726-5125, www.pastamoon.com, lunch Mon.–Fri. 11:30 A.M.–2:30 P.M., Sat.–Sun. noon–3 P.M., dinner Sun.–Thurs. 5:30–9:30 P.M., Fri.–Sat. 5:30–10 P.M., $14–34) manages to be both casual and upscale all at once. The restaurant serves updated Italian cuisine with an emphasis on fresh, light dishes. The rustic dining room, with a view of the woods and creek, completes the experience.

THE BLUE LADY

With all its history, it's easy to get lost in the ghost stories that haunt the San Francisco. Yet two of the most famous Bay Area hauntings aren't anywhere close to Chinatown or Nob Hill. Instead, strange stories and creepy occurrences perch nearer to the perilous cliffs of the Pacific Coast, and lurk in the Santa Cruz Mountain forests.

Just north of Half Moon Bay, the **Moss Beach Distillery** (see *Food* in the *Half Moon Bay* section) has been featured on *Unsolved Mysteries* and written up in countless publications. Not for its food, but for its famous ghost: the Blue Lady. Rumor has it that a beautiful young woman walked the cliffs of Moss Beach from her home to the coastside speakeasy (now the Distillery) to meet her lover, a handsome piano player who worked in the bar. The Lady, whose name has never been discovered, perished one night on the cliffs under suspicious circumstances. Some say that her lover had left her, and she threw herself down onto the rocks out of grief; others claim that her seafaring husband came home, discovered his wife's infidelity, and shoved her to eternity. However it happened, in the middle of the 20th century,

odd things started occurring at the Distillery. A storage room with only one door and a barred-over window became stuck from the inside. Eventually, several men bashed it open, only to discover several heavy cases of spirits that had been shoved up against the door to keep it closed. But by whom? No one was in the room, and no one could have gotten out. Many years and a major reconstruction later (the building sits on a slowly eroding cliff that will eventually lie beneath the ocean), an accountant was working late one night in the restaurant's offices. She was startled to hear her printer turn itself on...startled because she was in another office using a different computer and was alone in the building. Upon examination, the printer yielded a single piece of paper with a tiny heart printed on it. The accountant believes this means the ghost likes her.

Today, the Distillery is a favorite with ghost-hunting groups, who often come to spend the night in an old building that gets decidedly creepy after the lights go out. Restaurant patrons rarely have ghostly experiences, unless you count those created by the owner for the entertainment of his customers.

As many people come to the **Moss Beach Distillery** (140 Beach Way, Moss Beach, 650/728-5595, www.mossbeachdistillery.com, brunch 11 A.M.–2 P.M., dinner daily $15–30) for the ghost stories (see *The Blue Lady* sidebar) as for the hearty food and terrific ocean views. The Distillery operated as a speakeasy in the 1930s, with the basement rooms in the cliffside building storing cases of illegal alcohol.

The restaurant offers something of a cross between traditional American food and California cuisine. Portions tend to be large, and service is friendly if occasionally slow during peak crowd times. Folks who want to soak up the old-school speakeasy atmosphere like to sit in the bar, while visitors who want to stare out over the ocean prefer the terrace.

When all you need is a quick bite or a casual lunch, the **Moonside Bakery & Cafe**

(604 Main St., 650/726-9070, www.moonside bakery.com, daily 7 A.M.–5 P.M.) can fix you up. Stop in the morning for breakfast pastries and espresso. In the afternoon and evening, expect sandwiches and hand-fired pizzas.

Practicalities

The best way to get to Half Moon Bay is to drive. Half Moon Bay sits on Highway 1 about 45 minutes south of San Francisco. Drivers can take the Great Highway down to Highway 35 (aka Skyline Blvd.) in Pacifica and catch Highway 1 from there.

An alternate route is to take I-280 from either the north or the south, then turn onto CA-92 west. This two-lane state highway goes over the Santa Cruz Mountains that separate the Valley from the coast. Because it's the major truck route over the hill, it can get jammed up even on weekdays, but it's worst on sunny summer weekends when everyone on the Peninsula wants to hit the beach.

Parking in downtown Half Moon Bay is usually a fairly easy proposition. Except, of course, if you're in town for the Pumpkin Festival, when parking is a nightmare of epic proportions; your best bet is to already be staying in town with your car safely stowed in a hotel parking lot before the festival.

The two local Coastside publications are the **Half Moon Bay Review** (www.hmbreview .com) and **CoastViews Magazine** (www.coast viewsmag.com). The *Review,* published weekly, provides the best information about live local entertainment. *CoastViews* comes out monthly and is free around the Coastside region. It's got more in-depth coverage of the region's attractions, restaurants, and farms.

The nearest major trauma centers are in San Francisco, Santa Cruz, and on the Peninsula, and helicopter transport may be involved. For less-serious health services, you can visit the **Coastside Family Medical Clinic** (225 S. Hwy. 1, Half Moon Bay, 650/712-7330, www.coastsidedocs.org, Mon.–Fri. 8 A.M.–5 P.M.).

Cell phones work fine in the town of Half Moon Bay, but coverage can be spotty up in the hills above town and out on the undeveloped coastline and beaches along Highway 1. For Internet access, head downtown to the local cafés or ask at your inn or hotel, since most offer some form of Wi-Fi or wired access.

PESCADERO

One of the last true small towns in the Bay Area, Pescadero is a tiny dot on the coastline, south of Half Moon Bay and well north of Santa Cruz. With one main street, one side street, and several smallish farms, in Pescadero pretty much everyone knows everyone else, and there's a strong sense of community. Despite its tiny size, many Bay Area denizens find reasons to visit Pescadero, including twisty roads that challenge motorcyclists and bicyclists, fresh produce, and, of course, the legendary Duarte's Tavern.

Año Nuevo State Reserve

The best sights in Pescadero are outside. Año Nuevo State Reserve (Hwy. 1 south of Pescadero, look for signs, 650/879-2025, www.parks.ca.gov, daily 8 A.M.–sunset, $8/ car) is world-famous as the winter home and breeding ground of the once-endangered elephant seals. The reserve also shelters Pomponio Native American remains and extensive dune and marshland. The beaches and wilderness are open all year. The elephant seals start showing up in late November and stay to breed, birth pups, and loll on the beach until early March. Visitors are not allowed down to the elephant seal habitats on their own and must sign up for a guided walking tour. Once you see two giant males crashing into one another in a fight for dominance, you won't want to get too close! Book your tour at least a day or two in advance since the seals are popular with both locals and travelers.

Pescadero Marsh Natural Preserve

Bird-lovers flock to Pescadero Marsh Natural Preserve (www.parks.ca.gov), located on Highway 1 right across the freeway from Pescadero State Beach. This protected wetland is home to a variety of avian species, including blue herons, great and snowy egrets, and northern harriers. For the best birding, visit the marsh in late fall or early springtime, when migration is in full swing.

Pigeon Point Lighthouse

South of Pescadero proper sits Pigeon Point Lighthouse (210 Pigeon Point Rd. at Hwy. 1, 650/879-2120, www.parks.ca.gov, daily 8 A.M.–sunset). First lit in 1872, Pigeon Point is one of the most photographed lighthouses in the United States. Sadly, visitors find the lighthouse itself in a state of some disrepair, and recent earthquakes have made climbing to the top unsafe. Yet the monument stands, its hostel still shelters travelers, and visitors still marvel at the incomparable views from the point. Winter guests can see migrating whales from the rocks beyond the tower.

© ROBERT HOLMES / CALTOUR

Pigeon Point Lighthouse

Beaches

Pescadero State Beach (Hwy. 1 just north of Pescadero Rd., 650/879-2170, www.parks .ca.gov, daily 8 A.M.–sunset, $8 parking, no fires) is the closest beach to the town of Pescadero. Though it's a great spot to walk in the sand and stare out into the Pacific, near-constant winds make it less than ideal for picnics or sunbathing. It does have some facilities, including public bathrooms.

North of Pescadero, at the intersection of Highway 84 and Highway 1, **San Gregorio State Beach** (650/879-2170, www.parks .ca.gov, daily 8 A.M.–sunset, $8/car) stretches farther than it seems. Once you're walking toward the ocean, the small-seeming cove stretches out beyond the cliffs that bound it to create a long stretch of beach perfect for contemplative strolling. San Gregorio is a local favorite in the summer, despite the regular appearance of thick, chilly fog over the sand. Brave beachgoers can even swim and body-surf here, though doing so without a wetsuit gets swimmers cold fast. Picnic tables and

bathrooms cluster near the parking lot, though picnicking can be hampered by wind.

Accommodations

Pescadero has a small but surprisingly good array of lodging options. If budget is a factor, try the **Pigeon Point Hostel** (210 Pigeon Point Rd. at Hwy. 1, 650/879-0633, http://norcal-hostels.org/pigeon, dorm bed $20–24, private room $55–100). This HI hostel has simple but comfortable accommodations, both private and dorm-style. And the locale can't be beat! Amenities include three kitchens, free Wi-Fi, and beach access. But the best amenity of all is the cliff-top hot tub, which makes the hostel more than special.

Another option in the **Costanoa Lodge and Campground** (2001 Rossi Rd. at Hwy. 1, 650/879-1100, www.costanoa.com, camping $55/night, lodge and cabin rooms $143–400). At this eco-lodge you can do anything from pitch a tent in the campground to rent a whirl-pool suite in the lodge. Other lodging options include log-style cabins with shared baths, small tent cabins with shared baths, and private rooms. Costanoa's many nature programs seek to educate visitors about the ecology of the San Mateo coast and the preservation efforts underway. A small general store offers s'mores makings and souvenirs. You'll pay for the privilege of staying at Costanoa, but the location is beautiful and the eco-chic atmosphere is all the rage these days.

For a little more luxury, the **Pescadero Creek Inn Bed & Breakfast** (393 Stage Rd., 888/307-1898, www.pescaderocreekinn.com, $209–264) sits conveniently in downtown Pescadero, an easy walk from Duarte's, the grocery stores, the local cemetery, and the creek. While the house isn't completely soundproof, the rooms are high ceilinged and prettily appointed. The owners serve up a delectable breakfast each morning, plus wine and cheese in the afternoon. If you ask nicely, you might get a bottle of the house vintage, handmade by the owner.

If you want something unique, Pescadero has lodgings available year-round. The **Pescadero Creekside Barn** (248 Stage Rd., 650/879-0868, www.pescaderolodging.com, call for rates) nestles in the loft of an old barn downtown. This studio-apartment style space sleeps two, has a TV with DVD player, a kitchen, and a clawfoot tub. The seclusion and charm make the space perfect for a romantic getaway or solitary weekend retreat.

Food

The one true restaurant in Pescadero is **⟨ Duarte's Tavern** (202 Stage Rd., 650/879-0464, www.duartestavern.com, daily 7 A.M.–9 P.M., $10–20). The rambling building features sloping floors and age-darkened wooden walls. The food is excellent, the service friendly, and the coffee plentiful. Almost everybody in the Bay Area comes to Duarte's eventually—whether it's for a bowl of artichoke soup, some great local fish, a slice of olallieberry pie, or just a drink at the dimly lit, often-crowded bar.

To enjoy the best of Coastside food, hit a local farm or two and put together your own picnic lunch (or dinner). **Harley Farms** (205 North St., 650/879-0480, www.harleyfarms .com, call for tour information) boasts of being the last working dairy on the San Mateo coast. Their goat cheese is locally famous, sold at high-end grocery stores and offered in restaurants around the Bay Area. Look for the small wheels with colorful edible flower petals pressed into pretty patterns—a Harley Farms trademark. You can even assist in the cheese-making process, taking a tour that teaches you how to milk a goat, then create fresh artisan cheese.

For scrumptious homemade bread and pastries, stop in at **Arcangeli Grocery** (287 Stage Rd., 650/879-0147, www.normsmarket .com/store) across the street from Duarte's. All breads are homemade and delicious, and the pastries (especially the raspberry twists) are to die for. The store also carries many grocery staples and plenty of cold drinks and California wines.

Practicalities

Pescadero Road lies 17 miles south of Half Moon Bay on Highway 1 at Pescadero State Beach. Watch for signs, and turn east, away from the ocean onto Pescadero Road. Town lies a few miles east of the ocean in a tiny valley. When you come to the stop sign (it's the only one in town), you've hit the town center. Turn left onto Stage Road to find most of the rest of Pescadero.

Parking is free and generally easy to find on Stage Road or in the Duarte's parking lot. On weekends, you might need to park down the road a ways and walk a block or two.

Pescadero maintains two local-style markets and a gas station with a mini-mart. That's pretty much it for services.

Cell phone coverage is spotty in Pescadero, and Internet service somewhat rare. Don't expect to be completely connected while you're visiting this tiny rural town.

WINE COUNTRY

Entering California's Wine Country is an unmistakable experience. From the crest of the last hill, sunlight paints golden streaks on endless rows of grapevines that stretch out in every direction for as far as the eye can see. Trellises run along both sides of every road, tempting visitors to question the unplucked weeds beneath the vines, the rose bushes capping each row, and the strange still fans standing guard high above. A heady aroma of earth and grapes permeates the area. Welcome to the Napa and Sonoma Valleys.

The area's beautiful grapevines are renowned worldwide for producing top-quality vintages and economical varietal table wines. But foodies also know the area as a center for stellar cuisine. Yountville, a tiny upscale town in the middle of the Napa Valley, is the favorite haven of celebrity chef Thomas Keller. The food served at his French Laundry restaurant is legendary (as is its price). Keller's influence helped to usher in a culinary renaissance, and today the lush flavors of local, sustainable produce are available throughout the region.

The Sonoma Valley has long played second fiddle to Napa in terms of viticultural prestige, but the wines coming out of the area are second to none. The Russian River Valley wineries are often friendlier and less crowded than their Napa counterparts, while the wineries in the southern Carneros region are few and far between. Each offers visitors a more personal experience than Napa and the chance to sample unique and amazing varietals. Sonoma County's craggy coastline and natural beauty provide great recreation

© LANCE SCOTT

HIGHLIGHTS

◖ Domaine Chandon: This Yountville winery offers a gorgeous setting in which to sample their premier champagne. Their wine- and champagne-making tour is one of the best in Napa (page 153).

◖ Mumm: This sophisticated yet down-to-earth winery excels in friendly service, sparkling wines, and generous pours (page 155).

◖ Grgich Hills: Home of the California Chardonnay that won the Paris Wine Tasting of 1976, Grgich Hills uses a biodynamic farming process to produce exquisite wines (page 159).

◖ Culinary Institute of America: The ancient gray stonework and quietly forested surroundings of the CIA belie the bevy of culinary activity inside. Stop by for cooking classes and demonstrations, to peruse the museum, or to indulge in a meal at the exemplary restaurant or café (page 163).

◖ Kendall-Jackson Wine Center: Kendall-Jackson's Food & Wine Pairing tasting option is the best example of this Wine Country trend: excellent small bites paired with a daily selection of wines and served in a elegant tasting room (page 182).

◖ A. Rafanelli: The best Sonoma reds are produced at this small, unpretentious appointment-only winery. Be sure to pick up one of their stunning Cabs (page 185).

◖ Mission San Francisco Solano de Sonoma: Sonoma is home to the last

California Mission, the centerpiece of Sonoma State Historic Park (page 203).

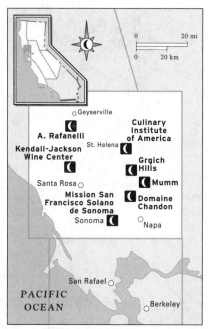

LOOK FOR ◖ TO FIND RECOMMENDED SIGHTS, ACTIVITIES, DINING, AND LODGING.

opportunities for visitors more fond of the outdoors than grapes.

PLANNING YOUR TIME

If you're coming to Wine Country for the first time, you'll probably spend most of your visit paying homage to the grape. After all, Napa and Sonoma form the beating heart of California's great Wine Country. Literally hundreds of wineries cluster within the relatively small valleys of Napa and the Russian River, while other wineries call the regions of

Carneros and outer Sonoma home. Most visitors plan a weekend in Napa, with weekend trips back to explore the outer valleys. If you come during the summer or fall seasons, you'll find a crush in almost every tasting room in the valley; even the smaller boutique labels do big business during the six-month high season (May–Oct.).

To make the most of your trip, do a little advance research. Plan out which wineries are must-sees, and which routes you'll take. Be aware that Highway 29 (which runs through

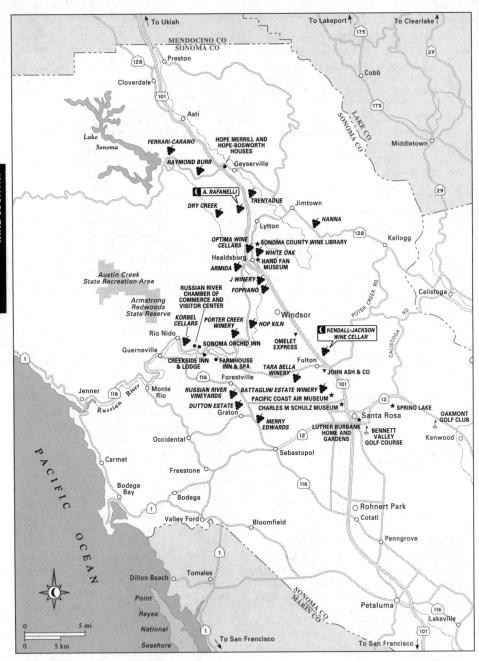

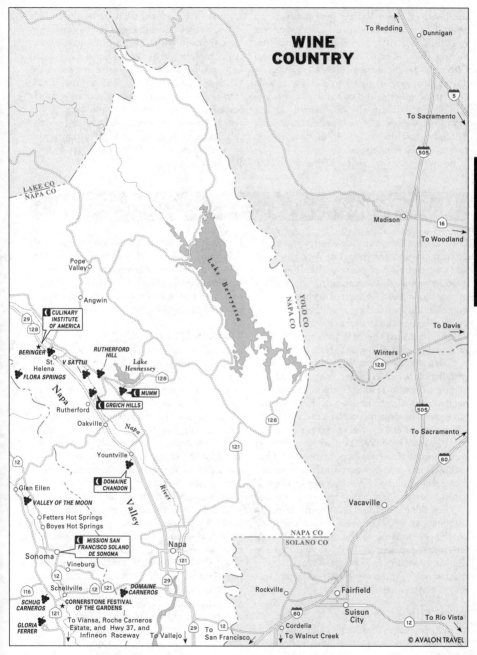

WINE COUNTRY

To Redding

Dunnigan

To Sacramento

5

505

Madison

16

To Woodland

LAKE CO
NAPA CO

Pope
Valley

Angwin

Lake Berryessa

YOLO CO
NAPA CO

To Davis

Winters

128

29
128

☾ CULINARY
INSTITUTE
OF AMERICA

BERINGER

St.
Helena

V SATTUI

FLORA SPRINGS

*RUTHERFORD
HILL*

Lake
Hennessey

128

Napa

☾ *MUMM*

☾ *GRGICH HILLS*

Rutherford

Oakville

Napa

505

To Sacramento

80

121

128

Yountville

☾ *DOMAINE
CHANDON*

River

Glen Ellen

VALLEY OF THE MOON

12

Fetters Hot Springs
Boyes Hot Springs

Valley

NAPA CO
SOLANO CO

Vacaville

☾ *MISSION SAN
FRANCISCO SOLANO
DE SONOMA*

Sonoma

Napa

121

Vineburg

12

Schellville

116

*SCHUG
CARNEROS*

12

121

*DOMAINE
CARNEROS*

121

Rockville

Fairfield

☾ *CORNERSTONE FESTIVAL
OF THE GARDENS*

*GLORIA
FERRER*

To Viansa, Roche Carneros
Estate, and Hwy 37, and
Infineon Raceway

To Vallejo

29

To
San Francisco

12

80

Cordelia

To Walnut Creek

Suisun
City

12

To Rio Vista

© AVALON TRAVEL

the heart of Napa Valley) gets jammed up around St. Helena and can be very slow on weekends. U.S. 101 slows through Santa Rosa during the weekday rush-hour commutes. Check to see whether any events are going on during your stay, as they can increase crowds both at the wineries and on the roads. If you're not up for driving, the downtown tasting rooms in the cities of Napa, Sonoma, and Santa Rosa are good alternatives to the slow trek up and down the wine roads.

Be aware that while wine tasting can be the ultimate vacation experience for adults, kids will not enjoy being dragged around all day to an activity in which they cannot participate. And children are not welcome at many small bed-and-breakfasts nor allowed in most of the Calistoga spas. Overall, a Wine Country vacation is a better adults-only trip than a family vacation. If you must bring your kids, plan a few activities that aren't food-, wine-, or spa-related, such as the Charles Schulz Museum in Santa Rosa, or enjoying the water at Lake Berryessa.

Napa Valley

Once upon a time, the Napa Valley was a hot, dry region with a few straggling wine vineyards and a whole bunch of prune orchards growing in its lowlands. A few pioneering winemakers in the 1960s and '70s started trying to make higher-quality wines here, and they were generally sneered at by the French wine establishment. Then came the 1976 Judgment of Paris tasting, and everything changed.

Today, the Napa Valley feels like Disneyland… with liquor. Wineries cluster along Highway 29 and the Silverado Trail, each trying to outdo its neighbors to win the business of the thousands of visitors who descend on Napa every weekend to taste of the endless river of fermented grape that's grown, aged, and bottled here. Tasting rooms boast souvenirs and logowear by the rackful, tours sell out hours in advance, special events draw hundreds of people to wineries that can comfortably seat two dozen.

Then there's the food. As the wine industry in Napa exploded, top-tier chefs rose to the challenge, flocking to the area and opening amazing restaurants in the tiny towns that line the wine trails. Even if you don't love wine, a meal at one of the many high-end restaurants makes Napa worth a visit.

WINERIES

Literally hundreds of wineries call Napa home. You could spend weeks tasting wine here and not hit every vintner. Know that you can't visit a dozen wineries in a day—tasting wine takes time and rubs your mouth raw. Following is a small selection of Napa wineries—some large, some small, all worth visiting—organized from south to north along (or near) Highway 29.

Trinitas Cellars

Situated in a cool cave beneath a hilltop vineyard, the Trinitas Tasting Room (875 Bordeaux Way, Napa, 707/251-1956, www.trinitascellars .com, daily noon–8 P.M.) functions as the resort wine bar for the Meritage Inn. The bar is open to both hotel guests and passersby, offering tastings of Trinitas wines and bites of cheese, fruit, and tiny gourmet goodies. Seats at the bar make it easy to get comfortable and stay awhile—which quickly becomes a possibility as soon as tasters get their nose inside a glass. Trinitas wines do not tend toward downmarket hotel freebies. These surprisingly balanced, well-crafted wines are more than worth your time, even if (or especially if) you're serious about your vintages. Expect a small list featuring one or two whites, a rosé, and one or two red wines, all sold at shockingly low per-bottle prices, especially compared to other Napa wines of similar quality. If you happen to be a guest at the inn, wander into the cave at about 5 P.M. for the free daily tasting of two wines—sometimes Trinitas, sometimes guest vintners.

© LANCE SCOTT

Wine Country is filled with scenic drives.

WINE COUNTRY

◖ Domaine Chandon

One of the premier champagneries in Napa Valley, Domaine Chandon (1 California Dr., Yountville, 707/944-2280, www.chandon.com, daily 10 A.M.–6 P.M., $16) offers one of the best tours in all of Napa—it's a perfect introduction to the process of wine- and champagne-making. Walk out into the vineyards to look at the grapes, head down to the tank- and barrel-filled cellars to learn about the champagne-making process, then proceed into the aging rooms to see the racked bottles, tilted and dusty, aging to the point of drinkability. Finally, you'll adjourn to the tasting room to sample the bubbly concoctions. Chandon also makes still wines, which you can also taste. Reservations are required for tours, and making those reservations in advance is a good idea.

Domaine Chandon also boasts lovely gardens, a stream, and an immense estate. Visitors can walk the open paths between vineyards, enjoy the delights of the tasting room (fee for tasting without a tour), and make a reservation for dinner at Étoile, the on-site California-French restaurant.

Hill Family Estate

Set right on Washington Street in the midst of downtown Yountville, the Hill Family Estate (6512 Washington St., Yountville, 707/944-9580, www.hillfamilyestate.com, daily 10 A.M.–6 P.M., $10) tasting room and antiques shop offers an elegant tasting and shopping experience. The most affordable item in the room is your tasting glass; you can get two tastes for free if you stop by the Yountville Visitors Center (on the next block) first, or just purchase your tastes for $5. Roam amongst the pricey French antiques as you sip, or stand at the bar to enjoy the company of the Hill family and a small selection of light, balanced red and white wines. The Cabernet Sauvignons are *not* made in the typical heavy-handed Napa style, so even tasters with delicate palates will find them drinkable. Ask about the Double Barrel Cab, which is sold in a box that the younger sons of the winery have blasted full of buckshot with their grandfather's double-barrel shotgun.

Jessup Cellars

Located in downtown Yountville, the tiny tasting room at Jessup Cellars (6740 Washington St., Yountville, 707/944-8523, www.jessup cellars.com, daily 10 A.M.–6 P.M.) offers tastes of incredible boutique red wines you'll have a hard time finding anyplace else. You'll get no tours here, no picnic grounds or fancy gardens. But you'll find lush, rich Zinfandels and deep, smoky Cabernets that are more than worth the sometimes-steep price tag. The tasting room boasts a cute little bar, a few shelves with items for purchase, and staff that love their jobs. If you chat them up, you may find yourself tasting rare Jessup vintages that are not on the usual list.

Robert Sinskey Vineyards

Robert Sinskey Vineyards (6320 Silverado Trail, Napa, 800/869-2030, www.robert sinskey.com, daily 10 A.M.–4:30 P.M., $20–60) is getting into the foodie act that's sweeping Wine Country, offering a menu of small bites alongside their list of current wines. They're

WINE COUNTRY

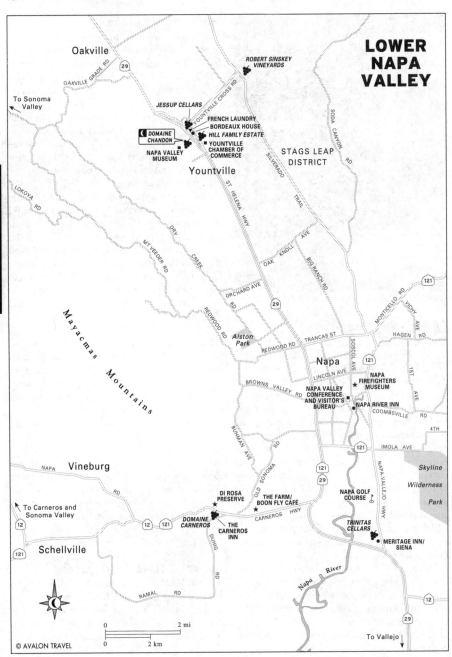

LOWER NAPA VALLEY

Oakville

OAKVILLE GRADE RD

29

To Sonoma
Valley

**ROBERT SINSKEY
VINEYARDS**

YOUNTVILLE CROSS RD

JESSUP CELLARS

FRENCH LAUNDRY
BORDEAUX HOUSE

**DOMAINE
CHANDON**

HILL FAMILY ESTATE

**YOUNTVILLE
CHAMBER OF
COMMERCE**

**NAPA VALLEY
MUSEUM**

Yountville

ST HELENA HWY

SILVERADO TRAIL

SODA CANYON RD

**STAGS LEAP
DISTRICT**

LOKOYA
RD

M a y a c m a s   M o u n t a i n s

MT VEEDER RD

DRY CREEK

OAK KNOLL AVE

BIG RANCH RD

MONTICELLO RD

VICHY AVE

121

ORCHARD AVE

REDWOOD RD

29

Alston
Park

REDWOOD RD

TRANCAS ST

HAGEN RD

SOSCOL AVE

121

Napa

LINCOLN AVE

1ST AVE

**NAPA
FIREFIGHTERS
MUSEUM**

BROWNS VALLEY RD

**NAPA VALLEY
CONFERENCE
AND VISITOR'S
BUREAU**

NAPA RIVER INN

COOMBSVILLE RD

BURNHAM AVE

OLD SONOMA RD

121

IMOLA AVE

4TH

NAPA RD

Vineburg

121

29

**NAPA GOLF
COURSE**

NAPA VALLEJO HWY

Skyline
Wilderness
Park

To Carneros and
Sonoma Valley

12

12

121

**DI ROSA
PRESERVE**

**THE FARM/
BOON FLY CAFÉ**

CARNEROS HWY

**DOMAINE
CARNEROS**

**THE
CARNEROS
INN**

**TRINITAS
CELLARS**

121

Schellville

DUHIG RD

**MERITAGE INN/
SIENA**

RAMAL RD

Napa River

12

29

0   2 mi

0   2 km

© AVALON TRAVEL

To Vallejo

To Vallejo

not quite there yet—the food is sometimes served cold and the pairings aren't yet perfect—but if you happen to snag something fresh off the chef's stove, you'll feel treated. Then again, the red wines themselves are worth a stop at this attractive stone-and-wood edifice. Whether you prefer a dusky Pinot Noir or a fruity Cabernet-Zinfandel blend, you'll find something delicious here that's worth taking home with you.

Opus One

Yup, that huge thing on the rise that looks like a missile silo really is a winery. Opus One (7900 Hwy. 29, Oakville, 707/944-9442, www.opus onewinery.com, daily 10 A.M.–4 P.M.) boasts a reputation as one of the most prestigious, and definitely one of the most expensive, vintners in Napa. The echoing halls inside the facility add to the grandeur of the place, as does the price of a tasting ($30 for a three-ounce pour of a single wine). You're unlikely to find a bottle of Opus One for under $250.

Peju

Peju (8466 St. Helena Hwy., Rutherford, 800/446-7358, www.peju.com, daily 10 A.M.–6 P.M., $10) embodies the ultimate success of the Napa Valley—a 25-year-old family winery that has through hard work created great wines that have garnered the attention of international magazines and judging bodies. Today, visitors to the Peju winery see gorgeous sycamore trees running up the drive (hand-pruned by Tony Peju himself), a fabulous garden tended by Herta Peju, and solar panels on the roof of the elegant winery building. Inside, you'll get tastes of an array of aromatic and award-winning red wines—from the lighter Bordeaux-varietal Cabernet Franc to the many vintages of classic California Cabernet Sauvignons. A few whites and perhaps a pink or a port round out Peju's list.

Rubicon Estate

As many movie buffs as wine lovers come to the grand tasting room and museum at Rubicon (1991 St. Helena Hwy., Rutherford,

707/782-4266, www.rubiconestate.com, daily 10 A.M.–5 P.M., $25), formerly Niebaum-Coppola. This estate winery, a pet project of Francis Ford Coppola himself, also houses a small but delightful museum showcasing famed Coppola movies. You'll see memorabilia from the *Godfather* series and other films, period costumes, some of Coppola's awards, and a few documents that film buffs find fascinating. Over in the large, elegant tasting room you'll find a generous bar area with plenty of staff to help you navigate the Rubicon wine list. Despite the famous name, this isn't just another star-owned vanity winery; the winemakers take their job seriously and the results can be spectacular. Rubicon offers a wide range of varietals, including a few whites. But the specialty of the house is the selection of big, heavy, serious reds that run like blood from the bottle into your glass. Appropriate, don't you think?

Miner Family Vineyards

The estate tasting room at Miner Family Vineyards (7850 Silverado Trail, Oakville, 800/366-9463, www.minerwines.com, daily 11 A.M.–5 P.M., tasting fee $15) provides Silverado Trail–ers with a typical taste of the Napa Valley. (You'll need to climb a flight of stairs or take the elevator up to the oddly small tasting room that still manages to display an array of hoity-toity souvenirs for sale.) The winery mostly makes standard Napa Valley varietal wines (Chardonnay, Cabernet Sauvignon, etc.) with a Viognier or a Sangiovese thrown in for interest. Most of the wines aren't bad, but they aren't remarkable either—certainly not as remarkable as the prices might indicate. If you've never tasted a California wine before, Miner Family might make for a good baseline. If you're an experienced oenophile, you can give this one a pass.

◖ Mumm

You may have already tasted the sparkling wines produced by Mumm (8445 Silverado Trail, Rutherford, 800/686-6272, http://mumm napa.com, daily 10 A.M.–5 P.M., tasting fee

WINE COUNTRY

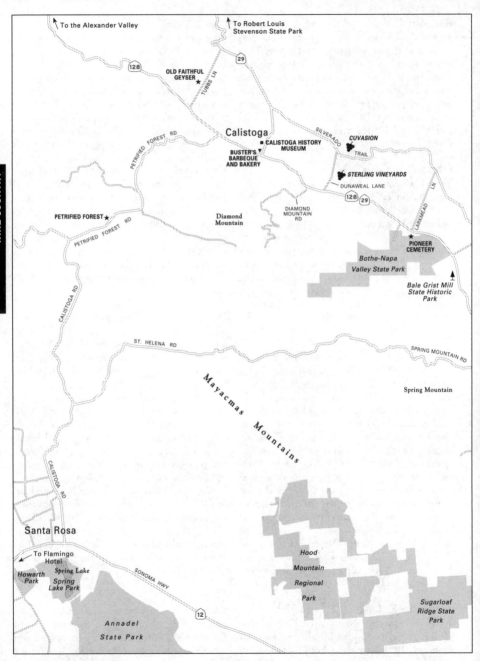

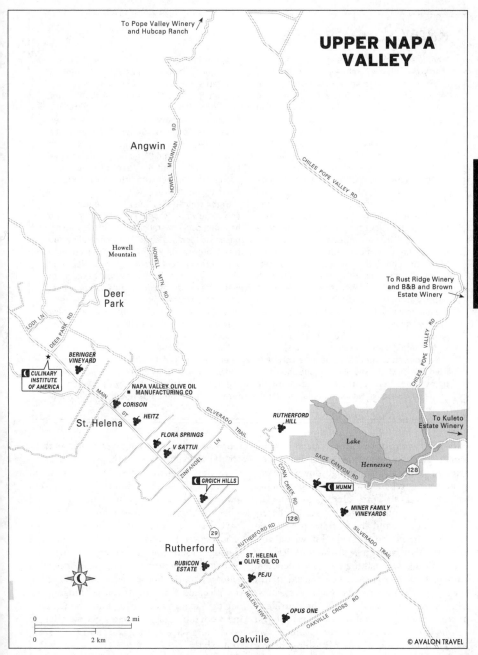

To Pope Valley Winery
and Hubcap Ranch

UPPER NAPA VALLEY

Angwin

HOWELL MOUNTAIN RD

CHILES POPE VALLEY RD

Howell
Mountain

HOWELL MTN. RD

Deer
Park

To Rust Ridge Winery
and B&B and Brown
Estate Winery

LODI LN

DEER PARK RD

BERINGER
VINEYARD

CHILES POPE VALLEY RD

CULINARY
INSTITUTE
OF AMERICA

NAPA VALLEY OLIVE OIL
MANUFACTURING CO

MAIN ST

CORISON

HEITZ

SILVERADO TRAIL

RUTHERFORD
HILL

To Kuleto
Estate Winery

St. Helena

FLORA SPRINGS

V SATTUI

Lake

Hennessey

128

ZINFANDEL LN

SAGE CANYON RD

GRGICH HILLS

CONN CREEK RD

MUMM

MINER FAMILY
VINEYARDS

29

RUTHERFORD RD

128

SILVERADO TRAIL

Rutherford

RUBICON
ESTATE

ST. HELENA
OLIVE OIL CO

PEJU

ST. HELENA HWY

OPUS ONE

OAKVILLE CROSS RD

0   2 mi

0   2 km

Oakville

© AVALON TRAVEL

KNOW YOUR GRAPES

Want to seem more knowledgeable about wine than you really are? Before you come to Napa and Sonoma, get to know your popular California grapes. While nearly every wine grape known to humankind is grown somewhere in the state, and different varietals go in and out of fashion almost as fast as clothing, California has a few distinctive and easy to find grapes that comprise the basics of vintning in the state.

Chardonnay. Most of the white wine made and sold in California is Chardonnay. The grapes grow best in a slightly cooler climate, which lends them well to the vineyards closer to the coast. Most Chardonnay wines are made from nearly 100 percent Chardonnay grapes. Chardonnay is typically fermented in steel tanks, then poured into steel or oak barrels to finish fermenting and to age just a little bit. Most California Chardonnays taste smooth and buttery and a bit like fruit; they often take on the oak flavor of the barrels they sit in. Chardonnay doesn't keep (age), so most Chards are sold the year after they're bottled, and consumed within a few months of purchase.

Sauvignon Blanc. This pale green grape is used to make both Sauvignon Blanc and Fumé Blanc wines in California. Sauvignon Blanc grapes grow well in Napa, Sonoma, and other warm-to-hot parts of the state. The California Sauvignon Blanc wine has a "food friendly" reputation – it goes well with salads, fish, vegetarian cuisine, and even spicy ethnic foods. Sauvignon Blanc has such a light, fruity, and floral taste it almost seems to float away. The difference between a Sauvignon Blanc and a Fumé Blanc is in the winemaking more than in the grapes. Fumé Blanc wines tend to have a strong odor and the taste of grapefruit. Fumes also pair well with fish dishes and spicy Asian cuisine.

Pinot Noir. Unlike the other California-favored red wine grapes, Pinot Noir grapes do best in a cool coastal climate with limited exposure to high heat. The Anderson Valley and the Monterey coastal growing regions tend to specialize in Pinot Noir, though many Napa and Sonoma wineries buy grapes from the coast to make their own versions of this popular wine. California vintners make up single-varietal Pinot Noir wines that taste of cherries, strawberries, and smoke when they're great, and of mold and fish when they're not.

Zinfandel. A good California Zinfandel is not what you think is it. For starters, it's not sweet and pale pink. A true Zinfandel is a hearty deep red wine. These grapes grow best when tortured by their climate; a few grow near Napa,

$16–30). Even for genuine wine snobs, it's worth spending an hour or two at Mumm estates, a friendly and surprisingly down-to-earth winery amongst the often pretentious estates on the Silverado Trail. First, get on the list and take the complimentary tour of the example vineyard and the working production facility. Then learn from the knowledgeable and articulate tour guides, who will describe the sparkling winemaking process in detailed, comprehensible English. All tours wind up in a special treat of a place—the only gallery showing off *original* Ansel Adams prints outside of Yosemite Valley. (Even if you skip the tour, you can hang out in the gallery for as long as you like.) Perhaps best of all, after finishing the free tour you'll get a tag that gives you 15 percent off all bottle purchases in the winery.

Tastings happen at tables, with menus and service in restaurant fashion. Yes, the prices look very Napa Valley, but you'll get more wine and service for your money at Mumm. Each pour is three ounces of wine—some of it high-end—and you get three pours per tasting. Good news for designated drivers: Nonalcoholic gourmet grape sodas or bottled water are on the house, as thanks for keeping the Silverado Trail safe. If you've brought your dog to Napa, you can bring him into the tasting room too. (Dogs get water, gourmet doggie bones, and plenty of petting from the tasting room staff.)

© LANCE SCOTT

wine grapes

producing grapes for nearly 100 years. A great Zinfandel wine boasts the flavors and smells of blackberry jam and the dusky hues of venous blood. Zinfandel often tastes wonderful all by itself, but it's also good with beef, buffalo, and even venison.

Cabernet Sauvignon. If you spend any length of time in Napa or Sonoma, you'll hear the phrase "Cab is King." This always means Cabernet Sauvignon, a grape from the Bordeaux region of France that creates a deep, dark, strong red wine. The grapes that get intense summer heat make the best wine, which makes them a perfect fit in the scorching Napa Valley. In France, Cabernet Sauvignon grapes mix with several other varieties to create the famed Bordeaux Blends. In California, especially in Napa, winemakers use Cabernet Sauvignon on its own to brew some of the most intense single-grape wine in the world. A good dry Cab might taste of leather, tobacco, and Bing cherries. Harsh tannins can create a sandpapery feeling in the mouth and an unpleasant tree-bark flavor, making Cabernet Sauvignon difficult for newcomers to the wine world to enjoy. Cabs age well, often hitting their peak of flavor and smoothness over a decade after bottling. (By then, the tannins have mellowed and the wine tastes less like chewing on an oak branch.)

but most make their homes in Gold Country and the inland Central Coast. Zinfandel was one of the first types of grape introduced in California, and a few lucky vineyards have "Old Vines," Zinfandel vines that have been

Rutherford Hill

If you're planning in advance to visit Rutherford Hill (200 Rutherford Hill Rd., Rutherford, 707/963-1871, www.rutherford hill.com, daily 10 A.M.–5 P.M., $15), book a spot on the winery and cave tour. The winery is pretty standard for a Napa facility, but the caves impress even jaded wine lovers. Dug back into the hillside, Rutherford's caves provide a natural temperature-controlled space in which to age their array of wines, mostly hearty reds. (If you're looking for a place to hold a special dinner or midsized event, Rutherford rents space in their caves.) Contrary to the myth perpetuated by the movie *Sideways,* Rutherford produces a fine

Merlot, as well as rich Cabernet Sauvignons and other tasty varietals.

◖ Grgich Hills

The tasting room at Grgich Hills Winery (1829 St. Helena Hwy., Rutherford, 800/532-3057, www.grgich.com, daily 9:30 A.M.–4:30 P.M., $10) isn't housed in the most elaborate building. The gardens aren't showy, and the working vineyards run right up to the back of the winemaking facility. Active aging barrels crowd the main building and narrow the path to the tasting room's restrooms. If you're looking for a showy Napa Valley "experience," this might not be the best place for you.

What you *will* find at Grgich are some of

the best wines in the valley, an entirely biodynamic winemaking operation, and the rich history of fine wine from California taking its rightful place alongside and even ahead of the great French vintages. Mike Grgich took his California Chardonnay to the Paris Wine Tasting of 1976 and entered it in the White Burgundy blind-tasting competition. It won. The French winemakers were incensed at the result and demanded that the contest be re-run. Grgich's Chardonnay won again. (That same year, Robert Mondavi's Cabernet Sauvignon also took top honors in its category at the same contest.) The quality of California wines could no longer be ignored by even the snottiest of French wine connoisseurs.

Today, you'll learn about this history when visiting Grgich Hills. You'll also see plenty of information about biodynamic farming, a process that takes organic to the next level, using all-natural processes and including phenomenon such as the phases of the moon in the growing and harvesting cycles of the vineyards. All Grgich wines are biodynamically grown and made. Their best wine might be the descendants of Mike's legendary Chardonnay—arguably the best Chardonnay made in Napa or anywhere else in California. But don't ignore the reds; Grgich offers some lovely Zinfandels and Cabernets. And the Violetta, a dessert wine named for Mike's daughter, is a special treat that's only made in years when the grape conditions are perfect. None of the Grgich wines are cheap, and there's a fee for tasting, but it's more than worth it when you sip these rare, exquisite elixirs.

V. Sattui

A boutique winery that distributes to no retailers at all, V. Sattui (1111 White Ln., St. Helena, 707/963-7774, www.vsattui.com, daily summer 9 A.M.–6 P.M., winter 9 A.M.–5 P.M., $5–15) won the "Best Winery" award at the California State Fair in both 2006 and 2007—a mighty feat in a state filled with excellent vintners. Sattui produces a wide selection of varietals—everything from light-bodied whites to full-flavored Cabernet Sauvignons. The dessert

Madeira is particularly fine—if it's not on the tasting menu, ask your pourer at the bar if they've got a bottle open and you might just get lucky.

The big tasting room on Highway 29 boasts three big bar areas, endless stacks and cases of wine out and ready for purchase, a separate register, and a full deli. The gardens surrounding the facility include a number of picnic tables and Sattui is a popular lunchtime stop for all-day tasters. But beware: All the recent good press makes even the big Sattui tasting room fill up on in-season weekends.

Flora Springs

This winery straddles the line between boutique and big-deal Napa player. You'll find Flora Springs (677 S. St. Helena Hwy., St. Helena, 707/967-8032, www.florasprings.com, call for hours) on a few menus in upscale restaurants and in their tasting room. The open, airy tasting room sweeps in a half-circle around its bar, with plenty of windows letting in the glowing Napa sunlight. You'll taste a variety of reds and whites, but the Cabernet Sauvignons are the Flora Springs standouts.

Heitz

One of the oldest wineries in the valley, Heitz (436 St. Helena Hwy., St. Helena, 707/963-3542, www.heitzcellar.com, daily 11 A.M.–4:30 P.M., free) brings a touch of class to the glitz and glamour of Napa. The elegant high-ceilinged tasting room is dominated by a stone fireplace with comfy chairs before it. (Be sure to say hello to Ruby, the small pampered dog rescued a couple years ago by the winery staff.) A low bar off to the right sets the stage for an array of Napa Valley Cabernet Sauvignons. To the happy surprise of many, Heitz's Cabernets are well balanced and easy to drink, and though costly, they approach affordable by Napa standards. Most of the grapes in these wines grow right in the Napa Valley. If you're lucky enough to visit Heitz in February, you can taste the current release of the Martha's Vineyard Cabernet—a vintage grown in the first wine-designated vineyard (i.e. the first vineyard to grow grapes for wine rather than eating) in all of Napa.

Corison

A rarity in the ritzy Napa Valley, Corison (987 St. Helena Hwy., St. Helena, 707/963-0826, www.corison.com, daily 10 A.M.–5 P.M., tasting fee $5–10) is the genuine article—a tiny single-proprietor winery producing great wines in small quantities. Technically, Corison takes tasters by appointment only, but in truth they've never turned away a drop-in during their regular business hours. After turning onto a short gravel driveway, you'll pass a vintage home to reach the small barn that serves as a tasting room. Open the huge white door (it's easier than it looks) and enter the tasting/barrel/stock room. A tiny tasting bar sits right next to the entrance, offering tastings from the 3,000 cases the winery produces each year. Expect the attentive staff to talk in loving and knowledgeable terms about the delicious wines they're pouring. Corison's flagship Cabernet Sauvignon tastes of luscious fruit and perfect balance. The other wines are not distributed—you must buy them then and there, join the wine club, or long for them from afar.

Beringer Vineyards

You may recognize the Beringer name, since this winery sells large quantities of inexpensive wines across the country. The palatial stone estate buildings of Beringer Vineyards (2000 Main St., St. Helena, 707/967-4412, www .beringer.com, daily 10 A.M.–5 P.M., $10–25) belie the reasonably priced vintages you see in your local supermarket. Inside, you'll find an array of wines for tasting, many of which are not commonly available outside the tasting room.

Outside, you can stroll in the beautiful estate gardens, which stretch for acres along the prime land next to Highway 29. Tours take you into the winemaking facilities and show off the highlights of the vast estate.

Sterling Vineyards

Sterling Vineyards (1111 Dunaweal Ln.,

Calistoga, 800/726-6136, www.sterlingvineyards .com, daily 10:30 A.M.–4:30 P.M., $20) is more appealing for folks who are touring Wine Country for the first time to see the sights than for serious wine aficionados. The jewel of the new "Disneyland with wine" culture of Napa, Sterling features a gondola ride and an enforced "tasting tour" through their estate rather than a traditional tasting room experience. It's expensive, and the lines can get long on in-season weekends.

To be fair, once you've stood in line and bought your tickets, the gondola ride up the mountain to the estate shows off Napa Valley at its best. Take advantage of the time to admire the stellar views of forested hills and endless vineyard lands. Once up at the estate, you'll be led around by signs to each tasting glass of wine. Frankly, the wine isn't worth the effort or the high per-bottle price tag. But the estate has some charm, and the views off the deck match those from the gondola.

Cuvaison

This small winery harkens back to the Napa of decades past. The intimate tasting room at

Cuvaison on the Silverado Trail

Cuvaison (4550 Silverado Trail N., Calistoga, 707/942-6266, www.cuvaison.com, Apr.–Nov. daily 10 A.M.–5 P.M., Dec.–Mar. Sun.–Thurs. 11 A.M.–4 P.M., Fri.–Sat. 10 A.M.–5 P.M., $10–15) doesn't hold busloads of tourists and the bar might show a few scars, but the tasting room staff know quite a bit about the wine they're pouring and they want to tell you all about it. The quaint building sits on the slope of the mountains bordering Napa Valley and shelters several friendly cats. A picnic area invites a longer stop to enjoy the vineyard views with your lunch and a nice bottle of Cuvaison Chardonnay, or just to relax and sip one of their light, tasty reds.

SIGHTS

Believe it or not, there are a few things worth seeing in Napa outside of the wineries. Granted, the major industry pervades even the museums here, but the arts and parks of Napa can make a wonderful break from tasting wine, or a whole-day adventure if vino isn't your thing.

di Rosa Preserve

At the unique di Rosa Preserve (5200 Hwy. 21, Napa, 707/226-5991, ext. 25, www.dirosa preserve.org, Wed.–Fri. 9:30 A.M.–3 P.M., Sat. tours 10 A.M.–noon, $10–15), you'll see the cutting edge of modern California art. With 217 acres at its disposal, the di Rosa Preserve has ample room for its three galleries, outdoor sculpture meadow, and on-site lake. Take in the festival of color and creativity in the galleries and sculpture garden, or wander the undeveloped portion of the preserve to soak in the colors and shapes nature chose for this area.

Napa Firefighters Museum

Need a wine break? Got someone in your party who's into firefighting, local history, old photos, or small museums? The Napa Firefighters Museum (1201 Main St., Napa, 707/259-0609, Wed.–Sat. 11 A.M.–4 P.M., free) makes a perfect 30-to-60-minute stop right in the midst of downtown Napa. The antique fire trucks and fire engines dominate the one-room museum, which is staffed by volunteers who truly love

history and firefighting. But don't let the cool equipment completely overwhelm you; small artifacts and collections of vintage photos tell the story of the Napa Valley, and the crucial part played by the area firefighting teams and equipment. Flip through poster-sized news shots of the many Napa Valley floods (including one that flooded the museum building!), examine the collection of old tools, and ask the docents about the incongruous collection of insurance-company plaques. Though there's no admission charge to come and check out all the neat stuff in this great small museum, it's nice to put a few dollars into the donation box to help keep the organization afloat.

Skyline Wilderness Park

Once you're on the trails of Skyline Wilderness Park (2201 Imola Ave., Napa, 707/252-0481, www.skylinepark.org, daily sunrise–sunset), you may forget you're even in the Wine Country. Up at this park, no vineyards encroach on the natural chaparral landscape of Napa's high country. This park includes the Martha Walker Garden—a botanical garden planted with California and Napa native plants in honor of a legendary figure in the local horticultural community. The rest of this 850-acre park is given over to multiple community uses. You'll find campgrounds, hiking trails, horse and bike paths, a disc golf course, halls suitable for events, and more. Be aware that it gets *hot* here in the summertime, and not all the campgrounds and trails offer adequate shade to cool visitors off. Even so, the natural beauty of this protected wilderness makes Skyline Park a favorite with both locals and travelers to the Wine Country area.

Napa Valley Museum

The small Napa Valley Museum (55 Presidents Cir., Yountville, 707/944-0500, www.napavalley museum.org, Wed.–Mon. 10 A.M.–5 P.M., $4.50) sits tucked away behind Domaine Chandon on the other side of Highway 29 in Yountville. Here you'll find perhaps the most complete description of the winemaking process available in all of Wine Country. The main feature of the downstairs gallery is a big high-tech multimedia display that categorizes each step and month in the life of a wine (and a winemaker). If you're interested in learning the details of the grape, plan on spending at least half an hour reading the left-hand wall. Next, you can test what you've learned with a variety of interactive "quizzes" on winemaking. Finally, you can examine information about how different types of wine taste and how to appreciate and drink them. A tiny exhibit tells the history of Napa Valley, from the earliest pioneers through the current wine boom. The upstairs gallery provides space for rotating exhibitions; you're likely to find the work of local artists or art depicting food and wine.

(Culinary Institute of America

The premier institute for professional chef training in America has only two campuses: one in upstate New York and one right here in the Napa Valley. The Culinary Institute of America at Greystone (2555 Main St., St. Helena, 707/967-1010, www.ciachef.edu, Sun.–Thurs. 11:30 A.M.–9 P.M., Fri.–Sat. 11:30 A.M.–10 P.M.) has it all: a restaurant, a café, a gourmet shop, one-day cooking classes and demos, a food history museum, and a stunning set of campus buildings nestled into the forests and vineyards near the town of St. Helena right on Highway 29. If Napa is the perfect place to introduce newcomers to the world of high-end food and wine, Greystone takes it to the intermediate and advanced levels. No matter who you are, you'll love the De Baun Café and the Spice Islands Marketplace, and you'll want to make a reservation in the Wine Spectator Greystone Restaurant. But if you're a for-real foodie or cork dork, consider signing up in advance to attend a cooking demo or even a seminar at this haven for haute cuisine. And be sure to take a few minutes to wander the charming grounds and marvel at the imposing structures of the campus—made from (of course) gray stonework.

Bale Grist Mill State Historic Park

Up under the cool shade trees of the Napa hills,

the gristmill at this state park (3369 N St. on Hwy. 29, 3 miles north of St. Helena, 707/942-4575, www.parks.ca.gov, grounds open daily, buildings Sat.–Sun. only) rests quietly now. The huge water wheel no longer turns, and the vast network of elevated and ground-level wooden pipes and ducts have dried out. Today, visitors can take a pleasant nature walk from the parking lot down to the site of Dr. Edward Bale's old wheel and its associated mill structures. On weekends, take a tour inside the flour mill with a docent who will tell the story of the gristmill and show off the facility that the good doctor built using local stone, redwood, and fir lumber. Once you've soaked in the local history and perhaps enjoyed a picnic on the scattered tables, take a hike further out into the woods along several shady trails.

Old Faithful Geyser

No, that's not a typo, and you haven't accidentally turned east into Yellowstone. The Napa Valley has its own Old Faithful Geyser (1299 Tubbs Ln., Calistoga, 707/942-6463, www .oldfaithfulgeyser.com, adults $8, seniors $7, children 6–12 $3, under 6 free). Unlike its more famous counterpart, this geothermal geyser was manmade. In the 19th and early 20th centuries, more than 100 wells were drilled into the geothermal springs of the Calistoga area, and many of these created geysers. Old Faithful is one of the few that wasn't eventually capped off, and it's the only one that erupts with clockwork regularity. When you visit the geyser, expect no more than a 40-minute wait to see it erupt 60 or more feet into the air. A grassy area surrounds the geyser, with benches and chairs scattered about to allow visitors an easy wait for the show. A bamboo garden surrounds the grassy spot (bamboo is one of the few plants that can tolerate the hot mineral water of this area). Also at Old Faithful you'll find an incongruous but cute petting zoo that shelters several "fainting goats," plus a few sheep and llamas. A coin-op feeder lets visitors feed and pet the animals—a perfect means of inspiring patience in children who may grow tired of waiting for the geyser to erupt. Note

WINE COUNTRY

Old Faithful gets ready . . .

Old Faithful erupts.

that the water in the pool from which the geyser erupts, as well as that of the geyser itself, is *very hot*. It's not safe to wade in the water, nor to stand too close when the geyser goes off. Keep an eye on small children when you visit.

Petrified Forest

The petrified trees of the Petrified Forest (4100 Petrified Forest Rd., Calistoga, 707/942-6667, www.petrifiedforest.org, daily 9 A.M.–5 P.M., summer until 7 P.M., adults $6, seniors/juniors $5, children $3) no longer stand—technically this is an archaeological dig that uncovered a forest that existed more than three million years ago. A volcano that no longer exists erupted, blowing over the trees and covering them with ash. Over hundreds of thousands of years, the minerals in that ash traded places with the contents of the cells that made up the wood of the trees, "petrifying" them. Now these long-dead trees are made of stone. When you visit the forest, you'll see plenty of live, upright trees. Follow your trail map along a 0.5-mile loop to visit the various excavated petrified trees and chunks of trees. You can touch some of the chunks of petrified wood, but most

of the large fallen stone trees enjoy the protection of fences to preserve their pristine state. You'll get to see one rare petrified pine tree, and a number of petrified Coast Redwoods, almost all of which have names. A fun note: All the trees fell in the same direction (and still face that way), showing us from which direction the blast came when the volcano blew up. Inside the visitors center and gift shop, you'll find lots of rocks and minerals, books on geology, and a few rare shards of the petrified trees from this very forest.

Calistoga History Museum

The Calistoga History Museum (1311 Washington St., Calistoga, 707/942-5911, www.sharpsteen-museum.org, daily 11 A.M.–4 P.M., donation suggested) is also known as the Sharpsteen Museum, after its founder Ben Sharpsteen. Sharpsteen, an Academy Award–winning animator for Disney, had a passion for dioramas. It was through his desire (and money) that the immense, exquisitely detailed dioramas depicting the 1860s Calistoga hot springs resort and life in 19th-century Calistoga were built. The other major

© LIZ HAMILL SCOTT

Petrified Forest

have full-sized oak trees growing through them. The whole area is covered by a dense canopy of forest foliage, making it a pleasantly cool place to visit on hot summer days. You can explore up the hillside, where the paths get more overgrown and some of the tombstones are still old wooden planks, their lettering worn away. If you're interested in genealogy, start at the front entrance of the cemetery, where a map and alphabetical survey of the cemetery are posted. One warning about visiting this cemetery: No, not ghosts—lack of parking. There's enough room at the front for one small car. Otherwise, you'll need to park elsewhere and walk carefully along and across Highway 29 to the gate.

SHOPPING
Galleries
Want to taste rare Napa vintages while sitting at an antique wooden table topped with a chunk of mammoth bone? Browse ultra-modern leather and metal furniture paired with objets d'art including an inlaid human

player in the museum, Sam Brannan, was the first pioneer to Calistoga to build a hot springs resort using the geothermal springs in the area. At the museum, you'll learn of Brannan's success and subsequent ruin in the resort business, as well as his unsuccessful attempt to convert the Napa Valley to Mormonism. Other museum exhibits highlight daily life in 19th-century Napa, complete with artifacts and a nod to the Wappo Native American tribe who were the first residents of this area.

Pioneer Cemetery
Looking for your Napa ancestors? Just like prowling through historic graveyards? Stop at the Napa Valley Pioneer Cemetery (Bothe-Napa Valley State Park, 3801 St. Helena Hwy. N., Calistoga, www.parks.ca.gov). Here you'll find the graves of many of Napa's earliest settlers and some of the more prominent early families. The cemetery seems to undergo regular maintenance, since paths between plots are kept clear and walkable. But many of the graves are overgrown with vines—some even

© LIZ HAMILL SCOTT

Napa Valley Pioneer Cemetery

skull? Step inside **Masonrie Napa Valley** (6711 Washington St., Yountville, 707/944-0889, tasting fee $20–40), an honestly unique art gallery and tasting room inhabiting the old stone building that was the Burgundy House. An ever-rotating collection of modern and antique decorative art has a distinctly industrial and almost macabre feel you won't find anywhere else in the Napa Valley. You'll also get the chance to taste local wines made by Napa vintners who don't have their own tasting rooms. Tastings aren't cheap, but you can get a 2-for-1 ticket from the Yountville Chamber of Commerce (6484 Washington St., 707/944-0904), and you'll have the undivided attention of your pourer, who will sit you down in a small gallery and discuss the wines with you as you sip. Tasting selections are forever changing, so frequent visitors to the region can keep coming back to try something new.

Olive Oil Tasting

All that wine can get monotonous, and even the most intrepid tasters need something different once or twice throughout the day. For a great way to get some food and check out some different Napa Valley and California products, visit local olive oil producers. The two olive oil companies look and feel as different as red and white, but each has both charm and great olive oil for sale. The **St. Helena Olive Oil Company** (8576 St. Helena Hwy., Napa, 707/967-1003, www.sholiveoil.com, daily 10:30 A.M.–5 P.M.) lies outside of town in a big warehouse-style space. Elegant displays offer tastes of more than a dozen different bottled-in-house olive oils and unique local vinegars. The tall, curving tasting bars offer the same oils, with commentary from a friendly attendant who'd love to sell you a few bottles. An array of delicious bath and body products sits in one corner of the tourist-friendly shop. You'll also find kitschy farm-style antiques from the United States and Europe for sale in the big facility, part of which is closed off for storage and olive oil bottling.

On the other end of the retail spectrum, the **Napa Valley Olive Oil Manufacturing Co.** (Allison and Charter Oak Sts., St. Helena, 707/963-4173, daily 8 A.M.–5 P.M.) is one of those amazing off-the-beaten-path treasures that travelers feel lucky to find. The tiny, funky old storefront sits two blocks off Highway 29 and features a motley collection of plastic-covered picnic tables sitting out front and a faded hand-lettered sign on the door. Inside, take care not to trip over the uneven floor in the cramped, meandering rooms of the shop. Those in the know dart in, grab at the plainly labeled quart jugs of olive oil, then pay cash for what's obviously a year's supply of the good stuff. You can't taste the oils and vinegars here—you'll just have to go on faith that this Italian-owned and- operated shop will sell you the best. The tiny store also sells fabulous cheeses and fresh-baked breads, making it a great stop for would-be picnickers who don't mind the less-than-elegant surroundings. Napa Valley Olive Oil Manufacturing Co. has its own bottling facilities just like St. Helena does—though here the "facility" consists of the cashier in the back room with a funnel.

ENTERTAINMENT AND EVENTS

A visit to Napa Valley is all about wine, but there are also plenty of events to suit every taste and desire. (But the focus of many of the festivals and festivities is, of course, wine and food.)

Bars and Clubs

Feeding the needs of the cocktail-dress and suit-and-tie crowd, **Étoile Lounge** (1 California Dr., Yountville, www.chandon .com) at Domaine Chandon offers drinks, dancing, and DJs most nights of the week. Sip Chandon's lovely bubbly as you enjoy the scene in this elegant wine bar. Snack food is served in the lounge if you need a nibble (though you won't if you started your evening in the Étoile restaurant).

Theater

More than 50 years ago, the **Lincoln Theater** (100 California Dr., Yountville, 707/944-1300, www.lincolntheatre.org) ran its first show at the Veterans Home in Yountville. Today, a packed year-round season brings top-end live entertainment of all kinds to the Wine Country. You can get tickets to touring Broadway shows, locally produced plays, stand-up comedy, dance productions, music nights, and more. Many of the productions at the Lincoln welcome family audiences. Though this large theater seats hundreds, purchase tickets in advance if you can—especially for one-night-only special performances or if you'll be in the area for only one weekend. Ticket prices range $10–125, depending on the seats and the show. The theater recommends arriving half an hour in advance of showtime to ensure that you've got time to park your car, walk from the parking lot, and find your seat before the curtain goes up.

Festivals and Events

By far, the biggest thing that happens in Napa every year is the grape harvest, sometimes called Crush because the grapes get crushed as part of the first stage of winemaking. During September and October (dates can vary depending on the weather conditions and growing season), events spring up all over Napa Valley. Many wineries host gala festivals for their wine club members, but you must be part of the club to join in the fun.

On the other hand, the **Napa County Fair** (1435 North Oak St., Calistoga, adults $7, children 6–12 $3, under 6 free) is held every July 4th weekend at the Napa County Fairgrounds and is open to all. The annual fair features live music, a parade, carnival rides for the kids, and plenty of food (and wine) for everyone.

If you prefer smaller crowds but bigger fun, consider coming to Napa in February or March to enjoy the events of the **Napa Valley Mustard Festival** (www.mustard festival.org). Each year in the not-so-dead of winter, wild mustard plants bloom brilliant yellow throughout the vineyards of Napa. (Mustard acts as a cover crop, protecting and nurturing the soil in which the precious grape vines grow.) Festival attendees can check the festival website and choose

the opening gala, closing gala, or any of the grand events that happen on the weekends in between. Restaurants and wineries open their doors for special dinners and tasting events. Do be aware that February and March are the rainy season in Napa, so the weather for this festival isn't always the best.

Another fun festival that takes advantage of the off-season, the **Festival of Trees** (707/226-6872, ext. 24) has opened the holiday season in Wine Country for the last 15 years. Put on by the Napa Valley Symphony League, this festival focuses on music as well as food and wine. Make your reservations early (starting in October) to attend the three days' worth of events that make up this festival.

SPORTS AND RECREATION
Spas
NAPA AND ST. HELENA

Rivaling the wineries for popularity in the Napa Valley, the Calistoga hot springs spas have been drawing visitors for over 150 years. Early pioneers to the area found a geothermal spring underneath Calistoga, and it wasn't long before that spring was channeled into pools—and thus the Calistoga spas began. Now, almost a dozen spas compete for the business of locals and tourists alike, offering an array of standard spa services, plus the famous Calistoga mud and mineral baths.

Spa Terra (875 Bordeaux Way, Napa, 707/251-3000, www.spaterra.com, $115/50 min.) is the jewel of the Meritage Inn's property. The interior of an artificial cave beneath a vineyard seems like an odd choice for a luxury spa, but the gorgeous cavern rooms will make a believer of even the most discerning spagoer. Begin your pampering with a warm greeting and a tour of the public areas from your (necessary) guide. Be sure to show up at least 30 minutes in advance of an appointment—you'll have the run of a tiled hot tub, steam room, and relaxation space both before and after your scheduled treatment. Grab a glass of lemon water, a cool moist cloth for your forehead, and warm out (it's not the least bit chilly in Spa Terra).

The menu of treatments includes a full-body scrub using grapeseed extracts, couples massages in two-person rooms, and an espresso-based facial.

An easy walk from anywhere in downtown Yountville, the newly reimagined **Spa Villagio** (6481 Washington St., Yountville, 800/351-1133, daily 7:30 A.M.–9 P.M.) has a beautiful space in which to pamper its patrons. You don't need to be a guest at the Villagio Inn to book a treatment at the spa, though you may wish for one of the five Spa Suites—private spaces where singles, couples, and friends can relax before, during, and after their treatments. Be sure to show up an hour early for your massage, facial, or treatment package—at the price you're paying for treatments here, you'll definitely want to take advantage of the saunas and hot tubs, relaxation rooms, and all the other chichi amenities. The spa recommends making reservations for your treatment at least three weeks in advance, especially during the summer and fall seasons.

CALISTOGA

The award-winning **Calistoga Oasis Spa** (1300 Washington St., 707/942-2122) offers a complete range of day-spa treatments and services. Their signature service, the mud bath, includes time in a tub full of Calistoga mud followed by a soak in a bubble bath of local mineral water and finishing with a few minutes wrapped in cotton blankets in a peaceful dark room. Each private treatment room is set up for two people. Throughout your treatment, an attendant will see to your every wish, providing cold cucumber water to drink and wrapping chilled towels around your neck to create a wonderful juxtaposition of hot bath and cool head. For a special treat, add a massage to the end of your mud bath for a full-fledged pampering session. At the Oasis, the therapists have training in an array of techniques, including reiki energy work. Or pick an herbal facial using your favorite scents to complete your perfect day.

For an old-school Calistoga spa experience, head down the main drag to **Dr. Wilkinson's**

Hot Springs Resort (1507 Lincoln Ave., 707/942-4102, www.drwilkinson.com, daily 8:30 A.M.–5:30 P.M.). Tucked into a charmingly run-down 1950s motel building, this spa was opened by "Doc" Wilkinson in 1952. Doc's proprietary blend of Calistoga mineral water and volcanic ash, Canadian peat, and lavender is still the gold standard for the Calistoga mud bath today. "The Works" includes the mud bath (complete with a soothing mud masque for your face), mineral bath, and finishing blanket wrap. And of course you can also get or add a facial and a massage to your treatment. The men's and women's spa areas are separated at Dr. Wilkinson's. If you're a guest of the hotel, be sure to take a swim or a soak in one of the three mineral-water pools (there are two outdoor pools and one huge spa inside).

At the **Calistoga Hot Springs Spa** (1006 Washington St., 707/942-6269, www.calistoga spa.com, Tues.–Thurs. 8:30 A.M.–4:30 P.M., Fri.–Mon. 8:30 A.M.–9 P.M.), indulge in a mud bath, mineral bath, or all the usual spa treatments. Also available to the public and guaranteed with a spa reservation is access to Calistoga Hot Springs' four outdoor mineral pools. The lap pool is the coolest at 80°F and set up for serious swimmers. The 90°F wading pool with fountains offers fun and health benefits for the whole family. Another large soaking pool is set to 100°F and meant primarily for adults. Finally, the 104°F enormous octagonal jetted spa sits under a gazebo—the perfect location to relax and enjoy the serenity of spa country.

Two other lovely Calistoga spas, both of which offer full mud and mineral baths as well as spa services, are **Golden Haven** (1713 Lake St., 707/942-8000, www.golden haven.com, daily 8 A.M.–11 P.M.) and **Indian Springs** (1712 Lincoln Ave., 707/942-4913, www.indianspringscalistoga.com, daily 9 A.M.–8 P.M.). The **Lincoln Avenue Spa** (1339 Lincoln Ave., 707/942-2950, www.lincoln avenuespa.com) does not have mud bath facilities, but offers a wider array of spa and esthetic treatments.

Bicycling

Biking is a popular way to see the vineyards, forests, and wineries of Napa. You'll get away from the highways and the endless traffic of the wine roads on two wheels under your own power. If you don't know the area, the best way to bike the area is to take a tour. **Napa Valley Bike Tours** (6795 Washington St., Yountville, 800/707-2453, www.napavalleybiketours.com, $149) offers standard and custom tours all over the area, from central Napa to Calistoga. You'll get a brand-name bike, a map, a helmet, and an orientation before beginning your trek. Then you'll be off on your chosen tour: a pedal through the vineyards, a half-day tour or a full-day tour including both wine tasting and meals, or a multi-sport "adventure package" that includes kayaking, a balloon ride, or a horseback ride.

If you prefer to go off on your own rather than follow a guide, you can also rent a bike from Napa Valley Bike Tours. Or you can select from a more diverse fleet at the **Calistoga Bikeshop** (1318 Lincoln Ave., Calistoga, 707/942-9687, http://calistogabikeshop.com, $35–80/day). With cruisers and touring bikes, mountain and road bikes, tandems and trailers, this shop has whatever you need to suit your travel plans. Ask at the shop for directions and maps for whatever kind of ride you want to take, from a simple couple of hours puttering through the vineyards up to the most challenging mountain-bike tracks in the area.

Boating and Fishing

Tired of the often dry land of Napa in the summertime? Get out into the water! If you like your water running, take a cruise on the Napa River with **Napa River Adventures** (Kennedy Park Boat Dock, Napa, 707/224-9080, www.napariveradventures.com, adults $40, children $20). Float along the river in a lovely small covered motor launch in cushy seats, enjoying the view out the massive wraparound windows. Bring along a picnic and a bottle of wine to make the most of your pleasure-cruising experience. The trip takes you right into the heart of downtown Napa and back to the dock.

If you're looking for a lake vacation adjacent to Wine Country, drive a few miles out to **Lake Berryessa** (Berryessa-Knoxville Rd., east of Rutherford). On this largish lake you can ride powerboats Jet Ski, kayak, canoe, and fish—or just sunbathe on the shore and splash about in the shallows with your family. If you've got your own boat, you can launch it at one of the marinas or the **Capell Cove Boat Ramp** (Knoxville Rd.). Or you can rent from one of the lakeside resorts. The **Markley Cove Resort** (7521 Hwy. 128, Napa, 707/966-4204, www.lakeberryessaboats.com) offers all kinds of boats, from patio cruisers to high-end ski-tow boats to personal watercraft to kayaks. Make reservations well in advance to get the boat you want! You can also rent water skis, wakeboards, and ski tubes.

Lake Berryessa also boasts some of the best fishing in California. You can fish for cold- and warm-water fish, including bass, rainbow trout, and kokanee salmon. Rent a boat from one of the resorts, launch your own, or enjoy some relaxed fishing from the shore. The resorts can sell California fishing licenses and bait, and advise you about the season's hottest fishing holes.

Golf

Since you're already in the land of upscale entertainment options, it seems only natural to enjoy a round of golf during your Wine Country vacation. At the par-72 **Napa Golf Course** (2295 Streblow Dr., Napa, 707/255-4333, www.playnapa.com, $33–43), golfers of all levels—even beginners—can enjoy a full 18 holes. More experienced players will enjoy (or curse!) the plethora of water and full-sized trees on this course, known locally as a bargain. Another charming, inexpensive course up north in the valley is the **Mt. St. Helena Golf Course** (Napa County Fairgrounds, Calistoga, 707/942-9966, www.napacountyfairgrounds.com/golf.htm, $18 Mon.–Fri., $24 Sat.–Sun.). This 9-hole, par-36 course offers a perfect spot to take your younger or less-experienced golfing buddies. It's flat and straight, with easier lines than some other courses. On the other hand, all those trees along the fairways and the small greens make it interesting for intermediate-level players.

Horseback Riding

If you don't want to use your own legs to get around Napa Valley, consider borrowing the four strong legs of a horse. Take a break from the endless vineyards and explore some of Napa's most beautiful parks with the **Triple Creek Horse Outfit** (707/887-8700, www.triplecreekhorseoutfit.com, $60–90). Choose from Jack London State Historic Park, Sugarloaf Ridge State Park, or Bothe-Napa Valley State Park in Calistoga. Rides run 1–3 hours and cover a variety of terrain where you can explore both the natural beauty and the historic significance of these parts of Napa. Whether you're an experienced rider or this is your first time on a horse, Triple Creek will find the right horse for you. Check with the ranch for limitations on rider age, fitness, and weight.

Hot-Air Ballooning

Another near-unique Wine Country experience is rising into the morning sun over the valley in a brightly colored hot-air balloon. Be sure to make your reservations in advance as trips can fill up quickly, especially during the high season (which extends well into fall in Napa). You must be an early riser, since most balloon trips depart shortly after dawn. You'll float serenely over the vineyards of Napa Valley on your trip, before a gentle descent into a predetermined spot.

Calistoga Balloons (888/995-7700, www.calistogaballoons.com) is the only company offering regular flights in the north end of Napa Valley, so they've got the lock on some of the prettiest scenery around. In addition to the vineyards, wineries, spas, and charming town of Calistoga, you'll get to see Mount St. Helena and the lush forests of the hills surrounding this lovely area.

On the other end of Napa, **Balloons Above the Valley** (800/464-6824, www.balloonrides.com) offers the full experience—from lodging

balooning over Wine Country

© LANCE SCOTT

packages that include transportation to the launch site to included-with-every-ride champagne brunch after you touch down. Be sure to bring your camera to capture those otherwise-impossible shots of the vineyards and wineries from above!

ACCOMMODATIONS
Napa
$100-150

The **Chateau Hotel** (4195 Solano Ave., 707/253-9300, www.thechateauhotel.com, $135) actually has a pleasantly unpretentious motel feel. The guest rooms are reasonably sized with colorful decor, carpet, and linens. Some rooms offer larger baths or sink areas where you can really spread out if you're staying several days. Choose from an array of room arrangements, including two-bed rooms that work well for families or couples traveling together who want to save money on lodgings. The Chateau Hotel even has some smoking-allowed rooms—a diminishing rarity in California. The building is only two stories, so it's easy to get to whatever room you've rented, even if it's been a long day wine tasting. The pool and spa beckon guests morning, noon, and night, and both remain heated even in winter.

$150-250
At the **Chablis Inn** (3360 Solano Ave., 800/443-3490, www.chablisinn.com, $175), the guest rooms include all the usual amenities: wet bar with mini-fridge, in-room coffee maker, TV with cable, and more. Rooms are simply decorated, but the beds are comfortable, the carpets are dark (perfect for drinking just a little bit of red wine in the rooms!), and the address is central to both the attractions of downtown Napa and the famous Highway 29 wine road.

The pretty, unassuming **Wine Valley Lodge** (200 S. Coombs St., 800/696-7911, www.wine valleylodge.com, $175) welcomes guests with its redbrick and adobe tiled exterior. Inside, guests enjoy the serene rooms with unobtrusive art, pale yellow walls, and soothing pastel comforters. The rooms are nicely sized, and you can get your choice of king bed, two doubles, or a suite depending on the needs of your party. The Wine Valley Lodge also boasts a significant past; in the late 1950s and early '60s, several movies were filmed in Napa, and various A-list stars, including Rock Hudson, Jean Simmons, and even Elvis himself stayed at the lodge during filming. If you're a movie buff, ask for the Elvis suite!

The C **Napa River Inn** (500 Main St., 877/251-8500, www.napariverinn.com, $225) has one of the best locations in Napa. It sits inside the historic Napa Mill, so you can practically fall out of your hotel room and hit the General Store (and restaurant), several galleries, the candy store, and at least one other restaurant on the way down. You're also located steps from the center of Napa's bustling downtown, and if you're lucky your room might afford you a view of the Napa River. Inside, this luxury hotel is crammed with high-end antiques and reproductions in the common area. Best of all, you can choose from three styles of interior decor: Historic Victorian rooms

come with canopy beds, floral prints, cushy chairs, and slipper tubs; the Nautical rooms (many of which face the river) look like the inside of a yacht, with wood paneling, port-hole-style mirrors, and rope-styled accents; the Wine Country rooms echo the natural wealth of the Napa Valley with floral linens, marble bathrooms, and oak moldings.

For a different style of historic lodging experience, stay at the **Napa Inn** (1137 Warren St., 800/435-1144, www.napainn.com, $175), which inhabits two Victorian houses, both painted blue, in the historic downtown Napa area. You can walk from either to downtown shops and restaurants, and take very short drives to the Wine Train depot. As bed-and-breakfasts go, the Napa Inn is a big one, with more than 10 rooms and suites. If you plan to travel with your pet, talk to the inn well in advance to get one of their two pet-friendly rooms. Elegant fabrics and lush modern textures moderate the florals and carved wood of the Victorian era. The nicest rooms have corner whirlpool tubs and king-sized beds. Breakfast at the Napa Inn is an event, with multiple courses served by candlelight. For the ultimate in pampering, book a spa treatment in the privacy of your room.

OVER $250
The king of Napa lodging is the **Silverado** (1600 Atlas Peak Rd., 707/257-0200, www .silveradoresort.com, $275). Your resort experience begins as you drive up and catch your first sight of the stately white colonial main building. You'll find the finest in modern amenities and decorations in your suite (all rooms at the Silverado are full suites with kitchens and dining rooms), from the high-thread-count linens to the complimentary Wi-Fi to the private patio or deck overlooking the grounds. Pale colors with eye-popping jewel-toned accents speak of the best current designers. Outside your room, there's so much to do at the Silverado that you'll find it hard to pry yourself off the grounds to go wine tasting. Choose from the immense spa with full fitness and salon services, the two 18-hole golf courses, the two

restaurants, the 17 tennis courts, the 10 pools, and—believe it or not—more.

Whether you call its locale Napa or Carneros, there's no doubt that **The Carneros Inn** (4048 Sonoma Hwy., Napa, 707/299-4900, www.thecarnerosinn.com, $550–720) is totally misnamed. This "inn" is actually an expansive and expensive cottage resort. The immense property, which backs onto the real Wine "country," has three restaurants, a spa, two pools, a fitness center, and even a small market. Upon arrival, follow the signs to Registration and then just keep driving—the lobby sits at the very top of the resort's hill. Your persistence will be rewarded by a charming greeting, complete with drinks, when you arrive to check in. The unprepossessing (from the outside) cottages spread out in small clusters for acres, each group surrounding its own garden paths and water features. Inside, the cozy (yes, that does mean "smallish" here) cottages sparkle with white linens, tile floors, and windows overlooking sizeable private backyards with decks and comfy chaises. But it's the bathrooms that bring Carneros Inn clients back again and again. The deep soaking tub sits beside a window overlooking the private fenced yard, and the stall shower opens from the back onto an outdoor wooden shower that beckons on hot summer evenings. In winter, it's the radiant-heated tile floor that warms both toes and hearts.

The **Meritage Inn** (875 Bordeaux Way, Napa, 707/251-1900, www.themeritageresort.com, $400–575) sits beside the small Napa Valley airport, convenient to businessmen and to travelers who want easy access to both the Napa Valley and Sonoma-Carneros wine regions. This big motel got a Wine Country makeover—now the grounds, common spaces, and guest rooms have the deep harvest colors and country-elegant style of Tuscany. The lush garden pool is the literal centerpiece of the property, which also includes a wine tasting room, a fabulous spa, and a refreshingly down-to-earth restaurant. The basic shape of the guest rooms remains true to the Meritage's motel roots, but the Tuscan-styled decor and trimmings make a play for elegance, with comfortable beds, deep soaking tubs in the bathrooms, and posh amenities. Expect a fridge stocked with free water and sodas, coffee maker, and a (better than average) complimentary bottle of wine to get you started on your vacation.

Yountville

If you've come to Napa Valley to dine at the French Laundry or immerse yourself in the food scene, you'll want to stay in Yountville if you can. Several inns sit within stumbling distance of the French Laundry, which is convenient for gourmands who want to experience a range of wines with their unearthly meal.

$100-150

A French-styled inn, the **Maison Fleurie** (6529 Yount St., 800/788-0369, www.foursisters.com, $140) offers the best of small-inn style for a more reasonable nightly rate. On Yount Street, the Maison Fleurie has a perfect location for walking to Bouchon, the Bouchon Bakery, and the many other amazing restaurants, boutiques, and tasting rooms in town. The 13 rooms in this "house of flowers" have an attractive but not overwhelming floral decorative theme. The more economical rooms, described as "cozy," are small but attractive. If you've got the budget to splurge, opt for a room in the Bakery Building, where you'll get a fireplace, jetted spa tub, and king bed. All guests enjoy a full breakfast each morning, afternoon wine reception, fresh cookies, and complimentary access to the inn's bikes.

OVER $250

The **C Bordeaux House** (6600 Washington St., 707/944-2855, www.bordeauxhouse.com, $325) has it all: a beautiful brick facade (an unusual sight this close to the fault lines!), lovely French Country interior design, and a location that's literally three doors down from the French Laundry. It's not cheap, but the amenities in each individually decorated room make you feel as though you're staying in a quaint country inn in the south of France.

WINE COUNTRY

Throughout your stay, take a stroll through the inn's gardens, enjoy a splash in the outdoor spa, and partake of the better-than-continental breakfast down in the common area each morning. Perhaps best of all, the location on Washington Street makes a walk from the inn through the best of downtown Yountville an easy prospect.

The **Napa Valley Lodge** (2230 Madison St., 888/455-2468, www.napavalleylodge.com, $285), a stunning Mediterranean-style hotel with stucco walls and red-tiled roofs, loves the sunshine and warmth of the Napa Valley summer. Guests are steeped in the luxury that the Wine Country in general, and Yountville in particular, is known for. Book a spa treatment either in your guest room or out beside the heated pool. Start each day off right with the complimentary champagne buffet breakfast, or order from the California cuisine room-service menu. And finish off each night in the luxury of your room—be it a Parkside Terrace room with a king bed topped with a European-style duvet, a Vineyard Courtyard Terrace room with its own patio and sweeping views of the surrounding vineyards, or a luxurious King Suite with a fireplace, two-person soaking tub, and the ubiquitous valley vineyard views.

At **The Cottages of Napa Valley** (1012 Darms Ln., two miles south of Yountville, 707/252-7810, www.napacottages.com, $460), you'll pay a princely sum to gain a home away from home in the heart of Wine Country. Each cottage has its own king bed, private garden, outdoor fireplace, and kitchenette. Every morning the quiet staff drops off a basket of fresh pastries from Bouchon Bakery and a pot of great coffee for breakfast to greet you whenever you feel like waking up. Simple yet luxurious country-cottage furnishings feel welcoming and homey, and the staff can help you plan and execute the ultimate Wine Country vacation—whatever that means to you.

If splurging on a no-expenses-spared trip to the Napa Valley, go ahead and enjoy the location and luxury of the **Vintage Inn** (6541 Washington St., 800/351-1133, www.vintageinn.com, $375–850). Your room in one of the elegant hexagonal buildings will feature the softest sheets ever, L'Occitane toiletries in a big beautiful bathroom with plenty of storage for longer stays, and a prettily hidden TV and fridge. The French Country–meets–Wine Country decor extends out to a private patio or deck overlooking the lush gardens. Once you make your way off the property (it's easy to get lost in the landscaping and identical structures of this big resort space), you're at the center of the main drag in Yountville. Walk to wine tasting rooms, galleries, and of course, the legendary restaurants. But before making reservations for lunch someplace pricey, take a look at the fabulous food offerings at the Vintage Inn. The dining room serves what might be the best complimentary hotel buffet breakfast in all of California, with buttery French pastries, fresh fruit, and made-to-order omelets. Then, at 3 P.M., the staff sets out a full-fledged free afternoon tea, complete with finger sandwiches, homemade scones, and organic teas. Plus wine, of course! As a sister property of the nearby Villagio, Vintage Inn guests get use of the Villagio's fitness center, tennis courts, and spa.

St. Helena

The charming small village of St. Helena sits right on Highway 29, and its stop signs and traffic signals are often the cause of the endless weekend Wine Country traffic jams. But if you're staying here, you can avoid the worst of the traffic and enjoy the wooded central Napa Valley area.

$150-250

At the **Zinfandel Inn** (800 Zinfandel Ln., 707/963-3512, www.zinfandelinn.com, $175), you'll find yourself inside a 1980s re-production of a Shakespearean castle. Lavish stonework coats the outside of this unique structure. Inside, you'll stay in one of three exquisitely decorated suite-like rooms. Each guest room boasts a unique design, complete with antique bedsteads and dressers, featherbeds, fireplaces, and tiled whirlpool tubs. All guests enjoy the full breakfast every morning of their stay, plus the rich amenities suitable to a Wine Country inn.

A less imposing structure, **The Ink House** (1575 St. Helena Hwy. at Whitehall Ln., 707/963-3890, www.inkhouse.com, $185) prides itself on its more casual elegance. A pretty yellow facade looks almost like a wedding cake. Inside, the breakfast room inhabits the 1st floor, all the guest rooms live on the 2nd floor, and the small 3rd-floor solarium is open as a parlor to all guests. There are many amenities to enjoy at the Ink House, from the full gourmet breakfast and afternoon wine social to the complimentary nightcaps and loaner bicycles. The lounge areas include a pool table and a TV with a VCR (plus a VHS library). Your room will be individually decorated, but every one of the rooms has a view of the surrounding forest and vineyards. Furnishings tend toward American and European antiques, and all beds are queen-sized.

Calistoga

A plethora of places to stay clusters at the north end of Napa Valley. Here's where you'll find most of the hotel-and-spa combos, plus plenty of mineral water pools and hot tubs for your pleasure.

$100-150

The **Calistoga Inn** (1259 Lincoln Ave., 707/942-4101, www.calistogainn.com, $90–140) gives guests an old-school hotel experience, complete with shared bathrooms and showers. The inn, in continuous operation for over 100 years, offers a continental breakfast each morning, an English pub downstairs that serves lunch and dinner, and perhaps the best bargain rooms in the whole of Napa Valley. Each of the 18 guest rooms provides a small, cozy haven with a queen bed, simple furnishings, and a view of the town. Be sure to make reservations in advance—at these prices, rooms go quickly, especially in summer and fall! And be aware that the pub downstairs has live music acts four nights a week, so the party can get loud (and fun!) on weekends.

$150-250

The **Roman Spa Hot Springs Resort** (1300 Washington St., 707/942-4441, www.romanspa hotsprings.com, $150–310 in high season) in the heart of downtown Calistoga has it all. Three mineral water pools, each set at a different temperature (no children under four are allowed in any pool, and the 105°F spa is adults-only), plus saunas inspire guests to relax and refresh themselves with daily soaks and swims. Guest rooms run the range from inexpensive motel-style rooms with floral comforters, to whirlpool rooms that include your own private two-person mineral bath, to kitchen suites (pots, pans, and dishes provided) that beckon families or groups who plan to stay a while. The Roman Spa connects to the Calistoga Oasis, which offers an array of spa treatments, including the famous mud baths.

If you're looking for a more traditional bed-and-breakfast experience, you can't miss **The Pink Mansion** (1415 Foothill Blvd., 800/238/7465, www.pinkmansion.com, $165–345). Literally. The 1875 mansion is painted bright, unmistakable pink from stem to stern, making it a local landmark. Each lush room features a unique theme suitable to romance and wine. The more economical rooms have queen beds and pretty antique furnishings; the larger suites are spacious enough to dwarf their king-sized beds, and you'll also find fireplaces, whirlpool tubs, and top-tier amenities. You'll get to enjoy the heated indoor pool and spa, a full breakfast each morning, and use of the various TVs and VCRs (plus movie library) secreted around the house.

Want to combine all the elements of a Wine Country vacation into one inclusive spot? Visit the **Silver Rose Resort Winery** (351 Rosedale Rd., 800/995-9381, www.silverrose .com, $175–325). Choose your favorite of the 20 individually styled rooms, each with its own theme and country-elegant appointments, where your queen or king bed will invite you to a comfortable night's sleep each evening. The Silver Rose has its own winery, where you can taste and tour. Or spend a few hours in the spa, getting a massage-and-mud-bath combo. If you prefer to get active on your vacation, check out the tennis courts, swimming pool (shaped like a wine bottle), putting green, or hiking and biking roads and trails. Whatever your dream for your trip in the Napa Valley, the Silver Rose can probably accommodate you.

Another fabulous spa and hotel is the **Mount View Hotel and Spa** (1457 Lincoln Ave., 800/816-6877, www.mountviewhotel.com, $175–375). Perfectly located on Calistoga's main drag, the Mount View offers more than 30 posh rooms in which to break for the night between wine tasting adventures and pampered spa days. You'll find rooms, suites, and cottages decorated with tasteful 19th-century antiques and soothing colors inspired by the vines and vintages of the local area. Rooms have either two twin beds, a queen, or a king, all softened with featherbeds and down comforters. The spa offers facials, body wraps, steam showers, and scrubs. Enjoy the outdoor pool and spa at your leisure.

FOOD

The restaurants of Napa garner almost as much fame as the wine. Some of the best food in California, and possibly the world, clusters near the vineyards of the Napa Valley. You'll find everything from kickin' barbecue to the hautest of haute French cuisine, all with an unforgettable California touch. And of course, most of it goes perfectly with wine!

Napa

The FARM (4048 Sonoma Hwy., 707/299-4880, www.thecarnerosinn.com, daily 11:30 A.M.–2:30 P.M. and 5:30–10 P.M., Sun. brunch 10:30 A.M.–2 P.M., $35–60) at the Carneros Inn serves up the expected upscale California cuisine, complete with a chef's tasting menu and big white service plates topped with tiny artistic piles of food. So why choose to dine at the determinedly all-caps FARM? The food may be a touch pretentious, but it's cooked perfectly, and the chef has put some imagination into his dishes that really works well. Expect unusual but deftly created flavor combinations, smaller portions appropriate to the

number of courses you'll get, and just a touch of molecular gastronomy thrown in for color and interest. The dining room feels more comfortable than many of its ilk, with cushy banquettes and padded chairs. Servers are friendly and good at their jobs, and can help you decipher anything on the menu that might be confusing. Do dress up just a little bit—despite its name, the FARM has a distinctly upscale vibe.

For classic breakfast dishes and almost down-to-earth salad and sandwich fare, the **Boon Fly Café** (4048 Sonoma Hwy., 707/299-4870, www.thecarnerosinn.com, daily 7 A.M.–9 P.M., $25–40) offers an upscale Californified diner experience at the posh Carneros Inn. (If staying at the inn, skip the mediocre service of the café itself and order the Boon Fly menu via room service—the price is the same in-cottage as in-diner.) Eggs are cooked competently, salads are enormous, and the carefully designed "down-home" dining room is cute. The half-booth banquettes are comfortable to sit in, and lingering over coffee or tea is tolerated. Wine tasters passing through will find the Boon Fly easily—it's got a nice big sign on the bright-red barn of a building. Sadly, the Boon Fly does *not* serve breakfast all day—be sure to arrive and order before 11 A.M. if you're dying for an omelet.

If expecting typical Wine Country cuisine at **Siena** (875 Bordeaux Way, 707/251-1900, www.themeritageresort.com, Mon.–Sat. 6:30 A.M.–3 P.M., Sat.–Sun. 5–10 P.M., Sun. brunch 6:30–10:30 A.M., $30–50), the restaurant at the Meritage Inn, you're in for a pleasant surprise. As its name suggests, the chef at Siena cooks mostly Italian food, much of it hot, hearty, and welcome after a long day of wine tasting. Choose from fresh salads, pasta dishes, and big entrées, though if you've been in Napa for a while you may not be able to resist a macaroni-and-cheese appetizer or a cheeseburger. Both of these comforting dishes stand out for their simplicity and their quality—the waiter can even suggest the right wine (or beer!) to accompany your burger. Desserts also tend towards the dense and filling—consider sharing one amongst your tablemates. The upholstered booths and dim lights make a romantic dining experience possible, but the vibe in the dining room manages to stay low-key enough to make jeans-clad diners comfortable.

When Napa locals need a birthday cake, a breakfast danish, or a diner-style breakfast or lunch, they head over to the **Butter Cream Bakery & Diner** (2297 Jefferson St., 707/255-6700, www.buttercreambakery.com, diner daily 5:30 A.M.–3 P.M., bakery Mon.–Sat. 5:30 A.M.–6:30 P.M., Sun. 5:30 A.M.–4:30 P.M., $10–15). It's not in the ritzy part of downtown, but the brilliant pink-and-white-striped building is hard to miss. On the diner side, the Butter Cream serves breakfast all day; choose between a small table in the fluorescent-lit linoleum dining room or a stool at the old-school counter. Service is indifferent, but you'll get decently cooked eggs, tasty sandwiches, reasonable portions, and best of all, *reasonable prices* (a real rarity in Napa Valley dining establishments). Over on the bakery side, mouth-watering turnovers, danishes, and fruit rings make it easy to get a good breakfast on the go. Dessert pastries, cookies, and cakes tempt even dieters to sin—the tasty homemade goods are worth just one little splurge, really!

Yountville

The tiny town of Yountville boasts perhaps the biggest reputation for culinary excellence in California—a big deal when you consider the offerings of San Francisco and Los Angeles! The reason for this reputation starts and finishes with Thomas Keller's indisputably amazing **C** **French Laundry** (6640 Washington St., 707/944-2380, www.frenchlaundry.com, daily 5:30–9 P.M., Fri.–Sun. 11 A.M.–1 P.M., reservation only, $240). Once you've gotten that all-important reservation, the fun begins! From the moment you walk in the door of the rambling Victorian, you're treated like royalty. You'll be led to your seat in one of the small dining rooms by one of the many, many pristine black-and-white-clad staff. Even if you're new to this level of dining (and most of us are), you'll be made to feel more than welcome here.

The menu, which changes often, offers two main selections: the regular nine-course tasting menu and the vegetarian nine-course tasting menu. You'll have a few either/or choices as you run down each list—usually you'll see two options for the fish course and two options for the entrée. The waitstaff can help you identify anything you don't recognize, or if you're having a crisis of decision-making. The sommelier is at your beck and call to assist you with a wine list that weighs several pounds.

Then the meal begins. From the first, waiters and footmen ply you with extras—an amuse-bouche here, an extra middle course there—and if you mention that someone else has something on their plate that you'd like to try, it appears in front of you as if by magic. Finally, the desserts come. And come. And come. After the fourth separate dessert course, you may want to ask for a white flag with which to signal your surrender. All together, a meal at the French Laundry can run up to 13 courses and take four hours to eat. Afterward, you might not eat normally for a couple of days, and you'll have spent a good chunk of rent money on a single meal, but it will seem worth it.

Departing from Yountville's ever-present Wine Country cuisine formula, **Bistro Jeanty** (6510 Washington St., 707/944-0103, www.bistrojeanty.com, daily 11:30 A.M.–10:30 P.M., $30–60) gets lots of recommendations from locals. Certainly the interior works on a theory of whimsy rather than prestige, with a life-sized toy man "riding" a bicycle down the middle of the front dining room. Parisian posters on the walls evoke just the sense the proprietors are going for—that of an authentic French bistro. The menu is Jeanty's heart, a single page devoted to the classics of Parisian bistro cuisine. Tomato bisque served with a puff pastry shell, traditional salads, cassoulet, coq au vin, even a croque monsieur are all crafted with obvious joy. Every local Yountville resident will lovingly describe his or her own favorite dish. Service is friendly, and you'll see a few locals hanging at the bar, watching the TV tuned to a sports channel—something of a non sequitur here. Jeanty has two dining rooms, making walk-in

RESERVATIONS FOR FRENCH LAUNDRY

Most people familiar with the world of high-end food know that the best restaurant in all of California, and possibly all of the United States, is the **French Laundry.** Thomas Keller's culinary haven in tiny Yountville was the only restaurant in the greater Bay Area to earn the hallowed three-star rating from the Michelin Guide in 2007. The restaurant sits inside a charming vintage house; its kitchen garden grows right across the street where anyone can walk down the rows of vegetables and herbs.

Sounds like foodie paradise, right? There's just one problem: getting a table.

The difficulty in getting reservations to the French Laundry is almost as legendary as the French Laundry itself. Rather than expecting to dine at the French Laundry during a planned trip to the Wine Country, savvy travelers expect to plan their whole trip around whatever French Laundry reservation they manage to get.

The bare facts: The French Laundry takes reservations two months in advance. *Precisely* two months. The restaurant accepts reservations by phone, online, and via local concierges. Reservations are accepted for parties of two, four, or six. No more and no less. Diners can choose between lunch and dinner seatings that offer the same menu. It's easier to get a table for lunch than it is for dinner. Lunch or dinner takes two and a half to four hours to consume. Budget $500 *per person* for your meal if you plan to drink wine, and $300–350 if you don't.

The French Laundry starts taking **phone reservations** at 9 A.M. daily. Between 8:30 and 8:45 A.M., program their number on your speed-dial and begin calling. Continue calling again and again until you get an answer. If you get a continuous busy signal past 11 A.M., you'll probably need to try again the next day. And maybe the day after that.

Making **reservations online** works much the same way as on the phone, only it's harder. The French Laundry offers only one table (for lunch) online per day. Go online at OpenTable (www.opentable.com) at about 8:30 A.M. and start trying to snag that table. If you're still trying at 9:30 A.M., it's probably already gone.

Hands down the low-stress way to get a coveted French Laundry table is to hire a concierge to do it for you. The French Laundry lets concierges walk downtown to the restaurant each day to put in bookings for their clients. Call or email a concierge and expect to pay a nominal fee ($20–30), but if you can afford to dine at the French Laundry, that's pocket change. Give your new best friend a range of dates and times that will suit you, and he or she will do their best to accommodate your request. Do not expect get your first choice of times; flexible diners will find themselves with a remarkably trouble-free reservation experience.

So is it *really* worth all this rigmarole just to get into one lousy restaurant, then pay a sizeable part of a month's salary for a single meal?

Yes.

From the gracious welcome at the door to the stunning service throughout the meal to the food that can be found nowhere else, dining at the French Laundry is worth both the hassle and the price tag. I speak from experience and am dying to go back!

---

dining easy on off-season weeknights, but definitely make a dinner reservation if you're in town on the weekend or in high season.

Étoile (1 California Dr., 707/204-7529, www.chandon.com, Thurs.–Mon. 11:30 A.M.–2:30 P.M. and 6–9:30 P.M., $32–41) is another high-end restaurant in Yountville, sitting inside the tasting facility at the prestigious Domaine Chandon champagnery. Lovely white tablecloths sparkle in the sunlight and overlook Chandon's lush green gardens. The menu at Étoile is inventive even for Napa, and each dish is prepared to utter perfection. Order the chef's tasting menu with wine pairings to sample Chandon's wine list at its best and enjoy the delectable cuisine as it was intended to be eaten.

If you can't quite manage the French Laundry, try Thomas Keller's other Yountville option, **Bouchon** (6534 Washington St.,

707/944-8037, www.bouchonbistro.com, daily 11:30 A.M.–12:30 A.M., $24–34). Reservations are still strongly recommended, but you can get one just a week in advance. Bouchon's atmosphere and food scream Parisian bistro. Order traditional favorites such as the croque monsieur or steak frites, or opt for a California-influenced specialty salad or entrée made with local sustainable ingredients.

If you're just looking for a breakfast pastry or a sandwich, walk from Bouchon to the **Bouchon Bakery** (6528 Washington St., 707/944-2253, www.bouchonbakery.com, daily 7 A.M.–7 P.M.) next door. This ultra-high-end bakery supplies both Bouchon and the French Laundry with pastries and breads, as well as operating a retail storefront. Locals and visitors flock to the bakery at breakfast and lunchtime, so expect a line.

Rutherford

The historic **Auberge du Soleil** (180 Rutherford Hill Rd., 800/348-5406, www.aubergedusoleil.com, daily 7 A.M.–11 A.M., 11:30 A.M.–2:30 P.M., and 5:30–9:30 P.M., tasting menu $98) has an inn where you can stay the night, but some visitors come to the Auberge just for the food. The charming Mediterranean-style dining room has drawn visitors from all over the world for decades. Sunny yellow tablecloths, a central fireplace, exposed wooden beams, and wall-to-wall picture windows welcome diners to the restaurant. Executive Chef Robert Curry, a legend of the Napa Valley culinary scene, uses the finest local ingredients to create his own take on Mediterranean/California cuisine. Choose one item from each course list on the short but exquisite tasting menu to create a four-course dinner. If you ask, they can also serve you à la carte items from any of the courses. After all that rich food and fine wine, you might find yourself at the inn's desk, begging to be allowed to stay the night within staggering distance of the restaurant.

Another long-standing Wine Country favorite is the **Rutherford Grill** (1180 Rutherford Rd., 707/963-1792, www.hillstone.com,

$10–30), which is more casual than many of its Napa Valley brethren. Some of the best seats in the house cluster outside the dining room on the wide deck; sheltered by a collection of umbrellas, guests enjoy the pretty gardens while they wait for their classic grill fare—cheeseburgers, salads (with grilled items), bangers and mash, and a whole array of grilled meats—as well as an extensive and impressive wine list. Perhaps the best news of all? You can escape from the Rutherford Grill for well under $100 per person.

St. Helena

A highlight of the St. Helena dining scene is the **Wine Spectator Greystone Restaurant** (2555 Main St., 707/967-1010, http://ciachef.edu, Sun.–Thurs. 11:30 A.M.–9 P.M., Fri.–Sat. 11:30 A.M.–10 P.M., $21–34), better known to its friends as "the restaurant at the CIA," where the world's top aspiring chefs practice their craft. It's easier to get a reservation here than in Thomas Keller's hallowed halls; with several big dining rooms, the CIA can seat large numbers every night. If you get the right table, you can watch your food being prepared in the open kitchen. The ever-changing menu highlights the best of each season and the wine list features the best of Napa Valley's vintages; the student chefs plan menus with an eye to wine pairings.

Calistoga

Small, homey Calistoga offers a pleasing combination of high-end California cuisine and simpler yet still delicious fare. If you need a break from rich, expensive food, a great place to stop for a meal sits right at the corner of Lincoln and Highway 29. **⟨ Buster's Barbecue and Bakery** (1207 Foothill Blvd., 707/942-5605, $4–10) brings unpretentious barbecue to Wine Country. You may find lines at this walk-up eatery at both lunch- and dinnertime—mostly locals looking for a good, quick meal. The simple fare includes huge hot dogs, homemade barbecued tri-tip sandwiches, barbecued pork, and chicken. You'll also have your pick of traditional sides (baked beans, slaw, potato salad, cornbread, and such) and Southern-style baked goods. The sweet-potato pie is a reputed local favorite. Portions are huge, the quality rocks even for Wine Country food, and when they say that the "hot" barbecue sauce is serious, they really mean it.

INFORMATION AND SERVICES
Tourist Information

If you hit only one visitors center during your whole stay in California, make it one in Napa Valley. Why? For the complimentary wine tasting passes. Tastings in the Napa region grow ever more expensive—you can easily spend $20–30 per person, per winery these days. But if you ask at the visitors centers, you can easily get up to six free passes for two tasters. That means you'll save $100–180 based on just 15 minutes spent chatting with a friendly local who can also direct you to the locals' favorite wineries, restaurants, and attractions, which tend to be cheaper and better than those that spend bucketloads of money on advertising.

The **Napa Valley Conference and Visitors Bureau** (1310 Napa Town Center, 707/226-7459, www.napavalley.org, daily 9 A.M.–5 P.M.), right in the middle of downtown Napa, is one good place to start; another is the **Yountville Chamber of Commerce** (6484 Washington St., 707/944-0904, http://yountville.com, daily 10 A.M.–5 P.M.), located right in the midst of the downtown main drag.

Media and Communications

A plethora of publications offer all the information you could ever use to tour Wine Country. Most of the free magazines, which can be overwhelming in number when you see them in the racks, are available in hotels, inns, visitors centers, wineries, restaurants—wherever you look, really. For current events, *Wine Country This Week* (www.winecountrythisweek.com) has the best up-to-date information.

If it's local news you're seeking, you can find it in the daily *Napa Valley Register* (www.napanews.com).

You will find a **post office** in most of the Napa Valley municipalities. In downtown Napa there's one at 1351 Second Street (707/255-0621).

Medical Services

For medical treatment (including alcohol poisoning), the **Queen of the Valley** (1000 Trancas St., Napa, 707/257-4038, www.thequeen.org) has both a 24-hour emergency room/trauma center and a by-appointment urgent-care clinic.

GETTING THERE AND AROUND
Car

Think you're going to enjoy a lovely weekend wine tasting tour at the height of harvest season, bopping quickly from winery to winery without a care in the world? Think again. Many thousands of visitors from the Bay Area and all over the world will be plying the same two major Napa Valley wine routes. **Highway 29** runs through the center of the valley and becomes something akin to a 20-mile parking lot on weekend afternoons. It can take a ridiculous amount of time to get just from one winery to the next. **The Silverado Trail** isn't much better.

To have the best experience with the least traffic headaches, make a few adjustments to your plans:

1. Take your tasting tour on Monday, Tuesday, or Wednesday. These are the least popular days with the Bay Area weekend hordes.

2. Get going early. If you can stomach wine with breakfast, start your tour at 9–10 A.M., right when the tasting rooms start to open. If you can finish up with the wineries by noon or 1 P.M., you might be able to grab lunch in Calistoga and then go for a mud bath or a walk in the woods while everyone else is sitting in gridlock.

3. Consider postponing your Wine Country trip until the rainy season (Nov.–Feb.). This is the least popular season in Napa, since the grape vines are hibernating and the dank weather doesn't show off the valley to its most scenic advantage. But the wines still taste

fabulous, and you'll avoid the worst car traffic and crowding in the tasting rooms. Heck, you might even get a chance to *talk* to your pourer about the vintages you're tasting!

Be sure to bring a map along for the drive to Napa; it's not the most straightforward trip from the Bay Area or points east. From San Francisco, take the Golden Gate Bridge north across the bay to U.S. 101. From there, pick up Highway 37 in Novato (you'll see signs on U.S. 101 directing you to Napa), which takes you right into the city of Napa. If you're staying in Calistoga or someplace farther north, continue on U.S. 101 all the way to Highway 128, which will take you straight into Calistoga.

If you're driving down to Napa from Sonoma, U.S. 101 to Highway 128 is your best option. This route also works if you're coming from the North Coast.

Driving from the East Bay? Take I-80 and turn off at Highway 37; you'll see the Six Flags amusement park at this freeway interchange. Highway 37 will take you all the way to Napa. This route also works for travelers coming from Lake Tahoe or the Sacramento/Gold Country area.

Bus

The **VINE** bus (800/696-6443, www.nctpa .net/vine.cfm, Mon.–Fri. 5:20 A.M.–9:25 P.M., Sat. 6:30 A.M.–8:40 P.M., Sun. 8:30 A.M.–7 P.M., adults $1.25–2.75, children $1–2) provides public transportation to the Napa Valley. Check the website for routes, stations, and fares. You can pay cash when you get on the bus, but you must have exact change.

Wine Tours

A popular and wonderful way to tour the Napa Valley wineries is *not* to drive yourself. If you hire a limo or join up with a tour, no one in your party must abstain as the designated driver, and everyone has a better time because no one's worried about traffic. You'll find plenty of tour operators and limo companies in the area happy to take your reservations. Calling at least a few days in advance is recommended, or even earlier during late summer

and fall. Expect to spend $100–300 on your tour or limo service, depending on the size of your party and the level of service and tour customizing you want.

Napa Valley Wine Country Tours (707/226-3333, www.winecountrylimos.com, $79/person, 11 A.M.–5 P.M.) runs a luxury van to some of the most prestigious wineries, plus a few great boutiques you might not be familiar with. With a flexible schedule and a 13-passenger limit, this tour makes a great choice for serious oenophiles as well as Wine Country newcomers. A picnic lunch is included in this six-hour tour, though you're expected to pay your own tasting fees.

If you're in Napa with a small party or just your sweetie, consider hiring **Elegant Tours** (707/312-1352, www.elegantwinetours.com). Stretch limos in several styles are available, but so are smaller unobtrusive sedans that can take smaller parties on custom tours. They'll take you tasting, to dinner, and to the airport.

For visitors looking to meet new people on their travels, a seat on the bus with **California Wine Tours and Transportation** (800/294-6386, www.californiawinetours.com) might be the perfect choice. Leaving from either Napa or San Francisco, these large package tours offer a great overview of the biggest Napa wineries. You'll be seated in a comfortable bus for the duration of the trip, swapping tasting notes with your fellow travelers. Or if you prefer a smaller tour of the more intimate winemakers, consider hiring one of the company's smaller vehicles for your trip.

Walking Tours

Many Napa Valley towns invite walking tours—a great way to learn about the areas you're visiting and work off some of the rich food and wine at the same time. In downtown Napa, there's a short but fascinating self-guided walking tour at the **Historic Napa Mill** (500 Main St.). You can stroll the outer perimeter and then the inner corridors of this 100-plus-year-old building created by some of Napa's founders. Maps are available in front of some of the shops to guide you and teach you about the origins of each storefront.

Expect this tour to take 30–60 minutes, depending on whether you stop to shop.

Another great place to take a historical walk is **Yountville** (Washington and Yount Sts.). Stop in at the visitors center to get a Historical Walking Tour map, then take off to explore the history of the town that's turned into the culinary mecca of California. Along the two-mile loop you'll see parks, the local pioneer cemetery, original Victorian homes, century-old storefronts, wineries, and much more. If you do the full loop and stop to admire the various sights, this walk may take you as much as 2–3 hours.

Russian River Valley

The Russian River Valley may be the prettiest part of Wine Country. The Russian River runs through it, providing ample water for forests and meadows, as well as wide, calm spots with sandy banks. Rafting, canoeing, and kayaking opportunities abound on the zippier stretches of the river, making this area as much of a destination for outdoors enthusiasts as for wine fans. If you are visiting for the vino, the area called the "Russian River Valley" actually encompasses several prestigious American Viticultural Areas, including Dry Creek, the Alexander Valley, and of course the Russian River.

A little to the west of the area's concentrated wine region, you'll reach the river in Guerneville—a noted gay and lesbian resort destination. Even if you're straight (but not narrow) you'll love the kitschy downtown, clothing-optional resorts, and general sense of friendliness and fun that permeates this area.

WINERIES

Wineries are listed from south to north and are clustered along three main roads: the Gravenstein Highway (CA-116), River Road, and U.S. 101.

Merry Edwards Winery

Merry Edwards was the first woman to earn a degree in enology (winemaking) from the prestigious UC Davis program in 1993. After working as a winemaker for numerous Sonoma vintners and developing her own Pinot Noir grape clone with the help of the facilities and staff at UC Davis, Merry finally gave in and opened her own winery. The Merry Edwards Winery (2959 Gravenstein Hwy., Sebastopol, 707/823-7466, www.merryedwards.com, appointment only, free) offers tastings by appointment only in its two glass-walled tasting rooms (same-day appointments can be arranged). Anxious to avoid the overcrowded, underattended Napa tourist tasting model, each member of Merry Edwards' tasting staff will work with only one party of tasters at a time. Instead of forcing your way through a crowd to garner 12 inches of bar space, you'll be led to a table with comfortable chairs that's already set with four glasses ready to hold the four different Pinot Noirs you'll sip. (That's four examples of the same varietal, plus a bonus Sauvignon Blanc served at the end of the tasting.) It's easy to spend an hour at Merry Edwards, soaking up the luxury of a completely different tasting experience. Perhaps most amazingly of all, tasting at Merry Edwards is free. However, you probably won't make it out the door without purchasing at least one bottle of Merry's stellar wine.

Battaglini Estate Winery

Many large Russian River wineries make a wine out of every varietal under the hot Sonoma sun, but Battaglini Estate Winery (2948 Piner Rd., Santa Rosa, 707/578-4091, www.battagliniwines.com) has chosen instead to specialize. Inside the cute wood-paneled tasting room with the homey cluttered bar, you'll find only Zinfandels, Chardonnays, and Petit Sirahs. However, the expression of each of these grapes approaches perfection. You'll also see a few unusual manifestations, such as a late-harvest dessert Chardonnay. For the most fun you can have during the crowded harvest season, join Battaglini in the fall for a "Stomp" event, during which you'll literally take off your shoes and start stomping in a bucket of grapes.

Russian River Vineyards

Ironically, Russian River Vineyards (5700 Gravenstein Hwy., Forestville, 707/887-3344, www.russianrivervineyards.com, daily 11:30 A.M.–4:30 P.M., free) really isn't in the Russian River Valley; it sits in the coastal hills that nurture the Sonoma Coast vineyards and wineries. The property doesn't look like a typical high-end winery—the elderly wooden buildings seem almost to be falling apart. (Don't worry, the tasting room has recently been shored up.) Sadly, the funky old Victorian house behind the tasting room isn't open for tours—it's part of the private production facility.

For lunch, ask for a table in one of the two small dining rooms, divided by the brushed-metal tasting bar. The staff here are friendly, and create a classy small-winery tasting experience. Russian River Vineyard's small list of only red wines reflects their locale—tasters enjoy full-bodied, fruity Pinot Noirs and interesting varietals from the southern reaches of Europe. The Charbono tastes especially good.

Dutton Estate

Another small winery along the comparatively undiscovered Gravenstein Highway, Dutton Estate (8757 Green Valley Rd., Sebastopol, 707/829-9463, www.duttonestate.com, daily 11 A.M.–5 P.M., tasting fee $10) sits right in the midst of its own vineyards. (Please don't pick the grapes!) Tasters enjoy plenty of personal attention from pourers, along with a small list of white and rosé wines, moving into the red Pinots and Syrahs that do so well in this area. Dutton's Syrahs stand out among their offerings, which can include a few extra pours for people who seem genuinely interested in the wines.

◖ Kendall-Jackson Wine Center

The Kendall-Jackson Wine Center (5007 Fulton Rd., Fulton, 866/287-9818, www .kj.com, daily 10 A.M.–5 P.M., tours 11 A.M., 1 P.M., and 3 P.M., tasting fee $5–25) surprises even serious oenophiles with the quiet elegance of its tasting room and the extensive sustainable gardens and demonstration vineyards surrounding the buildings. Inside, choose between the moderately priced regular ol' wine tasting, and the $25 per person Food & Wine Pairing (order at the tasting bar, then wait to be seated at one of the small bistro tables nearby). KJ's Food & Wine Pairing might be the very best example of this new Wine Country tasting trend. A staff of full-time chefs prepares a fresh selection of small bites that pair with the day's selection of reserve and estate wines. The wines are delicate and tasty, but it's the food that stands out—brought out hot and perfect by one of the chefs, who will tell you all about the preparation of each luscious mouthful. (Expect one or two goodies that aren't on the menu.) Locals sometimes stop by the high-ceilinged tasting room and make a lunch out of the Food & Wine Pairing here. Just be aware that in high season you might need to make a reservation in advance—KJ doesn't boast too many tables. Take a tour of the gardens in the spring and the summer, and try a taste of fresh wine grapes during the fall harvest season.

Tara Bella Winery

You must call ahead to arrange a private appointment if you want to visit the tiny, exclusive Tara Bella Winery (3701 Viking Rd., Santa Rosa, 707/544-9049, www.tarabella winery.com). Tara Bella represents the ultimate in intimate family-owned wineries; the husband and wife team, Tara and Rich, tend their own vineyard, press their own grapes by hand, and make their own wine. From their eight-acre Russian River vineyard, they create *one* Cabernet Sauvignon each year. And each November, they release a new vintage to the public (most of which is snapped up by their wine club, though you can purchase a bottle if you taste at the winery). A visit to Tara Bella is a visit to the roots of California wine—family-owned and handcrafted, with a flavor all its own.

Korbel Cellars

Champagne grapes like cooler climates, so it makes sense that Korbel Cellars (13250 River Rd., Guerneville, 707/824-7000, www.korbel.com, daily 9 A.M.–4:30 P.M., until 5 P.M. May–Oct., first three tastes free), the leading producer of California champagnes, maintains a winery and tasting room on the Sonoma coast. The large, lush estate welcomes visitors with elaborate landscaping and attractive buildings, including a small area serving as a visitors center. Tours of the estate are offered several times daily for a fee. Inside the tasting room, visitors get to sample far more than the ubiquitous Korbel Brut that appears each New Year's. Korbel makes and sells a wide variety of high-end champagnes, plus a few boutique still wines and a line of brandies. You can't taste the brandy (that's a different and harder-to-obtain liquor license), but you can purchase it from the winery store. The facility also has a full-service gourmet deli and picnic grounds for tasters who want to stop for lunch.

Hop Kiln

Bringing truth in advertising to Sonoma, Hop Kiln (6050 Westside Rd., Healdsburg, 707/433-6491, www.hopkilnwinery.com, daily 10 A.M.–5 P.M.) winery is housed in an old hop kiln. Earlier in its history, the Russian River Valley grew more beer-making ingredients than grapes, and this distinctively shaped hop kiln dried the valley's crop each year. Today, you'll find an extensive wine tasting bar and gift shop inside the main kiln.

Porter Creek Winery

Serious cork dorks recommend the tiny tasting room at Porter Creek Winery (8735 Westside Rd., Healdsburg, 707/433-6321, www.portercreekvineyards.com, daily 10:30 A.M.–4:30 P.M., free), which casual tasters might otherwise miss at the bend on a twisting road. Turn onto the dirt driveway, passing a farm-

©LIZ HAMILL SCOTT

Hop Kiln winery, Russian River Valley

WINE COUNTRY

style house (that's actually the owner's family home), and park in front of a small converted shed—*that's* the actual tasting room. This is Sonoma wine tasting, old school. Porter Creek has been making its precious few cases of rich red wine each year for the last 30 years or so. You can find it at the occasional local restaurant, but if you like what you taste you'd better buy it right here at the winery. Porter Creek's wines are almost all red, made from grapes grown organically within sight of the tasting room. You might even see the owner-winemaker walking through his vineyards with his family on a sunny afternoon in the off-season.

Foppiano

One of the oldest wineries in the Russian River Valley, Foppiano (12707 Old Redwood Hwy., Healdsburg, 707/433-7272, www.foppiano .com) dates from 1896. Today Foppiano is still making a small list of premium red wines. Their signature wine is a legendary Petit Sirah, unusual for the area. They've also got a great Sangiovese, a Zin, a Cab, and a Merlot under the Foppiano label. A second label, Riverside, encompasses a few tasty but exceedingly inexpensive varietals that let drinkers on a budget enjoy Foppiano wines. Inside the farmhouse-style tasting room, enjoy sips of the various vintages. But also be sure to ask for Susan's recipes; the hospitality director and fourth-generation member of the Foppiano family creates and adapts dishes to match the family wines.

J Winery

Unlike many wineries that cling to Old World traditions, J Winery (11447 Old Redwood Hwy., Healdsburg, 888/594-6326, www .jwine.com, Thurs.–Tues. 11 A.M.–4 P.M., $10–55) loves the cutting edge of the California wine scene. J specializes in sparkling wines, California style. Their tasting room is a triumph of modern design, and their tasting experience gives visitors a taste of the best that Wine Country has to offer. Instead of the standard tasting bar and pouring staff, J has tables and waitstaff. And instead of just the standard

one-ounce pour of a bunch of wines, you'll be served the wines with specially paired small bites of high-end California cuisine prepared in J's own kitchens by their own team of gourmet chefs. You'll get the chance to taste the sparkly vintages as they are meant to be enjoyed—with an array of (often spicy!) foods.

Armida

Come to the Armida (2201 Westside Rd, Healdsburg, 707/433-2222, www.armida.com, daily 11 A.M.–5 P.M.) tasting room for the gorgeous scenery and the funky facilities, but stay for the wonderful wines. The driveway meanders up a Russian River hillside to a cluster of geodesic domes set amidst lovely and sustainable landscaping. Bring a picnic to enjoy on the big deck overlooking the duck pond and the valley beyond. Before you get to eating, wander into the tasting room to check out some of the truly tasty Russian River red wines. You'll get your choice of smoky Syrahs and jammy Zinfandels. The flagship wine, Poizin, is well represented in the wines and logowear in the small gift shop that shares space with the tasting bar. Armida sells Poizin in a coffin-shaped box—ask nicely and they might open a bottle for you to taste (even if they don't, it's still worth buying).

Optima Wine Cellars

Mike Duffy started making homemade wine with his dad when he was a kid. He got his degree in winemaking (enology) from the prestigious UC Davis program, and from then on it was only a matter of time before he opened his own winery. Today, Optima Wine Cellars (498 "C" Moore Ln., Healdsburg, 707/431-8222, www.optimawinery.com, by appointment only) makes a small list of premium wines from single appellations within the Russian River Valley wine area. These include Cabernet Sauvignon, Zinfandel, and Chardonnay. They also produce a luscious Zinfandel port—perfect for dessert, or at the end of a long day of wine tasting.

White Oak

At White Oak (7505 Hwy. 128, Healdsburg,

707/433-8429, www.whiteoakwinery.com, daily 10 A.M.–5 P.M.), you'll find a wonderful combination of whimsy and wine. This Spanish mission–inspired winery complex is surrounded by green gardens dotted with fun sculptures. Beyond the gardens, estate vineyards grow grapes for Old Vine Zinfandels and other fine wines. Go inside to taste some of those wines—the tasting list is small but prestigious. While white-wine drinkers enjoy the Sauvignon Blanc and Chardonnay, big reds are the specialty of the house. Cabernet Sauvignon and Zinfandel lovers flock to White Oak for the fabulous regular releases and occasional special library selections. Tours at White Oak give participants a special look at wine tasting, describing and illustrating the various components that make up a wine's fragrance.

Rosenblum Cellars Tasting Room

Just off the square in downtown Healdsburg is the attractive if slightly pretentious Rosenblum Cellars Tasting Room (250 Center St., Healdsburg, 707/431-1169, www.rosenblum cellars.com, daily 11 A.M.–6 P.M., tasting fee $8). In the regular tasting room, sip a selection of ports and late-harvest wines as Rosenblum's myriad ribbons and awards stare down at you from the walls. Unusually, Rosenblum wines aren't made locally—this Russian River tasting room features vintages grown in Contra Costa County (the Livermore area and beyond) and made in an airplane hangar in Alameda. If you'd prefer to take a seat and stay a while, ask (and be willing to pay) for a session in the adjacent reserve tasting room.

Hanna

The first thing you'll notice when you drive up to Hanna (5353 Occidental Rd., Santa Rosa, 707/575-3371, www.hannawinery.com, daily 10 A.M.–4 P.M.) is the stunning view down the hillside into the Alexander Valley. The tasting room is surrounded by vineyards climbing up the hills and flowing downward to the foot of the valley. The tasting room has plenty of windows and a broad wraparound porch to help you take in the vistas. But don't neglect

the wines! Hanna offers a large list, plus a reserve tasting of their finest vintages. In addition to the inevitable Cabernet Sauvignons and Chardonnays, you might find some unusual varieties such as Malbec—ask nicely and you might even sneak a taste!

Dry Creek Vineyard

It seems odd that a winery named Dry Creek should have sailboats on all its labels, but that's the signature icon on each bottle produced by Dry Creek Vineyard (3770 Lambert Bridge Rd., Healdsburg, 800/864-9463, www.dry creekvineyard.com, daily 10:30 A.M.–4:30 P.M., $5–15). This midsized winery focuses much effort within its own appellation (Dry Creek, of course), producing many single-vineyard wines from grapes grown within a few miles of the estate. Other wines include grapes from the Russian River Valley appellation. Dry Creek prides itself on both its classic California varietals such as Chardonnay, Cabernet, and Merlot, and on occasionally hopping out of that box and producing something unusual, like a Musque, a Chenin Blanc, or a Sauternes-style dessert wine. Try as many as you can when you enter the ivy-covered tasting room, styled after a French chateau.

◖ A. Rafanelli

Tasting at A. Rafanelli (4685 W. Dry Creek Rd., Healdsburg, 707/433-1385, www.arafanelli winery.com, appointment only) feels just about as different from the standard big-business high-end wineries of Wine Country as it's possible to get. You can't just walk in to A. Rafanelli, since they offer tastings by appointment only. There's no marble-covered bar, no chic tasting room. Instead, you'll walk into the barrel room of the working winery and stand on the concrete floor in the oak-and-grape-scented air. The owner-winemaker will hand out glasses to your group, and you'll begin to taste some of the best red wines produced anywhere in Sonoma County. In a region where the phrase "Cab is king" comes up at almost every winery, Rafanelli's Cabernet Sauvignons are still special. If you can't taste at Rafanelli, look for their Zins and Cabs at local Sonoma restaurants, to whom they sell the bulk of their wholesale wines.

Trentadue

As you walk up to the magnificent Italianate tasting room at Trentadue (19170 Geyserville Ave., Geyserville, 707/433-3104, www.trentadue .com, daily 10 A.M.–5 P.M., $5), the first thing you'll notice are the gardens sweeping out toward the vineyards. Many of Trentadue's vintages get made from estate-grown grapes, and the gorgeous grounds surrounding the winery get used for weddings and events almost every weekend. Inside the tall, narrow tasting room you'll find European-style decor, the usual gifts (including bottled water and nonalcoholic drinks), and a sometimes-too-small-for-the-crowd tasting bar. Trentadue offers a wide variety of still wines and a couple of sparklers. But the stars of Trentadue's show are unquestionably the ports. Trentadue makes an array of different styles and flavors of the famed fortified dessert wines. Any chocolate lover will need to take home a bottle of their Chocolate Amore. Trentadue offers a "port club" that sends members several bottles of different ports each year.

Raymond Burr

As well as portraying detective Perry Mason on the famous 1980s TV series, Raymond Burr had a second life as a wine connoisseur and orchid lover. He, along with his partner Robert Benevides, combined these loves to create the Raymond Burr Vineyards (8339 West Dry Creek Rd., Healdsburg, 888/900-0024, www.raymondburrvineyards.com, daily 11 A.M.–5 P.M. by appointment only). You'll drive up a bumpy driveway past the greenhouse to reach the parking lot. Wine seekers then enter the tiny (by Wine Country standards) tasting room to sip a few of the Burr label vintages. Frankly, most of the wines are tasty but not amazing compared to some other Sonoma products. But the staff and the winery's cats are fun and friendly, the views from the tasting room porch out over the valley are

stunning, and the tiny bar and small-town experience are reminiscent of an early time in the Wine Country.

Flower lovers must come on specific days or make an appointment in advance to take a tour of the greenhouses. Burr and Benevides have bred more than a thousand new orchid varieties, and you'll get to see many of them here on the estate.

Ferrari-Carano

One of the best large wineries in Dry Creek Valley, Ferrari-Carano (8761 Dry Creek Rd., Healdsburg, 707/433-6700, www.ferrari -carano.com, daily 10 A.M.–5 P.M., $5–35) provides great standard and reserve wines in an upscale tasting room and winery facility. Upstairs you'll get to taste from Ferrari-Carano's extensive menu of large-production moderately priced whites and reds. Downstairs, enjoy the elegant lounge area, which includes comfortable seating and a video describing the F-C winemaking process, from grape to glass. Look down into one of the major barrel storage areas, where F-C's wines age right before your eyes. And finally, open the glass doors and enter the reserve tasting room, where for an additional fee you can taste the best of F-C's vintages—smaller runs that are mostly bold, assertive reds. Back upstairs you can also browse the larger-than-average gift shop for gourmet edible goodies, wine and kitchen gadgets, and Ferrari-Carano logowear.

SIGHTS
Charles M. Schulz Museum

Charles Schulz drew the world-famous *Peanuts* comic strip for almost 50 years, and from 1958 until his death in 2000, he lived in Sonoma County. In honor of Schulz and the *Peanuts* gang, the Charles M. Schulz Museum and Research Center (2301 Hardies Ln., Santa Rosa, 707/579-4452, www.schulzmuseum.org, Mon. and Wed.–Fri. 11 A.M.–5 P.M., Sat.–Sun. 10 A.M.–5 P.M., adults $8, seniors/children $5) opened in 2002. Inside the 27,000-square-foot building, which somehow manages to look like it comes from a four-inch comic strip, you'll find an incredible wealth of multimedia art, original drawings, and changing exhibitions based on the works of Charles Schulz. No matter how many times you visit, you're likely to see something new in the ever-changing exhibits. Plenty of permanent collections provide stability and a base for the museum's theme. The museum owns most of the original *Peanuts* strips, a large collection of Schulz's personal possessions, and an astonishing array of tribute artwork (from everyone from other comic-strip artists to urban installation designers the world over). Outside the building, the grounds include attractive gardens, the Snoopy Labyrinth, and even the infamous Kite-Eating Tree.

Schulz's influence is felt outside the museum property as well. Across the street you can skate at Snoopy's Home Ice. (Schulz was an avid hockey player for most of his life.) And throughout downtown Santa Rosa, especially in Historic Railroad Square, you'll see colorful sculptures depicting favorite members of the *Peanuts* gang brightening the streets, making people smile.

Pacific Coast Air Museum

Even if you're not an aviation buff, the Pacific Coast Air Museum (2230 Becker Blvd., Santa Rosa, 707/575-7900, www.pacificcoastair museum.org, Tues., Thurs., and Sat.–Sun. 10 A.M.–4 P.M., $5 donation requested) is worth a stop. Through interpretive and photographic exhibits, learn about the history of aviation in America. Spend some time studying the cutaways and bits and pieces to enhance your understanding of the mechanics of powered flights. And finally, fantasize about flying the fine examples of F-series fighters and many other military and civilian aircraft on display. Many of the planes here are examples of modern war machines—such as those you'd see on the deck of an aircraft carrier in the Persian Gulf today. Or if you prefer to see civilian craft, check out the funky little Pitts aerobatic plane, the sort of thing you'll see doing impossible-looking tricks during the museum's annual **Wings over Wine Country** air show, held each August.

Luther Burbank Home and Gardens

If you love plants and gardening, don't miss the Luther Burbank Home and Gardens (Sonoma and Santa Rosa Aves., Santa Rosa, 707/524-5445, www.lutherburbank.org, gardens 8 A.M.–dusk year-round, free; tours Apr.–Oct. Tues.–Sun. 10 A.M.–4 P.M., fee). Luther Burbank personally created (using hybridization techniques) some of the most popular plants growing in California gardens and landscapes today. You don't have to go to his gardens to see examples of his famous Shasta Daisy—an incredibly hardy pure-white daisy hybrid that now covers vast areas throughout the state. But you will see them in the Luther Burbank gardens within the more than acre's worth of horticulture ranging from medicinal herbs through showy roses. Check the website for a list of what's in bloom during your visit, as something will be showing off its finest flowers every month of the year!

Sonoma County Wine Library

If you're a serious student of wine, don't miss out on the Sonoma County Wine Library (Piper and Center Sts., Healdsburg Regional Library, Healdsburg, 707/433-3772, www .sonomalibrary.org/wine). This public library extension contains a collection of over 5,000 books on wine, subscriptions to more than 80 wine periodicals, photos, prints, wine labels, and an online resource for wine lovers at http:// winefiles.org. Among the 1,000 or so rare wine books, you'll find treatises on the history, business, and art of wine from as far back as 1512. The library is a perfect place for wine drinkers who want to take their habit or hobby to the next level.

Hand Fan Museum

Yes, you really can visit a museum dedicated exclusively to the display and description of hand fans. The tiny Hand Fan Museum of Healdsburg (327A Healdsburg Ave., Healdsburg Hotel, 707/431-2500, www.hand fanmuseum.com, Wed.–Sun. 11 A.M.–4 P.M.) seeks to tell the cultural histories of Europe,

WINE COUNTRY

America, and Asia through the creation, decoration, and use of fans. It doesn't take long to view and enjoy both the permanent collection and seasonal exhibits at this fun little museum. You might be surprised to discover the level of artistry put into some of the fans here, be they paper or lace, antique or modern. And you'll learn a little bit about how fans were and are used in various societies (the 17th-to-19th-century courting practices and sexual invitations in some European countries included intricate movements of a lady's fan, directed at the gentleman of the hour).

ENTERTAINMENT AND SHOPPING
Bars and Clubs

One way to taste wines from a wider variety of vineyards is to stop in at a wine bar. **Willi's Wine Bar** (4404 Old Redwood Hwy., Santa Rosa, 707/526-3096, www.williswinebar.net, Tues.–Thurs. 11:30 A.M.–9 P.M., Fri.–Sat. 11:30 A.M.–10 P.M., Sun.–Mon. 5–9 P.M.) offers flights of small pours and bottles of high-end vintages from Sonoma, Napa, and around the world. To go with their wines, this upscale establishment offers cheese plates, charcuterie plates, and small plates of haute cuisine. Your server should be able to advise you as to which plates pair best with which wines. For a more casual wine bar atmosphere, drop in at **The Wine Shop** (331 Healdsburg Ave., Healdsburg, 707/433-0433, Mon.–Sat. 10 A.M.–6 P.M., Sun. noon–6 P.M.).

Want to find a bar that *doesn't* pander to the ubiquitous wine trade? Check out the **Russian River Brewing Company** (725 4th St., Santa Rosa, 707/545-2337, www.russianriverbrewing.com, Sun.–Thurs. 11 A.M.–midnight, Fri.–Sat. 11 A.M.–1 A.M.), which both makes and serves lots and lots of beer. And what goes better with beer than pizza? The food menu leans heavily on pizza and calzones to satisfy folks who build up their appetites trying the various (strong!) local brews. The brew pub also acts as a venue for local and regional blues, funk, and jazz bands—Saturday, Sunday, and Wednesday nights feature live music.

Holy pink neon, Batman! The **Lounge at the Flamingo** (2777 4th St., Santa Rosa, 707/545-8530, www.flamingoresort.com) draws a significant crowd even on weekday evenings. This retro-styled nightspot does have a good-sized dance floor (bathed in fuchsia light), plenty of seating, and an endless stream of live bands and nighttime fun that appeals to locals and visitors alike. Expect an older (but not senior) crowd for live jazz, oldies cover bands, and weekly West Coast Swing classes. The atmosphere exudes geniality, bar food is served all day, and the evening crowd isn't afraid to get out on the floor and dance. All in all, it's a fun scene.

Guerneville wouldn't be a proper gay resort town without at least a couple of good gay bars creating a proper nightlife for visitors and locals alike. The most visible and funky looking (from the outside) of these is the **Rainbow Cattle Company** (16220 Main St., Guerneville, 707/869-0206, www.queersteer.com, daily 6 A.M.–2 A.M.). Mixing the vibes of a down-home country saloon with happenin' San Francisco nightspot, the Rainbow serves up cold drinks and hot men with equal abandon. Think cocktails in Mason jars, wood paneling, and leather nights. And yet this is just the kind of queer bar where you can bring your mom or your straight-but-not-narrow friends, and they'll have just as much fun as you do.

Both the ladies and the dudes, and even the straights, come out to dance and party at **Liquid Sky** (16225 Main St., Guerneville, 707/869-9910). Right across the street from the Rainbow, Liquid Sky lures DJs up from the Bay Area to spin for the dancing, groping crowds that populate the floor. Call or drop by to get the low-down on parties going on when you're in town.

Live Music

Live-music venues are few and far between in the Russian River region. But for big shows, you can get tickets for the **Wells Fargo Center for the Arts** (50 Mark West Springs Rd., Santa Rosa, 707/546-3600, http://wellsfargocenterarts.org, ticket prices vary by show).

This full-sized theater hosts any number of national acts each year (plus the occasional play or headlining comic). You might see Melissa Etheridge, the Beach Boys, or Donna Summer at this Santa Rosa concert hall.

Theater

Wine makes many people think of high art and high culture. Accordingly, Sonoma County supports a number of theater groups that put up everything from funky black-box originals to big-budget Broadway musicals. The **Sonoma County Repertory Theater** (104 N. Main St., Sebastopol, 707/823-0177, http://the-rep .com, adults $23, seniors/children $18) sits in Sebastopol, producing a mix of beloved classics like *Taming of the Shrew* and *A Christmas Carol,* plus a generous helping of newer works such as *Rabbit Hole.* While the weekend prices are reasonable, the Sonoma Rep also has "Pay What You Can" Thursdays; you walk up to the door on Thursday evening, and if tickets are left for the show, you can get in for whatever price you deem to be reasonable.

The **Raven Players** (115 North St., Healdsburg, 707/433-6335, www.ravenplayers .org, adults $18–25, seniors/students $15) ply their art in the boutique town of Healdsburg. This ambitious company stages five plays per year—primarily award-winning and established works, such as Arthur Miller's *After the Fall* and Christopher Durang's *Beyond Therapy.* For their last show each season, the Ravens produce a big, dramatic musical; recent productions include *Evita* and *Miss Saigon.*

Festivals and Events

One of the biggest annual events in this agricultural region is the **Sonoma County Fair** (1350 Bennett Valley Rd., Santa Rosa, 707/545-4200, www.sonomacountyfair.com), held over two weeks at the end of July. Even the biggest Sonoma wineries prize the awards they win at their local county fair, and you'll see fair ribbons displayed proudly in many a Russian River tasting room. If you're lucky enough to be able to attend, you'll find far more than just wine—live entertainment acts, family shows,

and an amazing array of contests and exhibitions featuring the work of folks from all over the Sonoma region. Live horse racing and an adjacent golf course round out the many attractions.

On the other hand, the **Harvest Fair** (1350 Bennett Valley Rd., Santa Rosa, www.sonoma countyfair.com, Oct.), also held on the Sonoma County Fairgrounds in Santa Rosa, focuses almost exclusively on competition between wineries and farmers in Sonoma County. All the growers and vintners gather their finest produce and pit it against their local competitors' items.

Shopping

The eensy-weensy **Chadwick's of London** (300 Center St., Healdsburg, 707/431-9001, www.chadwicksoflondon.com, Mon.–Fri. 10:30 A.M.–5:30 P.M., Sat. 10:30 A.M.–6 P.M., Sun. 11 A.M.–5 P.M.) on the square is worth squeezing into if you like to admire pretty ladies' underthings. The store carries mostly British imported brands of lingerie (Jezebel's, Felina, etc.) at fairly reasonable prices. Pick up a fancy teddy or a lacy nightgown, but you can also stock up on, er, necessities you've forgotten to pack.

SPORTS AND RECREATION
Biking

Bicycling is a popular way of exploring Wine Country, and Sonoma is a major bicyclists' mecca, boasting some of the finest road biking anywhere in the world. Out in the Russian River Valley, you can find easy tours, more strenuous trail rides, and even some mountain biking possibilities.

Newcomers to bike touring in the area can choose from several reputable touring companies that will get them up on the saddle and pointed in the right direction. **Wine Country Bikes** (61 Front St., Healdsburg, 866/922-4537, www.winecountrybikes.com, $129/person) sits right on the square in downtown Healdsburg. Its Classic Wine Tour starts at 10 A.M. and runs until 3:30 P.M. During your leisurely pedal through the Dry Creek region, you'll get to stop and taste wine, take walks in vineyards, and learn more about the history of wine in this small, proud appellation. A gourmet picnic lunch is included with your bike tour. From there, the tours get longer and/or more luxurious—check the website for information about multi-day bike tour packages that include accommodations. For independent souls who prefer to carve their own routes, Wine Country Bikes also rents road bikes, tandem bikes, and hybrids that you can also take out on moderate park trails that permit biking.

To become a part of the larger bicycling culture in the area, consider participating in the annual **Harvest Century Bicycle Tour** (www .healdsburg.com/chamber/bike_tour, July). This event requires some degree of physical fitness, since riders must register to ride a 23-, 37-, or 60-mile route. The roads are moderate, however; while you'll find some inclines, experienced cyclists won't be tortured so much as to preclude enjoying the rest of the day with great food, wine, and the companionship of plenty of like-minded souls.

Hiking

The Russian River Valley offers a wide variety of hiking trails suited to everyone from sedate walkers to brawny backpackers. Many of these lie away from central Wine Country, out in the mountains near the river itself and Guerneville. One of the best of these spots is undoubtedly **Armstrong Redwoods** (17000 Armstrong Woods Rd., Guerneville, 707/869-2015, www.parks.ca.gov, daily 8 A.M.–sunset, $7 per vehicle), an easy five-minute drive from Guerneville on one mostly straight road. This little redwoods park often gets overlooked, which makes it a little bit less crowded than some of the most popular North Coast and Sierra redwood forests. But you can still get a fabulous hike in here—either a short stroll in the shade of the trees or a multi-day backcountry adventure. The easiest walk ever to a big tree is the 0.1-mile stagger from the visitors center to the tallest tree in the park, named the **Parson Jones Tree.** If you saunter

another half mile you'll reach the **Armstrong Tree,** which grows next to the Armstrong Pack Station—your first stop if you're doing the heavy-duty hiking thing. From the Pack Station, another quarter mile of moderate hiking gets you to the **Icicle Tree.** If you want more advice on the trails here, stop in and talk to the rangers at the visitors center; they're both knowledgeable and helpful, and love to share information about their park.

Bored with redwoods and yearning for a different landscape? Right next to Armstrong sits the **Austin Creek State Recreation Area** (17000 Armstrong Woods Rd., Guerneville, 707/869-2015, www.parks.ca.gov, 8 A.M.– sunset, $7 per vehicle). It's rough going (2.5 miles of steep, narrow, treacherous dirt road) to get to the main entrance and parking area (no vehicles over 20 feet long and no trailers of any kind are permitted). But once you're in, some great—and very difficult—hiking awaits you. The eponymous **Austin Creek Trail** (4.7 miles one-way) takes you down from the hot meadows into the cool forest fed by Austin Creek. To avoid monotony on this challenging route, create a loop by taking the turn onto the **Gilliam Creek Trail** (4 miles one-way). This way you get to see another of the park's cute little creeks as you walk back to your starting point.

Hot-Air Ballooning

Just as in Napa, one of the popular ways to get a great view of the Russian River Valley is from the basket of a hot-air balloon. Granted, you and your hangover must fall out of bed *before* dawn for this particular treat—so you might want to make this a first-day adventure before you start wine tasting. **Above the Wine Country** (meeting site at Kal's Kaffe Mocha, 397 Aviation Blvd., Santa Rosa, 707/538-7359, www.balloontours.com, flights daily, adults $225, children $195) can get you up in the air to start the day high above Wine Country. This big company maintains a whole fleet of balloons, which can carry 2–16 passengers. Expect your total experience time to be 3–4 hours, with 1–1.5 hours in the air.

Water Sports

Between the various creeks, Spring Lake, Lake Sonoma, and the Russian River, it's no wonder that many people view the Russian River Valley as a recreation destination as much as a wine region.

Guerneville and its surrounding forest land act as the center for fun on the river. **Russian River Adventures** (www.rradventures.info) offers guided paddles down a secluded section of the river in stable, sturdy inflatable canoes. Dogs, children, and even infants are welcomed by Russian River Adventures. The trip usually lasts 4–5 hours, with little whitewater and lots of serene shaded pools.

Fly-fishers can cast their lines out into the Russian River, hunting for some seriously enormous trout. A couple of recommended spots include the Wohler Bridge (9765 Wohler Rd., Forestville) and Steelhead Beach (9000 River Rd., Forestville).

At the north end of the valley, **Lake Sonoma** (3333 Skaggs Springs Rd., Geyserville, 707/433-2200, www.parks .sonoma.net/laktrls.html) sprawls in a series of skinny fingers, holding water for both recreation and more practical uses. A public boat launch at Warm Springs Bridge lets you launch your own ski or fishing boat for a $3 fee. A marina (Stewart's Point Rd.) offers boat rentals (plus slip rentals) for guests who don't have their own. Bass anglers school at the Warm Springs Creek and Dry Creek fingers of the lake, where trees shade the water and create a hospitable home for bass, perch, catfish, and sunfish.

A smaller but also less crowded lake, **Spring Lake** (391 Violetti Dr., Santa Rosa, www .sonoma-county.org/parks/pk_slake.htm, parking $6) has a bit more in the way of quiet and solitude than its bigger brethren. Anglers out to stalk the wily largemouth bass can launch electric-motor boats (but not gas-powered boats) into Spring Lake. Lifeguards watch over a cordoned swimming lagoon that's perfect for kids, and the nearby concession stand rents paddle boats and canoe-like craft during the summertime.

ACCOMMODATIONS

It's easy to find a place to stay in the Russian River Valley. Even the smaller towns perched along the state roads host any number of inns and cabins. For a more elegant hostelry, plan to stay in one of the luxury hotels or resorts in Santa Rosa or Healdsburg.

Santa Rosa

In the big city of Santa Rosa, you'll find all the familiar chain motels you can imagine. You'll also see a few charming inns and upper-tier hotels that show off the unique aspects of the city that divides the Bay Area from true Northern California.

The **Sandman Motel** (3421 Cleveland Ave., 707/544-8570, www.sonoma.com/lodging/ sandman, $90–135) offers clean, comfortable motel rooms for pleasantly reasonable prices. The guest rooms are decorated in a standard motel style, with dark carpets and floral bedspreads. Amenities include a big heated swimming pool, outdoor whirlpool tub (heated year-round), coffee and continental breakfast in the lobby each morning, and in-room refrigerators and satellite TVs. The Sandman is a great place to bring the family.

At the corner of Historic Railroad Square, **Hotel la Rose** (308 Wilson St., 800/527-6738, www.hotellarose.com, $110–300) exemplifies the luxury hotel concept as it has evolved over 100 years. The stone-clad main building rises high over Railroad Square, with more rooms available in the more modern carriage house just across the street. Because Hotel la Rose has only 47 guest rooms, you'll see an attention to detail and level of service that's missing in the larger motels and hotels in the area. The carriage house offers modern decor and amenities, and each large room and suite feels light and bright. In the main building you'll find an older style of elegance, with antique furniture and floral wallpaper appealing to guests who want a taste of what the hotel might have been like back in 1907. A quick trip downstairs takes you to the breakfast room, where a complimentary continental breakfast is served each morning.

WINE COUNTRY

At the north end of Santa Rosa, convenient to the major Russian River wine roads, you can stay at the lovely upscale **Vintners Inn** (4350 Barnes Rd., 800/421-2584, http://vintners inn.com, $225–500). The low, attractive red-tiled-roof buildings that comprise the inn and the fabulous John Ash & Co. restaurant sit adjacent to a large stretch of vineyard. Every room has a king-sized bed, fluffy down bedding, and patio or balcony overlooking a cute gardenlike courtyard. Many rooms boast fireplaces and spa tubs, and all feature luxurious appointments. Your stay includes a full breakfast each morning, plus access to the inn's outdoor whirlpool tub and the common den with fireplace. The only downside to the Vintners Inn is its regrettable proximity to a local power station; just try to look in the other direction when admiring the view.

Don't panic—the inside of your room at the kitschy **Flamingo** (2777 4th St., 707/545-8530, www.flamingoresort.com, $239–400) will be decorated in a soothing modern style, without a hint of virulent pink. The heavy-duty '50s styling stays at the front of the property inside the lobby and lounge, and, of course, on the giant rotating neon sign with the flamingo perched atop. Guest rooms sit in "spokes" surrounding a central garden and immense swimming pool. Each sizeable motel-style room has comfortable beds, a clean bathroom, and nearby parking. The Flamingo is a great place to bring the kids during the hot Sonoma summer—they'll love the pool, while grownups will love the easy access to the Russian River wine roads.

Sebastopol

In Sebastopol, the best place to stay is the expensive but lovely **Avalon, a Luxury Bed and Breakfast** (11910 Graton Rd., 707/824-0880, www.avalonluxuryinn.com, $375). With only three rooms, the Avalon offers the ultimate in private and romantic accommodations. All rooms have king beds, a hot tub or access to the garden hot tub, a fireplace, air-conditioning, and many luxurious amenities. Because Avalon was purpose-built as a bed-and-breakfast, each room is actually a suite, with plenty of space to

spread out and enjoy a longer stay. At breakfast time, you'll be served an organic feast, with produce purchased from a local CSA and loving attention to the details of preparation.

Guerneville

Because it's the major resort town for lovers of Russian River recreation, you'll find a couple dozen bed-and-breakfasts and cabin resorts in town. Many of these spots are gay friendly, some with clothing-optional hot tubs and such.

The **Creekside Inn & Lodge** (16180 Neeley Rd., 800/776-6586, www.creeksideinn.com, $125–270) sits right along the Russian River outside of downtown Guerneville. The river floods fairly regularly, hence the entire resort perches on stilts that provide pretty views as well as dry carpets. Cabins and cottages at the lodge run short on posh amenities, but long on woodsy kitsch. Every cabin, even the studios, has a full kitchen with refrigerator, plenty of space, a comfortable bathroom, and some of the best complimentary coffee you'll ever drink in a hotel room. Choose from economical studios, multibedroom family units, and brand-new "eco-cabins" that were designed and constructed to create the minimum possible impact on the delicate local environment. The property is large and has a swimming pool for summertime refreshment, but it does *not* have good river frontage for swimmers. The owners, who know and love their area, will give good suggestions for local "beaches." They'll also make appointments for wine tastings at their favorite private local wineries; if you're in town for the wine, definitely make use of this service as you won't necessarily find the best appointment-only tasting rooms on your own.

The **Sonoma Orchid Inn** (12850 River Rd., 888/877-4466, www.sonomaorchidinn .com, $165–270, pets welcome) experience is made by its amazing owners. They've created beautiful guest rooms with elegant linens and furniture, plus just enough tchotchkes to keep things interesting. The best (and spendiest) rooms have satellite TVs with TiVo as well as

DVD players and VCRs, and microwaves and small refrigerators. On the economy end of the spectrum the rooms are tiny but cute, with private baths and pretty decorations. But best of all, the owners of the Orchid will offer to help you with absolutely everything you need. They not only recommend restaurants and spas, they'll make reservations for you. They've got opinions about the local wineries, hikes, river spots, and just about everything else in the region. The Orchid makes a perfect inn for visitors who've never been to the area before—they're dog friendly, clothing mandatory, and welcoming to travelers of all persuasions.

A darling of the *San Francisco Chronicle,* the **Farmhouse Inn & Spa** (7871 River Rd., Forestville, 707/887-3300, www.farmhouse inn.com, $250–350) lies along River Road out in the midst of prime wine tasting country. The yellow-painted farmhouse is the inn's restaurant and contains the two most luxurious rooms; most of the guest accommodations march up the gently sloped hillside in the form of a row of cottages. These cute little cabins have upscale decor, warm fireplaces, private bathrooms, and precious little space. The pool area and restaurant aren't big either, but make up what they lack in size with charm and an adorable outdoor fireplace area. A gourmet breakfast is included, but make reservations for dinner in the evening.

On the gay resort end of the spectrum, there's the **Russian River Resort** (16390 4th St., 707/869-0691, www.russianriverresort .com, $110–220, two-night minimum May–Oct.). This absolutely adults-only resort offers economical but comfortable accommodations, a popular pool, a hot tub, and a near-endless stream of entertainment and events on-site and in town. An equal-opportunity resort, both gay men and lesbians (and a few liberal straights) stay here regularly. Granted, many of the pool parties tend toward the masculine, but there's plenty of fun for anybody who's interested in finding it here. The RRR isn't clothing optional, because it's got two restaurants and a bar on-site. It is dog-friendly, though it's got a no-dogs-on-holiday-weekends policy.

Healdsburg

Travelers planning to stay a night in Healdsburg had best get their credit cards ready. None of the boutique inns and hotels in this utterly yuppified town come cheap. But if you pick a room at the **Honor Mansion** (14891 Grove St., 707/433-4277, www.honormansion.com, $245–660), you probably won't feel like all that cash went to waste. Each of the 13 rooms and suites has been furnished and decorated with exquisite attention to even the smallest details. Whatever room you choose, you'll be overwhelmed with luxury, and want to spend all day every day in the soft cocoon of your oversized elegant featherbed. All rooms have private baths (at these prices, they'd better!) stocked with high-end toiletries, TVs, CD players, bathrobes, phones, air-conditioning, turn-down service, and more. Naturally, all rooms come with a full gourmet breakfast each morning. The Honor Mansion also has a lap pool, tennis court, croquet lawn, bocce pit, and outdoor professional massage service.

Set on the central town plaza, the **Hotel Healdsburg** (25 Matheson St., 800/889-7188, www.hotelhealdsburg.com, $290–870) is a local icon. The 55-room boutique hotel offers the most posh amenities, including Frette towels and linens, TVs with DVD players, soaking tubs and walk-in showers, and beautiful decor. Your guest room will great you with shining wood floors and furniture, Tibetan throw rugs, and spotless white down comforters. All rooms include free Wi-Fi and a gourmet breakfast, among other amenities, and guests can enjoy the outdoor pool, fitness center, and full-service day spa.

Raford House Bed and Breakfast Inn (10630 Wohler Rd., 800/887-9503, www.raford house.com, $165–260) offers Healdsburg-level luxury at slightly less stratospheric prices than its nearby competitors. Each of the six rooms has a queen bed, air-conditioning, a CD player, and a private bath. Some have fireplaces, oversized showers, and other luxury amenities. All rooms have been decorated with an attractive minimalist-Victorian style that feels historic but doesn't overwhelm a modern guest. Every morning, the Raford serves up a hearty country breakfast—the perfect start to a day of wine tasting.

Geyserville

In tiny Geyserville, the bed-and-breakfasts to visit are the **((** **Hope-Merrill and Hope-Bosworth Houses** (21238 and 21253 Geyserville Ave., 800/825-4233, www.hope-inns.com, $165–310). This Victorian charmer, which does in fact include two separate historic houses across the street from one another, harkens to classic bed-and-breakfasts on the East Coast. The owners come from Back East, and they've brought their traditions and aesthetics with them out to the Alexander Valley. If loud floral wallpaper covering every surface of your bedroom causes nightmares and hallucinations, this might not be the inn for you. But true aficionados of the Victorian style will love the flowers, lace, frills, and geegaws. Amenities include a pool and two hot tubs, plenty of common space in both houses, Friday-evening wine tastings out in the yard, and an enormous multicourse homemade breakfast each morning. At breakfast, the owners preside over the tables, offering touring advice to guests. Each room has its own private bath—most in the same room, and one or two lying just across the hall from your room. The most comfortable rooms with the good mattresses tend to be the spendier rooms—if you're in a less-expensive room, you may find yourself with less-than-plush pillows. But overall, the Hope Houses make for a great base from which to explore the Alexander, Dry Creek, and Russian River Valley wineries.

FOOD
Santa Rosa

((**John Ash & Co.** (4350 Barnes Rd., 707/527-7687, www.vintnersinn.com, Sun.–Thurs. 5–9 P.M., Fri.–Sat. 5–9:30 P.M., $30–50) stands out as one of the best high-end California cuisine restaurants in the Russian River region. This large dining room is part of the Vintners Inn, and the only unappetizing thing about it is its location across the street from a power plant. The elegant dining room is done up in the Mediterranean style and the food runs to pure California cuisine, with lots of local and sustainable produce prepared to show off its natural flavors. The menu runs fairly short, making it easy to choose from each of the three courses (often highlighting seafood, beef, lamb, and seasonal specialties). And of course, the wine list at John Ash & Co. is something special with some amazing local vintages that are tough to find anywhere outside of the Russian River Valley.

Josef's (308 Wilson St., 707/571-8664, www.josefsrestaurant.com, lunch Tues.–Fri., dinner daily, $20–32), a quiet little restaurant inside the historic Hotel la Rose, offers fine French food in a romantic setting. The low-key decor belies the elegance of the cuisine served here. The menu offers a mix of truly classic French dishes, such as mussels, sole amandine, and beef bourguignon, and interesting California twists like dishes with Asian or Middle Eastern spices. While the wine list has lots of great local selections, it includes fine vintages from around the world as well. Open for lunch during the week and serving breakfast to hotel guests only, Josef's offers opportunities to enjoy fine meals in smaller portions and at smaller prices.

Need something a bit more casual? Get in line for breakfast (or brunch, or lunch) at the **((** **Omelette Express** (112 4th St., 707/525-1690, www.omelette.com, Mon.–Fri. 6:30 A.M.–3 P.M., Sat.–Sun. 7 A.M.–4 P.M.). Owned by local character Don Taylor, who might even be acting as host at the front door on weekends, this spot is definitely ruled by locals. Don calls many of his customers by their first names, but he also welcomes newcomers with enthusiasm. The ultra-casual dining rooms are decorated with the front ends of classic cars. The menu runs to—surprise—lots and lots of omelets. Dishes are huge, and come with a side of toast made with homemade bread, so consider splitting with a friend.

Syrah (205 5th St., 707/568-4002, www.syrahbistro.com, Tues.–Sat. 11:30 A.M.–2 P.M. and 5:30 P.M.–close, Sun.–Mon. 5:30 P.M.–close,

$30–70) sits right in the midst of Santa Rosa, making it easy to experience high-end Wine Country cuisine in a nice downtown locale. The chef-owner often works the exposed grill area to one side of the small dining room, putting a perfect char on the meats to be served in the imaginative entrées on the tasting menus and the à la carte list. But it's the appetizers, salads, and sides that really make Syrah's offerings great. Salads are fresh and imaginative, and entrée plates include side dishes that both balance and enhance the main meats. The pastry chef does a fantastic job on the final course, creating a selection of classic chocolate and local seasonal desserts. The California-centric wine list evolves constantly—expect a different array of vintages each time you return.

Sebastopol

A great break from the endless fancy food is to find yourself a nice ethnic restaurant. In Sebastopol, one of the best of these is the **Himalayan Tandoori and Curry House** (969 Gravenstein Hwy. S., 707/829-2679, Mon.–Sat. 11 A.M.–2:30 P.M. and 5–9 P.M., $10–16), which serves up Indian food in the Himalayan style. You'll find both vegetable curries and meat tandoori here, both properly spicy, as well as fresh naan, spicy rice pudding, and all sorts of Eastern treats. You'll even get a break from the endless river of wine, since there's plenty of beer on the drinks menu.

The **Underwood Bar and Bistro** (9113 Graton Rd., Graton, 707/823-7023, www .underwoodgraton.com, Tues.–Sat. 11:30 A.M.– 2:30 P.M. and 5–10 P.M., Sun. 5–10 P.M., $11.50–26.50) serves *the* upscale cuisine in the tiny town of Graton. Plush red velvet and dark wood tables grace the Underwood's dining room, which is recommended by many locals as the best spot in this wine region to sit down to a serious dinner. With a heavy seafood focus (including raw oysters on the half shell) and an emphasis on top-quality meats and produce, Underwood does in fact exemplify ideal Wine Country cuisine. The so-called "tapas" are actually small plates and appetizers, meant to be shared around the table, but

you can share the larger salads and entrées just as easily. The wine list leans heavily on small local vintners; ask your server to recommend some of the best local wines with dinner. One especially spiffy thing about Underwood—on Friday and Saturday nights the bar stays open late, serving a pared-down but still satisfying late-night menu from 10 P.M.–2 A.M.

Calling the **Willow Wood** (9020 Graton Rd., Graton, 707/823-0233, www.willow woodgraton.com, Mon.–Sat. 8 A.M.–9:30 P.M., Sun. 9 A.M.–3 P.M., $10–25) a deli is somewhat misleading. Sure, they've got a counter, a take-out business, and well-trodden old wooden floors. But really, Willow Wood is an upscale California-Italian restaurant for lunch, featuring souped-up versions of traditional deli sandwiches accompanied by pasta and pickled veggies. Diners sit on wooden benches to enjoy the *big* meals, which can also include giant salads and tureens of fresh soup. You can get a beer or a glass of Sonoma wine with your meal, or use the sugar found in the silver alien pod on your table to sweeten the locally beloved hot teas. If you're having trouble making a choice, the open-faced hot sandwich with egg salad and pesto is a favorite with both locals and tourists.

Guerneville

At **Charizma Wine Lounge & Deli** (16337 Main St., 707/869-0909, www.charizmawinelounge .com, Mon.–Tues. 11:30 A.M.–9 P.M., Wed. 11:30 A.M.–4 P.M., Thurs. 11:30 A.M.–10 P.M., Fri.–Sat. 10 A.M.–10 P.M., Sun. 10 A.M.–9 P.M., $10–19), you can get a cheeseburger with your 2001 Cabernet. Milkshakes are also a specialty of this fun, casual spot. Wine geeks can sip wine and nibble brie on comfortable sofas, or belly up to the redwood bar. Culinary enthusiasts might even find a cooking class held on the premises!

A focal point of downtown Guerneville, **Main Street Station** (16280 Main St., 707/869-0501, www.mainststation.com, daily 11 A.M.–11 P.M. May–Oct., daily noon–10 P.M. Nov.–Apr., $15–30) offers a big menu filled with homey, casual grub. The mainstay is handmade pizzas; you can grab a quick slice for lunch, or bring friends and order a whole pie for dinner. In the evenings, locals and visitors come down to munch sandwiches and pizza, drink beer, and listen to live entertainment on the small stage. Though live folk, jazz, blues, and even comedy happen every single night, this tiny venue gets crowded when a popular act comes to town. Consider making reservations in advance to assure you'll get a seat.

Pat's Restaurant (16236 Main St., 707/869-9904, www.pats-restaurant.com, daily 6 A.M.–3 P.M., $10) is the kind of diner that travelers hope to find. It's homey, casual, and the place the locals come to sit at the counter and have breakfast all day long. It sure doesn't look like much from the outside—a small storefront in the middle of downtown Guerneville—but when you peer in the plate windows you'll notice quite a number of diners inside. Classic diner food (eggs, sandwiches, burgers) is served fresh by a single waitress who makes managing two dining rooms full of customers look easy. She and the guy at the counter greet regulars by name, but have a friendly demeanor that extends to visitors and newcomers as well. The eggs are done perfectly, the hash browns are homemade, and the kitchen actually runs out of favorites like sausage gravy because it's made from scratch daily.

Healdsburg

In a sea of self-conscious chichi restaurants, the **Healdsburg Charcuterie & Cafe** (335 Healdsburg Ave., 707/431-7213, Mon.–Thurs. 11 A.M.–3 P.M. and 5:30–9 P.M., Fri.–Sat. noon–3:30 P.M. and 5:30–9:30 P.M., Sun. noon–3:30 P.M. and 5–9 P.M., $13.50–21.50) makes diners feel at home. With a cute-but-not-annoying pig theme, local art on the walls, and a softly romantic atmosphere, the Charcuterie makes a great option for a romantic but not overwhelming dinner out. The house-cured pork tenderloin sandwich is the house specialty, but vegetarians certainly can find a tasty and well-prepared meal here. The Charcuterie pours some lovely local vintages and offers wine flights.

The most famous restaurant in Healdsburg is probably the **Dry Creek Kitchen** (317 Healdsburg Ave., 707/431-0330, www.charliepalmer.com/dry_creek/home.html, Mon.–Thurs. 5:30–9:30 P.M., Fri.–Sat. 11:30 A.M.–2:30 P.M. and 5:30–10 P.M., Sun. 11:30 A.M.–2:30 P.M. and 5:30–9:30 P.M., $26–38). This chic Charlie Palmer dining room takes the concept of California cuisine to the next level. Expect to see foam, froth, jus, and coulis splattered across the menu, which can range from upscale-but-recognizable to totally bizarre. Dry Creek Kitchen serves brunch and lunch on the weekends, offering its own unique take on eggs Benedict, sliders, and other standards. This is a great place to check out some Dry Creek appellation vintages.

For an ecofriendly upscale California restaurant *without* the green propaganda, head to fabulous ❰ **Zin** (344 Center St., 707/473-0946, www.zinrestaurant.com, Mon.–Thurs. 11:30 A.M.–9 P.M., Fri. 11:30 A.M.–9:30 P.M., Sat. 5:30–9:30 P.M., Sun. 5:30–9 P.M., $15–30), just off the square in downtown Healdsburg. The cavernous dining room takes advantage of its existing antique features for decor, the tables are made with recycled and repurposed materials, and the art on the walls comes from local artists and is for sale. But the real reason to eat lunch or dinner at Zin is undoubtedly the food. The chef creates cuisine that fuses upscale Wine Country with Mexican, giving Zin a unique twist that sets it apart from a plethora of other upscale restaurants in the region. Most locals recommend starting with the Mexican beer-battered green beans—fabulous french fries with a guilt-reducing green-vegetable interior. If you've OD'd on haute cuisine, check out the Blue Plate specials for dinner, offering something down-home at a reasonable price each night—think spaghetti with meatballs, or chicken and dumplings. For dessert, the homemade jelly donuts bring home the best of Wine Country. The chef makes his own jelly out of local Zinfandel grapes each fall, and the donuts ooze with deliciousness you won't find anyplace else.

For an independent cup of coffee in

Healdsburg, saunter across the town square to **Flying Goat Coffee** (324 Center St., 707/433-8697, www.flyinggoatcoffee.com, Mon.–Sun. 7 A.M.–7 P.M.). This attractive West Coast coffee house serves above-average lattes, defaults to "no whip" on their mochas, and doesn't make 'em too sweet either. The relaxed feel and pleasant seating area make it easy to stop and stay awhile.

Oakville Grocery (124 Matheson St., 707/433-3200, www.oakvillegrocery.com, daily 8 A.M.–6 P.M.) sells high-end groceries and local gourmet products to well-heeled customers. It's a great place to pick up gifts for friends back home—they carry fine (and expensive) local olive oils, vinegars, soaps, and bath products. You can also get the goods for a proper picnic here, with a great selection of cheeses, fresh local breads, an upscale deli counter, plus a somewhat redundant wine selection and a few fine nonalcoholic beverages.

Geyserville

The restaurant offering in Geyserville is **Taverna Santi** (21047 Geyserville Ave., 707/857-1790, www.tavernasanti.com, Mon.–Sat. 11:30 A.M.–2 P.M. and 5:30–9 P.M., Sun. 11:30 A.M.–2 P.M. and 5–9 P.M., $18–35). This elegant Italian eatery allows only the teensiest of California twists to interfere with its cuisine. Even truly Italian staples that rarely make American menus (such as tripe) can be found here. Santi cures many of its own sausages and meat products, and makes much of its own pasta. For a serious Italian feast, order a full four-course meal with one item from each menu category. Lighter eaters might enjoy a "first course" dish of pasta as their entrée. Service at Santi can be spotty (but not awful), though the dimly lit, softly colored dining room makes it easier to pay attention to your sweetie across the table and forget for a few minutes that your appetizers are overdue.

INFORMATION AND SERVICES

In the Russian River region, you'll find a number of different visitors centers, though not necessarily in the spots you'd expect. Yes, there's a California Welcome Center in Santa Rosa, but frankly it's not the best source of local Russian River Wine Country information. A better spot, though it's off the beaten wine paths, is the **Russian River Chamber of Commerce and Visitor Center** (16209 1st St., Guerneville, 707/869-9000, http://russianriver.com) in downtown Guerneville. Here you'll find local staff who can give you serious local recommendations not only for wineries, but for river recreation, restaurants, and other less-traveled local attractions.

The serious local daily newspaper is the *Santa Rosa Press Democrat* (www.pressdemocrat.com). Check the Living and Entertainment sections for tourist information. You can also check out the many Wine Country guides that proliferate in the tasting rooms, motels, and inns of the Russian River region.

As a major city, Santa Rosa has plenty of available medical services. If you need help, try to get to **Santa Rosa Memorial Hospital** (1165 Montgomery Ave., Santa Rosa, 707/546-3210, www.santarosamemorial.org), which includes an emergency room.

GETTING THERE AND AROUND

To reach the Russian River Valley, take U.S. 101 from the north or south right into the midst of the valley. U.S. 101 runs through Santa Rosa, Windsor, Healdsburg, and Geyserville, making access to the restaurants, inns, and shopping easy enough—in theory.

So what's the problem? In a misguided (and failed) attempt to discourage traffic in the area, Sonoma has refused for years to widen U.S. 101 in key areas through the Russian River Valley. The too-narrow highway leads to traffic slowdowns at commute hours and massive jams when accidents happen. Expect slow traffic through and south of Santa Rosa most of the time.

The good news is that you leave U.S. 101 to get to the Russian River wineries. To get to Guerneville, your best route is Highway

116. In that direction less traffic and pretty forests make for a more serene on-the-road experience.

For wine and kitsch, you can take a horse-drawn carriage tour, stopping to taste wine along the way. The **Flying Horse Carriage Company** (707/849-8989, www.flyinghorse .org, $145) will take you off the paved roads and out into the vineyards of the Alexander Valley region. Here you'll get to see the wine grapes growing right in front of you as you slow down to really enjoy the sights and scenery of the Wine Country. Enjoy a picnic lunch (complete with dessert) in between stops at various tasting rooms to sample the local wines. Your tour starts at 12:30 P.M. and lasts four hours. This is an especially romantic pick for couples celebrating an anniversary or birthday.

Sonoma and Carneros

The Sonoma and Carneros wine regions lie in the southeast part of Sonoma County. The scenery here features oak forests and vineyard-covered open spaces. The last California mission in the great chain and the terminus of El Camino Real sits in the small city of Sonoma, which includes the famed Sonoma Mission Inn. Wineries cluster here, though not as many as in the Russian River Valley; the tasting rooms still see plenty of traffic, but the crowding can be less vicious than in the ultra-popular Napa and Dry Creek Valleys.

WINERIES

The Carneros region might be described as the "lost" area of Wine Country. Though the wines are spectacular, the wineries are a bit more spread out than in the Napa and Russian River Valleys, and fewer visitors cram into the tasting rooms every weekend. And yet some prestigious California names make their homes here, and some small boutique vintners quietly produce amazing varietals you won't find anywhere outside their tasting rooms. If you come to Carneros on a weekday, you might be the only person in a few of the tasting rooms, able to chat in depth with the staff about each wine you taste!

Gloria Ferrer

For a taste of some of the upscale sparkling wines Sonoma can produce, take a long drive through immense estate vineyards to the tasting room at Gloria Ferrer (23555 Carneros Hwy. 121/Arnold Dr., Sonoma, 707/996-7256, www.gloriaferrer.com, daily 10 A.M.–5 P.M., glass $2–10). Ferrer adheres to the popular format for sparkling wineries—there's no traditional "tasting." Instead, visitors order one or more full flutes of sparkling wine, then take a seat at an available table either inside the tasting room or out on the patio overlooking the Sonoma Valley. This style of tasting isn't cheap, but the sparklers here make the high cost worth it for any serious champagne lover. Just be sure that someone is designated as driver—they don't pour stingy flutes at Ferrer.

Schug Carneros Estate

You might recognize the labels at the Schug Carneros Estate (602 Bonneau Rd., Sonoma, 800/966-9365, www.schugwinery.com, daily 10 A.M.–5 P.M., $5–10). One of the Carneros region's elder statesmen, Walter Schug has made wine that's set the tone for California vintages for many years. The estate itself is worth a visit; the Tudor-esque barn sits in the middle of barns and fields of mustard (the brilliant yellow flowering plants) on the valley floor, with views of the surrounding mountains all around. Schug's hallmarks are Chardonnays and Pinot Noirs, grapes that grow well in this cooler region, so be sure to try the latest releases of both.

Domaine Carneros

The Sonoma-Carneros region has perfect conditions for champagne-making grapes, and so

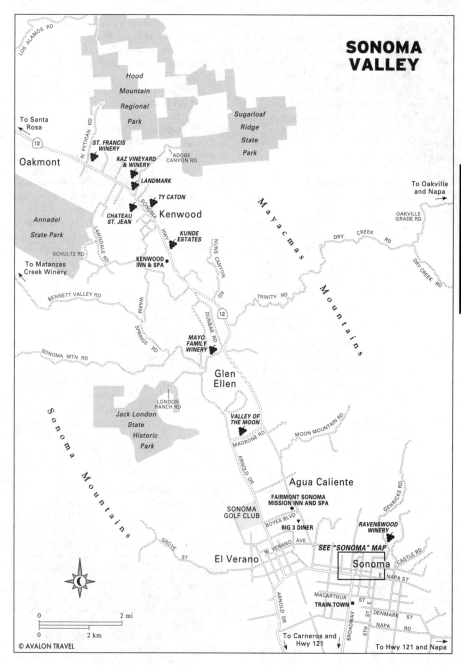

SONOMA VALLEY

To Santa Rosa

Oakmont

Hood Mountain Regional Park

Sugarloaf Ridge State Park

To Oakville and Napa

LOS ALAMOS RD

N PYTHIAN RD

ST. FRANCIS WINERY

KAZ VINEYARD & WINERY

ADOBE CANYON RD

LANDMARK

TY CATON

CHATEAU ST. JEAN

Kenwood

SONOMA HWY

Mayacmas Mountains

OAKVILLE GRADE RD

DRY CREEK RD

DRY CREEK RD

Annadel State Park

LAWNDALE RD

SCHULTZ RD

KUNDE ESTATES

NUNS CANYON RD

To Matanzas Creek Winery

KENWOOD INN & SPA

TRINITY RD

BENNETT VALLEY RD

WARM SPRINGS RD

DUNBAR RD

12

MAYO FAMILY WINERY

SONOMA MTN RD

Glen Ellen

LONDON RANCH RD

Jack London State Historic Park

VALLEY OF THE MOON

MOON MOUNTAIN RD

Sonoma Mountains

MADRONE RD

ARNOLD DR

Agua Caliente

GEHRICKE RD

FAIRMONT SONOMA MISSION INN AND SPA

SONOMA GOLF CLUB

RAVENSWOOD WINERY

BOYES BLVD

BIG 3 DINER

GROVE ST

W. VERANO AVE

SEE "SONOMA" MAP

CASTLE RD

El Verano

Sonoma

E

MACARTHUR ST

TRAIN TOWN

ARNOLD DR

BROADWAY

5TH ST W

NAPA ST

DENMARK ST

NAPA RD

To Carneros and Hwy 121

To Hwy 121 and Napa

0   2 mi
0   2 km

© AVALON TRAVEL

the glorious Domaine Carneros (1240 Duhig Rd., Napa, 800/716-2788, www.domaine.com, daily 10 A.M.–6 P.M.) makes its estate home here. Visitors rarely fail to be impressed by the grand estate structure, styled in both architecture and garden setting like the great chateaux of France. Even more impressive are the finely crafted sparkling wines (Domaine Carneros prefers not to use the term "champagne") and a few still Pinot Noirs the winery creates using grapes from the Carneros region.

Charles Creek Vineyard

Conveniently located on the square in downtown Sonoma, the tasting room at Charles Creek Vineyard (483 1st St. W., Sonoma, 707/935-3848, www.charlescreek.com, daily 11 A.M.–6 P.M.) beckons visitors with a giant cork cow standing proudly in the middle of its floor. This only-in-Wine-Country objet d'art was won at a charity auction, and now entices people to wander into the tasting room to take a closer look. Once inside, it's worth your time to taste the wines, too. This smaller-production winemaker purchases grapes from Napa and Sonoma to create boutique Chardonnays, Merlots, and Cabernet Sauvignons. The winemaker takes care to produce vintages that are easy to drink, especially with food.

Sebastiani Vineyards and Winery

The Sebastiani family has owned and operated Sebastiani Vineyards and Winery (389 4th St. E., Sonoma, 707/933-3230, www.sebastiani .com, daily 10 A.M.–5 P.M.) since 1904, making it the winery in longest continuous operation in Sonoma County. When visiting the cavernous tasting room and hospitality center, you'll get to taste from the huge portfolio of Sebastiani wines, which are meticulously crafted from grapes grown in different parts of Sonoma County. Sebastiani prides itself on the care with which the vineyard managers and growers select the right grapes to grow in the right parts of the diverse Sonoma region. This care shows in the wines, which you'll also find on menus around California. While you're at the winery, be sure to check out the sizeable

gift shop, the famous carved casks, and the retail kitchen and wine specialty marketplace. Or take one of two tours (Thurs., Fri., Sat. 2 P.M., $7.50/person, 1 hr): a historical walking tour of the Sebastiani estate or an open-air trolley tour through historic Sonoma and three of Sebastiani's local vineyards.

Ravenswood Winery

Ravenswood Winery (18701 Gehricke Rd., Sonoma, 888/669-4679, www.ravenswood -wine.com, daily 10 A.M.–4:30 P.M., $10–15) prides itself on making "no wimpy wines." Though the company is now owned by a large conglomerate, Ravenswood wines are still overseen by the original winemaker, Joel Peterson, who began making California Zinfandel in 1976. To this day, Zinfandel remains the signature varietal under the Ravenswood label. Many of the prized Zins come from individual vineyards in Sonoma County, while others are blends of grapes purchased from growers throughout California. When you come to taste, you won't find a stereotypical winery. Unlike many Napa and Sonoma wineries, Ravenswood sponsors a racecar, hosts a bevy of summer barbecues (yep, you can drink Zin with ribs!), and strives to make tasters of all types feel at home in the winery. Tours and barrel tastings teach newcomers the process of winemaking, while "blend your own" seminars beckon to serious winos. Perhaps best of all, Ravenswood wines are easy on the pocketbook, ranging $13–50 per bottle.

Valley of the Moon

At Valley of the Moon (777 Madrone Rd., Glen Ellen, 707/939-4510, www.valleyofthemoon winery.com, daily 10 A.M.–4:30 P.M., $2), 150 years of history juxtaposes with the highest winemaking technology California has to offer. Since the Civil War era, this Sonoma institution has passed through many hands and produced hundreds of wines. The circa-1860s stone buildings house late-model stainless-steel fermentation tanks as well as classic oak barrels. In the tasting room, you'll find a small list of boutique wines, from an unusual Sangiovese rosé to a classic California Cabernet. Valley of the Moon takes pride in its awards, and you'll find that almost every wine you taste has its own list of medals. Check the website for a list of upcoming wine events that show off this great Sonoma landmark at its best.

Mayo Family Winery

The Mayo Family Winery (13101 Arnold Dr. at Hwy. 12, Glen Ellen, 707/938-9401, www .mayofamilywinery.com, daily 10:30 A.M.– 6:30 P.M.) breaks from the Chard-Cab-Merlot juggernaut of Sonoma, producing an array of interesting Italian varietals. Here you might taste your first smoky rich Carignane or Barbera, enjoy a fruity white Viognier, or savor the Chianti-based Sangiovese. Mayo Family boasts a big presence in the region, with an at-the-winery tasting room, a small store-front tasting room in downtown Sonoma (on Sonoma Plaza), and the prized reserve tasting room up north in Kenwood (9200 Sonoma Hwy., Thurs.–Mon. 10:30 A.M.–6:30 P.M., reservations recommended, fee). At the reserve tasting room, your experience includes seven tasting pours of Mayo's very best wines, each paired with a small bite of gourmet California cuisine created by on-site chefs. Bon appetit!

Kunde Estates

One of the large wineries on Sonoma's major tasting road, Kunde Estates (10155 Hwy. 12, Kenwood, 707/833-5501, www.kunde.com, daily 10:30 A.M.–4:30 P.M., tasting fee $10– 20) has the typical enormous and elegant tasting room, hilly estate vineyards, and tasty but not spectacular wines. What Kunde offers that others don't is a sense of humor and fun. Be sure to look out for Blossom—the gaily painted fiberglass cow that the staff moves to different places all over the property. (Just please don't climb or sit on her! She has been broken several times by careless visitors.) Tours through the caves underneath the vineyards occur daily for a fee. Belly up to the broad bar to get not only a few sips of Kunde's wines, but a few stories from the often entertaining characters working the tasting room.

Muscardini and Ty Caton

These two tiny wineries maintain a cosponsored tasting room in a stylish strip mall in the village of Kenwood. As you drive down the highway it's easy to miss the tiny bar, which would be a crime for any true oenophile. Muscardini and Ty Caton (8910 Hwy. 12, Kenwood, 707/833-0526, www.tycaton .com, www.muscardinicellars.com, daily 11 A.M.–6 P.M.) pour some of the best wines in all of Sonoma. Ty Caton's $17 per bottle "pizza wine" puts $50 Cabernets from the bigger estates to shame. And their big Syrahs, perfect Pinots, and astonishing Cabernets are off the charts. Beware: If you seem interested in the wines you're sipping, the tasting room staff will not only give you the long story about each vintage they pour, they'll start opening and pouring everything they've got in the shop. If you're visiting on an off-season weekday, you may find yourself alone in the shop, discussing the wine regions of California and various varietals for more than an hour. Even in season, this small tasting room preserves the kind of wine tasting experience that wine lovers have been coming to Sonoma for decades to enjoy.

Chateau St. Jean

True to its name, Chateau St. Jean (8555 Hwy. 12, Kenwood, 707/833-4134, www.chateau stjean.com, daily 10 A.M.–5 P.M., tasting fee $10–15) is built in the style of a miniature French chateau, with flat graveled walks marching in straight lines through formally styled gardens. Stroll under the arbors to reach both tasting rooms—the regular (on the right) and the reserve (on the left). In the "regular" (read: cheaper) tasting room, you'll find the story of the first winemaker to come to Sonoma and a selection of traditional California wines— Chardonnay, Cabernet, Pinot Noir, and the like. Though Chateau St. Jean wines are sold in stores and at restaurants, the single-vineyard varietals tasters enjoy at the estate cannot be purchased anywhere but at the winery. Visitors can tour the winery's grounds, but not the production facilities for the winery.

WINE COUNTRY

Landmark

It seems appropriate that Landmark (101 Adobe Canyon Rd., Kenwood, 707/833-0053, www .landmarkwine.com, 10 A.M.–4:30 P.M. daily) provides wine to the entire United States. Owned and operated by the descendents of John Deere, Landmark seeks to continue the agricultural traditions of America while producing top 21st-century wines. In the tasting room, you'll find premium Chardonnays and Pinot Noirs—wines that grow best in the cooler region of Sonoma. Outside the tasting room, you can walk in some of the most spectacular gardens in a region noted for its landscaping. If you're visiting in the summer, take a horse-drawn wagon ride through the vineyards. Or bring a picnic and enjoy a game of bocce ball (a popular local pastime) on the grassy court surrounded by flowers and fountains and grapes. You can also arrange in advance to stay in either the guest suite or the cottage on the estate grounds.

Kaz Vineyard and Winery

At the other end of the spectrum from the big boys of Wine Country that produce many thousands of barrels, there's Kaz (233 Adobe Canyon Rd., Kenwood, 877/833-2536, www .kazwinery.com, Fri.–Mon. 11 A.M.–5 P.M.). This tiny winery is a family affair from start to finish—in the vineyards, the winery, and the tasting room. Inside Kaz, you'll find a broad array of ultra-small-production wines—sometimes only one barrel of a particular wine gets made. Reds are the Kaz specialty, including a number of blends and unusual varietals you just don't see at other Sonoma wineries. (Think Mouvedre, Grenache, and Barbera-Tannat blend.) Kaz also makes several unique ports—even whites and rosés! Inside the simple brown barn that's been made over into a tasting room, you'll get 6–9 tastes for $5, and if you're lucky, Kaz himself will be pouring and commenting on his wines.

St. Francis Winery

It is believed that the Franciscan order of monks brought wine production to California. In their honor, the St. Francis Winery (100 Pythian Rd. at Hwy. 12, Santa Rosa, 888/675-9463, www .stfranciswine.com, daily 10 A.M.–5 P.M., $10–30) sells thick, rich wines that appeal to reds

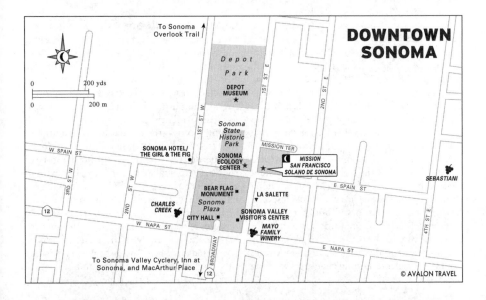

lovers. The estate is built in the light-adobe-with-red-roof style of the California missions, complete with square bell tower. Inside, visitors drink classic Sonoma Chardonnays and an array of yummy reds that show off the lush flavors of Sonoma grapes in both single varietals and blends.

SIGHTS
◖ Mission San Francisco Solano de Sonoma

Mission San Francisco Solano de Sonoma (114 E. Spain St., Sonoma, 707/938-9560, www.parks.ca.gov, daily 10 A.M.–5 P.M.), or the Sonoma Mission to its friends, is the northernmost of the California Missions. It sits at the corner of the historic plaza in downtown Sonoma—a low, surprisingly unpretentious block of buildings without much in the way of decoration or crowds. The last Mission (established in 1823) and one of the first restored as a historic landmark (finished in 1926), the Sonoma Mission isn't the prettiest or most elaborate of the California Mission chain. But

visitors can see museum-style exhibits depicting the life of the later Missionaries and Native Americans who lived here, and a unique series of watercolor paintings depicting all the California Missions. Outdoors, guests can rest on benches by the fountain, observe a moment of silence at the Native American mortuary monument, or check out the cactus "wall" that's been living on the property since the Mission days.

Bear Flag Monument

It's a little-known fact that California's state flag—the Bear Flag depicting a now-extinct California grizzly bear—first came to be in the tiny rural Mission town of Sonoma. To commemorate this historic beginning, the Bear Flag Monument (Sonoma Plaza at E. Spain St. and 1st St. E.) was erected. Visit the monument as you stroll the plaza or explore the various sites that comprise the Sonoma State Historic Park.

Cornerstone Gardens

For a break from all the history of Sonoma's

© LIZ HAMILL SCOTT

Mission San Francisco Solano de Sonoma

WINE COUNTRY

main attractions, take a walk in the ultra-modern gardens of Cornerstone Place (23570 Hwy. 121, Sonoma, 707/933-3010, www .cornerstonegardens.com, 9 A.M.–5 P.M.). This unique installation combines an art gallery with the work of the foremost landscape and garden designers in the world. Stroll these un-usual gardens, which range from traditional plantings to post-modern multimedia instal-lations, then finish up your excursion with a crawl through the boutiques, upscale foodie shops, and wine bars that have recently sprung up around the gardens. Daily wine tastings and various snacks and nonalcoholic drinks pro-vide welcome refreshment, especially on hot Sonoma summer afternoons.

Depot Park Museum

For a glimpse into the history of the ground you're treading, visit the Depot Park Museum (270 1st St. W., Sonoma, 707/938-1762, www .vom.com/depot, Wed.–Sun. 1–4:30 P.M., free). The museum hosts a small set of exhibits inside a reproduction of the historic Northwestern Pacific railroad depot, hence the name. Inside are reconstructions of the active depot in the Rand Room, a showcase of the Bear Flag Rebellion, and the life of the native Miwok people. Depot Park makes a great half-hour break from the endless wine tastings and spa treatments of Sonoma.

Jack London Historic State Park

Literary travelers come to Sonoma not just for the fine food and abundant wine, but for the chance to visit Jack London Historic State Park (2400 London Ranch Rd., Glen Ellen, 707/938-5216, www.parks.ca.gov, $6 entrance fee). Famed author Jack London did in fact live and write in the midst of rural Sonoma at the beginning of the 20th century. On week-ends, docents offer tours of the park, which include talks on the life and history of Mr. London. Explore the surviving buildings on London's prized Beauty Ranch or hike up Sonoma Mountain and check out the (artifi-cial) Lake and Bath House. The pretty stone House of Happy Walls, the creation of Jack

London's wife, houses a small museum (daily 10 A.M.–5 P.M.). Though there's no camping at Jack London State Park, you can bring a picnic to enjoy on the attractive grounds.

Sonoma Ecology Center

Many Sonoma wineries boast of the unique characteristics of their environment, such as being organic, biodynamic, or sustainable. To get deeper into the character and issues of Sonoma's landscape, check out the Sonoma Ecology Center (20 E. Spain St., Sonoma, 707/996-0712, www.sonomaecologycenter .org). Much more than just a visitors center, this organization works throughout Sonoma county to study, manage, repair, and restore as much of the land as possible to a pristine, healthy state. Their office includes displays and materials about their work and the landscape of Sonoma.

Train Town

Got a young (or not-so-young) train enthu-siast in your family? Take them to Sonoma's own Train Town (20264 Broadway, Hwy. 12, Sonoma, www.traintown.com, June–Sept. daily 10 A.M.–5 P.M., Sept.–May Fri.–Sun. only, $4.25). Ride the 15-inch scale railroad that winds through the park's 10 cool forested acres, take a spin on the roller coaster or the Ferris wheel, or climb the clock tower for a magnificent view of the park and beyond.

ENTERTAINMENT AND EVENTS

For a fun evening of drinking and live enter-tainment, head on down to **Murphy's Irish Pub** (464 1st St. E., Sonoma, 707/935-0660, www.sonomapub.com) on Sonoma Plaza. Grab an imported Irish pint or a glass of local wine, some barbecued oysters or a fine-dining entrée, and sit back to enjoy an evening of live music, literary entertainment, or perhaps a lively trivia game. Unlike many pubs and wine bars in Wine Country, Murphy's welcomes kids in its dining room, so feel free to bring the whole family for a meal and a good time.

Vineyards and olive groves have been

associated with one another for thousands of years. Celebrating the symbiosis of these two historic staple crops is the **Sonoma Valley Olive Festival** (www.sonomavalley.com, Dec.–Feb.). Sonoma hosts a variety of annual events that highlight the growth, curing, pressing, and many uses of the noble olive. Check the online calendar for a list of olive-curing classes, olive-themed winemaker's dinners, and other celebrations. The "hot" olive weekend each year is the festival finale on President's Day weekend. Expect to make your lodging reservations early and buy tickets to your favorite events in advance—this popular time is rife with classes, dinners, parties, and crowds.

SPORTS AND RECREATION
Spas

The most famous spa in the area is the **Fairmont Sonoma Mission Inn & Spa** (100 Boyes Blvd., Sonoma, 707/938-9000, www.fairmont.com/sonoma, Sun.–Thurs. 8 A.M.–7 P.M., Fri.–Sat. 8 A.M.–9 P.M.). Its eminence literally springs from beneath the rocks on which it stands. A natural mineral hot spring lies beneath the Sonoma Mission Inn, lending its warm water to the indoor and outdoor pools and whirlpools that create the center of the spa's signature Bathing Ritual. Whether you choose a relaxing massage or a challenging yoga class, be sure to arrive at least an hour early to allow time for each step of the Ritual, which will relax and focus you for your next treatment or activity. The spa offers an almost bewildering variety of massages, scrubs, wraps, facials, and even more rarified treatments designed to pamper even the most discerning spagoers. A snack bar in the spa feeds the body, and the spa's facilities are surrounded by the inn and a gourmet restaurant, both of which draw visitors from around the world all on their own.

You can also get pampered for the day in downtown Sonoma at the **Sonoma Spa on the Plaza** (457 1st St. W., Sonoma, 707/939-8770, www.sonomaspaontheplaza.com, 9 A.M.–9 P.M.). This luxury day spa, sitting steps from the pretty shops and wine bars of Sonoma Plaza, offers a complete range of massage options and facials. Their signature treatments—several different flavors of mud and cream masks—include a relaxing period in an aromatherapy sauna and an exfoliating scrub. For the ultimate downtown spa experience, pick a multiple-treatment package. If you're on a honeymoon or anniversary trip, go for the couples' massages or therapies, which you'll get together in a private room.

If you're looking for a lift to your face, visit **The Pampered Pout** (678 Broadway, Sonoma, 707/938-9396, www.thepamperedpout.com). Here you'll choose from among a dozen different 30-to-90-minute facials to beautify your skin. Esthetician and owner Bridgene Raftery can do anything from a classic European pampering facial to a series of microdermabrasion treatments to makeup lessons for teenagers. Specialty facials for teens and men, plus eyebrow designs, round out a complete menu of face-perfect services.

Golf

On the few acres of land in the Carneros region where vines don't grow, you can find a few great golf courses to help you pass the time. Between Kenwood and Santa Rosa, check out the **Bennett Valley Golf Club** (3300 Yulupa Ave., Santa Rosa, 707/528-3673, www.bvgolf.org, $26–47). This 18-hole medium-length par-72 course provides challenging play for beginners and intermediates, and some fun for advanced golfers too.

Practically next door are two 18-hole courses at the **Oakmont Golf Club** (7025 Oakmont Dr., Santa Rosa, 707/539-0415, www.oakmontgc.com, $32–64). The Oakmont East course offers executive-length par-63 play—perfect for a shorter or slightly easier game. Oakmont West is a little bit bigger and more challenging, coming in at regulation length and par 72.

If you're lucky enough to be staying at the Sonoma Mission Inn, you can access the **Sonoma Golf Club** (17700 Arnold Dr., Sonoma, 707/939-4100, www.sonomagolfclub.com). This private 18-hole par-72 course offers tee times only to guests of Sonoma Mission Inn

WINE COUNTRY

or its spa. On the other hand, the public **Los Arroyos Golf Club** (5000 Stage Gulch Rd., Sonoma, 707/938-8835) is open to all comers. Great for newer players, Los Arroyos offers nine holes, par 29, and good fun for golfers.

Hiking

Several fabulous hikes lurk in Sonoma County. One of the best of these is the easy two-mile **Overlook Trail.** You can reach it from the center of downtown Sonoma by following 1st Street West to the Veteran's Hall and Cemetery, then looking for the signs describing the trail route. As you walk this gentle path you'll get fabulous views of Sonoma, plus the chance to see the locals out on a favorite jogging route. In wetter (or recently wet) weather, wear sturdy hiking boots to combat the clay.

Horseback Riding

With its vineyards, open spaces, and state parks, the Sonoma-Carneros region begs to be explored on horseback in homage to its pioneering history. The **Triple Creek Horse Outfit** (707/887-8700, www.triplecreekhorseoutfit .com, $60) offers guided rides at Jack London

State Historic Park and Sugarloaf Ridge State Park. These rides, which can last from an hour up to half a day, take you beyond what you can see from the windows of your car. A ride through Jack London Park takes you through the writer's life in Sonoma and the literary history of the region. Up on Sugarloaf in the Mayacamas Mountains, you'll ride along the ridge and get glimpses of both the Sonoma and Napa Valleys. Or if you prefer, you can enjoy the forests and wildlife of Sugarloaf by moonlight on a two-hour full-moon ride.

Motor Sports

Not every inch of ground in Sonoma County grows grapevines or houses inns and restaurants. One huge plot of invaluable dirt has long been given over to the **Infineon Raceway** (29355 Arnold Dr., Sonoma, 800/870-7223, www.infineonraceway.com). This massive motor-sports complex hosts almost every sort of vehicular race there is. With several NASCAR events each year, various AMA motorcycle races, an Indy car race, and of course an NHRA drag race, Infineon sees more action than many of the country's most popular

INFINEON RACEWAY POST-RACE TRAFFIC

Don't give a darn about auto or bike racing? Think you can safely ignore Infineon's schedule during your travels in Sonoma? Not if you're wise in the ways of event traffic. The turnoff to Infineon Raceway lies roughly at the intersection of Highways 37 and 121. These charming and scenic two-lane roads are great for motoring and sightseeing – unless, of course, you're stuck in bumper-to-bumper race traffic. The absolute worst time to try to drive either of these roads (particularly Hwy. 37 out of Sonoma) is when a major race event has finished. The wretched traffic jams, which truly are more stop than go, can last for hours as people try to exit the racetrack into the unprotected intersection. In the summer, the sweltering heat causes both engines and tempers to overheat, to no good end.

So what can you do?

- Check the race schedule (www.infineonraceway.com), and avoid the roads in question for at least four hours after the scheduled or estimated end of a big race.

- Plot another route to your next destination, or stick around in Sonoma until well after the traffic is likely to have unsnarled. (Give it about six hours post-race.)

- Escape via Highway 12 east to Napa or north to Santa Rosa. From Santa Rosa, catch Highway 101 south to the Bay Area or north toward the Russian River. If heading to Napa, pick up Highway 37 at a less crowded spot and then follow it south to Highway 80. Highway 80 will either take you south to the East Bay or east into Sacramento and beyond.

racetracks. It has events scheduled literally 340 days per year, though many of these run to local track days and small-time club races. Ticket prices vary hugely, so check the website to learn the cost of your favorite event.

ACCOMMODATIONS
Sonoma

For a charming room at a reasonable price within the town limits of Sonoma, stay in the **Sonoma Creek Inn** (239 Boyes Blvd., 888/712-1289, www.sonomacreekinn.com, $90–160). The whimsical, colorful decor and unique art pieces brighten each guest room and each guest's stay. Amenities include cable TV, free wireless Internet access, a refrigerator, and private garden patios. Located a few minutes away from downtown Sonoma and convenient to the Carneros wineries, the Sonoma Creek Inn is perfect for travelers who want to spend their money on the wine and dining of the region rather than their motel room.

Right on Sonoma Plaza in the heart of Sonoma, **Les Petites Maisons** (1190 E. Napa St., 800/291-8962, www.lespetitesmaisons.com, $130–325) offers four cute cottages for a homey stay in the Wine Country. Each cottage has its own style, but all have warm colors and comfy furniture to evoke the relaxation needed for a perfect vacation. All the cottages have fully equipped kitchens (one with kitchenette) that let you visit the fabulous Sonoma farmers markets and cook your own fresh food. Or you can eat at the girl and the fig or one of the other wonderful restaurants on the plaza.

In 1850, one of the first Spanish settlers to the Sonoma area built a home for his family on the town square. For almost the last 100 years, the **Swiss Hotel** (18 W. Spain St., 707/938-2884, www.swisshotelsonoma.com, $110–250) has offered a bed and a meal to travelers from near and far. With a renovation in the 1990s, the guest rooms have plenty of modern amenities, while the outside of the building and the public spaces retain the historic feel of the original adobe building. You'll find your room light, bright, and airy with fresh paint and pretty floral comforters. Downstairs, take a meal at the restaurant or have a drink at the historic bar—or both! Step outside to take a walk around the historic plaza.

Glen Ellen and Kenwood

With its wraparound porches and lush gardens, the **Beltane Ranch** (11775 Hwy. 12, Glen Ellen, 707/996-6501, www.beltaneranch.com, $150–220) looks like it belongs outside of Savannah, Georgia, rather than Sonoma, California. But this Valley of the Moon charmer sits right in the middle of Wine Country, offering five guest rooms and a detached cottage to wine lovers from around the world. After a good night's sleep in the pristine country-style rooms, guests enjoy a sumptuous breakfast in the dining room or on the porch overlooking the gardens and vineyards beyond.

For a fabulous wine-and-spa retreat away from anything resembling a city, stay at the **Kenwood Inn & Spa** (10400 Hwy. 12, Kenwood, 707/833-1293, www.kenwoodinn.com, $250–400, no children under 18, no pets). This Tuscan-style villa has 29 posh guest rooms, a world-renowned spa, and a rustic-elegant Italian restaurant on-site. The only problem with the Kenwood Inn is that you may have trouble prying yourself away long enough to go wine tasting. Expect to pay premium room prices during the summer and fall high season.

Got lots of money to blow on one of the best-reviewed inns in all of Wine Country? Do it at the **Gaige House Inn** (13540 Arnold Dr., Glen Ellen, 707/935-0237, www.gaige.com, $700), where comfort and luxury have been built into the design of guest rooms and common spaces, and special attention paid to every detail. Each of the 23 guest rooms and suites resembles a spread in an interior-design magazine; suites have bathrooms the size of bedrooms and their own tiny garden spaces. Be aware that breakfast and spa treatments cost extra.

FOOD
Sonoma

A favorite with the local-sustainable-organic

food crowd, ☾ **the girl and the fig** (110 W. Spain St., Sonoma, 707/938-3634, www.the girlandthefig.com, daily 11:30 A.M.–10 P.M., $20) sits right on Sonoma Plaza. The menu changes often to take advantage of the finest local seasonal ingredients; for a special treat, order one of the amazing cheese plates. If you love the sauces and jams here, look for the girl and the fig products both on-site and at wineries and high-end food shops throughout Wine Country.

Another California cuisine hot spot with a beautiful outdoor patio and a seasonal local-focused menu is the **Harvest Moon Café** (487 1st St. W., Sonoma, 707/933-8160, www.harvest moonsonoma.com, Sun.–Thurs. 5:30–9 P.M., Fri.–Sat. 5:30–9:30 P.M., $17–25). The menu of this charmingly casual restaurant changes daily to take advantage of the best ingredients available.

It's rare when locals and tourists agree on the best restaurant in any given town. The fact that this one's a traditional Portuguese place navigating in a sea of California cuisine just makes it all the more special. ☾ **LaSalette** (452 1st St. E., Sonoma, 707/938-1927, www .lasalette-restaurant.com, Mon.–Thurs. and Sun. 11:30 A.M.–2:30 P.M. and 5–8:30 P.M., Fri.–Sat. 11:30 A.M.–9 P.M., $17–24) has a simple, charming atmosphere with a wood-fired oven facing a curving bar that serves drinks and friendly chatter to regulars, as well as a full dinner menu. A large outdoor patio is the most popular seating area in summer, though the meandering tile-floored dining room offers plenty of easy appeal plus a bonus view of the open kitchen. The undisputed star of LaSalette is the food. The unrelentingly Portuguese menu features fresh fish and hearty meat dishes, plus some good meat-free options. Simple yet delectable preparations let the flavors of the principle ingredients shine through. Need an ingredient substituted or removed? Just ask—they're happy to accommodate special requests.

Need a hearty breakfast or down-home lunch before you get going on a full day of wine tasting? Stop in at the **Big 3 Diner** (18140 Hwy.

12, Sonoma, 707/939-2410, www.fairmont .com, daily 7 A.M.–5 P.M. and 5:30–9:30 P.M., $8–18). The restaurant is part of the Fairmont Sonoma Mission Inn property, which explains both the tip-top prices and the upscalified diner cuisine. But it's good stuff—the kitchen uses high-quality (often organic and local) ingredients to create its fancy Benedicts and sandwiches. Even the locals approve, coming in to be greeted by name by the friendly and efficient service staff. If staying at the Sonoma Mission Inn, order room service from Big 3 or walk over to the big friendly dining room, sparkling with wooden chairs and tables and a pleasant casual atmosphere.

If you just need a cup of coffee and maybe a quick pastry, stop in at the **Barking Dog Coffee Roasters** (201 W. Napa St., Sonoma, 707/996-7446, www.barkingdogcoffee .com, Mon.–Fri. 6 A.M.–8 P.M., Sat.–Sun. 7 A.M.–8 P.M.). Barking Dog is the spot where the locals go to get their morning mochas. Sip a latte or indulge in a scoop of Caffe Classico gelato, take a seat on a comfy old couch, and maybe even enjoy some live music.

For travelers fixing most of their own meals, or folks looking for gluten-free grains to take home with them, the **Fruit Basket** (24101 Arnold Dr, Sonoma, 707/938-4332, daily 7 A.M.–7:15 P.M.) open-air market has a great selection. This isn't a local farm stand—much of the produce is emphatically not local, especially in the winter. But the array of dried beans and grains would put a San Francisco health-food store to shame, making it easy for celiacs and those with food allergies to find great make-it-yourself food options here. Despite its suggestive name, the Fruit Basket actually serves as a fully stocked market, selling imported Italian and Mexican foods, dairy products, somewhat superfluous wines, and of course fresh fruits and vegetables. The only thing they don't stock is fresh meats. Prices are reasonable, and the market is easy to see and access at the south end of the Sonoma-Carneros wine region.

Glen Ellen and Kenwood

At the **Glen Ellen Inn Restaurant** (13670

Arnold Dr., Glen Ellen, 707/996-6409, www
.glenelleninn.com, Fri.–Tues. 11:30 A.M.–9 P.M.,
$20), haute California cuisine meets small-
town kitsch. You'll find this self-described oyster grill and martini bar's dining room inside
a cute low building in the tiny hamlet of Glen
Ellen. In addition to the seafood-heavy gourmet menu, the Glen Ellen Inn boasts a full bar
and a wine list worthy of its location.

the fig café (13690 Arnold Dr., Glen
Ellen, 707/938-2130, www.thegirlandthefig
.com, daily 5:30 P.M.–close, Sat.–Sun. brunch
10 A.M.–2:30 P.M., $13–20) serves the same
excellent food as its namesake restaurant in
Sonoma, with a warm interior and the weekend brunch a sure bet.

Despite its Hispanic name, the cuisine at
Dóce Lunas (8910 Sonoma Hwy., Kenwood,
707/833-4000, www.docelunasrestaurant
.com, Wed.–Sat. 11:30 A.M.–2:30 P.M. and
5–8:30 P.M., Sun. 10 A.M.–2:30 P.M. and
5–8:30 P.M., $17–20) has a distinct Wine
Country flair. Downstairs, enjoy a delectable
meal in a country-style dining room. Upstairs,
take a ramble through the Dóce Lunas antique
store, which sells country-style kitsch and
collectibles.

INFORMATION AND SERVICES

Before you begin your Sonoma and Carneros
wine tasting adventure, stop in at the
Sonoma Valley Visitors Center (453 1st St.
E., Sonoma, 866/996-1090, www.sonoma
valley.com, Mon.–Sat. 9 A.M.–5 P.M., Sun.
10 A.M.–5 P.M.). Ask the volunteers for advice
on which wineries to hit, and be sure to pick up
some complimentary tasting passes.

One of the local papers in the Sonoma
Valley is the **Sonoma Index-Tribune** (www
.sonomanews.com). Turn to the Do and Shop
sections for visitor information.

For medical attention in Sonoma, head for
the **Sonoma Valley Hospital** (347 Andrieux
St., Sonoma, 707/935-5000, www.svh.com),
which has a full-service emergency room.

GETTING THERE AND AROUND

The town of Sonoma lies over the mountains west of the Napa Valley. The main route
through the valley is Highway 12, also called
the Sonoma Highway. From Napa, drive south
on Highway 29, turning west onto Highway
12/121. Turn north on Highway 12 to reach
downtown Sonoma.

If driving from the Bay Area, take U.S.
101 north, then Highway 37 east. It becomes
Highway 121, then Highway 116 as it winds
into the city of Sonoma. If you're driving south
on U.S. 101, you can turn off onto Highway 12
south in Santa Rosa and take a scenic journey
down into the Sonoma-Carneros wine region.

Parking in downtown Sonoma is easy in
the off-season and tougher in the high season
(summer and fall). Expect to hunt hard for a
spot during any local events, and prepare to
walk several blocks. Most wineries provide
ample free parking on their grounds.

For your public transit needs, use the buses
run by **Sonoma County Transit** (707/576-
7433, www.sctransit.com, $1.15–3.10). Several
routes service the Sonoma Valley on both
weekdays and weekends. You can use SCT
to get from Sonoma Valley to Santa Rosa,
Guerneville, and other spots in the Russian
River Valley as well.

It's fitting that in Wine Country, a place at
the bleeding edge of sustainable agriculture in
a state known for its eco-mindedness, you can
take a vineyard tour on a Segway. **Sonoma
Segway** (524 Broadway, Sonoma, 707/938-
2080, www.sonomasegway.com, $99/tour,
$40/hour rental) offers a 2.5-hour tour that
includes a visit to a local winery, a stop at a
local food-based business, and a full-fledged
visit to historic Sonoma. You'll start off with
a lesson on the Segway, and when you finish
you'll get a complimentary bottle of wine (if
you're of age, of course). If you'd prefer to traverse the Sonoma streets and paths on your
own, rent a Segway—for just two hours or up
to a month at a time.

WINE COUNTRY

NORTH COAST

The rugged north coast of California is a spectacular place. Its wild beauty is in many places unspoiled, and almost desolate. This is not the California coast of surfer movies, though hardy souls do ride the chilly Pacific waves all the way up to Crescent City. Cliffs are forbidding, beaches are rocky and windswept, and the surf thunders in with formidable authority.

The North Coast also means redwood country. South of the pretty college town of Eureka, the famously immense California redwood trees loom along the highway. Redwood National Park and the Humboldt Redwoods State Park boast some of the biggest, oldest trees on the continent.

Wending back toward the edge of the ocean to the south, nature-lovers traverse the 80-mile, highway-free Lost Coast. Accessed by steep, narrow roads and bereft of amenities, the scenic California Coastal Trail runs for 64 miles over mountains and across beaches. Finally, for the best mix of natural and cultural California, Mendocino County and the Sonoma coast offer lovely beaches and forests, top-notch cuisine, and a friendly, uncrowded wine region.

PLANNING YOUR TIME

The outdoors is the primary attraction here, though Eureka offers some indoor attractions as well. Driving is the way to get from place to place, unless you're a hardcore backpacker. Plan some time on the beaches (in nice warm clothes) and some time in the forest as well. Hiking is the one don't-miss activity. Close second is some time fishing or whale-watching out on the cold, majestic café.

HIGHLIGHTS

◖ Blue Ox Historic Park: The rambling buildings of this working lumber mill and historic park are filled with 19th-century tools used to customize historic homes. A school offers opportunities to learn about the lives and work of these craftsmen and even turn a piece of your own (page 220).

◖ Patrick's Point State Park: This tiny coastal park harbors prominent landscapes of coastal history, such as a re-creation of a Yurok Village. The cool climate is perfect for year-round hiking (page 235).

◖ Mendocino County Botanical Gardens: Stretching out to the sea, these 47 acres of botanical gardens portray a vast variety of flowers and plants and the butterflies who love them (page 246).

◖ Glass Beach: Spend the day combing for "sea glass" on Mendocino's most well-known beach (page 246).

◖ Fort Ross State Historic Park: For a taste of historic California, explore this fortified outpost that served as a wayfaring point between 19th-century traders (page 247).

LOOK FOR ◖ TO FIND RECOMMENDED SIGHTS, ACTIVITIES, DINING, AND LODGING.

Many residents of the Bay Area consider Mendocino to be the perfect spot for a romantic weekend retreat, and indeed a weekend is about the perfect length of time to spend on the Mendo Coast or in the Anderson Valley wine country. (You might want to extend your trip for a day or three once you fall in love with the beautiful country.) You can also spend an active weekend hiking and exploring the Redwood National Park and state parks. If you want to explore the North Coast in more depth and make stops in more than one destination, plan to spend a full week here.

HISTORY

True human history in the North Coast began long before white men came to the region. Rich with natural resources, this area was home to more than a dozen Native American tribes who made great use of the fishing, hunting, and gathering grounds so abundant near and on the coast. Chief among them were the Yurok and the Wiyot people. It is only recently that the rich cultures of these people have begun to be appreciated by visitors and residents alike. Many still live here on the various reservations and rancherias, and an encouraging number of museums and historical parks are being dedicated to the study and celebration of North Coast Native American heritage.

The gold rush brought white settlers to the North Coast of California—gold mines in the Trinity area in 1850. Soon after, entrepreneurs saw the potential wealth in the forests and the

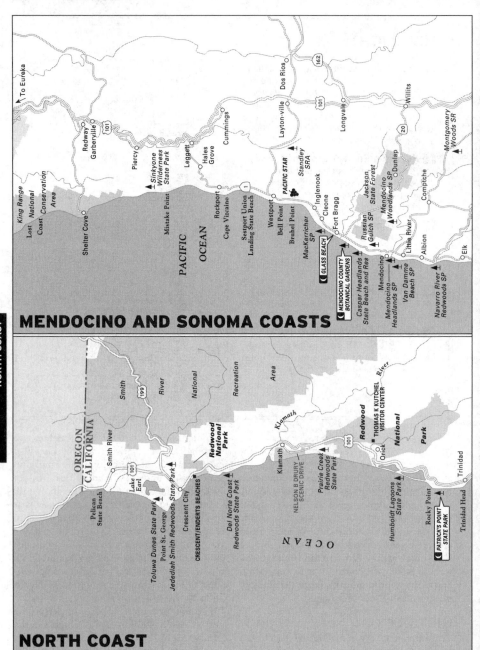

MENDOCINO AND SONOMA COASTS

NORTH COAST

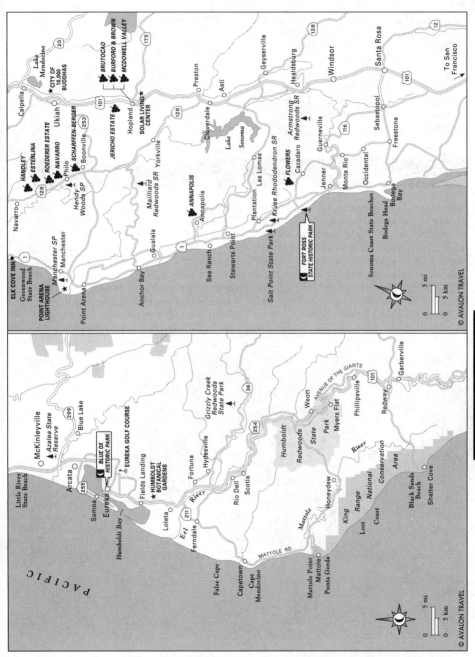

sea and began creating the now legendary lumber and fishing industries. The principal city of Eureka was founded in 1850, and the prosperity of the times is still visible in the elaborate Victorian shops and homes built along Humboldt Bay. Inland, a variety of Europeans emigrated to the rich farmland. Dairy cattle flourished, and so communities grew to support the ranchers.

In 1964, a tsunami from Alaska mangled Crescent City, but largely spared Eureka, Mendocino, and points south. The later 1960s brought a flood of a different kind—hippies and artists—to Mendocino. These rare creatures and their works can still be viewed in the area today, though the rise of the area as a tourist destination makes it more difficult for younger artists to find affordable living here.

Crescent City

The northernmost city on the coast of California perches on the bay whose shape gave the town its name. Cool and windswept, Crescent City is a perfect place to put on a parka, stuff your hands deep in your pockets, and take a long contemplative walk along a wide, beautiful beach. Serious deep-sea fishing lovers will find fishing to their hearts content, and lovely and uncrowded redwood forests beckon hikers.

In 1964, much of Crescent City was destroyed in a tsunami caused by an Alaskan earthquake. The damage, estimated at $7–15 million, plus those who died and were injured in the disaster, amounts to the most severe tsunami damage ever recorded on the West Coast of the United States. More than 40 years have passed, but the ripples of the event still shudder through the small community. Look to the tops of phone poles to see old tsunami warning sirens, now rusted with disuse, but not yet removed.

© LIZ HAMILL SCOTT

the beach at Crescent City

SIGHTS

Point St. George

The wild, lonely, beautiful Point St. George (end of Washington Blvd.) epitomizes the glory of the North Coast of California. Walk out onto the cliffs to take in the deep blue sea, wild salt-and-flower scented air, and craggy cliffs and beaches here. On a clear day, you can see all the way to Oregon. Short (but steep) trails lead across wild beach prairie land and down to broad, flat, nearly deserted beaches. In spring and summer, wildflowers bloom across the cliffs and swallows nest in the cluster of buildings on the point. On rare and special clear days, you can almost make out the St. George Reef Lighthouse sitting lonely on its perch far out in the Pacific. Helicopter trips (707/464-8299) to this lighthouse are available from October 16 to June 1 each year.

Battery Point Lighthouse Park

West of the middle of downtown Crescent City you'll find the Battery Point Lighthouse Park (at foot of A St., 707/464-3089, open Apr.–Oct. daily 10 A.M.–4 P.M. tides permitting) past the visitors center. Plan carefully and pick up a recent schedule, since the lighthouse is not always accessible to tourists. At high tide, the causeway that connects the city to the lighthouse is under water. But if you catch the tide at low or medium, you'll get an unadvertised treat as you walk to and fro: tidepools. The Battery Point tidepools are rife with life, from sea stars and sea anemones to worm colonies and barnacle clusters. Small fish are trapped by the receding tides, and hunt for food in the pools until the waters rise again. Up in the lighthouse, built in 1856, a tiny bookstore features local- and lighthouse-themed books and souvenirs. The guided tour takes visitors through the lighthouse, which is set up as a museum, though it is also a working private light station.

Ocean World

Are the kids bored with all the gorgeous

© LIZ HAMILL SCOTT

Battery Point Lighthouse, Crescent City

NORTH COAST

scenery? A great family respite is Ocean World (304 Hwy. 101 S., 707/464-4900, www.ocean worldonline.com, 8 A.M.–8 P.M. daily, $9.95 adults, $5.95 kids). Tours of the small sea park depart about every 15 minutes, and last about 40 minutes. Featured attractions are the shark petting tank, the half-million gallon aquarium, and the sea lion show. After the tour, take a stroll through the immense souvenir shop, which sells gifts of all sizes, shapes, and descriptions, many with nautical themes.

Del Norte County Historical Society Museum

The Del Norte County Historical Society Museum (577 H St., 707/464-3922, open May–Sept. Mon.–Sat. 10 A.M.–4 P.M.) provides an educational respite from the chilly sea breezes. The Historical Society maintains this small museum featuring the local history of both the Native Americans who once inhabited Del Norte County and the encroaching white settlers. Featured exhibits include the wreck of the *Brother Jonathan* at Point St. George, the story of the 1964 tsunami, and artifacts of the local Yurok and Tolowa tribes.

ENTERTAINMENT AND EVENTS
Bars and Clubs

If you're looking for a varied and rockin' night life, Crescent City is not your town. But a few options exist for insomniacs. Most of the hot action after 9 P.M. takes place at the **Elk Valley Casino** (2500 Howland Hill Rd., 888/574-2744, open 24 hrs) at the eastern edge of town. The Elk Valley is a bit more upscale than other local Native American casinos, with genuine aluminum-siding walls, poker and blackjack tables, a VIP card room, and a small nonsmoking slots area.

The **Tsunami Lanes Bowling Center** (760 L St., 707/464-4323, Mon.–Thurs. 11 A.M.–11:30 P.M., Fri.–Sat. 11 A.M.–midnight, Sun. 11 A.M.–10 P.M., $2 games before 6 P.M., $3 after 6 P.M.) is a straight-up bowling alley, serving beer and greasy fries to all comers late into

the night. For a more active evening, take a wheeled spin around the polished floor at the **Rollercade** (421 Hwy. 101 N., 707/465-0412, call for hours and rates).

A more civilized evening is available at performances of the **Lighthouse Repertory Theater** (707/465-3740). The **Del Norte Association for Cultural Awareness** (P.O. Box 1480, 707/464-1336) hosts several live musical acts and other entertainments each year. Check this year's schedule for upcoming shows, all of which take place at the Crescent Elk Auditorium (994 G St.). If all else fails, you can take in a first-run movie at the **Crescent City Cinemas** (375 M St., 707/465-4567).

Festivals and Events

A must for serious birders, the **Aleutian Goose Festival** (www.aleutiangoosefestival.org) takes place each spring when the once endangered but now plentiful geese come to Crescent City during their annual migration. The highlight of the festival is the dawn viewing of tens of thousands of Aleutian geese rising all at once from their island sleeping grounds to come ashore to feed. Almost 100 other events highlight area avian diversity, natural education and appreciation, and celebration of the indigenous peoples of Del Norte County. This festival is sponsored by and centered in the Crescent City Cultural Center (1001 Front St.).

For almost 50 years, the Yurok tribe has held a festival to honor a creature most precious to them: the mighty salmon. The **Klamath Salmon Festival** (www.yuroktribe.org) takes place in August of each year and includes a parade, live music, games, and of course salmon dinners served all day.

SPORTS AND RECREATION
Beaches

The sands of Crescent City are a beachcomber's paradise. Wide, flat, sandy expanses invite strolling, running, and just sitting to contemplate the endless crashing Pacific. **South Beach** is located, as advertised, at the south end of town. Long, wide, and flat, it's perfect for a romantic stroll, so long as you're bundled up. The adventurous and chill-resistant can try surfing and boogey-boarding here. Farther south, **Crescent** and **Enderts Beaches** (Enderts Rd.) offer picnic spots, tidepools, and acres of sand to walk and play on. The sand is dark colored, soft, and perfect for families. The trails down to the beach are steep and rocky, so take care getting to the beaches. Hikers enjoy the trails that lead away from the beach and into the national forest.

It might look tempting on the rare sunny days, but swimming from the beaches of Crescent City is not for the faint of heart or body. The water is icy cold, the shores are rocky, and as elsewhere in Northern California, undertow and rip currents can be dangerous. No lifeguards patrol these beaches, so you and your family are on your own.

Bird-Watching

Birders flock to Crescent City since the diverse climates and habitats nourish a huge variety of avian residents. The parks and preserves have become destinations for enthusiasts looking for "lifers" hard to find anyplace else. Right in town, check out **Battery Point Lighthouse Park** and **Point St. George.** For a rare view of an Aleutian goose or a peregrine falcon, journey to **Tolowa Dunes State Park** (1375 Elk Valley Rd., 707/464-6101 x5151, www.parks .ca.gov) specifically the shores of Lake Earl and Kellog Beach. South of town, **Enderts Beach** is home to another large bird habitat.

Surfing

For surfers and bodysurfers willing to don heavy wetsuits and brave the cold North Coast waters, some great waves are there for the catching. It may not be paradise, but **South Beach** is a longboarder's mecca. Longboard legend Greg Noll hosts an annual longboard contest here, and his son's **Noll Surf & Skate** (275 L St., Crescent City, 707/465-4400, www.noll .net) perches on the nearby wharf. The beach

at **Point St. George** is but in the right condition break.

Fishing and Whale-

Anglers can choose betw sea fishing and exciting river trips. The Pacific yields ling cod, snapper, and salmon, while the rivers are famous for Chinook (king) salmon, steelhead, and cutthroat trout. Mammal-loving travelers can choose whale-watching over fishing. The **Tally Ho II** (1685 Del Mar Rd. at the harbor, 707/464-1236) is available for a variety of deep-sea fishing trips, whale-watching, and a combination of the two.

River fishers have a wealth of guides to choose from. **Ken Cunningham Guide Service** (10515 Salmina Rd., Kelseyville, 707/928-4762) and **North Coast Fishing Adventures** (1657 Childrens Ave., McKinleyville, 707/839-8127) cover the Klamath and Smith Rivers as well as smaller waterways.

Hiking

The redwood forests that nearly meet wide sandy beaches make the Crescent City area a fabulous place to hike. The hikes at **Point St. George** aren't strenuous, and give hikers stunning views of the coastline and surrounding landscape. **Tolowa Dunes State Park** (1375 Elk Valley Rd., 707/464-6101 x5151, www .parks.ca.gov), north of Point St. George, offers miles of trails winding through forests, across beaches, and meandering along the shores of Lake Earl.

Horseback Riding

The rugged land surrounding Crescent City looks even prettier from the back of a horse. Casual riders can rent horses from **Fort Dicks Stable** (2002 Moorehead Rd., 707/487-3014). A great place to ride is **Tolowa Dunes State Park** (1375 Elk Valley Rd., 707/464-6101 x5151, www.parks.ca.gov), which maintains 20 miles of trails accessible to horses. Serious equestrians with their own mounts can ride in to a campsite with corrals at the north end of the park off Lower Lake Road.

MMODATIONS

...mmodations in Crescent City are afford-
...e even during high season (midsummer) and
can be surprisingly comfortable.

Under $100

The aptly named **Curly Redwood Lodge**
(701 Hwy. 101 S., 707/464-1655, www.curly
redwoodlodge.com, $64–89) is constructed of
a single rare curly redwood tree. You'll get to
see the lovely color and grain of the tree in your
large, simply decorated room. A 1950s feel pervades this friendly, unpretentious motel that's
located right on the freeway conveniently near
some of the area's best restaurants.

Few frills decorate the family-owned **Pacific
Inn** (220 M. St., 707/464-9553, $60) but the
rooms are clean, inexpensive, and comfortable.
Located right downtown, access to restaurants,
museums, and points of interest is easy.

$100-150

The **Lighthouse Inn** (681 Hwy. 101 S.,
877/464-9035, www.lighthouse101.com,
$99–119) brings more than a touch of class
to this fisherman's town. An elegant, eclectic
lobby filled with dolphins and dollhouses welcomes guests, and the enthusiastic staff can
help with restaurants recommendations and
sights. Stylish appointments and bold colors
grace each room. Corner suites with oversized
whirlpool tubs make a perfect romantic couples' retreat at a reasonable nightly rate, while
standard double rooms are downright cheap
given their comfort.

The **Anchor Beach Inn** (880 Hwy. 101 S.,
800/837-4116, www.anchorbeachinn.com) at
the south end of town offers great access to
South Beach, the harbor, and several good
seafood restaurants. The ocean views require
guests to overlook (literally) a wide swath of asphalt RV park, but the in-room decor is attractive, the rooms are clean and well maintained,
and there's free Wi-Fi.

For a more personal, intimate experience,
try the **Castle Island Getaway** (1830 Murphy
Ave., 707/465-5102, www.castleislandgetaway
.com, $85–125). Offering lodgings to only one

party of up to four people at a time, the inn-
keepers take special care of guests here. You'll
get to choose your breakfast from a menu of
options, and it will be served at your convenience. Light, bright, private rooms and a short
walk to Pebble Beach (no, not that one!) make
for a delightful romantic getaway.

Over $150

Perhaps the best lodging location in town
is the **Cottage By the Sea** (205 S. A St.,
707/464-9068). Downtown and right on
the coast, both the honeymoon cottage and
the house rooms overlook the Battery Point
Lighthouse. A nontraditional B&B, the owner
stocks the fridge with food you can cook yourself, or the owner will cook breakfast upon request. Special rates are available for stays of at
least three days.

FOOD

Unsurprisingly, standard fare in Crescent City
runs toward seafood, but family restaurants
and even one or two ethnic eateries also offer
tasty fare.

American

The **Apple Peddler** (308 Hwy. 101 S.,
707/464-5630, $8–18) is a 24-hour family
restaurant with an extensive, classic American
menu and great local dessert specials like
summertime blackberry cobbler. Right next
door to Ocean World, it's the perfect place to
take the weary family for a hearty lunch or a
mid-afternoon slice of pie. The service can be
spotty, and the place can get crowded on summer weekends, but it's still the favored diner
in the area.

Seafood

Much of the fish is fresh and locally caught,
so dig in! The **Beachcomber** (1400 Hwy. 101
S., 707/464-2205, $10–18) is the only beach-
front restaurant in town, sitting in the middle
of South Beach. The glass-front dining room
is the perfect place to view the sun setting over
the crescent-shaped bay while dining on delectable parmesan halibut or smoky pit-barbecued

beef. Extra-friendly service makes even the first-time visitor feel like a local. Be aware that weekend evenings can be crowded.

Northwood's Restaurant (675 Hwy. 101 S., 707/465-5656, $8–20) prides itself on serving the freshest fish available, and in Crescent City that can mean the fillet you're eating for dinner was caught that very morning by a local fisherman. The varied menu also includes imported exotic fish, plus a number of land-based entrées to appeal to every palate. Northwood's is open for breakfast, lunch, and dinner.

The Fisherman's Restaurant (700 Hwy. 101 S., 707/465-3474) is a great place to walk into wearing jeans and sandy sneakers to grab a bite of great fresh fish. A local favorite is the **Harbor View Grotto** (150 Starfish Way, 707/464-3815, $6–20). While the steaks and sides are good, it's the seafood that stands out here and Clam chowder, shrimp appetizers, and fish are all favorites here.

Coffee
The **Java Hut** (437 Hwy. 101 N., 707/465-4439, daily 5 A.M.–10 P.M., $5) is a drive-thru and walk-up coffee stand that serves a wide array of fancy coffee drinks, including some alcoholic treats. (Yes, at the drive-thru!) Beware of long lines of locals during morning hours. Downtown, check out **Coffee Corner** (530 L St., 707/464-9255, daily 5 A.M.–3 P.M.). Excellent pastries and sandwiches make this local shop stand out.

Markets
Small, family-owned, award-winning **Rumiano Cheese Co.** (451 Hwy. 101 N., 707/465-2873, www.rumianocheese.com, call for hours) has been part of Crescent City since 1921. Come to the tasting room for the cheese, stay for, well, more cheese. The dry Jack cheese is a particular favorite, though lots of varieties are available.

Like most California towns, Crescent City runs a **farmers market** (451 Hwy. 101 N. at the Del Norte County Fairgrounds, 707/464-7441, June–Sept. on Sat.). While the harvest season is more restricted here than in points south, veggie lovers can still choose from an array of fresh local produce all summer long.

INFORMATION AND SERVICES
The Crescent City **visitors center** (Mar.–Oct. daily 9 A.M.–5 P.M., Nov.–Feb. 9 A.M.–4 P.M.) is located at the Chamber of Commerce at 1001 Front Street. Here you'll find young but knowledgeable staffers who can advise you on "secret" local sights as well as the bigger tourist attractions advertised in the myriad brochures lining the walls.

The Daily Triplicate, the local newspaper of Crescent City, is published Tuesday through Saturday. At the visitors center and many local businesses, you can pick up a Del Norte County Map and a copy of *101 Things to Do in Del Norte County and Southern Oregon.*

GETTING THERE AND AROUND
Air
Jack McNamara Field (5 miles northwest) serves as Crescent City's only airport. Commuter flights are available on several airlines from major airports in California and Oregon. Major Internet ticketing sights cover CEC.

Bus
Redwood Coast Transit (RCT) (707/464-6400, $1 adults, $0.50 seniors/disabled, $10 punch passes) handles bus travel in and around Crescent City. Four in-town routes and a coastal bus from Smith River down to Arcata provide ample public-transit options for travelers without cars. Pick up a schedule at the visitors center (1001 Front St.) or local stores for current fares and times.

Car
The main routes in and out of town are U.S. 101 and Highway 199. Though both are well maintained, they can get twisty in spots so take care, especially at night. Traffic isn't a big issue in Crescent City, and parking is free and easy to come by throughout town.

Eureka

The town of Eureka began as a seaward access point to the remote gold mines of the Trinity area. Almost immediately, settlers realized the worth of the redwood trees surrounding them and started building the logging industry. In the late 19th century, men got rich here, and built a wealth of lovely Victorian homes and downtown commercial buildings. Today, lumber is still a major industry in Eureka. But tourism is another draw, with people coming to enjoy the waterfront wharf, the charming downtown shopping area, and the Victorian lumber-baron history that pervades the town. Active outdoors lovers can fish, whale-watch, and hike, while history buffs can explore museums, Victorian mansions, and even a working historic millworks.

SIGHTS
◖ Blue Ox Historic Park

Even in a town that thrives on the history of man using wood, the Blue Ox Millworks and Historic Park (1 X St., 800/248-4259, www .blueoxmill.com, tours Mon.–Fri. 9 A.M.–5 P.M., Sat. 9 A.M.–4 P.M., adults $7.50, children $3.50) is unique. Blue Ox is at once a working lumber mill, upscale wood and cabinetry shop, ceramics studio, blacksmith forge, old-fashioned print shop, shipbuilding yard, school, and historic park. Owner Eric Hollenbeck didn't

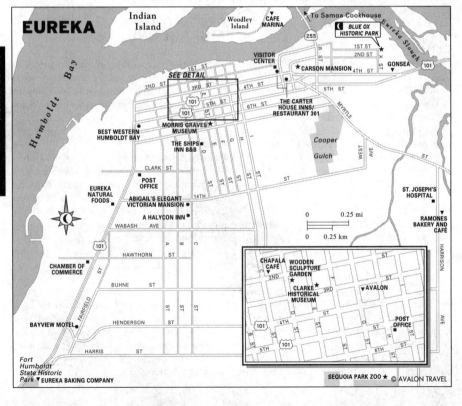

Eric, founder of the Blue Ox Millworks

intend to start an immense historic enterprise. He simply couldn't afford fancy new power tools for his shop, so he rescued and rehabilitated 19th-century human-powered jigsaws, routers, and other woodworking tools. Today, his rambling buildings are filled with purchased, donated, and rehabbed tools of all kinds, which his craftsmen use to create ornate custom items for homes and historic buildings across the country. The school teaches high school students everything from digging their own clay to make pottery to hand-setting type to print their own yearbooks. Visitors to the Blue Ox can't help but learn about the real lives and times of craftsmen of the last centuries as they tour the facilities and examine the equipment. If you ask, you might even be allowed to touch and even turn a piece of wood of your own. Also, be sure to stop in at the gift shop—a converted lumberjack barracks—to check out the ceramics and woodwork the students have for sale.

Clarke Historical Museum

The privately owned and maintained Clarke Historical Museum (240 E. St., 707/443-1947, Tues.–Sat. 11 A.M.–4 P.M., free) is dedicated to preserving the history of Eureka and the surrounding area. Visitors get a view of changing exhibitions that illustrate Victorian life in Eureka from the gold rush through the logging era and on to the 20th century. The Nealis Hall annex displays one of the best collections of Northern California Native American artifacts anywhere in the state.

Fort Humboldt State Historic Park

Established in 1853 to protect white settlers from the local Native Americans, the original Fort Humboldt lasted only 17 years as a military installation. Today, Fort Humboldt State Historic Park (3431 Fort Ave., 707/445-6567, www.parks.ca.gov, daily 8 A.M.–5 P.M.) gives visitors a glimpse into the lives of 19th-century soldiers and loggers. The original fort hospital now serves as a museum. A sedate (but fairly long) walking tour takes you through re-creations of historic fort buildings, then out to the logging display. Here you'll find several "steam

equipment that revolution-
dustry as well as examples
e of redwood trees loggers
moving from 19th-century
can spend a few minutes
enjoying the tranquil historic garden, where
master gardeners maintain the type of garden
fort residents kept a century and a half ago.

Sequoia Park Zoo

The Sequoia Park Zoo (3414 W St., 707/442-
6552, summer Tues.–Sun. 10 A.M.–7 P.M., winter Tues.–Sun. 10 A.M.–5 P.M., free) might
seem small, but its mission is a big one. This
zoo seeks not only to entertain visitors, but to
preserve local species and educate the public
about their needs. The Secrets of the Forest
exhibit re-creates the ecology of the Northern
California forest while letting children of all
ages see the inner workings of the various species that live there. Be sure to say hi to Bill the
Chimpanzee while you're there!

Wooden Sculpture Garden

Conveniently located right downtown in the
shopping district, Romano Gabriel's Wooden
Sculpture Garden (315 Second St.) sits behind
a glass wall for all to see. Gabriel created the
bright, colorful artworks over many years and
placed them in his front yard. Each piece has
its own meaning; many are political.

Humboldt Botanical Gardens

Brand new in 2008, the Humboldt Botanical
Gardens (south of Eureka near College of the
Redwoods, 707/442-6634, www.hbgf.org) are
the product of years of work by staff and volunteers to create gardens that celebrate the ecosystems of Humboldt County.

ENTERTAINMENT AND EVENTS
Bars and Clubs

The biggest, most popular restaurant and
bar in Eureka is definitely the **Lost Coast
Brewery** (617 Fourth St., 707/445-4480,
www.lostcoast.com, daily 11 A.M.–1 A.M.). The
tall-for-its-street cream-and-green building

perches off by itself on the main drag, easy
even for casual drivers passing through town.
The Brewery draws crowds, especially on the
weekends. One thing that makes it special is
that the Brewery makes all the beers you can
get on tap at the bar, all of which are award
winners in various microbrew competitions
and the California State Fair. Come to eat
tasty brew-pub style food and drink one or
more of the delicious beers.

For a good solid dive bar experience on the
North Coast, complete with occasional live
music, spend an evening at **The Shanty** (213
Third St., 707/444-2053). You'll find all the
proper dive bar accoutrements—older locals,
loud young drinkers, vintage arcade games,
funky decor (including light-up penguins),
and plenty of cheap booze. On the rare warm
evenings in summer, you can lounge outside on
the patio for a smoke. Be sure to stop in for a
pre-dinner drink during happy hour, when the
prices are rock bottom and some of the beers
and liquors are top shelf.

Even in far-out Eureka, you're still in
California. So if you're looking for a gay bar,
head on down to the aptly named **Auntie Mo's
Lounge** (535 Fifth St., 707/442-0772, http://
auntymoslounge.com, Mon.–Fri. 4 P.M.–close,
Sat.–Sun. 6 P.M.–close). This newish venue
hosts plenty of live music, drag and theme
events, and of course nightly drinks and fun
in downtown Eureka. Folks of all orientations
are welcome here, so long as they get into the
fun and fabulous spirit of the lounge.

Theater

Don't confuse Eureka's **North Coast Repertory
Theater** (300 Fifth St., 707/442-6278, www
.ncrt.org, cash only) with the San Diego theater
company of the same name. Here in Eureka,
the company performs a mix of musicals, comedies, and the occasional Shakespeare or heavy-
duty drama. Many performances benefit local
charities.

Festivals and Events

Eureka hosts a number of great festivals and
events each year. The most unusual of these

is the **Kinetic Sculpture Race** (www.kinetic kingdom.com), which runs from Arcata down to Main Street in Ferndale each year on Memorial Day Weekend. Even if creating your own colorful, ridiculous human-powered locomotive sculpture isn't your thing, it's worth taking a spot along the racecourse to see what the artists have come up with this year. Be prepared for dinosaurs, donkeys, dung beetles, and other sublimely silly things not often seen outside of the Nevada playa. The sculptures cross pavement, sand, water, and mud over the course of the three-day race. While nowadays other towns have their own kinetic sculpture races (and yes, there's one at Burning Man), the North Coast is the origin of the event, and remains the grand championship of them all. For a great view, try to get a spot to watch Dead Man's Drop or the Water Entry.

Music lovers flock to Eureka each year for any one of a number of big music festivals. **Blues by the Bay** (www.bluesbythebay.org) is one of the largest. Held at Halvorsen Park right on Humboldt Bay, the two-day summer festival features many of the finest blues musicians alive playing in a spectacular setting. Accompanying the wailing blues are art, food, and microbrew booths. Another big event is the **Redwood Coast Jazz Festival** (www .redwoodjazz.org). For four days in mid-spring, music lovers can enjoy every style of jazz imaginable, from Dixieland to zydeco to big band. Dance contests and side events such as silent movie screenings are crowd favorites.

SHOPPING
Antiques
Even the cosmopolitan antique dealers of San Francisco and Los Angeles respect the Eureka antique scene, which is the largest California antiques market north of the Bay Area. In Old Town, seekers find lumber baron–era and Victorian antiques, from tiny porcelain figurines to huge pieces of furniture. **Vintage Home Antiques** (531 Third St., 707/443-1323, Tues.–Sat. noon–5:30 P.M.) specializes in vintage linens and laundry products. **Heritage Antique & Coins** (505 H St., 707/444-2908,

Mon.–Sat. 10 A.M.–5 P.M.) is a coin shop that also carries jewelry and Native American artifacts. Music lovers must visit the **Antique Annex** (208 F St., 707/443-9113, Mon.–Sat. 11 A.M.–5 P.M.) to peruse the collection of vintage vinyl and antique sheet music. Generalists will love rooting through the huge **Antiques and Goodies** (1128 Third St., 707/442-0445, Mon.–Sat. 10 A.M.–5 P.M.) and **Old Town Antiques** (318 F St., 707/442-3235, daily 10:30 A.M.–5:30 P.M.).

Books
For an afternoon of shopping in Eureka, head down toward the water to Second Street. Most of the buildings here are historic, and you might find an unassuming brass plaque describing the famous brothel that once inhabited what is now a toy store. Literature lovers have a nice selection of independent bookstores. **Eureka Books** (426 Second St., 707/444-9593, www.eurekabooksellers.com, Mon.–Sat. 10 A.M.–6 P.M., Sun. noon–5 P.M.) has a big, airy room in which to browse the selection of new and used books. **Booklegger** (402 Second St., 707/445-1344), just down the street, is a small but well-organized used bookshop that has a specialty in antique books.

Clothing
Ladies have an array of clothing boutiques to choose from. As advertised, **Cotton Works** (420 Second St., 707/268-0895) sells stylish clothing made from cotton. Attractive undergarments are sold at the aptly named **Bliss** (527 Second St., 707/445-1733, Tues.–Sat. 10 A.M.–6 P.M.).

Galleries
Galleries and gift shops abound, highlighting all aspects of California culture. The **Shorelines Gallery** (434 Second St., 707/443-7272, www.shorelinesgalleryeureka .com, hours vary) specializes in fun, sea-themed art and jewelry. Prices here start out quite reasonable—handmade jewelry starts at $10—and run up to five figures for the whimsical glass octopus coffee table. Native American

art, including blankets, pottery, clothing, and jewelry is sold at **Indian-West Emporium** (326 Second St., 707/442-3042). Catering to a more modern California sensibility, the **Art of Wine Gallery and Tasting Room** (308 Second St., 707/268-0626, www.humboldtartofwine.com, Tues.–Fri. noon–6 P.M., Sat. noon–9 P.M.) offers photographs, mixed-media artwork, glass, and of course wines. **Many Hands Gallery** (438 Second St., 707/445-4700, www.many handsgallery.net) contains eclectic, hippie-style gifts and art items, including pleasantly inexpensive tea towels, potholders, note cards, candles, pottery, and drums.

SPORTS AND RECREATION
Fishing
Eureka is a serious fishing destination. Oodles of both ocean and river fishing opportunities abound all over this region, and several fishing tournaments are held each year. As everywhere else in California, you must have a valid state fishing license to fish in either the ocean or the rivers surrounding Eureka. Be sure to check with your charter service or guide to be sure they provide a day license with your trip. If they don't, you may have to provide your own.

For deep-sea fishing, **Celtic Charter Service** (Woodley Island Marina, Dock D, 707/442-7115) has daily trips leave at 6:30 A.M. each morning. They rent tackle and sell day licenses as well. **Full Throttle Sportfishing** (Woodley Island Marina, 707/498-7473, http://fullthrottlesportfishing.com) supplies all needed tackle and can take you out to fish for salmon, rockfish, tuna, or halibut. Trips last all day and most leave at 6:30 A.M. If you're launching your own boat, public launches are the **Samoa Boat Ramp** (New Navy Base Rd., 707/445-7651, daily 5 A.M.–midnight) and the **Fields Landing Boat Ramp** (Railroad Ave., 707/445-7651).

Eureka also has good spots for pier fishing. In town, try the K Street Pier, the pier at the east end of Commercial Street, or the per at the foot of Del Norte Street. Farther north, the north jetty (Hwy. 255 across the Samoa Bridge) also has a public pier open to fishing.

If an exciting fight with a steelhead trout is more your game, ample opportunities exist on the Klamath and Trinity Rivers. For a guided trip, check out **Jet Stream Guide Service** (707/826-2926).

Kayaking and Rafting
The water is cold, but getting out on it in a kayak can be exhilarating. If you're new to the sport or just want a guided trip of the area, guided paddles, lessons, rentals, and kayak fishing trips are available through **Humboats Kayak Adventures** (Woodley Island Marina, 707/443-5157, www.humboats.com). Guides lead a huge variety of tours, from serene paddles in the harbor suitable for children or dogs to 30-plus-mile trips designed for experienced kayakers.

River rafters and kayakers have great opportunities for rapid fun on the Klamath and Trinity Rivers. **Bigfoot Rafting Company** (Willow Creek, 530/629-2263, www.bigfoot rafting.com, $35–85) leads half-, full-, and multi-day trips of both these rivers as well as the Cal-Salmon and the Smith. Experts can take inflatable kayaks down the Class IV rapids, and newcomers can find a gentle paddle with just enough white water to make things interesting.

Bird-Watching
The national, state, and county parks lacing through the Eureka area create ideal bird-watching conditions. Hundreds of species live here, and more migrate through seasonally (thespring and fall migrations are the best times to bird-watch around Eureka). Especially good spots for birding include the **Arcata Marsh and Wildlife Sanctuary** (foot of I St., Arcata, 707/826-2359, www.cityofarcata.com), the **Humboldt Bay National Wildlife Refuge** (1020 Ranch Rd., Loleta, 707/733-5406, www .fws.gov/humboldtbay) and the **Headwaters Forest Reserve** (707/825-2300, www.blm .gov/ca).

Hiking and Biking
In addition to the vast trail systems in the state

and national parks, the city of Eureka maintains a number of multi-use (biking and hiking) trails. Most familiar is the Old Town Boardwalk, part of the **Waterfront Trail** which includes other disconnected sections along Humboldt Bay. **Sequoia Park Trail** begins at the Sequoia Park zoo and wends through redwood forests, past a duck pond, and through a meadow. This trail is paved and friendly to strollers and wheelchairs. The unpaved **Elk River Trail** (foot of Hilfiker Lane) stretches for a mile through wild meadows along the coast. **Cooper Gulch Trail** is more a sedate stroll than a strenuous hike, circling the Cooper Gulch park playing fields.

Golf

With a surprisingly mild climate (it's not warm, but it doesn't snow much either), Eureka golf courses stay open all year long. Try the **Eureka Golf Course** (4750 Fairway Dr., 707/443-4808, public, 18-hole, par 70) or make the short drive north through Arcata to McKinleyville to visit the **Beau Pre Golf Course** (1777 Norton Rd., 707/839-2342, public, 18-hole, par 71).

Casino Gambling

Just north of Eureka and Arcata, the **Blue Lake Casino** (777 Casino Way, Blue Lake, 877/252-2946, www.bluelakecasino.com) boasts the best gaming on the North Coast. In addition to its 700 slot machines, Blue Lake Casino has 16 card tables with a variety of games, plus bingo. For non-gamblers, the casino also features two restaurants, a lounge with live music and an open dance floor, and a large-act entertainment venue.

ACCOMMODATIONS

With such a wealth of Victorian homes, Eureka is a natural location for classic bed-and-breakfast accommodations. Chain motels are also available in abundance, many of them quite cheap. But for a real taste of the town, try one of the many charming inns.

$100-150

A Halcyon Inn (1420 C St., 888/882-1310, www.halcyoninn.com, $115–165) welcomes guests to a small Victorian house and a friendly, intimate Eureka experience. The brown-shingled exterior and verdant well-kept lawns give way to a gracious home. Only three guest rooms guarantee a quiet and uncrowded experience. Each room has its own four-poster bed and collection of antique furniture, floral bedspreads, and private bathroom. In the morning, come to the cozy dining room to enjoy a breakfast both sumptuous and health-conscious. Then wander out into the small but pretty gardens with summer flowers blooming and tables and chairs set up to encourage reading, card games, or just lounging with an extra cup of coffee or glass of wine.

The Ship's Inn B&B (821 D St., 877/443-7583, www.shipsinn.net, $130–175) is a newer B&B in an older, recently restored Victorian home on the east side of town. Few rooms and a friendly innkeeper make a stay at this inn delightfully like staying in a friend's grand home. Breakfast is particularly good here, and the small garden is the perfect place to sit out in the afternoon reading a good book. Each of the four rooms has its own decoration and theme; the Captain's Quarters take the inn's name to heart with a blue and gold nautical design, while the other rooms tend more toward classic Victorian florals. Unlike many B&Bs, you'll find televisions in every room, along with fireplaces, plush robes, and private bathrooms.

If B&Bs just aren't your style, get a room at the **Bayview Motel** (2844 Fairfield St., 866/725-6813, www.bayviewmotel.com, $100–175). This hilltop motel has lovely views of Humboldt Bay from many rooms and from the grounds. Rooms are spacious, and decorated in slightly more elegant colors and fabrics than the average chain motel room. You'll find wonderful whirlpool suites, free Wi-Fi, cable TV, wet bars, and coffee makers. If you're traveling with your family, you can rent a double-suite—two rooms with an adjoining door and separate bathrooms. Though not right in the midst of downtown Eureka, it's an easy drive from the Bayview for dinner, shopping, and strolling by the harbor.

$150-250

For the most Victorian experience you can have, book a room at  **Abigail's Elegant Victorian Mansion** (1406 C St., 707/444-3144, www.eureka-california.com, $180–300). Originally built by one of the founders of Eureka, the inn has retained many of the large home's original fixtures. The owners took pains to learn the history of the house and town, and has added appropriate decor to create a truly Victorian mansion, right down to the vintage books in the elegant library. Anyone with an interest in Victoriana need only ask for a tour, and the owners will gladly give an hour or more of his time to describe the artifacts in each room. Each of the three rooms comes with its own story and astonishing collection of antiques. All rooms have private baths, though the bathroom might be just across the hall. While you're not encouraged to bring small children to this romantic inn, families and groups traveling together can request combined rooms with additional beds.

Come morning, all guests adjourn to the dining room for a sumptuous breakfast.

The **Carter House Inns** (301 L St., 800/404-1390, www.carterhouse.com, $200–335) encompass two inns and two smaller cottage, the larger mansions easily seen on either side of the street in the heart of downtown Eureka. The unusual smaller butter-yellow mansion is not the true Victorian dwelling it seems, but instead is a reproduction built in the 1980s. The rooms in each building are elegantly appointed, the dark wooden furniture evocative of the Victorian era while the minimum of floral geegaws caters to modern sensibilities. Standard rooms are small and stylish with particularly attractive baths. Larger suites are decorated with antiques and some have gorgeous soaking tubs set into windowed alcoves. Between the two buildings, the large inn offers nearly 30 rooms. Enjoy a truly magnificent dinner at the attached Restaurant 301, book an in-room massage, or even go for a wine-tasting package that delves into the Carter House's remarkable cellars.

Abigail's Elegant Victorian Mansion

© LIZ HAMILL SCOTT

FOOD
American
The **Samoa Cookhouse** (511 Vance Rd., Samoa, 707/442-1659, www.samoacookhouse .net, breakfast, lunch, and dinner daily) is an historic Eureka institution. Red-checked tablecloths cover long rough tables to re-create a logging-camp dining hall atmosphere. Meals are served family-style from huge serving platters. Diners sit on benches and pass the hearty fare down in turn. Think big hunks of roast beef, mountains of mashed potatoes, and piles of cooked vegetables. This is the place to bring your biggest appetite! After dinner, browse the small Historic Logging Museum and gift shop.

California
C Restaurant 301 at the Carter House Inns (301 L St., 800/404-1390, www.carter house.com, $18–29) seems like a top-shelf San Francisco or Los Angeles eatery lost on the distant North Coast. But in truth, the local ingredients and award-winning wine list are right at home in downtown Eureka. The chef creates an ever-changing menu of delectable delicacies, with tasting menus that give diners the best chance to experience this great restaurant. You'll find everything from exotic duck dishes to simple local seafood preparations to items out of the restaurant's own on-site kitchen garden on the succession of plates served at a relaxed pace. For a special treat, try the wine flights suggested with the menus.

Another high-end Eureka restaurant that impresses even the snootiest Bay Area–trained palates is **Avalon** (601 Third St., 707/445-0500, www.geocities.com/avaloneureka, Tues.–Sat. from 4:30 P.M., $20–28). This restaurant speaks to the hearts of eco-conscious carnivores, with sustainably-sourced steaks, mixed grills, and game meats prominent on the menu.

Chinese
Looking for classic Chinese food in Eureka? Try **Gonsea** (2335 Fourth St., 707/444-8899). You'll find a fairly typical style of Americanized Chinese food here, complete with Hunan, Szechuan, and Mandarin dishes. (You might find

it a bit unvaried if you're from a major metropolitan area.) Whether you come for lunch or dinner, the best way to order is family style so that you can try a variety of foods. Do be aware that portions are huge, so order lightly unless you've got a place to stash and chill the leftovers.

Mexican
Some of the best Mexican food in Eureka can be had at **Chapala Café** (201 Second St., 707/443-9514, www.chapalacafe.com, daily 11 A.M.–9 P.M.). The large menu offers many Mexican classics, all available in both meat and vegetarian versions. The atmosphere at Chapala is friendly and festive, and you can't miss the gorgeous and colorful mural or the live entertainment on weekend evenings. Whether you order a classic taco-enchilada combination or one of the house-made slow-cooked chilis, be sure to get yourself a margarita to go with it. Kids and alcohol-free diners may prefer the imported Mexican Jarritos sodas. Chapala prides itself on its fast and excellent service, actually promising a free meal should your food not arrive in a timely fashion. The fish tacos are highly recommended.

Seafood
Café Marina (601 Startare Dr., Woodley Island, 707/443-2233, www.samoacook house.net/cafe-marina.html, open daily) provides the right California coastal dining experience. Located on Woodley Island overlooking the harbor, diners can sit outdoors on rare sunny days and watch the sea lions lazing about between the docks as the fishing boats come and go. The seafood is good here, and the menu also includes an array of burgers and sandwiches, plus a few entrées at dinnertime. Portions are large and preparations are basic but tasty. The service is decent and the prices are reasonable, but the main reason to come out to the Café Marina is the location.

Bakeries
Ramone's Bakery and Café (2223 Harrison Ave., 707/442-1336, http://ramonesbakery. com) is a genuine local North Coast chain.

All locations (including 209 E St. and 430 N. St. in Eureka, one in Arcata and one in McKinleyville) all sell fresh, made-from-scratch baked goodies and candies. Come in the morning to enjoy a fresh cup of coffee roasted in-house and a danish or a scone, indulge in an afternoon pastry, or even get a whole tart or cake to save for evening dessert. You can even buy a loaf of fresh-baked bread to take out for an afternoon picnic.

INFORMATION AND SERVICES

The Eureka-Arcata corridor forms the urban center of the far-north coast of California. If you need urban services, you'll probably find them here.

Tourist Information

Eureka's **visitors center** (1034 Second St., 707/443-5097, http://redwoods.info, Mon.–Fri. 9 A.M.–5 P.M.) covers the whole Redwood Coast region. Check out the website before you visit to get the scoop on lodgings and create an itinerary, then come into the office to grab a map and get recommendations for local restaurants.

Media and Communications

The local daily paper is the *Times-Standard* (www.times-standard.com). It covers both national and wire news, as well as local news and events for the whole North Coast region. Check the entertainment section for the latest hot spots and live events during your stay.

There's also plenty of Internet access in and around Eureka. Your inn or motel may have Wi-Fi for free or for a fee, and Internet cafés abound.

Banks and Post Office

As the big urban area on the North Coast, Eureka (and Arcata) has the major services travelers sometimes need. You'll find branches of most major banks, complete with ATMs, plus more ATMs at supermarkets, pharmacies, and other businesses.

Naturally, you'll find post offices in Eureka

(337 W. Clark St. and 514 H St.) that can help you with any letters or packages.

Medical Services

If you need medical assistance, Eureka has a full service hospital with both an emergency room and urgent care center (for less serious emergencies). For immediate health care needs, **St. Joseph Hospital** (2700 Dolbeer St., Eureka, 707/445-8121, www.stjosepheureka.org) can take care of you.

GETTING THERE AND AROUND
Car

Eureka lies right along U.S. 101, easily accessed by car from either the north or the south. If you're driving from the Bay Area, expect to spend six or so hours on the road. From Crescent City, Eureka is less than an hour without stops.

In Eureka, you'll need to drive if you're not staying downtown and if you want to head out to Woodley Island. You can easily traverse the Second Street shops and restaurants on foot. Parking downtown is by meter or is free on the streets, and not too difficult except on holiday or event weekends.

Bus

Bus service in and around Eureka is operated by the Humboldt Transit Authority (www.hta.org, adults $1.30, children/seniors $1). The HTA's Eureka Transit System (ETS) runs within town limits, and the Redwood Transit System (RTS, adults $2, children/seniors $1.75) can take you up and down the coast, from Eureka up toward Crescent City or down to Ferndale, and out east to Willow Creek. Check the website for route maps and up-to-date schedules.

Air

Eureka has a small commercial airport, **Arcata/Eureka Airport** (http://co.humboldt.ca.us/aviation) that serves the North Coast region. You can fly in and out on either Horizon Air (a division of Alaska), Delta, or United Airlines. Expect such flights to be expensive but convenient.

Redwood National and State Parks

From Crescent City to the edge of Humboldt County run an interlocking series of national and state parks that feature the majestic Sequoia—redwood trees that can grow hundreds of feet high and live to be hundreds of years old. Though each park listed here has its own unique character and offerings, their proximity enables the park service (and the folks who paint the highway signs) to refer to them all as one: Redwood National and State Parks. The lone exception is Humboldt Redwoods State Park, which is farther south and treated separately from the other North Coast parks.

Practicalities

Visitors centers abound in these parks. The largest is the **Thomas K. Kutchel Visitors Center** (U.S. 101 at Orick, watch for signs, 707/465-7765, Mar.–Oct. daily 9 A.M.–5 P.M.,

© LIZ HAMILL SCOTT
coast redwoods

Nov.–Feb. daily 9 A.M.–4 P.M.) situated on Redwood National Park land on the coast. Here friendly and knowledgeable rangers can assist you with maps, directions, and recommendations for the best and least crowded trails and beaches throughout the park system. More detailed information is available at the **Prairie Creek Visitors Center** (Newton B. Drury Scenic Pkwy., 707/465-7354, Mar.–Oct. daily 9 A.M.–5 P.M., Nov.–Feb. daily Wed.–Sun. 9 A.M.–5 P.M.), **Jedediah Smith Visitors Center** (U.S. 101, 707/465-2144, May 20–Sept. 30 daily 9 A.M.–5 P.M., winter Fri.–Sun. 10 A.M.–6 P.M.) in the parks, and the **Hiochi Information Center** (Hwy. 199, 707/458-3209, June–Sept. daily 9 A.M.–5 P.M.) and the **Crescent City Information Center** (1001 Front St., Mar.–Oct. daily 9 A.M.–5 P.M., Nov.–Feb. 9 A.M.–4 P.M.) located in their respective towns.

Most of the major park areas can be accessed via U.S. 101 and Highway 199. Follow the signs to the smaller roads that take you farther from civilization. To get to the redwood parks from the south, simply drive up U.S. 101 or the much slower but much prettier Highway 1. The two roads become one at the tiny town of Leggett north of Fort Bragg, then proceed north into the trees. Public transit options run to the Redwood County Transit bus system (707/464-6400), which runs daily from Smith River to Arcata.

Folks camping in the Redwood National and State Parks usually pack in their own food and cook at their campsites. To restock, you can drive into Crescent City to find a market or Eureka for a true supermarket.

JEDEDIAH SMITH REDWOODS STATE PARK

The northernmost of the parks, Jed Smith (U.S. 199, nine miles east of Crescent City, 707/458-3018, www.parks.ca.gov) as it's known to locals, sits north of Crescent City along the Smith River, right next door to the immense Smith River National Recreation Area (Hwy.

199 west of Hiouchi). The State Park visitors center sits on the east side of the park, doubling as the Hiouchi Information Center.

Sights

The best redwood grove in all the old growth of Jed Smith is **Stout Memorial Grove.** This bunch of coastal redwood trees are, as advertised, stout—though the grove was named for a Mr. Frank Stout, not for the size of the trees. These old giants make humans feel small as they wander in the grove. These are some of the biggest and oldest trees on the North Coast, somehow spared the loggers' saws. Another great thing about this grove is the lack of tourists, since its far-north latitude makes it harder to reach than some of the other big redwood groves in California.

Hiking

The trails running through the trees make for wonderful summer hiking that's cool and shady. Many trails run along the river and the creeks, offering a variety of ecosystems and plenty of lush scenery to enjoy. Just be sure that wherever you hike, you stay on the established trails. Wandering into the forest, you can stomp on the delicate and shallow redwood root systems, unintentionally damaging the very trees you're here to visit.

The **Simpson Reed Trail** (1 mile, easy) takes you right from U.S. 199 (six miles east of Crescent City) down to the banks of the Smith River.

To get a good view of the Smith River, hike the **Hiouchi Trail** (2 miles, intermediate). From the visitors center and campgrounds, cross the Summer Footbridge then follow the river north. The Hiouchi Trail then meets the Hatton Loop Trail and takes you off away from the river and into the forest.

SAVE THE REDWOODS

The stereotype of a tree-hugging conservationist usually brings to mind dirty, long-haired college students living on tarp-covered platforms and tying themselves to trees. Many visitors (and heck, residents) of California might imagine that it was a bunch of dreadlocked hippies and starving artists that saved the huge swaths of redwoods lining the North Coast region.

Nothing could be further from the truth. The California redwoods were saved by some very rich people.

Powerful rich white men poured their power, political connections, and, in some cases, millions of their own dollars into a group called the **Save the Redwoods League** (www.savethe redwoods.org). The three founders were a U.C. professor named John Merriam, and fellow conservationists Madison Grant and Henry F. Osborn. After surveying the destruction of the forests surrounding brand-new Highway 101 in 1917, the three men decided that something had to be done. And thus the League was born.

For 90 years, the Save the Redwoods League has aggressively pursued the conservation of redwood forests in California. Using high-level political connections, the League has successfully lobbied the U.S. government to create the Redwood National Park and to expand the territory protected by Sequoia National Park. They're also major players at the state level, creating and expanding state parks all over the landscape.

So how did they get hold of all those groves? They bought them. Large donations plus the resources of League members have given the League the ability to buy thousands of acres of redwood forest, then donate them to various parks. They're still doing it to this very day, and in the 21st century the League has made several major purchases to expand Sequoia National Park, Redwood National Park, and several state parks.

Got some spare change in your ashtray? You can donate to Save the Redwoods and help the group preserve and expand California's fabulous redwoods. Donate your life savings, and they might even name a grove after you! (No promises though.)

If you're looking for a longer and more aggressive trek, try the **Mill Creek Trail** (7.5 miles round-trip, difficult). A good place to start is at the Summer Footbridge. The trail then follows the creek down to the unpaved Howland Hill Road.

If it's redwoods you're looking for, take the **Boy Scout Tree Trail** (5.2 miles, difficult). It's a bit more of a trek out to the trailhead along an unpaved road, but rumor has it that's part of the beauty of this hike.

Fishing

With the Smith River and numerous feeder and offshoot creeks running right through Jed Smith, it's not surprising that fishing is one of the most popular activities here. Chilly winter fishing draws a surprising number of anglers out to vie for king salmon up to 30 pounds and 20-pound steelhead.Seasons for both these fish run from October through February. In the summertime, cast out into the river to catch cutthroat trout.

Boating and Swimming

You'll find two boat launches in the park: one at Society Hole and one adjacent to the Summer Footbridge that's open in the wintertime only.

Down by the River Beach Trail, you'll find **River Beach** (immediately west of the visitors center), a popular spot for swimming in the river. Swimming is allowed throughout the park, but please be very careful! Rivers and creeks move unpredictably, and you might not notice deep holes until you're upon them. Enjoy the cool water, but keep a close eye on your kids and loved ones to ensure that a good and safe time is had by all.

Camping

The **Jedediah Smith campground** (Hwy. 199, Hiouchi, 800/444-7275, www.reserve america.com) clusters near the river, with most sites near the River Beach Trail (immediately west of the visitors center). There are 106 RV and tent sites for $15–20 per night, depending on the season (hike-in primitive sites are $3).

Facilities include plenty of restrooms, fire pits, and coin-op showers. Reservations are advised in advance, especially for summer and holiday weekends.

Information and Services

Jed Smith has a **visitors center** (U.S. 199, 1 mile west of Hiouchi) where you can get park information and purchase souvenirs and books. Ask for a schedule of nature programs and guided hikes.

DEL NORTE COAST REDWOODS STATE PARK

South of Crescent City and Jedediah Smith State Park, Del Norte Coast Redwoods State Park (U.S. 101, accessible via Mill Creek Rd., 707/465-2146, www.parks.ca.gov) encompasses a variety of ecosystems, from eight miles of wild coastline to second-growth redwood forest to virgin old-growth forests. One of the largest in this system of parks, Del Norte is a great place to "get lost" in the backcountry with just your backpack and fishing rod ready to camp and ply the waters of the meandering branches of Mill Creek.

Hiking

Guided tours, nature trails, and wheelchair-accessible trails and campgrounds are all amenities here. Dress in layers to hike at Del Norte, as it can get down into the 40s even in the summertime.

Camping

The **Mill Creek** campground (Hwy. 101, 7 miles south of Crescent City, 800/444-7275, www.reserveamerica.com, May 1–Sept. 30, $12–20) sits in an attractive setting along its namesake creek. There are 145 sites for RVs and tents and facilities include restrooms and fire pits. Feel free to bring your camper to the Mill Creek campground; it's got spots for RVs and a dump station on-site. Call in advance to reserve a spot and to be sure that your camper does not exceed the park's length limit.

Information and Services

Del Norte State Park has no visitors center.

Minimal restroom facilities are available at the campgrounds, and the park has an RV dump station but no RV hookups.

PRAIRIE CREEK REDWOODS STATE PARK

At the junction of the south end of the Nelson B. Drury Scenic Drive and U.S. 101, Prairie Creek Redwoods State Park (25 miles south of Crescent City on Nelson B. Drury Dr., 707/465-7347, www.parks.ca.gov) boasts large campgrounds and shady hiking trails through redwoods. Just beyond the entrance, the visitors center includes a small interpretive museum describing the history of the California redwood forests. A tiny bookshop adjoins the museum, well stocked with books describing the history, nature, and culture of the area. Many ranger-led programs originate at the visitors center.

Sights

One of the cool things that make a drive to Prairie Creek worth the effort is the herd of **Roosevelt elk** that live there. The big guys with their huge racks hang out at—where else?—the Elk Prairie. This stretch of open grassland lies right along the highway. The best way to find the viewing platform is to watch for the road signs pointing you to the turnoff. The best times to see the elk out grazing in the field are early morning and around sunset. Please stay in the viewing area and let the elk enjoy their meals in peace.

A gorgeous scenic cutoffs through the redwoods, the **Nelson B. Drury Scenic Drive** (about 5 miles south of Klamath) cuts off U.S. 101 features old-growth trees lining the roads, a close-up view of the redwood forest ecosystem, and a grove or trailhead about every hundred yards or so. A great place to turn off is at the **Big Tree Wayside.** The namesake tree is only a short walk from the parking area, and several trails radiate from the little grove.

Hiking

Perhaps the single most famous hiking trail along the redwood coast is **Fern Canyon** (2 miles of U.S. 101 on Davidson Rd. to Gold

Yurok home, Prairie Creek Redwoods State Park

© LANCE SCOTT

Bluffs Beach). This hike takes you through a narrow canyon carved by Home Creek. Ferns, mosses, and other water-loving plants grow thick up the sides of the canyon, creating a beautiful vertical carpet of green that made the perfect setting for Steven Spielberg's *Jurassic Park 2* and *The Return of the Jedi.*

A longer and tougher loop can take you from the visitors center on a more serious foot tour of the park. Start out on the **James Irvine Trail,** but don't follow it all the way to the coast. Instead, make a right onto the **Clintonia** and cut across to **Miner's Ridge.** The hike runs a total of about six miles.

If you're working on the **California Coastal Trail,** you can do a leg here at Prairie Creek. The Coastal Trail runs along the northern coast of this park. Another way to get to the campground is via the **Ossagon Creek Trail** (2 miles round-trip, north end of Newton B. Drury Dr., moderate). Though it's not too long, the steep grade makes it a tough haul in spots, but you'll get to see many lovely old-growth redwood trees along the way.

Camping

The **Elk Prairie Campground** (Newton B. Drury Scenic Parkway, 800/444-7275, www .reserveamerica.com, $15–20) has 75 sites for tents or RVs and a full range of comfortable camping amenities. You can get a shower and purchase wood for your fire ring. Several campsites are wheelchair-accessible, so be sure to ask for one if needed when you reserve your site. A big campfire area sits to the north of the campground, an easy walk for campers interested in the evening programs put on by rangers and volunteers.

For a sand camping experience, head out to **Gold Bluffs Beach Campground** (Davidson Rd., 3 miles north of Orick, www.nps.gov/ redw, no reservations, $14–15). There are 25–29 sites for tents or RVs. Amenities include flush toilets, water, solar showers, and wide ocean views. (The surf can be quite dangerous here, so be extremely careful if you choose to go into the water at all.)

Information and Services

Stop in at the **visitors center** at the south end of the Nelson B. Drury Scenic Parkway. Enjoy the exhibits, chat with the rangers, or grab a field guide in the small bookstore. Campfire programs are held by rangers at the campfire area adjacent to the Elk Prairie Campground. Check with the visitors center for a schedule.

REDWOOD NATIONAL PARK

The lands of Redwood National Park meander along the coast, abutting the various state parks that crowd to cover the bulk of California's northern redwood forests. The main bulk of Redwood National Park lies just south of Prairie Creek State Park along U.S. 101 to the north, meandering east away from the coast and the highway. In the south, driving access to the park runs along Bald Hills Road.

Sights

Generations of kids have loved spotting the gigantic wooden Paul Bunyan and his blue ox Babe from U.S. 101. And the **Trees of Mystery** (15500 U.S. 101 N., 800/638-3389, www.treesofmystery.net, June–Aug. daily 8 A.M.–7 P.M., Sept.–May daily 9 A.M.–5 P.M., adults $13.50, children $6.50) doesn't disappoint as a great place to take a break from the road to let the family out for some good cheesy fun. Visitors can enjoy the original Mystery Hike as well as the Skytrail gondola ride through the old-growth redwoods and the palatial gift shop. Perhaps best of all, at the left end of the gift shop rests a little-known gem: the Native American museum. A large collection of artifacts from tribes across the country and native to the redwood forests grace several crowded galleries.

Hiking

For an easy, fun little walk around the park, try the **Lady Bird Johnson Trail** (Bald Hills Rd., 1 mile, easy). This level loop can give you a lovely view of the redwood and fir forest that informs this region. Another easy-access and pretty trail goes out to **Trillium Falls** (Davidson Rd. at Elk Meadow). In

Paul Bunyan and his blue ox, Babe, at the Trees of Mystery

© LIZ HAMILL SCOTT

truth, you're likely to see more elk than trillium flowers, and find the redwood trees more exciting that the small waterfall. But it's still an attractive trail, best in the spring when the falls flow at their peak.

The **Lost Man Creek Trail** (1 mile off U.S. 101, east of Elk Meadow, 0.5 mile, easy–difficult) has it all. The first half-mile is perfect for wheelchair-users and families with small children. But as the trail rolls along, the grades get steeper and more challenging. You can spend all day trekking from the picnic grounds by the creek around and down to Bald Hills Road almost to the Redwood Creek Overlook.

Another fabulous long hike is the **Redwood Creek Trail** (Bald Hills Road spur off U.S. 101, difficult). This trail follows Redwood Creek all the way down to the **Tall Trees Grove.** If you've got someone willing to act as a shuttle, you can pick up the **Tall Trees Trail** and walk it to the **Dolason Prairie Trail,** which will take you back out to Bald Hills Road. For visitors who'd prefer to spend two days out on the trail, you can stop at either **Elam Camp** or **44 Camp,** both hike-in, primitive campgrounds.

Accommodations

The **Redwood Hostel** (14480 U.S. 101 at Wilson Creek Rd., Klamath, 707/482-8265, www.norcalhostels.org/redwoods, $21–52) has fabulous views, abundant charm, and worthwhile amenities. South of Eureka along U.S. 101, the Redwood Hostel has ready access to parks, beaches, and trails. On the outside, you'll see an old green building that's obviously been around for a while. Inside, you'll find the casual clutter that defines most hostel common areas. Linens are included with the bunk rates, dorm rooms are small and have pretty wooden bunk beds, and private family rooms are available. Kitchen and laundry facilities are well lit and spacious. The cheerful young owners can help with transportation, food, and the nearest great hiking spots.

Information and Services

If you're new to the Redwood National and State Parks region, the **Thomas H. Kuchel Visitors Center** (U.S. 101, west of Orick, 707/465-7765, Mar.–Oct. daily 9 A.M.–5 P.M., Nov.–Feb. daily 9 A.M.–4 P.M.) is your main stop. This big center includes a ranger station, clean restrooms, and a path right out to the shore. You can get maps, advice, permits for

WOODSY TOURIST TRAPS

As you wend your way up U.S. 101 through the verdant forests filled with rare trees, you'll become aware of something besides parks and trails luring visitors to pull over and rest awhile. You'll know them by the collections of tacky chainsaw carvings, the kitschy hand-painted signs, and the cheap, shiny toys out front. Whether you've found a Redwood Sculpture Emporium, a Drive-Thru Tree, or a Mystery Spot, hang on to your wallet when you stop at one of the infamous redwood coast tourist traps.

The granddaddy of all tourist traps – it's even an example of the concept in Wikipedia – is the **Trees of Mystery** (see *Sights*). Trees of Mystery has it all: tacky wood sculptures, a "mystery" visual-trickery trail, and a gondola ride. But most of all, it's got a gift shop the size of a supermarket selling some of the tackiest souvenirs you can possibly imagine and perhaps a few that will make you shriek softly with horror. Imagine a cheap build-a-bear machine sitting next to a display of varnished redwood slices painted with images of Jesus and the Virgin Mary.

The various Drive-Thru Trees are usually privately owned tourist traps, and you'll pay $10-20 to drive a tiny one-way street through a large mutilated tree. Why would anyone do this? Well, the novelty of finding trees big enough to create drive-thru tunnels catches the attention of many out-of-state visitors. And families on long road trips often shell out for the drive-thru trees to sidetrack their utterly bored kids for just five more minutes.

Finally, you can't miss the roadside redwood sculpture stands, even if you try. They dot the sides of the highway, selling the tackiest in wooden animals lovingly sculpted by chainsaw artists. You'll also find T-shirts, coffee mugs, shot glasses, and dozens of other tacky souvenirs. Little animal figurines made out of petrified moose and elk turds are a particular favorite with the children.

backcountry camping, and books here. Picnic tables perch here, or you can walk just a short way up to Redwood Creek.

◖ PATRICK'S POINT STATE PARK

Patrick's Point State Park (U.S. 101, 25 miles north of Eureka, 707/677-3570, www.parks .ca.gov) is a rambling coastal park replete with campgrounds, trails, beaches, landmarks, and history. It's not the biggest of the many parks along the North Coast, but it might be the best. The climate remains cool year-round, making it perfect for hiking and exploring, if not for ocean swimming. Because Patrick's Point is tiny in comparison to the other parks, it's easy to get around by requesting a map at the gate and by following the signs along the tiny and often nameless park roads.

Sights

Prominent among the landmarks is park namesake **Patrick's Point,** which offers panoramic Pacific views and can be reached by a brief hike from a convenient parking lot. Another popular spot is **Wedding Rock,** adjacent to Patrick's Point in a picturesque cove. People truly do hike the narrow trail out to the rock to get married and you might even see a bride and groom stumbling along holding hands on their way back from their ceremony.

Perhaps the most fascinating area in all of the park is **Sumeg Village.** This re-creation of a native Yurok village is based on an actual archaeological find that lies east of the "new" village. Visitors can crawl through the perfectly round hobbit-like hole-doors into semi-subterranean homes, meeting places, and storage buildings. Or check out the native plant garden, a collection of local plants the Yurok people used for food, basketry, and medicine. Today, the local Yurok people use Sumeg Village as a gathering place for education and celebrations, and request that visitors tread lightly and do not disturb this tranquil area.

Hiking

Only six miles of trails thread their way through

Patrick's Point. Choose from the **Rim Trail,** which will take you along the cliffs for a view of the sea and if you're lucky a view of migrating whales. On the other hand, tree-lovers might prefer the **Octopus Tree Trail,** which shows its walkers a great view of an old-growth Sitka spruce grove.

Beaches

For those who want to dip a toe in the ocean rather than just gaze at it from afar, Patrick's Point encompasses a number of accessible beaches. The steep trail leading down to **Agate Beach** deters few visitors. This wide stretch of coarse sand bordered by cliffs shot through with shining quartz veins is perfect for lounging, playing, and beachcombing. The semi-precious stones for which it is named really do cluster here. The best time to find good agates is in the winter, after a storm.

Camping

The campgrounds at Patrick's Point meanders through the park. It can be difficult to determine the difference between **Agate Beach, Abalone,** and **Penn Creek,** so be sure to get good directions from the rangers when you arrive. Most campsites are pleasantly shaded by the groves of trees; all include a picnic table, a propane stove, and a food storage cupboard. You'll find running water and restrooms nearby, plus showers.

Information and Services

Patrick's Point does not have a visitors center. You can get a map and information at the entry gate, and information about nature walks and campfire programs is posted on the bulletin board. The nearest one sits to the north at Thomas H. Kuchel Visitors Center (U.S. 101, west of Orick, 707/465-7765).

The Lost Coast

So how did this stretch of California become Lost? In the state that made the personal automobile a necessity, the area known as the Lost Coast is not accessible by any state or Interstate highway. In fact, much of the Lost Coast hasn't got so much as a gravel lane nearby. Many native Californians have never been anywhere near this region; others heft their backpacks and spend weeks hiking the Sinkyone and King's Mountain Range backcountry wilderness. A precious few towns service the general area, providing food, lodging, and lots of local history.

FERNDALE

Ferndale was built in the 19th century by Scandinavian immigrants who came to California to farm. Dairy pastures and farmland still surround the town today, and many of the "happy cows" in California munch grass near Ferndale. In town, little has changed since the immigrants constructed their fanciful gingerbread Victorian homes and shops.

Sights

The main "sight" in Ferndale is the town itself, since the whole thing is a designated historical landmark. Ferndale is all Victorian, all the time—just ask about the building you're in and you'll be told all about its specific architectural style, its construction date, and its original occupants. Even the public restrooms in Ferndale are housed in a small Victorianesque structure, surrounded by Main Street's shops, galleries, inns, and restaurants—all set into scrupulously maintained and restored late 19th-century buildings. Architecture buffs can spend hours just strolling through downtown.

Inside the historic facades, two fascinating little museums open their doors to anyone who cares to come inside. The **Ferndale History Museum** (Shaw and Third Sts., 707/786-4466, June–Sept. Tues.–Sat. 11 A.M.–4 P.M., Sun. 1–4 P.M., $1) is a block off Main Street and tells the story of the town. Life-sized dioramas depict period life in a Victorian home, and an array of antique artifacts brings history to life. Downstairs, the implements of rural coast

© LIZ HAMILL SCOTT

Lost Coast beaches

history vividly display the reality that farmers and craftspeople faced in the pre-industrial era. On the other hand, the **Kinetic Sculpture Museum** (580 Main St., 707/786-9259, Mon.–Sat. 10 A.M.–5 P.M., Sun. noon–4 P.M.) salutes wacky modernity in all its colorful, weird glory. As the endpoint of the region's annual Kinetic Sculpture Race, Ferndale has the honor of housing a number of the kinetic sculptures. No docents interpret the art displayed here, so visitors must make what they can of the duckies, froggies, aeroplanes, and bicycles.

To cruise further back into the town's history, consider wandering out into the **Ferndale Cemetery** on Ocean Street. Well-tended tombstones and mausoleums wend up the hillside that back the town. Genealogists will love reading the scrupulously maintained epitaphs that tell the human history of the region.

Entertainment and Events

Expectedly, Ferndale is a quiet town where the sidewalks roll up early. But for visitors who like to be out and about after 6 P.M., a few fun options await. Locals collect in the bar at **Curley's Bar and Grill** (400 Ocean Ave., 707/786-9696, Mon.–Sat. 11:30 A.M.–9 P.M., Sun. 8 A.M.–9 P.M.), sipping the dangerously delicious signature cocktails and enjoying local live music several nights each week. The **Ferndale Repertory Theater** (447 Main St., 707/786-5483, www.ferndale-rep .org, $12–15) puts on a number of shows each year. Most are wholesome and well suited for the whole family, and many are put on by local kids and teens, but be sure to check what's on when you're in town. Also check the schedule for special events and performances. Late into the night, you can fill the slots at the **Bear River Casino** (11 Bear Paws Way, 707/733-9644, www.bearrivercasino.com).

Ferndale hosts the **Humboldt County Fair** (1250 Fifth St., www.humboldtcountyfair. org) each August. For 10 days, people from all around the county come to celebrate at the down-home fair, complete with livestock exhibits and horse racing, competitions, a carnival, musical entertainment each night, and a variety of shows for kids and adults on the fairground stages. If you're in the area, come join the fun!

Shopping

A tour of Ferndale's Main Street shops makes for an idyllic morning stroll. The Victorian storefronts house antique stores, jewelry shops, clothing boutiques, and art galleries. Ferndale is also a surprisingly great place to buy a hat.

The **Golden Gait Mercantile** (421 Main St., 707/786-4891) has it all: antiques, candies, gourmet foodstuffs, clothing, hats, souvenirs, and more. Antiques and collectible tend to be small and reasonably priced. By comparison, **Silva's Fine Jewelry** (400 Ocean Ave., 707/786-4425, www.silvasjewelry.com), on the bottom floor of the Victorian Inn, is not a place for the faint of wallet. But the jewels, both contemporary and antique, are classically gorgeous. Another jewel is the **Blacksmith Shop** (455 Main St.707/786-4216, www.ferndaleblacksmith.com), which displays a striking array of useful art made by top blacksmiths and glass blowers around the country. Few art galleries can compare to the unique array of jewelry, furniture, kitchen implements, fireplace tools, and metal things defying common description. A gentler warmth comes from the **Golden Bee** (441–451 Main St.), a purveyor of fine products made with honey and beeswax. The candles, soaps, and much more make the whole store smell delicious.

Accommodations

In Ferndale, lodgings run to (of course) Victorian-style inns, mostly bed-and-breakfasts. Guests of the **Shaw House B&B** (703 Main St., 800/557-7429, www.shawhouse.com, $125–275) must walk a block or two to get to the heart of downtown Ferndale. But the reward for staying outside of the town center is a spacious garden well worth a stroll of its own. In the heat of the afternoon, huge shade trees and perfectly positioned garden benches make a lovely spot to sit and read a book, hold a quiet conversation, or just enjoy the serene beauty of garden and town. A lush morning breakfast fortifies shoppers ready to walk up and down Main Street, as well as adventurers preparing to head out to the deserted beaches of the Lost Coast or the trails into the nearby redwood forests.

The **Victorian Inn** (400 Ocean Ave., 888/589-1808, $100–400) is an imposing structure at the corner of Main Street, which also houses Curley's Bar and Grill and Silva's Jewelry. The inn includes 13 rooms, all uniquely decorated with antique furnishings, luxurious linens, and pretty knickknacks. Package deals are available, including a rare chance to spend the night in the famous (private and inaccessible) Carson House in Eureka.

Hotel Ivanhoe (315 Main St., 707/786-9000, www.ivanhoe-hotel.com, $95–145) is cattie-corner across from the Victorian Inn. (Nothing in Ferndale is far from anything else in Ferndale.) In a town full of history, the Ivanhoe is the oldest hostelry still standing in town. Plaques on the outside of the building describe its rich legacy. Fully refurbished in the 1990s, the four guest rooms are done in rich colors that revive the western-Victorian atmosphere of the original hotel.

Two other great B&Bs in Ferndale are the award-winning **Collingwood Inn B&B** (831 Main St., 800/469-1632, www.collingwoodinn.com, $125–215), with uniquely decorated rooms, and the **Gingerbread Mansion Inn** (400 Berding St., 800/952-4136, www.gingerbread-mansion.com, $135–340), with lush antiques, luxurious linens, and turn-down service.

If bric-a-brac and scented soaps make your skin itch, an inexpensive not-an-inn accommodation option in Ferndale is the **Redwood Suites** (332 Ocean Ave., 707/786-5000, www.redwoodsuites.com, $75–105). Only a block off Main Street, the Fern Motel's rooms are simple yet comfortable. Family suites with full kitchens are available, and the price is right.

Food

Curley's Grill (400 Ocean Ave. 707/786-9696, Mon.–Sat 11:30 A.M.–9 P.M., Sun. 8 A.M.–9 P.M. $13–30) is part of the Victorian Inn complex. Here California cuisine meets good old-fashioned bar-and-grill-style food. Salads are delicious, and so are the heartier entrées. Signature cocktails are big and potent, served in both the bar and the dining room. The dining room is a high-ceilinged, dimly lit barn of a place that somehow manages to be charming. Service is warm and timely, and both couples and family groups are welcome.

The restaurant at the **Hotel Ivanhoe** (315 Main St., 707/786-9000, www.ivanhoe-hotel .com) is a favorite for folks as far away as Eureka. It's all about the hearty homemade Italian dishes and friendly personal service. A more casual Italian dining experience can be had down the street at the **Ferndale Pizza Co.** (607 Main St., 707/786-4345, Tues.–Thurs. 11:30 A.M.–9:30 P.M., Fri.–Sat. 11:30 A.M.–10 P.M., Sun. noon–9:30 P.M.).

The **Candy Stick Fountain and Grill** (361 Main St., 707/786-9373) harkens back not to the 19th century, but to the 1950s. Come sit on a shining red vinyl bench at a big booth table, or on a matching stool at the old-fashioned counter. Enjoy retro-style soda fountain fare like burgers, fries, and ice cream treats. If your accommodations don't furnish breakfast, stop in at local favorite **Poppa Joe's** (409 Main St., 707/786-4180). The interior is dim and narrow, but the breakfast and lunch fare is yummy.

If you need to grab some grub and go, **Valley Grocery** (339 Main St., 707/786-9515) stocks staples and also maintains a deli; it's a perfect last stop on the way out to a beach picnic. Don't forget to stop at the heavenly candy store **Sweetness and Light** (554 Main St., 707/786-4403, www.sweetnessand light.com, Mon.–Sat. 10 A.M.–5 P.M., Sun. 11 A.M.–5 P.M.).

Practicalities

Ferndale's paper, the *Ferndale Enterprise,* is published weekly and also puts out a souvenir edition aimed at tourists once a year. Many inns and shops carry the souvenir edition, which is free, all year long.

If you need medical care, the **Humboldt Medical Group** (528 Washington St.,

707/786-4028) can assist you. The **post office** is at 536 Main Street.

Ferndale, like much of the Lost Coast, is not directly accessible from the freeway. Leave U.S. 101 at Fernbridge and follow CA-211 right into town. Mattole Road leads out of town south toward the Sinkyone Wilderness area, while Centerville Road heads out to the beach. Walking provides the best views and feel of the town itself.

MATTOLE TO SHELTER COVE

This is the true "Lost Coast," the remote rugged coastline accessible by few roads and no highways at all. Even GPS navigators lose connectivity out here, so bring an old-fashioned map if you plan to explore the unspoiled wilderness from Mattole to Shelter Cove. The reason to make the arduous trek out to the Lost Coast is to hike the miles of wilderness trails.

Sights

One of the few drivable routes to view the Lost Coast is via **Mattole Road.** This narrow, mostly paved two-lane road affords views of remote ranchland, unspoiled forests, and a few short miles of barely accessible cliffs and beaches. In good weather, the vista points from Mattole Road are spectacular. This road also acts as the connecting access to the even smaller tracks out to the trails and campgrounds of the Sinkyone Wilderness.

Big Black Sands Beach is one of the most beautiful and accessible features of the Lost Coast. Just north of the town of Shelter Cove, you can enjoy a walk with your family along the dark sands of the wide beach. This beach also serves as the south end of the Lost Coast Trail.

At **Mal Coombs Park** in Shelter Cove, the tower of the **Cape Mendocino Lighthouse** now rests quiet and dark. It began its life on Cape Mendocino—a 400-foot cliff that marks the westernmost point of California—in 1868. In 1951 the tower was abandoned in favor of a light on a pole, and in 1998 the tower was moved to Shelter Cove, becoming a museum in 2000. The original first-order Fresnel lens is now on display in nearby Ferndale.

Hiking and Backpacking

Easier day hikes include the long walk across **Big Black Sands Beach** to either Horse Creek or Gitchell Creek. Even kids can make these easy, pretty walks. **Mattole Beach** is another spot with a broad sandy beach that's perfect for an easy, contemplative stroll of any length you choose. The **Chemise Mountain Trail,** only 1.5 miles long, gives hikers beautiful views of beaches and mountains from the top of Chemise Mountain. For guided day hikes, contact the **Sanctuary Forest** (hike@sanctuaryforest.org) organization for their summer schedule of interpretive hikes.

Serious Lost Coasters bring their backpacks and spend days on the trail, enjoying the serenity of a place where few others come to disturb them. The ultimate Lost Coast experience, **Lost Coast Trail** (trailheads at Usal Campground, Big Black Sands Beach, Mattole Beach) takes about three days to traverse. Plenty of drinking water is a must, as is a current tide table since the beach areas of the trail dwindle and in some spots disappear at high tide. Campsites, many with restroom facilities (and small usage fees), cluster along the trail, making it easy for backpackers to rest when they need to. Be sure to pick up your backcountry permit at one of the ranger stations (Usal and Mattole have them), and apply for fire permits if you need them.

For another great hike, take the **King Crest Trail,** a mountain hike from the southern Saddle Mountain Trailhead to stunning King Peak and on to the North Slide Peak Trailhead. A good solid one-day round-trip (about 10 miles) can be done from either trailhead. An arduous but gorgeous loop trail, the eight-mile Hidden Valley–Chinquapin–Lost Coast Loop Trail can be done all in one day or in two with a stop at water-accessible Nick's Camp. **Buck Creek Trail** includes an infamous grade, descending more than 3,000 feet down an old logging road to the beach. The many other trails include **Rattlesnake Ridge, Kinsey Ridge, Spanish Ridge,** and **Lightning.**

Surfing

Big Flat is a legendary surf spot about eight miles north of Shelter Cove. While the hike in is challenging, hardcore surfers will find it worth the effort. Other surf breaks along the Lost Coast are **Deadman's, No Pass,** and **Gale Point.**

Fishing and Whale-Watching

The Lost Coast is a natural fishing haven. The harbor at Shelter Cove offers charter services for ocean fishing. **Salmon King Charters** (707/986-7521, www.innofthelostcoast.com) can accommodate up to six people for salmon (of course), rockfish, and other local delicacies—they'll even clean and fillet your catch for you. Another reputable charter service is **Shelter Cove Sport Fishing** (707/923-1668, www.codking.com). This company offers trips to hunt halibut, albacore, and salmon, as well as whale-watching trips.

If shellfish is your favorite, come to the Shelter Cove area in the springtime to enjoy the Northern California abalone season. Ask locally for this year's best diving spots.

Camping

For many, staying on the Lost Coast means camping on the trails. Dozens of campgrounds welcome tired trekkers in need of respite. Some of the larger BLM camping areas (www.blm.gov/ca, no reservations) in the King Range include **Wailaki** (Chemise Mountain Rd., $8), **Nadelos** (Chemise Mountain Rd., $8), **Tolkan** (King Peak Rd., $8), **Horse Mountain** (King Peak Rd., $5), and **Mattole Campground** (end of Lighthouse Rd., $8). Sites are semi- or fully developed with restrooms, grills, fire rings, picnic tables, bear boxes, and on-site water. Trailers and RVs up to 20 feet are allowed at these sites, though it's wise to check road conditions beforehand.

In Sinkyone Wilderness State Park (707/986-7711, www.parks.ca.gov), you can stay at **Usal Beach, Needle Rock,** or the **Sinkyone Wilderness Campground.** Sites are first come, first served.

Accommodations

Shelter Cove offers several nice motels for folks who aren't up for roughing it in the wilderness overnight. At the **Shelter Cove Beachcomber Inn** (412 Machi Rd., 800/718-4789, $65–105), each room has its own character along with views of the coast or the woods. The inn is an easy stroll to the airstrip and downtown. **The Tides Inn of Shelter Cove** (59 Surf Point, 888/998-4337, www.sheltercovetidesinn.com, $95) has standard rooms and luxurious suites with fireplaces and full kitchens. Most rooms face the sea, which is only steps from the inn. The Tides Inn is centrally located within walking distance of the airstrip, local shops, and restaurants.

The **Inn of the Lost Coast** (205 Wave Dr., 888/570-9676, www.innofthelostcoast.com, $150) boasts an array of rooms and suites to suit even luxurious tastes. Rooms are large and airy, with stellar views. Ask about discounts for AOPA, AAA, and package deals with Salmon King Charters. The **Cliff House at Shelter Cove** (141 Wave Dr., 707/986-7344, www.cliffhousesheltercove.com, $150–170) perches atop the bluffs overlooking the black sand beaches. Only two suites are available; each has a full kitchen, living room, bedroom, gas fireplace, and satellite TV. These suites are a perfect spot from which to enjoy a romantic vacation or family getaway.

Food

Most Lost Coast dining options cluster in Shelter Cove. For a delicious seafood meal, visit the glass-fronted A-frame **Chart Room** (210 Wave Dr., 707/986-9696, www.chartroom.cc, Sat.–Wed. 5–9 P.M.). In addition to seafood, the Chart Room serves hearty meat and pasta dishes, as well as vegetarian fare, sandwiches, and soups. Be sure to check out the nautical and aeronautical gift shop while you're there. At the **Cove Restaurant** (10 Seal Ct., 707/986-1197, www.sheltercoverestaurant.com, Thurs.–Sun. 5–9 P.M., Sun. 11:30 A.M.–3:30 P.M., $13–30), a solid hearty American menu, heavy on the seafood, looks perfect after a hard day of hiking, fishing, and beachcombing. A slice of pizza or a whole pie are on the menu for takeout only at **Costa Cucina** (707/986-7672, Tues.–Sun. 11:30 A.M.–1:30 P.M., 4:30–8 P.M.).

For a quick bite of lunch or the ingredients for a trailside picnic, stop by the Campground Deli (492 Machi Rd., 707/986-7474). And if what you need is a hot cup of coffee or tea before an active day, buy it at **Cape Mendocino Tea** (1176 Lower Pacific Dr., 707/986-1138, Sat.–Mon. 11 A.M.–4 P.M., $7–21) or **Angel of the Sea Coffeehouse** (205 Wave Dr., 707/986-7888, Thurs.–Mon. 7:30 A.M.–noon).

Practicalities

The **Sinkyone Wilderness State Park Visitors Center** (Usal Rd., 707/986-7711, www.parks.ca.gov) is the largest information center in the area. Mattole Campground and several of the other large campgrounds have information posted at the parking areas. Emergency services are coordinated through the Shelter Cove Fire Department (9126 Shelter Cove Rd., Whitethorn, 707/986-7507, www.sheltercove-ca.gov).

If you have access to a small airplane, consider flying in to the Shelter Cove Airport. If not, you can drive to the coast via Highway 1 or U.S. 101. Contact the State Parks department for maps and information about the trailheads in the Sinkyone and King's Range wilderness areas.

If you're up for a one-way journey through the Lost Coast Wilderness, look into a shuttle from one trailhead back to your car. **Lost Coast Trail Transport Service** (707/986-9909, www.lostcoasttrail.com) offers rides from the Shelter Cove Black Sands Beach to Usal Beach, Mattole Beach, and many other points along the trail.

HUMBOLDT REDWOODS STATE PARK

Surprisingly, the largest stand of unlogged redwood trees anywhere in the world isn't on the coast and it isn't in the Sierras. It's right here in Humboldt, bisected by U.S. 101. Come to this park to hike beneath 300-plus-foot old-growth trees that began their lives centuries before Europeans knew California existed. The visitors center for the park rests along the Avenue of the Giants (CA-254), between the towns of Weott and Myers Flat. Start here if you're new to the region or need hiking or camping information. You can also enjoy the theater, interpretive museum, and gift shop here.

While it's more than worth the time to spend a weekend in the Humboldt Redwoods, you can also spend as little as an hour or two here. A drive through the Avenue of the Giants with a stop at the visitors center and a quick nature walk or picnic can give you a quick taste of this lovely south end of the coastal redwood region.

Sights

The most famous stretch of redwood trees in the state, the **Avenue of the Giants** (look for signs on U.S. 101 to turnoffs, www.avenue ofthegiants.net) parallels U.S. 101 and the Eel River between Fortuna and Garberville. Visitors come from all over the world to drive this stretch of road and gawk in wonder at the sky-high old-growth redwoods that line the pavement. Campgrounds and hiking trails sprout among the trees off the road. The Avenue's highest traffic time is July and August, when you can expect a bumper-to-bumper, stop-and-go traffic jam for almost the whole of the 31-mile stretch of road. If crowds aren't your thing, try visiting in the spring or fall, or even braving the rains of winter to gain a more secluded redwood experience.

Hiking

With all that fabulous forest, it's hard to resist parking the car and getting out to enjoy the world of the big trees up close and personal. A great place to start is (duh!) Humboldt Redwoods State Park (707/946-2409, www .parks.ca.gov, day-use fee $6). Many visitors start with the **Founders Grove Nature Loop Trail** (0.5 mile, easy), located at mile marker 20.5 on the Avenue of the Giants. This flat nature trail gives sedate walkers a taste of the big old-growth trees in the park. Sadly, the one-time tallest tree in the world (the Dyerville Giant) fell. Now visitors can see it decomposing on the forest floor—a natural end to such a tree that feeds the newer life of the forest.

Right at the visitors center, you can enjoy

the **Gould Grove Nature Trail** (0.5 mile, easy)—a wheelchair-accessible interpretive nature walk that includes signs describing the denizens of the forest.

If you're looking for a longer walk in the woods, try out the lovely **River Trail** (Mattole Rd., 1.1 miles west of Ave. of the Giants, 7 miles round-trip, moderate). It follows the South Fork Eel River, allowing access to yet another ecosystem. Check with the visitors center to be sure that the "summer bridges" are installed before trying to hike this trail.

Hardcore hikers who want to spend all day testing their legs can also find the fun at Humboldt Redwoods. Start at the **Grasshopper Multiuse Trail Head** (Mattole Rd., 5.1 miles west of Ave. of the Giants) to access the newer **Johnson Camp Trail** (10.5 miles round-trip, difficult) that takes you to the abandoned cabins of railroad tie makers. Or pick another fork from the same trailhead to climb more than 3,000 feet to **Grasshopper Peak** (13.5 miles, difficult). From the Peak, you can see for 100 miles in any direction, overlooking the whole of the park and beyond.

Biking and Horseback Riding

Don't want to hoof it in the woods? You can bring your street bike up to the park and ply either the Avenue of the Giants or Mattole Road. A number of the trails throughout Humboldt Redwoods State Park are designated as multi-use, which means that mountain bikers can make the rigorous climbs and then rip their way back down.

Equestrians can also make use of the multi-use trails, and the Cuneo Creek Horse Camp provides a place for riders who want to spend more than just a day exploring the thousands of acres of forest and meadowland.

Swimming and Kayaking

The Eel River's forks meander through the Humboldt Redwoods, creating lots of great opportunities for cooling off on hot summer days. Check with the visitors center for this year's best swimming holes, though you can reliably find good spots at Eagle Point (near Hidden Valley Campground), Gould Bar, and

Garden Club of America Grove. In addition to all the usual precautions you must take for unprotected river swimming, you must take care in the months of August and September. A poisonous (if ingested) blue-green algae can bloom late in the summer, making swimming in certain parts of the river hazardous.

In the springtime when the river flows high, kayakers and canoeists bring their craft out to launch into the Eel. Just call ahead to get river conditions before you strap your boat to the top of your car, as the flow can be unpredictable even in spring.

Entertainment and Events

The Humboldt Redwoods State Park area is quiet in general, but a few events draw visitors and locals alike. The **Humboldt Redwoods Marathon** (www.redwoodsmarathon.org), fondly known to participants as the Redwood Run, takes place each fall. Runners of all ability levels can participate; events include a full marathon, half-marathon, and 5K run.

Accommodations

Few lodging options are really close to Humboldt Redwoods State Park other than the

NORTH COAST

HUMBOLDT'S TOP CASH CROP

Some people might not think first of pretty trees or cool coastlines when hearing the words "Humboldt County." Instead, many folks of a certain persuasion think of a lesser-seen plant that grows well in the damp temperate climate here. To be honest: Humboldt's (sub) culture is all about the pot.

Indeed, the climate, soil, and altitude of Humboldt County, as well as conditions in neighboring Mendocino and Trinity, are great for marijuana farming. And the dense forests make good cover for marijuana gardens in danger of discovery by DEA and CAMP helicopters. Better botanical knowledge of marijuana plants has led to a much bigger kick than pot smokers got back in the 1960s and '70s. Much of that knowledge has been gleaned right here in the redwoods as the counterculture hippies and artists of previous decades fled the increasingly hostile and overcrowded neighborhoods of San Francisco and Los Angeles to enjoy a "simpler" life on the land. That simplicity included green smoke as soon as the hippies arrived and growers have been making a living on the North Coast ever since. What was once a backyard-of-the-commune industry for the hippies has become a big business. Most of the pot smoked in the United States (and perhaps the world) comes from California.

The presence of Mexican drug cartels in the Humboldt redwoods is hotly debated these days. Whether you believe they're there or not, it's a good bet that if you stumble upon a remote pot garden, you should leave – quickly and quietly. It's a known fact that some major gardens, which can be worth billions of dollars on the open market, are guarded by big men with big guns who will shoot anyone trying to steal from their crop. South Humboldt County is rife with large farms, and even the locals recommend that hikers avoid trekking anywhere other than maintained, in-park trails to stay safe.

The state legalized medical marijuana by popular vote more than a decade ago, creating a pitched battle with the Feds over pot clubs and medical growers. CAMP, a state agency, leaves known medical marijuana growers alone.

Despite the roughly $4 billion per year the U.S. government spends on "marijuana suppression" these days, usage rates remain the same as they were during the Summer of Love.

Certainly marijuana plays a role in the lifestyle of many Humboldt residents. Most of the larger towns support at least one head shop, and local glassblowers can make a living creating and selling pipes that are works of art. The presence of Humboldt State University helps to bring in the next generation of pot smokers, and the local smokin' surf-and-arts crowd has been entrenched for decades. Several publications dealing with cannabis culture originate here, and the issue of marijuana never leaves the city and county governments.

campgrounds in the park itself. For car and RV campers, you'll find plenty of options, including **Burlington Campground** adjacent to the visitors center, **Albee Creek** (Mattole Rd., 5 miles west of Ave. of the Giants), and the large and ever-popular **Hidden Springs Campground** (5 miles south of the visitors center, Ave. of the Giants). Minimalist campers will enjoy seclusion of the hike-in trail camps at **Johnson** and **Grasshopper Peak.** Reservations are strongly recommended for campsites, as this region is quite popular with weekend campers.

Folks on moderate budgets can find accommodations in nearby Garberville. Several small motels offer reasonable rooms, and many have outdoor pools where weary guests can cool off during the heat of summer. The best of these is the **Best Western Humboldt House Inn** (701 Redwood Dr., 707/923-2771, book.bestwestern.com, $143–165). Rooms are clean and comfortable, the pool is sparkling and cool, and the location is convenient to restaurants and shops in Garberville. You'll get the usual comforts of the Best Western chain. Most rooms have two queen beds, making this motel perfect for families and couples traveling together on a budget.

The place to stay in the Humboldt Redwoods area is the **Benbow Inn** (445 Lake Benbow Dr., 800/355-3301, www.benbowinn.com, $195–660). A swank resort backing onto Lake Benbow, this inn has it all: a gourmet restaurant, an 18-hole golf course, and a woodsy atmosphere that blends perfectly with the idyllic redwood forest surrounding it. Rooms glow with polished dark woods and jewel-toned carpets and decor. Wide king and comfy queen beds beckon to guests tired after a long day of hiking in the redwoods or golfing beside the inn.

Food

The restaurant at the **Benbow Inn** (445 Lake Benbow Dr., 800/355-3301, www.benbowinn.com, dinner 6–9 P.M.) matches the lodgings for superiority in the area. It serves upscale California cuisine and features an extensive wine list with many regional wineries represented. The white-tablecloth dining room is exquisite, and the expansive outdoor patio overlooking the water is the perfect place to sit as the temperature cool on a summer evening. The only downside to this usually terrific restaurant is that service can lag on weekday nights when the dining room isn't full.

For travelers who can't spend a month's grocery money on one meal, Garberville proper has several modest eateries that appeal to weary travelers and families with kids. Drive or stroll down Redwood Drive and take your pick of a variety of restaurants. One of these is the **Woodrose Café** (911 Redwood Dr., 707/923-3191, www.woodrosecafe.com). You can get a traditional American-style breakfast and lunch at this small independent eatery, though it won't come cheap. The touristy nature of the locale has driven up the prices, but the food is usually palatable and the service acceptable.

Calling **Sicilito's** (445 Conger St., 707/923-2814, www.asis.com/sicilitos) "world cuisine" might be pushing it, especially when you see the funky signs out front advertising pizza and Mexican food. But the pizzas and taco salads are tasty (if unusual) and the beer and wine selection helps make diners happy with their choices. The small dining room's walls are crowded with American memorabilia, and the establishment sometimes gets filled with biker types making their way up U.S. 101.

Need a lift? You won't find too many Starbucks around here, so enjoy a taste of locally owned java instead. Grab a cup of coffee at **Signature Coffee** (3455 Redwood Dr., Redway, 707/923-2661).

Practicalities

A few tiny towns dot the Humboldt Redwoods region, but they can be short on services such as gas stations. Top off in Fortuna or Willits if you can. There is a 76 station in Garberville, well off the highway at 790 Redwood Drive.

There's a supermarket, **Ray's Food Place** (875 Redwood Dr., 707/923-2279), in Garberville. You can also find ATMs and even some Internet service in town. The easiest post office to access is at 3400 Redwood Drive in Redway.

The nearest hospital with an emergency

room is **Redwood Memorial Hospital** (3300 Renner Dr., Fortuna, 707/725-3361).

The best way to get to Humboldt Redwoods State Park from either the north or the south is via U.S. 101. You can also approach the center of the park from Mattole Road if you've been traversing the Lost Coast. Road signs direct visitors to the Avenue of the Giants. Bicycles are not permitted on U.S. 101, but you can ride the Avenue and Mattole Road.

Mendocino and Sonoma Coasts

The coastline stretching from Sonoma County through Mendocino is the most popular retreat on the North Coast for locals. Weekends see Bay Area residents flock north to their favorite hideaways to enjoy the windswept beaches, secret coves, and luscious cuisine. This area has something for everyone, from dedicated deep-sea sport fishermen to wine aficionados to luxury spa lovers. Art is especially prominent in the culture here; from the 1960s onward, aspiring artists have found supportive communities, sales opportunities, and homes in Mendocino County. A wealth of galleries display their beautiful, often unusual work.

WINERIES

The Pacific coastline is not an ideal climate for most wine grapes, thus you won't find dozens of wineries hugging the shore, even in famous Sonoma County. However, a few wineries persevere, growing grapes more suited to the cooler temperatures and using the salt air to create unique flavors in their wines.

Pacific Star Winery

The only winery on the Mendocino Coast, Pacific Star Winery (33000 N. Hwy. 1, 707/964-1155, www.pacificstarwinery.com, daily 11 A.M.–5 P.M., tasting free) prides itself on using its unique location to create unique wines. Barrels of wine are left out in the salt air to age, incorporating a hint of the Pacific into each vintage. Friendly tasting room staffers will tell you how much they like their bosses, the winemaker, and which of the winery cats most likes to be picked up. Wines are tasty and reasonably priced, and the picnic grounds sit on a bluff overlooking the ocean.

Annapolis Winery

A small winery up in the hills near Sonoma, Annapolis Winery (26055 Soda Springs Rd., Annapolis, 707/886-5460, www.annapolis winery.com, daily noon–5 P.M.) sits just east of Sea Ranch. At this little family-owned winery, you'll find a pleasant coastal hill climate and a small list of classic California wines. You can taste sauvignon blanc, chardonnay, zinfandel, and cabernet here, all under the funky rooster-emblazoned label. Take a glass outside to enjoy the views from the estate vineyards out over the forested mountains.

Flowers Vineyard

So what kind of grapes could possibly grow in the chilly, drippy air of the northern California coast? Pinot noir and chardonnay grapes not only survive in such a climate, they thrive in the cool moist conditions. Flowers Vineyard (28500 Seaview Rd., Cazadero, 707/847-3661, www.flowerswinery.com) makes the most of its locale by specializing in these varietals. In fact, that's all you'll find when you come to taste at Flowers, except for one annual red blend. To fill their list, Flowers creates single-vineyard estate vintages, selecting from their favorite blocks of grapes.

Gourmet au Bay

Gourmet au Bay (913 Hwy. 1, Bodega Bay, 707/875-9875, www.gourmetaubay.com, Thurs.–Tues. 11 A.M.–7 P.M.) isn't a winery; it's a shop and tasting bar in the coastside town of Bodega Bay. The good news is that you get to taste wines from a variety of different vintners, some major players in the Napa wine scene, some from wineries so small that they don't have tasting rooms of their own. You might even get to taste the odd French or Australian varietal when you "wine surf," tasting three wines poured and laid out on a miniature "surfboard" for you to carry out to the deck to admire the view. Inside, you can sip as you peruse the gift shop, which includes some local artisanal foods plus plenty of handmade ceramics and pottery and an array of toys for wine lovers.

SIGHTS

The shores of Mendocino are clustered with state beaches and picturesque secluded coves. While many of the major tourist attractions are well worth a visit, as a traveler along this stretch of coastline, seek out that perfect spot of sand and make it your own.

Skunk Train

One of the famed attractions to Mendocino County, the Skunk Train (depot at foot of Laurel St., Fort Bragg, 800/866-1690, www .skunktrain.com, office daily 8 A.M.–8 P.M.) is perfect for rail buffs and traveling families alike. The restored steam locomotives pull trains from the coast of Fort Bragg through the redwood forest to the town of Willits and back. The adventure lets everyone see the true majesty of the redwoods, while giving a hint about life in Northern California before the state highways. The gaily painted trains appeal to children, and the historic aspects and scenery call to adults. You can board in either Fort Bragg or Willits, making a round-trip to return to your lodgings for the night. Check the website for special rides featuring the food of local chefs, the wines of local vintners, and even locally brewed beers.

Point Arena Lighthouse

Though its magnificent Fresnel lens no longer turns through the night, the Point Arena Lighthouse (45500 Lighthouse Rd., Point Arena, 877/725-4448, www.pointarenalight house.com, daily summer 10 A.M.–3:30 P.M., winter 10 A.M.–3:30 P.M., $5 adults, $1 children) remains a Coast Guard light and fog station. But what makes this unusually-shaped beacon special is its history. When the 1906 Earthquake hit San Francisco, it jolted the land all the way up the coast, severely damaging the Point Arena Lighthouse. When the structure was rebuilt two years later, engineers devised the above-ground foundation that gives the lighthouse both its distinctive shape and additional structural stability.

Visitors can enjoy an the Lighthouse's extensive interpretive museum housed in the fog station beyond the gift shop. Docent-led tours up to the top of the lighthouse are well worth the trip, both for the views from the top of the lighthouse and for the fascinating story of its destruction and rebirth through the earthquake as told by the knowledgeable staff. Tour groups also have the opportunity to climb right up to the Fresnel lens, taking a rare close look at an astonishing invention that reflected pre-electric light far enough out to sea to protect passing ships.

◖ Mendocino County Botanical Gardens

No tiny space carved out to nurture a few precious plants, the Mendocino County Botanical Gardens (18220 N. Hwy. 1, 707/964-4352, www.gardenbythesea.org, Mar.–Oct. daily 9 A.M.–5 P.M., Nov.–Feb. daily 9 A.M.–4 P.M., $10 adult, $7.50 senior, $4 youth) is a vast expanse of land bearing an astonishing variety of vegetation. Stretching 47 acres down to the sea, these gardens offer literally miles of walking and hiking through careful plantings and wild landscapes. The gardens' map is also a seasonal guide, useful for folks who aren't sure whether it's rhododendron season, or whether the dahlia garden might be in bloom. Butterflies flutter and bees buzz, and good labels teach novice botany enthusiasts the names of the plants they see.

◖ Glass Beach

The most famous beach in the Mendo area, Glass Beach (Elm St. and Glass Beach Dr., Fort Bragg) is *not* a miracle of nature. The dubious origin of this fascinating beach strewn with "sea glass" was the Fort Bragg city dump. As the ocean rose over the landfill, the heavy glass that had been dumped there stayed put. Years of pounding in the surf polished and smoothed the broken edges, and now the surf returns our human refuse to the shore.

Beachcombers can collect smooth, coated shards of glass in hues of green, blue, brown, and clear. The trail down to Glass Beach is steep and treacherous, so don't wear sandals! Good walking or hiking shoes and attention to safety are a must.

◖ Fort Ross State Historic Park

In the 19th century, Russians came to the wilds of Alaska and paired with the native Alaskans to ply the fur trade, killing seals, otters, and sea lions as well as land mammals for their pelts. The enterprise required sea travel, as the hunters chased the animals all the way to California. Eventually, a group of fur hunters and traders came ashore on what is now the Sonoma coast to create a wayfaring point for their brethren. This fortified outpost became known as Fort Ross (19005 Coast Hwy. 1, Jenner, 707/847-3286, www.parks.ca.gov, hours vary), named for the "Ross-ians" who built it.

Today, visitors can walk into the reconstructed fort buildings and see how the settlers lived. (U.S. 101 was originally built right through the middle of the fort area, but it was moved to make way for the historic park.) The only original building still standing is the captain's quarters—a large, luxurious house for the era and situation. The other buildings, including the large bunkhouse, the chapel, and the two cannon-filled blockhouses, were rebuilt using much of the original lumber used by the Russians. Be aware that a serious visit of the whole fort and the beach beyond is a level but long walk; wear comfortable shoes and consider bringing a bottle of water.

Salt Point State Park

Stretching for miles along the Sonoma coastline, Salt Point State Park (25050 Hwy. 1, 707/847-3221, www.parks.ca.gov, visitors center open Sat.–Sun. 10 A.M.–3 P.M., day use $6) provides easy access from U.S. 101 to over

Fort Ross State Historic Park

© ROBERT HOLMES / CALTOUR

a dozen sandy state beaches. You don't have to visit the visitors center to enjoy this park and its many beaches—just follow the signs along the highway to the turnoffs and parking lots. If you're looking to scuba or free dive, head for **Gerstle Cove,** accessible from the visitors center just south of Salt Point proper. The cove was designated as one of California's first underwater parks, and divers who can deal with the chilly water have a wonderful time exploring the diverse undersea wildlife here. For a more genteel experience at Salt Point State Park, head east off the freeway to the **Krause Rhododendron State Reserve.** Here you can meander along the China Gulf Trail in the springtime, admiring the profusion of pink rhododendron flowers blooming beneath the second-growth redwood forest. If you prefer a picnic, you'll find tables at many of the beaches—just be aware that the North Coast can be quite windy in the summertime. Campers throng to Salt Point in the summertime, and a number of campgrounds serve both tent campers and RVs stretch along the shore. Check the park website for campsite reservation information.

Kelley House Museum

The mission of the lovely, stately Kelley House Museum (45007 Albion St., Mendocino Village, 707/937-5791, www.mendocinohistory.org, summer Thurs.–Tues. 11 A.M.–3 P.M., winter Fri.–Mon. 11 A.M.–3 P.M., admission free, tours $10) is to preserve the history of Mendocino for future generations. The newer addition to the historic home houses the village archives, which include thousands of photos. In the museum proper, antique furniture and fixtures grace the rooms. A rotating collection of Victorian clothing is displayed, as are photos and documents that tell the story of historic Mendocino. To help tell that story, knowledgeable docents hang out in the house. Ask about the town's water-rights issues for a great lesson in the untold history of the Mendo Coast. For a special treat, come on a weekend and ask about a tour of the nearby Presbyterian Church.

Triangle Tattoo Museum

Warning: This is not your grandmother's art museum, so enter at your own risk. For more than 20 years, the Triangle Tattoo Museum (356B N. Main St., Fort Bragg, 707/964-8814, www.triangletattoo.com, from noon) has displayed the implements of tattooing and photos of their results. To enter, walk up a flight of narrow stairs and stare at the walls completely covered with photos of tattoos. All kinds are represented, from tribal to carnival to prison. In glass cases upstairs, all types of tattooing apparatus, some antique and many tribal, stare out as if to dare passersby to allow them out onto live human skin. More photos grace the walls of the warren of small rooms in a never-ending collage. The street-side rooms comprise the working tattoo parlor, and you can find intrepid artists and their canvases working late into the evenings. If you're brave enough, talk to an artist about scheduling an appointment.

© LANCE SCOTT

Kelley House Museum

ENTERTAINMENT AND EVENTS
Bars and Clubs

Not too many happening nightclubs make their homes on the Mendocino coast. If you're looking for a local-style night out, get tickets to one of the live theater performances, find a winemaker's dinner or bundle up for a moonlit stroll on the coast. But if all you need is a pint of beer or a good stiff drink (or maybe a hot toddy after that beach stroll), the towns along the coastline have a number of pubs, breweries, and bars that open their doors into the night. The **North Coast Brewing Company** (455 N. Main St., Fort Bragg, 707/964-2739, www .northcoastbrewing.com, daily from noon) opened in 1988, aiming at the then-nascent artisanal beer market. Come in, grab a classic brewpub meal, then check out the latest beers. Whether you choose an Acme, a Red Seal Ale, or an Old Rasputin (yes, really), you'll definitely enjoy.

For a place to hunker down over a pint in Mendocino proper, saunter on over to **Patterson's Pub** (10485 Lansing St., Mendocino Village, 707/937-4782, www .pattersonspub.com). This traditional Irish-style pub sits in the former rectory of a 19th-century Catholic church. It nods to the 21st century with six plasma TVs that screen the current games. You can order a blessedly simple and filling meal either at the tables or the bar here. You'll find a dozen beers on tap, a full-fledged wine list, and hard liquors imported from around the world.

So where do the locals go for a drink in tourist-heavy Mendocino? That would be **Dick's Place** (45080 Main St., 707/937-5643, daily until 2 A.M.), sometimes called Richard's by the Sea. It's easy to find, just next to the Hotel with the only neon sign on Main Street. (It's a martini glass). The vintage-y decor pales next to the colorful array of resident drinkers perched around the bar at Dick's.

For nightlife lovers who don't need copious liquor to lubricate a good time, **Headlands Coffee House** (120 Laurel St., Fort Bragg, 707/964-1987, www.headlandscoffeehouse .com, Sun.–Thurs. 7 A.M.–10 P.M., Fri.–Sat. 7 A.M.–11 P.M.) makes a perfect destination. The pale blue walls and woven French-style chairs make this a light and bright place to grab coffee and a sandwich during the day. The coffee house really heats up with live entertainment every single night—usually a local jazz group. Order a cuppa, sit back, and enjoy a chill-out evening filled with music and conversation.

Theater

The **Mendocino Theater Company** (707/937-4477, www.mendocinotheatre.org, $10–25, shows Thurs.–Sat. 8 P.M., Sun. 2 P.M., $15–20) offers a genuine small community theater experience. All plays are put up in the 81-seat Helen Schonei Theater (45200 Little Lake St., Mendocino), which definitely makes for an intimate night of live drama or comedy. The small, weathered old building exudes just the right kind of charm to draw lovers of quirky community theater inside its door. But this little theater company has big goals, and they show mostly newer works by playwrights who take on some of the toughest issues that resonate with modern audiences. You might see *Gross Indecency* or *Rabbit Hole* or another thought-provoking contemporary work here. Do keep in mind that this is a community theater company; don't expect Broadway quality, but do expect lots of fun and surprises.

The **Gloriana Opera Company** (210 N. Corry St., Fort Bragg, 707/964-7469, www .gloriana.org) focuses more on musicals than true operas, but their shows still delight young and old theatergoers alike. Gloriana seeks to bring music and theater to young people—accordingly, they produce major musicals that appeal to kids, such as *The Aristocats*. On the other hand, *Into the Woods* appeals mostly to kids who are past their second decade. Local performers star in the two major shows and numerous one-off performances that Gloriana puts up each year.

Cinema

If you prefer your entertainment on a screen but still like a little atmosphere, take in a show at the **Arena Theater** (210 Main St., Point Arena, 707/882-3456, www.mendocino .com). This one-time vaudeville theater was also a "movie palace" of the old school when it opened in 1928. In the 1990s, the old theater got a restorative facelift that returned it to its art deco glory. Today, you can see all kinds of films at the Arena, from recent box office toppers to new documentaries to fun independent films. If the cinema isn't playing, you might find a live musical or theatrical show.

Festivals and Events

Perhaps nowhere in California are festivals so much a part of life as in Mendocino. It's difficult to find a weekend in the region without something going on. Whether you prefer wine, art, music, or wildlife, you'll find a celebration of it somewhere on Mendo's packed festival and events calendar.

Art is a big deal in Mendocino. Accordingly, the area hosts any number of art events each year. **Art in the Gardens** (www.gardenbythesea.com, $20 at the door) takes place at the Mendocino County Botanical Gardens, for which it is an annual fundraiser. Each August, the gardens are decked out with the finest local artwork, food, and wine. Music entertains the crowds who come to eat, drink, view, and purchase art.

For folks whose tastes run more toward the musical arts, the annual **Whale and Jazz Festival** (www.mendocino.com) takes place all around Mendocino in April of each year. Some of the nation's finest jazz performers play in a variety of venues, while the whales put on their own show out in the Pacific. Point Arena Lighthouse offers whale-watching from the shore each day, and the wineries and restaurants of the region provide refreshment and relaxation every evening of the festival weekend.

In July, musicians of all types descend on the temporarily warmish coast for the **Mendocino Music Festival** (www.mendocino.com). For two weeks, live performances dot the landscape. Take your family to a children's matinee or your sweetie to a dance. Enjoy the soft relaxation of a chamber music performance or

the lively beats of the famed big band concert, an annual fixture of the festival.

If restaurants are the heart of the Mendocino food scene, festivals are its soul. **Taste of Mendocino** (www.mendocino.com/ mendocino-crab-wine-days-festival.html), also sometimes known as the Mendocino Crab and Wine Days, takes place from November through March each year. The Dungeness crab season, the wild mushroom season, and wine releases converge to create a fabulous time to visit the blustery Mendo Coast. Just about every restaurant in the area, plus all the wineries of Hopland and the Anderson Valley, gets in on the action for the weekends of the festival run. Check the website for the year's plethora of wine dinners, mushroom-hunting seminars, crab feeds, and special events. Take a cooking class put on by a local celebrity chef, deepen your knowledge of local wine varietals, or even head out onto the ocean to learn how the crab fishermen do their jobs.

SHOPPING

On the coast, the best place to browse is **Mendocino Village.** Not only are the galleries and boutiques welcoming and fun, the whole downtown area is beautiful. It seems that every shop in the Main Street area has its own garden, and each fills with a riotous cascade of flowers in the summertime. Even if you hate to shop, make the trip down to the village just to (literally) smell the roses.

Books

On the other end of the spectrum, pick up a new-to-you tome to read in your cushy bed at the **Main Street Book Shop** (990 Main St., 707/937-1537). Next door to the funky Sweetwater, this used bookshop harkens back to Mendocino's days as an art colony. The books are vaguely organized into sections—the fiction and nonfiction at least seem separated on the cluttered tables and overstuffed shelves. It's easy to spend an hour in here, hunting bargains or for your next throwaway thriller.

Galleries

Panache (45110 Main St. and 10400 Kasten St., Mendocino Village, 707/937-0947, www .thepanachegallery.com) displays and sells beautiful works of art in all sorts of media. You'll find paintings and jewelry, sculpture and art glass. Much of the artistic focus reminds viewers of the sea crashing just outside the large multi-room gallery. The wooden furniture and boxes are a special treat—handmade treasures using rare woods combined and then sanded and polished to silk-smooth finishes.

Even folks who find most art galleries pretentious can find the fun at the **Leedy Art Gallery** (45000 Main St., Mendocino Village, 707/937-1354, www.leedyart.com). Billed as "Art That Makes You Laugh," the pastel originals and reproductions in this smallish gallery really are that funny. You'll find the lawyer series, the golf series, and many other vividly colorful paintings that depict the human condition and American life just a little bit too well. If you're really lucky, you might find artist Jeff Leedy in the gallery when you visit. Laugh a bit and he'll gladly tell you all about the picture you're looking at and take you for a tour of the gallery.

Gift and Home

The lavish B&Bs of Mendocino get many guests thinking about upgrading their home boudoirs. Knowing this, the **Golden Goose** (45094 Main St., 707/937-4655) offers all the linens and accessories that a (wealthy) shopper might need to create a soft and luxurious bed and bath all her own. The shopkeepers encourage you to pet the Egyptian cotton sheets and towels, sniff the sachets and soaps, and try on the thick spa-style robes. You'll find yourself longing for (and perhaps purchasing) a Mendocino inn sleep experience for every day of the week.

SPORTS AND RECREATION

Resist the urge to spend all your time in Mendocino inside your inn, shopping at the galleries, and eating endless plates of fine food. Spend at least a few hours outdoors in the verdant wilderness and on the wild seashore that so beautifully define this region.

Fishing and Whale-Watching

The Mendocino coast is an ideal location to watch whales dance, or try to land the big one (salmon, halibut, rockcod, or tuna). During Dungeness season, you can even go out on a crab boat, learn to set pots, and catch your own crab feed's worth of the delectable delicacy.

Many charters leave out of Noyo Harbor in Fort Bragg. The *Trek II* (Noyo Harbor, 707/964-4550, www.anchorcharterboats .com) offers five-hour fishing trips and two-hour whale-watching cruises. Aboard the *Rumblefish* (Noyo Harbor, 707/964-3000, www.fortbraggfishing.com), you can watch a demonstration of crab fishing or spot for whales in the winter from the comfort of the heated cabin, or fish for various deep-sea dwellers in the summer (and year-round for cod). The crew can even clean and vacuum-pack your catch on the dock before you leave.

Canoeing and Kayaking

Kayak and canoe trips are a popular summertime activity on the Mendo coast. To explore the more sedate waters of the Big River estuary, consider renting an outrigger or even a sailing canoe from **Catch a Canoe & Bicycles Too!** (Hwy. 1 and Comptche Ukiah Rd., 707/937-0273, www.stanfordinn.com) at the Stanford Inn. For an adventurous day on the ocean, consider taking a sea cave tour by kayak. **Lost Coast Kayaking** (707/964-7480, www .lostcoastkayaking.com) launches three two-hour tours each day from Van Damme State Park. Because these tours use sit-on-top kayaks, no previous experience is necessary.

Hiking and Biking

A wealth of smaller state parks makes hiking and biking on the Mendocino coast a pleasure. At **Van Damme State Park** (Hwy. 1, 3 miles south of Mendocino Village, 707/937-5804, www.parks.ca.gov), take a walk to the park's centerpiece: the wheelchair-accessible **Pygmy**

Forest (0.25 mile, easy) loop trail. Here you'll see a true biological rarity: mature yet tiny cypress and pine trees perpetually stunted by a unique combination of always-wet ground and poor soil nutrient conditions. You can get to the Pygmy Forest from the **Fern Canyon Trail** (6 miles one-way, difficult), or drive Airport Road to the trail parking lot (opposite the county airport) directly to the loop.

Perhaps the most popular hiking trails in coastal Mendocino wind through **Russian Gulch State Park** (Hwy. 1, 2 miles north of Mendocino Village, 707/937-5804, www .parks.ca.gov). Russian Gulch has its own **Fern Canyon Trail** (3 miles round-trip), winding into the second-growth redwood forest filled with lush green ferns. At the four-way junction, turn left to hike another 0.75 mile to the ever-popular waterfall. Be aware that you're likely to be part of a crowd visiting the falls on summer

SWEATPANTS, PARKAS, AND NORTH COAST BEACHES

The Hollywood view of California beaches includes long, flat stretches of sugary white sand drenched in warm sunshine, populated by beautiful blondes in teeny bikinis and studly surfer boys riding the moderate waves.

Nothing could be further from the reality of the Northern California coast. Make no mistake – you'll find an overwhelming number of gorgeous beaches in the north, but it's a different kind of beauty. Craggy cliffs rise up to tower over narrow, rocky sand spits teeming with tidepools and backing into ever-changing sea caves. Wide swaths of beach become covered with driftwood, semiprecious minerals, and even fossils. Nonetheless, hardy beachgoers bring out their folding chairs, umbrellas, coolers, wetsuits, and surfboards to these beaches to enjoy a day on the sand and surf. If you aim to become one of these, here are some tips for equipment and preparation for your North Coast beach trip:

- **Dress in layers.** North Coast beach temperatures can hover in the 50s even in the middle of summer. Wear a sweatshirt and warm pants over shorts and T-shirt and wear that over your swimsuit.

- **Prepare for dampness.** Fog and drizzle often coalesce right on the coastline, even when it's sunny and hot only a few miles inland. Bring a hat and possibly a parka.

- **Bring appropriate footwear.** Most North Coast beaches are *not* barefoot friendly.

Exploration of rocky beaches and tidepools demand either specialized shoes or good, broken-in hiking boots. Jellyfish sometimes wash ashore on California's northern beaches, making bare feet or even beach sandals a painful idea. And on fire-legal beaches, some folks just cover over an abandoned fire with a little sand, making for hot footing for the next beachcomber to walk by. Even if you choose to go on a barefoot walk on the sand, carry a pair of closed-toed shoes with you, just in case the going gets tough farther down the beach.

- **Going swimming or surfing?** That water is cold. Wear a wetsuit and booties if you don't want to experience hypothermia and possibly even the hospitality of the California Coast Guard rescue teams.

- **Learn about fire restrictions.** Fires are illegal on many California beaches. Check restrictions on the beach you are visiting before lighting up a nice big driftwood bonfire to keep warm.

- **Wear sunscreen!** Even if a layer of fog covers the sun, you are still at risk of a nasty sunburn. (California natives call it a "cloud tan.")

- **Prepare your kids.** Bring plenty of beach toys and talk up tidepool walks, but *do not* promise the little ones a swim in the ocean. The reality is that is may be too cold or just generally unsafe to swim.

weekends. To the right at the four-way junction, you can take a three-mile loop (bringing your total hike to six miles) that brings you to the top of the small attractive waterfall. If you prefer the shore to the forest, hike west rather than east to take in the lovely wild headlands and see blowholes, grasses, and even trawlers out seeking the day's fresh catch.

Just north of Fort Bragg, tiny **MacKerricher State Park** (Hwy. 1, 3 miles north of Fort Bragg, 707/964-9112, www.parks.ca.gov) boasts cute Cleone Lake and miles of sand dunes and shoreline. *The* hike to take here is the **Ten Mile Beach Trail** (14 miles round-trip, moderate), starting at the Beachcomber Motel at the north end of Fort Bragg and running up an ironic seven miles to the Ten Mile River. Most of this path is fairly level and paved. It's an easy walk you can take at your own pace and turn around whenever you feel comfortable. Don't want to walk? Street bikes and in-line skates are allowed on this trail.

Horseback Riding

What better way to enjoy the rugged cliffs, windy beaches, and quiet forests of Mendocino than on the back of a horse? **Ricochet Ridge Ranch** (24201 N. U.S. 101, 707/964-7669, www.horse-vacation.com) has short trail rides departing four times a day, morning and afternoon. They also offer longer beach and trail rides, sunset beach rides, and full-fledged riding vacations by reservation. **Ross Ranch** (707/877-1834, www.rossranch.biz) provides horses and guides *by reservation only* for private treks at the south end of the county. Ross's horses are well cared-for and will please even the most discerning advanced rider.

Diving

The best abalone in the region usually clusters in the waters of **Van Damme State Park** (Hwy. 1, 3 miles south of Mendocino Village, www.parks.ca.gov), which also makes a good entry point for shore divers. Another is **The Blowhole** (at the end of Main St., Mendocino Village), a favorite summer lounging spot for locals. In the water, you'll find tons of abalone

and their empty shells, colorful tiny nudibranches, and, occasionally, overly friendly seals. The kelp beds just off the shore attract divers who don't fear cold water and want to check out the complex ecosystem.

Check with the park service or online for the abalone season opening and closing dates, limits, licensing information, and the best spots to dive each year.

Spas

Relaxation is key to any Mendo coast vacation. A variety of spas can help out with this goal. The **Sweetwater** day spa (44840 Main St., Mendocino Village, 800/300-4140, www.sweetwaterspa.com) rents indoor hot tubs by the hour and offers a range of massage services at reasonable rates. The rustic buildings and garden setting complete the experience. In Fort Bragg, the **Bamboo Garden Spa** (303-C N. Main St., 707/962-9396, www.bamboogardenspa.com) pampers its guests with a wide array of massage, skin, and beauty treatments. Two-person hot tubs can be rented for $45 per hour.

Would you prefer a massage in the luxury of your own accommodations? In Mendocino, you can do that too. Call **The Body Works** (707/877-3430, www.massagetime.biz, $85/hour) for an appointment for a foot rub, herbal facial, full-body massage, or all of the above.

ACCOMMODATIONS

Wherever you choose to stay in the Mendocino coast region, be aware that with the dozens of festivals all year long and the proximity to the Bay Area, the most popular inns fill up fast on many weekends throughout the year. Fall and winter can be high season, with the Crab Festival, the Mushroom Festival, and the various harvest and post-harvest wine celebrations. The moral of all this: If you want to stay someplace specific on the Mendocino coast, book your room early—at least a month ahead of time for weekdays and six months or more in advance for major festival weekends.

So what's up with the range of room rates? The truth of it is that you'll only get the cheap end of the spectrum on unpopular weeknights.

If you're visiting for a weekend—or worse, during a festival—expect to pay the premium room rates.

$100-150

You'll find the bulk of less-expensive lodgings in and around Fort Bragg. The **Beachcomber Motel** (1111 N. Main St., Fort Bragg, 707/964-2402, $132–300, pets allowed) is clean and decent, boasting many rooms with an ocean view. Amenities are minimal but acceptable—about what you'd find at a low-end chain motel. Expect shampoo and soap in your tiny bathroom, but little else. Guest rooms are big enough to satisfy, though some visitors find them a bit dark and sparsely furnished; certainly the decor is nothing to write home about. Thin walls and shared patios make noise a problem, especially if a biker group is sharing the motel with you. At the north end of town, the Beachcomber isn't too convenient to downtown Fort Bragg, but it's a short drive to restaurants and services. What makes the Beachcomber worthwhile, besides its lower-than-a-B&B prices, is its location. It sits right on the beach so ground-floor guests can walk right out of their back doors, across the busy pedestrian and bike path, and onto the sand.

If the crowds in Mendocino Village and Fort Bragg aren't your style and you prefer a more secluded getaway, the **(Elk Cove Inn** (6300 S. Hwy. 1, 800/275-2967, www.elkcoveinn.com, $135–395) is the perfect spot. This inn's unpretentious exterior barely hints at the luxurious room appointments inside. Choose from an antique-furnished room in the historic main building or a posh spa cabin overlooking the lawn. The attached day spa pampers guests with organic products and treatments especially designed for couples. Best of all, the tiny restaurant holds a secret: a chef worthy of the top San Francisco dining scene. The innovative dinner menu impresses even jaded big-city foodies, and a sumptuous breakfast is included with a stay at the inn. To work off all that rich cuisine, take a hike down to Elk Cove—the not-quite-private-but-close-enough secluded beach cove that foots the inn and lends it a spectacular view.

Fun and funky, the **Sweetwater Inn and Spa** (44840 Main St., Mendocino Village, 800/300-4140, www.sweetwaterspa.com, $125–300) harkens back to the days when Mendocino was a starving artists' colony rather than a yuppie weekend retreat. A redwood water tower was converted into a guest room, joined by a motley connection of detached cottages that guarantee guests great privacy. Every room and cottage has its own style—you'll find a spiral staircase in the water tower, a two-person tub set in a windowed alcove in the Zen Room, and fireplaces in many of the cottages. The eclectic decor makes each room unique, and many return guests request their favorite room again and again. Thick gardens surround the building complex, and a path leads back to the Garden Spa. The location, just past downtown on Main Street in Mendocino Village, is perfect for dining, shopping, and art walks.

$150-250

The **Little River Inn** (7901 N. Hwy. 1, Little River, 888/466-5683, www.littleriverinn.com, $143–400) appeals to a more coastal vacationer, boasting a 9-hole golf course and two lighted tennis courts. All of the recreation areas overlook the Pacific, crashing into the shore just across the highway from the inn. The sprawling white Victorian house and barns hide the sprawl of this inn, which also has a great restaurant and a charming sea-themed bar. The inn can cater to all sorts of travelers, from families looking for the privacy of a detached cottage to luxury-loving travelers to pet lovers who've brought their furry friends with them. Special guest room treats can include a fireplace, a spa, and a view of the ocean. Want to relax even further? Make a reservation for a massage or a manicure at the in-house Third Court Salon and Day Spa.

If you've got money to spare, the place to stay is **MacCallum House** (45020 Albion St., 800/609-0492, www.maccallumhouse.com, $150–395). With several properties in addition to the main hotel in Mendocino Village, MacCallum is the king of luxury on the Mendo coast. Choose from private cottages with hot

© LANCE SCOTT

Sweetwater Inn and Spa

tubs, suites with jetted baths, and regular rooms with opulent antique appointments. The woodwork gleams and the service pleases here. Note that a two-night minimum is required on weekends, and a three-night minimum goes into effect for most holidays.

The **Stanford Inn** (Comptche Ukiah Rd., about 0.5 mile past the Hwy. 1 intersection, 800/331-8884, www.stanfordinn.com, $225–500) is one of the largest accommodations in the Mendocino area. This resort hotel sits up away from the beaches, surrounded by redwood forest. Gardens surround the resort (in fact there's a nursery on the property), perfect for an after-dinner stroll. The location is convenient to hiking and only a short drive down to Mendocino Village and the coastline. Guest room have beautiful honey wood-paneled walls, pretty furniture, and puffy down comforters. You'll get the feel of an upscale forest lodge, whether you choose a basic Big River Room or one of the many varieties of suites. If you're traveling with a larger group, consider one of the elegant two-bedroom suites. (Be aware that

here "executive suite" means "junior suite.") All rooms include breakfast at Ravens, a wood-burning fireplace, a TV with DVD player, a stereo, and Internet access.

One of the few true inns in Fort Bragg, the **Grey Whale Inn** (615 N. Main St., Fort Bragg, 800/382-7244, www.greywhaleinn .com, $165–215) was once a community hospital. The blocky Craftsman-era building was erected by the Union Lumber Company in 1915. Today, 13 spacious, simply appointed guest rooms welcome travelers. Whether you get a view of the water or a more pedestrian city view, you'll get a lovely individually decorated room with a private bath and queen or king bed, perhaps covered by an old-fashioned quilt. The inn prides itself on simplicity and friendliness, and its perfect location in the heart of downtown Fort Bragg makes visitors feel right at home walking to dinner or the beach.

The **Auberge Mendocino** (8200 N. Hwy. 101, Little River, 800/347-9252, www.auberge mendocino.com, $160–325) is an elegant Victorian with a sweeping common area and four generous guest rooms. The lovely room appointments mix antiques and modern items, and the beds are supremely comfortable. You'll feel relaxed and at home with the designer-style fabrics, original artwork, and real plants and flowers. Be prepared for a huge breakfast in the morning, and if you can snag a slice of the owner's pear bread, take it—in fact, take two! A pretty garden leads out to a path that in turn picks up a trail right out to the ocean. On a nice summer day, you can walk from the inn to the secluded beach with a picnic lunch and enjoy yourself without ever getting in your car.

Over $250

Making a refreshing change of pace from the endless North Coast Victorian inns, **Stevenswood Spa Resort** (8211 N. Hwy. 1, Little River, 800/421-2810, www.stevenswood .com, $166–1,000) offers contemporary lodgings in a contemporary lodge. The emphasis here lies in relaxation and pampering. Two restaurants and a day spa help towards this end, as do the convenient beaches and forestlands of Van Damme State Park, which surrounds the resort on three sides. When you book your room, also be sure to book one of the outdoor in-ground hot tubs at the spa for a relaxing evening with your sweetie. After your tub appointment, your ultra-luxurious room with its bright white linens, memory foam mattress, sparkling picture windows, modern furniture, and peaceful appointments will seem the perfect haven in which to snuggle down and sleep.

FOOD

Mendocino prides itself on leading the California art scene, and the art of food is no exception. Some of the best cuisine in the state hides in small restaurants on the Mendo coast. It's hard to catch it all, so just try to hit as many different dining spots as you can.

American

Visitors and locals alike can find themselves growing weary of the endless parade of haute cuisine served on the Mendocino coast. For a more down-to-earth meal, try the **Mendocino Café** (10451 Lansing St., Mendocino Village, 707/937-6141, lunch daily from 11 A.M., dinner daily from 5 P.M., $12–26) for a bowl of soup, salad, or filling sandwich. Granted, this is simpler food California-style; the lunch menu's focal point is its burrito bar, while Asian flavors populate the salad menu. At dinnertime, you'll find things like Thai burritos and barbecued ribs on offer. The café has a small kid's menu, a wine list, and a beer list. The café sits right in the midst of the gardens of downtown Mendocino Village—yes, that's a giant American flag with Rosie the Riveter on the side of the older building.

California

It's strange that one of the best restaurants in an area known for its haute California cuisine is an open, airy bistro. **❰ Mendo Bistro** (301 N. Main St., Fort Bragg, 707/964-4974, www.

© LANCE SCOTT

breakfast, Auberge Mendocino

mendobistro.com, nightly 5–9 P.M., $10–28) wins with an unusual menu, dedication to local ingredients, and just plain great food. An unusual and fun culinary option is to create your own entrée from a pick-it-yourself menu of meats and vegetables you can mix and match with different sauces and cooking methods. In season be sure to try the award winning crab cakes. The restaurant sits upstairs on the balcony of the historical multi-use building, and no walls block your view of the other upstairs shops or the entrance below. The whole bistro feels completely open and airy, with a casual atmosphere that makes diners in jeans feel just as comfortable as those in dress clothes. If you're lucky, you might catch a glimpse of local celebrity chef-owner Nicholas Petti—he's the one in the chef's whites, funky cap, pirate's beard, and gold hoop earring.

French

Café Beaujolais (961 Ukiah St., Mendocino Village, 707/937-5614, www.cafebeaujolais .com, lunch Wed.–Sun. 11:30 A.M.–2:30 P.M., dinner nightly from 5:30 P.M., $24–42) is a stand-out French-California restaurant in an area dense with great upscale cuisine. This charming out-of-the-way spot sits a few blocks away from the center of downtown Mendocino Village in a creeper-covered older home. Despite the white tablecloths and fancy crystal, the atmosphere here is casual at lunchtime and gets only a little bit more formal at the dinner hour. In step with California trends for sustainability, the giant salads and delectable entrées are made with organic produce, humanely raised meats, and locally caught seafood. Beware: The portions can be enormous, but you can get half-sized portions just by asking. Having trouble deciding what to order? Ask the wait staff, who are friendly, helpful, and quite knowledgeable about the menu and wine list, and the attractions of the local area, for that matter. Online reservations are available directly from the restaurant's website.

Mexican

Perched improbably beside the entrance of MacKerricher State Park, the reputed best margaritas in all of Mendocino county are blended at the **Purple Rose Mexican Restaurant** (24300 N. Hwy. 1, Fort Bragg, 707/964-6507). While many locals find the food only average, it's said that if you just have a 'rita or two beforehand, you won't care too much about the cuisine.

Seafood

Along the coast and with the small fishing and crabbing fleet of Fort Bragg's Noyo Harbor, it's natural that lots of seafood restaurants cluster nearby. For the most authentic, fresh, and simple fish preparations, head down to the harbor to any one of the several ultra-casual restaurants and fish markets. This harbor deals in salmon, mussels, and, of course, Dungeness crab, all in their seasons. You can try the regrettably named **Nemo's Fish Market & Grill** (32410 N. Harbor Dr., Fort Bragg, 707/964-1600) or the ratty-looking but tasty **Carine's Fish Grotto** (32430 N. Harbor Dr., 707/964-2429)—try the clam chowder! Another option is **Sharon's by the Sea** (32096 N. Harbor Dr., Fort Bragg, 707/962-0680, www.sharonsbythesea.com, daily 11:30 A.M.–3 P.M., 5 P.M.–close, $16–26), which boasts expensive prices, good service, and fabulous views.

Vegetarian

Vegetarians and omnivores alike rave about **Ravens** (0.5 mile past Hwy. 1 on Comptche Ukiah Rd., 800/331-8884, www.stanfordinn .com/ravens.html, breakfast daily from 7:30 A.M., dinner daily from 5:30 P.M., $17–25) at the Stanford Inn. Inside the lodge-style building surrounded by lush organic gardens, you'll find a big open dining room. Many of the vegetarian and vegan dishes served here use produce from the inn's own organic farm; otherwise, Ravens purchases from local organic and sustainable farmers whenever possible. At breakfast, enjoy delectable vegetarian (or vegan with tofu) scrambles, omelets, and Florentines, complete with homemade breads and English muffins. At dinnertime, try one of the unique salads or a seasonal vegetarian entrée. Even the wine list reflects the restaurant's commitment to its cause—most vintages come from organic, biodynamic, and sustainable-practice wineries. (Luckily for wine lovers, some of the best and most prestigious wineries in California use such practices.)

Bakery and Dessert

Despite the often drizzly overcast weather, denizens and visitors to the Mendocino Coast crave ice cream in the summertime. **Cowlick's Ice Cream** (250 N. Main St., Fort Bragg, 707/962-9271, www.cowlicksicecream.com) serves delectable handmade ice creams in a variety of flavors. Yes, they really do serve mushroom ice cream during the famous fall Mendo mushroom season. You can get the perennial favorite flavors, such as vanilla, chocolate, coffee, and strawberry. If you're lucky, you might also find your favorite sometime-specialty flavor (banana daiquiri, cinnamon, green tea) on tap when you visit. If you're not in downtown Fort Bragg, you can also find this ultra-local family-owned chain at the Mendocino Botanical Gardens, Frankie's Ice Cream Parlor in Mendocino Village, and on the Skunk Train.

An unusual but tasty place to grab a latte and a pastry is the **Mendocino Cookie Company** (301 N. Main St, Fort Bragg, 707/964-0282, www.mendocinocookies.com). Their house special is obvious and baked on-site, making the storefront smell heavenly each morning. They prepare more than a dozen types of cookies, plus scones and croissants and other breakfast pastries. You'll usually find a line out the door of the tiny spot (which sits in the same building as the Mendo Bistro) as locals favor the coffee and espresso drinks. Most of the cookies lean heavily on the chocolate, but the cinnamon-sugar and ginger spice varieties are the bomb.

Farmers Markets

Local, sustainable produce is a staple of Mendocino County food culture. On the coast, you can choose between three weekly farmers markets, open May through October.

Fort Bragg hosts a market at Laurel and Franklin Streets 3:30–6 P.M. on Wednesdays. **Mendocino's** market appears on Fridays noon–2 P.M. at the corner of Howard and Main Streets. And farther south, the **Gualala** market opens 10 A.M.–12:30 P.M. on Saturdays at the Gualala Community Center.

INFORMATION AND SERVICES

As a major tourist destination, the Mendocino coast region offers more services than you might expect for a string of small towns on a craggy stretch of coast. For the most urban atmosphere, complete with supermarkets and big-box stores, head for Fort Bragg.

The **Mendocino Coast Chamber of Commerce and Visitors Center** in Fort Bragg (332 N. Main St., 707/961-6300, www.mendocinocoast.com) gets travelers the maps, brochures, and information they need to have a great time in Mendocino County.

The major daily newspapers you might find in Mendocino are the *San Francisco Chronicle* and the *Santa Rosa Press Democrat.* In the visitors center and many of the inns and businesses, you'll find a wealth of tourist and travel publications. Both Mendocino Village (10500 Ford St.) and Fort Bragg (1605 Reilly St.) have **post offices,** as do Little River (7748 N. Hwy. 1) and Albion (3350 Albion Ridge Rd.).

The **Mendocino Coast District Hospital** (700 River Dr. at Cypress St., Fort Bragg, 707/961-4652, www.mcdh.org) has the closest full-service emergency room.

GETTING THERE AND AROUND
Car

Most folks travel around the Mendocino coast by automobile. Highway 1 is the main drag all the way from Elk up through Mendocino to Fort Bragg and beyond. If you're in Mendocino Village on a festival weekend, expect to have trouble finding parking downtown. Be prepared to pay premium event and lot fees, or to walk a good distance into the downtown area.

Coming up to Mendo from the Bay Area

or from the northern reaches of California? The "short way" takes you up U.S. 101, then across the mountains to the coast via one of the passes. CA-20 takes you from Willits to Fort Bragg in the north, which is the shortest route from U.S. 101 to Highway 1. The longer route, CA-128, runs from Cloverdale to a spot south of Albion on the coast. Beware, especially if you're traveling at night, that these pass roads are narrow and twisty. Slow down and take your time getting through to be safe. All together, it takes about 2.5 hours to get from the City up to Mendo.

The longer but undeniably more beautiful way to get to Mendocino is to jump on Highway 1 just past the Golden Gate (or at any point north of Mendo). Expect to spend several hours traversing the cliffs and beaches, taking time to stop and take photos if you've gotten lucky enough to pick a sunny day.

Air

The nearest major airports to Mendocino are San Francisco and Oakland International. You can also fly in to the **Sonoma County Airport** (2290 Airport Blvd., Santa Rosa, 707/565-7243, www.sonomacountyairport.org) on Horizon Air from Los Angeles, Seattle, Portland, or Las Vegas.

Bus

The **Mendocino Transit Authority** (800/696-4682, www.4mta.org) runs bus service throughout the county. Ukiah acts as the hub for the MTA, but you can catch buses in Mendocino Village and Fort Bragg as well.

Mendocino Wine Region

Mendocino's interior valley might not be quite so glamorous as the coast, but it is home to history, art, and liquor. The Anderson Valley is the apex of Mendocino's wine region, though the tiny town of Hopland also boasts its share of tasting rooms. Ukiah, the county seat, is home to a number of microbreweries and a thriving agricultural industry. The apples from the Anderson Valley and the pears from Ukiah are some of the best fruit in the state. Up in determinedly funky Willits, a late 1960s art vibe thrives in the 21st century.

Unlike the chilly, windy coast, the interior valleys of Mendocino get *hot* in the summertime. Bring shorts, a swimsuit, and an air-conditioned car if you plan to visit in the months from June to September.

WINERIES

The two best areas in which to taste wine in Mendocino County are the Anderson Valley and the miniscule town of Hopland. You can cover either one thoroughly in half a day, or do both in one long day.

Anderson Valley

The Anderson Valley wine trail, also known as CA-128, begins in Boonville and continues northwest toward the coast. Watch for wild turkeys and flocks of quail scuttling in the vineyards. The largest of these is **Navarro** (5601 Hwy. 128, 707/895-3686, www.navarrowine.com, daily 10 A.M.–5 P.M.). A broad-ranging winery with a large estate vineyard and event center, Navarro offers a range of tasty wines as well as some interesting specialty products such as verjuice. Another big name in the Anderson Valley, **Scharffenberger Cellars** (8501 Hwy. 128, 707/895-2957, www.scharffenbergercellars.com, daily 11 A.M.–5 P.M., tasting $3) makes chocolate in Berkeley and wine in Mendocino. While the wine isn't much to write home about, the tasting room is elegant and unusually child-friendly.

Small boutique wineries cluster in the Anderson Valley, enjoying an area less crowded than Napa or Sonoma. Any of these are worth a visit to seek out gem wines that aren't available in shops. **Handley Cellars** (3151 Hwy. 128, 707/895-3876, www.handleycellars.com, daily 10 A.M.–5 P.M., until 6 P.M. May.–Oct.) offers a complimentary tasting of hand-crafted wines you probably won't see in your local grocery store. The intriguing Handley tasting room features folk art from around the world for show and sale. Books on wine are sold too, especially those that focus on women making and drinking wine. **Esterlina** (1200 Holmes Ranch Rd., 707/895-2920, www.esterlina vineyards.com, tastings by appointment only) boasts the best view in the valley—come close to sunset if you can. Beyond the spectacular vineyard vistas, Esterlina tastes a unique selection of sparkling and still wines that make it well worth the trip to the top of its hill.

In a valley full of great wineries, **Roederer Estate** (4501 Hwy. 128, 707/895-2288, www .roedererestate.com, daily 11 A.M.–5 P.M., tasting fee) sparkles. The California sparkling wines they create are some of the best you'll taste. The large tasting room features a bar with sweeping views of the estate vineyards and huge cases filled with Roederer's well-deserved awards. Pourers are knowledgeable here, and you'll get to taste from magnum bottles—a rarity in any winery. Be sure to ask for a taste of Roederer's rarely seen still wines—you might find something wonderful.

For visitors who prefer a cold beer to a glass of wine, **Anderson Valley Brewing Company** (17700 Hwy. 253, 707/895-2337, www.avbc .com, Sat.–Mon. 11 A.M.–6 P.M., Thurs. 1–6 P.M., Fri. 11 A.M.–7 P.M., with longer hours in summer) serves up an array of microbrews that changes each year and each season. The warehouse-sized beer hall has a bar, a number of tables, and a good-sized gift shop. A beer garden out back is comfortable in spring and fall, and a disc golf course out back is popular with tourists and locals alike.

Hopland

To get to the best wineries in Hopland, you never need to leave U.S. 101. The highway runs right through the center of town, and almost all the tasting rooms sit right against it. The star of this mini-region is **Brutocao Cellars** (13500 S. U.S. 101, 800/433-3689, www.brutocao cellars.com). Their vineyards crowd the land surrounding the town, and they took over the old high school to create their tasting room and restaurant complex. The wide, stone-tiled tasting room houses exceptional wines poured by knowledgeable staff. A sizeable gift shop offers gourmet goodies under the Brutacao label.

Can't get enough of Brutocao? They've got

BOONTLING: THE NORTH COAST DIALECT

Take your oddly broken English, throw in some old Scottish and Irish, add a pinch of Spanish and a dash of Pomo, then season with real names and allusions to taste. Speak among friends and family in an isolated community for a dozen years or more. The results: Boontling.

Boontling is a unique and almost dead language developed by the denizens of the then-remote town of Boonville in the Anderson Valley late in the 19th century. The beginnings of Boontling are obscured by time since all the originators of the language are "piked for dusties – that is, in the cemetery. And many Boonters – speakers of Boontling – are intensely protective of the local lingo. But in the 1960s, Professor Charles C. Adams of Cal State Chico came to town to study the language. He gradually gained the trust of the locals, and was able to write a doctoral thesis eventually published as a book, *Boontling: An American Lingo*. The book documents the history and acts as a dictionary for the more than 1,000 Boontling terms on record.

So if you find yourself in the Horn of Zeese (a café named for the Boontling term for "cup of coffee") and hear older folks speaking a language like none you've ever heard, you might just be listening to a rare and endangered conversation in Boontling.

another tasting room out in the Anderson Valley (7000 Hwy. 128).

For folks who love wine but hate crowds, the tiny wineries and tasting rooms in Hopland are the perfect place to relax, enjoy sipping each vintage, and really chat with the pourer who just might be the winemaker and owner too. **Burford & Brown** (13265 S. U.S. 101, Ste. 5, 707/744-8781, www.burfordandbrown.com) is one of these. Step into the narrow tasting room to get the real story of each wine poured. Right next door, **Graziano** (13251 S. U.S. 101, 707/744-8466, www.grazianofamilyofwines .com, daily 10 A.M.–5 P.M.) provides another great small winery experience. Across the street, **McDowell Valley Vineyards** (13380 S. U.S. 101, 707/744-8911, www.mcdowellsyrah .com, Mon.–Fri. 11 A.M.–5 P.M., Sat.–Sun. 10 A.M.–5 P.M., free) inhabits a weathered old general store, complete with a central counter that's now the wine bar. Check out the cool kitchen kitsch as you enjoy your tasting.

Driving north out of town, the highway passes through acres of vineyards spreading out toward the forest in all directions. Many of these grapes belong to **Jeriko** (12141 Hewlitt and Sturtevant Rd., 707/744-1140, www.jer-iko.us, Apr.–Dec. daily 10 A.M.–5 P.M., Jan.–Mar. daily 11 A.M.–4 P.M.). Visitors drive right between the chardonnay and the cabernet to get to the immense Napa-style tasting room. A glass wall exposes the barrel room with aging wines stacked high, tempting tasters to learn their secrets.

SIGHTS
City of 10,000 Buddhas

Treat respectfully when you visit the Sagely City of 10,000 Buddhas (4951 Bodhi Way, Ukiah, 707/462-0939, www.cttbusa.org). This active Buddhist college and monastery asks that guests wear modest clothing (try to avoid short shorts and short skirts, bare chests, and skimpy tank tops) and keep their voices down out of re-spect for the nuns and monks who make their lives here. Still, there's plenty for the spiritually curious to see here. The showpiece is the tem-ple, which really does contain 10,000 golden Buddha statues. An extensive gift and book shop provides slightly silly souvenirs as well as serious scholarly text on Buddhism. For a treat, stop in for lunch at the vegan restaurant on the grounds, open to the public most afternoons.

Solar Living Center

The Solar Living Center (13771 S. U.S. 101, Hopland, 707/744-2017, www.solarliving.org) successfully demonstrates what life might be like without petroleum. In Hopland, it's pretty darn good. The center presents a wide array of per-maculture exhibits, from the organic garden to the solar-powered water system to the showpiece gift shop. The completely recycled bathrooms are worth a look even if you just went. If your vehicle happens to run on biodiesel, you can fill your tank here. For all travelers interested in ecological living, the center is a must-see.

Grace Hudson Museum and Sun House

One of the few truly cultural offerings in Ukiah is the Grace Hudson Museum (431 S. Main St., Ukiah, 707/467-2836, www.gracehudson museum.org, Wed.–Sat 10 A.M.–4:30 P.M., Sun. noon–4:30 P.M.). This small set of galler-ies focuses on the life and work of artist Grace Hudson and her husband Dr. John Hudson. The couple's life work revolved, among other things, around the history and culture of the Pomo and other Native Americans. The per-manent collection of the museum includes many of Grace's paintings, a number of Pomo baskets, and the works of dozens of other California artists. For visitors whose imagi-nations are captured by the Hudsons' work, the museum offers docent-guided tours of the Sun House, which sits adjacent to the main museum building. This 1911 Craftsman-style house was in fact the eclectic and Bohemian Hudsons' home.

ENTERTAINMENT AND EVENTS
Bars and Clubs

While the daytime in Mendocino wine country is given over to the vino, the nightlife focuses around beer. Ukiah has a couple of top-notch brewpubs where you can a delicious pint of handcrafted brew.

The **Hopland Brew Pub** (13351 S. U.S. 101, Hopland, 707/744-1361, www.mendobrew .com, Wed.–Mon. noon–7 P.M.) serves some of the best local beer in the region. Mendocino Brewing Company produces one of California quaffers' favorite beers: Red Tail Ale. But don't stop at the Red Tail, and try some of the brewery's other great bird-named beers. Step inside the old red-brick square in downtown Hopland and you'll find a true traditional bar. It's dark, the wood is smooth and well worn, and regulars perch on barstools knocking back their favorite local brews.

For a later night out on the tiny town of Hopland, head for the bar downstairs in the **Hopland Inn** (13401 S. U.S. 101, Hopland, 800/266-1891, www.hoplandin.com, Sun.–Tues. and Thurs. 4–10 P.M., Fri.–Sat. 4–11 P.M., closed Wed., bar may be open later). Grab a barstool (if the locals don't have them all) and order a glass of local wine, a pint of local beer, or one of the wonderful single-malt scotches. On weekends, the restaurant often hosts local musical acts, livening up the night for restaurant and bar-goers alike.

The **Ukiah Brewing Company** (102 S. State St., Ukiah, 707/468-5898, www.ukiah brewingco.com, Sun. 11:30 A.M.–9 P.M., Mon.–Thurs. 11:30 A.M.–11 P.M., Fri.–Sat. 11:30 P.M.–1 A.M.) offers good beer and good entertainment several nights each week. Settle in with a pilsner or an amber ale and enjoy the live music and other weekend evening entertainment. You might even get a chance to strut yourself at an open mic night.

Festivals and Events

For the last 12 years, the Solar Living Center of Hopland has taken a weekend in August to put on "the greenest show on earth": **SolFest** (www.solfest.org). The hundreds of displays, demonstrations, and workshops go far beyond just solar power to teach and exemplify the ever-expanding world of permaculture and renewable energy. Keynote speakers each year include top names from the world of ecological activism and science. But it's not all serious business at SolFest; musicians perform on the main stage and the Saturday Night Moondance features entertainment and DJs for eco-lovers who love to dance deep into the night.

SPORTS AND RECREATION
Boating and Fishing

Even though a dry heat pervades inland Mendocino County in the summertime, a surprising range of water recreation is available. **Lake Mendocino** (www.lakemendocino .com) is an artificial lake along the Russian River that's held in place by Coyote Dam. It sits just off U.S. 101 north of Ukiah, allowing residents and visitors the chance to powerboat and water-ski, as well as canoe, kayak, and fish. Shockingly uncrowded even on the hottest summer afternoons, this locals' favorite is a great spot to cool off. You can even find a few beaches and lawns on which to spread out a blanket and lie down and shaded picnic tables where you can enjoy lunch.

You can access the lake from Lake Mendocino Drive, Calpella Drive, and a few other local roads off the freeway. Five marinas and two boat ramps sit along the shores of the lake, catering to boaters. A number of campgrounds also circle the lake—some are boat-in only.

Hiking and Biking

The best hiking and biking trails in the area run in and around the Anderson Valley, where evergreen forests shade hikers from the worst of the summer heat. At **Hendy Redwoods State Park** (a half-mile south of CA-128 on Philo-Greenwood Rd., 707/895-3141, www.parks .ca.gov), you can hike to two old-growth redwood groves. For an easy shaded walk, visit the **Big Hendy** grove via its self-guided nature trail. This trail is wheelchair-accessible and perfect for folks looking for a sedate forest walk. Another fun little hike with some slope is the moderate **Hermit's Hut Trail**—yes, Hendy used to have its very own hermit. No one resides in the tree-stump hut anymore, though it remains a curiosity for hikers. Fit hikers who love longer treks can weave around the whole of the park; Big Hendy Loop connects to the Fire Road, which connects to the Hermit's Hut Trail, which intersects to the Azalea Loop and on down to the Little Hendy Loop for a complete survey of the park's best regions.

Another great place to take a nice, cool, shady hike is **Montgomery Woods State Nature Reserve** (Orr Springs Rd., 13 miles west of Ukiah, 707/937-5804, www.parks.ca.gov). This remote redwoods park is less crowded than its more accessible and popular brethren. The quintessential hike at Montgomery runs along **Montgomery Creek** (3 miles, moderate). Here you get a chance to see something special and unusual—both the Coastal and Giant Sequoia varieties of redwood tree growing in the same park. Montgomery's location and climate make it hospitable to both types of tree, which usually grow hundreds of miles apart.

Spas

Wine and spas seem to go together naturally—perhaps it's the luxury factor. The most famous and historic spa in all of California sits tranquil and serene at the edge of Ukiah. Since its establishment in 1854, **Vichy Springs** (2605 Vichy Springs Rd., Ukiah, 707/462-9515, www.vichysprings.com, treatments $100–150 per hour, $40 non-resort all-day guest access to baths) has been patronized by Mark Twain, Jack London, Ulysses S. Grant, Teddy Roosevelt, and Jerry Brown. The hot springs, both mineral-heavy and naturally carbonated, closely resemble the world-famous waters of their namesake at Vichy in France. Spa-goers can view the source of the water bubbling out of the ground adjacent to the private bathhouses and the open-air hot pool. The water fills the baths, hot pool, and Olympic swimming pool. Day spa services include Swedish massage, hot stone massage, and facial-plus-massage treatments.

At the north end of the county in the artsy town of Willits, the **Baechtel Creek Day Spa** (101 Gregory Ln., Willits, 707/459-9063) offers a wide range of spa and aesthetic treatments. The

serene woodsy retreat completes a relaxing day of pampering and beautifying. In the heart of downtown Ukiah, **Tranquility Day Spa** (203 S. State St., Ukiah, 707/463-2189, http://tranquilitydayspaukiah.com) caters to the hippie side of this culturally divided town. Swirling curtains match well with the sandalwood incense that pervades the big warehouse space. Tranquility has both salon and spa services—what's better than a new haircut *and* a relaxing massage?

ACCOMMODATIONS

Accommodation options in and around the Anderson Valley vary widely. In the Valley proper you're more likely to find funky hotels and cabins, or forest-shaded campgrounds. Ukiah specializes in generic national chain motels from the modest to the mid-tier, and Hopland and Willits run to old-school independent hotels and motels.

Camping

Stylish lodgings aren't thick on the ground in the Anderson Valley proper, but you can still find a pleasant place to stay near the wineries. For wine and nature lovers on a budget, the campgrounds at **Indian Creek County Park** (Hwy. 128 at mile marker 23.48, 1 mile east of Philo, 707/463-4267, $10) and **Hendy Woods State Park** (8 miles northwest of Boonville, 0.5 mile south of Hwy. 128 on Philo-Greenwood Rd., 707/895-3141, www.parks.ca.gov, $20–25) provide woodsy, shady camp sites.

Under $100

The **Anderson Valley Inn** (8480 Hwy. 128, Philo, 707/895-3325, www.avinn.com, $85–200), between Boonville and Philo, makes the perfect spot from which to divide your time between the Anderson Valley and the Mendocino coast. Eight small rooms are done up in bright colors and attractive appointments. Expect a small space with homey bedspreads that match the casual exterior of the small multi-building inn. A butterfly-filled garden invites guests to sit out on the porches reading the paper and sipping coffee. The two

two-bedroom suites have full kitchens and are perfect for travelers looking to stay in the area a bit longer. The friendly owners welcome children and dogs (both must be attended at all times) and can be incredibly helpful with hints about how best to explore the region. This inn often books up fast on summer weekends, as it's one of the best value accommodations in the region. There's a two-night minimum on weekends May–October.

$100-150

⊞ The Hopland Inn (13401 S. U.S. 101, 800/266-1890, www.hoplandinn.com, $120–150) was the original hostelry of Hopland. In 1890, William Wallace Thatcher strove to create an elegant hotel to rival those in San Francisco, so he built a large structure with more than 40 guest rooms, soaring ceilings, and elegant woodwork. Visitors today will find the creature comforts—such as air conditioning, huge bathrooms, and luxurious linens—updated to suit modern tastes. But the large rooms themselves remain as they were more than 100 years ago, with Victorian floral wallpaper and large antique furniture. Suites are also available. The bar and dining room welcome guests to enjoy a leisurely evening of drinking and dining, while the library filled with books to appeal to guests who prefer quiet literary contemplation. A complimentary buffet breakfast in the dining room each morning completes the inn experience.

In Ukiah, the plentiful lodging options run to standard chain motels. Out by the airport, the **Fairfield Inn** (1140 Airport Park Blvd., 707/463-3600, www.marriott.com, $115–165) is a comfortable choice. With an elegant lobby, indoor pool and spa, small exercise room, and generous complimentary continental breakfast, guests are comfortable and content in this motel. The guest rooms are about what you'd expect of a decent mid-priced chain: floral spreads, durable nondescript carpets, and comfortable and clean bathrooms. Next door, the **Hampton Inn** (1160 Airport Park Blvd., 707/462-6555, www. hamptoninnukiah.com) offers attractive rooms, an outdoor pool and spa, high-speed Internet access, and a buffet breakfast.

$150-250

In the midst of Boonville, the quaint **Boonville Hotel** (14050 Hwy. 128, 707/895-2210, www .boonvillehotel.com, $140–310) pulls a switcheroo. The rough, weathered exterior belies the updated, comfortable guest rooms hiding inside this small-town hotel. Each of the 10 rooms is bright and airy, with light-colored, up-to-date furniture and an attractive collection of mismatched decorations. If you're traveling with children or pets, request one of the rooms that's set up to accommodate them. Downstairs, you'll find big, comfortable common areas and a huge garden suitable for strolling. Amenities include a book and gift shop, a good-sized bar, and a dining room. For a relaxing treat, book one of the rooms with a balcony—they come with a hammock set up and ready for napping.

FOOD
American

A locals' favorite, the **Maple Restaurant** (295 S. State St., Ukiah, 707/462-5221, breakfast and lunch daily, $10) serves excellent and inexpensive breakfast and lunch fare. Excellent service complements good, uncomplicated American-style food. Shockingly good coffee makes a final charming touch to this lovely find.

The **Highpockety Ox** (14081 Hwy. 128, 707/895-2792, $10–20) touts itself a "civilized saloon." Indeed the atmosphere is about the best thing about this eatery. Meal prices are high and fare is basic, and clearly the dining room caters to the wine-tasting tourist crowd. But the bar is another high point. Most of the beer served at the Ox is locally brewed—just down the road at the Anderson Valley Brewing Company, in fact. Locals cluster at the bar and greet the bartender and wait staff as old friends, and visitors might even catch a syllable or two of Boontling.

California

The tiny town of Hopland boasts few restaurants, but those available are worth the stop. The restaurant at the **Hopland Inn** (13401 S.

U.S. 101, 800/266-1891, www.hoplandinn
.com) serves dinner to inn guests and visitors
alike. Locals prefer the big bar area, while diners
are ushered in to the cavernous dining room or
out to the pleasant two-level patio area. For late
evening dining in the summertime, the patio
is absolutely the place to be—the Inn hosts live
musicians several times each week, and as the
air cools into evening, the temperature becomes
perfect. The menu is an innovative selection of
California cuisine, and the wine list is a who's-
who of local vintners. You might easily buy a
bottle of something you tasted just across the
street earlier in the afternoon.

Of the dining options in Ukiah, one of
the very best is **Patrona** (130 W. Standley
St., Ukiah, 707/462-9181, www.patrona
restaurant.com, Tues.–Sat., 5:30–9 P.M., $15–
30), where especially innovative California
cuisine is served in a bistro-casual atmosphere
by attentive servers. Portions are good-sized
but not enormous, and the attention to detail
from the kitchen is impressive. The wine list
features all sorts of Mendocino County vintages, plus a good range of European wines.
Most wines are available by the bottle only,
but the servers will gladly cork an unfinished
bottle for you and let you take it home to enjoy
the following day.

Italian

The Crushed Grape (13500 S. U.S. 101
Hopland, 707/744-2020, www.brutocaoschool
houseplaza.com, Tues.–Sat. 11 A.M.–9 P.M.,
$10–20) is attached to the Brutocao tasting
room. This elegant bistro features upscale
Italian cuisine and house wines. The Lion
Bistro is also part of the Brutocao complex,
offering diners a more casual experience.

Farmers Markets

A picnic makes a perfect lunch in the Anderson
Valley, and farmers markets and farm stands
can supply fresh local ingredients. The farmers market happens in Boonville on Saturday
mornings 9 A.M.–1 P.M. It draws a crowd, so
be prepared to hunt for parking. For fresh
fruit and vegetables every day, try **Gowan's**

Oak Tree Farm Stand (Hwy. 128, 2.5 miles
north of Philo, daily 8:30 A.M.–5:30 P.M.). The
stand belongs to the local farm of the same
name, and sells only in-season local produce
and homemade products made with the same
fruits and veggies.

INFORMATION AND SERVICES

If you need assistance with local lodgings, dining, or wine tasting, one place to find it is at
the **Ukiah Chamber of Commerce** (200 S.
School St. Ukiah, 707/462-4705, www.ukiah
chamber.com). As the county seat, it offers
plenty of information about both the city of
Ukiah and the county of Mendocino.

For national news, most Mendocino residents read the *San Francisco Chronicle.* But
if you want a paper with more local flavor, pick
up a copy of the *Ukiah Daily Journal* (www
.ukiahdailyjournal.com). This local daily paper
can give the best in up-to-date entertainment
and events throughout your visit.

The **Ukiah Valley Medical Center** (275
Hospital Dr., Ukiah, 707/462-3111, www
.uvmc.org) has a 24-hour emergency room as
part of its full service hospital, just in case.

As a good-sized city, Ukiah has branches of
many major national banks. You'll find ATMs
in many of the usual places: bank branches,
supermarkets, pharmacies, and such. Internet
access is available (often for a fee) at many of
the chain motels and of course at the various
Starbucks and other cafés.

You can find one or two ATMs in Hopland
and more in Willits, which has a more modern
big-box retail area at its south end. Check with
your lodgings for Internet access, or stop by a
café in Willits.

You can find **post offices** in Ukiah (224 N.
Oak St.), Willits (315 S. Main St.), Hopland
(13400 S. U.S. 101), and Boonville (14170
Hwy. 128).

GETTING THERE AND AROUND
Car

To get to the Mendocino wine country from

NORTH COAST

either the south or the north in California, find U.S. 101. Drive until you get to Willits in the north or Hopland in the south, then stop.

The Anderson Valley wine road is CA-128, with most of the wineries clustering between Boonville and Philo. You can get to CA-128 from U.S. 101 either directly out of Hopland or from Ukiah on CA-253.

Air

The closest major commercial airports to the Mendocino wine country are San Francisco and Oakland International. General aviation fliers can land at **Ukiah Municipal Airport** (1411 S. State St., Ukiah). From there, it's an easy trip to the heart of the local wine country.

Bus

The **Mendocino Transit Authority** (800/696-4682, www.4mta.org) runs bus service throughout the county. Ukiah acts as the hub for the MTA, but you can catch buses in Mendocino Village and Fort Bragg as well.

Tours

Many of the major wine country touring outfits that operate from San Francisco and the Napa Valley also offer trips in the Anderson Valley. Otherwise, try the folks at **Mendo Wine Tours** (888/805-8687, www.mendowinetours .com), a regional specialist offering a Lincoln Town Car for small groups and an SUV limo for groups of up to 10. Tours include a picnic lunch and expert knowledge of the region.

LAKE TAHOE AND THE NORTHERN SIERRA

The mountains in the far north reaches of California are perhaps the most unspoiled areas in the state, protected by a wealth of national and state parks and forest lands. This region calls to all outdoor recreation enthusiasts—from downhill skiers to wakeboarders to serious hikers and backpackers.

Crystal-blue Lake Tahoe offers some of the best winter and summer outdoor recreation opportunities to be had statewide. Visitors who think that all of California consists of year-round warm, sunny beaches are often shocked to learn that Tahoe's ski resorts are some of the finest in the nation—second only to the Rockies for vertical drop, quality of snow, and number of resorts. In summer, wakeboarders, waterskiers, and families all bring out their favorite toys to play in the pristine waters of the lake and to enjoy the stunning views of the wilderness areas that surround it.

Two mountains are notable as the most prominent features of this region: Shasta and Lassen. The snow-capped peak of Mount Shasta is a familiar picture-postcard sight, and is easily reached on I-5. Mount Shasta is quiet in contrast to Lassen—or at least it is for now. But Mount Shasta is not an extinct volcano; it is merely dormant and scientists are unsure as to when it will erupt again. South of Mount Shasta, its namesake Shasta Lake serves as a major resort area and boating vacation destination for Californians and visitors alike, with plentiful outdoor and indoor pursuits.

Mount Lassen, one of only two active volcanoes in the continental United States, is the more remote of the two and thus more of an

© PETTIT GILWEE / TOM ZIKAS

HIGHLIGHTS

◖ **The Village at Squaw Valley:** This adorable mountainside village, part of the Squaw Valley ski resort, is the perfect place to while away a winter day amid the numerous boutiques, galleries, restaurants, and entertainment (page 276).

◖ **MacArthur-Burney Falls:** Touted as the "the most beautiful waterfall in California," these cascades run year-round and are accessible via a short, easy path (page 297).

◖ **Lake Shasta Caverns:** A quick boat ride across Shasta Lake leads to these wonderful cathedral-like caverns, filled with natural limestone and marble stalactites, stalagmites, and new formations all their own (page 306).

◖ **Loomis Museum and Manzanita Lake:** This interpretive museum offers a history of Lassen's volcanic eruptions through a series of stunning and informative pictorials (page 315).

◖ **Bumpass Hell:** A two-mile hike leads through this hot bed of geothermal activity, including boiling mud pots, fumaroles, steaming springs, and pools of boiling, steaming water (page 316).

LOOK FOR ◖ TO FIND RECOMMENDED SIGHTS, ACTIVITIES, DINING, AND LODGING.

adventure to visit. Here, visitors are exposed to many unique volcanic features, including boiling mud pots, steam vents, and sulfur springs.

South of this mountain region, the city of Redding provides ready access and comparatively cosmopolitan entertainment before heading out to explore these vast outdoor pursuits.

PLANNING YOUR TIME

Any of the major mountains make for a fabulous weekend getaway—particularly if you've got a three-day weekend to play with. Lake Tahoe has numerous recreation options and is usually accessible all year long. Many California residents take even longer trips to Tahoe; one or two week vacations to

this area aren't uncommon because there's so much here to see and do. Mount Shasta and Mount Lassen are far more remote; it takes several hours driving from Tahoe (or most anywhere else in the state) to reach either of these peaks.

Mount Shasta offers fairly easy and reliable year-round access off I-5, plus both winter and summertime outdoor recreation. The weather on and near Shasta can get extreme; expect winter storms half the year and brutally high temperatures in the summer months. Check the weather reports so you pack the right clothes for your trip. If you're planning to climb high up the mountain, be aware that it's high enough to be create its own weather.

The best time to visit Mount Lassen, out in

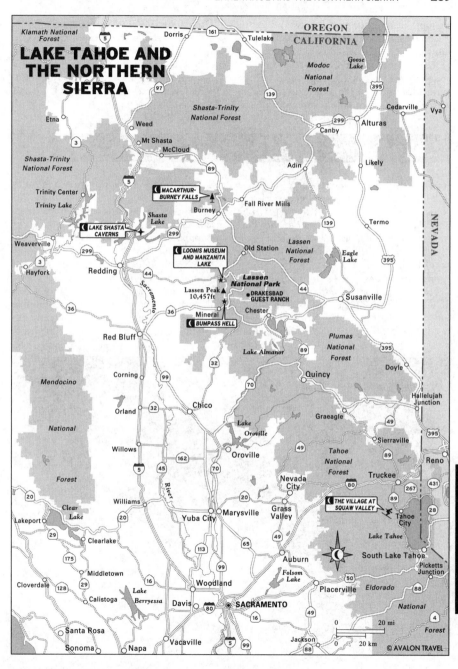

LAKE TAHOE AND THE NORTHERN SIERRA

OREGON
CALIFORNIA

Klamath National Forest

Dorris 161 Tulelake

5

97

Modoc National Forest

Goose Lake

395

Cedarville

Vya

139

Shasta-Trinity National Forest

Etna

Weed

Mt Shasta

McCloud

299 Alturas

Canby

Likely

89

Adin

Termo

Shasta-Trinity National Forest

5

Trinity Center

Trinity Lake

MACARTHUR-BURNEY FALLS

Shasta Lake

Burney

Fall River Mills

139

LAKE SHASTA CAVERNS

299

Old Station

Lassen National Forest

Eagle Lake

395

Weaverville

299

LOOMIS MUSEUM AND MANZANITA LAKE

3

Hayfork

Redding

44

Lassen National Park

Lassen Peak 10,457ft

DRAKESBAD GUEST RANCH

44

Susanville

Sacramento

36

36

Mineral

BUMPASS HELL

Chester

Red Bluff

32

Lake Almanor

89

Plumas National Forest

395

Doyle

Corning

99

Mendocino

Orland

32

Chico

70

Quincy

Hallelujah Junction

Lake Oroville

Graeagle

49

National

Willows

162

70

Oroville

49

Sierraville

395

Tahoe National Forest

89

Reno

Forest

5

45

Nevada City

Truckee

80

267

431

20

Clear Lake

Williams

River

20

20

Marysville

Grass Valley

THE VILLAGE AT SQUAW VALLEY

89

Tahoe City

28

Lakeport

Yuba City

65

49

Lake Tahoe

29

Clearlake

113

Auburn

South Lake Tahoe

Picketts Junction

175

99

Folsom Lake

50

Eldorado

88

Cloverdale

128

29

Middletown

16

Woodland

Placerville

National

Lake Berryessa

Davis

SACRAMENTO

80

4

Santa Rosa

Calistoga

16

Forest

20 mi

Sonoma

Napa

Vacaville

5

99

Jackson

88

0   20 km

© AVALON TRAVEL

a remote eastern corner of the state where the weather gets serious, is the middle to end of summer. It can still be snowy on Lassen as late as June, so keep that in mind when you make your camping plans. During the winter the main road through the park closes, making your visit the region far less interesting.

Don't try to see all three mountains unless you've got a week or so to explore. If you do want to make a California mountains trip, start at Lake Tahoe and make your way up Highway 395 to Susanville and then across to Lassen. Hit Redding next, adding Shasta Lake and Mount Shasta.

Lake Tahoe

Ask a California resident where to go for regular vacations or weekend getaways, and chances are high that at the answer will be 22-mile long Lake Tahoe. Tahoe's azure-blue waters and boulder-strewn shore draw visitors in summer while a plethora of snowy ski hills and forested wilderness draw winter sports enthusiasts.

Californians from the flatlands refer to Lake Tahoe as Tahoe. But the real locals get more specific—it's all about the North Shore versus the South Shore. Drive to the South Shore and you'll find a large town sprawling south along the huge lake, with glittering casinos just across (and I do mean *just* across) the state line. The South Shore offers great lakeshore parks with opportunities to access the water in the summertime.

The North Shore boasts the most downhill ski resorts, many of them clustered around the small, historic town of Truckee. It's possible to drive all the way around the lake, stopping at both shores, state parks, and sights in both California and Nevada.

the shore of Lake Tahoe

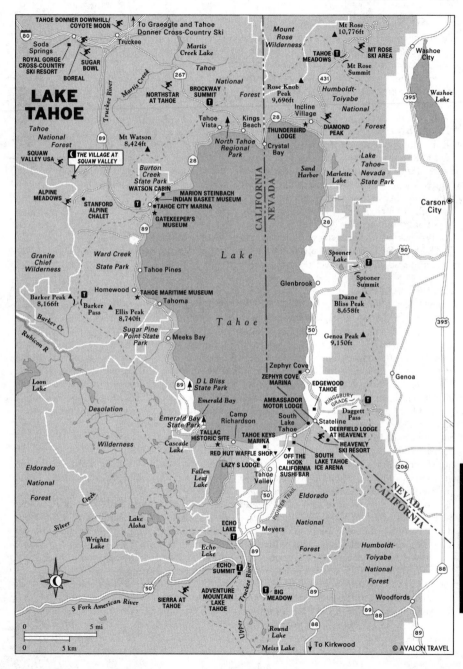

SKI RESORTS

The number-one reason folks come to Tahoe is for the snow. Whether you're a skier or a snowboarder, into cross-country skiing or snowshoeing, or even just want to play in the snow with your kids, Tahoe's got a resort that's perfect for you.

North Shore

Of the more than a dozen ski resorts surrounding Lake Tahoe, most of them sit on the North Shore. Tahoe regulars tend to divide into two camps: those faithful to Squaw Valley, and those in exclusive love with Alpine Meadows. Ne'er the two shall meet. (But skiing at any of the other resorts is acceptable.) Each resort has its own charms, strengths, and weaknesses. The best way to approach them is to try one or more and find your own favorites.

SQUAW VALLEY

Squaw Valley (1960 Squaw Valley Rd., Olympic Valley, 530/583-6985, www.squaw.com, adults $55–73, youth $55, children under 12 $10) was the headquarters of alpine sports during the 1960 Winter Olympic Games. Today it is perhaps *the* most popular ski resort in California. The resort has every amenity you could possibly want and plenty of other activities, but skiing and boarding maintain their number-one precedence here. Squaw has a great ski school with plenty of fun on tap for new skiers and boarders of all ages, and a wide selection of fun intermediate slopes. Some of these, such as those serviced by the Squaw Creek, Red Dog, and Exhibition/Searchlight lifts are long—perfect for skiers who want to spend more time on the snow than on the lifts. But the jewels of Squaw are the many black diamond and double-black diamond slopes and the three terrain parks. Whether you prefer trees, moguls, narrow ridges, or wide open vertical bowls, you'll find your favorite at Squaw. The slopes off KT-22 are legendary with skiers around the world. If you want to try freestyle for the first time, head for Belmont Park. Hardcore freestylers go for The Ford Freestyle Park & Superpipe.

the mountain at Squaw Valley

© LIZ HAMILL SCOTT

Squaw Valley offers night skiing free with a daytime lift ticket, or for a limited nighttime-only fee. During the day, especially on weekends and holidays, expect long lines at the lifts, crowds in the (nice, big) locker rooms, and still more crowds at the (numerous) restaurants and cafés.

ALPINE MEADOWS

The other grand ski resort at Tahoe, Alpine Meadows (2600 Alpine Meadows Rd., Tahoe City, 530/583-4232, www.skialpine.com, mid-Nov.–mid-May, adults $44–63, youth $44–49, children 5–12 $10), sits just one ridge over from Squaw. This sprawling resort encompasses both sides of its two Sierra peaks: Scott and Ward. While Alpine has a ski school and a token small handful of green runs, it is not a beginner's resort. In fact, Alpine devotes considerable area to what it refers to as "Adventure Ski Zones." These are large clusters of black diamond and double-black bowls and runs intended for expert skiers only. A dozen lifts service the mountains, including three high-speed chairs.

An intermediate skier can have a great time at Alpine, especially coming off the Summit Six or the Roundhouse Chairs. Or try the south side—from Scott Peak off the Lakeview Chair, all runs are blues. If you're an expert, well, take just about any chair up the mountain and you'll find hair-raising excitement. The Scott Chair leads to a bunch of single blacks on the front of the mountain, as does the Summit Six Chair at the back of Ward Peak. Summit Six also

GETTING DISCOUNT LIFT TICKETS

The prices for skiing the famous mountains at Tahoe have garnered their own unique infamy. New skiers quickly learn that spending a day on the slopes of Squaw, Alpine, or Heavenly can cost almost as much as spending the night in the nearby hotels. So what's a budget-conscious boarder to do?

Go coupon hunting. Check the racks full of leaflets in Tahoe hotels, or go to the visitors centers. The advertisements for the various ski resorts often include discount coupons for lift tickets, or free rides on the resort ski shuttles. In supermarkets and pharmacies, look at the soda cans and popular snack products – some of these include a lift ticket coupon with proof-of-purchase. (This type of coupon gets popular every winter down on the flat land of Sacramento and the Bay Area.) Mine the Internet by entering "discount coupon [ResortName]" to find any online discounts or tips to find physical coupons.

Ski in the afternoon. If you're a casual skier who only needs a couple of hours on the slopes to feel satisfied, check with your favorite resort for its afternoon rates. Most resorts offer lower-priced lift tickets after 2 or 3 P.M.

Ski a lot in one place. Find your favorite resort and stick to it, taking advantage of the discounts built into two- and three-day (or more) lift passes.

services the famed Granite Chief area double-black slopes. Get to Art's Knob from Sherwood Express or possibly the Alpine Bowl Chair. Terrain parks aren't Alpine's long suit, but you can find three—not too creatively named Small, Medium, and Large—towards the bottom of the front side of the mountain.

NORTHSTAR AT TAHOE

One of the best intermediate resorts in Tahoe, with over 60 percent blue slopes, is Northstar at Tahoe (100 Northstar Dr., Truckee, 800/466-6784, www.northstarattahoe.com, 8:30 A.M.–4 P.M., adults $60–75, youth $52–64, children $19–28). This smaller resort is often a bit less crowded than the big boys, and the slopes can be a bit friendlier here. At Northstar, even beginners can head way up the mountain on the fast Vista Express quad chair and still find green slopes heading gently all the way back to the Village. A "Slow Zone" creates a perfect spot for young children fresh out of ski school and wobbly adults who haven't spent their whole lives on the slopes. Intermediate runs crisscross the front of the mountain starting at the very peak off Comstock and running all the way down the mountain in what seems like every direction. The back side of the mountain, reachable via the Comstock Express quad chair and serviced by the Backside Express, is reserved for black diamond skiers, though adventurous intermediates can test their ski legs here. Freestylers will find the most terrain right off the Vista Express quad, though a couple of other small areas dot the mountain elsewhere.

SUGAR BOWL

Another great mid-tier ski area is Sugar Bowl (629 Sugar Bowl Rd., Norden, 530/426-9000, www.sugarbowl.com, Nov.–May daily 9 A.M.–4 P.M., adults $60–70, youth 12–18 $50–60, children 6–12 $15). With lots of ski-able snow spread across a wide area and plenty of vertical drop, Sugar Bowl can satisfy skiers and boarders of all ability levels. The mix of blue and black runs toward the top of the peaks offers intense variety, with a scattering of double-blacks out toward the edges and down the ridges. At the base near each lodge, green runs make it easy for younger and newer athletes to have a good time in the mountains. This resort offers two base lodges, one at Judah and the other at The Village. The Gondola takes visitors from a lower parking lot up to The Village.

BOREAL

If you can't afford nearly $75 per day to ski, consider one of the smaller resorts near Truckee. Boreal (19659 Boreal Ridge Rd., Soda Springs, 530/426-3666, www.rideboreal .com, Apr.–May daily 9 a.m.–9 p.m., Thanksgiving–Apr. daily, 9 a.m.–4 p.m., adults $44–47, youth $39, children 5–12 $12) feels low-rent compared to Squaw or Alpine, but many Californians found their snow legs at this resort. Boreal offers beginners' ski and snowboard lessons, and a kids' (and adults') ski racing school. From Claimjumper at the center of the resort all the way over to Cedar Ridge at the east edge of the resort, beginner skiers and boarders can have a great time on a number of runs and small bowls. The Accelerator chair serves Boreal's Superpipe and its night skiing area, while the 49er chair services the intermediate and advanced "Core," an area designed for boarders and freestylers. The small back-of-the-mountain offers fun for intermediate skiers who want to avoid the major boarding hot-doggers who favor the front of the mountain. Even on weekends, the lines at Boreal seem pleasingly short compared to the bigger resorts. While the services are minimal, you can get a hot meal, a cup of coffee, and a place to sit at the rather basic ski lodge at the bottom of the hill.

TAHOE DONNER DOWNHILL

Another great beginner hill is Tahoe Donner Downhill (11603 Slalom Way, Truckee, 530/587-9444, 9 a.m.–4 p.m., adults $25–35, children $10–15). With only four lifts (two of them conveyor belts) and 120 skiable acres, Donner seems miniscule. But it's a great spot to bring your family and get a feel for your board or your skis, take a lesson, and enjoy the California snow in the beautiful Tahoe forest.

South Shore

HEAVENLY

On the less-skied South Shore, the queen bee of the few resorts is undoubtedly Heavenly (Wildwood and Saddle, South Lake Tahoe, 775/586-7000, www.skiheavenly.com, call for current hours and prices). Perhaps the most sprawling of any Tahoe ski resort, avid skiers can choose from four lodge/village access points up to the ski area: Heavenly Village and California Lodge down by the lake and in the South Shore downtown area, and Boulder Lodge and Stagecoach Lodge up inland. Zillions of runs snake down the mountainside, taking advantage of the more than 2,500 vertical feet of drop you'll enjoy at Heavenly. Beware: Even the lowland ski area near the California Lodge has mostly black diamond runs. Approach the Killbrew and Mott Canyons with prejudice—gates at the head of these runs underscore the fact that only expert skiers should even try to take them on. Frankly, Heavenly doesn't have tons of green runs, but most of the beginner areas is served by the Gondola and the Powderbowl Express Six Chair. Freestylers can find a number of terrain parks, none of which are named other than the traditional and uninspired Small, Medium and Large.

Heavenly enjoys its status as an intensely popular resort, so prepare to find parking a challenge at whatever lodge you choose. Crowding and lines at the lifts, especially those at the bottom of the mountain, can get bad on weekends and holidays. On the other hand, once you're out of your car and on the mountain you'll have access to nearly every service and amenity you need.

KIRKWOOD

The South Shore's mid-tier resort is Kirkwood (1501 Kirkwood Meadows Dr. off Hwy. 88, 209/258-6000, www.kirkwood.com, lifts daily 9 a.m.–4 p.m.) offers dozens of downhill runs, plus everything from pipes to a cross-country space. Both the easiest runs and the children's ski school center are located around the Timber Creek Day Lodge. The Kirkwood Mountain Lodge lifts lead up to more intermediate and advanced runs; the back of the mountain is devoted to double-black-diamond runs. Kirkwood specializes in terrain parks for skiers and boarders, including a Cross Course, half-pipes, beginner terrain features, and areas with sound systems to complete the atmosphere. For a more sedate adventure, check out the snowshoe and cross-country park; you can rent equipment for both at the lodges.

You'll find plenty of sustenance in and around Kirkwood. Both lodges include restaurants and bars that serve lunch, dinner, and, in some cases, drinks to starving skiers and boarders. If you prefer to stay where you ski, look into Kirkwood's array of lodges and vacation rentals, most situated to make it easy to get to the slopes.

SIERRA-AT-TAHOE

For a smaller and less crowded South Shore ski experience, check out Sierra-at-Tahoe (1111 Sierra-at-Tahoe Rd., Twin Bridges, 530/659-7453, http://sierraattahoe.com, weekdays 9 A.M.–4 P.M., weekends 8:30 A.M.–4 P.M., adults $55–65, youth $45–55, children $14–16). Sierra-at-Tahoe offers plenty of long, sweeping advanced runs, as well as many fun intermediate tracks. The many beginners' green slopes run right down the middle of the mountain, all the way from the top. Take the Tahoe King or Grandview Express quad chairs or the Nob Hill double chair to the upper greens, or the Rock Garden or Easy Rider Express to stay lower on the mountain. It's all black diamonds on the east side of the big quads, and mostly blues with a few black diamonds for spice in the west, coming off the West Bowl Express quad or the Puma triple chair. A few more beginning and intermediate runs flow down the back of the mountain. For a nice, hot cup of coffee and a hearty meal, ski down either to the Base Lodge or the Baja Grill. Some skiers think Sierra-at-Tahoe is the best-kept secret in the area.

Nevada Side

If you're staying over the state line in Incline Village or out in Reno, you can choose between two nearby ski resorts.

MT. ROSE

Mt. Rose (22222 Mt. Rose Hwy., Reno, NV, 800/754-7673, http://skirose.com, 9 A.M.–4 P.M., adults $48–62, youth $42, children 6–12 $17) has the most to choose from in terms of both variety and beginner routes. Lots of different ski school packages and private lesson options are offered for children as young as three on up to senior citizens who want to cut it up on a snowboard. You can even sign your kids up for ranger-guided exploration programs and ski or board camps where they'll have a great time, learn lots, and make ski buddies their own age.

Beware of the center of Mt. Rose, an area called Chutes with a morass of double-black runs with fun names like Detonater and Yellow Jacket. If you're on your own looking for the green runs, park at the Main Lodge and then take the Ponderosa or the Galena chairs up to beginner territory. For lots of great, long, intermediate tracks, start at Slide Lodge (the second access point for the Mt. Rose resort) and take the Blazing Zephyrs Six-Chair almost to the top of the mountain. You can grab a hot cocoa and a meal, or make a pit stop at either lodge.

DIAMOND PEAK

The smaller Diamond Peak (1210 Ski Way, Incline Village, NV, 775/832-1177, http://diamondpeak.com, 9 A.M.–4 P.M., adults $37–48, youth $29–38, children $14–18) is easy to access from the town of Incline Village. It has two—count them, two—green run at the bottom of the hill. Probably not the best place to bring young children or yourself if you're on your first ski trip. (You can go to ski school here for sure, but you won't find much in the way of route variety.) But if you're even an intermediate skier or boarder, be sure to take the Crystal Express quad up to the top of the peak. Stop for a moment and enjoy the amazing vistas down to Lake Tahoe before you take a wonderfully long run down the blue Crystal Ridge, continuing to enjoy the views, or cut in to one of the black chutes that branch off through the forest. You'll start your day down at the Base Lodge, where you can also eat, drink, make merry, or even stop in for a non-denominational prayer on Sunday mornings before you start skiing. In the middle of the day, the Snowflake Lodge on the ridge lets you spend all the time you like looking out onto the lake as you sip a drink or just sit with your feet up.

SIGHTS

Most folks don't come to Tahoe to see its historic or cultural sights—which is a shame, really, because many of them are worth your time. Just be aware that sightseeing and museum-going in Tahoe are summertime activities. Most museums and cultural sights go to limited hours in the spring and fall, and close entirely in the wintertime. It's not that they're afraid of the weather, it's that the staff are all out skiing!

◖ The Village at Squaw Valley

You might think of The Village at Squaw Valley (1750 Village East Rd., Olympic Valley, 530/584-1000, www.thevillageatsquaw.com) as a ski area, but in truth it's an upscale small town designed to mimic a European Alpine village (but not quite succeeding). In fact, there's no need to ever hit a slope to enjoy the all The Village has to offer. You can spend hours just rambling around the colorfully painted clusters of buildings. Want to shop? Stroll the cute, exclusive boutiques and galleries, which are scattered throughout The Village. Souvenir seekers can go straight to **Squaw One Accessories** or the **Squaw Valley Clothing Company.** More than half a dozen restaurants, snack bars, and coffee shops offer everything from sushi to pizza to high-end wines. You can even stay at The Village if you've got enough cash.

The entertainment options are obvious; you can ski in the winter, hike in the summer, and take the **cable car** (adults $10–22, youth $10–17, child $5–6) up to **High Camp**

(1960 Squaw Valley Rd., Olympic Valley, 800/403-0206, www.squaw.com). There you can ice skate, browse in the **Olympic Museum** (1960 Squaw Valley Rd., 800/403-0206, www.squaw.com/olympic-museum, admission free with cable car ride), or just stand outside and enjoy the tremendous views. Live music often makes its way up to the base of the mountain, as do other events that offer fun to adults and kids alike.

Tahoe Maritime Museum

The Tahoe Maritime Museum (5205 W. Lake Blvd., Homewood, 530/525-9253, www.tahoe maritimemuseum.org, May 24–Sept. 30 daily 11 A.M.–5 P.M., Oct. 1–Dec. 20 daily 10 A.M.–5 P.M., adults $5, children free) seeks to illuminate the significant marine history of the large lake. On the West Shore of the lake, a shining new museum building was designed to resemble an old boathouse (a *big* old boathouse). It contains a fantastic collection of photos, artifacts, and a number of historic watercraft, some of which still run on the lake each summer. You'll learn about the "gentlemen's racing" history of the lake, the steam ferries that plied the waters, and the fishing that's been part of the lke's culture for over a century. The museum has the largest collection of outboard motors in the country, plus an exhibit on the history of water skis, from the days when they were handmade up to modern design and styling. You'll also find a children's area where younger visitors can enjoy interactive exhibits as they learn more about small and mid-sized boats, water skis, and more.

Historical Society Museums

Serious museum buffs will be thrilled to learn that the Lake Tahoe Historical Society owns and operates three separate museums in and around Tahoe City. The **Gatekeeper's Museum** (130 West Lake Blvd., Tahoe City, 530/583-1762, www.northtahoemuseums.org, open year-round, schedule varies, adults $3, children $1) offers the most in-depth history of society around the lake. You'll find transcribed oral history, photos, artifacts, costumes, and more inside this funky local museum. If your tastes run more towards Native American artifacts, check out the **Marion Steinbach Indian Basket Museum** (130 West Lake Blvd., Tahoe City, 530/583-1762, www.northtahoe museums.org) at the same site as the Gatekeeper's Museum. Guess what its star collection consists of? In addition to a wonderful array of baskets exemplifying the work of tribes from across the country, you'll also see dolls, costumes, and many other artifacts displayed in attractive and unusual (for a museum) pine-and-glass cases that match the wooden floors of the attractive galleries.

Finally, you can visit an authentic early 20th-century log cabin: the **Watson Cabin** (560 North Lake Blvd., 530/583-8717, www .northtahoemuseums.org, Memorial Day–Labor Day, schedule varies) at Tahoe City. Unlike many historic California buildings, especially cabins, this one sits on its original building site. Inside, you'll find diorama-style displays of pioneer life in early modern Lake Tahoe.

Tallac Historic Site

It sounds like something to do with Native American culture, but in fact the Tallac Historic Site (Hwy. 89, 3.1 miles north of Hwy. 50 intersection, South Lake Tahoe, 530/541-5227) pays homage to the lavish mansions built by white men in the early 20th century around Lake Tahoe. True, the centerpiece of the complex, the **Tallac Museum** (June 15–Labor Day, Tues.–Sun. 10 A.M.–4 P.M., free) in the Baldwin Estate, does include an exhibition focusing on the life and times of the local Washoe tribe. But most of this complex of 33 different buildings, including three major mansions, are all about wealth and privilege. In the Baldwin Estate, you'll find featured the importance of Lucky Baldwin and his family to the history of California. Walk the grounds of the Pope and Heller Estates, checking out the attractive gardens and many small cottages and outbuildings. If you make reservations in advance, you can take a tour of the interior of the **Pope Mansion** (Tues., Thurs., Fri. 1 P.M.

and 2:30 P.M., $1.50). The Heller Estate has been set aside to showcase the arts and music of the Tahoe region. The smaller cabins spend each summer acting as galleries for photographers, fiber artists, and other local craftspeople. Check into children's workshops when you're in town. Out on the grounds, summer concerts rule the weekends, so you might hear jazz, bluegrass, or even classical music with the crystalline lake as your backdrop.

In addition to the history and grandeur, you'll find the Pope-Baldwin Recreation Area, a number of easy-to-walk nature trails, a picnic ground, and beach access with swimming permitted. It seems only proper, as these were beach resorts/retreats, after all!

Thunderbird Lodge

The Nevada side of the lake boasts the Thunderbird Lodge (5000 Hwy. 28, Incline Village, NV, 775/832-8750, www.thunderbird lodge.org). Once again, if you're seeking Native Americana, you're in for a surprise. The Thunderbird Lodge was built in 1936 by a Tahoe resident locally called The Captain, who intended to create a luxury hotel and casino on his vast lakeside acreage. It was one of the last great posh residential mansions constructed alongside the lake. The property includes several outbuildings and a 600-foot underground tunnel from the mansion proper to the boathouse and card house.

When you visit the Thunderbird Lodge, you won't be able to drive to the property. Instead, park at the Crystal Bay Visitors Center in Incline Village and meet your tour guide and bus for the land tour (adults $39, children 6–11 $19). You'll be driven out to the lodge and take an hour-and-change walking tour through several of the buildings and the landscape. The tunnel is one of the tour highlights, especially for kids. Another highlight is the unbelievable 1930s-era mahogany yacht, *The Thunderbird,* which still floats in the boathouse.

If you're staying on the west side of the lake, you can book a boat tour (Tahoe Keys Marina, 775/588-1881, www.tahoeboatcruises.com/ tbirdlodgetours.htm, adults $110, children

6–11 $55) on a historic wooden powerboat that will take you across the lake and along the eastern shore. The boat docks at the Thunderbird Lodge, and you'll take the walking tour from there. Snacks and a cold lunch spread are included with this tour package. Children under six years old are not permitted on any tour of the Thunderbird Lodge. Both tours operate in the summertime only.

ENTERTAINMENT AND SHOPPING
Bars and Clubs

With the youthful snowboarding crowd packing the Tahoe lodgings in the winter and the wakeboarders in the summertime, it's no surprise that some noticeable nightlife crops up around the lake. For the obvious reasons, the favorite clubs tend to be inside the Stateline casino resorts. Often you'll find that the hip dancing crew spills out of the clubs and onto the casino floor throughout the evening.

Many locals' favorite nightclub is **Vex at Harrah's** (15 Hwy. 50, Stateline, NV, 775/586-6705, Thurs.–Sat. 10 P.M.–close). This swank late-night watering hole features girls, girls, girls as the entertainment, the staff, and the clientele—every Friday night is "Ladies Night" (free cover for female guests). Whether the entertainment is a high-flying aerial act or just the Vex Girls dancing on the upper walkways, both locals and visitors alike have a great time here. You can shake it on the dance floor, sip a cocktail at the bar, or if you've got the money, get waited upon by the lovely cocktail staff in a posh VIP booth.

Even though **The Opal Ultra Lounge at MontBleu** (55 Hwy. 50, Stateline, NV, 775/586-2000, Wed.–Sun. 8 P.M.–close, cover varies) is technically in Nevada, you'll find a serious California-style fusion of cuisine and nightlife. The idea is for club-goers to start out with a nice sushi dinner, then move seamlessly into cocktails and the lounge scene. Each evening includes different featured entertainment—just don't mix up Wednesday night's lingerie party with Thursday's VIP professional mixer! Live drumming spices up Friday

night, and "exotic" belly and fire dancers make Saturday intensely sexy.

Comedy

If you crave more structure, more laughter, and less booty shorts in your evening's entertainment, get tickets to **The Improv at Harvey's** (15 Hwy. 50, Stateline, NV, 800/786-8208, www.harrahs.com, Sun. and Tues.–Fri. 9 P.M., Sat. 8 P.M. and 10 P.M., $25–30). Each night, an old-school Budd Friedman comic showcase goes up. You'll see national acts like Wendy Liebman and Dan Levy, as well as young up-and-coming comics who are building their careers. Once upon a time, Jay Leno, Jerry Seinfeld, Jim Carrey, and any number of famous comics whose names don't begin with "J" performed on this stage.

Festivals and Events

Each year Lake Tahoe hosts a number of big festivals in both summer and wintertime, though undoubtedly summer is high festival season. One of the biggest of these is the **Lake Tahoe Music Festival** (www.tahoe music.org). Players like Kenny Loggins and Big Bad Voodoo Daddy perform alongside symphony orchestras over a three-week stretch in late July and early August. Concerts are held at a number of venues—often ski resorts such as Homewood, Alpine Meadows, and Tahoe Donner. Check the festival website for this year's concert dates, times, venues, and ticket prices.

If you enjoy costumes and want to dive into the living history of the early 20th-century wealth and privilege that surrounded Lake Tahoe, hit the **Great Gatsby Festival** (http://tahoeheritage.org, Aug.) at the Tallac Historic Site. In the heat of August each year, actors and volunteers dress in period attire and stroll the grounds of the estates, mimicking 1920s vacationers. The most popular event of this two-day festival is the Gatsby Tea on Saturday afternoon. For $30, you'll enjoy a sumptuous afternoon high tea spiced up by entertainment that culminates in a vintage fashion show. On both days, additional entertainments, tours, and vendors selling early 1900s-styled items draw folks onto the estates.

California theater-lovers have been known to drive for hours to see the shows of the **Lake Tahoe Shakespeare Festival** (www.lake tahoeshakespeare.com, July–Aug.). In 1995, a new stage facility was built at the classic **Sand Harbor State Park** beach location (three miles south of Incline Village on SR-28). Festival-goers can still flop onto a towel in the sand, but the play they'll watch will be a world-class Shakespearean production. (In truth, you'll be much comfier if you bring a low beach chair to sit in for the show.)

Shopping

Lots of shopping opportunities cluster in South Lake Tahoe. If you're in need of basic necessities or discount factory outlet stores, head for the **Stores at the Y** (Intersection of Hwy. 89 and Hwy. 50, South Lake Tahoe, http://shopthe-y.com). For athletic equipment and apparel, check out **Adidas** (daily 10 A.M.–6 P.M.) and the **Great Outdoor Clothing Company** (daily 10 A.M.–6 P.M.). For après-ski apparel for the ladies, **Blue Willow** (daily 10 A.M.–6 P.M.) offers silky, sexy lingerie.

If it's ski equipment or apparel you need, the upscale **Shops at Heavenly Village** (1001 Heavenly Village Way) can hook you up. Guess what **Powder House Ski & Snowboard** (530/541-6422, www.tahoe powderhouse.com, Sat.–Thurs. 7 A.M.–10 P.M., Fri. 7 A.M.–midnight) sells? Granted, you'll pay a premium for equipment here. For the summertime sportsters, **Tahoe Boot 'n' Bike Works** (530/542-1388, www.tahoebootnbike .com) specializes in hiking and biking gear.

Snowboarders are one of the major communities served in Tahoe. And if you know snowboarding culture at all, you know what that means: head shops! Head shops are easy to find in South Lake strip malls. Redundantly named **Tahoe Hemp Company (THC)** (3117 Harrison Ave., South Lake Tahoe, 530/544-4367, http://lp8.tahoehemp.com, daily 10 A.M.–5 P.M.) sits next to Sprouts and Rude Brothers, selling all the usual pipes and glassware, stickers

and T-shirts. You can also get yourself a stylin' hemp tuk and a couple of local alternative newspapers with semi-underground entertainment information.

SPORTS AND RECREATION
Skiing and Snowshoeing

There's far more land surrounding Tahoe that's available for cross-country skiing and snowshoeing than there is for downhill sports. In fact, Tahoe is something like heaven for strong-legged snow lovers of all types. It's hard to go more than five miles without tripping over a snowshoe trail or a cross-country track.

The granddaddy of Tahoe cross-country ski areas, the **Royal Gorge Cross Country Ski Resort** (Summit Station, Soda Springs, 800/500-3871, www.royalgorge.com, daily 9 A.M.–5 P.M., adults $15–29, youth 13–17 $15–16, children under 12 free) has a truly tremendous chunk of the Sierras within its boundaries. Striving to provide a luxurious ski experience comparable to what downhillers expect, the Royal Gorge offers lodgings, food, drink, a ski school, equipment rentals, equipment care facilities and services, and much more. Expect more than 185 miles of groomed trails, all with two stride tracks and a skate track to allow easy passing. Royal Gorge even offers four surface lifts for skiers who'd like to rest for a few minutes while getting from one area to another. Another option is to start out at the Soda Springs downhill ski resort gondola and spend the day exploring the Van Norden Track System, which connects down to the Summit Station.

The Royal Gorge Summit Station is the central Lodge for Royal Gorge. However, you'll also find four restaurants, two overnight lodges, and eight warming huts dotting the cross-country wonderland. Do be sure to grab a map before you head out for the day. Patches of mountains are off limits due to avalanche danger, and it's best to know where they are before you get deep into your cross-country ski adventure.

North Shore regulars say that **Tahoe Donner Cross Country** (15275 Alder Creek

Rd., 530/587-9484, www.tdxc.com, adults $13–22, children under 12 free) offers some of the better cross-country skiing action in the area. It's true that Donner has a separate day lodge just for cross-country skiers, and another restaurant halfway up the mountain, the Euer Valley Cookhouse. It's also got almost 5,000 acres crisscrossed with trails ranging from easy greens all the way up through double-black diamonds. A cross-country ski school teaches newcomers to the sport and helps more experienced skiers expand their skills. This is more of a cross-country paradise than a big snowshoe area, and you'll find only two snowshoe-only trails at Donner.

If you're up for some cross-country skiing on the Nevada side of the lake, check out the **Spooner Lake** (Hwy. 28, 0.5 mile from Hwy. 50, 775/749-5349, www.spoonerlake.com, adults $10–21, teens $10, children under 12 free) cross-country and snowshoe resort. You can stride and glide by two small lakes in this region: Spooner and Marlette. Less experienced and more sedate skiers tend to stick to the well-groomed easy and moderate trails near Spooner Lake, Spooner Meadow, and the Lodge. The buns-and-thighs of steel crowd can head up North Canyone to Saints Rests beside Marlette Lake, or go all out and circle the aptly named Big Loop—a 21-mile advanced monster that will definitely give you a full day's workout. All cross-country ski trails at Spooner are snowshoe-accessible (be courteous by staying on the outside edges), and the resort maintains narrow marked snowshoe-only trails throughout the area. If you'd like to stay right at Spooner Lake, inquire about rental cabins, which are available year-round.

Many cross-country skiers and snowshoers eschew the groomed and crowded resorts for more virgin territory. At Tahoe, a number of cross-country trails that really do cross some country are maintained by the Forest Service. Some of these trails offer short, single-day excursions, while others go miles back into the ominously named Desolation Wilderness and appeal to hardcore ski-campers who want a multi-day adventure. Beginner explorers can have the safest fun at **Taylor Creek** (just north of Camp Richardson, Hwy. 89), an uncongested but reasonably populous area with many flat, marked trails to help newcomers get the feel for the forest. Lots of trails for skiers of all levels range out along the **South Shore** and the **West Shore** of Lake Tahoe. If you're planning to camp in Desolation Wilderness, the most popular trailhead first takes you past **Echo Lakes** (Hwy. 50 at Echo Lake Rd.) and then on into the backcountry along the Pacific Crest Trail.

A $5 Sno-Park parking pass is required for many forest ski trailheads, and can be purchased at places like Longs Drugs at the South Shore Y and the Chevron in Meyers. Folks planning overnight ski-camping trips must first get a wilderness permit from the El Dorado Information Center in Camino on Highway 50. While snow conditions are generally best in the mornings, nighttime "moonlight skiing" is allowed and even encouraged in some areas.

Snowmobiling

There's enough room around Tahoe to create space to satisfy every different kind of snow activity—even snowmobiling. While you can't take your mad machine anywhere and everywhere, you'll find vast acreage at your disposal, whether you're a lifelong rider or want to go out for your very first guided tour. A number of companies offer snowmobile rentals, maps, groomed terrain, open fields, and guided tours of the winter scenery.

Operating out of the town of Meyers on the South Shore, **Lake Tahoe Adventures** (3071 Hwy. 50, Meyers, 530/577-2940, www.laketahoeadventures.com, Nov.–Apr. daily 9 A.M.–5 P.M.) specializes in group snowmobile tours on the Nevada side of the lake. A shuttle takes riders from the tour center up to the base camp in Hope Valley, where the fleet of Arctic Cat snowmobiles waits to ply the high-elevation backcountry Sierra terrain. First-time drivers and families with children should pick one of the more sedate trail tours or the snowmobile track, while expert snowmobile enthusiasts prefer the "Ultimate" off-trail tours that get deep into the backcountry and rougher riding. Children are welcome, but snowmobile drivers must be at least 15 years old. Reservations are required for all tours.

If you're up on the North Shore, check out **Lake Tahoe Snowmobile Tours, Inc.** (Hwy. 267, south of Northstar, 530/546-4280, www .laketahoesnowmobiling.com, daily, $90–250). Boasting a fleet of Sea-Doo snowmobiles and more than 20 years of guided touring experience, this outfit offers everything from 90-minute easy tours that give you gorgeous lake views (aptly named Lakeview Adventures) up through private three- and four-hour adventures geared toward expert riders up for tackling ungroomed backcountry terrain. You'll see sweeping North Shore views and drive through miles of unspoiled (if slightly singed) forest. Reservations are highly recommended, drivers must be 16 or older and have a valid driver's license, and no children under five may ride with this company for safety reasons.

Several snowmobiling outfits operate west of Truckee along the main roads—you'll see the tracks as you drive in and out of town. One company, **Cold Stream Adventures** (11760 Donner Pass Rd., Truckee, 530/582-9090, www.coldstreamadventures.com, daily, $130–155 for 2-hour tour), also offers tours into the mountains, promising climbs up to 2,000 feet above your starting point. These guided tours take routes through the forest that are private to this company—that is, you'll see forested landscapes available to you no other way. Make reservations, grab your sunglasses, and come on out!

Down south on the Nevada side, it's hard to miss the presence of the **Zephyr Cove Snowmobile Center** (760 Hwy. 50 at the Zephyr Cove Resort, 775/589-4906, www .laketahoesnowmobiles.com, $110–250). The free shuttle runs right along the freeway for all to see, and for all reserved riders to use at their convenience. A Lakeview or Sierra Summit tour on a new Sea Doo snowmobile will include breathtaking views, easy riding on groomed trails, and plenty of stops that let you take pictures. Advanced riders can work with the guides to create a challenging personal tour.

Sledding and Snow Play

You don't need to be under the age of 12 to have a blast flying down a hill on a specially designed snow tube or saucer, or grabbing a handful of fresh powder and starting a roaring snowball fight. Any number of hills all around Tahoe become designated or impromptu play areas each season once the snow gets deep. A good way to find one near your accommodations is to ask a few locals; they'll be able to tell you which spots are the best for small children and which ones appeal more to big kids-at-heart. Many of the ski resorts, including Boreal and Donner, offer snow-play areas as well as their trademark steep ski slopes.

Just a couple of miles from Heavenly Valley in a cute residential area sits the **Tube & Saucer Hill at Hansen's Resort** (1360 Ski Run Blvd., 530/544-3361, daily 9 A.M.–5 P.M., $6/hour, $12 for 3 hours). One of the annual favorites, this hill offers more in the way of features than many impromptu play spots. Don't bother stacking a bunch of equipment in the car, since Hansen's requires that you use their saucers and tubes. With constructed runs, you'll definitely get some thrills as you slip down the hill through the scattered pine trees. The resort also makes a snack bar and a redwood hot tub available to fee-paying snow-lovers.

In the South Shore area past Meyers on Highway 50, **Adventure Mountain Lake Tahoe** (21220 Hwy. 50 at Echo Summit, 530/577-4352, www.adventuremountaintahoe .com, Dec.–Apr. daily 10 A.M.–5 P.M., $15/car) boasts the best groomed sledding area in all of Tahoe. With 40 acres of sled runs and play areas, plus restrooms and a concession stand that sells hot coffee and new sleds, Adventure Mountain works to make good on its promise. It's also got access to the Pacific Crest Trail and a few other cross-country skiing and snowshoeing trails for those who want a more quiet buy labor-intensive day in the snow. Feel free to bring your own sleds and tubes.

Up on the North Shore, the **North Tahoe Winter Adventures** (Donner Rd., Tahoe Vista, 530/546-0605, daily 9 A.M.–5 P.M., $5/all day) is part of the North Tahoe Regional Park. This fully developed seasonal recreation area includes warm restrooms, groomed hills, a snack bar, snowmobile tracks (plus on-site snowmobile rentals), and several miles of cross-country trails. Whatever kind of playing in the snow you want, you can do it here—and all within sight of the lovely north end of the lake.

Sleigh and Sled Rides

Oh, what fun it is to ride in a one-horse open sleigh! No, really. You can take an old-school sleigh ride at several locations around Tahoe. Just over the state line, across the street from the Harrah's and MontBleu casinos, seek out **Sleigh Rides by the Borges Family** (50 Hwy. 50, Stateline, NV, 775/588-2953, www.sleighride.com, $20 adults, $10 children). These folks have been giving sleigh rides on the South Shore for more than 30 years. They've got five sleighs (seating 2–20 passengers) and some lovely blond Belgian draft horses. Each ride lasts 35 minutes and takes you through the woods to grandmother's spectacular lake view. Blankets to cuddle under are included with each ride, as are stories and songs, but you'll need to bring your own thermos of cocoa.

Over on the other side of the lake, you can catch a similar ride with **Wilderness Sleigh Rides at the Camp Richardson Corral** (530/541-3113, $25). Call ahead for reservations, and meet your horse and sleigh at the corner of Emerald Bay Road and Fallen Leaf Road on the west side of the lake.

If you prefer dogs to draft horses, make a journey with **Wilderness Adventures Dog Sled Tours** (530/550-8133, www.tahoedogsledtours.com, daily 10 A.M.–5 P.M., $95–110 passengers over 60 lbs., $45–55 passengers under 60 lbs.). Most tours last one hour, but if you're not afraid of cold and around on a weekday, you can sign up for a two-hour or more Wilderness Expedition that takes you 15–20 miles through the snows of the backcountry.

Any time you want to sled, you can choose either Sugar Bowl (629 Sugar Bowl Rd., Norden) or the Resort at Squaw Creek (400 Squaw Creek Rd., Olympic Valley) as your starting point. Whichever you choose, you just won't be able to resist those adorable fuzzy Huskie faces!

Ice Skating

Ice rinks proliferate all year, though wintertime is the most popular for visiting skaters.

It ain't cheap, but on a clear day skating at **High Camp at Squaw Valley** (1960 Squaw Valley Rd., Olympic Valley, 530/452-7246, www.squaw.com, adults $26, youth $22, children under 13 $14) can be a beautiful thing. You'll take the big cable car ride up to High Camp. At the Ice Pavilion, lace up your skates and enjoy the Olympic-sized rink with its panoramic views out over the Sierra forests and peaks.

At the South Shore, **Heavenly Gardens** (1021 Heavenly Village Way, South Lake Tahoe, 530/542-4230, www.theshopsatheavenly.com/skating, daily 10 A.M.–close) turns part of its landscape each year into a winter wonderland. This outdoor, winter-only rink appeals more to tourists and kids than serious skaters, but it definitely offers fun and a partylike atmosphere.

For more hardcore skaters and hockey players who want to indulge their obsession while vacationing in Tahoe, the **South Lake Tahoe Ice Arena** (1176 Rufus Allen Blvd., S. Lake Tahoe, 530/542-6262, www.recreationintahoe.com, adults $9, youth $8, children $6) can hook you up. This year-round ice center offers drop-in hockey, public skating hours, and even an "Adult Coffee Club" skating hour.

Waterskiing and Wakeboarding

Once the summer sunshine has warmed the air—if not the waters of the lake—visitors' thoughts turn to those other kinds of skiing and boarding. The vast clear waters of Lake Tahoe are irresistible to water skiers, wakeboarders, Jet Skiers, and powerboaters. You've got miles of open water to cross, a number of docks and marinas, and a lovely coastline to explore. If you dive deeper than about a foot and a half, you'll find the water of Tahoe ice-cold (in the 40s) even in the height of summer. But that's no matter if you're sunning yourself on the bow of a speedboat or flying along behind the boat on a wakeboard.

Be aware that Tahoe takes the water quality of not only Lake Tahoe, but Falling Leaf, Echo, and the other small area lakes very, very seriously. Especially if you plan to bring your own powered watercraft, it's wise to familiarize yourself with the rules and restrictions governing all waterways in the Tahoe Basin. Check http://boattahoe.com/trparegs.htm for more information.

South Lake Tahoe's **Tahoe Keys Marina** (2435 Venice Dr., South Lake Tahoe, 530/541-2155, www.tahoemarina.com, powerboats $100–150/hr, $600–1,000/day) looms large as the only "inland" marina on the lake. This full-service marina sells gas, provides launch access, and rents slips, as well as offering boat rentals of all kinds and charter fishing trips. You can rent an array of ritzy Reinell powerboats, some of which seat up to 10 people and can work for either cruising, fishing, or skiing and wakeboarding. Yamaha personal watercraft come a bit cheaper and are all legal on prissy Lake Tahoe. For an extra fee, you'll get a pile of water toys, sets of water skis, or a high-class wakeboard. Just don't expect anything here to come cheap!

On the Nevada side, **Zephyr Cove Marina** (750 Hwy. 50, Zephyr Cove, NV, 775/589-4901, www.zephyrcove.com/marina/index.cfm, ski boats $150–175, WaveRunners $115–150) offers a full complement of services and watercraft rentals. For skiers and wakeboarders, Zephyr Cove has a small fleet of 22–24 foot Sea Ray open-bow ski boats, plus skis, boards, and toys. Personal watercraft riders can rent one of the marina's three-person WaveRunners. Truly adventurous visitors can also sign up for a parasailing session with the professional drivers from Zephyr Cove.

On the North Shore, **Tahoe City Marina** (700 N. Lake Blvd., Tahoe City, 530/583-1093, www.tahoecitymarina.com, ski boats $130–160/hr) has not only full marina facilities, but a shopping mall with a number of restaurants and boutiques. But if your main focus is out on the water rather than the shore, the marina can hook you up with one of three ski boats.

Boating and Fishing

Among the most popular warm-weather activities on the waters of Lake Tahoe are fishing and pleasure boating. Many visitors also enjoy taking small human-powered watercraft out near the shore (or farther out for the stronger paddlers).

To rent a pontoon boat for a nice cruise around the lake, make a reservation at the Tahoe Keys Marina (see above) either with the **Tahoe Keys** rental company or with the **Ski Run** outfit. Each of these also offers a wide array of kayaks, canoes, and pedal boats. Ski Run even rents some truly weird apparatus, and for a small fee you can try an hour on a hydrobike or a water trike. Zephyr Cove also has a fleet of "beach craft" running to kayaks, canoes, pedal boats, and funky pedal kayaks.

Want to go fishing, but don't know where the good holes are or have tackle and the initiative to go out on your own? Several companies offer charter trips on Lake Tahoe for anglers looking to score Mackinaw lake trout, rainbow and brown trout, or kokanee salmon. Operating out of the **Ski Run Marina** (900 Ski Run Blvd.), **Tahoe Sport Fishing** (800/696-7797, www.tahoesportfishing.com, $85–135) offers halfday and full-day fishing trips tailored to suit all styles of lake fishing. Choose from among six fishing boats, all of which have heated cabins and modest bathroom facilities. Your trip will include all the trimmings: bait and tackle, cleaning and bagging services, cold beer and soda on board, and a choice of morning or afternoon half-day trips.

Mickey's Big Mack Charters (800/877-1462, www.mickeysbigmack.com, $65–85) operates out of the Sierra Boat Company in Carnelian Bay. The 43-foot fishing boat goes out twice daily, once for an early-morning trip

© PETTIT GILWEE / TOM ZIKAS

sailing on Lake Tahoe

and again for a late-afternoon cruise that includes spectacular sunset views. The cabin and restroom on board add to the comforts of your trip as you fish for Mackinaw, rainbows, and browns.

Down at Zephyr Cove, book a fishing trip with **O'Malley's Fishing Charters** (775/588-4102, $110). The cozy 22-foot boat guarantees an intimate angling experience. You can fish summer or winter with O'Malley's.

Do you prefer fly-fishing to lake fishing? With the proliferation of rivers and streams surrounding Lake Tahoe, it's easy to find a good place to cast. **Tahoe Fly Fishing Outfitters** (2705 Hwy. 50, South Lake Tahoe, 877/541-8208, http://tahoeflyfishing.com, $110–300) can take you on an expert guided fly-fishing or spin fishing trip on one of the smaller lakes, Walker Rivers, Carson Rivers, Truckee and Little Truckee Rivers, or the Pleasant Valley Fly Fishing Preserve.

Hiking

In the summertime, many trails frequented by snowshoers and cross-country skiers turn into perfect paths for hiking. In fact, wonderful hikes abound all around the lake, up in the mountains, and out by the smaller alpine lakes surrounding Tahoe.

Along the South Shore, hikes range from easy walks along the shore at the Tallac Historic sight to hardcore treks up the **Mount Tallac Trail** (Hwy. 89 at Baldwin Beach, South Lake Tahoe, 10 miles round-trip, difficult). This long hike starts out easy, taking casual strollers past the Floating Island and Cathedral Lakes, then gets steeper and harsher as it ascends up the front face of the mountain. To access the trail, turn off the highway away from the beach toward the dirt road, which takes you to the trailhead parking lot. For a more moderate but equally beautiful hike, choose the **Echo Lakes Trail** (Johnson Pass Rd. at Lower Echo Lake, 5–12 miles, moderate to strenuous, wilderness permit may be required). You can pick your distance on this route, depending on how many small pristine alpine lakes you want to see. You'll start with a short walk to Upper Echo Lake, where you have an option to catch a water taxi rather than continuing on the trail along the lake. If you keep on going, you'll see Tamarack Lake, Lucille and Margery Lakes, Lake in the Woods, and maybe even Aloha.

Up North Shore way, the great hiking continues. For a quick easy walk, head up to the **State Lookout** (Forest Service Rd. 1601 at the iron pipe gate, 1 mile, easy). At the lookout, you'll find summer volunteers who can give you information about the region, including the short, self-guided nature trail that surrounds the lookout proper. For a heftier hike, try the **Marlette Lake Trail** (Spooner Lake Trailhead, 10 miles, moderate to difficult). The trailhead sits inside the Lake Tahoe Nevada State Park at the junction of Highways 50 and 28. You'll be charged a parking fee at the gate. The hike itself slopes uphill all the five miles up to the Marlette Dam. While you're free to enjoy the beauty and serenity of this manmade lake, no fishing is allowed because the lake serves as a fish hatchery.

Serious hikers challenge themselves with the **North** and **South Rim Trails** (www.tahoe rimtrail.org, 40 miles total, difficult). These two trails put together encircle all of vast Lake Tahoe (minus a couple of spots where connectors have been proposed but not yet built). Check the map on the website for the various trailheads; about half a dozen fan out around the lake. To do the whole Rim Trail takes two or three days for a fit, experienced hiker who expects to camp along the way. Contact the visitors center for information about wilderness permits and backcountry camping along the Rim Trails. More casual day-hikers can pick one portion of the trail and tackle it, either doing a back-and-forth, or using some sort of shuttle service to get back home again at the end of the day.

Biking

A great place to get out and walk or bike is summertime **Kirkwood** (1501 Kirkwood Meadows Dr. off Hwy. 88, Kirkwood, www.kirkwood .com, 209/258-7360). Without snow covering them, the slopes of the ski resort become great mountain biking tracks. For $30 (adult) or $15 (youth) per full day, you can take two different lifts up the mountain with your bike, then ride your way down. You can rent bikes from Kirkwood on the weekends, and hone your skills at the clinics held several times each season. The bike terrain opens for business in late June every year, and closes after Labor Day.

If you prefer your own two feet, take the lifts up (or don't, if you're strong and energetic), and hike down the multi-use trails to the lodge any day of the week during the summertime. Check the Kirkwood website for scheduled guided hikes and wildflower walks throughout the season.

Horseback Riding

For travelers who prefer to explore the forests and trails on horseback, a few stables offer guided rides. On the west side of the South Shore, find the **Camp Richardson Corral** (Emerald Bay Rd. and Fallen Leaf Rd., 530/541-3113, $32–65). Choose between

horseback riding

a one- or two-hour trail ride to explore the meadows and the forest, or a ride with a meal included. Camp Richardson offers an early morning ride that culminates in a hearty hot "cowboy-style" breakfast and an evening barbecued steak dinner ride. Riders must be at least six years old and weigh 225 pounds or less. Camp Richardson also offers horse boarding by the day, week, and month.

Over on the Nevada side, sign up for a ride with the **Zephyr Cove Resort Stables** (on Hwy. 50, 775/588-5664, http://zephyrcove stables.com, summer daily 9 A.M.–5 P.M., spring and fall daily 10 A.M.–4 P.M., $35/hour). Enjoy your lovely scenic trail rides, complete with panoramic views of the lake through the pine trees. Zephyr Cove also has "food rides" at breakfast, lunch, and dinnertime each day. Bring your appetite for these one-hour rides. (You'll need to make advanced arrangements if you're a vegetarian or have dietary restrictions.) As at most stables, restrictions include a 225-pound weight limit and a minimum rider age of seven.

LAKE TAHOE

Want to get out and see the Sierra Foothills and mountains from the back of a horse? Summertime at **Kirkwood** (1501 Kirkwood Meadows Dr. off Hwy. 88, Kirkwood, 209/258-4600, www.kirkwood.com, mid-June–Labor Day, $46) has what you need. Take a gorgeous guided trail ride out into the Mokelumne Wilderness. Pick a 1.5-hour or 2.5-hour ride, depending on your skill level and rear-end stamina. For kids who want to get more serious about their riding while on vacation, check out the children's Wrangler for a Day program. Kids spend most of the day caring for the horses with the experienced wranglers, plus they take a 90-minute ride through the forest.

Golf

Amongst all the other summertime recreation available in and around Lake Tahoe, a number of golf courses offer surprisingly good games, plus a few unique lake and mountain views.

The championship George Fazio course at **Edgewood Tahoe** (180 Lake Pkwy., Stateline, NV, 775/588-3566, http://edgewoodtahoe.com, daily May.–Oct., $150–250) has been compared to the Pebble Beach Golf Links—and called *better*. Not everyone agrees with that bold statement, but the consensus is definitely that Edgewood is one of the top courses in the West, if not the nation. As you walk the course, you'll see views of the lake and mountains that are so wonderful that you may forget all about that pesky putting for a moment or two. Several holes sit right along the shores of Lake Tahoe—one of the bigger water hazards you'll find in California.

After your game, enjoy lunch and a stiff drink at the Brook's Golf Bar & Deck. You can call or go online to reserve a tee time ahead of time. Your rather hefty fee includes a golf cart, and you can rent clubs and hire a caddie as well.

On the other side of the lake, **Coyote Moon** (10685 Northwoods Blvd., Truckee, 530/587-0886, www.tahoemountainclub.com, $160) also imposes a hefty green fee, but according to expert golfers and writers, it's more than worth the money you'll lay down. Coyote Moon boasts fairways dotted with granite boulders and lined by dense natural forest. No, the builders didn't make it that way—instead, the designer created a layout that takes advantage of the natural features of this unique locale. While Coyote Moon tends to beckon more to advanced golfers, even beginners can play an enjoyable round here.

For golfers looking to play a few holes on the cheap, **Tahoe Paradise Golf Course** (530/577-2121, www.tahoeparadisegc.com, daily 6 A.M.–7 P.M., $20–60) offers a pleasant course as well as pleasantly small green fees. On the South Shore, in fact right off Highway 50, this convenient course has pretty mountain views and plenty of lovely pine trees—and 18 holes of moderate golf that provides a fun game for beginners and intermediate golfers. There's also a pro shop, practice area, and a modest snack bar that runs to hot dogs and beer.

Spas

It's tough to go more than a block or two in South Lake Tahoe, Tahoe City, or even Truckee without tripping over some sort of day spa or massage parlor (the real kind, not the other kind). If you're staying at one of the big ski resorts or casinos, you're likely to find a spa attached to your accommodations, and perhaps even the option of in-room spa services. Campers and motel-goers can choose from the resort spas or pick out an independent provider for massages, facials, scrubs, and mani-pedis.

On the north side, one of the most popular day spas is the **Lighthouse Spa** (850 N. Lake Blvd. #20A, Tahoe City, 530/583-8100, www.lighthousespa.com, daily 9 A.M.–8 P.M.). Just look behind the Safeway (perhaps an unlikely spot for a spa). Inside, you can choose from Swedish, deep tissue, and hot stone massages, or get a special prenatal massage for your favorite expectant mom. Lighthouse also offers facials, body wraps, luxurious foot treatments, and aesthetic services including manicures, pedicures, and waxing. While they don't have the biggest spa menu ever, the services offered exemplify the heart of good California day spa care. Late appointments, up until 8 P.M., are available for those in desperate need of après-ski TLC.

Tired feet after a day of hiking, skiing, or snowshoeing? Walk them over to **Wish Hair & Skin Salon** (12030 Donner Pass Rd. Ste. 2, Truckee, 530/550-1319, www.wishsalon.com). You can also bring your tired hair, hands, face, and skin to this salon that doubles as a mini-mum-services day spa. Wish offers a full range of aesthetic services, including their signature four-hour mani-pedi with facial that creates a fabulous half-day of pampering. Book an appointment to get your hair done, your legs waxed, your face buffed and peeled, or even a full-body scrub. The website includes a full menu of services and prices, as well as an online appointment scheduler.

Among the wealth of day spas in South Lake Tahoe, **Shannon's Day Spa** (3600 Lake Tahoe Blvd., South Lake Tahoe, 530/542-4095, www .shannonsdayspa.com) stands out. You'll get plenty of personal attention here, plus a massage, facial, or luxurious body treatment that will leave you feeling refreshed and ready for another day out on the lake or up on the slopes. For the best experience at Shannon's, go for one of the packages that puts several treatments together for a full day of pleasure and well-being. Shannon's really is a spa, so don't expect to find waxing or nail services here.

So if you do want your nails done, head for **Tahoe Nail Spa** (2176 Lake Tahoe Blvd., #8, South Lake Tahoe, 530/541-1230). Be aware that it's a tough one to ferret out in the strip mall/plaza complex it's part of, but don't give up! The aestheticians at this small salon will give you great attention as they work on your feet and hands, clipping, buffing, and polishing to perfection.

Casino Gambling

Think that casinos are disgusting smoke-filled holes sheltering nothing but lonely senior citizens pouring their Social Security into slot machines? Not in Tahoe! On the South Shore, just over the state line, the various casinos beckon to a young crowd looking for a lively, hip night out.

The gaming floor of the **MontBleu Casino** (55 Hwy. 50, Stateline, NV, 888/829-7630, www.montbleuresort.com) is great fun on weekend evenings, with its go-go dancers and youthful gamblers taking the free drinks as they hammer the slots and place bets on the tables. Since it (and all the other casinos listed here) are in Nevada, you'll find all the full-fledged table games of a Vegas casino: craps, roulette, blackjack, and Texas Hold 'Em, among others. "The Zone" contains the sports book and the poker room. And as with most casinos, the slots and video poker machines are everywhere. MontBleu's casino is better lit and less smoky than many, making it easy to stay and play late into the night. Or if you get tired of tossing your money away, wander around and you'll find a lingerie shop, an art gallery, and a hip nightclub.

Gambling fans should definitely bring their frequent-player cards to the casino floor at **Harrah's Lake Tahoe** (15 Hwy. 50, Stateline, NV, 800/427-7247, www.harrahs .com/). They've got all the Vegas gaming favorites, like classic craps, Rapid Roulette, and of course Keno pads and monitors scattered all over the place. The atmosphere is a bit more "classic casino" here, with fairly dim lights in the evenings and a warren of slot machines that make it easy to get lost and keep on spending money. Now that Harrah's has absorbed former neighbor Harvey's, it's got a solid lock on its block. Once you're done with gaming, check out the live entertainment or the locally popular nightclub.

ACCOMMODATIONS

As a major vacation destination, you'll have no trouble finding a place to stay around Lake Tahoe. Some visitors camp around the lake, which can be beautiful in the summertime and frigid in winter, but most folks get rooms in the cute inns, historic hotels, budget motels, and upscale resorts that cluster in Tahoe's towns. Or they hook up with a rental agency and find a fully furnished vacation cabin or condo to call their own for the duration of their stay.

North Shore

$100-150

The **Truckee Hotel** (10007 Bridge St., 530/587-4444, www.truckeehotel.com, $55–187) offers a fabulous period ambiance for reasonable nightly rates. The hotel has been welcoming guests to the North Shore for more than 125 years. Rooms show their age with a gentle, shabby grace, and high ceilings, claw-foot tubs, and little Victorian touches delight visitors who appreciate a little history along with a comfortable bed. Part of the historic "charm" includes third- and fourth-floor rooms without an elevator on the premises, so prepare to climb and to haul luggage up narrow flights of stairs. One reason the rates are so reasonable here is that most of the 37 rooms have shared hall bathrooms. These are clean and comfortable, with either a shower or a bathtub and a lock for privacy. The few rooms with private baths are pricier. All rooms come with breakfast each morning. The Truckee Hotel building also shelters Moody's (the best restaurant in town) and sits only steps from historic downtown Truckee.

Be sure to listen to the friendly staff at the Truckee Hotel, especially when they tell you to move your car around to the back parking lot on winter evenings. If the police find your car blocking the snow-removal equipment in the dead of night, they will tow you without a second thought.

Mother Nature's Inn (551 N. Lake Blvd., Tahoe City, 800/558-4278, www.mothernaturesinn.com, $56–127) strives to bring a Tahoe camping experience inside, while still providing the creature comforts travelers expect in indoor accommodations. Guest rooms have a distinct theme based on a wild creature, and you can expect plenty of decorative tchotchkes in keeping with your room's animal totem. You'll also find lodge-style furnishings and linens arranged in cozy and somewhat cluttered arrangements. All rooms have private baths, refrigerators, and coffee makers. Pets are welcome for a small additional fee. The inn is only a few steps from the shores of the lake and the conveniences of downtown Tahoe City.

If you prefer to rent a condo with full kitchen facilities, especially for a longer stay, call the **Donner Lake Village Resort** (15695 Donner Pass Rd., #101, Truckee, 530/587-6081, www.donnerlakevillage.com, $140–170), situated right on the shores of Donner Lake. You can choose from regular motel rooms without kitchens, studio condos, and one- or two-bedroom condos. Inside your room, you'll find all the amenities of a nicer motel, including tea and coffee, private bathrooms, phones, and TVs with DVD players. But once you get a peek at the lake in summer or the mountains in winter, you won't want to stay inside for long. Donner Lake Village has its own marina with rental ski boats, fishing boats, and slips if you've brought your own watercraft. A bait and tackle shop across the street from the resort can hook you up with all the fishing equipment you need. And all the nearby North Shore ski resorts beckon in wintertime, an easy drive from your condo. After a long day out on the slopes, the fireplaces in the common rooms overlooking the lakes seem like the perfect location for a relaxing après-ski nightcap.

$150-250

Devotees of Alpine Meadows vie for rooms at the exclusive and beautiful ◖ **Stanford Alpine Chalet** (1980 Chalet Rd., 530/583-1550, $220–270), situated right at the base of Alpine's mountain. With only 14 rooms, you'll feel like a rock star when you stay here. Guest rooms are done up in simple yet elegant style, with lots of real wood; all rooms have private baths and many have striking mountain views. Meals are served family or B&B style, at big communal tables. In the summertime, the chalet offers a heated swimming pool, sports courts, and horseshoe pit, while in the winter guests can enjoy a private ski shuttle and the warmth of a giant great room fireplace. The outdoor hot tub lures guests to its bubbling warmth year-round. Oh, and if you happen to be a Stanford grad, you can get a discount with your alumni membership number.

From the outside, the **Cedar House Sport Hotel** (10918 Brockway Rd., 866/582-5655, www.cedarhousesporthotel.com, $210–330) looks just like a lodge in a town called Truckee ought to look. Think all-exposed wood exterior, landscaped with live trees, fallen stumps, and a great big rusty steel girder. But don't let the rustic charm or the name fool you, since the guest room interiors are all about the luxury. All rooms boast ultra-modern decor that would look great even in San Francisco or Los Angeles, such as light wood platform beds, designer leather chairs and sofas, and shining stainless steel fixtures in the private bathrooms. Choose from comfortable rooms with queen or king beds, or fancy suites with flat-screen TVs and every possible amenity. So where does the "sport" part come in? The staff at Cedar House have the expertise to help you create your Tahoe dream expedition, and if you call in advance they'll be happy to put together guided hikes, bike rides, and rafting or kayaking trips.

For travelers who prefer an intimate inn to a big impersonal condo block, there's the **Donner Lake Inn** (10070 Gregory Pl., Truckee, 530/587-5574, www.donnerlakeinn .com, $176–200). This five-room and one-cabin B&B offers simple charm in pretty, rustic Truckee. Each guest room has its own simple, homelike decorating scheme, without too many flowers or Victorianoid geegaws. You'll find your own private bathroom with shower, a private entrance to your room, a queen bed, a TV set with DVD player, and free wireless Internet. Unlike many B&Bs, the Donner Lake Inn even has a "family" room with bunk beds to accommodate a couple with two children. Each morning, the friendly and hospitable owners serve up a delicious full breakfast down in the dining room. Just ask them, and they'll be happy to help you set up everything from ski days to in-room spa treatments.

For the ultimate convenience in ski vacations, you can get a condo at **The Village at Squaw Valley** (1750 Village East Rd., Olympic Valley, 866/818-6963, www.thevillageatsquaw .com, $260) and never leave the vicinity of the lifts. Elegant, modern condos can be anywhere from compact studios perfect for singles or couples up through three-bedroom home-away-from-homes that sleep up to eight people traveling together. The Village condos have full kitchens with all appliances, fully stocked with utensils, and you might even get granite countertops. Each condo also has a living room with TV, maybe even a fireplace, and a dining table at which to serve home-cooked meals. Of all the posh amenities in The Village condos, the skiers' favorite is almost always the heated tile floors in the private bathrooms and the kitchen.

South Shore

Lots of chain motels cluster in the town of South Lake Tahoe, competing with the dozens of independent inns and lodges for the tourist trade. Despite the plethora of rooms available on the South Shore, it's still a good idea to make reservations well in advance for holiday weekends in both winter and summertime.

UNDER $100

For inexpensive year-round rooms, check in to the **Ambassador Motor Lodge** (4310 Manzanita Ave, South Lake Tahoe, 530/544-6461, www.ambassadorcapritahoe .com, $72–100, children under 16 free with adult). With its private beach access and associated water recreation options, rates are a touch higher in the summer months and bargain basement in the wintertime. Guest rooms have that basic motel feel, but a few soft touches make them appear prettier than the average bargain chain room. Amenities are also reminiscent of low-end chain motels; you will find coffee and a coffee maker, a TV set, and a private bathroom, but little else in the way of extras. The good news is that the Ambassador is on the lake for summer visitors, and only a short walk to the Heavenly gondola for winter guests.

$100-150

The small, rustic **Lazy S Lodge** (609 Emerald Bay Rd., South Lake Tahoe, 530/541-0230, www.lazyslodge.com, $105–140) has a great location away from the center of town, and some of the most reasonable room rates in the region. The 20 guest rooms all have microwaves, wet bars, TVs, phones, and private baths. You can choose from a studio room, with a nice bed, bath, and bar. Or choose a two-room cabin with sleeping room for several people, a kitchenette, and a nice warm fireplace that's perfect for chilly winter evenings. Facilities of this small lodge include a year-round hot tub, summer swimming pool, barbecue grills and outdoor picnic tables, and easy access to hiking and biking trails, warm lake swimming, and Heavenly ski resort.

Perhaps *the* most famous accommodation on Lake Tahoe is ◖ **Camp Richardson** (1900 Jameson Beach Rd., South Lake Tahoe, 800/544-1801, www.camprich.com, $145–275). Whether you just need a spot to pitch your own tent, or you want a luxurious private two-bedroom cabin to call your own, you can find the right space for you somewhere at Camp Richardson. Choose a room in the refurbished hotel or one of the many individual cabins, and you'll find rustic-style furnishings smoothed out by the luxurious fabrics and appointments. The hotel rooms are comfortable and quaint, with private baths and nice upscale amenities. Cabins offer full kitchens and linens, but no TVs or phones. (Note that all cabins are rented by the week in the summer months.) Outside your room, is a group recreation area, a beach, a marina, a restaurant, and the southern edge of the Tallac Historic Site, all on Camp Richardson's property.

For a condo on the South Shore, head on over to **The Lodge at Lake Tahoe** (3840 Pioneer Trail, South Lake Tahoe, 800/874-9900, www.lodgeatlaketahoe.com, $132–190). As Tahoe condo complexes go, it's not much to look at from the outside, and you might mistake it for a budget motel. But inside, the rooms have the elegant look of proper vacation condos, with colorful furnishings and tasteful prints on the walls. And the price is right for moderate budget travelers who want to save a few dollars by cooking for themselves. The smallest studios have only kitchenettes, but the larger condos offer fully equipped kitchens with utensils provided, as well as a nice table and chairs. Complex amenities include a summertime pool and spa, swing set, horseshoe pit, and outdoor barbecues near the pool area. Heavenly skiers will have easy access to the resort, and gamblers can get to the Stateline casinos in a few minutes.

$150-250

Spruce Grove Cabins (3599–3605 Spruce Ave., South Lake Tahoe, 800/777-0914, www.sprucegrovetahoe.com, $165–330) boasts a gay-friendly, dog-friendly Tahoe vacation experience. With only seven cabins on the property, you're guaranteed peace and privacy throughout your stay. Choose from one-bedroom and two-bedroom cabins, all with full kitchens, dining rooms, and living rooms with pull-out sofas to accommodate extra guests. Each cabin has its own wilderness-based decoration theme, from Snowshoe to Steamboat to Washoe Native American. You'll get your own bathroom, plus proper accommodations for your favorite furry friend. As one of the closest resorts to the Heavenly ski resort (right at Ski Run Blvd.), Spruce Grove gets its heaviest traffic in the wintertime.

OVER $250

Dedicated B&Bers enjoy the hospitality of the **Black Bear Inn** (1202 Ski Run Blvd., South Lake Tahoe, 877/232-7466, www.tahoeblackbear.com, $250–480). Located right on the road to Heavenly, you'll be thrilled when you spy the lovely large building with lodgepole and river-rock exterior accents. A giant fireplace dominates the great room, echoed by smaller but equally cozy river-rock fireplaces in the upstairs lodge guest rooms. Each unique room features a king-sized bed, posh private bathroom, free Wi-Fi, and an energy-building full breakfast. Appointments throughout the lodge rooms and cabins breathe luxury, from the cushy comforters to the rustic-elegant furniture. But the most beautiful spaces of all lie outside of the lodge and cabins, so be sure to take a few moments to stroll on the tree-lined paths and serene green lawns surrounding the inn.

Hardcore skiers who prefer to sleep as close to the slopes as possible book their rooms at the **◖ Deerfield Lodge at Heavenly** (1200 Ski Run Blvd., 888/757-3337, www.tahoedeer fieldlodge.com, call for rates). This resort drips luxury, from the whirlpool tubs in every slate-and-granite bathroom to the stone fireplaces in the spacious living areas of each guest room. Contemporary furniture and striking black-and-white linens compliment the ultra-comfy beds, while TVs, DVD players, and wireless Internet access combine to create the perfect home away from home. A kitchenette makes it easy to make coffee for your morning enjoyment, while the aromatherapy bath products lure tired skiers and swimmers into their bathrooms to soak the evening away. A yummy buffet continental breakfast is served in the common areas, and drinks and snacks form a tasty après-ski happy hour for guests. Just be sure to bring your credit card to the Deerfield, since all this luxury doesn't come cheap.

Nevada Side

The casino resorts are some of the spiffiest places to stay over on the Nevada side. In hopes of convincing you to come spend lots and lots of time gambling, they offer upscale, attractive hotel rooms, often at less-than-it-looks-like prices. You'll also find the occasional non-casino lakeshore resort that focuses more on the sports than the slots.

$100-150

The most popular casino resort on the Nevada side, **Harrah's** (15 Hwy. 50, Stateline, NV, 800/417-7247, www.harrahs.com, $110) offers upscale accommodations, all the nightlife and entertainment you need, and easy access to Heavenly and the other South Shore ski resorts in the winter, and to the lakeshore in the summer. The high-rise hotel has more than 500 posh rooms; even the lowest-end rooms have ample space, a California king or two double beds (your choice), two bathrooms (his and

hers), Wi-Fi, a TV with cable and premium movies (for a fee), mini-bar, and more. For (of course) more money, ask for a Premium Room that sits above the treeline to allow for excellent views of the lake and the mountains. Guest room decor is upscale and contemporary, with white linens and comforters, bright colorful accents, and sleek furnishings and wall art. With its variety of entertainment packages, Harrah's makes for a good location for both families and adults-only travelers. Be aware that rates vary hugely depending on the season, local events, and the weekday or weekend you plan to visit.

If you prefer the Nevada ski resorts, or you just want a change of scenery from Tahoe City or Truckee, try the **Inn at Incline** (1003 Tahoe Blvd., Incline Village, NV, 775/831-1052, $75–150). This budget inn offers 38 rooms in a mid-century-style modest motel. Guest rooms also feel reminiscent of a low-end motel, with older furniture and amenities. Notwithstanding the inn's age, the rooms are clean, and the private baths are adequate for their task. The amenities include an indoor pool and hot tub that are available year-round, TVs in all the rooms, and Wi-Fi in public areas.

$150-250

Club Tahoe (914 Northwood Blvd., Incline Village, 775/831-5750, www.clubtahoe.com, $165–275) at Incline Village is a great place to rent a condo on the Nevada side of the lake. Each condo here is a three-story, two-bedroom townhome with a loft with twin beds that serves as the bonus "third floor." These condos are perfect for families, or for a group of couples traveling together on a budget. Certainly the decor isn't the most contemporary, and expect 1970s- or '80s-era sofas, bargain-basement wooden furniture, and old-style paneling on the walls. But the kitchens come fully stocked with appliances and utensils and a full-sized fridge, the mattresses are newer than the rest of the furnishings, and a second bathroom off the "guest" bedroom makes sharing the condo much easier. Exterior amenities include an outdoor pool and spa, tennis court, racquetball court, arcade, and full bar with pool table for adults looking to unwind in the evening.

OVER $250
The **MontBleu Casino** (55 Hwy. 50, Stateline, NV, 888/829-7630, www.montbleuresort.com, $220–250) definitely shines when it comes to attractive hotel rooms with top amenities. Your tower room will include a comfortable bed, loud decor and fabrics, black-out curtains, room service, shiny clean private bathrooms, and all the conveniences you'd expect at an upper-tier chain. For extra luxury, try a Spa Room, which includes a pink marble bathroom, walk-in shower, and two-person hot tub in the bedroom. The one big downside in the MontBleu is the paper-thin room walls, so bring earplugs or expect to learn more than you ever wanted to know about your neighbors.

Perhaps the best-advertised Nevada-side non-casino resort is the **Zephyr Cove Resort** (750 Hwy. 50, Zephyr Cove, NV, 888/896-3830, www.zephyrcove.com, $220–375). This resort has it all: lakefront property, lodge rooms and individual cabins, its own full-service marina, a winter snowmobiling shuttle and park, restaurants, and evening entertainment options. Guests of Zephyr Cove can choose between a room inside the big lodge, or their own cabin down by the lake. The four lodge rooms all have private baths, attractive modern appointments and fabrics, TVs, microwaves, small fridges, and coffee makers. For a special treat, ask for the room with the spa tub. The 28 cabins run from cozy studios for couples to multi-story chalets that sleep up to 10 people. Though they look rustic and woodsy from the outside, indoors you'll find modern furniture, phones, TVs with cable and movie channels, and all the amenities you'd expect of a nice lakeside resort. Because Zephyr Cove bills itself as a rental resort rather than a full-scale hotel, maid service is provided only every other day inside the lodge, and every third day in the cabins. Zephyr Cove offers pet-friendly lodgings, but you'll need to let them know which furry friends you're bringing when you make your reservations.

FOOD
North Shore
CAFE
To fuel up for a day out on the lake or in the mountains, head over to the **Fire Sign Café** (1785 W. Lake Blvd., 530/583-0871, daily 7 A.M.–3 P.M., $8–15). This breakfast-and-lunch spot, a favorite with locals, serves up an enormous menu of hearty fare. Choose from a whole-grain waffle with fruit to a kielbasa omelet, crepes to blueberry coffee cake. Expect a wait for a table on weekend mornings.

CALIFORNIA
The best restaurant in Truckee, and possibly in all of the Tahoe region, is undoubtedly ◖ **Moody's** (10007 Bridge St., Truckee, 530/587-8688, www.moodysbistro.com, Mon.–Thurs. 11:30 A.M.–9:30 P.M., Fri. 11:30 A.M.–10 P.M., Sat. 11 A.M.–10 P.M., Sun. 11:30 A.M.–9:30 P.M., $22–30). This casual-elegant eatery with fresh herbs decorating its tables adjoins the historic Truckee Hotel, just off the main commercial drag in town. The warren of tiny rustic dining rooms show a few traditional French prints on the walls, plus a handwritten plug for the local CSA program. On weekends, strains of live jazz permeate from the lounge—just enough to be a charming background but not so loud as to forbid conversation. You'll definitely want to make reservations for weekend evenings since locals pack in here, making table space a premium. The reason everyone comes here isn't the lovely atmosphere—it's the food. Moody's puts together a menu that makes visiting chefs swoon with joy. Ingredients are seasonal, local, sustainable, and organic, while the preparations show off the chef's vivid imagination. You might find antelope on the menu, or local fish. For dessert, the cook-it-yourself s'mores brought to your table with a burner and skewers are the hands-down favorite. The alcoholic coffees are *not* old standards and are well worth your time; just imagine proper drinking chocolate laced with homemade peppermint schnapps! In the state that invented California cuisine, and that's filled to the brim with great

upscale restaurants of all kinds, Moody's still manages to stand out and shine.

The combination of ethnic cuisines may seem catch-all and bizarre, but the taste tells the tale at **Wolfdale's** (640 N. Lake Blvd., Tahoe City, 530/583-5700, www.wolfdales .com, Wed.–Mon. 5–10 P.M., $15–25). Billing it as "cuisine unique," the Wolfdale serves dishes that fuse Western and Far Eastern foods to create tastes you can't find elsewhere. The small seasonal menu leans heavy on seafood, though you can also find some tasty beef and game meats at the right time of year. Lighter diners often prefer the homemade soups, salads, or unusual appetizers. Be sure to save room for the delicious desserts, most made in a light California style.

After a long day of skiing, the **Terrace Bar & Restaurant** (800/403-0206, www.squaw .com/terrace-bar-restaurant) at The Village at Squaw Valley can feed even the hungriest skiers. Non-skiers and casual visitors favor the Terrace because of its floor-to-ceiling windows offering fabulous views of the mountains. Everyone enjoys the casual California-style fare of mostly soups, salads, and sandwiches. If the Terrace isn't your preference, you can also try one of several other Squaw Valley eateries, including the **Wildflour Bakery & Café** (1960 Squaw Valley Rd., 530/583-1963, www .squaw.com/winter/wildflour/wf1.htm) and **Alexander's Café & Bar** (1960 Squaw Valley Rd., 530/581-7278, daily 5–9 P.M.).

ITALIAN
Zano's Pizza (11401 Donner Pass Rd., 530/587-7411, www.zanos.net, daily 11:30 A.M.–2 P.M. and 4–9:30 P.M., Fri.–Sat. open until 10 P.M., $12–30) can hook you up with huge pizzas and tremendous salads in a big, casual dining room with the latest games playing on the TVs over the bar. A mural depicting the Italian countryside (complete with cows) graces the rear wall, and glass block semi-walls break up the sweeping dining space for a cozier feel. The full menu includes pastas and Italian entrées. At lunchtime, the hot, crisp paninis taste great. But it's the thin-crust pizzas that rule the house here, and you can pick one of Zano's interesting combinations or build your own from the list of fresh ingredients. Should the kids get bored, an arcade at the back can provide easy entertainment.

South Shore
BREAKFAST
For a classic American breakfast, it's tough to do better than the **Red Hut Waffle Shop** (2723 Lake Tahoe Blvd., South Lake Tahoe, 530/541-9024, $5–12, cash only). This down-home waffle spot serves classic crispy, thin waffles (if you're looking for huge, fat Belgian waffles, this isn't your place), plus biscuits and gravy, omelets, and plenty more. Locals recommend the waffle sandwich, which is a complete breakfast in a single dish. Expect to wait for a table or a seat at the counter on weekend mornings, as this spot gets popular with both visitors and residents.

CAFÉ AND DELI
For an unusual combination of hardcore health food and budget dining, check out **Sprouts Cafe** (3123 Harrison Ave., South Lake Tahoe, 530/541-6969, daily 8 A.M.–9 P.M., $8–15) in town at South Lake Tahoe. This cute, casual walk-up eatery offers an array of ultra-healthy dishes make with all-fresh, mostly organic produce and ingredients. Despite the wheatgrass growing on purpose-built shelves and the giant juicer on the rear counter, Sprouts has a pleasantly surprising number of items that appeal to non-health-food nuts. Breakfast is served all day, and the lunch and dinner menus run on for pages. Choose from salads, burritos, rice bowls, and even tasty vegetarian and vegan desserts. If you're truly brave, start your day with the legendary Hot Shot. You'll take your order to one of the rough-hewn tables and spice it yourself from the array of condiments over to the side of the restaurant. From there, sit back and linger over your tasty guilt-free grub, herbal tea, or organic, fair-trade coffee.

Rude Brothers Bagel & Coffee Haus (3117 Harrison Ave., Ste. B, 530/541-8195) looks and feels just about right for an indie coffee shop and sandwich bar. It's got a big open room for hanging out, and a tasty array of lunch goodies on tap for hungry visitors. They've also got all the usual espresso drinks available at the counter. This is definitely a locals' hangout.

ITALIAN
If the crowds at Heavenly have got you longing for a more intimate evening, book one of the seven tables at **Café Fiore** (1169 Ski Run Blvd., #5, South Lake Tahoe, 530/541-2908, www .cafefiore.com, daily from 5:30 P.M., $17–35) for dinner. This tiny bistro serves upscale Italian fare with a fabulous wine list. The exterior charms with its alpine-chalet look, while the inside defines the concept of "romantic restaurant." Right on Ski Run Boulevard, Café Fiore is convenient to both the Heavenly ski resort and to the lakeshore resorts of South Lake Tahoe.

SEAFOOD
Serious sushi aficionados might be concerned about trying raw ocean fish way out east in Tahoe. But the **Off the Hook California Sushi Bar** (2660 Lake Tahoe Blvd., #E., 530/544-5599, www.offthehooksushi.com) offers good rolls and fresh nigiri for vaguely reasonable prices. Don't expect too much from some of the traditional Japanese dishes, and you'll have an enjoyable dining experience here.

Nevada Side
The **Ciera Steakhouse at the MontBleu** (55 Hwy. 50, Stateline, NV, 800/648-3353, www.montbleuresort.com, Sun.–Thurs. 5:30–10 P.M., Fri.–Sat. 5:30–10:30 P.M., $20–35) provides precisely the experience diners expect from a mid-grade casino steakhouse. The dining room boasts blocky modern decor in soothing colors, an exposed wine cellar window, and big raised booths with plush red curtains that can be drawn to create a private dining experience. On the menu, you'll find plenty of steak and non-steak options, with preparations designed to appeal to visitors from across America. Sadly, the kitchen doesn't always get it quite right, and steaks tend to be overdone by California standards. But hang in there, since the coolest part of the Ciera dining experience comes in right at the end. Even if you don't usually do it, order coffee at the end of your meal. It comes with a fabulous tray of fixings, including delicious flavored whipped creams. And finally, you'll be presented with a complimentary dish of chocolate-covered strawberries resting atop a frothing container of dry ice. It's fabulous!

Sometimes, it's what a guidebook *doesn't* recommend that's most important. When you're driving up the backside of the lake in Nevada, the restaurant choices become thin for many miles. You may find yourself starving, and the only thing that you can find that's open is the **Café at the Biltmore Hotel and Casino.** You're better off scrounging from your leftover snacks. The only thing worse than the food here is the service. It's special to find a spot where the waiters actually hide from the customers. Granted, you can get coffee here, which might help you wake up enough to push on to Incline Village or even Tahoe City.

INFORMATION AND SERVICES
Tourist Information
The different regions around Lake Tahoe each have their own visitors centers. The **South Lake Tahoe Visitors Center** (Hwy. 50 at Tallack, 775/588-5900, www.bluelaketahoe.com) sits adjacent to the tiny Lake Tahoe Museum. It's got every brochure and leaflet you can possibly imagine, plus some good discount coupons. Sadly, the counter help tends towards younger folks who don't have as many decisive recommendations as might be helpful.

Media and Communication
The Lake Tahoe region has its own daily newspaper, the *Tahoe Daily Tribune* (www .tahoedailytribune.com). Pick up a copy at any newsstand, or ask for it at your hotel.

Lots of Internet access graces the cities around Lake Tahoe, since most youthful snowboarders expect to be able to hit the Wi-Fi on their Blackberries. Ask at your hotel, or find one of the dozens of Internet cafés that clutter the landscape. Most of the casinos have access as well.

Banks and Post Office

To get cash, you'll need to hit the ATMs in Truckee, Tahoe City, South Lake Tahoe, or Stateline. Naturally, all the casinos on the Nevada side proffer plenty of cash machines as well.

You can get to post offices easily in South Lake Tahoe (3180 Hwy. 50), Truckee (10050 Bridge St.), Tahoe City (7005 N. Lake Blvd., Tahoe Vista, 530/546-5600), and Stateline (223 Kingsbury Grade, 775/588-1943).

Medical Services

Plenty of medical facilities open their doors to luckless skiers in the cities around Tahoe. The major ski resorts also tend to have high-tech and extremely functional medical facilities on-site. If you injure yourself on the slopes, your best bet is to let the ski patrol take care of you rather than trying to take care of yourself.

If you need medical attention off-slopes in the North Shore, the **Tahoe Forest Hospital** (10121 Pine Ave., Truckee, 530/587-6011, www.tfhd.com) in Truckee has a full-service emergency room and plenty of services. On the South Shore, you can go to **Barton Memorial Hospital** (2170 South Ave., South Lake Tahoe, 530/543-5605, www.bartonhealth.org).

GETTING THERE AND AROUND
Air

The closest commercial airport to Lake Tahoe sits in Reno. The **Reno International Airport** (2001 E. Plumb Ln., Reno, NV, 775/328-6870, www.renoairport.com) offers flights on many major airlines and a few smaller carriers. This airport is open year-round, but be sure to check your flights in advance in the winter-time since storms delay and sometimes cancel flights here. Once you're in Reno, it's easy to rent a car or a truck in the airport from any of the major agencies.

Bus

You can't get to Tahoe by train, but **Amtrak** (1000 Emerald Bay Rd., 800/872-7245, www.amtrak.com) does run a bus service to South Lake Tahoe down at the South Y transit center.

Car

The main roads to Lake Tahoe from points west (the Bay Area, Sacramento, Wine Country, the Central Coast) are I-80 and state Highway 50. I-80 takes you to the North Shore and Highway 50 to the South Shore. It takes about five hours to drive up to Lake Tahoe from the San Francisco Bay Area in good weather without traffic. From Sacramento, it's only about two hours. But don't expect good weather or light traffic if you're planning to drive up to Tahoe on a Friday in winter. Everybody else will be on the road with you, significantly slowing down the routes. Generally, Highway 50 runs a bit faster than I-80, but you'll want to check traffic reports before you hit the road to see which way will work best.

Visitors doing a full tour of the eastern California mountains starting in the Eastern Sierra will take state Highway 120 from Yosemite or Mammoth up to Tahoe. As always, check road conditions before attempting this route in winter. Storms may cause chain requirements or even wholesale road closures.

Carry chains that fit your vehicle in winter, unless you're driving a four-wheel drive *and* know how to navigate in snow. Chains are often required near and around Tahoe in winter. There are lots of spots to pull off and attach your chains on I-80 and Highway 50. You can also buy chains on the road, but the closer you get to Tahoe, the more expensive chains get.

In winter, even the highways can close during major storms. And the smaller roads surrounding the lake can shut down for weeks at a time. Again, traffic reports both on the radio and online can give you information about road closures and alternate routes. If you're planning a winter trip, be aware of the weather and plan for a certain amount of uncertainty.

Ski Resort Shuttles

Parking at the ski resorts, especially on weekends, can be a serious hassle. A much better option, if you're staying in one of the towns, is the resort shuttles. Most of the major ski resorts maintain shuttles that bring skiers and their equipment up to the mountains in the morning and back down to their hotels in the late afternoon. You can usually find seasonal brochures for the shuttles in all the major hotels and resorts. If not, you can call or go online for the shuttles for Squaw Valley (www.squaw.com/getting-squaw), Heavenly (www.skiheavenly.com/mountain/services/shuttle_system), Alpine Meadows (www.skialpine.com/winter/plan/shuttle_schedule), and Kirkwood (www.kirkwood.com/winter/busshuttle.php), among others.

Tours and Cruises

If exploring on your own isn't enough, or you're not comfortable driving your own boat and you really want to get out on the water, a number of cruises and tours are offered all around Lake Tahoe.

If you want to get out on the water in a bigger boat, book a cruise with **Lake Tahoe Cruises** (800/238-2463, http://laketahoe-cruises.com, http://zephyrcove.com, adults $40–70, children $20–40). Two honest-to-goodness paddlewheel riverboats make cruises on Lake Tahoe on a near-daily basis—even in the wintertime! In the south, the *Tahoe Queen*

sails from Ski Run Marina and offers an array of cruises, several with meals, live music, and dancing. You can even take a ski shuttle-cruise that buses you up to Northstar in the morning, then takes you home across the breadth of the lake—an on-board après-ski party you'll enjoy whether you're up for dancing or just want a drink while sitting at one of the windows watching the water go by. The *MS Dixie II,* a rear paddlewheeler, was imported from the Mississippi River. It sails from the Zephyr Cove Marina, and you can choose from breakfast and brunch cruises, dinner and dancing cruises, and even on-the-water showings of the oh-so-appropriate musical *Show Boat.*

Another company that can take you to see the lovely Emerald Bay is **Bleu Wave** (866/413-0985, www.tahoebleuwave.com, adults $59–65, children $29.50), which operates from the **Round Hill Pine Beach & Marina** (325 Hwy. 50, Zephyr Cove, NV, 775/588-3055, www.rhpbeach.com) in Stateline. You'll see many of the most popular sights on the lake as you take a two-hour lunch cruise with an all-you-can-eat buffet and drinks included. For winter cruises, you'll enjoy the on-board fireplace and the spacious heated cabin. In the heat of summer, most folks prefer to sit outside in the fresh mountain air.

Mount Shasta

Star of photo and video, and perhaps the most iconic single mountain peak in all California, is majestic Mount Shasta. Gorgeous views of the tremendous dormant volcano are available along more than a dozen miles on I-5. In the wintertime, snow covers much of the huge mountain, while in the summertime glaciers decorate only the upper reaches near the peak.

To truly appreciate Mount Shasta, either come and camp in the cool forest or get a room at one of the quaint inns or relaxing retreat centers in the tiny town that also goes by the name of Mount Shasta. Numerous small towns spread out away from the mountain in

all directions, providing a few minutes of sightseeing or a spot to eat or lay your head.

Shasta makes for a great weekend trip all on its own, or it can be a fun overnight (or more) stop if you're making a trip up to the northern reaches of the California coast and want to loop back on a different set of roads.

SIGHTS

Hands down, if you're going to Mount Shasta, the one sight you must see is…Mount Shasta. Not that it's easy to miss; the 14,000-foot-tall cluster of volcanic peaks creates a unique shape high on the skyline. Ample spots exist all around the mountain for great photo opportunities.

But don't get too blown away by the mountain, since many other beautiful sights await you around Mount Shasta, from waterfalls to lava beds to cute museums. Take a few minutes away from the drama of the peak and peek into a landscape even many California residents don't know exists.

◰ MacArthur-Burney Falls

Often billed as the most beautiful waterfall in California, even by regular visitors to Yosemite, MacArthur-Burney Falls (Hwy. 89, 6 miles north of Hwy. 299, 530/335-2777, www .parks.ca.gov) draws the young and old alike. Unlike many California waterfalls, Burney Falls (as it's known to its friends) flows strong and true all year long and is just as beautiful in September as it is in April. The best news of all, you don't have to hike to reach the falls; they're right there as soon as you hit the parking lot. Still, it's more than worth your time to get out of your car and take a walk around the wide sheets of water that are almost reminiscent of Niagara in miniature. It's only a quick walk to the pool at the base of the falls. For the best set of views, take the one-mile-and-change hike around the 129-foot waterfall. The trails are well developed, with nice flat surfaces and low stone walls.

So how do the falls manage to keep falling all year long? Much of the water feeding Burney Creek bubbles up from springs created during periods of local volcanic activity. The creek grows wide and then cascades down to the perennially misty green-blue pool. You'll love that mist more than anything if you're visiting in the height of summer. It gets very hot here, but please don't try to swim beneath the falls. The force and currents can be quite dangerous.

McCloud Falls

Another wonderful regional waterfall to visit is McCloud Falls (www.waterfallswest.com) on the—surprise!—McCloud River. You'll find the name accurate—in truth you've got the opportunity to see three separate waterfalls here. The Lower McCloud Falls acts as the prelude, with roiling white water pouring over a 30-foot rock wall into an aerated river pool below. Next, the Middle McCloud Falls resembles a tiny half-Niagara, a level fall of water that's wider than it is tall. (A lot of these types of waterfalls cluster around the mountains.) Finally, Upper McCloud Falls cascades powerfully but shortly down into a chilly but occasionally welcome pool that can double as a swimming hole.

To get there, exit I-5 on Highway 89 east toward McCloud. After about five miles, start looking for signs to Fowler's Camp and Lower McCloud Falls. After about a mile, you'll come to the Lower Falls picnic area, where you can park.

Mossbrae Falls

Rather than one big gush of water through a narrow slot, Mossbrae Falls (Scarlett Way, Dunsmuir, www.waterfallswest.com) flows like a wild woman's hair—loose and all over the place. Just past the bridge and railroad tracks, these unique falls shower down into the deep blue-gray of the Sacramento River. The constant mists nourish an unbelievable cascade of greenery, from ferns to full-sized trees. You get to the beautiful and oddly pristine jungle by walking about 2.5 miles along the train tracks, then looking to the right just before you come to the railroad bridge.

Lava Beds National Monument

Some of the best views of volcanic activity in extreme Northern California lie within Lava Beds National Monument (Hill Rd., www .nps.gov/labe, Memorial Day–Labor Day daily 8 A.M.–6 P.M., Labor Day–Memorial Day daily 8:30 A.M.–5 P.M.). Over hundreds of millennia, the Medicine Lake shield volcano has created an amazing landscape. In amongst the Modoc battle sites, campgrounds, and desert-like wilderness, you'll find numerous caves created by ancient lava tubes. Some of these have been developed with ladders and walkways, others remain in their original difficult-

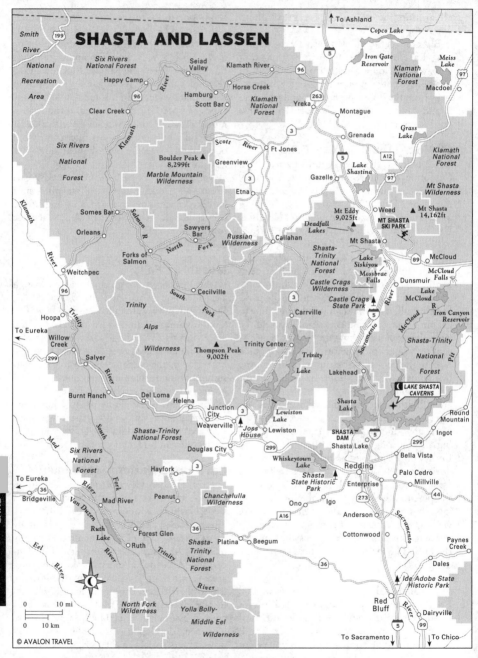

SHASTA AND LASSEN

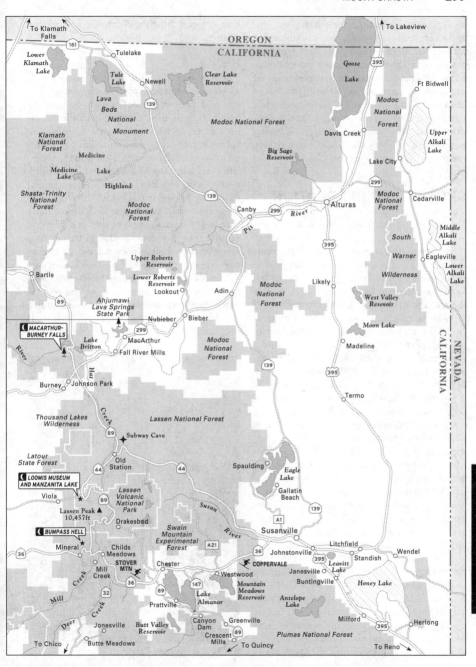

to-explore state. But they're worth your time and energy, even if you're not usually a spelunker. Not all of the lava tubes have remained empty for all these years; some have become home to whole ecosystems that thrive in the dark and the damp. Bring a flashlight, but be kind to the bats that dwell in these caves while you're checking out the ferns, mineral formations, and other unique features. Whether you've been into volcanoes in the past or not, the Lava Beds stand a good chance of winning you over.

SPORTS AND RECREATION

The main reason folks come to the Mount Shasta region is to enjoy its outdoor wonders and challenges. Shasta offers nearly unlimited sporting opportunities year-round. Just be sure to prepare for whatever activities you plan to tackle and enjoy, as Shasta gets blisteringly hot in the summertime (well, except at the peak of the mountain) and frigid in the winter.

With all the climbing and skiing and hardcore hiking available on and around Mount Shasta, it's not surprising that you'll find a number of outdoor athletic stores in the town of the same name. **The Fifth Season** (300 N. Mt. Shasta Blvd., Mt. Shasta, 530/926-3606, www.thefifthseason.com, open daily) has not only mountain bikes, it's got ski and snowboard equipment and other recreation gear. Most of all, it's got all the mountain climbing equipment and advice you need to scale the peak of Mount Shasta. You can start at their website before you come, then go into their storefront in town to rent or purchase everything from boots to ice axes to crampons; before you start up the mountain, call 530/926-5555 for a recording that describes the current conditions approaching Mount Shasta's summit.

If it's ski and snowboard equipment, adjustment, rental, or repair you need, your best choice might be **The Sportsman's Den** (402 N. Mt. Shasta Blvd., Mt. Shasta, 530/926-2295, www.mtshastasports.com, daily 8 A.M.–6 P.M.). This shop specializes in fine-tuning high-end snowboards and fitting skis to a perfect T. In the summer, the Sportsman's Den offers fishing tackle and some sporting equipment.

Hiking

The best way to see the Mount Shasta area is to get out of your car, onto your own two feet, and walk back into the wilderness. Some of the best hiking in all of California can be found on and around Mount Shasta. This beautiful region abounds with waterfalls, pine forests, rivers, streams, and fascinating geology. Informal camping and backpacking (wilderness permits required) can create a wonderful multi-day hiking trip. Day hikes offer everything from easy strolls great for kids and older travelers to strenuous miles that can take you up to minor mountain peaks for tremendous views of the whole southern Cascade mountain region.

The Shasta-Trinity National Recreation Area (www.fs.fed.us/r5/shastatrinity/recreation/nra/index.shtml#Recreation) encompasses quite a bit of land. Unlike many parks, the trailheads of Shasta-Trinity tend to be spread out. You'll

MacArthur-Burney Falls

© ROBERT HOLMES / CALTOUR

need to do some highway driving between many of them.

DAY HIKING

For an unlikely extension of a story that flowers way down on the Central Coast, take a walk along the **Ah-Di-Na Historic Trail** (0.25 mile, easy). Follow the signs from Squaw Valley Creek Road at the Reservoir to this odd little resort area along the McCloud River. The William Randolph Hearst family created a retreat here and you'll see photos of their property on the interpretive signs marking the short, flat trail. It's a bit of a drive out to Ah-Di-Na, and while you can take a passenger car, plan to traverse dirt roads and spend some time getting out there.

While the name of the **Sims Flat Historic Trail** (Sims Rd., south of the river, 1 mile, easy) refers to the name of the former logging town here, the trail itself is flat too. Sims Flat was once a bustling logging town, with the railroad running through it to carry products of the busy sawmill away to the big cities that needed fresh lumber. Nearly a century later, a few historic signs tell the story of this diverse ex-town. Another great thing about this walk are the up-close views of Mount Shasta, which looms over Sims Flat, offering many photo opportunities.

BACKCOUNTRY HIKING

Way over on the other end of the hiking spectrum, heavy-duty hiking buffs seek out the **Sisson-Callahan National Recreation Trail** (North Shore Rd., 18 miles round-trip, difficult); just past Deer Creek Bridge, take the left fork and park off the road. Starting near Lake Siskyou, this trail gains almost a mile in elevation, peaking at over 8,000 feet at Deadfall Summit, then dropping 1,000 feet to Deadfall Lakes. Be sure to dress in layers, since you might start out in the intense summer heat of the lower elevations only to end up making snowballs up on the summit. Because it's long and steep and challenging, many hikers prefer to do this trail over more than one day. Any number of campsites lie along the North Fork

of the Sacramento River and beyond, welcoming weary travelers with a spot to pitch a tent and enjoy a night's rest. In fact, the Sisson-Callahan links up with the Pacific Crest Trail down near Deadfall Lakes, letting backpackers keep on packin' if they choose to.

For a lovely long hike that takes you up to views of the whole of the Far North mountain region and into Oregon, trek up to **Mount Eddy** (Forest Service Rd. 17, 530/926-4511, 10 miles round-trip, difficult). You'll find a steep trail that takes you up to the 9,000-foot peak, where you can spin around and around, checking out various and sundry Cascade mountains: Shasta, Lassen, the Trinity Alps, and even Mount McLaughlin up in Oregon. The trail up from the Deadfall Lake trailhead is hot and dry, and you'll want to bring plenty of water as you'll find none here. You will find granite at the bottom of the mountain and green serpentine toward the top, lots of shade from the fir and pine trees proliferating on the mountainsides, and the clear waters of Deadfall Lake and Deadfall Creek on your way up to the lovely peak. (A number of hikers claim you can drink from the creek, but check with the rangers first and consider bringing purifiers if you plan to try this.) If you're not up for such a long day hike, consider an overnight camping trip; the lake makes a great informal primitive campground.

You know that cool brown-black cinder cone that sits close to the bottom of the mountain? Originally called Muir's Peak by humble naturalist John Muir, this "cinder cone" was created about 10,000 years ago during the same slow, thick magma eruption that created the Shastina crater. Believe it or not, you can scale the slick-looking sides of **Black Butte** (5 miles round-trip, difficult). It really is pretty slick. The trail ascends almost 1,900 feet in about 2.5 miles, with serious steep and rocky spots. In recent years, vegetation has started taking root in Black Butte, but the trail still offers precious little in the way of shade and no water at all. Bring plenty of water, and plan your hike for early morning if you're visiting in the summertime.

Climbing

Climbers come from all over the world come to tackle Shasta's majestic 14,162-foot peak. Be sure to pack your sturdiest hiking boots and your strongest leg muscles; less than one-third of the 15,000 intrepid mountaineers who try to conquer **Mount Shasta** (www.climbing mtshasta.org) each year actually make it to the top. If you're serious, you'll get plenty of help from the locals. Mountaineering and glacier classes are available, and several guides and outfitters can provide equipment and even lead you up the mountain. Take that help! You'll be required to negotiate Shasta's year-round icy glaciers, steep and rocky slopes, and extreme altitudes that thin the air to make the climb just that much tougher.

So what's the good news? There are more than a dozen routes you can take to ascend to the top. You can pick a quick, hardcore climb that takes you from the base camp up to the top in a single day, or choose a longer and more leisurely trail and spend two days making the trek, camping overnight in the ultimate California wilderness. The most popular route runs along Avalanche Gulch, and for the healthy and hearty, this can be the adventure of a lifetime. You'll see Mount Shasta up close in ways that most casual tourists could never even imagine. The peak climbing season is June through August.

If you are a casual tourist, exercise care accessing even the trailheads that lead to Shasta's peak. Some of the dirt roads around the base of the mountain require a four-wheel drive, and the weather conditions can severely impact the roads. To make this climb safely and successfully, you must be prepared, so check the web, talk to locals, and gather maps and equipment.

Nearby, the formation at **Castle Crags State Park** (on I-5, 6 miles south of Dunsmuir, 530/235-2684, www.parks.ca.gov) offers more than 40 established climbing routes, plus plenty of wide, open formations for explorers who prefer to climb where no one has climbed before. You'll get to tackle domes, spires, and walls of granite that reach 6,000 feet up toward the sky.

The crags first thrusted upward, then broke off and were scrubbed by glaciers into the fascinating, climbable formations visible today. Some of the known favorite climbs at Castle Crags are the Cosmic Wall, Castle Dome East, and Six Toe Crack.

Fishing

The rivers, streams, creeks, and lakes surrounding Mount Shasta make for some of the best freshwater fishing in all of California.

Fishing is permitted in Trinity Lake, Whiskeytown Lake, and most of the smaller lakes in the Shasta-Trinity National Recreation Area. You can bring your powered fishing boat to Trinity and Whiskeytown (be prepared to have it inspected for invasive mussels). Types of fish in these lakes include rainbow trout, German brown trout, kokanee salmon, and Mackinaw, among others. All you need is a California fishing license, tackle, and plenty of bait. Check with the bait and tackle shops in the area to learn what type of bait is working this season, and where the best spots are.

Almost all the major rivers and feeder streams running through the Mount Shasta region are open to fishing. You can tie your fly on and cast out into the McCloud River, the Sacramento River, the Trinity River, and many more. These rivers carry salmon, steelhead, and trout. If you want a guide to help you navigate these waters, contact one of the many services that can take you out to the perfect fishing holes. For fly-fishing, call **Jack Trout International Fly Fishing Guide Service** (530/926-4540, www.jacktrout.com). Jack's guides can both take you out to the rivers and help you improve your fly-casting technique. **Outdoor Adventures Sport Fishing** (800/670-4448, www.sacriverguide.com) not only takes trips out to the major NorCal rivers, it can guide you on a deep-water trip to Shasta Lake as well.

Rafting and Kayaking

In the Cascades, the best whitewater rafting to be had is definitely on the **Trinity River.** And a good guide service to take you out onto the big white waters of this river is (naturally) **Trinity River Rafting** (800/307-4837, www.trinityriverrafting.com, $54–125). In addition to its flagship runs on the Trinity, this major rafting company runs on the Klamath, the Salmon, the Upper Fork Sacramento, and Canyon Creek. So depending on where you're staying and what level of rafting you're up to handling, you can choose your favorite river to paddle. Anywhere from half-day to three-day trips are available on various rivers, and you can choose from placid Class I and II float suitable for the whole family to an aggro Class IV–V run for fit, experienced rafters only. Trinity Rafting also rents small rafts and one- and two-person kayaks for paddlers who want to go off on their own.

Another major player in the northern mountains rafting scene is the **Bigfoot Rafting Company** (800/722-2223, www.bigfoot rafting.com, $85). With day trips on the Trinity and Salmon, and multi-day rafting campouts on the Trinity and the Klamath, Bigfoot presents a depth of knowledge of the rivers it runs. Your guide will know a great deal about the history and natural surroundings of your chosen river, and as a bonus can cook you up fabulous meals on full-day and multi-day trips. Bigfoot also rents equipment.

New to river rafting? You probably won't meet at the rafting company's office. When you book your trip, you'll be given a spot to arrive at along your chosen river. The company will most likely also give you a list of items to bring with you, such as swimsuits, sweaters, specific shoes, waterproof cameras, and other such things. Be sure to ask questions when making your reservation.

Skiing and Snowboarding

The snow pack on Mount Shasta each winter creates a haven for downhill skiers, cross-country skiers, snowboarders, and snowshoers. The place to go for all this is the **Mount Shasta Ski Park** (Ski Run Hwy., 530/926-8610, www.ski park.com, Dec.–Apr. Wed.–Sat. 9 A.M.–9 P.M., Sun.–Tues. 9 A.M.–4 P.M., lift tickets: adults $25–39, youth $15–20, children/seniors $5).

This small but fun downhill park has 425 skiable acres, three chair lifts, and a tow rope. Nearly half the runs are open for night skiing, and the Marmot beginner area makes a perfect spot for beginners of all ages to gain their snow legs (at a fraction of the cost they'd pay in Tahoe). Half-day discount lift tickets and night-skiing-only lift tickets make skiing here even more attractive for snow-loving bargain hunters.

Cross-country lovers can also get their fix at the **Mt. Shasta Nordic Center** (Ski Park Hwy., 1 mile before downhill park, 530/926-2142, www.mtshastanordic.org, Dec.–Apr., free). With 15 miles of groomed trails, plus ample skiable backcountry, everyone from casual cross-country skiers and beginners to hardcore trail-breakers can have a good time here.

Horseback Riding

The wilderness around and on Mount Shasta beckons to equestrians with a penchant for trail rides. Many of the hiking trails in the Shasta-Trinity wilderness and the surrounding regions also allow horseback riders. You can bring your own horse up to the majestic mountain region, or you can look to one of the local stable spread across the countryside.

Shasta Cove Stables (800/662-3529, www.visitsiskiyou.org/shastacovestables, $35/hour, $155/day) can take you on the ride of your dreams, whether that's a brief tour created by the stables or a multiday excursion into the back country planned by you and the stable together. Camps and lessons are available, focused on children.

Another outfit sits all the way up in Yreka is the **Rockin Maddy Ranch** (11921 Cram Gulch Rd., 530/340-2100, www.rockinmaddyranch .com, $45–175). Choose from the 90-minute Shasta View ride that features grand vistas of the mountain, or the 90-minute Shasta Lake ride. For a more intense experience, take a full-day ride through the mountains, including tracks along rivers, past waterfalls, and with time to stop to fish while you're out. Rockin Maddy allows smaller children to ride double on the same horse, and has a small herd of ponies for very small children. You can even book a hayride or a carriage ride.

Mountain Biking

Some of the best and most unusual scenic mountain biking in all of California sits way up at **Lava Beds National Monument** (Hill Rd., www.nps.gov/labe, Memorial Day–Labor Day 8 A.M.–6 P.M., Labor Day–Memorial Day 8:30 A.M.–5 P.M.). You can bike on (relatively) recent lava flows, explore lava tubes, and check out the craters and calderas the volcano left behind. Or for an easier ride, explore the territory of the **Medicine Lake Highland** (530/233-5811, www.fs.fed.us/r5/modoc/recreation/mountain-biking.shtml) east of McCloud in the Modoc National Forest. This region contains Native American sacred sites, so please be respectful. Call the park for more information and the best spots to enter the mountain biking area.

ACCOMMODATIONS
Under $100

The cute **Dream Inn** (326 Chestnut St., 530/926-1536, www.dreaminnmtshastacity.com, $88–176) offers bed-and-breakfast accommodations right at the base of the magnificent mountain. The four small, inexpensive upstairs rooms have unique furnishings and shared hallway bathrooms. Downstairs, a bigger white antique bedroom has its own private bath and a view of Mount Eddy out of the lace-curtained window. Right next door, two large suites share space in a Spanish-adobe-style home; each has its own living space, bathroom, and truly homelike, cluttered decor. Rooms at the Dream Inn include a scrumptious full breakfast each morning.

The ultimate in clean, comfortable, and cheap lodgings at Shasta is the **Mount Shasta Ranch Bed and Breakfast** (1008 W. A. Barr Rd., 877/926-3870, www.stayinshasta.com, $66–130). The budget-friendly rooms in the Carriage House offer small spaces, queen beds, and shared bathrooms. The separate Cottage is the largest room in the house, with two bedrooms that can comfortably sleep up to six people. The four rooms in the Ranch

House proper are spacious and comfortably furnished with a clutter of country-Victorian antiques and tchotckes, and each has its own big private bathroom. All rooms include a full country breakfast served just before 9 A.M. to get you up, moving, and fueled for a long day out in the Shasta wilderness.

$100-150

To get a real sense of life in this remote region, book one of the rooms in the **(Shasta MountInn Retreat & Spa** (203 Birch St., 530/926-1810, www.shastamountinn.com, $138–195). The big white farmhouse exterior fits perfectly into its semi-alpine setting, while the rooms ooze country charm and modern comforts. Each of the four rooms has its own private bath and high-end memory foam mattress, which tempts guests to loll about in bed all morning rather than heading downstairs for a healthy continental breakfast and a cup or two of organic coffee. The "spa" part comes in with on-site massage therapy services and a funky barrel-shaped redwood sauna. And if you're serious about taking a spiritual retreat into the local woods and waterways, your hosts can guide you to the sacred spots that dot this area, or you can strike out on your own to find your own holy places.

$150-250

Perched between scenic Lake Siskiyou and its own 18-hole golf course, the **Mount Shasta Resort** (1000 Siskiyou Lake Blvd., 800/958-3363, www.mountshastaresort.com, $195) offers attractive lodgings and on-site sports to its guests. For a budget vacation, stay in one of the motel-style Woodland Rooms, each of which has a private bath with shower and two queen beds, making it perfect for families or couples traveling together. For a more private luxury experience, book one of the lovely individual chalets. Some of these sit right down by the lake, so you'll hardly ever want to leave your own front porch. Chalets can have private bathrooms, one or two bedrooms (sleeping up to six people), and full kitchens to make staying for a week or more a pleasure.

For more standard motel-style

accommodations, check in to the **Mt. Shasta Inn and Suites** (710 S. Mt. Shasta Blvd., 530/918-9292, www.mtshastainn.com, $225–375). They're not unique, but the king, two-queen, and family suites here offer lots of space and the comfort of familiar surroundings. You'll get a standard-issue motel bathroom, a TV, a phone, and a good location central to town and close to both I-5 and Highway 89. An all-year outdoor hot tub welcomes weary sportsters after a long day out on the mountain or in the woods and lakes. The family suites are actually adjoining king and two-queen suites, offering sleeping spots for six people comfortably and two separate bathrooms.

FOOD
American
For diners, the best in the area is the local iteration of the **Black Bear Diner** (401 W. Lake St., Mount Shasta, 530/926-4669, www.blackbeardiner.com, $15–30).

Asian Fusion
KenZen Sushi Bar and Exotic Cuisine (315 N. Mt. Shasta Blvd., 530/926-2345, www.kenzensushi.com/index.html, Tues.–Sat. 5–9:30 P.M., $8–20) can hook you up with some decent sushi and other Asian cuisine. Granted, if you've been eating in the Bay Area or Wine Country, the "exotic" items won't seem terribly uncommon to you. The menu features a pleasant array of Asian-themed soups and salads, a few steaks and grilled fish dishes, and a long (if fairly standard) sushi list. On the walls of this casual-elegant eatery you'll find the work of a number of local artists.

Brewpub
For a yummy casual meal and a good beer, stroll on in to **Billy Goats Tavern** (107 Chestnut St., 530/926-0209, www.billygoatstavern.com, Tues.–Sat. 11:30 A.M.–10 P.M., $10–15). Here you'll find a great selection of imports and microbrews, plus a full menu of California-ized pub treats, including sandwiches, salads, and appetizers. This friendly spot welcomes locals and visitors alike, and you can wear your favorite jeans and battered T-shirt and feel right at home.

Italian
If you're carbo-loading in preparation for climbing Mount Shasta, or carbo-loading to celebrate a successful climb, hike, swim, or ski, get a table at **Mike & Tony's Restaurant** (501 S. Mount Shasta Blvd., 530/926-4792, www.mikeandtonys.net, Mon. and Thurs. 5–9 P.M., Fri.–Sat. 5–10 P.M., Sun. 4–9 P.M., $13–22). This casual eatery serves up hearty Americanized Italian favorites, from big bowls of spaghetti to hefty broiled steaks. There are white cloths on the tables, so it's probably best to wear your clean T-shirt to this restaurant, but otherwise the atmosphere encourages family and friendliness and fun.

Coffee and Groceries
Need a cup of coffee to get you going? Grab one at the **Seven Suns Coffee & Café** (1101 S. Mount Shasta Blvd., 530/918-9022, daily 8 A.M.–4 P.M., $10). This coffee house offers plenty of fair trade and organic coffees, plus tasty sandwiches and such for lunch.

To stock up on groceries for camping and picnics, stop by the **Berryvale Grocery** (305 S. Mount Shasta Blvd., 530/926-1576, www.berryvale.com, Mon.–Sat. 8:30 A.M.–7:30 P.M., Sun. 10 A.M.–6 P.M.). You can pick up high quality international foods here, grab a cup of coffee at the café, and then feast like a king back at your campsite.

INFORMATION AND SERVICES
Tourist Information
Need a leg up on your visit to Shasta? Start at the **Mount Shasta Visitors Bureau** (300 Pine St., Mt. Shasta, 800/926-4865, http://mtshastachamber.com). Here you can get information about hotels, restaurants, and local recreation.

On the other hand, if you need wilderness permits and trail advice, head for one of the local ranger stations. The **Mount Shasta Ranger Station** (204 W. Alma St., Mt. Shasta, 530/926-4511) can supply you with both

LAKE TAHOE

wilderness and summit passes, plus park maps and information about current mountain conditions. Another station is the **Castle Crags Ranger Station** (Castle Creek Rd. and Castle Crags State Park Rd., 530/235-2684).

Media and Communications

Believe it or not, the Mount Shasta region has its own daily newspaper. In fact, the *Siskyou Daily News* (www.siskiyoudaily.com), published in Yreka, has been serving up current events to the mountain region for 150 years. Grab a copy and read up on the latest happenings around Mount Shasta and its surrounding towns and wilderness.

The Internet has made it even to the wilds of Mt. Shasta. Many of the quaint inns and small motels offer wi-fi in rooms or at least in common areas. You might also find access in local cafes.

Banks and Post Office

The local **Mt. Shasta Post Office** (530/926-1343) is easy to access at 301 South Mount Shasta Boulevard.

Several banks have branches in Mount Shasta, and you'll have ample access to ATMs and possibly even the service of actual humans. Bank of America (100 Chestnut St., 800/346-7693) sits near many motels downtown. A branch of Washington Mutual (168 Morgan Way, 530/926-8910) graces the town of Mount Shasta.

Medical Services

The town of Mount Shasta has a full-service hospital: **Mercy Medical Center Mt. Shasta** (914 Pine St., 530/926-6111) has a 24-hour emergency room and all the doctors you'll need.

GETTING THERE AND AROUND

Mount Shasta is remote and to get here, you're going to need a car. The main road to Mount Shasta is I-5. This major thoroughfare can get you to the mountain from the north or from the south, and it's plowed constantly in winter to keep it open to trucking.

Parking in the town of Mount Shasta is usually easy—just beware of local events in town that might draw numerous visitors. The various parks and wilderness areas usually have parking lots, though some of the trailheads do not. In these cases, you can often park alongside the road, so long as you're not on a major highway.

SHASTA LAKE

A good 45-minute drive down I-5 south from Mount Shasta, Shasta Lake sits shining and serene behind Shasta Dam. As you drive, you'll cross the lake twice. How is that possible? Rather than one big bowl, Shasta Lake is actually a series of fingers that connect at big, deep spots, then collect at the dam. Several of the fingers are actually incoming rivers that feed the reservoir. To create this mammoth spread-out lake, not one but *five* towns were drowned. The remains are still down there, most sunk so deep that even scuba divers cannot explore them.

Surrounding many fingers of the lake and some of the bigger pools are marinas, campgrounds, resorts, cabins, restaurants, and all the paraphernalia necessary for hundreds of people to enjoy lakeside vacations. Full powerboat access is permitted on Shasta Lake, and native Californians know that its size and variety of views make it a prime spot for weekend houseboating.

Not shockingly, most of the recreation at Shasta Lake centers around...the lake. Whether you want to paddle a kayak, tear it up on a wakeboard, or enjoy all the comforts of home on a houseboat, Shasta's got the water activities for you. Marinas dot the shores of the lake's fingers, offering boat rentals, gas, snacks, water, ice, and more. For those few folks who don't want to spend all day, every day on the water, hiking trails and four-wheel-drive roads thread through the forested wilderness areas surrounding the lake.

◖ Lake Shasta Caverns

Summer lake visitors can find themselves longing for cool air—hard to come by at Shasta in August! Perhaps the best natural air conditioning in the region can be had inside the Lake Shasta Caverns (20359 Shasta Caverns Rd., 530/238-2341, www.lakeshastacaverns .com, year-round daily). Your tour begins across the lake from the caverns, at the Caverns Park and gift shop. During the summertime, tours leave every half-hour starting at 9 A.M. When your tour is called, you'll walk down to the boat launch and board a broad, flat-bottomed ferry with plenty of bench seats and a canopy. As you take the quick ride across a narrowish section of the lake, your driver will regale you with tales of the caverns. Pay attention; though there isn't a test, the tour is more fun if you know more about what you're looking at. At the dock (where boaters can meet their tour groups if they prefer), you'll get on a bus and take a staggeringly steep drive up 800 feet to the cavern entrance. The road permits some fabulous views out over the lake and all the way up to Mount Shasta.

Your cavern tour guide will meet you at the entrance, then lead you into a manmade tunnel. You'll head up a whole bunch of stairs and into the series of natural limestone and marble caverns. The guide will describe the amazing formations that spring from the walls, the ceiling, and even the floor. The guides have spent a lot of time in the caverns and have found shapes within the formations that they've named. The cathedral size of most of the cavern areas and the railed walkways help to remind visitors not to touch the delicate stalactites, drapes, pancakes, and ribbons of "cave bacon" that decorate each space. You're welcome to bring a camera to try to record the marvels you'll see here, but memories often provide better lighting.

Both kids and adults enjoy the tour of the Lake Shasta Caverns, but you'll want to keep an eye on younger children throughout the trip for their safety. No matter how hot it is outside, bring a jacket or sweater for your tour; the caverns remain a constant 50-something degrees all year long. While the tour isn't incredibly strenuous, you need to be able to walk and to climb over 100 stairs at a time.

Shasta Dam

When you approach Shasta Dam (Shasta Dam Blvd., 530/275-4463) by water, it looks like, well, a big concrete dam. (Also, you're not allowed terribly close.) To learn what the pipes and structures actually *do,* you must get to the dam by car and take a tour of the facility. Even if hydro-engineering isn't your thing, it's worth your time to check out the dam, for the views of both lake and Mount Shasta if nothing else. But don't bother bringing a camera inside; for security reasons, no photography is allowed inside the dam. The tour lasts one hour and explains both the construction and the current function of the second-biggest dam in the United States.

Shasta State Historic Park

Believe it or not, the Shasta region was once more populous than it is now;the area was once rich with 19th-century gold miners and all the folks providing goods and services to the miners. Today, the Shasta State Historic Park (Hwy. 299, 530/243-8194, www.parks.ca.gov, Wed.–Sun. 10 A.M.–5 P.M.) displays and honors that regional history. Two on-site museums, the **Litsch Store Museum** and the **Courthouse Museum,** allow history buffs to dig deeper into the life and times of early Shasta residents. See everything from an extensive collection of California landscape paintings to the original area gallows. Outdoors, you'll get the chance to wander through the remains of historic cottages and read the human history of Shasta through the grave markers in the cemeteries.

Houseboating and Marinas

Most of the marinas inhabiting the Shasta Lake shores provide all the rentals and services you'll need while on the lake. If you've got a vacation rental or a campsite on or near the lake, you'll probably want to pick one of the marinas near your lodgings for convenience. (Shasta Lake really is that big and definitely that spread out.) But not all marinas offer public gas docks or public launch facilities, and one or two of them are primarily maintained for the owners of private slips. Just be sure that the marina nearest

housebouating on Shasta Lake

© ROBERT HOLMES / CALTOUR

to home has everything you need—including a good reputation!

Note: The marinas listed here offer a variety of amenities and services appropriate for a day on the lake. Folks staying up at the north end of the Sacramento River Arm of the lake might be tempted to rent from the wide selection of boats available at Antlers Marina and Resort. Resist that temptation if you're looking for a peaceful vacation without frustration, irritation, and angst. Unfortunately, Antlers is regarded by many respectable California publications as *the worst* marina anywhere on the lake and renters are advised to look elsewhere when possible.

SUGARLOAF MARINA

Of the marinas on the Sacramento River Arm, **Sugarloaf Marina** (19761 Lakeshore Dr., Lakehead, 877/468-7326, www.houseboats .com, May–Oct.) offers the best customer service. Sugarloaf rents small aluminum fishing boats, personal watercraft, speedboats, patio boats with barbecue facilities, and a range of

houseboats. It's easy to get to Sugarloaf from I-5, and the launch ramp is free to Sugarloaf guests (non-guests pay a launch fee). You can keep your own boat at Sugarloaf by renting a slip in one of the modern, wheelchair-accessible concrete docks. If you're houseboating, it's always best to bring your own supplies. But if you've forgotten anything, Sugarloaf offers a newly expanded convenience store that can provide paper towels and potato chips, live bait, an extra life jacket, cold beer, or whatever else you need. Out on the water, Sugarloaf sits away from the biggest boating areas on the lake, making it a little quieter and easier to get the hang of piloting your rental craft before you must contend with serious traffic. The one downside to Sugarloaf is its lack of a public fueling dock; you can get gas farther up the Sacramento Arm at Antlers if you're desperate.

SHASTA MARINA RESORT

If your trip will focus on a visit to the Shasta Caverns, you'll find that one of the nearest marinas to the Cavern gift shop and loading dock is the Shasta Marina Resort (18390 O'Brien Inlet Rd., Lakehead, 800/959-3359, www.shastalake .net). Easily accessed from I-5 towards the south end of the lake, this marina offers mid-sized houseboats and SeaSwirl BowRider ski boats with wakeboard towers. The marina facilities include a gas dock, convenience and souvenir store with ice and swimsuits (sold separately), and a boat launch (free with moorage or houseboat rental). This middle-of-the road rental spot definitely offers friendly service, so be sure to ask about good houseboating spots if you're new to Shasta Lake.

PACKERS BAY MARINA

The Packers Bay Marina (16814 Packers Bay Rd., Lakehead, 800/331-3137, http://packers-bay.com) is located in (surprise) Packers Bay, which sits a couple of miles west of I-5 near the big bridge. Getting to the marina from Redding is kind of tricky; you must get off I-5 at Shasta Caverns-O'Brien, then get *back on* going south to reach the Packers Bay Road exit. A small independent operator, this marina offers some of the rare, honest-to-goodness modest houseboats on Shasta Lake. These can sleep 10 people but are really comfortable for groups of 4–6 and are less expensive than the bigger models. Packers Bay Marina offers only houseboats, and fewer services than the larger places. But houseboat renters can expect more personal service, and nicer boats, here

HOUSEBOATING ON SHASTA LAKE

The denizens of the Shasta Lake PR agencies have named the lake "the houseboating capital of the world." That bold statement may or may not be true, but Shasta Lake certainly is California's most popular houseboating lake. Most of the houseboats rented on Shasta Lake run in size from "silly" to "absurd" – it's quite difficult to find a houseboat that sleeps fewer than 10 people, and most sleep 14-18, with a few true leviathans that can hold more than 20 partying people. Granted, the beds aren't big and the private bedrooms few, so for true comfort, pile in no more than half to two-thirds the number of recommended overnight guests.

You can rent a houseboat at almost any marina on the lake. No special boating knowledge is required to rent a houseboat, though you may be required to provide a valid driver's license upon rental. The www.houseboats.com website makes it a little bit easier to shop for the houseboat rental of your dreams and it works with three of the lake's marinas: Jones Valley, Sugarloaf, and Lakeview. Whichever marina you rent from, expect to pay anywhere from $850 per weekend for a minimal smaller craft to $8,500 per weekend for a huge luxurious new boat. Weekly rates (which include one weekend) are often a bargain at double or less the cost of a single weekend.

Expect to find a fair amount of luxury; many Shasta houseboats come with upper-deck hot tubs, waterslides, barbecues, satellite TVs, and high-end entertainment systems. Your houseboat will also come with some necessities – most have fully equipped kitchens, basic cleaning supplies, and basic sanitary supplies (please read here: toilet paper). But you'll need to bring a bunch of your own stuff too, such as pillows, towels, sheets, paper towels, folding chairs, ski-quality life jackets, and first-aid kits. (And food and booze, of course.) See your renter for a full list of supplies they recommend bringing with you.

Piloting a mammoth houseboat on the waters of Shasta Lake is a bit like driving a big rental RV up I-5. Take it slow and careful, follow all the instructions you're given at your marina, and you'll do fine. Most Shasta houseboaters pull their craft into small inlets and moor them for the night. Your marina staff can advise you on how to safely maneuver your houseboat in toward shore in the evening and back out again the next morning.

Many Shasta houseboats have the equipment to tow smaller watercraft along behind them. If you choose, you can rent a ski boat, personal watercraft, or fishing boat and bring it along with you as you explore Shasta Lake.

LAKE TAHOE

than at those big marinas. No pets are allowed on any boats.

BRIDGE BAY MARINA
You can see the Bridge Bay Marina (10300 Bridge Bay Rd., Redding, 800/752-9669, www.sevencrown.com/lakes/lake_shasta/bridge_bay/index.htm) from the big bridge on I-5. This huge marina is part of a full-scale resort that sees some of the biggest crowds on the lake. Bridge Bay Marina has a large rental fleet, which includes small-to-medium houseboats, closed-bow speedboats, personal watercraft, and patio boats. You can also moor your own boat in one of their many slips. From the water, this marina isn't too friendly to put into unless you're a customer, so if you need gas, ice, or snacks, you'll have to navigate carefully to avoid the renters-only area. But once you're in to the marina proper, you will find a fuel dock, a basic grocery store, a bait and tackle shop, and even a restaurant (Tail o' the Whale).

JONES VALLEY MARINA
One of the few year-round marinas on Shasta Lake, the Jones Valley Marina (22300 Jones Valley Marina Dr., Redding, 877/468-7326, www.houseboats.com) is situated on the secluded Pit River Arm, away from the higher traffic areas near the bridge but is still easily accessible from Redding and I-5. The McCloud Arm and the Squaw Creek Arm adjoin near this marina, which is one of the few that sells gas in this part of the lake. Jones Valley Marina is part of a larger resort, and includes a floating recreation area in addition to wheelchair-accessible docks and houseboats. Should you find yourself needing a three-deck houseboat with eight flat-screen TVs that sleeps 22 people, you can rent one at Jones Valley. They've also got a few more modest houseboats, plus the usual array of patio party boats and smaller craft, including a top-tier wakeboard-set speedboat.

Waterskiing and Wakeboarding
The vast acreage and many distinct sections of Shasta Lake make it an ideal place to water-ski and wakeboard—even on crowded weekends, chances are good that you'll find someplace to ski. Just be sure to abide by the speed limit buoys surrounding the marinas and the "No Ski" buoys that warn of shallow water or other hazardous conditions.

If you've got your own tow boat, you can put it in at any number of public launches and rent a slip from one of the marinas. For renters, again, most of the marinas around the lake rent both speedboats and personal watercraft. You'll find a wide selection—everything from championship-quality late-model tow boats with towers for wakeboarders to older, open-bow speedboats that are perfect for cruising the lake with your family. Personal watercraft are mostly WaveRunners, with the occasional Sea-Doo for variety. (If you can get a Sea-Doo, do. They're better machines.) Prices run about $70–120 per hour, with good half-day, full-day, and full-week rates available at most marinas. Do be aware that no matter what marina you work with, these are high-performance rental boats, and problems sometimes crop up. The good news is that no matter where you rented, you can bring a busted boat into any nearby marina and they'll help take care of it for you.

Usually you'll need to rent your skis, boards, and other toys for a minimal extra fee. You can get double and slalom skis, wakeboards of different brands and sizes, purpose-built ski tubes, and even ridiculous "ski bananas" and other five- and six-seat towable toys that will definitely get you noticed all over the lake.

Fishing and Patio Boating
If you just want to go out and putter on the lake for a day or host a sunset on-lake cocktail party, and all those beds and kitchens in the houseboats seem like overkill, what you want is a patio boat. These flat-bottomed, pontoon-style boats rent by the hour and by the day, and are much cheaper than the houseboats. Most come with plenty of seating and canopies for shade. Larger patio boats might have barbecues and storage chests as well. You're free to bring your own well-stocked coolers, fishing gear,

stereo, and friends. Check with your favorite marina about renting one.

Entertainment and Events

The main entertainment in the Shasta Lake area centers on the lake itself. The cool thing to do is to rent a patio boat or houseboat and throw your own party on the water. As with cars, it's necessary to designate a boat driver for your party to keep your friends and everyone else on the water safe.

The major annual festival at Shasta Lake each year is the **Shasta Damboree** (www .shastadamboree.com). Each May, a three-day weekend is devoted to family-friendly events that bring out the community and draw visitors to the region. The events feel typical of a good small-town celebration, with spaghetti feeds, pancake breakfasts, an arts-and-crafts area, and a parade and evening party with fireworks and live music. Check the website for dates and events for the coming year.

Some of the best drinking, pool playing, and occasional live music happens up on the northern Sacramento River Arm, just off the I-5 at **The Basshole** (20725 Lakeshore Dr., 530/238-2170, www.bassholebarandgrill.com, grill daily 11 A.M.–10 P.M., Tues. until 5 P.M., bar open until closing). Yeah, really, they went there. This bar, restaurant, pool hall, and bait shop comprise a single large hall for dining, drinking, and recreating, with the bait shop hiding in a tiny room just off the dining area. The food is nothing special—burgers and dogs and fairly tasty hot fries are the house specialties, though for dinner they do put out an array of slightly fancier entrées. Locals don't come here to eat, they come here for beer. Expect to find the occasional co-ed wet t-shirt contest and other such adult entertainment on summer weekend evenings.

Two other options are the **Wonderland Tavern** (15041 Wonderland Blvd., 530/275-2397) just off I-5 and the **Idle Hour Bar and Grill** (14961 Bear Mountain Rd., 530/275-0230), which sits south of the Silverthorn Resort, close to the intersection of Bear Mountain Road and Silverthorn Road.

Accommodations

Many of the visitors who come to Shasta Lake rent houseboats or lakeside cabins in which to enjoy their vacation. (See *Houseboating and Marinas* for more information about these types of rentals.)

$100-150

Because it's out in the woods a mile south of the lakeshore, the **Fawndale Lodge & RV Park** (15215 Fawndale Rd., 530/275-8000, www .fawndale.com, $80–130) offers comfy lodge rooms and cabins at bargain prices. Though you can't see the lake from the lodge, the surrounding forest has its own charm and the garden and pool offer plenty of beauty and comfort. All rooms include a fridge, microwave, and private bathrooms. Suites have full kitchens, bed space for six people, and (oh, true heaven!) air conditioning. The decor runs to rustic wood walls and furniture and simple amenities, and small TVs offer minimal entertainment and encouragement to get outside and play.

Tent campers and RV travelers are welcome at Fawndale; check the website or call for information about full-hookup RV spots and tent campsites, and make a reservation in advance to guarantee your spot.

Towards the north end of the lake, the **Shasta Lake Motel** (20714 Lakeshore Dr., Lakehead 530/238-2545, www.shastalake motel.com, $83–150) is a favorite for regular visitors. For the small prices, you'll get some bigger lodge amenities, including air conditioning, cable TV, microwave, mini-fridge, and coffee maker. Each room glows softly with dark, honey-colored wood-paneled walls and furniture, and the decor runs to rustic prints and artifacts. One special amenity will thrill taller travelers; all the twin and double sized beds are "extra long," making them far more comfortable for folks over six feet tall. Outdoors, you can enjoy the motel pool, or take a quick walk down to the shores of the lake. The motel is only a few minutes off I-5, close enough for convenience but not so near that you'll be listening to the trucks all night.

LAKE TAHOE

The **Bridge Bay Resort** (10300 Bridge Bay Rd., 800/752-9669, www.sevencrown .com/lakes/lake_shasta/bridge_bay/index.htm, $130–210) has one of the best locations of any resort on the lake, right where the big I-5 bridge crosses the lake. It's close to the center of the lake's arms, making it a perfect spot to launch a boat from the resort's full-service marina. Bridge Bay also includes a restaurant, a small grocery store, and a bait and tackle shop. The lodgings aren't terribly stylish, and the rooms are decorated in average budget-motel chic with colorful bedspreads, particle-board furniture, and generic prints on the walls. You'll definitely find a family-friendly vibe here—many of the guest rooms sleep 4–6 people, and some have full kitchens.

$150-250

Some travelers simply cannot do without their creature comforts. For those, on Shasta Lake there's the **O'Brien Mountain Inn** (18026 O'Brien Inlet Rd., 530/238-8026, www .obrienmountaininn.com, $154–330). This casual-elegant bed-and-breakfast inn eschews the woodsy-lodge theme that most lodgings in the area use. Instead, the eight rooms and suites are painted in soft pastels with attractive matching furnishings and amenities. Some suites have kitchenettes, and some have fabulous whirlpool bathtubs, perfect for relaxing after a long day out playing on the lake! Breakfast includes fresh coffee and baked goodies delivered to the door of your room at 8 A.M., then a full meal is served in the dining room at 9 A.M. The only real downside of the O'Brien is its location. It's not right on the lakeshore, so the views and access won't be right there. But the drive to the lake is minimal, and Lake Shasta Caverns sits nearby.

OVER $250

Well east of I-5 out on the tip of a small peninsula in the Pit River Arm, the **Silverthorn Resort** (16250 Silverthorn Rd., 530/275-1571, www.silverthornresort.com, $1,210–2,200 per week) definitely has the advantage of a location right on the water. The views from the common areas and guest cabins are phenomenal

and the resort has its own full-service marina with houseboats for rent. Just don't expect to blow in and get a cabin for a single night in the midst of high season. At Silverthorne, cabins rent *only* by the week in summer and require a three-day minimum for the rest of the year. Each cabin sleeps 4–6 people, except for the large family cabin that can handle eight. Inside, you'll find the ubiquitous wood-paneled interior walls and simple but attractive lodge-style decor. All cabins include a full kitchen (thus making the by-the-week rental requirement a bit more attractive) with full-sized refrigerator, plus private bathrooms. Expect bedrooms to be small but cute, and the atmosphere to be woodsy and restful. Be sure to book your boat rentals with the marina at the same time you book your cabin to ensure that you get what you want, when you want it. A small grocery store and a "pizza pub" offer easy dining and shopping on-site for visitors who don't feel like driving far away for dinner.

Food

The **Tail O' the Whale** (10300 Bridge Bay Rd., Redding, 800/752-9669, www.sevencrown .com/lakes/lake_shasta/bridge_bay/restaurants .htm) at the Bay Bridge Resort west of I-5 offers three meals daily in a casual dining room that's perfect for lakeside vacationers. The lengthy menu has plenty of American resort mid-scale favorites, with something to please almost everybody.

On the east side, the Silverthorn Resort boasts the only pizza along the lake at the **Silverthorn Pizza and Pub** (16250 Silverthorn Rd., Redding, www.silverthornresort.com/resort-svcs/pizza.html, Mon. 11 A.M.–10 P.M., Tues.–Wed. noon–10 P.M., Thurs. 11 A.M.–10 P.M., Fri.–Sat. 11 A.M.–1 A.M., Sun. 11 A.M.–9 P.M.). This ultra-casual eatery boasts ice-cold beer, piping hot pizzas, and other homey fare. A huge deck overlooking the lake lures folks out for cocktails, then bar games like pool and live music bring them back inside as night falls.

For supplies, Lakehead boasts the **Lakeshore Village Market** (20750 Lakeshore Dr., Lakehead, 530/238-8615) with plenty of food, plus basic camping, fishing, and outdoor recreation supplies for visitors staying at the north end of the lake.

A few miles north of the lake on I-5, where any hint of civilization disappears, you'll come upon the tiny "town" of Pollard Flat. This flat spot beside the road has one odd, rambling, blocky building, **The Restaurant at Pollard Flat** (24235 Eagles Roost Rd, Lakehead, 530/238-2534, $10), as well as a bar, mini-mart, and gas station. But what the restaurant at Pollard Flat has the most of is atmosphere. A few stools sit at a bar or counter (it's anyone's guess as to which it really is) just inside. Turn left and you'll be in the first of a warren of dark dining rooms, fitted out with ancient wooden tables and black vinyl booths. Just to sit down in this place and ask for a menu and a glass of water requires a degree of courage. To have a meal is the test of a genuine adventurer. A safer option might be the minimal packaged snacks and sodas sharing space with the bait and NRA stickers in the equally dim and creepy adjoining mini-mart.

Information and Services

New to the Shasta Lake area? Stop in at the **Shasta Lake Visitor Information Center** (Holiday Rd., Mountain Gate, 530/275-1589, Memorial Day–Labor Day Wed.–Sun. 8 A.M.–4:30 P.M.). This small ranger station can provide you with information and local guidance, plus information on this year's hot fishing spots.

Believe it or not, Shasta Lake does boast its own tiny local paper: the **Shasta Lake Bulletin** (www.shastalake.ws). Check the "Visitor's Guide" section for basic traveler's information, and the "After Five Magazine" for local entertainment and event options.

Not all cell phone providers offer coverage out in the Shasta Lake region. If you plan to rely on your cell phone while you're here, check with your carrier before you arrive.

Some places do offer Internet access, but they can be few and far between. Certainly none of the houseboats offer DSL. Some of the lodges and inns offer Wi-Fi, but the nearest Starbucks is all the way down in Redding. Ask

before you arrive to determine whether you'll have in-room Internet where you're staying, or check at www.shastalake.com/internet.

Another option is to leave the laptop and the Blackberry behind, unplug, and enjoy the beauty of the Shasta Lake region unspoiled by incessant beeping and buzzing and chirping.

There is a **post office** up at Lakehead (20856 Antlers Rd.), but the nearest major medical facilities are in Redding (see *Information and Services* in the *Redding* section for more information).

Getting There and Around

The nearest full-service airport to Shasta Lakes is Redding Municipal. (See *Getting There* in the *Redding* section for more information). From there, you can rent a car at the airport to drive out to the lake.

Most folks come to Shasta Lake by car or RV via I-5, which runs right over the lake in two different places. Bridge Bay is one of the more popular (and populous) spots on the lake, due to its proximity and easy access to I-5. The Sacramento Arm to the north is also easily accessible from the freeway.

Shasta Lake is big and spread out. As big as it might look from the bridge, you're seeing only a small part of the lake. A network of smaller (but mostly paved) roads encircle most of the other arms of the lake, allowing access to the marinas and resorts and campgrounds.

Parking isn't generally a problem around Shasta Lake, except possibly on holiday weekends in the summertime. Parking at the resorts is usually free.

Many people bring their own boats to Shasta Lake rather than paying the high fees to rent from the marinas. Check the *Houseboating and Marinas* section of this chapter and local maps to find the public launch nearest to your accommodations. (Expect to pay a small launching fee.) Before launching, your boat may be inspected both for proper state licensing and for pernicious mussels.

No special license is required to pilot a boat in California. All drivers of boats over 15 horsepower must be age 16 or over (that includes personal watercraft). Youth ages 12–15 can drive if directly supervised by an adult. All children under 12 must wear a life jacket at all times when on board a boat. Drunk boating laws are the same as drunk driving laws. The legal limit is BAC 0.08. Penalties for drunk boating can be severe. For more information about boating rules, visit www.co.shasta.ca.us/departments/sheriff/boatingsafety.htm.

Lassen Volcanic National Park

Mount Lassen is an active volcano with a recorded history of eruptions, the last of which took place in 1914 and 1915. The mountain is a remote and beautiful sight, one that's only accessible to large numbers of visitors in the short summer months when the temperatures rise and the snow melts. A wonderful loop drive through Lassen Volcanic National Park (530/595-4444, open daily year-round, Headquarters Information Desk open Mon.–Fri. 8 A.M.–4:30 P.M.) takes you from the stark slopes and jagged brand-new rocks of the most recent eruption, around the back to an enormous ancient crater, the remains of a long-gone volcano as big or bigger than Mount Shasta.

Ample hiking trails, wonderful pristine ponds, and many campsites that let visitors settle in and really enjoy the amazing panoramas of Mount Lassen. Beyond the bounds of the state park, national forest lands allow for additional exploration. Do be aware that the "lower" elevations of Mount Lassen trails sit more than 7,000 feet above sea level. If you're planning serious hiking, come up a day early and camp on the mountain to acclimate to the elevation. The next day you'll be better able to take the longer and higher trails without succumbing to altitude sickness.

For true, unspoiled California wilderness, it's hard to beat the backcountry at Lassen. Even the most traveled roads and "front side" sights will seem empty to travelers who've visited Yosemite Valley or Lake Tahoe. *But* (you knew there had to be a catch to such an

Mount Lassen

amazing place), the only time to visit Lassen is the height of summer. Snow chokes the area from as early as October until as late as June, closing the main road through the park and making even the lower altitude campground snowy and cold. Most determined mountain-lovers pick August and early September as the best time to come to Lassen. On the other hand, active snow lovers will make the trek up the mountain in the wintertime to enjoy snowshoeing and cross-country skiing, or bring their sleds and their kids for a fun afternoon playing on the mountain slopes.

SIGHTS

Lassen Volcanic National Park is one of the oldest national parks in the United States. It is also one of the most remote and primitive. On the other hand, a good (and paved) main road runs through the middle of the park, letting visitors enjoy many of the major attractions—including the park's active volcanic features.

The good news is that the rugged weather and isolated location mean that a visit to Lassen Volcanic National Park is a visit to an unspoiled wilderness area rather than an overdeveloped, Disney-fied amusement park with rocks. A good half of the park has only minimal dirt road access and offers its rugged beauty only to those travelers willing to hike for miles into the backcountry. Even the trails and campgrounds accessible by paved road maintain a kind of charm that's hard to find in the more popular California parks.

◖ Loomis Museum and Manzanita Lake

As you enter the northwest edge of the park on Highway 89, you'll almost immediately find the Loomis Museum (at the visitors center) and Manzanita Lake. Inside the museum, you've got a wonderful opportunity to learn about the known history of Mount Lassen, focusing heavily on the eruptions photographed by Mr. B. F. Loomis. Prints of those rare and stunning photos have been blown up and captioned to create these exhibits; the museum was named for the photographer, who later became a major

player in the push to make Mount Lassen a national park. This interpretive museum offers a rare chance to see, through photos, the devastation and following stages of regrowth of the ecosystem of volcanic slopes.

Chaos Jumbles

So this broken and decimated area is another spot that was overcome by the 1915 eruption of Mount Lassen, right? Nope! Lassen National Park is full of surprises, and the aptly named Chaos Jumbles is often the first that visitors stumble upon. Instead of volcanic activity, it was a massive avalanche that damaged this small part of the park about 300 years ago. The results seem quite similar to the regions that had the volcano erupt on them, with the devastation of the living ecosystem, the displacement of massive rocks, and the general disorder of the landscape. The avalanche that occurred here was so big, and came straight down so fast that it actually trapped a pocket of air underneath it, adding to the destruction. Now, visitors enjoy a wealth of new life, including a bigger-than-average variety of coniferous trees. The newness of the living landscape has allowed more competing types of plants to get a foothold here.

Devastated Area

It seems like an odd name for a point of interest, but in fact the Devastated Area is one of the most fascinating geological and ecological sites anywhere in California. When Lassen blew its top in 1915 after nearly a year of sporadic eruptions, a tremendous part of the mountain and all the life on its slopes was destroyed. Boiling mud and exploding gases tore off the side of Lassen's mountain peak and killed all the vegetation in the area. A hail of lava rained down, creating brand-new rocks, from gravel to boulders, across the north side of the mountain.

Today visitors can easily see how a volcano's surface ecosystem recovers after an eruption. First, park at the Devastated Area lot and take the interpretive walk through a small part of the recently disrupted mountainside. You'll see everything from some of the world's youngest rocks to grasses and shrubs up through tall pine trees. Also be sure to check out the photos in the Loomis Museum that depict the area during and immediately after the eruption for a great comparison to the spot as it looks now.

The Devastated Area offers ample parking, and the interpretive walk is flat and wheelchair accessible. Please don't pick up any of the red and black volcanic rocks here; they are part of the redeveloping ecosystem and necessary to the area's recovery.

Hot Rock

No, it's not hot anymore. But this huge boulder started out untouchable when the Loomises explored the eruption zone soon after the 1915 blast. Frankly, the site isn't all that amazing now, except when you think about that big rock remaining warm to the touch for months, so recently it was written about and even photographed. The Hot Rock turnout also offers more great views of the Devastated Area.

Lassen Peak

It's not as tall as it used to be, but Lassen Peak still reaches over 10,000 feet up toward the sky. Even if you're not up to climbing it, it's worth stopping at the significant parking lot at the trailhead to crane your neck and enjoy the view. The craggy broken mountain peak is what's left after the most recent eruption—hence the lack of much in the way of vegetation. The elevation (more than 8,000 feet at the parking lot) makes the Lassen Peak trailhead cool even in the heat of summer when the temperatures only 1,000 feet below hit the 90s. You may need to break out a light windbreaker or sweatshirt if you plan to explore at length.

It's not marked on the park maps, but the Lassen Peak trailhead includes a huge parking lot and a spot to rest off the road. You'll find adequate chemical toilets and a trailer-housed concessionaire in this parking lot. Head into the store for souvenirs, that sweatshirt you forgot, or a snack. Minimal hot food (hot dogs, mostly) and plenty of drinks are available, and a few picnic tables outside the trailer make a decent spot for a picnic.

Summit Lake

Lassen National Park is dotted all over with tiny lakes—most are more like ponds or even puddles than true lakes. One of the most popular and most easily accessible of these is Summit Lake, which sits right along the main road. The shining bright small lake attracts many campers to its two forest-shaded campgrounds. There's an easy walk around the lake that lets you see its waters and the plants that proliferate around it. Or find one of the small trails down to the edge of water and eke out a spot on the miniscule beach with all the other visitors who come to escape the blinding heat. You can swim and fish in Summit Lake, and even take rafts and canoes out to paddle around. (No powered boats are permitted on any lake at Lassen.)

◖ Bumpass Hell

The best and most varied area of volcanic geothermal activity on Lassen is at a location called Bumpass Hell (located six miles from the southwest entrance). The region was named for a Mr. Bumpass (no, really, this is the story) who, in his explorations, stepped through a thin crust over a boiling mud pot and severely burned his leg, ultimately losing the limb. In fact, the tale of the unfortunate Bumpass makes a good point for travelers visiting the mud pots and fumaroles here: *stay on the paths!* The dangers at Bumpass Hell are real, and if you step off the boardwalks or let your children run wild, you are risking serious injury and even death.

That said, a hike down to Bumpass Hell will prove fun enough to make the risks worthwhile. You'll need to walk about two miles from the parking lot and trailhead out to the good stuff—boiling mud pots, fumaroles, steaming springs, and pools of boiling, steaming water cluster here. Prepare for the strong smell of sulfur, more evidence that this volcano is anything but extinct. Boardwalks meander through the area, creating safe walking surfaces for all visitors.

The spacious parking lot also offers stunning views out east and south, giving you a hint at

© ROBERT HOLMES / CALTOUR

Bumpass Hell

the scope of the ancient volcano that once stood here. Or if you need to, you can take advantage of the primitive but usable facilities.

Sulphur Works

For visitors who can't quite manage the trek out to Bumpass Hell, the Sulphur Works offer a peak at the geothermal features of Lassen right on the main road. A boardwalk runs along the road and a parking area is nearby, allowing visitors to get out of their cars to examine the loud boiling mud pots and small steaming stream here. The mud pots both look and sound like a washing machine, sending up steam and occasional bursts of boiling water. Keep hold of your children!

As of the writing of this guide, the small loop trail and longer path out to Ridge Lake were closed. Check with the rangers on the status of these trails during your visit.

SPORTS AND RECREATION

The reason to haul yourself and your family and your friends and your gear all the way out to Mount Lassen is to get out and experience this amazing scenic wilderness. Whether you prefer short nature walks or intense multi-day hikes, swimming in the little crystalline lakes

or fishing for dinner in them, outdoor recreation calls to all Lassen visitors.

Day Hiking

Most of the easy interpretive walks and short day hikes run out to the sights of Mount Lassen Volcanic Park. For hikers who want to get out away from the more touristy areas but still make it back to their cars before dark, moderate-to-difficult hiking trails offer adventure, challenge, and maybe even a touch of solitude.

The **Kings Creek Falls** (Road Marker 32, 3 miles round-trip, moderate) starts out easy. Your initial walk will be downhill to the falls. Be sure to stop to admire the small cascade and pool, perhaps sit down and have a drink and a snack to prepare for the 700-foot climb back up to the trailhead. This makes for a good hike for fitter day-hikers who've been on the mountain for a couple of hours.

It's the length of the trail that runs from **Summit Lake to Echo and Twin Lakes** (east side of Summit Lake, 8 miles round-trip, moderate to difficult) that makes it hard to do. But you can choose how many little lakes you really want to see as you run short on breath. Happily, the ascent over this long trail is only

500 feet total—a gentle slope in these mountainous reaches. If you just walk out to Echo Lake, you'll have a pleasant and sedate four-mile walk. It's another two miles to get out to Upper Twin Lake and back, and a final two miles to reach Lower Twin Lake. You might want to wear a swimsuit under your hiking clothes on hot summer days, and cool off in one of the lakes before trekking back to base.

One trail that does not offer much in the way of solitary communion with nature is the path up to **Lassen Peak** (difficult). A large parking lot with a gift/snack shop and chemical toilet facilities sits at the barren trailhead. In the parking area sit the cars of the many visitors who want to climb up to the highest point on Mount Lassen. It's not a pretty hike; the recent (by geologic standards) eruption and prevailing weather conditions leave this peak virtually bereft of plant life. Expect an utterly steep climb that winds up the barren peak to the sounds of gasping hikers and their screaming leg muscles. But at the top, the views will make you forget the torturous climb, if only for a few moments. Be sure to turn all the way around to get 360° views back down to the newest volcanic landscape, then across to the remains of the giant caldera of an extinct huge volcano, then out west toward Cascade Range neighbor Mount Shasta.

For a good, solid, all-day, steep hike, climb up **Brokeoff Mountain** (Road Marker 2, 7.5 miles round-trip, difficult). Brokeoff makes a good second or third day Lassen hike—with an unrelenting 2,600-foot ascent from an already mile-high starting point, thin air and altitude sickness can be a real concern for out-of-shape, unacclimated hikers. On the other hand, if you're ready for it, this can be one of the prettiest and most serene hikes in the populous section of the park. Enjoy the pretty mountain streams and stellar views out over the mountains and valleys of far-Northern California.

Backcountry Hiking

Some of the most beautiful and interesting remote hiking in California can be found in Lassen's spreading expanse of backcountry.

While you might not be the only backpacker out there, you'll definitely leave the crowds on the main road behind and find yourself with more trees, birds, and other mountain critters than people to talk to. You might even get lucky enough to have a pristine lake or mountain stream all to yourself.

Backcountry camping is permitted at Lassen, and several hike-in campgrounds offer some minimal facilities and a way to minimize your impact on the landscape. Check with the ranger station when you enter the park to obtain backcountry permits and get the season's scoop on trail and campground conditions. Be sure to bring your fishing gear! Tasty trout swim the lakes and streams of the remote Lassen wilderness, offering the chance at a fresh dinner or breakfast.

No major park in California would be complete without a hunk of the **Pacific Crest Trail** running through it. This high-altitude piece (17 miles, difficult) of the continent-spanning trail offers lots of challenge and solitude, and a fairly short window of months in which you can traverse this part of California. If you're doing the California leg of the Pacific Crest Trail, try to hit Lassen sometime between June and September, and be prepared for extreme weather conditions from blistering heat to snowstorms.

For a radical change of scenery, take the **Cinder Cone from Butte Lake** (west end of Butte Lake Campground, 4–5 miles, moderate). Be sure to wear your sturdiest ankle-covering hiking boots on this adventure, since the ground on the Cinder Cone is…well…cinders. Watch your footing so you don't slide down; even cold cinders can cut you up. The cone rises 800 feet over two miles; to lengthen the hike, walk down the south side of the cone. Geology and photography buffs particularly like this hike, which is accessible by dirt road and shows off some of the more interesting and less-seen volcanic history of Mount Lassen.

If you can't get enough of Lassen's geothermal features, enter the park from Warner Valley Road and take a hike to **Boiling Springs Lake** (Warner Campground Parking Lot, 3 miles, easy to moderate). You'll get to see bubbling mud pots and check out (from a safe distance) the waters of boiling springs. The walk out and back is reasonably short and non-strenuous. Just be *very* careful once you reach the geothermal area. Unlike Bumpass Hell, this region has no nice safe boardwalks encircling the mud pots and fumaroles. These features, along with the hot springs, can be extremely dangerous. This might not be a great hike for young, spirited children. But it's heaven for serious nature-lovers who want to see what volcanic geothermal features look like in their wild state. Needless to say, trying to swim in (sulfurous, acidic, 125°F) Boiling Springs Lake is a *very bad idea*.

Looking for a more serious backcountry trek that will take you more than a day? Check the park's website for maps, and feel free to call the park to get advice on route planning and necessary equipment before you come. Once you're in the park, the visitors centers can issue you a free wilderness permit for backcountry hiking and camping, and give you last-minute pointers and current trail information.

Boating and Fishing

If you've got a canoe, a kayak, or a rowboat, bring it on up to Lassen in the summertime. Many of the small to midsized lakes on the mountain allow unpowered boating and fishing. While most of the lakes on the west side of the park near the road are too small to boat, out east Juniper, Snag, and Butte Lakes have plenty of space to row or paddle out and enjoy the serenity of water and earth. No boat rentals are available inside Lassen National Park.

Several varieties of trout inhabit the larger Lassen lakes. All you need is a pole, some bait, and a valid California fishing license. Manzanita Lake offers catch-and-release fishing only, but at all the other fishable lakes you're welcome to take a state limit of rainbows and browns. Fishing from several campgrounds makes it easy to enjoy the freshest dinner possible.

Swimming

You're free to splash to your hearts content in Summit Lake, Manzanita Lake, King Creek, and almost all of the eastern backcountry lakes.

Beware: These lakes can be icy cold! Summit Lake tends to get crowded with water-lovers on summer weekends.

CAMPING

If you're planning to camp, please review the regulations and Leave No Trace guidelines at the Lassen camping website (www.lassen.volcanic .national-park.com/camping.htm) to help you get organized and pack for your trip.

Paved Road Accessible Camping

Closest to the park entrance along Highway 89 you'll find the pleasant and serene **Manzanita Lake Campground** (179 sites, May–Sept., reservations recommended, $14). By far the largest campground in Lassen, Manzanita Lake has a full slate of amenities, including flush toilets, showers, potable running water, fire rings or pits, picnic tables in all campsites, and an RV dump station. Trailers and campers up to 35 feet are allowed at this campground.

Five miles south of Manzanita Lake, the more primitive and less expensive **Crags Campground** (45 sites, June–Sept., $8) offers a more out-in-the-woods style of camping. Crags does have potable running water and pit toilets, but no showers. Each site has its own table and fire pit.

Farther along Highway 89 at Summit Lake, the **Summit Lake North and South Campgrounds** (92 sites, June–Sept., $12–14) are among the most popular in the whole park, so reservations are recommended. Visitors can swim in Summit Lake, easily accessing its banks from campsites and paths. These two developed campgrounds have flush toilets, fire pits, and tables, but to be safe bring your own potable water, enough for the length of your trip for drinking and dishwashing. At 6,650 feet altitude, the Summit Lake campgrounds are among the highest in the park. Be sure to take it easy setting up camp on your first day so that you can get used to the thinner air.

Dirt Road and Walk-In Camping

Out in the backcountry, well away from the main road, the **Butte Lake Campground** (turn off Hwy. 44 toward Butte Lake/Lassen, 42 sites, May–Sept., $10) shows off the beauty of Lassen to its best advantage. Despite its remote location at the northeast corner of the park, you'll find this to be a fairly well-developed campground, with pit toilets and running water. (Check with the park service to be sure water at this campground is drinkable.) Each site has a fire pit and table. Trailers and RVs up to 35 feet that can negotiate the road can camp at Butte Lake. To reach the campground, take Highway 44 up to the dirt road, then drive six miles to the campground. Reservations are recommended.

The **Juniper Lake Campground** (dirt road from Chester, 18 sites, June–Oct., $10) takes campers farther off the beaten path. Since the campground is located in the east side of the park, at the end of a rough dirt road, you'll do much better if you're a tent camper rather than an RVer or trailer-tower. This small campground beside beautiful Juniper Lake has pit toilets, fire pits, and tables, but the water here isn't drinkable. Either bring purifying agents or your own drinking water in containers. Because it sits at almost 7,000 feet, definitely take it easy during your first day at Juniper Lake. Reservations are recommended.

If you're bringing your horses on vacation with you, you can reserve a space at the Juniper Lake Corral ($4/animal).

Warner Valley (one mile off Warner Valley Rd., 18 sites, June–Oct., $12) lies along the south edge of the park. Another smaller gem of a semi-developed campground, Warner Valley has pit toilets and drinking water, as well as tables and fire pits at each site. No trailers, please! Though the dirt road is only a mile long, it's too rough for large campers and RVs to navigate.

ACCOMMODATIONS

Indoor accommodations on Mount Lassen are few and far between. Most folks either camp or stay in Redding and day-trip up to the park. Expect little in the way of luxury or amenities if you do choose one of the indoor Lassen lodgings.

The one lonely non-camping lodging option in or even near Lassen National Park is the ◖ **Drakesbad Guest Ranch** (Warner Valley Rd., Chester, 530/529-1512, ext. 120, www .drakesbad.com, $155–179, summer only). This all-inclusive ranch includes three meals per day included with your room rate, though the national park fee is not included. The big brown barn of a lodge hints at the focus of this guest ranch—energetic exploration of the outdoors. The ranch maintains its own stable, making horseback riding all throughout Lassen Volcanic National Park an easy proposition. (Horseback rides cost extra.) You're also within easy reach of any number of trails, many of which are not accessible from the park's main paved roads. Bring your tackle along on a walk or a ride to take advantage of the fishing available in the local lakes and streams. Some anglers enjoy the guided fly-fishing program offered by the ranch, which teaches fly-fishing and practices catch-and-release sustainable fishing. (One-day California fishing licenses are available on-site.) The ranch even has a wonderful pool that's fed by the water from a local hot spring, making it healthful for soaking as well as for swimming laps.

A vacation at Drakesbad Guest Ranch is like few other retreats in all of California. The countryside really does have a wild feeling, with lots of backcountry riding and hiking trails and a general sense of solitude and serenity.

For inexpensive indoor lodgings that leave you free to explore on your own, check out **Lassen Mineral Lodge** (Hwy. 36E, Mineral, 530/595-4422, www.minerallodge.com, $72–85, open year-round) to the southwest of the park proper. The lodge offers small, cute, motel-style rooms with private baths and few frills. The lack of TVs and phones encourages visitors to get out and really visit Lassen National Park, just nine miles away, and its surrounding landscape. Hiking, fishing, and park exploration are favorite pastimes of guests here. The lodge does have its own casual family restaurant, which serves three meals each day to motel guests, campers, and passersby. A full bar satisfies the thirst of adult patrons well into the evening.

FOOD

Mount Lassen boasts precious little in the way of dining options. If you're camping, shop in Redding and bring in *lots* of food. And don't expect to get to a restaurant during your stay unless you're willing to drive a good long ways. But the national park does allow a couple of vendors to sell a few basic food items in the park.

In the summertime, a trailer at the parking lot for the **Summit Trailhead** acts as a gift shop and small snack shack. You can get a hot dog or a basic sandwich, chips, drinks, a few packaged items, and very little else. But if you've been hiking and exploring for half the day, a nice dog and a soda will taste fabulous. This snack bar doesn't exactly have operating hours or a phone; it's open when it's open and it's not when it's not.

INFORMATION AND SERVICES

The new **Kohm Yah-mah-nee Visitor Center** (Hwy. 89, year-round) is scheduled to open in fall 2008 at the south entrance station of the park. A ranger's station is located at the Highway 44/89 entrance. At each of these you can obtain wilderness permits for backcountry camping, any other necessary permits, and advice about where you can and should (and cannot and should not) hike, ride, swim, fish, and camp in Lassen.

Park rangers can provide first aid and help you get phone access to emergency services in Redding. If you're planning to hike seriously or camp, bring a well-stocked first-aid kit for minor injuries and illnesses.

GETTING THERE AND AROUND

On Mount Lassen, winter begins in November and continues through May. Highway 89 through the park closes from about October to May, June, or July depending on the weather and snowfall in any given year. Highway 89 serves as the main road through the park, and the visitors center, campgrounds, trailheads, and lakes cluster along it. You can actually get a decent feel for Lassen just by taking a day trip along Highway 89.

On the northeast side of the park, Highway 44 brings in visitors from the remote town of Susanville; dirt roads lead from Highway 44 into the park.

South of Lassen, roads run out of the tiny town of Chester up to the park. The Warner Valley Road is paved, but other roads out of town to the park are good old-fashioned dirt.

However you get to Lassen, be sure to bring a good map and possibly a GPS device as well. (Garmin GPS does work even on the dirt roads of Mount Lassen. I got lost up there once and was glad to have mine!)

Note that there are no gas stations in the park. Gas up in Redding, Chester, or Susanville before driving up to Mount Lassen.

REDDING

The good-sized city of Redding acts as a gateway town to the whole Shasta and Lassen region. Set right in the middle of the I-5 route, Redding has every major service you might need on your travels.

Sundial Bridge

The best-known sight in the Redding region is undoubtedly the magnificent and unusual Sundial Bridge (daily 6 A.M.–midnight, free). Part of the Turtle Bay Exploration Park, the Sundial Bridge crosses the Sacramento River. It's a beautiful bit of architecture designated for pedestrians only, with a single large pylon structure anchoring the suspension cables that fan out over the bridge. Most folks get to the bridge from Turtle Bay and walk north across it. When you begin your stroll across the bridge, you'll see more of the unique design of the structure. You'll be walking on blocks of green glass, strips of granite, and ceramic tiles from Spain. The overall effect is breathtaking, and you'll probably stop a few times just to take in the details of the design.

On the other side of the bridge, you'll see how it got its name. The brilliant white pylon acts as a huge sundial; brass plaques embedded in the north side lawn act as timekeepers. You'll see that the bridge keeps pretty good time on sunny days; the shadow hits the 20-minute markers right about on time!

LAKE TAHOE

Turtle Bay Exploration Park

Turtle Bay Exploration Park (840 Auditorium Dr., 800/887-8532, www.turtlebay.org) is also worth your time, though it (along with the rest of Redding) gets blisteringly hot in the summertime. To escape the heat, spend some quality time in the Turtle Bay Museum, with its air conditioning, art and nature displays, Native American exhibits, and traveling exhibits and shows. Turtle Bay gets great shows, like the Titanic history exhibit and Body Worlds 2. Much of the museum is geared for younger visitors, allowing kids to learn by listening, touching, and occasionally even smelling. Adults might be more fascinated by the information about California's water usage and management—one of the state's biggest ongoing natural, environmental, and political issues.

Outside of the museum, the Exploration Park includes the spacious **McConnell Arboretum and Gardens,** a 20-acre botanical garden that's perfect for spring and fall strolling, though it gets a bit hot in high summer. Beautiful plantings and areas include a children's garden, a medicinal garden, and two charming water features. Lots of butterflies are attracted to the flower plantings, so you'll get to see swallowtails, monarchs, and many other species. The arboretum is a 200-acre expanse of trees, and you can enjoy their shade as you explore the sustainable forest. The gardens have their own parking area on the west side, or you can reach them from the museum via the Sundial Bridge. Children enjoy the play areas and equipment in **Paul Bunyan's Forest Camp,** and one of the most interesting historical sites is the **Monolith**—a remnant of one of the plants that helped to build Shasta Dam.

Entertainment and Events

To break the monotony of life along the I-5, the town of Redding hosts a number of monthly and annual events. The annual **Redding Rodeo** (715 Auditorium Dr., 530/241-8559, www.reddingrodeo.com, admission $11.50) acts as the annual star, with a weeks' worth of events each May. The rodeo itself runs from Thursday through Saturday and includes all the traditional riding, roping, and racing events. For a slightly more refined day out in Redding, come out to the **Beer and Wine Festival** (530/243-7773, www.vivadowntownredding.org/services.html, late Sept.) and **Blues by the River** (Lake Redding Park, www.shastablues.com, late Sept.)—two great festivals that are deliberately held together.

Accommodations

If you're doing the long drive on I-5 and you need a place to lay your head for the night, Redding offers a wide array of clean and comfortable chain motels right off the freeway. If you're seeking a more quaint and unique inn experience, you can find that too in limited quantities. Folks who want to ply the waters of Shasta Lake but don't want the hassle of a rental cabin in the woods also often stay in Redding.

UNDER $100

The **Motel 6 Redding South** (2385 Bechelli Ln., 530/221-0562, www.motel6.com, $55–75) is known to regular travelers as one of the best examples of a Motel 6 anywhere—it's definitely better than the other two in the Redding area. Sure, it's a Motel 6, so your room will be plain and you won't get a lot of frills or extras. What you will get is a clean bedroom with a clean bathroom and a comfortable bed for the night. Even the pool is clean and totally swimmable!

$100-150

One tier up in the hierarchy of chain motels, the **Redding Travelodge** (540 N. Market St., 800/243-1106, www.reddingtravelodge.com, $94–115) offers a few more amenities for only a little more money. The pleasant light facade welcomes guests who need a comfortable bed in a clean room. Guest rooms have flowery comforters, dark carpets, white walls, and plenty of space. You can get queen or king beds and rooms with full refrigerators and partial kitchens. Free Wi-Fi graces the property—a rare amenity in the wilds of Northern California. You can take a dip in the outdoor pool in the summer months, or soak in the indoor whirlpool tub at any time of year.

If you're looking for something better than a corporate-issue motel room, book a room at the **Tiffany House B&B** (1510 Barbara Rd., 530/244-3225, www.tiffanyhousebb.com, $121–165). Sitting high on a hill in a quiet residential neighborhood, the Tiffany House shows off the best of Redding's views, accommodations, and people. Even if you're making your reservations on the spur of the moment, it's worth giving friendly owners Susan and Brady a call to see if any of the inn's four rooms are available. Each room has its own delightful decorations, including stunning handmade bedspreads created by Susan and members of her family. All the rooms offer charm and comfort, as well as views out over Redding and all the way out to Mount Lassen on a clear day. The spacious Cottage room has a huge spa tub, separate bathroom, private porch, and comfortable amenities. The common spaces of the inn include shady gardens and an outdoor pool, a music room, a parlor, and plenty of cozy nooks to sit and read a book. For great advice on the best sights, entertainment, and activities in town, be sure to ask Susan or Brady. Their suggestions, filled with civic pride, remind visitors that Redding can be much more than a waypoint on I-5, and for some it's a vacation destination in its own right.

Another lovely little inn is the **Bridge House Bed and Breakfast** (1455 Riverside Dr., 530/247-7177, www.reddingbridgehouse.com, $135–180). The distinctive steep-pitch-roofed yellow house sits along the Sacramento River just a block or two from historic downtown Redding. You can walk to some of the nicest restaurants and quirkiest shops on Market Street. Inside, you'll find a tranquil haven in one of four unique guest rooms. Each room is named after a bridge, and each is decorated with prints of its namesake, complementary colors, and attractive furniture. For folks who fear the plethora of flowers that often decorate B&B guest rooms, the Bridge House is a welcome surprise, with its quiet soothing solid colors and understated accessories. All rooms offer TVs, spa bathrobes, and lots of great amenities. The two largest rooms boast fancy "massage tubs" in the bathrooms. The Bridge House acts primarily as a romantic retreat for couples, so babies and small children are not always welcome.

Food

After a day outdoors, sometimes you just need a big ol' steak. **Jack's Grill** (1743 California St., 530/241-9705, www.jacksgrillredding.com, Mon.–Sat. 5–11 P.M., $13–31) can hook you up. This locally owned favorite has been serving steaks for more than 70 years. Don't expect the ultra-high-end cuts and preparations of big-city steakhouses. Instead, look for tasty and less expensive steaks, ground steak, and skewers. All meals come with soup or salad and baked potato or fries. Jack's includes a full bar that serves beer, wine, and cocktails.

Want a hearty diner-style meal of noticeably higher quality than your average giant national chain beginning with D? Head straight for the **Black Bear Diner** (2605 Hilltop Dr., 530/221-7600, www.blackbeardiner.com, open daily). This NorCal chain began in the mountain reaches you're now visiting, offering classic American dishes made fresh with better ingredients than most similar restaurants. Today, they still do; travelers will go miles out of their way or wait an extra hour for lunch just to eat at Black Bear. Menus are printed in the style of a local newspaper. Choose from American breakfast classics, salads, sandwiches, chicken and meat entrées, fries and potatoes…the list goes on. Breakfast is served all day, as are the thick (and real) ice cream milkshakes—try the huckleberry flavor. Service is friendly, though the Redding Black Bear Diner can get incredibly crowded on weekends.

In the mood for a hearty Italian meal? **Gironda's Restaurant** (1100 Center St., 530/244-7663, www.girondas.com, Mon.–Thurs. 11 A.M.–9 P.M., Fri. 11 A.M.–10 P.M., Sat. 4:30–10 P.M., Sun. 4:30–9 P.M., $13–25) serves an array of raviolis, pastas, and big Italian-style entrées for lunch and dinner. Choose between dining in the casual-elegant white tablecloth dining room, or ordering take-out to enjoy elsewhere—even at your campsite.

LAKE TAHOE

If you're planning to camp on Lassen or Shasta, or houseboat on the lake, your cheapest options for groceries lay in Redding. The **Grocery Outlet** (2235 Churn Creek Rd., 530/221-4209, www.groceryoutlets.com, Mon.–Fri. 8 A.M.–9 P.M., Sat. 8 A.M.–8 P.M., Sun. 9 A.M.–7 P.M.) sits only a couple of blocks off I-5 for easy access for passers-through. The chain offers lots of prepared foods and frozen items at rock-bottom prices. For an array of slightly higher-end groceries, head for **Safeway** (2275 Pine St., 530/247-3030; 1070 E. Cypress Ave, 530/226-5871). With slightly higher prices comes the ultimate convenience: 24-hour shopping, which can be a lifesaver on road trips and camping expeditions.

Information and Services

For visitors who intend to camp at Shasta Lake or Mount Lassen, Redding is the last outpost of serious civilization before the trek to the more remote reaches of the state. Especially if you're on your way out to Lassen, consider availing yourself of the shopping and services in Redding while you can.

If you're new to the Shasta and Lassen area, the **Redding Convention and Visitors Bureau** (777 Auditorium Dr., 530/225-4100, http://ci.redding.ca.us) is a good first stop. You'll find information and advice about the must-see sights, the best roads to travel, and good spots for impromptu meals.

The local daily newspaper of Redding is the *Record Searchlight* (www.redding.com). This paper covers national and local news, and devotes lots of space to local outdoor recreation. It's worth your while to grab at least one day's paper to find out what's happening while you're in the region.

In all the Shasta and Lassen region, the best place to find ATMs and even bank branches is Redding. A Bank of America (1300 Hilltop Dr., 530/246-5992, Mon.–Thurs. 9 A.M.–5 P.M., Fri. 9 A.M.–6 P.M.) and a Wells Fargo (830 E. Cypress Ave., 800/865-3997, Mon.–Fri. 9 A.M.–6 P.M., Sat. 9 A.M.–4 P.M.) sit right

along I-5 for easy access. ATMs abound; you can find them in big grocery stores, pharmacies, and big-box department stores.

The **post office** in Redding sits at 2323 Churn Creek Road (530/223-7523).

Most of the chain motels in Redding offer Internet access (with or without a fee, depending on the motel). Redding also has a few Starbucks and other cafés with Internet access, and the occasional for-fee Wi-Fi network. Again, if you need to send urgent email from the Shasta-Lassen region, it's a good idea to get it done while you're in Redding.

Redding has the only major medical services available in the entire Shasta-Lassen region. **Mercy Medical Center Redding** (2175 Rosaline Ave., 530/225-6000, http://redding.mercy.org) has a 24-hour emergency room with a full-fledged trauma center for major medical problems.

Getting There and Around

Most Californians get to Redding via I-5, whether they're coming from the north or the south. It's right on the freeway, with plenty of exits leading to the different parts of town. Watch for signs to take you where you need to go in town.

Redding also boasts a municipal airport with some commercial service. The **Redding Municipal Airport** (6751 Airport Rd., 530/224-4320, http://ci.redding.ca.us/transeng/airports/rma.htm) offers flights on Alaska-Horizon and United-Sky West airlines. Flying in and out of such a small airport ain't cheap, but you've got the advantage of far shorter ticketing and security lines.

Redding is an easy town to navigate, and parking tends to be a breeze (and free). You might have to hunt for a spot in historic downtown on summer weekends or during local events, but otherwise don't sweat it. Turtle Bay has two huge parking lots that make visiting a snap, and all the motels have private, ample lots.

SACRAMENTO AND GOLD COUNTRY

The state capital of California, Sacramento, is a cosmopolitan city with a friendly vibe and a low-key, fun entertainment scene. The city of Sacramento grew along the Sacramento River during the Gold Rush era and provided a vital transit link between the mining country and the port of San Francisco. Today, politics is the new gold and it rules Sacramento with a constant presence—you might even spy the "Governator," Arnold Schwarzenegger, in his fleet of Hummers outside the historic Capitol building.

Most California mining history, however, rests outside the big city, in the small boom towns that sprang up throughout the 19th century near major mines. With the closing of the mines, these towns declined for decades, but were eventually rediscovered by tourists and travelers. A wealth of mining museums in the Gold Country region teaches guests about the backbreaking work of gold mining, while ghost stories entertain locals and visitors alike. For travelers who want less history and more action, this is also prime whitewater rafting and kayaking country.

While Sacramento pumps California's political heart, down south in the Central Valley lies its agricultural artery and the staple of the state's economy. The huge flat valley is where the majority of California's crops grow, as it offers a prime climate for a huge array of foods, especially citrus.

History buffs will enjoy visiting the Capitol Building and the historic sights around Old Sacramento, before taking a road trip through the various Gold Rush towns and mining

HIGHLIGHTS

◖ Capitol Building: Sacramento's iconic State Capitol building is the epicenter for the city's political history – past and present. Be sure to check out the museum's impressive collection of art and antiques (page 328).

◖ Old Sacramento: Take a tour of Old Sacramento for a new sense of how the state capital of California grew up over its 150 year existence (page 328).

◖ Empire Mine State Historic Park: The best example of Gold Country mining is this living history museum and park (page 344).

◖ Apple Hill: East of Sacramento lies this 20-mile swath of grower heaven. The Apple Drive Scenic tour takes in dozens of orchards, vineyards, and pit stops for dining and relaxing along the way (page 346).

◖ Daffodil Hill: This private ranch is carpeted in golden color every March, the rare time when visitors can explore the more than 300 species of daffodils on offer (page 347).

◖ Columbia State Historic Park: A former Gold Rush town, Columbia is now a state park. The indoor-outdoor museum experience includes exhibits, shops, and even a saloon – all preserved in homage to the area's mining history (page 364).

LOOK FOR ◖ TO FIND RECOMMENDED SIGHTS, ACTIVITIES, DINING, AND LODGING.

museums along Highway 49. Outdoor lovers can start with a multi-day river rafting trip, then work their way north, hiking, kayaking, and spelunking as they go. Epicureans and wine lovers will find new delights along the farm trails of El Dorado County, through the Shenadoah Valley and Fair Play, and down to Fresno and the Citrus Belt. Whatever your pleasure, this diverse region of California has something for you.

PLANNING YOUR TIME

Sacramento makes a nice day trip or weekend getaway from the Bay Area, or a fun one- or two-day start to a longer Gold Country and Sierra adventure. Winters are mild in Sacramento, while summers get blisteringly hot.

Gold Country is too big, physically, to take in all in one day, or even in one weekend. Highway 49 runs more than 100 miles through the precious-metal-bearing Sierra Foothills,

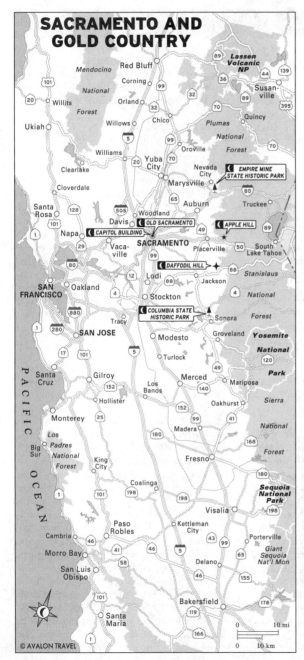

SACRAMENTO AND GOLD COUNTRY

and it's impossible to resist side trips to smaller towns and specific caverns, mines, and museums along the way. If you've got one day, pick a specific Gold Country town as your destination, and one or two of the major parks and attractions nearby. In a weekend, you can get an overview of either northern or southern Gold Country, driving from town to town and making short stops along the way. With a whole week (or even five days) to play with, you can get serious about the region—tasting wine, sampling produce, spelunking, hiking, rafting, and catching up on your Gold Rush history.

Visiting season in Gold Country runs from late spring through late fall, when the weather is best. Winter brings snow to many of the Sierra Foothill towns, which draws skiers and other winter sports enthusiasts.

the State Capitol Building

Sacramento

Many people outside the state don't realize that Sacramento is the state capitol of California. Despite the fact that hundreds of miles lay between this river town and Hollywood, many actors have made their homes here—the office of governor has belonged to the likes of B-movie actor Ronald Reagan and, more recently, big, buff Arnold Schwarzenegger. This surprisingly lovely town has lots to offer visitors, from whitewater rafting along the namesake river to one of the best jazz festivals in the state.

SIGHTS

There's plenty to see in Sacramento, especially if you have an interest in the history of the state of California. From the State Capitol complex to the Railroad Museum, all aspects of California's growth from a (mostly) peaceful oasis for dozens of Native American tribes, through a Spanish colonial settlement, on to a land of opportunity for tremendous wealth in the gold mines, towards its modern persona as an agricultural, radical, fame-loving, innovative, expensive place to live, work, play, and visit.

◖ Capitol Building

The California State Capitol Building (10th and L Sts., 916/324-0333, http://capitolmuseum.ca.gov, daily 9 A.M.–5 P.M., free) displays a grandeur befitting the great state of California. On the ground floor, the museum's magnificent art collection includes California art and artifacts, oil portraits of the state's governors, two murals, and a collection of antiques. You can take in a free tour that highlights the Neoclassical architecture of the building, or learn about the most important legal decisions made in and for the state.

Once you've finished absorbing the history of California from inside the museum, go outside and take a stroll around the grounds. At the rear of the building you'll find an unusual treat, the **Arbor Tour.** An amazing array of trees from around the world are planted in the sweeping space, creating a garden that's perfect for exploring if you love botany, or just for finding a nice place to sit and relax in the shade.

Governor's Mansion

Schoolchildren from all over the state journey to Sacramento to tour the Governor's Mansion (1526 H St., 916/323-3047, www.parks.ca.gov, daily 10 A.M.–5 P.M., adults $4, children $2). No, Arnold doesn't live here. In fact, the mansion served as the actual home of California governors for fewer than 100 years, 1903–1967. Governor Ronald Reagan and his wife Nancy were the last governing couple to live in the mansion—and they stayed only three months. Since then, the mansion has become an educational tool and a tourist attraction. To enter the Governor's Mansion, you must buy tickets and sign up for a guided tour, which happen frequently throughout the day. Guests get to see the ornate European interior decor, the evidence of different tastes and different generations, and the grandeur that has traditionally surrounded the governors of the great state of California.

◖ Old Sacramento

Sacramento became an important town as the Gold Rush progressed and supplies were sent up the Sacramento River from San Francisco. The most important part of the early town were the piers along the river, and that's where Old Sacramento (visitors center, 1002 Second St., 916/442-7644, daily 10 A.M.–5 P.M.) still sits today. The charming cobblestone streets and clattery wooden sidewalks pass old-time shops, restaurants, and attractions. You can take a carriage ride through the streets or walk the wharf and wander the decks of the Delta King. Check out the tiny **Wells Fargo Museum** (1000 Second St., 916/440-4263) and **Old Sacramento Schoolhouse Museum** (Front and L Sts., 916/483-8818, www.oldsac schoolhouse.org) or lighten your wallets in the

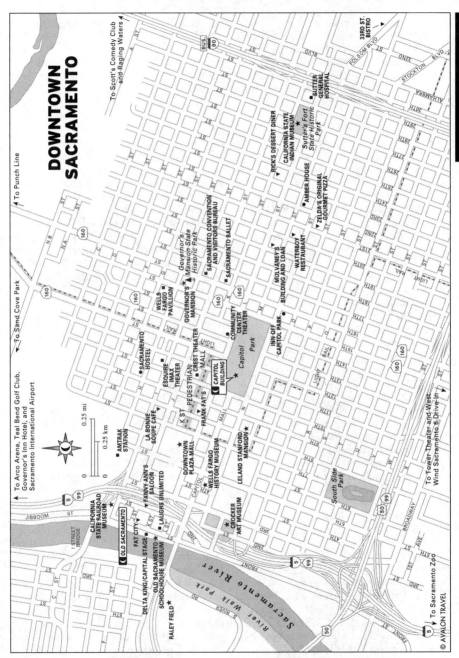

DOWNTOWN SACRAMENTO

To Punch Line

To Scott's Comedy Club and Raging Waters

33RD ST. BISTRO

To Arco Arena, Teal Bend Golf Club, Governor's Inn Hotel, and Sacramento International Airport

To Sand Cove Park

SUTTER GENERAL HOSPITAL

RICK'S DESSERT DINER

CALIFORNIA STATE INDIAN MUSEUM

Sutter's Fort State Historic Park

AMBER HOUSE

ZELDA'S ORIGINAL GOURMET PIZZA

WATERBOY RESTAURANT

MULVANEY'S BUILDING AND LOAN

Sacramento State Historic Park

Governor's Mansion State Historic Park

SACRAMENTO CONVENTION AND VISITORS BUREAU

SACRAMENTO BALLET

WELLS FARGO PAVILLION

GOVERNOR'S MANSION

SACRAMENTO HOSTEL

ESQUIRE IMAX THEATER

CREST THEATER

COMMUNITY CENTER THEATER

INN OFF CAPITOL PARK

Capitol Park

CAPITOL BUILDING

FRANK FAT'S

PEDESTRIAN MALL

AMTRAK STATION

LA BONNE SOUPE CAFÉ

DOWNTOWN PLAZA MALL

WELLS FARGO HISTORY MUSEUM

LELAND STANFORD MANSION

South Side Park

To Tower Theater and West Wind Sacramento 6 Drive-In

CALIFORNIA STATE RAILROAD MUSEUM

OLD SACRAMENTO

FANNY ANN'S SALOON

LAUGHS UNLIMITED

FAT CITY

DELTA KING/CAPITAL STAGE

OLD SACRAMENTO SCHOOLHOUSE MUSEUM

RALEY FIELD

I STREET BRIDGE

CROCKER ART MUSEUM

River Walk Park

Sacramento River

To Sacramento Zoo

To Avalon Travel

0 0.25 mi

0 0.25 km

© AVALON TRAVEL

shops and boutiques. Grab a bite at one of the many restaurants. To really get into the spirit of the location, look for the Old Sacramento Living History (916/445-3101, www.oslhp.net) activities that take place every month of the year. From May through October, join in on a Living History walk (May Sat.–Sun., June–Oct. Wed.–Sun.) with a costumed guide who'll tell you the story of this area from the point of view of a 19th-century resident. Enjoy the vintage-style clothes, the historic merchants, and the re-enactors engaging in period arts and crafts.

California State Railroad Museum

If you've ever felt a lick of romance at the sight of a steam locomotive, or ever longed for an adventure on the rails, you've got to stop at the California State Railroad Museum (111 I St., 916/445-7387, www.parks.ca.gov, daily 10 A.M.–5 P.M., adults $8, children $3). Inside the mammoth museum buildings are artifacts and models that illustrate the building of the railroads to the West, especially the all-important Transcontinental Railroad. The main floor plays host to the museum's fabulous collection of rolling stock—locomotives, freight and passenger cars, and cabooses. It's strange to see mammoth locomotives standing still inside walls; these creations that made so much industry possible seem to belong outdoors. (And indeed, the museum occasionally lends its stock for photography and films.)

You can look in on the stylish appointments of the private rail cars of the rich and stand next to the immense wheels of mighty steam locomotives. Climb aboard the open cars and locomotives for a look inside the railroad that made the growth and expansion of California possible. Along the edges of the room, are memorabilia from the heyday of the railroads, from timetables to fine china. A gift shop offers souvenirs for visitors of all ages, including Thomas the Tank Engine toys for young kids, replica china for collectors, and thick tomes of railroad history for history buffs.

Cross the plaza to board the steam-powered **Excursion train** (916/445-6645, Apr.–Sept.

Sat.–Sun. 11 A.M.–5 P.M., $8) for a 40-minute ride along the riverfront.

Sutter Fort State Historic Park

For a visit into the history of the European settlement of California, come to Sutter Fort State Historic Park (2701 L St., 916/445-4422, www.parks.ca.gov, daily 10 A.M.–5 P.M.). Situated right in the middle of downtown Sacramento, the fort was originally the center of John Sutter's "New Helvetia" settlement. A tour of the park begins with the mazelike museum at the entrance. Inside the fort structure, the story of John Sutter is called out in photos, artifacts, and placards. After perusing the interpretive area, wander outside into the sunlight and enjoy the living history taking place all around you. Wander the inner walls of the fort to see how the early settlers lived—from dragging their luggage from the East to their bedrooms at the settlement. Denizens of the park, dressed in costumes of the 19th century, engage in the activities that filled the days of California's settlers. With their help, you can try your hand at making rope, baking bread, and doing all sorts of pioneer activities. Listen to the music of the era as you learn about the history of Sutter and his followers by living it for a few hours. Afterwards, stop at the gift shop, which evokes a small 1800s store, filled with historic costume patterns, books, and period toys.

Leland Stanford Mansion

Railroad baron and Stanford University founder Leland Stanford and his family spent a number of years living in the capital city, close to Mr. Stanford's business interests, at what is now the Leland Stanford Mansion State Historic Park (800 N St., 916/324-0575, www.leland stanfordmansion.org, fee for mansion tours). Some years after Leland Stanford's death, his wife Jane Stanford donated the family mansion to the Catholic Church for use as a children's home. It was eventually purchased by the state, and the current museum was constructed beginning in 1991. Your tour will begin in the visitors center, which sits next to the museum

Store outside the mansion proper. From there you'll journey inside the lavish main building, admiring the lovingly restored furnishings, carpets, walls, and antiques. Visitors get a hint of what it might have been like to live as one of the wealthiest men in the country in some of the most exciting years of California's history.

Mansion tours are wheelchair accessible, and assistive listening devices and other aids are available upon request. You must be part of a tour to explore the mansion; however, the visitors center, store, and parts of the gardens can be visited for free during open hours.

Crocker Art Museum

For a detour from history into art, visit the Crocker Art Museum (216 O St., 916/808-1179, www.crockerartmuseum.org, Tues.–Sun. 10 A.M.–5 P.M., Thurs. until 9 P.M., adults $6, children $3). Ten centuries of fine arts are collected here, and traveling exhibitions visit on an ongoing basis. (Check the website for the latest and upcoming exhibitions.) The original gallery was donated to the city of Sacramento by the Crocker family— one of the Big Four railroad and industry barons who built California's infrastructure and made a fortune doing so. That fortune paid for the international art collection that Margaret Crocker donated to the public. Today, wander the galleries filled with paintings from Europe and Asia, ceramics from around the world, photography, drawing, and specifically California art. The galleries—housed inside Victorian mansions—are works of art themselves. Be sure to spend some time examining the floors, ceilings, and woodwork as you explore this wonderful world-class museum.

Sacramento Zoo

Ready for a break from all those museums? Take a trip to visit the animals at the Sacramento Zoo (Sutterville Rd and Land Park Dr., 916/808-5888, http://saczoo.com, daily 9 A.M.–4 P.M., adults $9, children $6.50). A fabulous array of animals await you, including big kitties and other mammals, funky frogs and amphibians, big ol' snakes, a small-fish

aquarium, and many more. Take cover from the summer heat under the shade of the century-old oak trees, as the critters enjoy their own custom-grown garden habitats. Check the website for a list of zoo activities each month, including educational talks, guided walks, special festivals, and other events—many of which center around fun and education for the younger set.

ENTERTAINMENT AND EVENTS
Live Music

For a night of impeccable classical music, buy tickets for a concert performed by the **Sacramento Philharmonic Orchestra** (916/264-5181, www.sacphil.org). The Philharmonic performs all over the greater Sacramento area, most often in the Community Center Theater (1301 L St.), the Mondavi Center at Davis (University of California Davis, 530/754-2787, www.mondaviarts.org), and the Magic Circle Roseville Theater (241 Vernon St., Roseville, 916/782-1777, www.mcircle .org). The comany plays a wide range of music, with something of a specialty in newer works by composers from around the world. You can also see occasional historic masterworks such as Berlioz's *Symphonie Fantastique.*

Each May, jazz lovers from all around the state flock to the capital for the **Sacramento Jazz Jubilee** (www.sacjazz.com). Over four days of Memorial Day Weekend, more than 100 jazz acts descend on Sacramento to perform in venues ranging from the lush Convention Center stage to the wooden planks of the Old Sacramento sidewalks. Check the website for a list of performers, which can include the top jazz musicians in the world today, with headliners like Kermit Ruffins and featured artists such as Joe Ascione, Harry Allen, and John Allred. Bands play every style of jazz imaginable—classic, zydeco, big band, western, skiffle, funk, and so much more. It seems amazing that a small city like Sacramento can handle so much raw talent, but it can—with the easy grace of a jazz riff. If you're already planning to come to Sacramento on Memorial

Day anyway, be sure to get tickets to shows in advance. If you've been looking for a reason to visit the state capital, this is one of the best Sacramento has to offer.

Comedy

Need a laugh while you're in Sacto? You can find one at any of the city's three major comedy clubs. The **Punch Line** (2100 Arden Way, 916/925-5500), sister club to the San Francisco Punch Line, brings top national talent to the state capital. If you know you'll be coming in advance, buy tickets online. If not, calling ahead for reservations for popular comics is always your best bet for getting in. You might see the likes of Dana Carvey live and in person. Shows run nightly from Wednesday through Sunday every week, with hot local and up-and-coming national acts such as Gabriel Iglesias and Amy Schumer. All tickets are general admission, so you'll be able to find a seat at a table when the doors open. Come early for seats nearest the stage (not always recommended at a live comedy show).

Right in the midst of Old Sacramento, **Laughs Unlimited** (1207 Front St., 916/446-8128, www.laughsunlimited.com, shows Thurs.–Sun.) brings hilarity to the waterfront. With comics such as Todd Paul and Chris Titus doing multi-night engagements every week, and occasional shows by comedy legends like Jack Gallagher, Shawn Wayans, and Alonzo Bodden, you'll have a great time at this classic comedy venue. There's a two-drink minimum for all patrons, and a reasonable appetizer and dessert menu can slake appetites grown large from laughing.

For a more intimate evening of chuckles, head to **Scott's Comedy Club** (2600 Auburn Blvd., 916/267-0502), now located inside Zigato's Bar and Grille. Here you're less likely to see a mega-star, and more likely to laugh at the never-before-told jokes of someone who's currently on their way up the ladder of comedic fame. Heck—*you* can take the stage at Scott's on open mic nights. See the website for details on making your Scott's debut. Despite its size and local flair, it's still a good idea to call for reservations in advance for the bigger shows.

Cinema

Sacramento is a great place to go to the movies. For a larger-than-life cinematic experience, get tickets for the **Esquire IMAX Theater** (1211 K St., 916/443-4629, www.imax.com/sacramento). The Esquire shows IMAX documentary films in traditional 2-D and mind-blowing 3-D. You can also see the occasional IMAX-remastered Hollywood blockbuster film here. Buy tickets online or at the box office.

On the other hand, if you're looking for a classic night out at the movies, drive in to the **West Wind Sacramento 6 Drive-In** (9616 Oates Dr., 916/363-6572, www.drive-ins.com/theater/catsac, $4.25–6.50). This six-screen drive-in plays first- and second-run Hollywood films. You won't get a speaker for your car, instead you'll tune into a radio channel. Bring your own pillows and blankets and convertible for a truly luxurious movie experience. The old-school circular building at the center of the facility sells inexpensive movie concessions and includes a fun, cheap arcade. The restrooms are nothing to write home about, so go before you drive in if you can. But the overall fun and inexpensive prices make up for any run-down amenities.

For your indie and classic film pleasure, go down to the Capital area and hit **The Crest** (1013 K St., 916/442-7378, www.thecrest.com, $8.50). The interior of the theater is a show in itself—it was restored in the 1990s to the glitzy heights of its 1940s Art Deco glory. Be sure to look around at the walls and up at the glorious ceiling of the single screen's theater before the show starts. Check the website calendar for a list of what's playing while you're in town. In addition to films, The Crest occasionally puts up a live stand-up comedy show with a major star like Carrot Top or Sam Kinison. The Crest also hosts the Sacramento Symphony's community music series, such as "Mocha and Mozart" or "Jeans and Beer."

The Tower (2508 Land Park Dr., 916/442-4700, www.thetowertheatre.com,

$8.50–11) is a quirky, three-screen art house that shows popular, foreign, and independent films. It's not quite as grand as The Crest, but at the Tower you can enjoy an old-fashioned, elegant cinematic atmosphere and a first-run Hollywood flick all at the same time.

Theater

In the tradition of historic Gold Country, live theater is an important part of the nightlife of Sacramento. In Old Sacramento, some of the best theater in the whole city happens on board the *Delta King*.

Performing aboard the *Delta King,* the **Capital Stage** (1000 Front St., 916/995-5464, http://capstage.org, $22–28) strives and succeeds at taking regional theater to the next level. This professional company has a small space to perform works by up-and-coming playwrights and classic, less-produced plays by heavy hitters like Sam Shepard. You'll feel like part of the action as you see great actors performing edgy "grown-up" shows. In fact, all the plays Capital Stage puts up are geared for the over-eighteen set, so they may include adult language and sexual situations. For a perfect night out on the town, have dinner on the *King* before the show.

Also on board the *Delta King,* **Suspects Murder Mystery Dinner Theater** (1000 Front St., 916/443-3600, $39.50) combines dinner and a fun show. As your dinner begins, gunshots ring out! You'll spend the rest of your meal laughing as you participate in an Agatha Christie–style murder mystery. You might find yourself a suspect, or possibly a victim. However the story plays out, you'll enjoy the comedy, the mystery, and the tasty food and drink at this fun, kitschy night of dinner theater.

If you just can't go more than a few days without a musical theater experience, get tickets for the latest show at **California Musical Theater** (916/557-1999, www.calmt.com, $15–70). CMT uses both the Wells Fargo Pavilion (1419 H St.) and the Community Center Theater (1301 L St.) for its productions. As advertised, the Broadway Series puts up iconic Broadway musicals—think *Phantom of the Opera* and *Mamma Mia.* On the other hand, the Music Circus shows off the classic musicals, from *Aida* to *Annie* to *The Best Little Whorehouse in Texas.* The high production values delight audiences at every show. Purchase single-show tickets online at the website, over the phone, or at the box office. You can also check out the seating charts for both theaters to pick out your perfect spot.

Dance

Classical dance lovers can enjoy a night out at the **Sacramento Ballet** (1631 K St., 916/552-5800, www.sacballet.org, performances Thurs.–Sun., adults $25–55, children $12.50–32.50). For 50 years, this company has brought high-level dance spectacles to the capital; the Sacramento Ballet went fully professional in 1986. For the last 20 years, they've produced an array of famous ballets, including such classics as *Sleeping Beauty* and *The Nutcracker,* as well as any number of new and interpreted works—such as the world premiere of *A Woman's Journey: The Tamsen Donner Story* and *A Streetcar Named Desire.* You can purchase individual tickets directly from the box office, by phone, or online via the ballet's website. Most performances go up at the Sacramento Community Center theater—a large space with multiple tiers of seats. Check the website for special events while you're in town.

Festivals and Events

Each year, the California State Fair takes place at the mammoth fairgrounds called the **California Exposition & State Fair Center** (1600 Exposition Blvd., 916/263-3000, www.calexpo.com), known to its friends as Cal Expo. The property is used all year long for every large-scale retail show imaginable, as well as shows and festivals that require plenty of exhibition space. The Quilt, Craft, and Sewing Festival comes here, as do RV shows, landscape shows, and boat shows. Year-round, horseracing fans can come to the Cal Expo Sports & Wagering Center at the Budweiser Grandstand to take a load off, enjoy a cold one, and place bets on their favorite ponies. Races play on the hundreds of flat-screen TVs set up all around the center. You've got access to free Wi-Fi at the Center as well.

The highlight of each year at Cal Expo is unquestionably the **California State Fair** (www.bigfun.org). The fair lasts for two weeks, usually at the end of August. During that period, nearly a million people pass through the gates of Cal Expo. They might come for the musical concerts performed by national acts, the horse races at the Budweiser Grandstand, the carnival, the exhibitions, or the contests. A major wine competition is held at the fair each year, and the biggest and most impressive wineries from around the state take it very seriously. If you want to taste the wines, along with top food, visit the SaveMart Supermarkets Wine Garden. A "Green Dreams" exposition shows off the best and brightest of ecologically friendly technology. For more classic fair fare, head for the concession stands at the Main Line or the Promenade. Everything from hot dogs on sticks to ice cream cones to Japanese food is served. Be sure to wear sunblock during the day and drink plenty of water any time you're there—it gets frighteningly hot in Sacto in August.

SHOPPING
Antiques
If you prefer the old to the new, come down to the **57th Street Antiques Mall** (875 57th St., 916/451-3110, www.57thstreetantiquemall .com, Tues.–Sun. 10 A.M.–5 P.M.). With more than 50 dealers selling here, you're likely to find whatever antique or collectible you're looking for. The Mall specializes in smaller items such as linens, jewelry, glass and china, and vintage clothing—perfect for non-local shoppers who'd like to pack their treasures into a suitcase. Inside the Mall, you'll find several unique antique shops with their own specialties. Discovery Antiques has furniture, Asian and French imported antiques, and a fine collection of estate jewelry. Seluka's features 20th-century vintage collectibles with a distinctive

West Coast/California bent. If you prefer the excitement of buying your antiques in an auction setting, head for The Auction Block Company, which holds live auctions once or twice each month.

Art Galleries
A plethora of galleries make Midtown home. Between H Street and Capitol Avenue you'll find any number of storefronts displaying works of local and worldwide artists working in all media. The best way to explore these is through **2nd Saturdays** (www.2nd-sat .com, 6–9 P.M., free), an art walk held the second Saturday of every month. Galleries stay open late and residents crowd the streets—usually Del Paso Boulevard or the Uptown Art District—filled with vendors, music, and food.

Clothing
The revitalized Midtown "Grid" (www .midtowngrid.com) offers an array of boutiques, galleries, and shops that please shoppers. Fashionistas have a range of choices, from the sleek **Cuffs Urban Apparel** (2523 J St., 916/443-2881, www.myspace.com/cuffs urbanapparel) to the truth-in-advertising **Cotton Club** (2331 J St., 916/442-2990) and **Dara Denim** (2404 K St., 916/444-1188), each of which specializes in clothing made from its named material. Thrift and vintage hunters head for **French Cuff Consignment** (2419 J St., 916/442-3724, www.frenchcuffbtq.com).

Department Stores
If you're looking for a standard urban-style shopping mall in Sacramento, go to the **Arden Fair** (1689 Arden Way, 916/920-1167, www .ardenfair.com, Mon.–Sat. 10 A.M.–9 P.M., Sun 10 A.M.–6 P.M.). It's perfectly placed near the junction of Highway 80 and Highway 50. In this typical American mall,—anchored by Sears, J.C. Penney's, Macy's, and Nordstrom—you'll find all your favorite midrange chain clothing stores, shoe stores, specialty shops, and a food court filled with junk food from around the world.

Gift and Home

If you're looking for gifts to bring home to family and friends, check **Something Fabulous** (1927 L St., 916/442-0185, www.saccenter.org /something-fabulous) for unusual international art and home furnishings, and **Zanzibar Imports & Jewelry** (1731 L St., 916/443-2057, www.zanzibartribalart.com) for tribal art.

SPORTS AND RECREATION

The Sacramento River and nearby delta are the center of recreation activities in Sacramento, but any number of other fun opportunities await adventurous visitors to this region.

Swimming and Fishing

The heat of Sacto summers can make anyone want to go jump in the lake—or the river, as the case may be. All through Sacramento proper, you'll find parks along the river, offering a variety of boat launches, swimming holes, and fishing areas.

For a fun and refreshing day out on the banks of the Sacramento River, head for **Sand Cove Park** (2005 Garden Hwy., 916/264-5200). Walk from the parking lot down the trail to the sandy river beach, which makes for a perfect spot to swim or fish. The park also offers a grassy lawn area, shade trees, hiking trails, and a boat dock at the north end. (There's no launch here, however.) Bring a picnic and while away the day alternately swimming in the water, sunning yourself, and fishing for your dinner. The river shelters bass, sturgeon, and salmon; you'll need a California fishing license to fish here. Amenities at this municipal park are minimal—expect no food vendors and portable toilet facilities, so prepare accordingly.

One of the more famous Sacramento-area parks actually runs through the separate town of West Sacramento. **River Walk Park** (651 Second St., www.cityofwestsacramento.org) features a paved pathway that runs along the river. As you walk the path, read the interpretive plaques to learn about the flora and fauna that inhabit this part of the Sacramento River ecosystem. Bring a cooler and have a picnic at

© LIZ HAMILL SCOTT

the Sacramento River

one of the various picnic areas along the path, or bring your rod and tackle and walk out onto the fishing dock. A major boat dock lets private boaters moor at the park. River Walk Park also encourages visitors to jump out into the water for a refreshing swim in the river.

Golf

You'll find more than a dozen golf courses in Sacramento and its surrounding lands and communities—not a surprise when you consider the relative density of politicians who live and work in town. With the endlessly mild weather of Sacramento winters and the heat of summer, it's always golf season in Sacto. Whatever skill level you play at, you can enjoy a round of golf while you're here. For information about public courses in the city proper, check the Capital City Golf website at www .capitalcitygolf.com. Perhaps you'll see Arnold himself as you tee off.

In town, perhaps the most beloved public course is the **Bing Maloney Golf Course** (6801 Freeport Blvd., 916/808-2283, www.bing maloney.com, $9.50–40). Bing Maloney offers two courses: the historic 18-hole course that's been on the property since 1952, and the 20-year-old 9-hole executive course. The par-29, 9-hole executive course can be a genuine bargain on weekdays and is perfect for beginners to the game. Make your reservations for a tee time up to eight days in advance online or over the phone for either course. The par-72, 18-hole course has been described as "what you see is what you get"—a straightforward course that will challenge your game with sloping greens and huge heritage oak trees, but not frustrate you with gimmicks or unwelcome surprises. If you're interested in taking a lesson at Bing Maloney, check the website for information and call in advance for a reservation.

A newer course in town, the **Teal Bend Golf Club** (7200 Garden Hwy., 916/922-5209, www.tealbendgolf.com, $29–65) has been around for only 10 years. Conveniently located near the airport and the river, you can

slip in a quick round of golf at Teal Bend no matter how little time you have in Sacto. As you walk and play, look out for the teal duck—the course's namesake—as well as deer, geese, and hawks, all of which make their home on the course. (You might want to watch your step in the rough, too.) This course, a locals' favorite, is famous for its many water features. Make your tee time reservations over the phone or online up to eight days in advance, or consider enrolling in one of the club's many annual tournaments. Check the website for Internet specials. After your game, relax at the Bar and Grille, enjoying a casual meal of a burger or a salad and a nice cold beer.

Just outside of town, still more golf courses invite politicians, pros, visitors, and amateurs alike. The **Empire Ranch Golf Club** (1620 E. Natoma, Folsom, 916/817-8100, www.empire ranchgolfclub.com, $29–67) is the suburb of Folsom's first golf course, designed by Brad Bell (also the designer of the Teal Bend). The 18-hole course offers challenging play, especially on a windy day, and spectacular views out toward the Sierras. If you're just looking to hone your skills, Empire Ranch offers a full range of practice facilities—putting greens, chipping ranges, and a driving range. Check the website for special Internet prices.

Spa

If you need to take a break, Sacramento has any number of spas to help you out. Midtown offers an especially dense spa concentration these days. **The Way Within Spa Retreat** (1722 J St., 916/446-4443) focuses its treatments on healing and retreat services for couples. Massages and foot treatments help weary travelers (and locals!) take a load off and get to feeling better. Baths, body scrubs, and steam treatments rejuvenate singles and couples. For a stretchy and wonderful California massage experience, book a Thai yoga massage.

Yoga

Looking for some directed tranquility during your stay in Sacramento? Inside the 57th

Street Antiques Mall, do a session of yoga at **The Yoga Solution** (887 57th St., Ste, B, 916/383-7933, www.theyogasolution.net). This studio offers classes each day, most in the Hatha and Iyengar schools.

Amusement Parks

Kids and adults alike can use a refreshing play day to escape the summer's heat in Sacramento. A perfect place to get cool is **Raging Waters** (1600 Exposition Blvd., 916/924-3747, www .rwsac.com, $20–24). With rides like Shark Attack, Dragon's Den, and Honolulu Half-Pipe, thrill-seekers can get a full day of excitement here. For a more sedate day at the water park, ride a slow tube down the Calypso Cooler river, play in Hook's Lagoon, or catch a wave at Breakers Beach. At lunchtime, get a meal at the ample snack bar, or bring your own picnic to enjoy at the picnic tables or on the lawns. If you don't mind the heat and you're tired of the waterslides, play a game of pickup volleyball on one of the provided courts.

Casino Gambling

Gamblers can take a spin through the slots and across the tables at the **Thunder Valley Casino** (1200 Athens Ave., Lincoln, 916/408-7777, www.thundervalleyresort.com, open daily), only a short drive from downtown Sacramento. You'll find more than 2,000 slot machines and nearly 100 table games here, along with a Vegas-style buffet and plenty of chain eateries. Be sure to stop for a drink at the Falls Bar for a drink, then head into the casino to play Ultimate Texas Hold 'Em, mini baccarat, or blackjack.

Spectator Sports

Sacramento is the treasured home of many professional sports teams at all levels. It's easy to take in a game while you're visiting.

Basketball is a local favorite sport here. The NBA's **Sacramento Kings** (www.nba.com/ kings, $10–165) play at the **Arco Arena** (1 Sports Pkwy.). A fast-paced basketball game can be a great way to unwind after a long day of historical sights and museums, so come on down and cheer for the purple and white! You

can get tickets for cheap if you're willing to sit in the nosebleeds. Tickets are available online, or right at the arena box office. The arena has ample parking ($10).

If you prefer the ladies of the WNBA, Sacramento's got a great team in the **Sacramento Monarchs** (www.wnba.com/ monarchs, $21–42). The Monarchs also call the Arco Arena home. Come and watch the most skilled women in basketball heat up the arena!

The hot, dry weather of the Sacto summer just begs for a baseball game. Take yourself out to one with the **Sacramento River Cats** (www.rivercats.com). The AAA (minor league) River Cats play **Raley Field** (400 Ball Park Dr., 916/376-4700, fee for parking), which appropriately sits right by the Sacramento River. At a River Cats game, you'll see serious baseball played by up-and-coming young men, many of whom have a serious eye on the majors. You can take a shuttle ($0.50) right to the field, buy a classic hot dog and a soda or a beer, sit back, and relax while the players do all the work. Ample pay parking is a short-to-medium walk from the stadium entrances.

ACCOMMODATIONS

Sacramento tends to be a workman's town, with folks coming in for meetings and conventions and staying at big-box chain motels and hotels. As the city remakes its Old Town and Midtown areas, more unique lodgings will appear. For now, however, your best bet at a cheap-and-easy room are the various Holiday Inns, Quality Inns, and Sheratons.

Under $100

For budget accommodations in Sacramento, you can't beat the **Sacramento Hostel** (900 H St., 916/443-1691, www.norcalhostels.org/ sac, $23–50). The hostel sits inside a grand old Victorian home right downtwon. You'll love the parlor, drawing room, and recreation room—all with high ceilings and historic-style moldings. A full kitchen welcomes cooks with all the equipment needed to create tasty and inexpensive meals. On warm evenings, take your dinner out to the wraparound porch to enjoy the weather as the sun goes down. Guest rooms include both co-ed and single-sex dorms, plus a few private rooms for a higher price. Note that only one private room includes a private bath—all other hall baths are shared. The attractive wooden bunks do not include linens, so you'll need to bring your own sheets or sleeping bag. However, the hostel does have free DSL and Wi-Fi, laundry, on-site parking, and 24-hour guest access.

The **Governors Inn** (210 Richards Blvd., 916/448-7224, www.governorsinnhotel .com, $95–145) sits in near the Capitol in Sacramento. Walk from the Governors to the Capitol, or take a five-minute drive to Old Sacramento or Midtown. Your room, with classic motel styling, creates a perfect base for your stay. Whether you book a standard room or a two-room suite, you'll enjoy the understated elegance of this motel. Kids enjoy the outdoor pool in the hot summer months, and adults take advantage of the fitness center, free Wi-Fi, continental breakfast, and more. Check the website or ask at the desk for a plethora of recommendations for shopping,

restaurants, golf courses, and sights to see throughout town.

$100-150

At the **Inn off Capitol Park** (1530 N St., 916/447-8100, www.innoffcapitolpark.com, $117), you'll find attractive luxury at moderate prices. The inn sits within easy walking distance of the Capitol and the Sacramento Convention Center. The linens, wall art, and paint all match tastefully, and the furniture and lighting feel more like home than a motel. With an eye toward business and pleasure travelers, amenities include free Wi-Fi and voicemail, plus a continental breakfast and dinner recommendations. If you're planning a stay in Sacramento during any major events, book a room at the Inn early—with only 38 rooms, this friendly boutique hotel can fill up fast during conventions. The Inn Off Capitol Park is 100 percent non-smoking.

If you want to stay on a piece of history, book a stateroom on the *Delta King* (1000 Front St., 916/444-5464, www.deltaking.com, $119–149). An integral part of the Old Town

© LIZ HAMILL SCOTT

Book a stateroom on the *Delta King* and step back in time.

neighborhood, the *Delta King* is at once a hotel, restaurant, theater, and gathering space. To stay on the *Delta King* means stepping back into the Prohibition era, when the *King* plied the Sacramento River between Sacramento and San Francisco. Drinks, jazz, and dancing were the order of the evening then. Today you can stay in the very same staterooms, albeit refurbished to modern, elegant standards. Be aware that the less expensive staterooms can be quite small, as is common onboard ships. All rooms have their own private bathrooms, and for a slightly higher fee you can stay in a much larger and more luxurious stateroom or suite. High-rollers can take advantage of the Captain's Quarters—a palatial space with its own private observation deck. Multi-bed rooms are available for families, and couples can enjoy a Romance Package complete with champagne and a coupon for dinner at one of the *King's* two restaurants.

$150-250

For a touch of luxury near the Capitol, stay at the **Inn and Spa at Parkside** (2116 Sixth St., 916/658-1818, www.innatparkside.com, $175–275). Each of the dozen rooms features unique decoration, with vibrant colors and sumptuous fabrics. Pick from rooms named Kiss, Passion, Refresh, and Extravagant. You'll feel as though you're in a cross between a small bed-and-breakfast and an elegant luxury hotel. Many rooms have spa tubs and showers, flat-screen TVs, balconies, fireplaces, and other great amenities. This inn is set up for romantic evenings for couples, so consider choosing a different lodging if you're traveling with children. To add extra pampering to your Sacramento stay, book a treatment at Spa Bloom—the attached luxury spa that offers beautifying facials (ask for microdermabrasion with any facial) and relaxing massages. Some rooms at the inn are set up for in-room massage; check when you book your reservations.

Over $250

If you've got the money for luxury, the best B&B in Sacramento has long been the 🌊 **Amber House** (1315 22nd St., 916/444-8085, www

.amberhouse.com, $190–310). It's located in a quiet residential street in Midtown within walking distance of shopping, restaurants, and nightlife. Consisting of two separate houses, the Amber House prides itself on a level of service you'd find at the Ritz. The owner and innkeepers will see to your every need from the moment you enter the front door. Once inside, you'll find that no matter what room you've reserved, you'll be treated to the best. Every room at the inn has either a Jacuzzi or deep soaking bathtub, a super-comfortable bed, a subtly tucked-away TV, and top-end amenities.

The stellar comfort and service extends to the food as well. If you indicate you want them, fresh, warm chocolate chip cookies will be waiting for you when you come in from dinner in the evening. The next day, coffee (or your favorite morning beverage) is delivered to your door along with the morning paper. Breakfast, which can be served in the privacy of your room, in the formal dining room, or out in the shaded garden, is a multi-course masterpiece of fresh ingredients and original dishes. After one night and morning at the Amber House, you'll want to stay for weeks.

FOOD

It might surprise new visitors to Sacramento to learn that the cuisine served in the smaller capital city can rival that of Los Angeles and even culinary heavyweight San Francisco. You'll find almost any kind of ethnic food you can imagine, upscale white-tablecloth bistros, and local favorite holes-in-the-wall with lines out the door. Whatever your tastes, you'll find dining in Sacto a welcome and tasty adventure.

American

An outgrowth of the original Frank Fat's is Old Sacramento's 🌊 **Fat City** (1001 Front St., 916/446-6768, www.fatsrestaurants.com/fatcity). Here, you'll imagine you've walked into an Old West saloon from the California gold mining heyday. Award-winning stained glass graces the windows, the lamps, and almost anything else they could affix it to. Dark furniture and linens complete the atmosphere in the high-ceiling dining room, which sits across the street from the *Delta King*. But it's the menu that makes Fat City stand out. A diverse selection of dishes appeals to any visitor's palate. You can get a plate of chow mein, an order of tacos, or an enormous gooey cheeseburger (the Bourbon Barbecue Burger is the best of these). At dinnertime, the entrées turn to American comfort food, including meat loaf, pot pie, and racks of ribs. Lighter eaters can get an entrée salad. Portions are enormous (perhaps appropriate given the restaurant's name), so consider splitting a meal with a friend. On weekend days, enjoy a mixed brunch menu that includes the best of the lunch menu, plus a number of Fat City breakfast specialties. Whenever you come in, you'll find the service friendly and helpful. Crowds can get heavy, especially during high tourist season, so you may have to wait a few minutes for a table. However, the large historic building accommodates plenty of diners, and the food is worth the wait.

Another good Old Sac burger joint is in **Fanny Ann's Saloon** (1023 Second St., 916/441-0505, www.fannyanns.com, $10–20). Enjoy classic American grub in an Old West setting.

Asian

Frank Fat's (806 L St., 916/442-7092, www.fatsrestaurants.com, Mon.–Fri. 11 A.M.–10 P.M., Sat.–Sun. 5–10 P.M.) lives up to its reputation as a legendary Sacramento institution. The oldest restaurant in Sacramento was opened by Frank Fat in 1939. From the beginning, Fat's served authentic upscale Chinese food—which it still does today. Also from the beginning, the cream of capital city society came to eat at Fat's. On the menu, you'll find steaks to satisfy even the heartiest appetites, Chinese delicacies with and without meat or poultry, and more. Vegetarians can get a fabulous meal at Fat's, even as carnivores can sate their appetites. The hardest part is choosing just enough for your table without going totally overboard. The dimly lit, rich atmosphere invites romantic couples on a night out, and of course politicians looking for a

quiet chat. Appropriately, Fat's sits near the Capitol complex.

For another side of Asian cuisine, have a tranquil Japanese meal at **Zen Sushi** (900 15th St., 916/446-9628, www.zen-sushi.com, Mon.–Thurs. 11:30 A.M.–2 P.M. and 5–9:30 P.M., Fri.–Sun. 11:30 A.M.–2 P.M. and 5–11 P.M., $5–15). This small, well-lit, casual sushi joint beckons visitors and locals with its wide array of house specialty rolls, fresh sashimi and nigiri, and plentiful vegetarian and cooked dishes. While Sacramento has no direct access to the sea, proximity to the San Francisco Bay Area guarantees the availability of the best fresh sushi-grade fish. Lunch and dinner combinations offer good value for plenty of food, plus lots of options for non-raw-fish eaters. But for the best Zen has to offer, look at the House Special Rolls list—that's where the good stuff hides. With your meal, quaff one of a variety of Japanese and American beers, a Japanese soda, or a glass of sweet fruity plum wine. Before you pick a time to eat, remember that Zen's downtown location makes it popular with the local business lunch crowd. Pick an off-time or the dinner hour for a smaller crowd.

Cajun

Hot & Spicy Café New Orleans (117 J St., 916/443-5051, Sun.–Thurs. 11 A.M.–10 P.M., Fri.–Sat. 11 A.M.–11 P.M., $20) brings a taste of Louisiana to Sacto. With exposed brick and ductwork and bright, colorful tablecloths, the atmosphere at this eatery is friendly and fun. As for the food…When they say "Hot & Spicy," they mean it. For real. The Cajun foods—jambalaya, gumbo, and many other New Orleans favorites—are riddled with hot peppers and other spices. Be careful of what you order! To put out the fire, go downstairs for an after-dinner drink at the attached SpeakEasy bar.

California

Calling the ◖ **33rd Street Bistro** (3301 Folsom Blvd., 916/455-2233, http://33rdstreetbistro.com, Sun.–Thurs. 8 A.M.–10 P.M., Fri.–Sat. 8 A.M.–11 P.M., $7–24) a "California cuisine" restaurant is somewhat misleading. In fact, the Bistro's menus are inspired by the foods of the Pacific Northwest—the training ground of executive chef Fred Haines—and favorite dishes from around the country. The panini selection speaks to the Northwestern connection, while the salads offer original and delectable healthy fare. In fact, most of the food at the Bistro tends toward the current trend for local, health-conscious cuisine. The casual dining room features exposed brick, an open kitchen and pizza oven, and a fun party atmosphere. Feel free to wear your favorite jeans and T-shirt when you eat at this Sacto locals' favorite, which is open late-ish for dinner on weekends to accommodate people out for a night on the town.

Mulvaney's Building & Loan (1215 19th St., 916/441-6022, www.culinaryspecialists .com/mulvaneybl.htm) is a product of the Midtown renaissance. This upscale eatery showcases the best of California cuisine. It's not cheap, but for a romantic night out, the original dishes at Mulvaney's are more than worth it. The menu changes often to take advantage of local, seasonal produce. You can go for a standard appetizer-and-big-ol'-main dish, or order small plates to share around the table or to satisfy a smaller appetite. The wine list offers a reasonable number of tastings and interesting vintages, some of which you may never have seen before. (Try the Kung Fu Girl Riesling if it's available—how can you resist a good wine with a name like that!) Pick between a seat in the lively and loud dining room or a quieter table on the gardenlike back patio, which is a great choice most days of the year in Sacto. Wherever you sit, you'll enjoy friendly, attentive service with a smile and a good understanding of both menu and wine list.

French

If you're looking for a tasty and inexpensive French lunch near the Capitol building, head for **La Bonne Soupe Café** (920 Eighth St., 916/492-9506, Mon.–Fri. 10:30 A.M.–2:30 P.M., $5–10). This is the kind of narrow-focus local favorite that visitors love to find. Beware, if you come right at noon, you'll likely spend some

time standing in line with local businesspeople who come from miles around to have lunch here. La Bonne Soupe serves fresh hot soups and handmade sandwiches on crusty French breads. Soups range from classics such as French onion to tasty treats made with fresh, in-season produce. Sandwiches made with fresh ingredients are far superior to supermarket standards. Best of all, the lunch you get at La Bonne Soupe will make you feel great during and after you eat it, since the soups and sandwiches here burst with healthy nutrients. Be sure to say hi to the chef as you wait—he's often found lovingly preparing sandwiches behind the counter as the line snakes out the door. If you usually eat a smaller lunch, consider splitting an order of soup and one sandwich with a traveling companion—portions are pretty hefty.

For a fancier French restaurant experience, dine out at the **Waterboy Restaurant** (2000 Capitol Ave., 916/498-9891, www.waterboy restaurant.com, Mon.–Fri. 11:30 A.M.–2:30 P.M., Sun.–Mon. 5–9 P.M., Tues.–Thurs. 5–9:30 P.M., Fri.–Sat. 5–10:30 P.M., $10–27). The light, bright dining room feels like something you'd walk into on the south coast of France. And in fact, the cuisine here takes much from the culinary traditions of Provence, as well as Tuscany and just a hint of California. If you've got a serious appetite, go for the full three courses: appetizer, first, and main. But if you've got a lighter appetite, the first course options can make adequate entrées and leave room for dessert. It's worth leaving room, since the dessert menu includes classical French favorites and interesting California innovations to tempt anyone with the slightest hint of a sweet tooth. Sit back in your white-and-black woven chair and finish off your meal with an espresso or a digestif to complete a near-perfect dining experience.

Italian

Zelda's Original Gourmet Pizza (1415 21st St., 916/447-1400, www.zeldasgourmet pizza.com, Mon.–Thurs. 11:30 A.M.–10 P.M., Fri. 11:30 A.M.–11 P.M., Sat. 5–11 P.M. Sun. 5–9 P.M., $10–20) serves deep-dish Chicago-style pies that locals just can't resist—despite the fact that the grease off the pizza may well soak through the thick crust, then through the bottom of the box before you get it to your table. You won't find much to help your cholesterol level or waistline at Zelda's, but if you've been on the road a while feasting on an endless stream of leafy green California cuisine, a Zelda's pizza might just be the perfect answer to your craving. The handwritten menus add to the charm of the great service and the amazing pizzas.

Bakeries and Cafés

Consider skipping dessert at whatever restaurant you dine in, just so you've got the appetite to hit **Ⓒ Rick's Dessert Diner** (2322 K St., 916/444-0969, http://ricksdessertdiner.com, Tues.–Thurs. 10 A.M.–midnight, Fri.–Sat. 10 A.M.–1 A.M., Sun. noon–11 P.M., Mon 10 A.M.–11 P.M.). This unique eatery delivers everything it promises—all desserts, all the time in a 1950s diner–style restaurant. Open late, Rick's finds favor with local teenagers as well as plenty of older patrons and there's often find a line out the door on weekends after 10 P.M. Rick's serves desserts and coffee only, so prepare to indulge yourself. The pies are nothing special, but the impossibly high layer cakes have wonderful flavor and texture in a wide variety of styles. An ice cream freezer makes pie and cake è la mode possible, as well as hot fudge sundaes and banana splits. You can take your choice out, or eat in the diner at one of the rather small booths clad in sparkling red vinyl upholstery.

INFORMATION AND SERVICES

Sacramento offers all the services of a major metropolitan American city. You'll find hospitals, entertainment publications, an ATM on every corner, and Internet access all over the place. In fact, if you're out in Gold Country and need city-style services, Sacramento may be your closest destination.

Tourist Information

Need help from local experts for your time in Sacto? Visit the **Sacramento Convention and Visitor's Bureau** (1608 I St., 916/808-7777, www.sacramentocvb.org, Mon.–Fri. 8 A.M.–5 P.M.). Call or check the website in advance for deals on hotels, advance reservations for attractions, and information about what's in and around the city. Or drop by the office while you're in town to get the locals' take on the best restaurants, the must-see museums, and more.

Media and Communications

The major metropolitan daily paper for Sacto is the *Sacramento Bee* (www.sacbee.com). With the proximity to the hottest California politics, you'll find better-than-average coverage of local current events. You'll also get information you can use in the Food/Wine, Entertainment, and Outdoors sections.

All major banks are represented in Sacramento. You'll find ample ATMs and branches downtown near the capital and in Midtown. In Old Sacramento, you'll find the Wells Fargo Museum, plus Wells Fargo branches all over the city.

As a major metropolitan area, Sacramento has plenty of **post office** branches. On the grid, you can mail out from the Metro office at 801 I Street, Room 149. Just off I-80, the Broadway office sits on 2121 Broadway. In Old Sacramento, the post office shares space with the visitors center at 1303 J Street.

Medical Services

Plenty of hospitals make Sacramento home, should you need medical services while you're in town. **Sutter General Hospital** (2801 L St., 916/454-2222, suttermedicalcenter.org) is located right downtown and has an emergency room. Another local emergency center is run by **UC Davis** on 10th Street between G and H Streets.

GETTING THERE AND AROUND

As is the case in most major California cities, cars are the One True Way locals get around. You'll have the most flexibility to travel out to Gold Country if you've got access to a private car. But inside Sacramento, ample public transit makes getting around without your own wheels a viable option. Getting to and from Sacramento works fairly well via planes and trains.

Air

Most major carriers fly into **Sacramento International Airport** (SMF, 6900 Airport Blvd., 916/929-5411, www.sacairports.org), which is your best bet for flying in to any location in and around Gold Country.

Train

If you're coming into Sacramento from the San Francisco Bay Area, one of the best ways to do it is on the Capitol Corridor Amtrak train (www.amtrak.com). Serving the centrally located Amtrak station (401 I St.), this train runs from Sacramento to Oakland and down to San Jose and back several times each day. The trip lasts a little more than three hours. You can also get to or from Sacramento on the California Zephyr, which crosses the country, from Chicago to the Bay Area, or the Coast Starlight, which travels from Seattle all the way to Los Angeles. The San Joaquins runs right up the middle of California, from Sacramento to Bakersfield.

Bus

Sacramento has a busy and reasonably extensive public transit system that includes both buses and a light rail train system: **Sacramento Regional Transit** (www.sacrt.com, single ride $2, day pass $5). Including the downtown trolley and the light rail lines, SACRT offers nearly 100 routes. Check the website for routes, schedules, and maps.

Car

I-80 runs through Sacramento roughly east–west, and the Business 80 adjunct goes right into downtown by a slightly different route. I-5 splits the city on an east–west route. Highway 50 takes you east to Lake Tahoe, and Highway 99 runs south down to Los Angeles.

Parking in town can get difficult during major events, but otherwise spots aren't ridiculously hard to come by. Near the Capitol

building, bring change to feed the meters. In Old Sacramento, spots right in the middle of the action can be at a premium during high season—you may have to walk a few blocks to get to Front Street. The theaters and arenas tend to have ample parking lots, though you'll pay at many of those. Most hotels offer on- or off-street parking free with your room.

Tours

A number of tours can give you views high and low, distant and close, of Sacramento. Take a self-guided walking tour of Old Sacramento, or a fly-over of the whole city and delta region.

Enjoy sightseeing as you dine aboard the **Sacramento RiverTrain** (800/866-1690, www.sacramentorivertrain.com, $37–69). Outside the window or on the open-air observation deck, look down on the river and out at the stunning Fremont Trestle. Choose from a variety of rides, from a standard weekday lunch up to a fancy weekend Dinner Party, or even a re-enactment of the Great Train Robbery, complete with costumed robbers and a Western-style barbecue lunch. Most rides last 2–4 hours; check the website for departure times, ride lengths, and special event rides that happen several times each year.

To see all of Sacramento in only an hour, make a reservation with **Delta SeaPlane Tours** (Sacramento Executive Airport, 877/378-3597, http://deltaseaplanes.com, $250–600). You'll get a bird's-eye view of the Delta, the Sacramento River downtown area, and various Sacramento historic sights. If you're really into flying, consider extending your tour out to the Bay Area as well.

For an amphibious tour of the river and city sides of Sacramento, book a tour aboard the **Golden Dawn** (916/552-2933, www.sacramentoyachtcharters.com). This funky-looking trolley-boat takes its passengers to many of the major sights of downtown and Old Town Sacramento, then out onto the river for a view of the riverfront from the water. This tour lasts about an hour, and is a great way to see the major sights of Sacramento if you've only got one day in town.

If you're looking for a laugh with your sidewalk tour, try one of the three **Hysterical Walks & Rides** (117 J St., 916/441-2527, www.hystericalwalks.com). The walking tours are evening affairs; the standard Hysterical tour leaves on Friday and Saturday evenings at 7 P.M. and lasts for one hour. Standup comedian-guides give you the story of Old Sacramento in the funniest way possible. At 8:30 P.M. on the same evenings, a costumed guide starts the Hysterical Walk of the Dead tour. On this hour-long walk through the back alleys of Old Sacramento, you'll alternately giggle and shiver as your guide relates all the best ghost stories from this historic area.

If you prefer a sleek, smooth ride to your own two feet, sign up for the daily Segway tour that takes you through Old Town, to the Capitol building and gardens, and past other historic Sacramento sights. Your standup comedian will share the history of the city as you glide across the sidewalks on your personal transport vehicle. This tour lasts 2.5 hours, and all riders must be at least 16 years old. Segway tours depart at 9:30 A.M. and 1:30 P.M. each day.

Northern Gold Country

California's Gold Country is not a small area surrounding a single city. It's a great sprawling network of small towns and roads crisscrossing the Sierra Nevada foothills. (Technically, Sacramento can be considered part of Gold Country as well.) Here begins much of California's written history. It was the gold in these hills that drew immigrants from the East Coast and around the world to come and work the fields, build the railroads, and drag the wild California land into the modern era.

When visiting, it's easiest to traverse Gold Country from north to south. The northern Gold Country extends from Nevada City down to the famed Sutter Creek. The I-80 freeway can get you from Sacramento (or even the Bay Area) to the northern Gold Country town of Auburn. Here you can pick up Highway 49 North to Grass Valley and Nevada City. On Highway 49 South, head down to Placerville, Plymouth, Amador City, and finally to Sutter Creek. From here, small state highways and roads can take you east to Volcano, Pioneer, and other tiny dots on the map.

SIGHTS
◖ Empire Mine State Historic Park
Arguably the best mining museum in Gold Country is the Empire Mine State Historic Park (10791 E. Empire St., Grass Valley, 530/273-8522, www.empiremine.org, May–Aug. daily 9 A.M.–6 P.M., Sept.–Apr. daily 10 A.M.–5 P.M., adults $3, children $1, tours $1.50 extra). Walking into the yard, you can see and feel the life of the 19th- and 20th-century miners who extracted tons of gold from the earth below your feet. Kids can run and

the main shaft at Empire Mine

© LIZ HAMILL SCOTT

shout in the yard, enjoying the open spaces and strange tools and machines. (Keep a close eye on children; the museum contains many obvious and hidden dangers.) Adults can enjoy the history of the place and imagine a hard-rock life in the mine, or a privileged existence up in the owner's cottage.

The mine yard holds a vast collection of tools and equipment used in the hard-rock mine shafts; the shop that kept the mine machinery functioning still works. If you come on the right day (weekends, usually), you might find a blacksmith working away inside. Duck inside for a glimpse of the main mineshaft itself. You can go a few feet down into the shaft, then look deep down and imagine what it was like to perch in a metal car and shoot down thousands of feet into the darkness. To get a real idea of

the scale of the mine shafts and tunnels, go inside the museum. The showpiece of the collection is the scale model of the Empire Mine and the various nearby interconnected mines' tunnels. This model was top secret when it was first built—only the mine owner and select executives and guests could view it. Today, turn on the lights surrounding the mammoth glass case to highlight and hear the stories of the different parts of the overwhelmingly vast and complex underground maze.

For something completely different, leave the mine yard and take the path up the slight rise to the "cottage"—the mine owner's home. In stark contrast to the dust, rust, and timber of the yard, here you'll see acres of sweeping green lawn dotted with flowering shrubs and bisected with gently curving pathways.

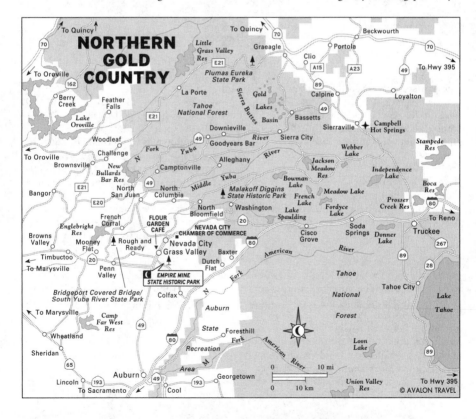

machinery in the mine yard, Empire Mine

© LIZ HAMILL SCOTT

The garden leads up to the mammoth brick mansion. Check the park schedule inside the museum for regular tours of the inside of the cottage and the surrounding gardens, as well as occasional living history events.

Gold Bug Park

If you're traveling with your kids and want them to experience a gold mining museum, visit Hangtown's Gold Bug Park (Bedford Ave., Placerville, 530/642-5207, www.goldbug park.org, Apr.–Oct. daily 10 A.M.–4 P.M., Nov.–Apr. daily Sat.–Sun. noon–4 P.M., adults $4, children $2, audio tour $1). This smaller mine, originally called the Hattie, dates from the 1850s. Today, the museum offers lessons in history, including tours of the mine, an interpretive museum, a gift shop, and more. For a small fee, you can pan for gold in a manufactured sluice. Many of the tour features and exhibits are designed for children, combining education and entertainment as kids don their hard hats, check out the mine shaft, and learn the function of a stamp mill.

◖ Apple Hill

Aptly named, Apple Hill (north of Hwy. 50, btwn. Placerville and Pollack Pines, 530/644-7692, www.applehill.com) produces many of the apples grown in California. Dozens of orchards cluster in the apple-friendly climate of this part of the Sierra Foothills. More recently, some of the orchards and vacant land have been converted to vineyards to help feed California's insatiable appetite for fine wines. For a scenic tour, download a map from the website or take Exit 48 or 54 from Highway 50 onto Apple Hill Scenic Drive. When you go out to Apple Hill, you'll drive charming country roads and pull up at the cute farm buildings that front the orchards filling out the landscape. At some orchards, you can pick your own apples in season. At others, you'll find a large shop stuffed with homemade pies frozen and ready to be baked, preserves, cookbooks, and every type of apple product you can imagine. Come in the middle of summer to enjoy the orchards' berry crops (raspberries, blackberries, blueberries), and later in the summer through the fall for the best of the dozens of varieties of apples grown in the region. Check the website for information about events and festivals that draw crowds out to Apple Hill to enjoy country fair–style activities, arts and craft shows, food and drink tastings, and more. The wineries get into the act as well, offering specials in their tasting rooms. If you have the slightest interest in California food and wine, you can't miss Apple Hill!

Sutter Gold Mine

Though the stereotypical picture of a California miner is an old man panning for gold nuggets in a river, most of the gold found here was dug out of rock and quartz veins deep underground. The best way to really experience gold mining is to take a tour of the Sutter Gold Mine (Hwy. 49, Sutter Creek, 888/818-7462, www.caverntours.com). Even dedicated local cave experts love this tour, which takes you deep into the heart of a modern hard-rock gold mine. The Sutter Gold Mine was built in the 1980s, but only operated as a mine for 10 years before becoming a touring and park facility. It connects underground to historic mine shafts.

The Sutter Gold Mine experience includes plenty of kid and tourist-friendly activities, such as geode-breaking and panning for gemstones, but the real gem here is the rare chance to see the inside of a hard-rock mine. You'll take a brief safety course before heading down. Next, you'll don your required hard hat and jump into a specially designed vehicle that takes you deep into the mine shafts. Once down inside, a guide will explain the sights you're seeing on your hour-long tour. While it's best to be able to walk around to see everything, if you call ahead to make arrangements, Sutter Gold Mine's underground tunnels are accessible to visitors who need to sit through the tour. However, safety requirements make this underground adventure unsuitable for children under four.

Amador Flower Farm

Ever wondered where pretty daylilies come from? Over 800 different kinds grow at the Amador Flower Farm (22001 Shenandoah School Rd., Plymouth, 209/245-6660, www.amadorflowerfarm.com, daily 9 A.M.–4 P.M.). Take a serene and colorful walk through the eight acres of farmland and four acres of demonstration gardens, enjoying the flowers and perennials. If you've got a picnic packed, enjoy it in the gardens shaded by heritage oak trees. In the gift shop, get a single lily for your sweetheart, or pick up a bundle of bulbs to take home and plant in your own garden.

Black Chasm

If you're looking for a natural underground experience, take an easy one-hour tour of the Black Chasm Caverns (Volcano-Pioneer Rd., Volcano, 866/762-2837, www.caverntours.com, daily May–Oct. 9 A.M.–5 P.M., Nov.–Apr. 10 A.M.–4 P.M., adults $12.95, children $6.50). Though this tour isn't accessible to strollers or wheelchairs, walking-age kids enjoy the reasonably sedate stroll into the immense chasm filled with amazing calcite formations. In the Landmark Room, you'll get a chance to check out the rare helictite formations (a crystalline cave formation) that made Black Chasm famous. On your way out or as you wait for your tour, enjoy the new visitors center. Many guests enjoy the video that describes the use of the look and feeling of Black Chasm by the creators of *The Matrix* films. You can even see some of the immense stalagmite props made for the movies!

Daffodil Hill

Spring is the time to visit the famed Daffodil Hill (Rams Horn Grade, Volcano, 209/296-7048, www.amadorcountychamber.com, daily late Mar.–mid-Apr., free). Perfect for travelers who love the greenery above ground as much as the minerals beneath it, Daffodil Hill explodes each March into a profusion of sunny yellow that lasts for about a month. Daffodil Hill is actually the private working ranch of the McLaughlin family, who have been planting daffodil bulbs on their property since they first acquired the land in 1887. Today, you'll see more than 300,000 flowers blooming, and more are planted each year. In addition to the more than 300 different species of daffodil, other bulb flowers and plants help create carpets of color across the meadows and hills. Even among the many fabulous landscapes and gardens of California, Daffodil Hill is special; out here, you can't help but feel the joy and promise of spring.

Daffodil Hill opens to the public *only* during daffodil season. Exact opening and closing dates vary each year. Call to get the latest information on this year's blooms.

Small Museums

If you're a history buff with a few extra minutes on your hands, you can find a wealth of "15-minute museums" in northern Gold Country. In these tiny galleries, you can learn about little-explored aspects of California pioneer life. The **Shenandoah Valley Museum** (14430 Shenandoah Rd., Plymouth, 209/245-4456, www.sobonwine.com, free) describes the winemaking process that began in Gold Country almost as soon as the first miners arrived. It's part of the Sobon Estate—a winery that's been in continuous operation in the Shenandoah Valley since 1856.

Miners, their wives, and everybody else who came to live in the bustling boom towns of Gold Country needed supplies: food, cloth, tools, medicines, etc. In 19th-century California, many of those supplies were sold at the general store. The **Monteverde Store Museum** (11A Randolph St., Sutter Creek, 800/400-0305, www.suttercreek.org) sold staples to Sutter Creek residents for 75 years. After its last shopkeepers, Mary and Rose Monteverde, passed on, the city took over the building. The sisters had stipulated that it was to become a museum and so it is—a look into the hub of town life in the 19th century. Perhaps miners bought Sobon wines here 100 years ago?

WINERIES

In the 21st century, the real gold in the Sierra Foothills flows from a bottle. The major tasting patch lies in the Shenandoah Valley, but you'll also find gems in the El Dorado, Amador, and Fair Play regions and appellations. Best of all, you'll find some fabulous wines, intriguing tasting rooms, and knowledgeable staff and winemakers in northern Gold Country—*without* the vast crowds you'll run into in Napa and Sonoma.

The truth is, there's been wine in them thar hills for almost 150 years. When European emigrants came to California to ply the gold fields, they found themselves longing for the wines they drank at home. The Italian miners who found no luck with gold began planting grapes, since the climate was similar to the Italian highlands. Vineyards grew around the mines, supplying wine to the hard-working miners and townsfolk of the Sierra Foothills. Then came the "noble experiment" that was Prohibition, and most of the Gold Country wineries ceased production. The vineyards languished for decades, until the growing California wine boom centering around Napa began spreading to other grape-growing regions of the state. By the 1990s, many of the wineries were back in business. Today, more than 100 wineries make their home in California's Gold Country.

Apple Hill

The Apple Hill region grows more than just Fujis and Granny Smiths. This region, which runs just northeast of Placerville, also plays home to a number of vineyards that feed the local wineries.

BOEGER WINERY

Among the largest of the Apple Hill wineries is Boeger Winery (1709 Carson Rd., Placerville, 800/655-2634, www.boegerwinery.com, daily 10 A.M.–5 P.M., tasting free). Just outside of Placerville proper, visit the elegant new tasting room for a regular or reserve tasting of Boeger's best current release wines. Better yet, bring a lunch and have a picnic in the redwood grove or out by the cracked white facade of the historic wine cellar. Owner and vineyard manager Greg Boeger bought his vines to follow a family tradition; more than a century ago, his grandfather had a winery in the Napa Valley to serve the new residents of California during the Gold Rush. Today, Boeger's specialties tend to be big, hearty reds, though you can taste the occasional delicate white wine here too. Beware of crowds on Apple Hill event days!

FENTON HERRIOTT VINEYARDS

At the opposite end of the spectrum, tiny Fenton Herriott Vineyards (120 Jacquier Ct., Placerville, 530/642-2021, www.fenton herriott.com) makes only a few hundred cases of wine each year. When you visit the little tasting room out off the main drag, you'll get to try a small variety of tasty and reasonably priced red wines you won't find in your local BevMo. The tasting staff knows lots about the wines they're pouring, and can tell you the story of each one. Fenton Herriott Vineyards gives you the perfect opportunity to see another side of the California wine scene: no huge souvenir shops, no fancy mostly-for-show estate, just good wine in small quantities made by folks who care more about grapes than anything else.

PRIMUS VINEYARDS

Towards the east end of Apple Hill you'll find Primus Vineyards (2875 Larsen Dr., 530/647-9463, www.primuswinery.com, daily 11 A.M.–5 P.M.). The cute red barn shelters a surprisingly elegant tasting room, complete with a wooden tasting bar and shelving to hold bottles for sale. The elegance extends to the wines—all small-lot reds. Primus releases only about five wines each year. While you're sipping, be sure to check out the collection of antique wine tools—an unusual and extensive array. Finally, if you like laughter with your vino, check the winery website for information about Primus' regularly scheduled comedy nights.

WOFFORD ACRES VINEYARDS

Wofford Acres Vineyards (1900 Hidden Valley Ln., Camino, 530/626-6858, Thurs.–Sun. 11 A.M.–5 P.M.), another red specialist, exemplifies the new era of small family wineries in California. Open for five years, Wofford Acres is owned and operated by the Wofford family, and you're likely to run into one or more Woffords when you visit the small tasting room. Look for low-priced but high-flavored red table wines, red varietals, and possibly even a yummy dessert port to finish off your tasting experience.

Shenandoah Valley

The best known wine region in Gold Country is the Shenandoah Valley—and not just because this corner of Amador County takes its name from a famous part of the South. Dozens of wineries make their homes here, most using locally grown grapes that show off the best of what the Sierra Foothills can produce.

STORY WINERY

Arguably the best of the small-to-medium Shenandoah wineries is Story Winery (10525 Bell Rd., Plymouth, 800/713-6390, www .zin.com, Mon.–Fri. noon–4 P.M., Sat.–Sun. 11 A.M.–5 P.M., tasting free). Here you can begin to taste the true history of Amador County wines. Some of the Story vineyards have lived nearly 100 years, and still produce grapes (albeit in tiny quantities) for wines being made today. The specialty of the house at Story is Zinfandel—in fact, this winery comes close to being all Zinfandel, all the time. Check out the amazing selection of old-vine, single-vineyard Zins to please any red-loving palate. You'll taste these in a charming, casual environment, where you'll be made to feel right at home—even if you're new to high-end wine. Walk outside to admire the estate vineyards ranging down the hills; those gnarled old tree-trunk like things create the special tastes adored by connoisseurs.

BRAY VINEYARDS

If you want something different in a tasting experience, visit Bray Vineyards (10590 Shenandoah Rd., Plymouth, 209/245-6023, www.brayvineyards.com, Fri.–Mon. 10 A.M.–5 P.M.). With only the barest of nods to California favorite varietals, Bray instead goes its own way, pouring wines made from grapes even savvy wine lovers won't find familiar. Take a taste of a wine made from Verdelho, Tempranillo, Alicante Bouschet, or an intriguing blend of largely unknown-in-America Portuguese grapes. Or if you must, stick with the old faithful varietals, such as Syrah, Zin, and Cabernet Sauvignon. But to really get a feel for what Bray does, go outside of the tasting room and into the vineyards; Bray grows its own grapes, plus olives for estate olive oil, and has a number of native oak trees.

MONTEVINA

One of the biggest names in the Shenandoah Valley, Montevina (20680 Shenandoah School Rd., Plymouth, 209/245-6942, www .montevina.com, daily 10 A.M.–4:30 P.M.) lives up to its reputation. Montevina prides itself on its Zinfandels, boasting that it makes "the best in the world." That's a bold claim in Amador County, which is the Zinfandel heartland. But Montevina doesn't box itself in—you can taste white wines, light red wines, medium red wines, blends, and more at this fun tasting room. Check out something from each of the three labels: the standard Montevina, reserve Terra d'Ors, and the fun, inexpensive Wild Bunch blends.

DEAVER VINEYARDS

For a small winery experience, hit the cute small barn at Deaver Vineyards (12455 Steiner Rd., Plymouth, 290/245-4099, www .deavervineyard.com, daily 10:30 A.M.–5 P.M.). Grab a bottle of something fine and some tasty picnic foods and take the whole lot down to the local lake for lunch. Deaver produces a couple white and rosé wines and some flavored sparklers, but reds are unquestionably the mainstay of this winemaker. At the tasting bar, you can sip a range of intense, layered Zins and Syrahs, or get bold with a Carignane or a Barbera. Even if you're not a wine fan, you can't help but be charmed by the farm-style atmosphere, complete with decrepit outbuildings and sweeping green fields (under the vines, of course).

WILDEROTTER VINEYARD

Wilderotter Vineyard (19890 Shenandoah School Rd., Plymouth, 209/245-6016, www .wilderottervineyard.com) brings great grapes from a loving grower out of the vineyard and into the tasting room. Wilderotter started as a vineyard that sold all its grapes to various winemakers, and only transformed into a winery in its own right in 2002. Even more recently, the charming stone facade of the tasting room was constructed, and the winery got going in earnest. The production is limited both in quantity and in scope. Zinfandel, Grenache, Viognier, and Barbera are what's planted in the vineyards, so that's what's available in the bottles.

Fair Play
FITZPATRICK WINERY & LODGE

Fitzpatrick Winery & Lodge (7740 Fairplay Rd., 530/620-6838, www.fitzpatrickwinery .com, Wed.–Mon. 11 A.M.–5 P.M.) was Fair Play's first winery, opened in 1980. Fitzpatrick focuses on "earth-friendly" wines, using organically grown grapes and producing wines in small lots to preserve the essence of the terroir from which the grapes come. Going further, the wine is bottled in recycled glass with untreated cork, then stored in a warehouse running almost entirely on solar energy, on land maintained with tractors running 90 percent vegetable oil. All in all, Fitzpatrick has created an eco-conscious wine-lover's dream winery. The lengthy wine list features some California classics in the way of Zinfandels, Chardonnays, and Merlots. But to get into this winery properly, try some of the less common vintages, which can range from Irish-styled white and red blended wines to a surprisingly complete array of ports in both red and white.

If you love Fitzpatrick so much that you just have to stay, you can. The estate also operates a bed-and-breakfast inn. On weekends between noon and four (or until the food runs out), stay for the Ploughman's Lunch—hearty hot fare that will set you up right for an afternoon of tasting elsewhere in Fair Play and northern Gold Country.

CHARLES B. MITCHELL VINEYARDS

Charles B. Mitchell Vineyards (8221 Stoney Creek Rd., 530/620-3467, http://charlesbmitchell

.com, Mon.–Fri. 11 A.M.–5 P.M., Sat.–Sun. 10:30 A.M.–5 P.M.) is one of the more recognizable names in the Fair Play appellation. In the tasting room, you'll get a chance to try a wide variety of wines, from sparklers to whites to Amador County–grown reds to lush dessert ports. You can take a tour of the winery as well. But for a special treat, plan ahead to bottle your own wine. Check the website for upcoming bottle-your-own events, which include wine and food during the working day, plus a deep discount on the bottles you create yourself.

TOOGOOD ESTATE WINE CAVES
A winery with a great name, Toogood Estate Wine Caves (7280 Fairplay Rd., 530/620-1910, www.toogoodwinery.com, Fri.–Sun. 11 A.M.–5:30 P.M.) beckons visitors with its unique winery and its distinctive wines. To get to the tasting room, you must enter the famed Toogood caves. All wines here are aged in the 5,000 square feet of underground space, which maintains a perfect cool temperature year-round. (Bring a coat into the tasting room if you're sensitive to cold.) You'll find almost all red wines in the caves, with a number of intriguing blends, some fun varietals like Barbera and and Cab Franc, plus a couple of unusual dessert wines. (Malbec port—really!) Bottle prices range from a moderate $20 up to $80 for the rarest ports. And finally, with a name like Foreplay (and underpants with matching labels in the gift shop), you know the red table wine has to be good!

CANTIGA WINEWORKS & DELI
Cantiga Wineworks & Deli (5951 Mt. Aukum Rd., 530/621-1696, www.cantigawine.com, Fri.–Sun. 11 A.M.–5 P.M., tasting free) brings innovation and history to the world of small-batch winemaking. If you're lucky, you'll find one of the owners and winemakers in the tasting room, and learn of the true passion that goes into Cantiga's wines. Many of the whites and several of the reds here are *not* malolactically fermented—highly unusual for California wines. Ask at the unpretentious tasting bar and you'll get the whole story of how each wine gets

made and why Cantiga's gone anti-malolactic. Some grapes are grown on the Cantiga estate, but most are lovingly chosen from vineyards around California, especially Lodi (where Cantiga maintains a second tasting room) and Monterey County. During the day, you can grab lunch at the attached deli to help soak up all that fabulous Fair Play wine.

ENTERTAINMENT AND EVENTS
Bars and Clubs
Nightlife in northern Gold Country runs to the classic saloons dotted along the main streets of each little town.

In Grass Valley, the saloon that sits on the ground floor of the historic Holbrook Hotel offers some of the best drinks and company in town. The **Golden Gate Saloon** (212 W. Main St., 530/273-1353, http://holbrookehotel.net/saloon) boasts of being the oldest continually operating saloon west of the Mississippi River. Yup, the Golden Gate braved possible Federal raids and kept on serving liquor throughout Prohibition. Today, this old-time saloon has a light lunch and dinner menu, a full bar with beer on tap, high-end wines, and plenty of cocktails. It's also got lots of locals, many of whom stop in to enjoy the live music that entertains patrons on Wednesday–Saturday nights.

If you're looking for something in an old-school biker bar, try **PJ's** (5641 Mother Lode Dr., 530/626-0336) in Old Hangtown. Off the main drag, this place features cheap beer and shots, a small dance floor, and the occasional DJ or live band designed to drag drinkers off their barstools. Expect lots of Harleys out front, precious little light inside, and perhaps a whiff of green emanating from the back porch. Definitely a dive bar!

On the other end of the spectrum, ritzy Nevada City boasts its very own upscale wine bar. The **Citronee Bistro and Wine Bar** (320 Broad St., Nevada City, 530/265-5697, Wed.–Mon. from 5:30 P.M.) offers dozens of California wines, European vintages, wine and champagne cocktails, splits of many types of vino, and more. You can sit at a table and enjoy a glass of wine with a fine California-style meal, belly up to the bar to get your taste on, or peruse bottles in the adjoining wine and cheese shop.

Theater

Theater is a major aspect of the culture in Gold Country, and local residents devote significant time and energy to keeping their theaters alive and well.

Most regional theater in Gold Country is performed at the **Nevada Theater** (401 Broad St., 530/265-6161, www.nevadatheatre.com, adults $24–26, children $11–14, students $19–21) in Nevada City. Professional companies such as The Community Asian Theatre of the Sierras and LeGacy Productions produce big-name works in the historic 1865 theater, with an occasional show in Grass Valley as well. The regular season can include Broadway musical hits like *Urinetown,* classics such as *On Golden Pond,* and unusual newer works including *Doubt, A Parable* (by John Patrick Shanley). In the summertime, the Nevada Theatre Film Series, as well as current and independent films, grace the screen. Check the website for the upcoming season's shows. During the regular season, just visiting the historic Nevada Theater—the oldest operating original-use theater in California—is worth the price of a ticket to a show.

You'll find a mix of live theater and live musical performance at the **Sutter Creek Theatre** (44 Main St., Sutter Creek, 209/296-5495, www.suttercreektheatre.com). Music acts range from folk to flamenco to country-western—smaller-time performers who can really connect with the audience in this intimate venue. Plays go up several times a year, and are generally family-friendly classics such as *A Christmas Carol* and *The Velveteen Rabbit.* Occasionally you might get a chance to see a new work by a local playwright. Check the website for the schedule for the next quarter, and for prices and dates.

Only in Gold Country would a town as tiny as Volcano see a need to maintain its own theater company, complete with both indoor *and* outdoor performance spaces. At the **Volcano Theatre Company** (Main St., Volcano, 209/296-5495, www.volcano theatre.org, shows Fri.–Sat. 8 P.M., Sun 2 P.M.), the wall of the outdoor amphitheater spans nearly half of one side of Volcano's lone main street, and the indoor space uses a storefront on the other side of that street. Highly regarded throughout the region, the amateur Volcano Theatre Company takes on some serious plays, such as William Nicholson's *Shadowlands* and *Of Mice and Men,* plus unusual comedies like John Cecil Holm's *Gramercy Ghost* and Barbara Pease Weber's *Delval Divas.* You'll see the summer plays in the amphitheater; bring your own chairs, thermoses of warm beverage, and blankets and coats to bundle up as the night cools off. In the spring and fall, shows go up at the 50-seat Cobblestone Theatre, and you'll need to purchase tickets early if you want to get in!

Festivals and Events

If you crave more serious exercise, plan a trip to the northern Gold Country in late fall for the **Apple Hill Harvest Run** (Camino, www .applehillrun.org). This annual event includes an 8.5-mile loop, a 3.5-mile loop, and 0.25- and 0.5-mile kids' fun runs. Depending on your condition, pick one of the races and get running! The race starts early in the morning and finishes equally early—allowing racers to spend their afternoons perusing the orchards and wineries of Apple Hill. This race, which includes some major hills on the longer loop to challenge runners, benefits local schools.

SHOPPING
Antiques

Good retail opportunities abound on Main Street in Old Hangtown. The main shopping blocks run from the 300s through the 500s, and are easily walkable. Placerville is a great place to look for antiques and vintage collectibles. Half a dozen antique shops cluster on Main Street—for straight-ahead antique shops, hit **Empire Antiques** (432 Main St., Placerville, 530/642-1025) or the **Olde**

Dorado Antique Emporium (435 Main St., 530/622-4792).

Art Galleries

Like most Gold Country towns, Placerville has a smattering of art galleries that appeal to a variety of shoppers. The **Bennett Gallery** (440 Main St., Placerville, 530/621-1164) displays art in a variety of media, from modern painting to hand-blown glass pieces. Local artists only show and sell their work at the **Gold Country Artist's Gallery** (379 Main St., Placerville, 530/642-2944). These Foothill artists create everything from painting and sculpture to pottery and gourd art.

At **Chaos Glassworks** (121 A Hanford St., 209/267-9317, Sutter Creek, www.chaosglassworks.com, Wed.–Fri. noon–7 P.M., Sat. 10 A.M.–7 P.M., Sun. 10 A.M.–6 P.M.), you can purchase handmade works of glass art, and watch the glassblower as he creates new pieces before your very eyes.

Books

Just like the apparel shops, the bookstores of Placerville are unique to the town; get your reading material at either **The Bookery** (326 Main St., Placerville, 530/626-6454) or at **Hidden Passage Books** (352 Main St., Placerville, 530/622-4540).

Clothing

You won't find any big chain clothing stores in Gold Country. Instead, shop in cute one-off boutiques like **Velvet's Treasures** (434 Main St., Placerville, 530/626-6120), **Empress** (582 Main St., Placerville, 530/642-2555), or **Placerville Clothing Co.** (327 Main St., Placerville, 530/626-3554).

Gift and Home

To shop Sutter Creek, simply take a stroll down historic Main Street. You'll find cluttered antique shops filled with treasures great and small. For something from the Far East, walk into **Turning East** (205 C Amador Rd., 209/267-1121, Sutter Creek, daily 10 A.M.–5 P.M.). Peruse the lovely Asian furniture imported directly by the owners, plus hundreds of decorative items.

Gourmet Goodies

Placerville hosts a surprising array of sweet shops. You can take your pick of gooey candies from **Sweet Cravings** (374 Main St., Placerville, 530/295-9144), **CandyStrike - Old Tyme Candy & More** (492 Main St., Placerville, 530/295-1007), or **Copper Kettle Candy** (366 Main St., Placerville, 530/622-6100). For something heartier, get some great cheese and artisan bread from **Dedrick's Main Street Cheese** (312 Main St., Placerville, 530/344-8282).

Unique

If you prefer your art permanently affixed to your body, check out Placerville's tattoo shops, which include **Moontiger Tattoos** (438 Main St., Placerville, 530/295-3917) and **Hangtown Tattoo and Body Piercing** (537 Main St., Placerville, 530/642-9172).

SPORTS AND RECREATION

While the museums and mines and quaint scenic towns of northern Gold Country have their appeal, many Californians visit the Sierra Foothills for entirely different reasons. The mixed woods, wilderness, and rivers of the region call to outdoor lovers of all stripes. Whether you fancy a quiet walk through the woods or an ultra-exciting ride down a roaring river, you'll find it here.

Hiking

In addition to its fabulous historic park and museum, the **Empire Mine State Historic Park** (10791 E. Empire St., Grass Valley, 530/273-8522, www.empiremine.org) doubles as an outdoor hiking park. With 800 acres of former mining lands, this park offers both natural beauty and views of abandoned mines that are being overgrown as nature re-establishes dominance. The Hardrock Trail Area can run 1–3 miles, depending on how far you want to take it. Loop from the visitors center around to see the remains of the Pennsylvania, W.Y.O.D., and Orleans Mines before heading out to the Osborn Loop or back to the parking lot. The Hardrock Trail and its offshoots are reasonably flat and easy to hike, but be aware that you can hit rocky stretches and there are no bathroom facilities on the trails. Along the trail, you'll see, and in some cases climb on, the remains of the major hard-rock mines that once produced gold here. Grab a trail guide from the visitors center to get a better idea of what you're seeing while you're seeing it. A caution: While you're welcome to look and take photos of the mines along the trails, don't leave the trail to attempt to climb on, under, or through abandoned mine structures, and keep an eye on your children. These things can be incredibly dangerous.

Off the Hardrock Trail Area, you can head farther afield on the Osborn Hill Loop Trail Area to check out several more abandoned mines and their detritus. This loop runs about a mile on its own, and is a bit steeper and more challenging than the Hardrock trails.

Finally, if you prefer natural beauty to a manmade landscape, head off in the other direction to the Union Hill Trails. Here you'll find the Pipeline Trail, where the massive pipes that kept water pumping out of the mines still run—for fire protection now. The other Union Hill trails take you out into the Foothills wilderness that was the long-ago home of a Maidu Native American tribe.

For an easy leg-stretching walk, **Gold Bug Park** (see *Sights*) has 61 acres of forested parkland with marked trails. Enjoy the interpretive plaques that describe the local foliage and scenery.

Biking

If you're looking for a guided bicycle tour through Gold Country, check out **Escape Travel** (916/419-5203, www.escapesactours.com). For about $100 per day, you can take a road bike out into the Amador Wine Country, heading through the Shenandoah Valley and tasting along the way. Or pedal out on a scenic tour of Amador and Sutter Creek, getting a close-up view of the major mining sights. If

you prefer a mountain trek, head up into the Sierra Foothills and experience trails at whatever level you feel comfortable with. Advance reservations are required, and all experience levels are welcome.

Whitewater Rafting and Kayaking

Northern Gold Country doubles as whitewater country from spring through fall. The North, South, and Middle Forks of the vast American River offer great rafting, whether you're an experienced Class V paddler or you've never set foot in a raft. The South Fork also beckons to beginner whitewater rafters, with lots of rapids but none over a Class III. The Middle Fork gets wilder, with some Class III and IV rapids— it's better for intermediate (or adventurous and athletic beginners) paddlers willing to traverse the legendary Tunnel Chute. The season for both Forks usually runs from April to October, but check online for specific dates.

One of the best of outfitters is **All-Outdoors Whitewater Rafting** (925/932-8993, www.aorafting.com, Mon.–Fri. 9 A.M.–5 P.M.). All-Outdoors offers half-day up to three-day trips on the South and Middle Forks of the American River. If all you want to do is float, or you have small children who'll be coming rafting with you, consider the half-day or full-day Tom Sawyer Float Trips down the rapids-free section of the South Fork. All All-Outdoors trips include a life jacket, helmet, safety instruction on dry land, and a certified river guide. On full-day trips, your guides will put together a near-gourmet meal for your party. If budget and time are short, the half-day trips make a great adventure. But if you're interested in exploring the true wilderness of Gold Country, a 2–3 day trip is perfect.

With **Beyond Limits Adventures** (800/234-7238, www.rivertrip.com) you can take half-day up to two-day trips on the South and Middle Forks. Overnight trips include all meals, plus a grassy, shaded campground where you can pitch your own tent or pay extra for tent cabin or yurt accommodations along the river. Shop at the camp store or grab a bite at the on-site snack bar. Beyond Limits loves introducing young people to the fun of the American River—check their website for family trips and special youth rates. But if you're with an up-for-anything rafting party of adults, ask about trips on the North Fork of the Yuba River. Available in spring only, the Yuba offers Class IV and V rapids on the longest stretch of heavy-duty whitewater in the state.

American Whitewater Expeditions (800/825-3205, www.americanwhitewater .com) can take you out to the South or Middle Forks, and also to the faster and whiter North Fork of the American River—a Class V adventure run by few companies. Trips run from half a day to three days, and include delicious dinners (with brew for of-age rafters on two- and three-day trips), knowledgeable guides, beautiful scenery, and all kinds of fun.

O.A.R.S. (800/346-6277, www.oars.com) also offers trips on the South, Middle, and North Forks of the American River. With almost 40 years' experience in California rafting and the one of highest guide-to-guest ratios in the business, O.A.R.S. will give you a friendly, personal trip to remember. They've got all the standard half- to two-day trips you want, plus a few surprises. Take O.A.R.S.'s South Fork Wine and Raft trip or consider one of the multi-Fork trips.

Golf

Golf addicts can find plenty to keep themselves busy in northern Gold Country in the summer. One of the best courses in the area is the highly rated public **Castle Oaks Golf Club** (1000 Castle Oaks Dr., Ione, 209/274-0167, www .castleoaksgolf.com, $13–60). This 18-hole, par 71 championship course offers five different levels of tee, making it fun for golfers of any skill level. Lots of water features make the game interesting, and the relatively flat terrain makes for a lovely walk. Located in Ione, west of Jackson and Plymouth, Castle Oaks makes a perfect diversion from the endless museums, mines, and wineries of the area. Even if you're just looking for practice, Castle Oaks has a driving range, chipping green, and putting green for your use. The club recommends

that you book your tee time at least one week in advance.

East of Jackson on uncrowded Highway 88, enjoy a game at the **Mace Meadow Golf and Country Club** (26570 Fairway Dr., Pioneer, 209/295-7272, www.macemeadow .com, $10–32, carts extra). This public course offers 18 holes at par 72 for reasonable rates. Three tee levels provide action for beginners, intermediates, and advanced golfers. Check the website for a hole-by-hole description of this course, plus online tee-time reservation and Internet fee specials. Before (or after) your game, kick back and enjoy breakfast or lunch at the Country Club's restaurant, or just grab a quick snack at the Snack Shack.

ACCOMMODATIONS

The accommodations in northern Gold Country run to quaint bed-and-breakfast inns. Many are reasonably priced for the level of comfort you get, though you can also find some seriously upscale inns if you've got the money to shell out. If B&B decor gives you hives, you can find a few vacation rentals and historic hotels as well. For folks who absolutely must stay in a generic chain, Auburn is a good town to hit for a totally average Travelodge or Comfort Inn.

Under $100

For a budget hotel adventure deep in northern Gold Country, get off the highway and head for the **St. George Hotel** (16104 Main St., Volcano, 209/296-4458, www.stgeorge hotel.com, $66–140). The only hotel in the tiny town of Volcano, the St. George gives its guests a serious vintage Gold Country hotel experience. The attractively shabby building houses a hodgepodge of all-different second- and third-floor hotel rooms. You can also get an individual bungalow out in the back of the main hotel. As befits a 19th-century mining town hostelry, no rooms in the main building have private baths (though the bungalows do). You must share the hall baths with your fellow guests. Whatever bed configuration you need for your party, you'll find at the St. George—including an ultra-cheap room for solo travelers. In your room, you'll see polished wood floors, antique-styled bedsteads, and floral or quilt-style bedspreads. Take your morning coffee out onto the wraparound verandah each morning to enjoy the cool early hours before the Gold Country heats up in the summertime.

You don't have to go too far for food and entertainment if you're staying at the St. George. Some of the best food in Amador County is served in the restaurant downstairs, The Whiskey Flat Saloon sits right next door, and the Volcano Theatre Company performs in the amphitheater across the street and the small indoor theater down the block.

$100-150

With the ethos of a classic B&B and the fun touches of a hostel, you'll find the perfect lodging mix at **Hanford House** (61 Hanford St., Sutter Creek, 209/267-0747, www.hanfordhouse.com, $120–275). Unlike the endless Victorians you see in the various Gold Country towns, the Hanford House is a brick manor house. Nine guest rooms grace the interior, each decorated in a floral country style with unique furnishings and textiles. Beds are large and comfy, and bathrooms squeak with cleanliness and feel a little bit like home. When you come to enjoy the hearty breakfast in the morning, don't bother picking up a newspaper. Instead, pass your morning reading the walls and ceiling of the inn. Guests have signed and commented on the plain white walls over the years;they're almost full now, so if you feel a need to add your own John Hancock, you'll have to hunt for a bare spot.

The **Imperial Hotel** (14202 Hwy. 49, Amador City, 209/267-9172, www.imperialamador.com, $115–250) shows off the brick facade and narrow-column architecture of a classic Old West hotel. You'll get a true mining town hotel experience, getting one of six bedrooms on the second floor of the building, or one of three new rooms in the "cottage" out back. These rooms have been updated to include private baths, and are done in simple antique styles that make use of the redbrick

interior walls as part of the decor. Your guest room is a haven of peace of quiet, without a TV or even a telephone to bother you. Music and literature make the entertainment at the Imperial. Downstairs, you can take all your meals, including the full hot breakfast that's part of your room rate. Dinner is a special time, featuring gourmet California cuisine made with local organic produce, natural meats, and sustainable seafood.

The **C Amador Harvest Inn** (12455 Steiner Rd., Plymouth, 800/217-2304, www.amadorharvestinn.com, $140–160) brings a bit of uptown Napa to the Shenandoah Valley while retaining the down-home feel of Amador County. The outside of the inn feels perfectly unpretentious—a simple farmhouse set on a green lawn surrounded by trees and water. Inside you'll find four guest rooms named for wine grapes, each decorated in a charming country style. Yet the interior feeling is more elegant than the sum of its parts; you could imagine paying half again as much for the same room in Yountville. The dining room continues the farmhouse charm, with kitchen-style tables and chairs waiting for guests to sit and enjoy a home-cooked breakfast each morning. Nearby, you can visit the Deaver Winery and the Amador Flower Farm. The Amador Harvest Inn makes a perfect base from which to explore the whole of the Shenandoah Valley wine country and perhaps beyond.

For a more hippie-California experience in the backwoods of the Foothills, book a cabin at **Rancho Cicada Retreat** (10001 Bell Rd, Plymouth, 209/245-4841, www.ranchocicadaretreat.com, $106–159). The retreat offers both tent cabins and wood-sided cabins, most of which share common single-sex bathrooms. The main attraction of the Rancho runs along outside the tent cabins: the Cosumnes River. Visitors can swim, inner tube, and fish in the river, and your hosts will happily tell you about good spots to bag a trout and peaceful holes to enjoy a relaxing dip. Or you can visit the riverside hot tubs, perhaps after an old-fashioned sweat in the Mi-Wok sweat lodge.

Be aware that Rancho Cicada offers primitive

lodgings. You'll need to bring your own sleeping bags or bedding and pillows, towels, and food to cook, plus ice chests for drinks (refrigerators are provided for perishable foods).

If you're looking for casual accommodations at the right price, consider the **49er Village** (18265 Hwy. 49, Plymouth, 800/339-6981, www.49ervillage.com, $105–150 cabin rentals). Primarily an asphalt-covered RV park, the 49er Village also rents studio and one-bedroom vacation cabins for reasonable rates. Cabins include private bathrooms, full kitchens with utensils, private decks, and full access to park pools and amenities. One-bedroom cabins can sleep five or six people.

$150-250

For elegance in the land of Gold, you can't beat the **Emma Nevada House** (528 E. Broad St., Nevada City, 800/916-3662, www.emmanevadahouse.com, $190–275). History permeates this large Victorian house, which once belonged to the family of a noted opera singer named Emma Nevada. You'll see real antiquities in the front rooms, and charming collectibles in the guest rooms. The guest rooms all have comfortable beds, attractive appointments, and plush bathrooms, some with clawfoot tubs. Whichever of the six uniquely styled rooms you choose, you're sure to enjoy your stay here. Your hosts can help you with whatever you need, and they have plenty of real opinions about the restaurants and sights in their area. Breakfast is served each morning—come out early to get a seat in the sun room, definitely the best breakfast seat in the house. You'll get a gourmet multi-course treat to fortify yourself for a day out exploring El Dorado and Amador Counties.

For a more up-to-date bed-and-breakfast experience, plus great access to a fabulous wine region, book at room at **Lucinda's Country Inn** (6701 Perry Creek Rd., Fair Play, 888/245-8246, www.lucindascountryinn.com, $190–225). You'll drive up to a thoroughly modern large home, surrounded by green lawns, meadows, and forests. (Keep an eye out for deer!) With the stylings of a luxury hotel, each of the five guest rooms welcomes

visitors and convinces them to settle in and stay a while. You'll find classy understated room decor, a fireplace, your own fridge, microwave, and coffee maker, plush robes to relax in, and maybe even a two-person spa tub. Even folks who usually can't take the overwhelming floweriness of most B&Bs will feel comfortable at Lucinda's, with its simple breakfast tables and homelike common rooms. Outside the inn, you've got a great chance to delve into the Fair Play wine region, or to head not too far out to the Shenandoah Valley.

FOOD

Depending on which town you're in, you'll find everything from one lone hotel restaurant to an array of ethnic eats to a shocking plethora of high-end California cuisine. With relatively easy drives between clusters of towns, you don't need to eat where you're staying. Instead, pick something close to your favorite sights, or choose a restaurant for its own sake.

California

For some of the best dining in one of the smallest towns in northern Gold Country, have dinner at the **St. George Hotel** (16104 Main St., Volcano, 209/296-4458, www.stgeorgehotel.com, Thurs.–Sun. 5:30–9 P.M., Sun. 9:30 A.M.–2 P.M., $18–27). The white-tablecloth dining room feels fancy yet intimate, with homey touches throughout the violet-colored space. The menu includes an array of upscale entrées, complete with California-style preparations, sauces, and seasonings. Much of the produce comes from local farms, and the herbs are often snipped from the St. George's own backyard garden. The small but interesting wine list focuses heavily on Amador County vintages, though other parts of California and a few European wineries are represented as well. On Sundays, stop by for a hearty brunch.

Italian

For delicious and inventive Italian food, go to **Cirino's** (309 Broad St., Nevada City, 530/265-2246, lunch Fri.–Sun. 11 A.M.–4 P.M., dinner Sun.–Thurs. 5–9 P.M., Fri.–Sat. 5–10 P.M.). This

APPLE HILL EATERIES

There's plenty of good, healthy food to be had in the Apple Hill region. But what if you need more than a nice, fresh apple to keep hunger away? Stop at one of the orchard-based restaurant along the meandering trails. A number of these offer a variety of foods, from sandwiches to hot handmade apple pies. The area maps available at almost every orchard point out which establishments offer a restaurant.

Perhaps the best place for lunch in the whole of Apple Hill is the kitschy **Bavarian Hills Orchard** (3100 N. Canyon Rd., Camino, 530/642-2714, Sept.-Dec. daily 11 A.M.-5 P.M., June-Aug. weekends only). Oompah music blares from speakers outside of the white-gingerbread-trimmed brown barn buildings that house the store and the restaurant. Walk into the unprepossessing cafeteria-style restaurant, with its linoleum floor, walk-up counter with refrigerator cases, and tile-lettered menu on the wall. Order a sausage on a roll with some traditional German side dishes, and strap in for one of the best surprises you'll encounter on your trip to Gold Country. Your food will be brought on paper plates to whatever table you can find, inside or outside. The sausages are phenomenal,

and the side dishes – from the warm German potato salad to the sauerkraut to the braised red cabbage – are homemade from scratch daily. The owner brought the recipes to Apple Hill from her Bavarian home, and her dedication to creating great authentic German food shows. Finally, your dessert can be any sort of apple pastry, though there's little reason to avoid the homemade strudel from the orchard's own apples.

A "lunch" includes a sausage on a roll, a side dish, and dessert. Portions are eminently reasonable. If you've got a hearty appetite, order an extra side dish or two – they're tasty enough to make it worth it. Or you can get an extra portion of strudel for dessert!

If you're just looking for a fresh slice of pie, some of the best you'll find is sold at the **Apple Pantry Farm** (2310 Hidden Valley Ln., Camino, 530/295-1001, Sept.-Nov. Fri.-Sun. 10 A.M.-4 P.M.). First you'll see the attractive small store, selling apples and an array of frozen uncooked pies ready to be baked in your home oven. Just up and to the right of the main store, a small trailer exudes aromas that draw visitors as if by magic. You can buy just a slice or a whole apple, apple-blackberry, or

---

cute, locally favored restaurant offers plenty of tables, a full bar, a relaxed atmosphere, and a large, innovative, and reasonably priced menu. Start with a cocktail from the bar, which doubles as a local watering hole. Enjoy a salad or an appetizer off the antipasti menu, then move on to the main event. The portions, especially of the pasta, are enormous. Despite this, you'll have a hard time resisting the array of delectable pasta dishes, plus the yummy entrées made with seafood, poultry, and meat (even veal). The service is friendly and helpful with menu questions, and the overall feel of the place will encourage you to sit back and enjoy your meal without rushing.

Mexican

Looking for a good taco or burrito in the

northernmost end of Gold Country? Have a meal at **Las Katarinas Mexican Restaurant** (311 Broad St., Nevada City, 530/478-0275, Sun.–Mon. and Wed.–Thurs. 11 A.M.–9 P.M., Fri.–Sat. 11 A.M.–10 P.M.). Right in the middle of the main drag, Las Katarinas doesn't pretend to be anything fancy. You'll find all your favorite items on the menu: enchiladas, tacos, tostadas, and such, plus chile colorado and verde. Dishes are made with whole, fresh ingredients. Vegetarians can get lard-free dishes, while Mexican purists can enjoy the rich taste of traditionally prepared foods. Beware: The salsa's got some kick to it! For children with more sensitive palates, smaller and less spicy entrées populate the kids' menu. The full bar serves Mexican beers, California wines, and strong margaritas. The dining room exudes a casually other seasonal fruit pie the likes of which your grandmother wished she could bake. Ask the proprietress if she buys her crusts premade, and she'll look at you as though you'd asked her if she enjoys torturing puppies. Every crumb of every Apple Pantry pie gets made from scratch and slices are sold hot out of the industrial ovens in the trailer. While some say that the apple-blackberry with the crumble crust is the best, everyone has their own take on which pie rules the Pantry. (The frozen ready-bake pies in the shop below are made by the same team; if you've got the means to transport them, pick up as many as you can.)

© LIZ HAMILL SCOTT

welcoming feel, and you'll feel perfectly comfortable dining in jeans and a T-shirt.

Bakeries

Baked goods are the thing to eat in Gold Country. Between the traditional Cornish pastie–makers and the organic patisseries, this is a pastry-lover's heaven. You'll find a good bakery in most every town you visit—just look around and take a chance.

Unpretentious and unassuming, the **Flour Garden Café and Bakery** (999 Sutton Way, Grass Valley, 530/272-2043, Mon.–Sat. 5 A.M.–7 P.M., Sun. 6 A.M.–6 P.M.) serves homemade pastries, soups, sandwiches, cakes, and more to a mostly local crowd who prefer something good to something trendy. Part of what makes this Gold Country mini-chain great is that they use natural, organic ingredients in all their food. If you're looking for an early-morning continental breakfast, purchase an unbelievably flakey and delicious pastry—made with real butter and homemade fruit fillings—plus an espresso drink or a plain old cup of good Fair Trade coffee. For lunch, pick up any number of to-go prepared items, have a sandwich made, grab a baguette to make your own sandwich, or order a bowl of the fresh homemade soup of the day. A menu published monthly describes the hearty hot soups, which make a meal in themselves. Those with dietary restrictions are not left out; ask about vegetarian, vegan, and gluten-free options at the counter. The Flour Garden is beloved by locals, and there's often a line at mealtimes.

Best of all, the Flour Garden has three

locations in Gold Country to serve you. Also check out the downtown Grass Valley location at 109 Neal Street and the Auburn store at 340 C Elm Avenue.

If you're in tiny Volcano and you're just longing for a traditional Cornish pastie or a slice of homemade sweet pie, stop in at **Humble Pies** (16154 Main St., Volcano, 209/296-8066, Wed.–Fri. 8 A.M.–5:30 P.M., Sat.–Sun. 8 A.M.–5 P.M., $3–4 single serving). This tiny business has attained more success than even the owners anticipated, so come early for your favorite pie or you may find Humble Pies sold out. The Cornish pasties, whether beef or vegetarian, make a filling lunch. But don't let that stop you from getting a slice of in-season fruit pie or even an old-school, homemade fry pie for dessert. Round out your meal with a latte or a macchiato, and consider adding a "Panic Button" (extra shot of espresso) if you're having trouble getting started.

Coffee and Tea

Looking for a great cup of coffee from an indie coffee house? If you're in Sutter Creek, get in line at **Sutter Creek Coffee Roasting Company** (20 Eureka St., Sutter Creek, 888/219-4127, www.suttercreekcoffee .com, Mon.–Sat. 6:30 A.M.–5 P.M., Sun. 8 A.M.–2 P.M.). Choose from your favorite regular coffee, espresso drinks, cold blended coffee drinks, chai, and more. On a typically blistering summer day in Sutter Creek, enjoy a snow cone. Or if it's lunchtime, choose from the tasty sandwiches, daily hot dishes, salads, and desserts. For a special treat, stop by on Wednesday, Thursday, or Friday to inhale the intoxicating aroma of coffee beans roasting in-house.

Love your traditional afternoon tea? You can indulge your whims in Sutter Creek at the **Tea Eras Tea Room & Gifts** (34 Main St., Sutter Creek, 209/267-0333, www.teaerastearoom .com, daily 11 A.M.–3 P.M.). A charming alternative to a plain ol' lunch, you can order a full tea service with scones, finger sandwiches, salad, savories, and desserts. Plus tea, of course! Several alternative tea services cater to all appetite sizes, while the è la carte menu offers salads and sandwiches to those who need something

more substantial (or less substantial!) for their repast. All this is served in a Victorian atmosphere inside a cute, white wood-framed house in old downtown Sutter Creek.

INFORMATION AND SERVICES

As a spread-out array of small towns with undeveloped mountainous countryside in between, northern Gold Country doesn't have quite the same plethora of services you'd find in the Bay Area or the Los Angeles Basin. If you need the services of a major city, Sacramento is your closest bet. Out on Highway 49, Auburn is the largest town in this area.

Tourist Information

Many of the little burgs have their own small visitors centers, usually on or near the local Main Street. The **Nevada City Chamber of Commerce** (132 Main St., 530/265-2692, www.nevadacitychamber.com, Mon.–Fri. 9 A.M.–5 P.M., Sat.–Sun. 11 A.M.–4 P.M.) doubles as the visitors center. Visit while you're in town, or check the website ahead of time for a wealth of information, including a thoughtful and helpful list of public restrooms in town.

Media and Communications

If you're looking for a major daily paper, pick up the *Sacramento Bee.* For a more local take on Nevada City and Grass Valley, read *The Union* (www.theunion.com), the Nevada County daily. In Amador, the local twice-weekly paper *Amador Ledger-Dispatch* provides information about local entertainment happenings. Several of the little towns have their own weekly or biweekly papers as well, and many of these are free.

A great online visitors guide to the Nevada County area is **Nevada County Gold** (www .ncgold.com). Most of Gold Country is covered in the pages of *Sierra Heritage Magazine* (www .sierraheritage.com), a travel magazine dedicated to the Sierra Nevadas and the Foothill region.

Some of the tiny Gold Rush towns did not retain many services when they busted after the gold ran out. In Volcano, for example, you won't find much in the way of bank branches or gas stations. On the other hand, Auburn has all the amenities of a small city, complete with gas stations near the highways, ATMs, and even big-box stores. You'll find ATMs and the occasional bank branch in Nevada City and Grass Valley as well.

Much of Gold Country has cashed in on California's new gold: the Internet. You'll find Internet cafés, hotels with Wi-Fi, and even the occasional war-hackable spot in each of the little towns. Outside of the towns, you won't see much other than trees, grass, and abandoned mines.

Post offices sit in Nevada City at 29453 Highway 49 and in Grass Valley at 185 East Main Street. In Auburn, you can mail a letter at 13116 Lincoln Way, and in Placerville, there's a post office at 3045 Sacramento Street.

Medical Services

For medical assistance, **Sutter Auburn Faith Hospital** (11815 Education St., Auburn, 530/888-4500, http://sutterauburnfaith.org) offers an emergency room and a full range of hospital services. To the north, the major hospital with an emergency room is **Sierra Nevada Memorial Hospital** (155 Glasson Way, Grass Valley, 530/274-6000, www.snmh.org).

GETTING THERE AND AROUND

When you're in Gold Country, you're out of the big cities and into the California countryside. Your public transit options diminish the farther you get from Sacramento. However, you can still find your way, even with minimal driving. Bicycling in the spring and fall is a great green alternative.

Air

The closest major airport to the northern Gold Country is the Sacramento International Airport. (See the *Sacramento* section for more information.) General aviation airports abound in the area. You can fly into the **Nevada County Airport** (13083 John Bauer Ave., Grass Valley, 530/273-3347, www.nevadacountyairport.com). Car rentals are available here with Hertz and Enterprise.

Bus

The **Gold Country Stage** (http://new.mynevadacounty.com/transit, adults $1, children under 6 free, day pass $3) runs buses and minibuses through Nevada City, Grass Valley, down south to Auburn, and up to points north of Gold Country.

Car

To explore northern Gold Country in depth, your best bet is to rent a car or bring your own. The major thoroughfare, Highway 49, doesn't get city-level crowded even in the high season. Highway 88 delineates the south end of northern Gold Country in this book. To get out to Gold Country from Sacramento (or the Bay Area), you'll take Highway 80, which can get jammed up around the big city.

Parking in the little North Gold Country towns usually isn't too difficult. Most street parking is free or metered, so bring a few quarters on your tours. The historic parks include either complimentary parking or fee parking at the entrance gates.

Tours

Much of the history of Gold Country isn't found in its museums. To get a real flavor for the Gold Rush era, you need to get out into the little towns that dot the landscape. You can pretty much walk any of the historic downtowns in Northern Gold Country to get a sense of place. Most towns offer a historic tour map to help you pick out the coolest spots.

If you're interested in the mines, take a drive along the **Sutter Creek Gold Mine Trail** (www.suttercreek.org). Highways 49 and 88 are the main thoroughfares through the Amador County gold mining district—a commercial map of the area makes a good companion to the hand-drawn map in the official brochure.

Fall visitors to this area are in for a special treat not usually associated with California: fall colors. Nevada County limns itself in gold and red each October and November, beckoning visitors and locals alike out for walks in the brisk autumn air. For the best colors, take walks in the historic Victorian sections of Grass Valley and Nevada City. A tour map put out by the Nevada County Chamber of Commerce (www.ncgold.com) points to the best routes for the prettiest trees and shrubs.

If it's agriculture and eco-tourism you're after, take a tour of the **El Dorado County Farm Trails** (530/620-1415, www.edc-farm trails.org). You can get a map from most El Dorado town visitors centers, in the County Visitors Guide, or at the website. Including the famed Apple Hill as well as numerous other

agricultural areas stretching all the way up to South Lake Tahoe, the Farm Trails encompass more than 100 farms, ranches, wineries, nurseries, and orchards that make up this diverse growing region. Easily visible signs along the roads can point you to the farms that are part of this association-all of which you can visit. Pet an alpaca, smell the lavender or the Christmas trees, pick your own apples or berries, and sip the latest vintage wines on your Farm Trails tour. If you're really interested in agriculture, you could spend several days exploring the Farm Trails of El Dorado.

Southern Gold Country

Southern Gold Country runs from the town of Jackson down almost to the Yosemite Valley. You'll find that the Native Sons of the Golden West and other such associations must have gotten two-for-one deals at the Historic Monument store. Every few miles along Highway 49 and the roads through Sonora and Jamestown, you'll see a plaque affixed to a boulder commemorating some historic person or event. History buffs will enjoy a slow journey through the area, stopping to read each one. Some really are worth reading—you'll find bronze commemorations of everything from the local hanging tree to the ladies of the evening who made life more, um, bearable for the rough men working the mines.

You'll also find museums, caverns, mines, parks, wineries, and great restaurants and quirky hotels in this region.

Southern Gold Country includes the towns of Jackson, Murphys, Angels Camp, Columbia, Jamestown, and Sonora. Highway 49 can take you north–south through the region. Highway 4 runs northeast–southwest, intersecting Highway 49 at Angels Camp and running east to Murphys. Highway 4 also runs south from Vallecito to Columbia and then on down to Sonora. You can also drive Highway 49 all the way down to Jamestown, then pick up Highway 108 east to Sonora.

SIGHTS

From Native American life and times to historic hard-rock mines to natural deep underground caverns, southern Gold Country has something for everyone. Nature lovers can hike in the parks and spelunk in the caves, history buffs can explore the mining era, and everyone can join in the fun.

Calaveras Big Trees State Park

Can't get enough of the California redwoods? Take some time away from mining history and visit Calaveras Big Trees State Park (three miles east of Arnold on Hwy. 4, 209/795-2334, www.bigtrees.org, summer sunrise–sunset, winter 11 A.M.–3 P.M.). The highlights of the park are the North and South Groves of rare giant sequoia trees; be sure to take a walk in both groves to check out the landmark trees and stumps. Beyond the sequoias, you can hike and bike in the 6,000 acres of pine forest crisscrossed with trails and scattered with campgrounds (call 800/444-7275 for reservations) and pretty groves set up for picnicking. Feel free to take a dip in the cool, refreshing Stanislaus River running through the trees, or cast a line out to try to catch a rainbow trout. In the winter, break out the snowshoes and cross-country skis—the trails are marked for winter sports as well as summer.

Start your day at the visitors center, where

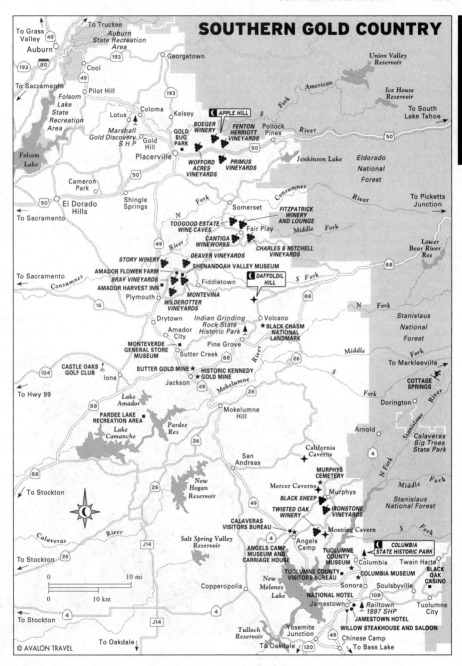

SOUTHERN GOLD COUNTRY

To Grass Valley
To Truckee
Auburn
Auburn State Recreation Area
To Sacramento
Cool
Georgetown
Union Valley Reservoir
Pilot Hill
Ice House Reservoir
Folsom Lake State Recreation Area
Lotus
Coloma
Kelsey
APPLE HILL
BOEGER WINERY
FENTON HERRIOTT VINEYARDS
Pollock Pines
To South Lake Tahoe
Marshall Gold Discovery SHP
Gold Hill
GOLD BUG PARK
Placerville
River
Folsom Lake
WOFFORD ACRES VINEYARDS
PRIMUS VINEYARDS
Jenkinson Lake
Eldorado National Forest
Cameron Park
El Dorado Hills
Shingle Springs
To Sacramento
Somerset
FITZPATRICK WINERY AND LOUNGE
To Picketts Junction
TOOGOOD ESTATE WINE CAVES
Fair Play
Middle
Fork
Lower Bear River Res
CANTIGA WINEWORKS
CHARLES B MITCHELL VINEYARDS
DEAVER VINEYARDS
To Sacramento
STORY WINERY
SHENANDOAH VALLEY MUSEUM
AMADOR FLOWER FARM
BRAY VINEYARDS
AMADOR HARVEST INN
Fiddletown
DAFFODIL HILL
Plymouth
MONTEVINA
WILDEROTTER VINEYARDS
Drytown
Indian Grinding Rock State Historic Park
Volcano
BLACK CHASM NATIONAL LANDMARK
Stanislaus National Forest
Amador City
Pine Grove
MONTEVERDE GENERAL STORE MUSEUM
Sutter Creek
To Markleeville
CASTLE OAKS GOLF CLUB
Ione
SUTTER GOLD MINE
HISTORIC KENNEDY GOLD MINE
COTTAGE SPRINGS
To Hwy 99
Jackson
Dorington
Lake Amador
Mokelumne Hill
Arnold
PARDEE LAKE RECREATION AREA
Lake Camanche
Pardee Res
Calaveras Big Trees State Park
To Stockton
San Andreas
California Caverns
To Stockton
New Hogan Reservoir
MURPHYS CEMETERY
Mercer Caverns
Murphys
Stanislaus National Forest
BLACK SHEEP
TWISTED OAK WINERY
IRONSTONE VINEYARDS
CALAVERAS VISITORS BUREAU
Moaning Cavern
Salt Spring Valley Reservoir
ANGELS CAMP MUSEUM AND CARRIAGE HOUSE
Angels Camp
COLUMBIA STATE HISTORIC PARK
TUOLUMNE COUNTY MUSEUM
Columbia
BLACK OAK CASINO
To Stockton
TUOLUMNE COUNTY VISITORS BUREAU
COLUMBIA MUSEUM
Copperopolis
New Melones Lake
Sonora
Soulsbyville
Twain Harte
NATIONAL HOTEL
Jamestown
Railtown 1897 SHP
Tuolumne City
To Stockton
JAMESTOWN HOTEL
WILLOW STEAKHOUSE AND SALOON
To Oakdale
Tulloch Reservoir
Yosemite Junction
Chinese Camp
To Oakdale
To Bass Lake

0   10 mi
0   10 km

© AVALON TRAVEL

you can talk to rangers about the best hikes for you, and pick up trail maps for several of the major hiking areas in the park. In the wintertime, you'll find many of the roads through the park closed, but drive in as far as you can and snowshoe or ski from there.

Columbia State Historic Park

A stroll down Main Street in Columbia State Historic Park (11255 Jackson St., Columbia, 209/588-9128) is a stroll into California's boomtown past. It's free to wander the streets of the park, which encompasses most of the downtown area. If possible, start with the **Columbia Museum** (corner of Main and State Sts.). Here you'll discover the history of this, one of the early California mining towns. Gold was discovered here in the spring of 1850, and the town sprang up as miners flowed in, growing to become one of California's largest cities for a short time. It inevitably declined as the gold ran out, and in 1945 the state took it over and created the State Historic Park. In the museum, you'll see artifacts of the mining period,

from miners' equipment and clothing to the household objects used by women who lived in the bustling city. After the museum, walk the streets, poking your head into the exhibits and shops selling an array of period and modern items. Examine the contents of the Dry Goods Store, imagine multiculturalism of another age in the Chinese Store Exhibit, or grab a bite to eat in the City Hotel Saloon.

This large indoor-outdoor museum experience is an easy flat walk, with plenty of wheelchair-accessible areas. The horses, carriages, and staff in pioneer costume delight children visiting the site. It can get hot in the summer and cold in winter, and you'll be on your feet a lot, so dress accordingly and wear sensible shoes. Docent-led tours happen each Saturday and Sunday at 11 A.M. Check the park schedule for dates of living history events held here.

Railtown 1897 State Historic Park

Where the State Railroad Museum in Sacramento brings the trains inside to you,

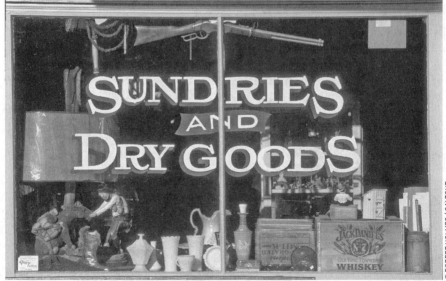

store window in Columbia State Historic Park

© ROBERT HOLMES / CALTOUR

Railtown 1897 (Hwy. 108, Jamestown, 209/984-3953, www.railtown1897.org, Apr.–Oct. daily 9:30 A.M.–4:30 P.M., Nov.–Mar. daily 10 A.M.–3 P.M., free, adults $2, children $1) invites you out to the trains. Much of this museum and oft-used film location is scattered on tracks outdoors. But the best plan is to start inside; the old depot waiting room includes artifacts and a video describing the filmography of the Railtown trains. You'll see signs from *Petticoat Junction* (a black-and-white "wild west" sitcom) and locomotives used in all sorts of films and TV shows. Prize locomotives sit in the century-old roundhouse. Some of the locomotives are undergoing active and messy restoration. Tools and parts lie all over the roundhouse and the large machine shop, and can be dangerous to small children and careless adults. Restoration buffs will drool over the work being done and the pieces of historic railroading strewn about the landscape. Train fans, history lovers, film buffs, and children all love this unusual indoor-outdoor museum. Behind the roundhouse you can check out the functioning turntable, then wander out to the rolling stock (some of it in fairly decrepit condition right now) and poke around a little.

Want to ride in the classic cars behind the great old steam locomotives you've seen? You can! From April through October, you can take a six-mile, 40-minute ride out into the woodsy Sierra Foothills. Trains depart on the hour 11 A.M.–3 P.M. If you're in town for the winter, check for holiday-themed rides in November and December.

Angels Camp Museum & Carriage House

Among the many museums that litter the ground in Gold Country, the Angels Camp Museum & Carriage House (753 S. Main St., Angels Camp, 209/736-2963, www .angelscamp.gov/museum.htm, Mar.–Dec. daily 10 A.M.–3 P.M. and Jan.–Feb. Sat.–Sun. 10 A.M.–3 P.M.) still offers a unique visitor experience. Inside the main museum building, you'll get to see meticulously preserved artifacts of the mining era. Outside, you'll find

old, and in some cases decrepit, mining equipment. The huge waterwheel sits in its original position in Angels Camp. A treat for transportation lovers, the Carriage House shelters more than 30 horse-powered vehicles of the 19th and early 20th centuries. Better restored than many similar displays, the carriages and wagons here show off the elegance and function of true horse-powered transportation.

Historic Kennedy Gold Mine

The Historic Kennedy Gold Mine (Hwy. 49 and Hwy. 88, Jackson, 209/223-9542, www .kennedygoldmine.com, guided tours Mar.–Oct. Sat.–Sun. 10 A.M.–3 P.M.) is a great place to bring your family to learn about life in a California gold mine. The Kennedy mine was one of the deepest hard-rock gold mines in the state, extending more than a mile down into the earth. Tour the stately Mine House, marvel at the size of the head frame, and learn how a stamp mill worked to free the gold from the rocks. For the best experience, take a guided tour and learn the true stories of the mine.

Indian Grinding Rock State Historic Park

Unlike most of the California State Historic Parks, Indian Grinding Rock State Historic Park (14881 Pine Grove-Volcano Rd., 209/296-7488) focuses on the history of the state before the European invasion. This park celebrates the life and culture of the Miwok, specifically the Northern Sierra Miwok who inhabited the Foothills for countless centuries. One of the central aspects of Miwok life was the grinding of acorns, the principal food. Women came to the grinding rock to grind and then soak their acorns for the day's meals. The park's focal point is a huge grinding rock, one used by all the women of the group who lived in the adjacent meadow and forest. The dozens of divots in the rock, plus the fading petroglyphs drawn over generations, attest to the lengthy use this chunk of marble. (The grinding rock's marble is frail; please don't walk on it!)

Follow the pathways past the grinding rock to the reconstructed roundhouse (a sacred space

© LIZ HAMILL SCOTT

Indian Grinding Rock State Historic Park

in current use by local Miwoks, so please be respectful). Then walk farther toward the Miwok village. Here, you can enter the dwellings to see how the Native Californians lived. If you're up for a longer hike, the North Trail winds around most of the total acreage of the park. For a deeper look into Miwok history, spend some time in the visitors center and museum.

Tuolumne County Museum

If you can hit only one "local" museum in your journey through southern Gold Country, make it the Tuolumne County Museum (158 Bradford St., Sonora, 209/532-1317, www .tchistory.org). The county fathers (and mothers) took entertaining advantage of the museum's location in the old Sonora jailhouse; a number of exhibits sit inside cells, and one cell has been re-created as an exhibit of what incarceration might have been like in 19th-century Tuolumne County. (Unpleasant.) Appropriate homage is paid to a Mr. Tom Horn, a prisoner who died in a jailhouse fire—one he set himself in an ill-conceived escape attempt. Oops! Throughout the rest of the museum, you'll find plenty of artifacts from the mines, shops,

and homes of the county. Interpretive areas describe the process of hard-rock mining, the arduous journey the would-be gold miners took to get from the East to California, and the history of the county.

Murphys Cemetery

Running up the hill outside downtown Murphys, the Murphys Cemetery (183 Jones St., Murphys) has been in continuous use since the 1860s. It sits adjacent to the old schoolhouse museum up on a small rising hill. You can drive through many parts of the graveyard, which is a good thing unless you've got several hours to spare wandering through the plots. A small fenced area denotes the space where members of the Masonic Order can be buried with their families. Despite its size and the obvious regular maintenance, this cemetery has plenty of ghostly atmosphere. An endless parade of slightly crooked marble and granite markers meander across the acres, and a few elderly oak trees provide light shade for the dead and their visitors. If you enjoy reading headstones, you'll find the graves of war veterans, Masons, miners, immigrants, wives, mothers, and children. You can piece together the Gold Rush history of Murphys by reading the town's collection of tombstones. Locals whose time in Murphys has finished can still be buried here, the modern markers standing in stark contrast to the softened lines of the older stones.

WINERIES

There's not as much wine in southern Gold Country as you'll find up north. But if you just can't manage without sampling the region's vintages, head for Murphys. A number of tasting rooms cluster in the low buildings downtown, and out in the countryside a few vineyards boast major estates.

The largest of the estates belongs to **Ironstone Vineyards** (1894 Six Mile Rd., Murphys, 209/728-1251, www.ironstone vineyards.com). The huge complex of vineyards, winery buildings, museum, amphitheater, and gardens can draw hundreds of visitors in a single day. If you're into live music, check

GOLD COUNTRY CAVERNS

Along with the tremendous network of artificial mine shafts, the southern Sierra Foothills are honeycombed through with natural tunnels and caverns. Children and adults love the cavern tours. If you choose to visit a cavern, be aware that you'll need to climb hundreds of stairs and squeeze through tight spots, and that the total walk may be more than half a mile. Check with the tour operators when you buy your tickets to be sure you're up for the trek. Also, the temperature inside the caverns hovers steadily at about 55°F, so bring a coat and hat to keep yourself warm!

Perhaps the most fascinating set of caves in the southern Gold Country is **Mercer Caverns** (1665 Sheep Ranch Rd., Murphys, 209/728-2101, www.mercercaverns.com, daily June-Aug. 9 A.M.-5 P.M., Fri.-Sat. 9 A.M.-6 P.M., Sept.-May 10 A.M.-4:30 P.M.). This network of rooms, tunnels, and river-connected underground lakes was discovered in 1885 by the gentleman who lent them his name. He began leading tours of the caverns almost immediately afterward, and Mercer Caverns have been a tourist draw ever since. The unusual aragonite formations found in several rooms improbably won a Grand Prize at the 1900 Paris World's Fair. Today, the custodians of the caverns require that you do not break off souvenirs, in fact they request that you do your best not to touch any of the numerous and delicate formations. This can be tough; you'll pass through some narrow spots where it's hard not to brush the calcite "angel wings" and stalactites. One of the neatest things about Mercer Caverns is the visible underground lake – a startling cerulean blue pool (lit artificially for your enjoyment) far below the tour pathway. The guides' descriptions of exploring the underground river flowing from lake to lake will make you wish for a reason to join in the research teams!

The popular **Moaning Cavern** (5350 Moaning Cavern Rd., Vallecito, 866/762-2837, www.caverntours.com, May-Sept. daily 9 A.M.-6 P.M., Oct.-Apr. Mon.-Fri. 10 A.M.-5 P.M., weekends and holidays 9 A.M.-5 P.M., adults $14.25, children $7.15) is still fun to visit, despite its sad history as a tourist attraction. Unlike the other caverns you can traverse in California, Moaning Cavern has only one major chamber, and it's a big one! Even folks with claustrophobia can get comfortable in the palatial chamber filled with great formations. You can take the basic 45-minute walking tour, rappel down 165 feet into the cavern (be in good shape), or sign up for a three-hour adventure tour that takes you through narrow passages to see things you'd miss completely from the regular tour (be in great shape and not claustrophobic!). But however you visit the Moaning Cavern, you'll never hear it moan. When it was first discovered and made into a tourist attraction, a big draw was the strange "moaning" sounds of air flowing through the cavern. It became so popular that the operators decided to widen the narrow mouth of the chamber to allow more tourists to enter at once. But when the rock was chiseled away and the mouth nice and wide and group-friendly, the famous "moan" disappeared. The shape of the rock had created the eerie sounds, which have never recurred. So come to Moaning Cavern for what you can see rather than what you can no longer hear.

© LIZ HAMILL SCOTT

Mercer Caverns

out their summer concert series. Buy tickets early, as the concerts tend to be local favorites. Or if you favor ore, visit the Heritage Museum and check out the astonishing 44-pound specimen of natural gold leaf.

Inside the vast tasting room, you'll find three bars and a pleasant surprise. The complimentary regular tasting includes any number of tasty wines, most priced at $10 per bottle. The reserve tasting bar shows off the higher-end vintages, but it's the lovely and shockingly reasonable "low-end" wines that make tasters want to buy their favorites by the case. If you're hungry, grab a bite at the deli inside the tasting room for lunch.

On the other end of the spectrum, the tiny, elegant **Black Sheep** (221 Main St., 209/728-2157, Murphys, www.blacksheepwinery.com, daily 11 A.M.–5 P.M.) tasting room offers higher-end red wines at a bar that can fit six people—if they're friendly. Black Sheep's specialty is Zinfandel made from Calaveras and Amador grapes, but they also make Cabernet Sauvignon, Cab Franc, and more unusual varietals like Cinsault. For a fun kick, be sure to taste the True Frogs Lily Pad blends—named for the celebrated jumping frog so famous in Calaveras.

For a fun third stop in Murphys, check out the **Twisted Oak Winery** (4280 Red Hill Rd. at Hwy. 4, Vallecito, 209/736-9080, www .twistedoak.com, daily 10:30 A.M.–5 P.M.). With a focus on Spanish and Rhone varietals and an unlikely mascot in a rubber chicken, Twisted Oak takes pride in being truly twisted. Their wines, however, are straight-up award-winners. From Viognier to Verdelho to the much-beloved percent@#$! Blend, you'll find a red or a white that's just perfect for you.

ENTERTAINMENT AND EVENTS

Want to enjoy a night out in southern Gold Country like the locals do? Like they have for the last 150 years? Head down to the local saloon and lift a cold one. You'll find a dearth of fancy lounges, but a wealth of *old*-school bars. Most every town in the area boasts at least one historic saloon that's still open and serving drinks.

Yes, it really does happen. Each May in

Angels Camp, the **Calaveras County Fair and Jumping Frog Jubilee** (209/736-2561, www .frogtown.org, adults $7, children $3) comes to town. During the fair each and every year, frogs jump on command in the contest that honors the famous Mark Twain story. You'll also find all sorts of other classic fair activities, such as livestock shows, baking contests, auctions, historic readings and exhibits. During the frog-jumping contest, you'll see literally thousands of frogs leaping toward victory. The top 50 from all heats compete in a final contest; all hope to beat the world record, a feat that carries a $5,000 reward. Practically speaking, visitors to the fair and jubilee will find lots of food at the concessionary, places to camp if they need, and ample restroom facilities.

SPORTS AND RECREATION

The outdoors beckons to many visitors to Gold Country. Between the land and the water in Calaveras and Tuolumne Counties, the recreation opportunities seem endless. The following lists just a few; talk to the locals and grab fliers and magazines to find the best spots for hiking, biking, kayaking, fishing, golf, and more.

Rafting and Kayaking

Southern Gold Country is home to a number of wild and turbulent rivers that make for fabulous and exciting river rafting and kayaking. Even if you've gone on float trips in other states, you need to prepare for rafting in California; this isn't a serene, slow paddle that gives you endless time to admire each mile of scenery. Instead, you'll spend a lot of time frantically paddling, screeching, and soaring over huge rapids, shooting through chutes, and hunting for the next restful eddy.

The Outdoor Adventure River Specialist, **O.A.R.S.** (209/736-4677, www.oars.com/california, one-day $147–227/person) operates out of Angels Camp, running rafting trips on the Stanislaus, the Merced, and the Tuolumne. This slick, all-amenities rafting chain offers everything from one-day trips on these popular river to five- and seven-day adventures that include multiple sports (mountain biking, rock climbing, kayaking) and trips into Yosemite proper. Do be aware that many of the rafting trips on these rivers include Class IV and even Class V rapids; be sure to check age minimums before signing up with your family.

All-Outdoors (925/932-8993, www.aorafting.com, Mon.–Fri. 9 A.M.–5 P.M.) offers trips on the North Fork Stanislaus, Merced, and Tuolumne, including a serious, adults-only, Class V ride down the Cherry Creek section of the Tuolumne. In addition, A-O Rafting makes regular trips down the Kaweah—a river just outside of Sequoia and Kings Canyon National Parks.

If you prefer to go out on your own with a kayak, check out www.riverfacts.com/rivers/10619.html for information about taking on the local rivers with your friends.

Boating and Fishing

For a peaceful fishing trip in the Gold Country, go to **Pinecrest Lake** (Hwy. 108 east of Sonora, www.fs.fed.us/r5/stanislaus/fishing/lakes/pinecrest.shtml). The National Forest permits boating, and a launch is available for your convenience. There's also a pier; bring your pole and bait and fish in peace from dry land. The Forest Service stocks the lake with rainbow trout. So long as you have a California fishing license, you're good to go.

A number of other lakes also allow fishing and boating. **New Melones Lake** (6850 Studhorse Flat Rd., Sonora, 209/536-9094) has beautiful hiking and biking trails along its edges. Dive in for a swim, go out on your boat, or cast a line out to catch your dinner. At **Lake Camanche** (2000 Camanche Rd., Iona, 209/763-5121, www.camancherecreation.com), zip around the lake on a personal watercraft, try your skills at waterskiing or wakeboarding, or enjoy a relaxing afternoon or evening of fishing. You can fish at Camanche all year. Beautiful scenery and beautiful fish combine at **Pardee Lake Recreation Area** (4900 Stony Creek Rd., Ione, 209/772-1472).

Hiking and Biking

If you want more challenging walks than those you'll find in the mine parks, head up

into the mountains. At Pinecrest Lake, take a gentle hike on the paved **Pinecrest National Recreation Trail,** or a sedate off-road bike trip on the three-mile **Sugar Pine Railroad Grade** (graded). For a stiffer bike trip, take the **Gooseberry-Crabtree Trail.** You'll ascend 2,000 feet over a difficult seven-mile stretch of gravel and dirt trails and roads.

More than a dozen hiking trails branch out from Pinecrest Lake. Most are easy to moderate and less than four miles long—perfect for day hikes with your family. A 0.25-mile walk takes you to the **Columns of the Giants** to check out the fascinating rock formations. Take a brisk one-mile hike to **Burst Rock** for fabulous views of the Foothills. Go another mile to reach Powell Lake, part of the Emigrant Wilderness. If you're willing to hike for your fish, start at the Kennedy Meadows Trailhead and hike out three miles (moderate) to **Relief Reservoir.**

In the summertime, the **Bear Valley** (Hwy. 4 at Hwy. 207, Bear Valley, 209/753-2301, www.bearvalley.com) ski resort turns its runs into tracks, its slopes into trails. Everyone, from the most sedate walkers and road bikers to the most aggro backpackers and 4x4 riders will find fun at Bear Valley. Check the website for maps and information about the acres of road biking areas, mountain biking tracks, and hiking trails.

Skiing and Snowboarding

When winter snows come to the southern Gold Country, the skiers and boarders come out to play. Only a few miles past Arnold, **Bear Valley** (Hwy. 4 at Hwy. 207, Bear Valley, 209/753-2301, www.bearvalley.com, daily 9 A.M.–4 P.M.) lures snow-lovers with a big mountain filled with great runs and tracks. Need a lesson? You can get one here on the wide, gentle beginner slopes near the lodge. If you prefer to take your chances, head up the hill to the array of intermediate and advanced trails that make up 75 percent of the skiable terrain at Bear. Ten different lifts make lines short on weekdays. If you're looking for something edgier, take your snowboard out to the "Cub" terrain parks.

Many native Californians cut their first turns in the snow at **Dodge Ridge** (209/965-3474, www.dodgeridge.com, daily 9 A.M.–4 P.M., adults $52, youth $39, children $10). Only a few miles from Sonora, Dodge Ridge is a reasonable drive from the Bay Area, and an easy one from Gold Country towns. A major bowl served by three different chairs has all beginner and advanced-beginner runs. The pee-wee area is reserved for kids learning to ski, while Ego Alley offers a chance for adventurous new skiers to try a slightly steeper slope. The rest of the mountain beckons to intermediate and advanced skiers and boarders. Intermediates love this resort, since you can get all the way down the mountain on blue slopes from almost every lift in the park. For experts, a few double-black diamonds nestle at the top of Chair 3. Freestylers have fun on the five terrain parks scattered throughout the park.

If you prefer cross-country to downhill, head for the trail areas at **Pinecrest Lake** (www.fs.fed.us/r5/stanislaus/summit/nordic.shtml). With a variety of terrain, including unmarked backcountry trails perfect for advanced adventurers, the area offers great fun. **Crabtree** sits only half a mile from the town of Pinecrest. The trails aren't groomed, but you'll find markers leading you in the right direction. Local amenities include restrooms and a small parking lot.

Adjacent to Dodge Ridge, the **Gooseberry** area calls to hardcore cross-country skiers. Trails range from "more difficult" to "most difficult" at this park. The tiny parking lot fits only about eight cars, but there is a restroom for weary skiers needing a break.

Casino Gambling

It's only fitting that the land where thousands gambled their futures on finding a fortune in gold should play host to a casino or two. If you're already in Sonora or Jamestown, take a detour to the **Black Oak Casino** (19400 Tuolumne Rd. N., 877/747-8777, www.blackoakcasino.com). This full-service, family-friendly casino features games for kids and adults alike. While the under-21 crowd bowl at the Black Oak Lanes or donate their quarters to the Underground Arcade, the grown-ups can play over 1,000 slots and video poker machines, plus a small array of table games. When you're ready for a break, you can eat and drink at any one of Black Oak's seven restaurants and bars, take in some live weekend entertainment at the Willow Creek Lounge, or even spin a few more slots in the smoke-free Manzanita Bar.

ACCOMMODATIONS

In southern Gold Country, you can stay at any number of charming Victorian B&Bs. Or for a change of pace, get a room in one of the historic downtown hotels in Jamestown or Sonora. These can be the most fun, with unique rooms, in-house restaurants and saloons, and often a great ghost story or two to lend additional atmosphere to the already fascinating inns.

Under $100

For a charming stay in an upscale Victorian inn, try the **Royal Carriage Inn** (18239 Main St., Jamestown, 209/984-5271, www.royalcarriageinn.com, $75–150). For a reasonable nightly rate, you'll find yourself staying in a uniquely decorated guest room furnished with antiques and collectibles. All rooms have private baths, and several have adjoining doors that make a perfect resting place for families or couples traveling together. You'll love the amenities and special extras in your room. Outside your room, enjoy the hospitality in the parlor by the fireplace or out on one of the two balconies overlooking the town.

If you're looking for history in your hotel room, you can't beat the **Gunn House Hotel** (286 S. Washington St., Sonora, 209/532-3421, gunnhousehotel.com, $75–120). The original home of Dr. Lewis Gunn—a gold prospector and newspaper owner—the building has been a home, hospital, and hotel in its more than 150 year existence. Renovated to create comfortable modern rooms and spaces, the Gunn House Hotel offers affordable luxury. A dozen rooms are done up in elegant jewel tones and rich fabrics, each with a king or queen bed. Upon each bed you'll find your companions for your stay—cute teddy bears that live at the Gunn House and welcome all guests with a whimsical touch of home. Unlike so many B&Bs, the Gunn House offers a TV with cable in every room, plus full heating and air conditioning—a welcome luxury when the summer weather turns scorching. Each morning, head down to the parlor to partake of the sumptuous Innkeeper's Breakfast, which is included with your room rate.

$100-150

The **C Jamestown Hotel** (18153 Main St., Jamestown, 800/205-4901, www.jamestown hotel.com, $100–195) looks just like the perfect Gold Country hostelry. With its brick exterior, long dim hallways trimmed in dark woods, and uniquely funky upstairs guest rooms, this hotel drips Gold Rush history. Each of the eight rooms bears the name of a famous entertainer or figure of the Old West or the Gold Rush—most are women. Whichever room you pick, be sure to read about its namesake during your stay. The hotel itself has been a boarding house, a bordello, a hospital, and the victim of two major fires. Is room 7 really haunted? Book a night in it and decide for yourself.

The rooms themselves have an unusual charm, with a combination of antique furnishings and modern fixtures. You might find a whirlpool bathtub in the same bathroom with a pull-chain toilet. While the appointments and amenities aren't perfect, somehow the little imperfections add to the hotel's character rather than detracting from it. In the mornings, head down the worn wooden staircase to the bar/breakfast room to enjoy a light, pleasant meal. Then go outside, and take a stroll up and down historic Main Street.

If you're looking for a more standard motel room, **Murphys Inn Motel** (76 Main St., Murphys, 888/796-1800, www.centralsierra lodging.com, $100–200) has what you need. Centrally located in sophisticated downtown Murphys, this motel makes a perfect base of operations for Gold Country wine tasting, as well as historical tours and outdoor adventures. Check the website for information about special packages that include visits to some of the area's attractions. Most of the 37 rooms have two queen beds, furnished and decorated in traditional motel style. Outside your room, you can take a cooling dunk in the pool or enjoy a hard workout in the small fitness room.

Over $150

The at-times infamous **C National Hotel** (18183 Main St., Jamestown, 800/894-3446, www.national-hotel.com, $155) has been operating as a lodging almost continuously since 1859. Granted, it's also had in its space a brothel, a small casino, and a "back bar" that was repeatedly raided during Prohibition. You'll find the nightlife at the National a bit more sedate than it was back in the 1920s. Today, an upscale gourmet restaurant sits downstairs, complete with an orange cat named Garfield out on the front porch welcoming diners. The Gold Rush Saloon serves up signature cocktails and California wines to a discerning local and visiting crowd each night.

Each of the nine guest rooms tends toward the luxurious, with antique furniture and soft, comfy linens and comforters. All rooms have their own baths with shower, and access to the soaking room, which the hotel describes as its "1800s Jacuzzi." Most rooms have only one queen bed—not the ideal setup or atmosphere for families with children. Indeed, both hotel and restaurant cater primarily to the romantic getaway crowd. Out back, be sure to check out (but do not try to enter!) the old gold mine tunnel, now filled with water most of the time. Or hunt through the hotel building for Flo, the resident friendly ghost.

The **Barretta Gardens Inn** (700 S. Barretta St., Sonora, 800/206-3333, www.barretta gardens.com, $155–425) seems like it ought to be in Sonoma rather than Sonora, with its elegant luxury and its wine-themed guest rooms. The highly polished wood floors of your room will be covered with antique Oriental rugs and an array of high-end antique furniture. Each florally decorated room has its own private bath, and many have two-person whirlpool or deep soaking tubs outfitted with candles and bath salts to create the perfect relaxing or romantic bath. Several multi-room suites are available for couples traveling together or for family groups. Located a few blocks away from downtown Sonora, the Barretta Gardens offers a haven of peace and privacy to Gold Country visitors looking for an upscale B&B experience. Every morning of your stay, you'll take a seat at the long dining table to enjoy a full hot breakfast. And if you're about in the afternoon, you can partake in a drink and a bite to eat downstairs in the common rooms.

From the outside, the blocky square structure of **Dunbar House, 1880** (271 Jones St., Murphys, 800/692-6006, www.dunbarhouse .com, $200–300) evokes a Dickensian air in the unlikely locale that is Murphys. Inside you'll find a plethora of modern comfort and Victorian elegance that calls to mind Dickens' richer characters. Each of the rooms boasts flowers, stripes, wallpaper, fabrics, and furniture reminiscent of the decorative excesses of the Victorian era. In the bathroom you might find an antique clawfoot tub and vintage shower, or the most modern of two-person whirlpool tubs. All rooms have English towel warmers—the very height of luxury on chilly winter mornings. For breakfast, you'll feast on homemade baked goods, a delicious hot entrée, coffee, tea, and specially blended hot chocolate. You can dine in the dining room, the garden, or (if you're in one of the suites) in the privacy of your own room.

If you're traveling with family or a group of friends, or you just want ample space to spread out, consider staying at the **Greenhorn Creek Resort** (711 Mccauley Ranch Rd., Angels Camp, 209/736-9372, www.greenhorncreek vacationcottages.com, $335). Here you can rent a condo or, better yet, a two- or three-bedroom "cottage" that's really your own full-fledged vacation home. Cottages have full kitchens, dining areas, and living rooms decorated in light, bright, homey styles. Each bedroom has its own separate bathroom; most bedrooms have king beds, though some have two twins. These cottages are perfect if you're planning a longer stay in the region and want to really settle in and get comfortable. The Greenhorn Creek Resort property offers every amenity imaginable, from an on-site restaurant to an 18-hole golf course to tennis courts. The pool facilities sparkle on hot summer days, with a shallow "family pool," large main pool, and nice hot whirlpool tub. The only downside to the Greenhorn Creek Resort is the exclusive country club price tag—it's up to you to decide whether it's worth it.

FOOD

A wealth of great dining awaits you in southern Gold Country.

American

Just next door to the Jamestown Hotel, you can get a hearty American breakfast or lunch at the **Mother Lode Coffee Shop** (18169 Main St., Jamestown, 209/984-3386). This local's spot offers traditional coffee shop fare: egg and pancake breakfasts, sandwiches, and burgers. The medium-sized dining room can get crowded on weekend mornings, with tourists vying for tables with the local community. Don't expect anything fancy here, but this is a good option if you need a good meal to get started on a long day of touring Gold Country.

One of the top locals' picks in the region, the **Diamondback Grill** (93 S. Washington St., Sonora, 209/532-6661, Mon.–Sat. 11 A.M.–9 P.M., $10) serves good grill food at extremely reasonable prices. Everyone loves the burgers at the Diamondback, but don't ignore the specials. Either the sweet potato fries or the garlic fries are a treat, but expect to feel the effects of the garlic fries for hours after your meal. Fresh salads feed lighter appetites, and everyone can enjoy a glass of California wine with their meal.

A recent move to a larger space increased seating capacity, but expect a wait, especially on weekends. You'll find the old bar present in the new dining room, which retains the great feel of old Sonora.

Italian

Carmela's Italian Kitchen (301 S. Washington St., Sonora, 209/532-8858) brings a tasty bite of Italy to Gold Country. Enjoy home-style food in a casual setting here—just be aware that the portions and full meals can get large.

Mexican

One of the best Mexican spots in the area is **Morelia** (18148 Main St., Jamestown, 209/984-1432), across the street from the Jamestown Hotel. Locals go to Morelia when they want enchiladas, Mexican grilled meat dishes, good beans and guac, and plenty of other tasty classic fare.

Steak

In a town thick with Gold Rush atmosphere, Jamestown's **Willow Steakhouse and Saloon** (Willow and Main Sts., Jamestown, 209/984-3998, $20–35) fits right in. The floor creaks as busy wait staff dash across the ancient wooden floor. Or is it the ghost that's reputed to haunt the craggy old building making the funky noises? Whichever it is, you'll hardly care once you dig into an order of the house special cheese fondue. To be honest, the steaks are only good rather than great, but the baked potatoes and the bucket of fixings make up for that. For an after dinner-cocktail, head into the Saloon and have a drink with the locals who frequent the bar area. You might have to wait for a table on weekend evenings; if you do, read the various plaques on the outside of the building to learn its history and the story of its ghost.

Bakery and Deli

For a truly homemade deli sandwich, go to the **Pickle Barrel** (1225 S. Main St., Angels Camp, 209/736-4704, Tues.–Thurs., Sun. 11 A.M.–4 P.M., Fri.–Sat. 11 A.M.–8 P.M.). The sandwich meats are barbecued out on the back porch of the deli, and the carrot cake is made from the owner's grandmother's recipe. If you're eating on-site, get a hot panini sandwich. If you're looking to carry out food for a picnic, choose from cold sandwiches, prepared salads, and other tasty treats.

Coffee and Tea

Do you care for a spot of tea? In southern Gold Country, the place to get it is inside **Babcia's Tea Room** (31 S. Washington St., Sonora, 209/532-1306). The Tea Room serves breakfast and lunch, but the best time to come is in the afternoon. You can order a full high tea, with finger sandwiches, scones, sweets, and, of course, a pot of good hot tea. Though you'll be sitting in elegant surroundings, feel free to wear your casual traveling clothes.

Need a cup of Fair Trade in the worst way? You can get it at **T E's Espresso Café** (1227 S. Main St., Angels Camp, 209/736-0927). Scallywag serves espresso drinks, plain ol' coffee, smoothies, baked goods, and more.

INFORMATION AND SERVICES
Tourist Information

Check each small town for its own municipal visitors center. For a larger center, head for the **Tuolumne County Visitors Bureau** (542 W. Stockton St., Sonora, 209/533-4420, www.tcvb.com). In Calaveras County, begin your trip at the **Calaveras Visitors Bureau** (1192 S. Main St., 800/225-3764, www.gocalaveras.com).

Media and Communications

The local southern Gold Country rag is the weekly *Calaveras Enterprise* (www.calaveras enterprise.com). This fun, ultra-local paper focuses on current events within the county and is a good place to find information about local nightlife, events, and festivals.

Some of the region's towns are *very* small, so it's sometimes difficult to find ATMs and Internet cafés. Take the opportunities you can to grab cash and check your email. In Angels Camp, hit the **Guaranty Bank** (479 S. Main St., 209/736-4561). They've got a 24-hour external ATM, plus you can cash travelers checks inside during regular business hours. In Murphys, try the **Mother Lode Bank** (150 Big Trees Rd., 209/738-3700) for ATMs and banking services.

For reliable free or inexpensive Internet access, your best bet is probably your lodgings; many inns, B&Bs, and motels offer wireless or high-speed wired connections. Outside your hotel, a local coffee shop (including the ubiquitous Starbucks in many towns) might be able to hook you up.

Each small town in southern Gold Country that has its own ZIP code has its own post office. In Sonora, the main **post office** sits at 781 North Washington Street (800/275-8777), easy to access for downtown visitors.

Medical Services

Be aware that not all towns in southern Gold Country have hospitals or any form of 24-hour emergency medical service. And if you're out in the backcountry, it might take help awhile to reach you.

One of the few major hospitals in the area is **Sonora Regional Medical Center** (1000 Greenley Rd., Sonora, 209/532-5000, www.sonorahospital.org, which has an emergency room with a helipad for emergency access.

GETTING THERE AND AROUND
Air

If you're lucky enough to have your own plane or access to one, you can fly in to the **Calaveras County Airport** (3600 Carol Kennedy Dr., San Andreas, 209/736-2501).

Train

Railroads in southern Gold Country tend toward tourist excursions rather than viable transportation these days. To access the area via Amtrak (www.amtrak.com), take the San Joaquins line to the Merced station, and make arrangements to catch a bus or get a car from there.

Car

Your main roads in southern Gold Country are running north—south and Highway 4 running west—east. Most of the towns have a main street (and it's often named Main Street), which can get crowded when a fair or event is happening. You can park on most town streets for free or a nominal meter charge. Unless you're in town for a major event or during a holiday weekend, you shouldn't have too much trouble finding a spot.

Central Valley

The Central Valley is the garden of California. Garden, not garden spot. Much of the legendary California agricultural industry makes its home out in the Central Valley. A number of ag towns cluster along the major highways (CA-99 and I-5), suffering through the sweltering summers that make the crops grow so well. No ocean breezes make it out here, since the Central Valley sits between the major coastal mountain ranges and the Sierra Nevadas, isolating it and creating a heat bowl each summer. As you drive I-5, you'll see everything from grapefruit trees to rice paddies to cornfields—California grows it all.

Culture and entertainment aren't very plentiful in these parts, though if you need a place to stay for the night on your way someplace else, any of the towns provide you with a motel room, a meal, and maybe even something to do to pass a few hours. If you're into the outdoors, head toward the many lakes and rivers for kayaking, rafting, and boating fun. Hardcore agricultural tourists might enjoy touring some of the massive orchards in the Orange Belt, and Fresno offers some agricultural tours.

Your safest lodging options in the Central Valley are the big chain motels—no quaint Victorian B&Bs or high-end boutique hotels ply their trade out in the great flat expanse.

STOCKTON

Stockton acts as a way-out commuter town with huge housing tracts that shelter workers who make the long, tortuous drive in to the Bay Area each day. While it's not an inspired tourist haven, Stockton sits at the confluence of several freeways, making it a convenient place to grab a tank of gas, a meal, or a cheap motel room if you find you're too tired to go on.

The **Stockton Asparagus Festival** (www.asparagusfest.com, adults $10, youth $5) takes place in the late spring of each year in downtown Stockton. Enjoy every tasty asparagus dish you can imagine, take in some live entertainment on the performance stage, and taste local vintages and brews at the Wine and Beer Pavilion.

Accommodations

Motel 6 (817 Navy Dr., 209/464-3948, www .motel6.com, $57) has some of the cheapest rooms with a good chance of reasonable sanitation. The best of the three Stockton locations is the one at Navy Drive; find another one right off I-5. Rooms have double or queen beds, including some set up for wheelchair accessibility. You can choose between smoking and non-smoking rooms. An outdoor pool completes a round of lower-end amenities, which also include free coffee from the office/lobby.

You can get a somewhat nicer room at the local **Best Western Stockton Inn** (4219 East Waterloo Rd., 209/931-3131, www.best westerncalifornia.com, $70), complete with basic amenities. This kid-friendly, low-rise motel has a pool, a wading pool, and a spa outdoors—perfect for getting the kids to relax and enjoy themselves or to cool off after a day in the legendary Central Valley summer heat. In your spacious guest room, you'll find jewel-toned carpets and matching bedspreads, a coffee maker, and high-speed Internet access. For travelers who really need a break, the Sutter Street Bar & Grill sits on the premises, making it easy to grab a drink or a meal.

La Quinta (2710 West March Ln., 209/952-7800, www.lq.com, $82) provides comparable lodgings to the Best Western. Grab a sizeable room with a king or two double beds, a coffee maker, and free high-speed Internet access. There's a pool, free continental breakfast, and pets are welcome.

If you want something a bit higher rent with nicer facilities, drop in on the **Residence Inn Stockton** (3240 March Ln., 209/472-9800, www.marriott.com, $140). Here you'll get a suite that includes a full kitchen with all appliances and pots and pans. The Wi-Fi is free, but the premium movies on TV are not. Step outside your room to enjoy the pool and spa or the

outdoor sports facility. Enjoy a free continental breakfast daily, do your laundry at the on-site coin-op machines, or take advantage of the valet dry cleaning and grocery shopping services.

Food

You can get some surprisingly good sushi in Stockton, specifically at **Cocoro Japanese Bistro & Sushi** (2105 Pacific Ave., 209/941-6053, www.cocorobistro.com, Mon.–Sat. 11:30 A.M.–2 P.M., 5:30–9 P.M., $10–30). The neat brick building houses a pretty, postmodern gold and crimson dining room. Take a seat at the table or up at the bar and order some of the fresh, original sushi. In addition to the fabulous rolls and variety of sashimi and sushi entrées, Cocoro offers lots of lovely hot food, including teriyaki, udon, donburi, tempura. Finish off your meal with a mochi ice cream or perhaps an apple tempura á la mode. Folks with lighter appetites can enjoy one of the great salads, many of which include fish.

Just jonesing for a burger? One of the best cheeseburgers in Stockton can be had **Chuck's Burgers** (6034 Pacific Ave., 209/473-9977, www.angelfire.com/biz/chuckshamburgers, Mon.–Sat. 6 A.M.–close, $10). This comfy downtown burger joint has vinyl booths, a counter with classic round stools, and eclectic decor. Chuck's serves more than just its famed gourmet and build-your-own burgers—you can get a down-home breakfast, a tasty sandwich, and even a low-cal dinner plate. Best of all, the owners hate the notion of "no substitutions," so you can create your own version of the perfect hamburger.

Practicalities

If you find yourself in Stockton, you probably got there on one of the major freeways. Stockon is bordered by I-5 and Highway 99; Highway 4 runs out from the Bay Area, and the 205 connector goes by to the south.

You can get to and from Stockton by **Amtrak** train (www.amtrak.com). The Stockton station services the San Joaquins line, which runs to Oakland, Sacramento, and down to Fresno and Bakersfield.

The **Stockton Record** (www.recordnet
.com) provides daily local and national news,
plus entertainment, food, and information on
things to do in Stockton.

For emergency medical care, go to **Dameron
Hospital** (525 W. Acacia St., 209/944-5550,
www.dameronhospital.org).

FRESNO

An agricultural town with aspirations, Fresno
sprawls in an ungainly fashion across the floor
of the Central Valley. It's the "big city" between
Sacramento and the passes down to Southern
California. Despite recent growth, the culture
of Fresno still revolves around the fields that
surround it. The Orange Belt starts here, and
any number of other warm-weather crops enjoy
the hot summer sunshine.

Beyond citrus, there's hockey. Catch a game
with the minor league pros of the **Fresno
Falcons** (700 M St., 559/485-7825, www
.fresnofalcons.com, tickets $12–28). The skat-
ing and amenities aren't quite up to NHL standards, but the fun and the energy rise up off the
ice like a mist. Join in with the locals for the

between-period festivities, which include events
like the infamous "Puck Chuck." Groan as the
announcer overstates yet another icing call.
Have a hot dog and a beer, and become part of
the loud cheering section for the Falcons!

Accommodations

You can get a clean, comfortable room at
EconoLodge Fresno (6309 N. Blackstone
Ave., 559/439-0320, www.fresnoeconolodge
.com, $87–154). The modestly decorated
rooms have a TV with DVD player, air conditioning, phones, and Internet access. A basic
but welcoming outdoor pool can help make a
steaming afternoon in Fresno more bearable.

The **Rodeway Inn Fresno** (6730 N.
Blackstone Ave., 559/431-3557, www.choice
hotels.com, $77–99) has reasonably clean, low-
end motel rooms and basic amenities. The free
Wi-Fi is a bonus and pets are welcome.

The **Picadilly Shaw Inn** (2305 W. Shaw
Ave., 559/226-3850, www.piccadillyinn.com,
$132–148) has several locations: the one de-
scribed here on West Shaw Avenue, another
out by the airport, and the third up at 4961

Welcome to Fresno.

© ROBERT HOLMES / CALTOUR

North Cedar near the university. These slightly more upscale motels offer rooms with a king or two-queen beds, decorated in fairly standard chain-motel chic. Amenities include free Wi-Fi, small refrigerator, coffee maker, and dual-head shower.

Food

A true local legend, you'll hear **Grandmarie's Chicken Pie Shop** (861 E. Olive Ave., 559/237-5042, $10) referred to as "Fresno's Chicken Pie Shop." The town feels a sense of ownership of this place, from the avocado green booths and matching giant plastic chickens to the unusually delicious pot pies. The vintage spot looks like it hasn't changed since the 1960s, but the pot pies and other delectable dishes are made fresh daily. You can get a sandwich, a meat dish, or an array of sides, but really the most obvious and best choice are the chicken pot pies. For dessert, grab a slice of homemade fruit pie. If you're looking for takeout for a picnic or a day on the road, Grandmarie's will pack full meals into containers for you. Or if you prefer to cook your own, you can buy unbaked frozen pies to take home with you.

For a great burger and fries, head for the **Dog House Grill** (2789 E. Shaw Ave., 559/294-9920, $10–30), a local favorite. You'll enjoy the classic American grill food in a casual bar and grill atmosphere. Beware that you're likely to run into a rowdier crowd on game days; the Dog House has big TVs and shows popular sporting events.

For something a little different, try the tasty Armenian cuisine at **Nina's Bakery** (2022 W. Shaw Ave., 559/449-9999, $10–20), an unlikely gem tucked in Fresno. If you're a newbie to the wonders of *lahmajoun, choreg,* and other Armenian treats, the staff will help you with suggestions. On the other hand, if you already know that you like your *lahmajoun* spicy, you won't be disappointed.

Practicalities

Fresno sits on the path of Highway 99. You can also get there on CA-41 (a north–south road) or CA-180, the major east–west thoroughfare.

The San Joaquin **Amtrak** route stops at the Fresno station (2650 Tulare St., www.amtrak .com). You can go north to Sacramento or Oakland, or south to Bakersfield from there.

Get into or out of Fresno by air through the **Fresno Yosemite International Airport** (5175 E. Clinton Ave., 800/244-2359, www .fresno.gov), which has the unenviable international designation FAT. almost every major airline operates in FAT, which is the major Central Valley air hub.

The local daily paper, the *Fresno Bee* (www.fresnobee.com), gets respect even from regular readers of the *San Francisco Chronicle* and the *Los Angeles Times.*

For medical services, go to **St. Agnes Medical Center** (1303 E. Hendon, www .samc.com) at the north end of town. In central Fresno, try the **Community Regional Medical Center** (2823 Fresno St., www.community medical.org), which has a 24-hour trauma center.

BAKERSFIELD

Bakersfield acts as a crossroads, separating the Central Valley from Southern California proper. It's the last major town on Highway 99 (also easily accessible from I-5) before you hit the infamous Grapevine and head down into the San Fernando Valley. It's a good place to stop for gas and a meal, and it can also be a necessary overnight stop if the Grapevine closes due to fog or snow.

For local entertainment, your best bet is the **Buck Owens Crystal Palace** (2800 Buck Owens Blvd., 661/328-7560, www.buck owens.com, Tues.–Sat. 5 P.M.–close, Sun. 9:30 A.M.–2 P.M., $10–30), where you can visit a museum, take in a live show, and grab a meal. In the museum, view Buck's favorite guitars and fabulous performance outfits, a collection of album covers, and endless photos and memorabilia chronicling Buck's lengthy music career. Fittingly, live music plays at the Crystal Palace almost every night of the week. Enjoy the lively dancing of the crowd in the dining room, or join in as country musicians play.

The restaurant serves up great American grill

food that matches perfectly with the music. Try the barbecue pizza, have a burger, or enjoy an only-slightly-lighter salad. Just don't expect too much in the Weight Watchers department—even the house salad has cheese and bacon on it. Be sure to save room for dessert, whether you favor the peach crisp or the house mud pie. And of course, you'll need a beer or a shot of Jack from the Buckmobile Bar to wash everything down.

Accommodations

The **Motel 6 Bakersfield Airport** (5241 Olive Tree Court, 661/392-9700, www.motel6.com, $50) is a good option for an overnight stay. Another reasonable choice is the **Rodeway Inn & Suites** (3400 Chester Ln., 661/328-1100, www.rodewayinn.com, $60).

For a few dollars more, you can get a few more amenities at the **Sleep Inn & Suites** (6257 Knudsen Dr., 661/399-2100, www.sleepinn.com, $90).

In Bakersfield, luxury appears at the **SpringHill Suites** (3801 Marriott Dr., 661/377-4000, www.marriott.com, $150).

Food

If you'd like to treat yourself to an upscale meal, try the **Valentine Restaurant** (3310 Truxtun Ave., Ste. 160, 661/864-0397, Mon.–Sat. 5–9:30 P.M., lunch Tues.–Sat., $10–30). You'll find treats like quail on the menu, and a great range of California vintages on the wine list. The small, elegant dining room set in an uninspiring strip mall seems almost out of place here—you'd be more likely to find a place like this in Los Angeles or San Francisco. Expect great service, both friendly and well timed, and plan to eat your fill if you order a full three-course meal.

For delectable home-style Mexican in a town that knows its Mexican food, you can't beat **Don Pepito's Restaurant** (1201½ Chester Ave., 661/326-1250, daily 11 A.M.–close, $10). In fact, Don Pepito's serves up both Mexican and Salvadoran dishes. The owner also acts as the chef, and occasionally as the waitress,

taking good care of the customers in her tiny dining room. The outside of this restaurant might seem forbidding—a run-down white and blue structure that may once have been Spanish Colonial Revival styled. Inside, there's little in the way of fancy decor, and the star of the show is rightly the food on your plate rather than the cloth on the table or the geegaws on the walls.

If all you need is a quick burger on your way through town, you can get one at **John's Burger** (2637 River Blvd., 661/873-8036, Mon.–Sat. 7 A.M.–11 P.M., Sun. 8 A.M.–11 P.M., $10). You can get a big ol' cheeseburger nearly any way you like it, sautéed mushrooms, fried zucchini, French fries, onion rings, and even a tri-tip sandwich. While it's been voted Best Burger in Bakersfield many times, rumor has it that customer service has gone downhill lately.

Practicalities

Highway 99 runs north right through the middle of town, and is one of the major corridors from Northern California to Southern California. From I-5, get to Bakersfield on the Stockdale Highway, which becomes CA-58 in the middle of town and heads east.

Bakersfield is also a stop on the **Amtrak** line (601 Truxtun Ave., www.amtrak.com), acting as the southern terminus for the San Joaquins line. You can take this train up to Stockton, Oakland, or Sacramento.

Meadows Field (3701 Wings Way, 661/391-1800, www.meadowsfield.com) is the local commercial airport. Delta, United, and US Airways all fly into and, more importantly, out of Bakersfield.

For the latest local news in Bakersfield, pick up a copy of the **Bakersfield Californian** (www.bakersfield.com), an independent, family-owned daily with plenty of local history.

For medical attention, try **Bakersfield Memorial Hospital** (420 34th St., 661/327-4647, www.bakersfieldmemorial.org), which has a full emergency room. On the other side of town, go to **Mercy Southwest Hospital** (400 Old River Rd., 661/663-6000).

YOSEMITE

Yosemite National Park might not be one of the seven wonders of the natural world, but its accessibility and beauty make it one of the most visited places in California. Ansel Adams' elegant black-and-white photographs turned Yosemite's stunning natural features—cascading waterfalls, striking granite cliffs, grand vistas—into international icons. Travelers come from all over the world to visit Yosemite, but other parks in the area beckon to those who prefer lighter crowds and a more unusual experience.

Mono Lake greets visitors with a serene stillness that seems almost eerie. No trees grow around this alkaline, salt-filled lake. Surrounded only by tough desert scrub, the still waters of Mono Lake have fallen and risen again amid endless state controversy. Throughout the lake and on the shore, odd calcite formations, called tufa, stand above the waterline, mute testament to the mineral content of the water. The rough High Sierra climate attracts few residents to the small towns nearby, though at one point the historic mining town of Bodie sheltered 10,000 gold-hungry residents.

The quiet, upscale town of Mammoth Lakes acts as the main access to the Mammoth Mountain ski area. Indeed, winter tourism to the mountain plays a big part in sustaining the local economy. But there's much more to do and see in and around Mammoth than just ski and snowboard. Hiking, biking, fishing, backpacking, and sightseeing are great in this part of the Eastern Sierra, and you can find bargains on lodgings in the summertime "off-season."

South of Yosemite, the Sequoia and Kings

© LIZ HAMILL SCOTT

YOSEMITE

HIGHLIGHTS

◖ **Yosemite Valley:** Yosemite Valley is the masterpiece of Yosemite National Park. Half Dome, El Capitan, Bridalveil Fall, Yosemite Falls, as well as miles of spectacular hiking trails can all be found here (page 382).

◖ **Mono Lake Tufa Preserve:** Free-standing calcite towers, knobs, and spires dot the alien landscape of Mono Lake. Several interpretive trails provide history and access to these unique formations (page 403).

◖ **Bodie State Historic Park:** A state of "arrested decay" has preserved this 1877 gold mining ghost town. Tours of the abandoned mine provide background on the settlement's sordid history (page 404).

◖ **Devil's Postpile National Monument:** One visit to these strange natural rock formations and you'll understand how they got their name. A mix of volcanic heat and pressure created these near-perfect straight-sided hexagonal posts that have to be seen to be believed (page 409).

◖ **Crystal Cave:** Well-lit tunnels venture into the grand chambers of this marble cavern, filled with dramatic calcite formations and polished marble (page 422).

◖ **Mount Whitney:** With a little bit of advance planning, you can climb or even day-hike California's tallest mountain (page 423).

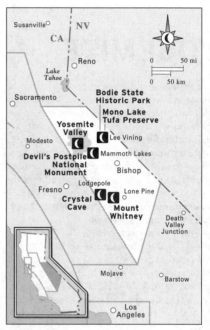

LOOK FOR ◖ TO FIND RECOMMENDED SIGHTS, ACTIVITIES, DINING, AND LODGING.

Canyon National Parks boast gorgeous rugged mountain scenery, immense redwood trees, and far smaller crowds than their more famous neighbor. The traveled part of this area actually encompasses two distinct parks and a forest: Sequoia National Park to the south, Kings Canyon National Park to the north, and Sequoia National Forest between the two in the west.

PLANNING YOUR TIME

This vast area deserves as much exploration time as you can give it. Both geographically huge and filled with sights and hikes and attractions, this is the perfect region to slow down and take your time.

Though summer is traditionally the high season and spring is best for the waterfalls, Yosemite is gorgeous at any time of year. During the high summer season, however, traffic jams and parking problems plague the park, just as though it were a major city. Seriously consider parking at the visitors center in Yosemite Valley and using the free shuttles to travel to different locations within the park. Tioga Pass is less congested, and parking more available, making it a viable summer option. Try to plan at least two or three days just in

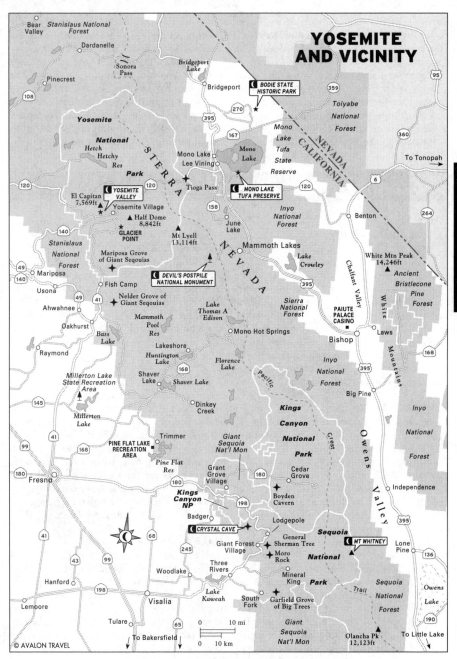

YOSEMITE AND VICINITY

© AVALON TRAVEL

Yosemite Valley, with an excursion to Glacier Point. Adding Wawona, Tuolumne, or Hetch Hetchy? Plan a week—though it will never be long enough!

Mammoth Lakes makes a great ski weekend getaway, but prepare yourself for a long drive to get there. In winter, take a break from touring and spend your time on the slopes; in summer a week will cover you.

For Mono Lake, plan another full weekend with time to walk around the lake and explore the tufa reserves. Be sure to save a half day for the drive up to Bodie State Historic Park.

When planning a visit to Sequoia and Kings Canyon, you have a couple of options. The parks could almost be done as a day trip if all you want to do is follow the main road and maybe take a couple short hikes. To explore the parks in depth, including longer hikes, plan anywhere from 3–4 days to a week.

Yosemite National Park

SIGHTS
◖ Yosemite Valley

The first place most people go when they reach the park is the floor of Yosemite Valley (Hwy. 140, Arch Rock Entrance). From the Valley floor, you can check out the visitors center, theater, galleries, museum, hotels, and outdoor historic exhibits. Numerous pullouts from the main road invite photographers to capture the beauty of the Valley and its many easily visible natural wonders. It's the most visited place in Yosemite, and many hikes, ranging from easy to difficult, begin in the Valley.

VISITORS CENTER

After the scenic turnouts through the park, your first stop in Yosemite Valley should be the visitors center (Yosemite Village off Northside Dr., 209/372-0200, www.nps. gov/yose, daily 9 A.M.–7 P.M., hours vary by season). Here you'll find the ranger station, as well as an intricate interpretive museum describing the geological and human history of Yosemite. Separate from the interpretive museum stands the Yosemite History Museum. Also a part of the big building complex are the theater, the Ansel Adams Gallery, and the all-important public restrooms.

A short flat walk from the visitors center takes you down to the re-created Miwok Native American village. The village includes all different types of structures, including those of the later Miwoks who incorporated European architecture into their building techniques. You can walk right into the homes and public buildings of this nearly lost culture. One of the most fascinating parts of this reconstruction is the evolution of construction techniques—as white settlers infiltrated the area, building cabins and larger structures, the Miwok took note. They examined these buildings and incorporated pieces that they saw as improvements.

EL CAPITAN

The first natural stone monument you encounter as you enter the valley is El Capitan (Northside Rd. west of El Capitan Bridge), comprised of Cretaceous granite that's actually named for this formation. This 3,000-foot craggy rock face is accessible in two ways: You can take a long hike west from the Upper Yosemite Fall and up the back side of the formation, or you can grab your climbing gear and scale the face. El Cap boasts a reputation as one of the world's seminal big-face climbs.

HALF DOME

At the foot of the valley perhaps the most recognizable feature in Yosemite rests high above the valley floor. Ansel Adams' famed photographs of Half Dome (visible from most of the valley floor) made it known to hikers and photo-lovers the world round. Scientists believe that Half Dome was never a whole dome—in fact, it sits now in its original formation. This

© LIZ HAMILL SCOTT

Half Dome

YOSEMITE

piece of a narrow granite ridge was polished to its smooth "dome" shape by glaciers tens of millions of years ago, giving it the fallacious appearance of half a dome. Want to climb Half Dome? See the *Hiking* section for information about this strenuous ascent.

BRIDALVEIL FALL

Bridalveil Fall is many visitor's first introduction to Yosemite's numerous waterfalls. A pleasantly sedate water-lovers' walk, the trail to Bridalveil Fall (Southside Dr. past Tunnel View) runs a half-mile round-trip. Though the falls run year-round, their fine mist sprays strongest in spring—expect to get wet!

The trailhead comes before the main lodge, parking, and visitors center complex, making it a great first stop as you travel up the valley.

YOSEMITE FALLS

Springtime and early summer are the best times to view the many waterfalls that cascade down the granite walls of Yosemite. You must hike to most of the falls, but Yosemite Falls are visible from the valley floor near Yosemite Lodge. Actually two separate waterfalls, Yosemite Falls together create one of the highest waterfalls in the world. But both Yosemite Falls are seasonal; if you visit Yosemite Valley during the fall or the winter, you'll see a trickle of water on the rocks or nothing at all. The best time to see a serious gush of water is the spring, when the snowmelt swells the river above and creates the beautiful cascade that makes these falls so famous.

MIRROR LAKE

You must walk or bike a gentle mile into the park from Yosemite Valley to get to still, perfect Mirror Lake (hike past end of Southside Dr., about 4 miles round-trip). This small lake reflects the already spectacular views of Tenaya Canyon and the ubiquitous Half Dome. But come early in the season—this lake is gradually drying out, losing its water and existing as a meadow in the late summer and fall.

Glacier Point

The best view of Yosemite Valley may not be

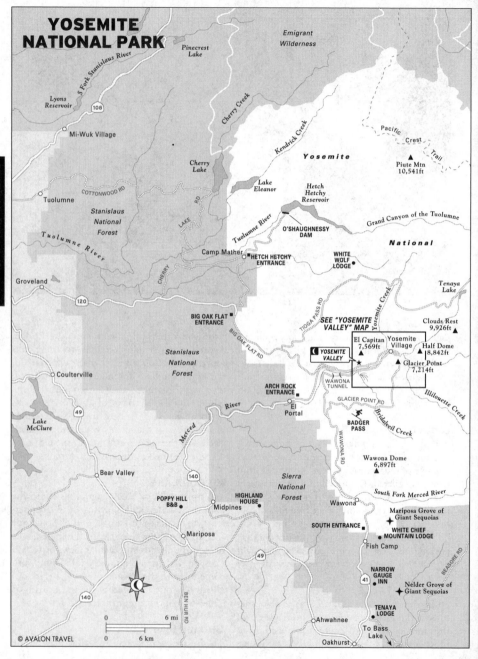

YOSEMITE NATIONAL PARK

S Fork Stanislaus River

Pinecrest Lake

Emigrant Wilderness

Lyons Reservoir

108

Mi-Wuk Village

Cherry Creek

Kendrick Creek

Yosemite

Piute Mtn 10,541ft

Pacific Crest Trail

COTTONWOOD RD

Tuolumne

Cherry Lake

Lake Eleanor

Hetch Hetchy Reservoir

Grand Canyon of the Tuolumne

Stanislaus National Forest

LAKE RD

Tuolumne River

Tuolumne River

O'SHAUGHNESSY DAM

National

Groveland

CHERRY

Camp Mather

HETCH HETCHY ENTRANCE

WHITE WOLF LODGE

Tenaya Lake

120

BIG OAK FLAT ENTRANCE

TIOGA PASS RD

BIG OAK FLAT RD

SEE "YOSEMITE VALLEY" MAP

Yosemite Creek

Clouds Rest 9,926ft

Stanislaus National Forest

Coulterville

49

Lake McClure

ARCH ROCK ENTRANCE

El Portal

YOSEMITE VALLEY

El Capitan 7,569ft

Yosemite Village

Half Dome 8,842ft

Glacier Point 7,214ft

WAWONA TUNNEL

GLACIER POINT RD

Illilouette Creek

River

Merced

BADGER PASS

Bridalveil Creek

Bear Valley

140

Sierra National Forest

WAWONA RD

Wawona Dome 6,897ft

South Fork Merced River

POPPY HILL B&B

HIGHLAND HOUSE

Midpines

Wawona

Mariposa Grove of Giant Sequoias

Mariposa

49

SOUTH ENTRANCE

WHITE CHIEF MOUNTAIN LODGE

Fish Camp

BEASORE RD

NARROW GAUGE INN

41

Nelder Grove of Giant Sequoias

BEN HUR RD

TENAYA LODGE

140

Ahwahnee

To Bass Lake

Oakhurst

0   6 mi

0   6 km

© AVALON TRAVEL

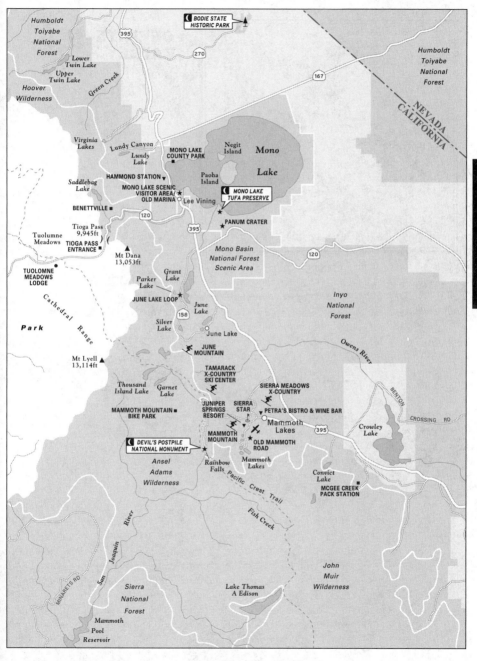

YOSEMITE

YOSEMITE

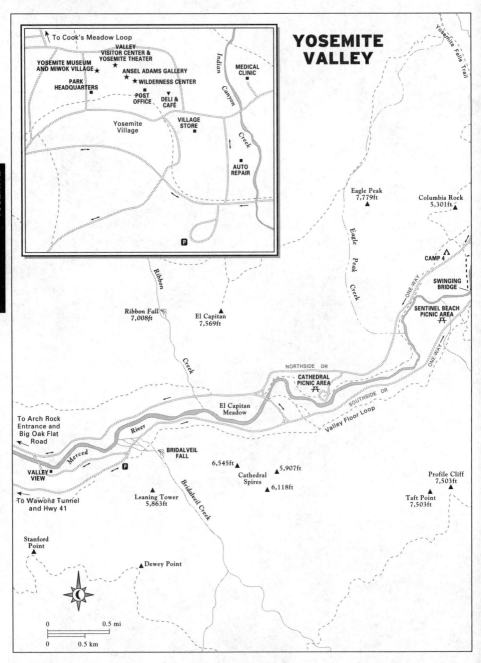

YOSEMITE VALLEY

To Cook's Meadow Loop

VALLEY VISITOR CENTER & YOSEMITE THEATER

YOSEMITE MUSEUM AND MIWOK VILLAGE

ANSEL ADAMS GALLERY

MEDICAL CLINIC

PARK HEADQUARTERS

WILDERNESS CENTER

POST OFFICE

DELI & CAFÉ

Yosemite Village

VILLAGE STORE

AUTO REPAIR

Indian Canyon Creek

Yosemite Falls Trail

Eagle Peak 7,779ft

Columbia Rock 5,301ft

Eagle Peak Creek

CAMP 4

SWINGING BRIDGE

Ribbon Fall 7,008ft

El Capitan 7,569ft

Ribbon Creek

ONE-WAY

SENTINEL BEACH PICNIC AREA

ONE-WAY

NORTHSIDE DR

CATHEDRAL PICNIC AREA

SOUTHSIDE DR

El Capitan Meadow

Valley Floor Loop

To Arch Rock Entrance and Big Oak Flat Road

Merced River

BRIDALVEIL FALL

6,545ft

Cathedral Spires

5,907ft

Profile Cliff 7,503ft

VALLEY VIEW

6,118ft

To Wawona Tunnel and Hwy 41

Leaning Tower 5,863ft

Bridalveil Creek

Taft Point 7,503ft

Stanford Point

Dewey Point

0   0.5 mi

0   0.5 km

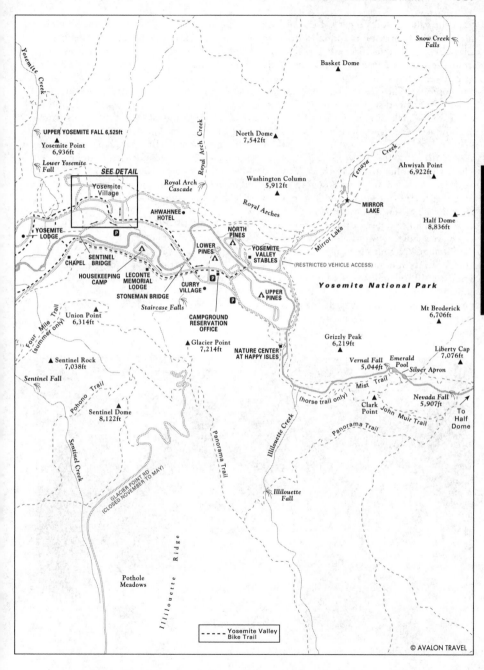

Snow Creek Falls

Basket Dome

Yosemite Creek

UPPER YOSEMITE FALL 6,525ft

Yosemite Point 6,936ft

Lower Yosemite Fall

North Dome 7,542ft

Royal Arch Creek

Tenaya Creek

Ahwiyah Point 6,922ft

SEE DETAIL

Yosemite Village

Royal Arch Cascade

Washington Column 5,912ft

Royal Arches

MIRROR LAKE

Half Dome 8,836ft

AHWAHNEE HOTEL

Mirror Lake

YOSEMITE LODGE

SENTINEL BRIDGE

CHAPEL

HOUSEKEEPING CAMP

LECONTE MEMORIAL LODGE

STONEMAN BRIDGE

LOWER PINES

NORTH PINES

YOSEMITE VALLEY STABLES

(RESTRICTED VEHICLE ACCESS)

Yosemite National Park

UPPER PINES

CURRY VILLAGE

Staircase Falls

CAMPGROUND RESERVATION OFFICE

Union Point 6,314ft

Four Mile Trail (summer only)

Sentinel Rock 7,038ft

Sentinel Fall

Glacier Point 7,214ft

NATURE CENTER AT HAPPY ISLES

Mt Broderick 6,706ft

Grizzly Peak 6,219ft

Liberty Cap 7,076ft

Vernal Fall 5,044ft

Emerald Pool

Silver Apron

Mist Trail

Nevada Fall 5,907ft

To Half Dome

Clark Point

John Muir Trail

Pohono Trail

Sentinel Dome 8,122ft

(horse trail only)

Panorama Trail

Panorama Trail

Sentinel Creek

Illilouette Creek

GLACIER POINT RD (CLOSED NOVEMBER TO MAY)

Illilouette Fall

Illilouette Ridge

Pothole Meadows

- - - Yosemite Valley Bike Trail

© AVALON TRAVEL

from the valley floor. To get a different look at the familiar formations and falls, drive up Glacier Point Road to Glacier Point. The trail from the road is any easy one—paved and wheelchair accessible—but the vista down into Yosemite Valley is anything but common. Glacier Point Road stays open all year (except when storms make it temporarily impassable) to allow access to the Badger Pass ski area.

Wawona

The small town-like area of Wawona (Wawona Rd./Hwy. 41, 1.5 hours from Yosemite Valley) sits only a few miles from the south entrance of Yosemite. The historic Wawona Hotel was built in 1917 and also houses a popular restaurant as well as a store. Wawona also plays home to the **Pioneer Yosemite History Center** (trail from Wawona information station, open daily). The first thing you'll see is a big open barn housing an array of vehicles used over a century in Yosemite, from big cushiony carriages for rich tourists to oil wagons once used in an ill-conceived attempt to control mosquitoes on the ponds. Onward, walk under the Vermont-style covered bridge to the main museum area. This rambling, not-overcrowded stretch of land contains many of the original structures built in the park—most over 100 years ago. Most were moved here from various remote locations. Informative placards describe the history of Yosemite National Park through its structures, from the military shacks used by soldiers who comprised the first park rangers, through homes lived in by early park settlers in the area presided over by stoic pioneer women. Check your *Yosemite Guide* for living history programs and live demonstrations held at the museum.

MARIPOSA GROVE OF GIANT SEQUOIAS

One of three groves of rare giant sequoia trees in Yosemite, the Mariposa Grove (Wawona Rd./Hwy. 41) offers a view of these majestic trees even to visitors who aren't up for long walks or strenuous hikes. During high season, a one-hour tram ride meanders through the grove, complete with an audio tour describing the botany of the trees, their history, and more.

© LIZ HAMILL SCOTT

carriage at the Pioneer Yosemite History Center

Or if you prefer, you can walk throughout the grove, taking your time admiring the ecology of the giant sequoia forest. The **Mariposa Grove Museum** (Upper Mariposa Grove, May–Sept. daily 10 A.M.–4 P.M.) brings still more information to grove visitors.

It's best to take the free shuttle to the grove from Wawona or Yosemite Valley in high season, to cut down on auto traffic and minimize use of limited grove parking areas.

Tioga Pass

Tioga Pass, a.k.a. California State Road 120 is Yosemite's own "road less traveled." The pass (as locals call it) crosses Yosemite from west to east, leading from the populous west edge of the park out toward Mono Lake in the east. To get to Tioga Pass from Yosemite Valley, take Northside Road to Big Oak Flat Road to the Highway 120 junction, and turn east. Its elevation and location lead to annual winter closures, so don't expect to be able to get across the greater park from November through May. Along the pass, you'll find a number of developed campgrounds, plus a few natural wonders many visitors to Yosemite never see. In the spring, walk out to view the wildflowers at **White Wolf,** which sits about 10 miles east of the junction—turn north on the dirt road to get to the parking lot. Another 10 miles along, bring out your camera to take in the vista at **Olmstead Point.** Or stroll on the sandy beach at **Tenaya Lake,** two miles east of Olmstead while staring up towards **Clouds Rest.**

TUOLUMNE MEADOWS

Once you're out of the valley and driving along Tioga Pass, you're ready to come upon Tuolomne Meadows (about 10 miles from the eastern edge of the park, accessible by road summer only). After miles of soaring rugged mountains, it's almost surprising to come upon these serene grassy High Sierra alpine meadows. Brilliant green and dotted with wildflowers in spring, gradually turning to golden orange as fall approaches, the waving grasses support a variety of wildlife. Stop the car and get out for a quiet, contemplative walk through the meadows. Or if you prefer a long trek through the backcountry, Tuolumne Meadows serves as base camp for high country backpacking.

Hetch Hetchy and O'Shaughnessy Dam

Perhaps the most disputed valley in all California, Hetch Hetchy (Hetch Hetchy Rd. past the Hetch Hetchy park entrance) was once a valley similar to Yosemite Valley, but is now a reservoir. Hetch Hetchy supplies famously clean, clear water (plus some hydroelectric power) to the city of San Francisco and other parts of the Bay Area. But many environmental activists see the reservoir's existence as an affront, and lobby continuously to have O'Shaughnessy Dam torn down and the valley returned to its former state of natural beauty.

HIKING

The hiking in Yosemite is second to none. From short interpretive walks on the valley floor to strenuous hikes up waterfalls and rock formations, there's something here for everyone who wants a little fresh clean air.

Yosemite Valley

Yosemite Valley is the perfect place to take a day hike, no matter how energetic you feel. Valley hiking maps are available at the valley visitors center (Yosemite Valley at Valley Village, Northside Dr.). Read your map and talk to the rangers. Though the hikes described here provide a good sample of what's available in the valley, plenty of other trails wind through this gorgeous area. Be aware that many people love the valley trails, so you likely won't be alone in the wilderness. If you're staying at Yosemite Lodge and want a gentle walk with a great view, take the one-mile **Lower Yosemite Fall** loop. Enjoy the wondrous views of both Upper and Lower Yosemite Falls, complete with lots of cooling spray! If you can, hike this trail in the springtime or early summer, when the flow of the falls is at its peak. This easy trail works well for families with kids who love the water.

Quintessential Yosemite Valley views are visible from the **Cook's Meadow Loop,** a one-mile walk through the heart of the valley. The point of this hike is to observe Ansel Adams' famous view of Half Dome from the Sentinel Bridge, then go on to gaze up at the Royal Arches and Glacier Point.

For walkers with a little more stamina, several trails in the valley are flat, but longer. To see **Mirror Lake** (end of Southside Dr., four miles, moderate), first take the short, wheelchair-accessible paved path. For a longer walk, take the connected loop trail two miles following Tenaya Creek. Read the exhibits around the lake to learn how and why Mirror Lake is transforming from a lake into a meadow (a natural process).

If you've got several hours and a desire to extend your visit to the valley floor, take the **Valley Floor Loop** (Northside Dr. and Southside Dr., paved path alongside road). For visitors who want a mid-length hike, the half loop runs 6.5 miles and takes about three hours to traverse, going over the El Capitan Bridge and following the path of many old wagon roads and historic trails. The full loop is 13 miles long and takes all day (about six hours) to hike. But it's worth it, since you'll see all the most beautiful parts of the valley while escaping the crowds on the roads. If you want to hike the Valley Floor Loop, it's a good idea to talk to the rangers at the visitors center; the route is not entirely clear on the trail map and getting lost in the meadows or forests is a distinct possibility.

Some of the more challenging hikes in Yosemite Valley are also the most rewarding. One of these is the trek up to **Upper Yosemite Fall** (trailhead at Camp 4). You can take the shuttle (Stop #7) to the Upper Yosemite Fall trailhead rather than walking up from Lower Yosemite Fall. From the trailhead, it gets steep—you'll climb 2,700 feet in three miles (seven miles round-trip) to reach the top of America's tallest waterfall. Your reward for the work will be some of the most astonishing aerial views to be had anywhere in the world. You can look down over the fall and out over the valley, with its grassy meadows so tiny far below. Plan all day (6–8 hours) for this hike,

and bring plenty of water and snacks to replenish your energy for the tricky climb down.

Perhaps the most famous hardcore climb in Yosemite Valley takes you to the top of the monumental **Half Dome** (Mist Trail to Half Dome Trail, trail parking at the east end of Northside Dr.). This hike can be dangerous! Attempt this climb only in the summer and early fall, when the cables are up (which you hold onto for balance and use to help pull yourself up the steep granite of the last 400 feet to the top of the dome). At a round-trip distance of 17 miles and with a 4,800-foot ascent, this arduous, all-day hike (10–12 hours) is not for small children, the elderly, or the out-of-shape. Take your pack with water, food, and essentials for safety. Once you stagger to the top, you'll find a restful expanse of stone on which to sit and rest and enjoy the scenery.

Starting at the Happy Isles Nature Center, the **Mist Trail** takes you first to Vernal Fall, then on to Nevada Fall over much steep, slick granite—including over 600 stair-steps up to the top of Vernal Fall. The total distance from Happy Isles to Nevada Fall and back is seven miles, with a 2,000-foot elevation rise and fall. Plan 5–6 hours for this hike, and consider taking a lightweight parka since this aptly named trail gets intrepid visitors very wet in the spring and early summer months.

Glacier Point Road

If you love the thrill of heights, head up Glacier Point Road and take a hike up to or along one of the spectacular (and slightly scary) granite cliffs. Hikes in this area run from quite easy to rigorous, but note that many of the cliffside trails aren't appropriate for hard-to-control children.

The two-mile round-trip hike up **Sentinel Dome** (trailhead just southwest of end of Glacier Point Rd.) makes for a surprisingly easy walk; the only steep part runs right up the dome at the end of the trail. You can do this hike in 2–3 hours, and you'll find views at the top to make the effort and high elevation (more than 8,000 feet at the top) more than worthwhile. On a clear day, you can see from

Yosemite Valley to the High Sierras and all the way out to Mount Diablo in the Bay Area to the west. Be sure to bring a camera! Be aware that there are no guardrails or walls to protect you from the long falls along the side of the trail and at the top of the dome.

Another not-too-long walk to a magnificent vista point is the hike to **Taft Point and the Fissures** (park 1–2 miles southwest of Glacier Point, Glacier Point Rd.). This two-mile round-trip hike takes you along some of Yosemite's unusual rock formations (the Fissures), through the always lovely woods, and on out to Taft Point. This precarious precipice boasts not a single stone wall—only a rickety set of guard-rails to keep visitors from plummeting off the point 2,000 feet down to the nearest patch of flat ground. Thrill seekers enjoy challenging themselves to get right up to the edge of the cliff and peer down. Happily for more sedate hikers, the elevation change from the trailhead to the point is only about 200 feet.

If you're looking for a mid-level or challenging hike, plus the most spectacular view of *all* of Yosemite Falls anywhere in the park, take the **Four Mile Trail** (Glacier Point to Southside Dr., eight miles round-trip) that connects Glacier Point to Yosemite Valley. The easiest way to take this hike is to start at the top, from Glacier Point, and hike down to the valley. You can then catch a ride on the Glacier Point Tour Bus (be sure to buy tickets in advance!) back up to your car. The steep climb up the trail from the valley can be much harder on the legs and the lungs, but it affords you an ascending series of views of Yosemite Falls and Yosemite Valley that grow more spectacular with each switchback.

For a longer high-elevation hike, take the 12.5-mile walk to **Ostrander Lake** (trail-head approximately two miles past Bridalveil Creek Rd., Glacier Point Rd.) and back. (You can cross-country ski to the lake in the winter and stay overnight at the local ski hut.) This trek can take all day if you're going at a relaxed pace-especially if you're visiting during June or July and stopping to admire the wildflowers in bloom all along the trail. The lake itself is a lovely patch of shining clear water surrounded by granite boulders and picturesque pine trees. Consider starting up the trail in the morning and packing a picnic lunch to enjoy beside the serene water. And remember to bring bug repellant since the still waters of the lake and nearby streams are mosquito heaven during hiking season.

Wawona

It's not quite as popular (or populous) as Yosemite Valley, but the hikes near Wawona in southern Yosemite can be just as scenic and lovely. Start with the **Wawona Meadow Loop** (Pioneer Yosemite History Center), a flat and shockingly uncrowded 3.5-mile sweep around the lovely Wawona meadow and somewhat incongruous 9-hole golf course. This wide trail was once fully paved, and is still bikeable, but the pavement has eroded over the years and now you'll find much dirt and tree detritus. Best in late spring because the wildflowers bloom in profusion, this trail takes about two hours to navigate. If you'd like a longer trip, you can extend this walk to five miles (with about 500 feet of climb/descent) by taking the detour at the south end of the meadow.

If you're up for a hardcore hike and a water-fall experience few who visit Yosemite ever see, take the difficult, 8.5-mile trail to **Chilnualna Fall** (trailhead near Pioneer Yosemite History Center). Plan 4–6 hours for this 2,300-foot ascent, and bring water, snacks, and a trail map. On this amazing hike, you'll see a few fellow hikers, and many tantalizing views of the cascades. Sadly, there's no created viewing area, so you'll need to peek through the trees to get the best looks and photos. The trail runs all the way up to the top of the falls, but be careful to avoid the stream during spring and summer high flow—it's dangerous in there, what with the waterfall and everything!

Tioga Pass and Tuolumne Meadows

For smaller crowds along the trails, take one or more of the many scenic hikes along Tioga Pass. However, be aware that they don't call it "the high country" for nothing; the altitude here *starts* at 8,500 feet and goes up on many trails. If you're not in great shape, or if you have breathing problems, take the altitude into account when deciding which trails to explore.

A great place to start your high country exploration, the loop trail to **Tenaya Lake** (Tioga Pass 20 miles west of the park's east entrance, right along the main road) offers an easy walk, sunny beaches, and possibly the most picturesque views in all of Yosemite. The trail around the lake runs about 2.5 miles, and the only difficult part is fording the outlet stream at the west end of the lake, since the water gets chilly and can be high in the spring and early summer. If the rest of your group is sick of hiking and scenery, you can leave them on the beach while you take this easy one- to two-hour stroll. Just remember the mosquito repellant!

If you're aching to see some giant trees, but you were put off by the parking problems at Mariposa Grove, try the **Tuolumne Grove of Giant Sequoias** (park and find the trailhead at the junction of Tioga Pass Rd. and Old Big Oak Flat Rd.). This 2.5-mile round-trip hike takes you down about 400 feet into the grove, which contains more than 20 mature giant sequoias. (You do have to climb back up the hill to get to your car.) While you'll likely see other visitors, the smaller crowds make this grove an attractive alternative to Mariposa, especially in the high season.

For non-athletes who just want a short walk to an amazing view, **Olmstead Point** (Tioga Pass 1–2 miles west of Tenaya Lake) may be the perfect destination. Only half a mile round-trip from the parking lot to the point, this trail exists to show off Clouds Rest in all its often-underrated grandeur. Half Dome peeks out behind Clouds Rest, and right at the trail parking lot a number of large glacial errata boulders draw almost as many tourists as the point itself.

Hikers willing to tackle somewhat longer, steeper treks will find an amazing array of small scenic lakes within reach of Tioga Pass. **Gaylor Lakes** (trailhead at the Yosemite Park border, Tioga Pass Rd.) starts high (almost 10,000 feet) and climbs a steep 600 feet up the pass to the Gaylor Lakes valley. Once you're in the valley, you can wander at will around the five lovely lakes, stopping to admire the views out to the mountains surrounding Tuolumne Meadows or visiting the abandoned 1870s mine site above Upper Gaylor Lake. The total hike spans about three miles if you don't wander around the valley. Crowd-haters will enjoy this trek, which is one of Yosemite's less crowded scenic hikes.

May Lake (one mile southwest of Tenaya Lake, Tioga Pass Rd.) sits peacefully at the base of the sloping granite of Mount Hoffman. While the hike to and from May Lake is only 2.5 miles, there's a steady, steep 500-foot climb from the trailhead up to the lake. One of Yosemite's High Sierra camps perches here, which makes this hike popular with the sorts of visitors who enjoy the much-less-known high-country areas. For truly hardcore hikers, a trail leads from the lake up another 2,000 feet (and six miles round-trip) to the top of Mount Hoffman.

The trail to **Elizabeth Lake** (trailhead at Tuolumne Gas Station and John Muir Trail) begins at Tuolumne Meadows and climbs almost 1,000 feet up to the lake, with most of the climb during the first mile of the 4.5-mile round-trip. Evergreens ring the lake and steep granite Unicorn Peak rises high above it. This stunning little lake makes a perfect photo op that your friends won't necessarily recognize as being Yosemite.

If altitude doesn't bother you and your legs are strong, Tioga Pass offers some stunning hikes good for a full day of hiking (or longer, if that's your thing).

For a different look at a classic Yosemite landmark, take the **North Dome** trail through the woods and out to the dome, which sits right across the valley from Half Dome. You'll hike almost nine miles round-trip, with a few hills thrown in, but getting to stare right at the face of Half Dome (and check out Cloud's Rest just beyond) at what feels like eye-level makes the effort worth it.

If you can't get enough of Yosemite's granite-framed alpine lakes, take the long walk out to one or both of the **Cathedral Lakes** (trailhead at Tuolumne Meadows visitors center, part of the John Muir Trail). Starting at ever-popular Tuolumne Meadows, you'll climb about 800 feet over 3–4 miles (depending on which lake you choose). These picture-perfect lakes show off the dramatic rocky peaks above, surrounding evergreens, and crystalline waters of Yosemite to their best advantage. Be sure to bring your camera, water, and munchies!

The **Glen Aulin Trail** (trailhead at Tuolumne Stables) to Tuolumne Fall and White Cascade is part of the John Muir trail, and several of its forks branch off to pretty little lakes and other nice spots in the area. From Tuolumne Meadows to Tuolumne Fall and back is 13 miles round trip, with some steep and rocky areas in the trail. But if you've got the lungs for it, you'll be rewarded by the fabulous views of the Tuolumne River alternately pooling and cascading right beside the trail. This hike may get a bit crowded in the high season. In the hot summertime, many hikers trade dusty jeans for swimsuits and cool off in the pools at the base of both White Cascade and Tuolumne Fall. A great way to do this hike is to enter the High Sierra Camp lottery and, if you win, arrange to stay the night at the Glen Aulin camp. If you do this, you can take your hike a few miles farther, downstream to California Fall, Le Conte Fall, and finally Waterwheel Fall.

SPORTS AND RECREATION

The whole point of coming to Yosemite is to get outside and enjoy it. If you're craving more than just endless hiking, the park offers plenty of different outdoor activities suited to all ages and fitness levels.

Horse and Mule Riding

Miles of trails let visitors of all ability levels take a load off their own feet and explore Yosemite from the back of a horse…or a mule! For some of Yosemite's more rugged terrain, especially in the high country, easygoing, surefooted mules are the best animals for the job of getting both people and gear around.

Three rides begin at the **Yosemite Valley Stable** (end of Southside Dr., 209/372-4386, www.yosemitepark.com/activities_mulehorse backrides.aspx, half-day $59–119). The sedate two-hour trek to Mirror Lake works well for kids and beginning riders. As part of the ride, your guide explains the geologic forces that are slowly drying out the lake. A half-day ride takes you out to Vernal Fall, where you can admire the views of Nevada Fall and the valley floor. This ride takes about four hours, but isn't terribly difficult. The all-day ride requires a great deal more stamina—going all the way out to Little Yosemite Valley and back.

You'll find more horses than mules at **Wawona Stable** (Wawona Rd. at Pioneer Yosemite History Center, $59–119), and more tourists, too—reservations for the rides out of Wawona are strongly encouraged. From Wawona you can take a sedate two-hour ride around the historic wagon trail running into the area. Or try the five-hour trip out to Chilanualna Falls—you'll get to tell your friends about a waterfall that few Yosemite visitors ever see. Be sure to bring a camera! Both of these rides are fine for less experienced riders, and the wagon trail ride welcomes children with its easy, flat terrain.

Out of **Tuolumne Meadows Stable** (Tioga Pass Rd. past Tuolumne Visitors Center, north side of the road, short dirt road to stables) you can get the perfect overview of the Yosemite high country by taking the introductory-level two-hour ride. For a longer ride deeper into the landscape, do the four-hour trip that passes Twin Bridges and Tuolumne Falls. An all-day ride with a variable route beckons the adventurous traveler, but you need to be both in good shape *and* an experienced rider for this one.

Bicycling

Biking is a great way to get out of the car and off the crowded roads, and to explore Yosemite at a quicker-than-walking pace. Twelve miles of paved trails are mostly flat. You can bring your own bikes, or rent (www.yosemitepark .com/Activities_Biking_BikeRentals.aspx, daily 8:30 A.M.–8:30 P.M., $9.50/hour, $25/day) from

Yosemite Village. Check at Yosemite Lodge at Yosemite Falls for more information about renting and to get a bike trail map.

Rock Climbing

The rock climbing at Yosemite is some of the best in the world. **El Capitan,** the face of **Half Dome**, and **Sentinel Dome** in the high country are challenges that draw climbers from all over. If you plan to climb one of these monuments, check with the Yosemite park rangers and the Mountaineering School well in advance of your planned climb for necessary information and permits.

But many of the spectacular ascents are *not* beginners' climbs. Go try to scale El Capitan for your first climb ever, and you'll fail (if you're lucky). The right place to start climbing in Yosemite is the **Yosemite Mountaineering School** (209/372-8344, www.yosemitepark .com/activities_mountaineeringschool.aspx). Here you'll find beginners' "Go Climb a Rock" classes perfect for older kids or adult team-building groups. You'll also find guided climbs out of Yosemite Valley and Tuolumne Meadows, and if you're looking for a one-on-one guided climb experience, you can get it through the school. Also available are guided hikes and backpacking trips, and cross-country skiing lessons and treks in wintertime.

Skiing

Yosemite prides itself on its 350 miles of cross-country skiing tracks and trails throughout the park. In fact, many places in Yosemite are accessible in winter only by cross-country skis or snowshoes. Check out the **Cross Country Ski School** (www.yosemitepark.com/ badgerpass_crosscountryskiing.aspx) for classes, rentals, and guided cross-country ski tours. If you're looking for a fun day out in the snow, the groomed tracks from Badger Pass to Glacier Point run 21 miles and are frequented by day skiers. You'll see fewer other skiers on the backcountry trails, which can also be traversed in a single day by a reasonably strong skier. For the hardcore XCer who wants a serious skiing experience, check out the overnight and multi-day tours—hiring a guide for these trips is recommended for most skiers.

Downhill skiing at **Badger Pass** (Glacier Point Rd., five miles from Wawona, mid-Dec.–Apr., daily 9 A.M.–4 P.M., prices vary) is another favorite wintertime activity at Yosemite. Badger Pass was the first downhill ski area created in California. Today, it's the perfect resort for families and groups who want a relaxed day or three of moderate skiing. With plenty of beginner runs and classes, Yosemite has helped thousands of kids (and adults!) learn to ski and snowboard as friends and family look on from the sun decks at the lodge. There are enough intermediate runs to make it interesting for mid-level skiers, too. Double-black diamond skiers may find Badger Pass too tame for their tastes since there are just a few advanced runs. But everyone agrees that the prices are more reasonable than much of what you'll find at Tahoe's huge resorts, and the focus is on friendliness and learning rather than showing off and extreme skiing.

Snowshoeing

Even if you're not up for hardcore skiing, you can get out and enjoy the snow-covered landscapes of wintertime Yosemite. Snowshoeing requires no experience and only minimal fitness to get started. "If you can walk, you can snowshoe," claims Yosemite's own website. You can rent snowshoes at several locations in Yosemite and acquire trail maps from the rental centers. The **Cross Country Ski School** (www.yosemitepark.com/badgerpass_snowshoeing.aspx) offers guided hikes and winter camping trips.

ENTERTAINMENT AND EVENTS
Photography and Art Classes

The unbelievable scenery of Yosemite inspires visitors young and old to create images to take home with them. Knowing this, Yosemite offers art and photography classes to help people catch hold of their inner Ansel Adams. In the summertime, art classes are offered for free out of the **Yosemite Art and Education Center** (Yosemite Village, Mon.–Sat. 10 A.M.–2 P.M.). Check the *Yosemite Guide* for a list of classes during your visit. You must bring your own art supplies, chair or cushion to sit on, and walking shoes (you'll take a brief walk out to a good location to see the scenery). If you don't have supplies, you can buy them at the Village Store just before class. Also check the *Guide* for guided tours of the **Ansel Adams Gallery** in the Village.

Theater and Music

The **Valley Visitors Center Auditorium** (Northside Dr. at Yosemite Village visitors center) in the heart of Yosemite Village acts as home to the Yosemite Theater. For an evening of indoor entertainment, check the copy of *Yosemite Today* you received at the gate for a list of what shows are playing during your visit. Most plays are one- or two-man productions; all center on the theme of the rich history and culture of Yosemite National Park. The John Muir Performances, starring resident actor Lee Stetson, have been running for 25 years.

It's worth making an evening trip out to Wawona one evening to listen to the delightful piano music and singing of legendary Tom Bopp. He plays vintage camp music (and requests, and whatever else strikes his fancy) in the **Piano Lounge at the Wawona Hotel**

YOSEMITE

YOSEMITE AT NIGHT

Yosemite National Park does not roll up its meadows and trails at sunset. In fact, parts of the park come alive at nightfall, showing off another side of Yosemite's natural wonders. Check your *Yosemite Today* guide for more information about these and other activity programs.

If you fancy a nighttime stroll, you can take one regardless of season or weather. In summer, **Night Prowl** (90 minutes, $5) takes you along easy trails near Yosemite Lodge at Yosemite Falls, explaining the nightlife of the inhabitants of the valley floor. This fun guided tour welcomes children and adults. It takes place once or twice a week, starting at different times and places. In winter, take a **Full Moon Snowshoe Walk** ($14.75 rental, $5 without, children over 8). This two-hour trek from the Badger Pass ski lodge takes you out into the sparkling white wonderland that is Yosemite in winter. These walks are offered five days per month – the four days leading up to the full moon, and the day of the full moon itself. Also be aware that the Badger Pass shuttle *does not* run in the evenings, so you must drive yourself to and from the lodge.

If astronomy is your favorite nighttime interest, join experienced guides out in the valley meadows for the **Starry Skies** ($5, summer and fall) program. Well suited for individuals and families, this one-hour program takes groups out to look at the unpolluted lights of stars and moon over the park. You'll learn about constellations, comets, and meteors, and enjoy the myths and legends surrounding the mysteries of the night sky. Starry Skies happens several times each week in Yosemite Valley, and once a week in Wawona.

For families who find themselves tired after a long day running around the park, plenty of non-hiking evening fun can be had at various semi-sedentary evening programs. The **Campfire Program** ($5) does it old-school – groups gather around a nice big campfire (bring blankets and bug repellant!) for stories, singing, and marshmallow toasting. You might need to take a short walk to get to the fire near Camp Curry. If you're out at one of the more primitive lodges or campsites, check with your local rangers or office for campfire programs at your site, since many spring up in the summer and early fall months. **Fireside Storytelling** (fall, winter, and spring, free) focuses on, well, telling stories around the big fire inside the Ahwahnee Great Lounge. Take refuge from the bugs and the cold and listen to great tales in a comfortable indoor environment during the off-season.

(209/375-1425) five nights a week. Older visitors especially love his old-style performance and familiar songs, but everyone enjoys the music and entertainment he provides. Even if you're just waiting for a table at the restaurant, stop in to say hello and make a request.

CAMPING

Many people come to Yosemite specifically to feel the great outdoors all around them all the time. Naturally, that experience includes camping out under the stars. Inside the park, you'll find 13 designated campgrounds and the High Sierra camps. If you prefer less expense and less need for advance reservations, try one of the campgrounds outside the park boundaries.

Inside the Park

For any Yosemite National Park campground, make reservations early! All the major campgrounds fill up from spring through fall, and reservations can be difficult to come by. Consider making your Yosemite campground reservation *at least six months in advance* to get the campsite you want. To make a reservation, go to www.nps.gov/yose/planyourvisit/camping.htm or call 877/444-6777.

YOSEMITE VALLEY

In Yosemite Valley, the campgrounds at **Upper, Middle,** and **Lower Pine** (reservations required, 375 campsites, $20/day) allow trailers and RVs, and you can bring your dog camping here with you. Upper Pine is open through the winter. Camp Curry offers plenty of food options within walking distance, and showers are available nearby. **Camp 4** (near Yosemite Lodge, no reservations required, 35 campsites, $5) stays open year-round. Yes, you can camp in the snow! Bring a tent—no RVs or trailers are allowed at Camp 4—but you'll find showers nearby and lots of food and groceries at Yosemite Lodge.

WAWONA

To the south, you can camp at lovely forested **Wawona** (one mile north of Wawona, reservations required Apr.–Oct., 93 sites, $20) year-round. RVs are welcome, though there are no

hookups on-site. If you want to camp with your horses, Wawona offers two horse sites. The small grocery store in town can provide a few basics, but most services (including showers) can't be found closer than Yosemite Valley. For a more picturesque southern Yosemite camping experience, check out **Bridalveil Creek** (Glacier Point Rd., no reservations required, 110 campsites, $14/night). You can reserve one of three horse sites if you're traveling with your mount. Mechanical beasts of burdens (RVs) are welcome as well.

TIOGA PASS AND TUOLUMNE MEADOWS

Yosemite visitors who favor the high country tend to prefer to camp rather than stay in a lodge. Accordingly, most of Yosemite's campgrounds sit north of the valley, away from the largest tourist crowds (excluding the High Sierra Camps, which are also up north). **◖ Tuolumne Meadows** (Tioga Pass Rd. at Tuolumne Meadows, reservations suggested, $20/night) hosts the largest campsite in the park, with over 300 individual campsites, plus four horse sites. Expect Tuolumne to be crowded for the whole of its season (July–Sept.). Tuolumne is RV-friendly and has most necessary services, including food and showers available at the Tuolumne Meadows Lodge. Other good-sized campgrounds off Tioga Pass include **Crane Flat** (reservations required, 166 campsites, $20/night, RVs ok, open mid-June–mid-Oct.), **White Wolf** (no reservations, 74 campsites, $14/night, open July–mid-Sept.), and **Hodgdon Meadow** (reservations required high season, 105 campsites, $20/night, open year-round) at the west edge of the park.

If you're looking to ditch the RV traffic and crowded central visitor areas, head for **Yosemite Creek** (no reservations, $10/night). This tents-only campground boasts only 40 campsites on a first-come, first-served basis from July through September. The creek flows right through the campground, perfect for cooling off on a hot day, and you can even drink the water if you first treat it properly. Yosemite Creek offers few amenities—no groceries, showers, or on-site potable water. It's just what many outdoorsy visitors want! Another option is **Tamarack Flat** (Tioga Pass Rd., no reservations, 52 campsites, $10/night). Here you'll be closer to Yosemite Valley but still in a more primitive environment.

The **High Sierra Camps** (www.yosemite park.com/accommodations_highsierra_how toapply.aspx) at Yosemite offer far more than your average backcountry campground. Rather than carrying heavy packs filled with food, tents, and bedding, multi-day hikers can plan to hit the High Sierra Camps, which provide tent cabins with amenities, breakfast and dinner in camp, and a box lunch to take along during the day. Choose from among the Merced Lake, Vogelsang, Glen Aulin, May Lake, and Sunrise Camp—or hike from one to the next if you get lucky. Why do you need luck? Because you can't just walk up to a High Sierra Camp one weekend at random and expect to find a bed. In the fall, a lottery takes place for spots at High Sierra Camps through the following summer. You'll need to submit an application if you want to join the lottery, and even if you get a spot there's no guarantee you'll get your preferred dates. You can check in at the website during the camping season (June–Sept.) to see if any dates are available.

The bottom line? If you want to take advantage of the Yosemite backcountry, plan for a summer when you can be flexible in your dates, and start making your arrangements a year in advance.

Outside the Park

Some campers prefer a bit more seclusion, lower campsite prices, or just a different atmosphere. They tend to go for the campgrounds outside Yosemite's boundaries, which abound in the woodsy wilderness surrounding the park.

GROVELAND

To camp in Big Oak Flat along Hwy. 120 near Groveland, try the Thousand Trails RV campground at **Yosemite Lakes** (31191 Harden Flat Rd., 800/533-1001, ranger station 209/962-0103, www.1000trails.com). This sprawling wooded campground beside the water has more

than 250 RV sites with full hookups, 130 tent sites, a few dozen cabins, tent cabins, and yurts, and a 12-bed hostel. It's only five miles from the park entrance, and it's got a full slate of recreational amenities, laundry facilities, and Wi-Fi. You're right on the Tuolumne River, you've got great access to the boating opportunities on Lake Don Pedro, and the Moaning Cavern (see the *Sacramento and Gold Country* chapter) is only a few miles away.

MARIPOSA

Several campgrounds surround the Arch Rock Entrance to Yosemite on Hwy. 140, near the border town of Mariposa. The **Yosemite Bug Rustic Mountain Resort** (6979 Hwy. 140, 866/826.7108, www.yosemitebug.com, $23/dorm bed, $35–55/tent cabin, $65–135/private cabin rooms) is part hostel, part rustic cabin lodge. This facility includes five hostel dormitories, a number of attractively appointed tent cabins with real beds, and a few cabins with private rooms, some with private baths. Solo travelers and families on tight budget favor Yosemite Bug for its comfortable and cheap accommodations. It's not the Ritz, but the bathrooms are clean and the linens are fresh when you arrive, and the location is great for Yosemite visitors who want to exit the park each night.

RVers aiming for the Arch Rock Entrance flock to the **Indian Flat RV Park** (9988 Hwy. 140, 209/379-2339, www.indianflatrvpark .com, tent sites $20–30, RV sites $35–40, tent cabins $60, cottages $110, pet fee $5). This park is a full-service low-end resort, with everything from minimal-hookup RV sites up through tent cabins and full-fledged cottages. Showers are available here, even for passersthrough who aren't staying at Indian Flat. The lodge next door has extended an invitation to all Indian Flat campers to make use of their outdoor pool. Because Indian Flat is relatively small (25 RV sites, 25 tent sites), reservations are strongly recommended. You can make your booking up to a year in advance, and this kind of planning is a really good idea for summertime Yosemite visitors.

SOUTH ENTRANCE

At the South Entrance down by the spread-out forest town of Fish Camp, book a site at the small, attractive **Summerdale Campground** (northeast of Fish Camp on Hwy. 41, 877/444-6777, www.reserveusa.com, two-night minimum weekends, three-night minimum holiday weekends, $19, June–Nov.). This lovely spot has only 29 campsites and a strict limit on RV size (24 feet), making it a bit quieter and less city-like than the mega-campgrounds. You'll have a fire ring and a grill at your site, plenty of room under mature shade trees for yourself and your friends, and maybe even a running water spigot (on some sites, boiling before drinking recommended).

INYO NATIONAL FOREST

Out east, near Highway 395 and Tioga Pass, campgrounds tend to cluster in the Inyo National Forest. You can stay at **Ellery Lake** (Hwy. 120 in Upper Lee Vining Canyon, 877/444-6777, www.fs.fed.us/r5/inyo/recreation/campgrounds.shtml, $17, no reservations, pit toilets, garbage cans), which boasts 21 campsites perched at 9,500-feet elevation with available running water. Get there at dawn if you want a site on a weekend!

Another option is **Sawmill Walk-In** (Saddlebag Rd., 1.6 miles from Hwy. 120, 877/444-6777, www.fs.fed.us/r5/inyo/recreation/campgrounds.shtml, $12, June–Oct.). This primitive, no-reservations, hike-in campground (no water) has an astonishing 9,800-foot altitude that will, after a day or two, prepare you for any high-altitude activity you want to engage in.

ACCOMMODATIONS
Inside the Park

All the lodges, hotels, and cabin-tent clusters in Yosemite are run by the same booking agency. Contact the Yosemite Park concessionaire (801/559-4884, www.yosemitepark.com) to make reservations. Coming to Yosemite in the summer high season? Make reservations early-6–9 months early, if you have a preference as to where you want to stay. If you wait until the week before your trip, you'll either find the park sold out or end up in a tent cabin at Curry when you wanted a suite at the Ahwahnee.

YOSEMITE VALLEY

Curry Village offers some of the oldest lodgings in the park. Locally called Camp Curry, this sprawling array of wood-sided and tent cabins was originally created in 1899 to provide affordable lodgings so that people of modest means could afford to visit and enjoy the wonders of Yosemite. At Curry Village, you can rent a hard-walled cabin or a tent cabin, with or without heat and with or without a private bath depending on your budget and your needs. The tent cabins ($95), the most affordable option, are small, fitting cot beds and a small dresser on the wood floor. Bear-proof lockers sit outside each tent cabin. Wood cabins ($179) have double beds (one or two) and electricity, but little else. The cabins with private baths are heated and boast daily maid services, but no TVs or phones. A few motel rooms and unique cabins have TVs and more amenities, but still no phones or significant distractions of the modern world. With its perfect location on the valley floor, a swimming pool in the summer and an ice skating rink in the winter, Camp Curry makes an inexpensive vacation at Yosemite a joyful reality.

Want to camp, but don't want to schlep all the gear into the park? Book a tent cabin at **Housekeeping Camp** ($76). Located on the banks of the Merced River, Housekeeping Camp has its own sandy river beach for playing and sunbathing. Cabins have cement walls, white canvas roofs, and a white canvas curtain that separates the bedroom from the covered patio that doubles as a dining room. Every cabin has a double bed plus two bunks (with room for two additional cots), a bear-proof food container, and an outdoor fire ring. You can bring your own linens, or rent a "bed pack" (no towels) for $2.50 per night. No maid service is provided, but you won't miss it as you sit outside watching the sun set over Yosemite Valley.

◀ **Yosemite Lodge at the Falls** ($150–250), situated near Yosemite Village on the Valley floor, has a location perfect for touring all over the park. The motel-style rooms are light and pretty, with polished wood furniture, bright-colored bed linens, and Native American design details. Lodge rooms with king beds offer romantic escapes for couples, complete with balconies overlooking the valley, while the standard rooms can accommodate singles, couples, or families. Enjoy the heated pool in the summertime and the free shuttle transportation up to the Badger Pass ski area in winter. The amphitheater at the middle of the lodge runs nature programs and movies all year. The lodge has a post office, ATM, and plenty of food options, and is central to the Yosemite shuttle system.

If you're looking for luxury amongst the trees and rocks, check in to the **(Ahwahnee Hotel** ($379–1,189). Built as a luxury hotel in the early 20th century, the Ahwahnee lives up to its reputation with soaring ceilings in the common rooms, a gorgeous stone facade, and striking stone fireplaces. Guest rooms, whether in the hotel or in the individual cottages, drip sumptuous appointments. The theme is Native American and you'll find intricate, multicolored geometric and zoomorphic designs on linens, furniture, and pillows. Rooms with king beds invite romance for couples, while those with two doubles are perfect for families.

WAWONA

Consider staying at the charming **Wawona Hotel** ($120–190) near the south entrance of the park. The black-and-white exterior of the hotel complex reminds onlookers of a 19th-century Mississippi riverboat. Indeed the hotel opened in 1879, and has been a Yosemite institution ever since. The interior matches the outside well, complete with Victorian wallpaper, antique furniture, and a noticeable lack of in-room TVs and telephones. The Wawona feels more like a huge European pension than an American motel, complete with shared bathrooms for the more economically minded traveler. (Rooms with private baths are also available.)

TIOGA PASS AND TUOLUMNE MEADOWS

In the high country, **Tuolumne Meadows Lodge** ($78, June 1–Sept. 16) offers rustic lodgings and good food in a gorgeous sub-alpine meadow setting. Expect no electricity, no private baths, and no other plush amenities. What you will find are small, charming wood-framed tent cabins that sleep up to four, central bath and hot shower facilities, and a dining room. The location is perfect for starting or finishing a backcountry trip through the high-elevation areas of the park.

Another rustic high-country accommodation, the **White Wolf Lodge** ($75–110, July–Sept.) sits back in the trees off Tioga Pass. Here you can rent either the standard wood-platform tent cabin with use of central bath and shower facilities, or a solid-wall cabin with a private bathroom, limited electricity, and daily maid service. All cabins and tent cabins at White Wolf include linens and towels, plus breakfast and dinner served family style in the dining room. You can order box lunches to take with you each day. Amenities are few, but breathtaking scenery is everywhere at White Wolf. Take a day hike to Hardens Lake, or a horseback ride through the backcountry. White Wolf works well for visitors who prefer a smaller crowd, since the lodge boasts only 28 cabins.

Outside the Park

If you seek a small inn or inexpensive motel for your visit to Yosemite, consider staying outside the park proper and driving in each day. A wealth of inns, lodges, and B&Bs cluster near both the west and south entrances to the park. If you prefer a standard chain motel, Oakhurst (south of Fish Camp on Highway 41) and Mariposa (to the west on Highway 140) have most of the usual suspects.

If you're planning an extended stay at Yosemite with friends or family, it might be more convenient and economical to rent a condo or house with a full kitchen, privacy, and the comforts of home. You can find these at the **Yosemite West Condominiums** (800/669-9300), rented through the Yosemite Four Seasons Vacation Rentals. Modular buildings can be divided into a number of separate units—or not, if you want to rent a large space for a big crowd. The studio and loft condos sleep 2–6 people and have full kitchen and access to all complex amenities. Luxury suites are actually one-bedroom apartments with full kitchens, pool tables, hot tubs, four-poster beds, and all sorts of other amenities. Two- and three-bedroom apartments sleep 6–12 people. And the full houses can fit up to 22 guests, so you can fit an entire family reunion or college ski party into one huge house!

MARIPOSA

You can't miss the **River Rock Inn and Deli Garden Café** (4993 7th St., Mariposa, 800/627-8493, www.riverrockncafe.com, $100–132) with its vivid orange-and-purple exterior in the heart of Mariposa. What was once a run-down 1940s motor lodge is now a quirky, fun motel with uniquely decorated rooms that make the most of modern Pottery Barn-esque wrought-iron and wood styling and the spaces the decorators had to work with. Never fear: The colors become softer as you step through the door of your reasonably priced guest room. Two suites provide enough space for families, while the other five rooms sleep couples in comfort. The River Rock is a 45-minute drive from the west entrance to Yosemite, and at the southern end of the long chain of Gold Country towns, making it a great base of operations for an outdoorsy, Western-style California vacation.

If you prefer cozy seclusion to large lodge-style hotels, stay at the **Highland House** (3125 Wild Dove Ln., 209/966-3737, www.highland housebandb.com, $127–165) outside Mariposa to the west of Yosemite. The house is set deep in the forest far from town, providing endless peace and quiet away from civilization. This tiny B&B has only three guest rooms, each uniquely decorated in soft colors and warm, inviting styles. All rooms have down comforters, sparkling clean bathtubs and showers, and TVs with DVD players.

Another lovely small B&B, **Poppy Hill Bed and Breakfast** (5218 Crystal Aire Dr., Mariposa, 800/587-6779, www.poppyhill .com, $137–165) sits 27 miles from the west

entrance to the park. The four airy guest rooms are done in bright white linens, white walls, lacy curtains, and antique furniture. No TVs mar the sounds of the expansive gardens surrounding the old-style farmhouse. But you can take a dip in the totally modern hot tub any time. A full gourmet breakfast served on your schedule puts the right start on a day spent exploring Yosemite or the Mariposa County area. This inn can be hard to find, especially at night. Double-check the directions on the website and consider using a GPS device if you have one.

SOUTH ENTRANCE

Near the south entrance to Yosemite on Highway 41, the **Narrow Gauge Inn** (48571 Hwy. 41, Fish Camp, 888/644-9050, www .narrowgaugeinn.com, $132–215) recalls the large lodges inside the park, in miniature. This charming 26-room mountain inn offers one- and two-bed guest rooms done in wood paneling, light colors, white linens, or vintage-style quilts. Each room has its own outdoor table and chairs to encourage relaxing outside with a drink on gorgeous summer days and evenings. The restaurant and common rooms feature antique oil lamps, stonework, and crackling fireplaces. Step outside your door and you're in the magnificent High Sierra pine forest. A few more steps takes you to the Yosemite Mountain Sugar Pine Railroad—the narrow-gauge steam train from which the inn takes its name.

For inexpensive lodge-style accommodations in Fish Camp, check in to the **White Chief Mountain Lodge** (east of Fish Camp, 559/683-5444, www.sierratel.com/whitechief mtnlodge, $112–118). The basic rooms feature light wood paneling, tribal-design textiles, and inoffensive accents and lighting. Small TVs offer in-room entertainment, but the woods outside your door invite you outside to enjoy all that the rich Sierras have to offer. The lodge has its own restaurant and offers packages that show off the best of the Wild West heritage of the area.

The **ⓒ Tenaya Lodge** (1122 Hwy. 41, 888/514-2167, www.tenayalodge.com, $345–400) sits just outside the south entrance of Yosemite, offering plush lodge-style accommodations at a more reasonable price than comparable rooms inside the park. Guest rooms are styled with rich fabrics in bright oranges and other bold, eye-catching colors. The modern wall art evokes the woods and vistas of Yosemite. The beds are comfortable, the baths attractive, and the views forest-filled. Tenaya Lodge focuses on guest care, offering a three-meal-per-day dining room, a full-service spa that specializes in facials, and daily (and nightly) nature walks complete with costumed guides. Check at the desk for events occurring during your stay.

If you plan to do some fishing during your trip to the Yosemite area, the **Pines Resort** (54432 Road 432, Bass Lake, 800/350-7463, www.basslake.com, $245–375) is perfectly located for your angling convenience right on the shores of Bass Lake; bring your boat! You can choose a suite (a split-level king room with dark floors, light walls, fireplaces, and mountain-y touches, some with spa tub) or rent a chalet (a two-story cabin in a rustic mountain style that sleeps up to six, with a full kitchen and outdoor mini-barbecue). The Pines is a full-service resort, with a restaurant (Ducey's), bar and grill, market, all-weather tennis courts, summer swimming pool, year-round hot tubs, spa services, shaded lakefront chaise lounges, and wedding and meeting facilities.

FOOD
Yosemite Valley
There's plenty to eat inside Yosemite National Park, but if you leave the valley floor you'll need to plan for meals. In Yosemite Valley, you have a number of dining options. The 𝄆 **Ahwahnee Dining Room** (Ahwanee Hotel, 209/372-1489, daily 7–10:30 A.M., 11:30 A.M.–3 P.M., 5:30–9 P.M., $20–35) enjoys a reputation for fine cuisine that stretches back to the 1920s. The grand dining room features expansive ceilings, wrought-iron chandeliers, and a stellar valley view. The restaurant serves three meals daily, with dinner the highlight. The California cuisine of an Ahwahnee dinner mirrors that of top-tier

San Francisco restaurants (with a price tag to match). Reservations are recommended for all meals, though it's possible to walk in for breakfast and lunch. Dinner requires more formal attire.

At the other side of the valley, you can enjoy a spectacular view of Yosemite Falls at the **Mountain Room Restaurant** (Yosemite Lodge, 209/372-1274, 5:30–9 P.M., year-round, $15–20), part of Yosemite Lodge at the Falls. The glass atrium lets every guest at every table take in the view. The menu runs to American food, and drinks are available from the full bar. A casual bar menu is available at the **Mountain Room Lounge** (noon–11 P.M., inexpensive) immediately across from the restaurant.

For more casual food options, head to Yosemite Village for **Degnan's Loft** (spring–fall) for hot pizza, soups, and appetizers, and **Degnan's Delicatessen** (daily 7 A.M.–5 P.M.) for an array of sandwiches, salads, and other take-away munchies.

Curry Village is where to go for (relatively) cheap, fast food. Hiking clothes are expected! The **Curry Pavilion** (daily Mar.–Nov., $10–15) hosts an all-you-can-eat buffet for breakfast and dinner. There is also a deck, with a full-service bar, a taqueria, pizza, ice cream, and coffee.

Wawona
If you can, plan a meal at the south end of the park in the 𝄆 **Wawona Dining Room** (Wawona Hotel, 209/375-1425, moderate-expensive). This lesser-known gem of a restaurant serves upscale homey California cuisine for reasonable prices to all comers. No reservations are accepted-all seating is first come, first served. The large, white painted dining room is family friendly, and the menu offers options for vegetarians as well as devout carnivores. Because you'll probably have to wait for a table on high-season weekends, a large common area invites seating, drinks, and live piano music by local legend Tom Bopp. The Wawona Dining room serves breakfast, lunch, dinner, Sunday brunch, and a weekly outdoor barbecue on Saturday evenings during the summer.

INFORMATION AND SERVICES

With the high density of visitors to Yosemite Valley, the Park Service has thoughtfully put in place any number of guest services, going above and beyond most other venues in the national park system.

Media and Communications

The print guide you absolutely need as you tour Yosemite is the monthly or biweekly published *Yosemite Guide*. This paper provides general information about the park's places and services. More importantly, it's got a detailed schedule of all classes, events, programs, and so on for the coming two weeks (in summer) or month (spring, fall, winter). You'll receive your copy when you enter the park at one of the entrance stations.

Limited Internet access is available in a few spots in Yosemite Valley. The only Wi-Fi to which you can connect your own laptop sits inside Yosemite Lodge. Kiosks are available in Degnan's Café and the Mariposa County Library—the library is free, while the café kiosks are available for a fee.

Banks and Post Office

A number of ATMs are available throughout Yosemite, making it easy to extract cash with which to pay for souvenirs, food, and more souvenirs. You'll find at least one ATM in Yosemite Village at the Art and Education Center, one in Yosemite Lodge, one at Curry Village, and one at Wawona.

Several post offices provide mailing services in Yosemite. Look for a post office in Yosemite Village (Mon.–Fri. 8:30 A.M.–5 P.M., Sat. 10 A.M.–noon), inside Yosemite Lodge (12:30 P.M.–2:45 P.M.), and in El Portal (Mon.–Fri. 8:30 A.M.–5 P.M., closed 12:30–1:30 P.M.).

Gas and Automotive Services

No gas is available anywhere inside Yosemite Valley. The nearest gas station sits at **El Portal** (24 hours, pay-at-pump). Limited seasonal gas is also available up at **Tuolumne Meadows** just past the visitors center on Tioga Pass. There's

also gas in Mariposa at a **Pioneer Gas/Texaco** (5177 Hwy. 140, Mariposa) that also has a mini-mart.

If your car breaks down, you can take it to the **Village Garage** (Yosemite Village off Northside Dr., 209/372-8320, daily 8 A.M.–5 P.M., towing 24 hours). Because it's the only game in town, expect to pay a high premium for towing and repairs here.

Laundry and Groceries

There are laundry facilities available to all comers at the Housekeeping Camp inside the Curry Village complex (Apr.–Oct. daily 8 A.M.–10 P.M.). Limited-stock, expensive grocery stores sit in Curry Village at the **Gift and Grocery** (daily 8 A.M.–10 P.M.) and in the **Housekeeping Camp Grocery** (Apr.–Oct. daily 8 A.M.–6 P.M.). For a better selection of goods and much lower prices, you're better off shopping outside the park. You can check out **Bear Valley Grocery** (7313 Hwy. 49 at Road J-16, North Mariposa, 209/377-8424) or the **Pioneer Market** (5034 Coakley Cir. 104, Mariposa, 209/742-5097).

Medical Services

Yosemite maintains its own **medical center** (209/372-4637) in Yosemite Village at the floor of the valley. It's got a 24-hour emergency room, 8 A.M.–7 P.M. walk-in urgent care center, and a domestic violence crisis center. **Dental services** (209/372-4200) are also available adjacent to the medical center.

GETTING THERE AND AROUND

Car

Almost all the most popular sights, attractions, and trailheads are accessible by road. The Arch Rock entrance to the west of the park is accessed via Highway 140. The Big Oak Flat entrance is accessed via Highway 120 from the north; it's about another 45 minutes to Yosemite Valley from there. Both entrances provide access to Tioga Pass Road via Big Oak Flat Road. Tioga Pass reconnects to Highway 120 at the Tioga Pass Entrance on the east side of the park. Tioga Pass closes in November or December each year and reopens in the spring, usually in May. Yosemite's south entrance is accessed via Highway 41 from Oakhurst. Wawona Road leads from the south entrance, through Wawona, and into Yosemite Valley. Glacier Point Road is reached from Wawona Road and allows access to the Badger Pass Ski Area. In winter, chains can be required on any road at any time, so check the website (www .nps.gov/yose) for current road conditions.

Train and Bus
Amtrak (www.amtrak.com) services Merced, an hour away from the park. From Merced,

bus service is available on **VIA Bus Lines** (209/384-1314, www.via-adventures.com); call for reservations. The **YARTS** (877/989-2787, www.yarts.com) bus system services Mariposa and Merced.

Shuttle Services
Yosemite runs an extensive network of shuttles in different areas of the park. One of the most-used travels through **Yosemite Valley** (daily 7 A.M.–10 P.M., year-round, free). The **El Capitan Shuttle** (mid-June to early Sept, daily 9 A.M.–6 P.M., free) also runs around certain parts of Yosemite Valley during the summer season.

YOSEMITE

Mono Lake

Mono Lake itself, eerie in its stillness, is the main attraction to this remote area of the Eastern Sierra. It might be enough just to sit on the edge of the lake and enjoy its beauty. Or in the summertime, enjoy an oddly buoyant swim in the heavily salted waters or even a boat trip out to some of the silent uninhabited islands. But if you'd prefer more adventure or exploration, a number of options await.

SIGHTS
Mono Lake Scenic Visitor Area
The large building that houses the visitors center for Mono Lake is easy to see from Highway 395, and only a short drive from the highway. The Mono Lake Scenic Visitor Area (Hwy. 395 just north of Lee Vining on the lake side, 760/647-3044, www.monolake.org) is the perfect place to start learning about Mono Lake, to start walking around the lake, and to start taking photos of the unique landscape. The interpretive museum inside the distinctive building describes in detail the natural and human history of the lake, from the way tufa towers form to the endless litigations surrounding the lake like papery ghosts. Walk out the back of the building to take your first closer look at the grassy meadows leading down to the shores of

the lake. Talk to the staff to learn about the best hikes and spots to visit, swim, launch a boat, or cross-country ski.

At the visitors center, you can also learn about various guided walks and hikes at Mono Lake, which can give you and your family a more in-depth look at the wonders of the area.

◖ Mono Lake Tufa Preserve
The tufa formations—freestanding calcite towers, knobs, and spires—make Mono Lake unique. The Mono Lake Tufa Preserve (Hwy. 395 just north of Lee Vining, 760/647-6331, www.parks.ca.gov, park hours and fees vary) educates and amazes visitors. A one-mile interpretive trail winds through the South Tufa area (southeast of the visitors center, adjacent to Navy Beach, fee for parking) describing the natural history of the area and formations. With some of the most spectacular tufa towers at the lake, this is a good place for newcomers to the lake to start exploring. A boardwalk trail (adjacent to the County Park) provides access to the North Tufa area. Enjoy wandering through the different chunks of this preserve, which appear along the shore all the way around the lake. Be aware that much of the land adjacent to the State Reserve areas is

YOSEMITE

© LIZ HAMILL SCOTT

Mono Lake

restricted—please care for this delicate terrain and do not venture out of the designated visiting areas. Also, to access some of the reserve at the east side of the lake, you'll need either a boat or a four-wheel-drive vehicle since no paved roads circle Mono Lake.

Old Marina

Years ago, the stillness of Mono Lake was broken by quite a bit of boat traffic. (Private boats and small tour operators still ply the salt-alkaline lake in the summer, but no major commercial water traffic remains.) The hub of this activity was the Marina a few miles north of Lee Vining. Today, the Old Marina is merely spot off Highway 395 north of town at which you can take a short stroll down to the edge of the lake. From here you can see the two large islands in the middle of the lake, several nearby tufa towers, and much of the lakescape itself. The boardwalk trail here is wheelchair accessible.

◖ Bodie State Historic Park

Bodie State Historic Park (end of Dirt Road 270, 760/647-6445, www.parks.ca.gov, daily 9 A.M.–4 P.M., weekends Memorial Day–Labor Day 8 A.M.–7 P.M., fees) is the largest ghost town in California. Preservation in a state of "arrested decay" means you get to see each home and public building just as it was when it was abandoned. What you see is not a bright shiny museum display. You get the real thing: dust and broken furniture and trash and all. It would take all day to explore the town on foot, and even then you might not see it all. Tours let you into the abandoned mine and gain a deeper understanding of the history of the buildings and the town.

The town of Bodie sprang up around a gold mine in 1877. It was never a nice place to live—at all. The weather, the work, the scenery, the people…all tended toward the bleak or the foul. By the 1940s, mining had dried up and the remote location and lack of other viable industry in the area led to Bodie's desertion.

A visit to Bodie takes you back in time, to a harsh lifestyle in an extreme climate at least 10 miles from the middle of nowhere. As you stroll down the dusty streets, imagine the whole

YOSEMITE

© LIZ HAMILL SCOTT

Bodie's historic ghost town

town blanketed in 20 feet of snow in winter, then scorched by 100° temperatures in summer with precious few trees anywhere around to provide shade or a hint of green in the unending brown landscape. In a town filled with rough men working the mines hundreds of miles from civilization, you'd hear the funeral bells tolling at the church every single day—the only real honor bestowed upon the many murder victims Bodie saw in its lifetime. Few families came to Bodie (though a few hardy souls did raise children in the hellish town), and most of Bodie's women earned their keep the old-fashioned way. The prostitution business boomed just as mining did.

Today, most of the brothels, stores, and homes of Bodie aren't habitable or even tourable. Structures have been loosely propped up, but it's dangerous to go inside so doors remain locked. However, you can peer in the windows at the remains of the lives lived in Bodie, and get a sense of hard-core California history.

Panum Crater

Even if you aren't a professional geologist, the volcanic Panum Crater (Hwy. 120 three miles east of Hwy. 395, short dirt road to parking) is worth visiting. This rhyolite crater is only 600 years old—a mere baby in geologic time! Take a hike around the rim of the crater, and if you're feeling up to it climb up the trail to the top of the plug dome. Be sure to slather on the sunscreen since no trees shade these trails and it gets quite warm in the summertime. Check the Mono Lake website for occasional guided tours of Panum Crater.

SPORTS AND RECREATION
Hiking

Mono Lake is not like Yosemite, with clusters of trailheads everywhere. But the hiking near Mono Lake affords things the big park can't: unusual scenery and plenty of solitude.

For an easy walk along the lake, go to the **Mono Lake County Park** (Cemetery Road, trailhead 0.5 mile east of the road) and take the boardwalk trail 0.25 mile down to the tufa formations. Wandering through the tufa will add distance to your walk, but the ground is flat and the scenery is diverting.

A lovely interpretive trail, the **Tioga Tarns Nature Walk** (Hwy. 120, east of Tioga Lake) spans about half a mile and includes numerous signs describing the flora, fauna, and geology of the area. Another nature walk is the **Lee Vining Creek Nature Trail** (Best Western Motel, Hwy. 395, moderate). This trail follows the Lee Vining Creek, currently under restoration, returning to its natural state after decades of diversion. The total walk is about three miles and takes an hour or two, depending on how much time you spend admiring the revitalized ecosystem.

You can find any number of moderate hikes in the Mono Lake vicinity. The **Lundy Canyon** (Lundy Lake Rd., dirt lot at trailhead) trail can be anywhere from 0.5 mile of fairly easy walking through Lundy Canyon to a strenuous seven-mile hike all the way out to Saddlebag Lake. Another variable hike takes you out to **Parker Lake** or **Parker Bench** (Parker Lake dirt road off Hwy. 158). This hike is a minimum of four miles round-trip, and can be 10 miles if you take the left trail fork out to Silver Lake and Parker Bench. Steep sections make this trek a bit more demanding, but you'll love the scenic, shady trail that follows Parker Creek out the shorter right fork to Parker Lake. If one or two lakes just aren't enough, take the longish but only moderately tough **20-Lakes Basin Trail** (Saddlebag Lake Rd., parking across from the dam). This six-mile loop trail will take you out past many of the lakes for which the basin is named. Or if you're tired of all that water, take a moderate two-mile round-trip pilgrimage out to the remains of the mining town at **Bennettville** (Junction Campground Rd.). You can prowl around the abandoned mine, but be careful! Old mine shafts and abandoned buildings can be extremely hazardous.

Boating and Swimming

Go ahead and bring your powered boat, canoe, kayak, or even sailboat out to Mono Lake. A parking lot near the water at Navy Beach makes launching lightweight kayaks and canoes reasonable. If you're putting a heavier boat into the lake, check with the staff at the Mono

Lake Scenic Visitor Area for directions to the launch ramp near Lee Vining Creek. Also note that no matter what kind of craft you're piloting, you cannot beach on the islands April 1–August 1.

During the summer, the **Mono Lake Boat Tours** (meet at Tioga Lodge, 760/647-6446, www.monolakeboattours.com, adults $70, children/seniors $65) offers water tours of the lake. You'll get an utterly experienced guide who's been traveling on the lake for ages.

Swimming is allowed (and even encouraged!) in Mono Lake in the summertime. You can swim from your boat, or from any of the unrestricted shore access points. You'll find yourself floating easily since the salt content of Mono Lake is several times that of the ocean. But take care and watch your kids closely, because no lifeguards patrol the area and you're swimming at your own risk.

ACCOMMODATIONS

You won't see any five-star resorts in the Mono Lake area. The outdoorsy and naturalist types who favor this region find the no-frills motels, lodges, and campgrounds perfectly suitable for their activities.

No camping is allowed on the shores of Mono Lake. Visitors can rent affordable rooms at several motels and lodgings in the lakeside town of Lee Vining.

Under $100

Rent clean, comfortable, affordable lodgings at **Murphey's Motel** (51493 Hwy. 395, 800/334-6316, www.murpheyyosemite.com, $58–118). Open all year, this motel provides double-queen and king beds with cozy comforters, TVs, tables and chairs, and everything you need for a pleasant stay in the Mono Lake area. Its central location in downtown Lee Vining makes dining, shopping, and trips to the visitors center and Chamber of Commerce convenient. If you plan to make a winter trip to Mono Lake, call to find out about Murphey's discounts for ice climbers.

The **El Mono Motel** (Hwy. 395 at Third St., 707/647-6310, www.elmonomotel.com) offers comfy beds and clean rooms at very reasonable prices. Enjoy the location in downtown Lee Vining, and start each morning with a fresh cup of organic coffee from the attached Latte Da Coffee Café.

$100-150

Just across the freeway from Mono Lake, the **Tioga Lodge** (54411 Hwy. 395, 760/647-6423, www.tiogalodgeatmonolake.com, $133–165) boasts an astonishing view of the lake from every room. This older lodge at the center of the town of Lee Vining offers the perfect location for sightseeing and outdoor adventures, plus heated rooms and comfortable beds. Guest rooms are simple and uniquely decorated, each with tile floors and a full private bath. Some rooms sleep two, others up to four in two-bedroom suites are perfect for families. Don't expect to find TVs or other digital entertainment here—in keeping with the area, you're encouraged to get outside to find your entertainment. Friendly, helpful staff can assist with everything from room amenities to local restaurants to great places to visit in the area.

At the intersection of Highways 120 and 395, stay at the comfortable and affordable **Lake View Lodge** (51285 Hwy. 395, Lee Vining, 800/990-6614, www.lakeviewlodgeyosemite .com, $138–220). This aptly named lodge offers both motel rooms and cottages. The cottages can be rented in the summer only, but the motel rooms are available all year. Whether you choose a basic room for only a night or two, or a larger accommodation with a kitchen for more than three days, you'll enjoy the simple country-style decor, the outdoor porches, and the views of Mono Lake. All rooms have TVs with cable and Internet access is available. Pick up supplies at the local market for a picnic on the lawns of the lodge, get yourself a latte at the on-site coffee shop, or enjoy one of the nearby restaurants in Lee Vining.

Named for its location only 14 miles from Yosemite's east gate, the **Yosemite Gateway Motel** (51340 Hwy. 395, 760/647-6467, www .yosemitegatewaymotel.com, $143–154) offers a charming rustic experience for travelers to

the Eastern Sierra. The red and white exterior echoes in the decoration of the guest rooms, supplemented with gleaming wood, new furnishings, and clean bathrooms. A TV and the Internet provide entertainment on chilly evenings, and of course the wonderful outdoor recreation opportunities of the Eastern Sierra are just outside the door. Enjoy your crystalline views of Mono Lake, or take a day trip to Bodie or indulge in some skiing at Mammoth Lakes or June Lake. Room rates are deeply discounted in the wintertime, making the trek worth the effort.

FOOD

Your food choices around the Mono Lake area might feel limited if you're coming right from Los Angeles or San Francisco. Nor will you see many of the standard fast-food chains. However, the town of Lee Vining offers a number of respectable eateries, plus adequate groceries for campers and picnickers.

Restaurants

The **C Hammond Station Restaurant** (54411 Hwy. 395, 760/647-6423, www.tioga lodgeatmonolake.com, $8–20) at the Tioga Lodge serves breakfast, lunch, and dinner. Choose from the health-conscious vegetarian/ spa menu (which includes a number of vegan items), the American menu, or the Mexican menu. If you're planning a day out hiking or sightseeing, get a sandwich or a wrap from the "Picnic to Go" menu before you leave for the day. If you're dining in, expect a small dining room with attractive wrought-iron furniture, plus an ample outdoor seating area perfect for warm summer evenings. The food is tasty, and the service makes you feel like a local even if you're from far out of town.

A classic American diner, **Nicely's** (Hwy. 395 and Fourth St., 760/647-6477, summer daily, winter Thurs.–Mon.) offers friendly service and familiar food to locals and visitors alike. Inside, you'll find a large dining room with half-circle booths upholstered in vinyl and many other diner-style touches. The cuisine runs to sandwiches, burgers, and egg breakfasts. Portions are generous, though the service can be slow when the restaurant is busy. Nicely's opens early and stays open through dinnertime, making it a viable dining option year-round—something of a rarity in the area. This is a good place to take the kids for burgers and fries.

If you're looking for a Wild West atmosphere and a good spicy sauce, have dinner at **Bodie Mike's Barbecue** (51357 Hwy. 395, 760/647-6432, summer only). Use your fingers to dig into barbecued ribs, chicken, beef, brisket, and more. A rustic atmosphere with rough-looking wood, red-check tablecloths, and local patrons in cowboy boots completes your dining experience. Just don't expect the fastest service in the world. At the back of the dining room you'll find the entrance to a small, dark bar populated by local characters. The good news is that the bar serves drinks to the dining room.

Bakeries and Delis

For a unique deli dining experience, stop in for a tank of gas and a meal at the **Whoa Nelly Deli** (Hwys. 120 and 395, 760/647-1088, Apr.–Nov. daily 7 A.M.–9 P.M.) at the Tioga Gas Mart. You'll get a full, hearty meal from the daily offering, be it ribs or meatloaf or something else. Sandwiches and drinks are also available for lighter noshing. Expect to wait in line for a while at the counter to order, then to wait to pick up your own food. Seating, both indoor and out, tends to be limited during high-traffic mealtimes, and heaven help you if you get there in conjunction with a tour bus. But still, compared to the so-called food offered in most gas station mini-marts, you'll find some great stuff at Whoa Nelly, and the rowdy cooks provide something of a show for the dinner crowd.

A great place to get a to-go breakfast or lunch is the **Mono Market** (51303 Hwy. 395, 760/647-1010, daily summer 7 A.M.–10 P.M., winter 7:30 A.M.–8 P.M.). An array of breakfast sandwiches and pastries are made fresh daily, as are the sandwiches, wraps, and messier napkin-requisite entrées you can carry out for lunch or dinner.

Coffee

Even dedicated outdoor lovers often need their morning coffee to get going on a long day of hiking, climbing, or kayaking. To that end, you'll find some charming independent coffee shops in Lee Vining. The **Latte Da Coffee Café** (1 Third St. at Hwy. 395, 760/647-6310) uses organic coffee and local fresh water to create delicious coffee drinks at the El Mono Motel. Over at the Lakeview Lodge, grab a cup of joe at the **Garden House Coffee Shop** (5185 Hwy. 395, Lee Vining, 760/647-6543, www.lakeviewlodgeyosemite .com, daily 7–11 A.M.). In addition to your favorite espresso drinks, you can pick up a smoothie or a fresh pastry to get a great start to your day.

Markets

In addition to prepared food, the **Mono Market** (51303 Hwy. 395, 760/647-1010, daily summer 7 A.M.–10 P.M., winter 7:30 A.M.–8 P.M.) offers standard grocery staples and a liquor section.

INFORMATION AND SERVICES

The **Mono Basic Scenic Area Visitors Center** (Hwy. 395 just north of Lee Vining on the lake side, 760/647-3044, www.mono lake.org) includes an interpretive museum that describes the creation of Mono Lake and the strange tufa formations that define it. This visitors center also has a ranger station with knowledgeable staff who can help you with the best seasonal trail and lake advice.

You can use mail services at the **Lee Vining Post Office** (121 Lee Vining Ave., 760/647-6371). Lee Vining boasts few ATMs, but you can find one or two places to grab cash (which you'll need, because many places out here don't take plastic). Try the gas stations, the visitors center, and the local grocery/ mini mart.

The nearest medical facilities to Mono Lake lie to the south in Mammoth Lakes at **Mammoth Hospital** (85 Sierra Park Rd., 760/934-3311, mammothhospital.com), which has a 24-hour emergency room.

GETTING THERE AND AROUND

Getting to Mono Lake from San Francisco or Los Angeles or anyplace else in California with a major airport is, frankly, a royal pain in the you-know-what. Mono Lake sits almost on top of the junction between Tioga Pass Road and Highway 395.

Tioga Pass is closed between November and May each year—check with the Yosemite website to get the exact closing and opening dates for this road. Highway 395 remains open all year (though storms can close it briefly until it is plowed). But accessing Highway 395 from the north or south involves long drives. You might want to consider flying in to Las Vegas or even Reno to get to Mono Lake as directly as possible.

Very little public transit of any kind gets as far as Lee Vining and Mono Lake. To adequately explore this region, you need a vehicle of your own. On the bright side, parking in Lee Vining and around the lake tends to be both easy and free. Few enough others are vying for spots that you won't spend much time looking for your own space.

Mammoth Lakes

SIGHTS
◖ Devil's Postpile National Monument

Compared to the area's other national parks, Devil's Postpile National Monument (Minaret Vista Rd., 760/924-5500, www.nps.gov/depo, summer only, daily 9 A.M.–5 P.M., adults $7, children $4) seems small. But what you'll see is unique to the region. The gem and namesake of the park is the strange, unbelievably natural rock formation called the Devil's Postpile. It's hard to imagine that the near perfect straight-sided hexagonal posts are a natural phenomenon, created by volcanic heat and pressure. You

PHOTO COURTESY OF THE MAMMOTH LAKES VISITORS BUREAU

Devil's Postpile National Monument

PHOTO COURTESY OF THE MAMMOTH LAKES VISITORS BUREAU

June Lake

have to see it to believe it. Less heavily traveled than many other parks, you'll also find hikes to serene meadows, unspoiled streams, and perhaps even see the occasional deer grazing in the woods. If you're lucky, you might get a trail all to yourself for a while.

Also part of the Monument is the crystalline, beautiful **Rainbow Falls.** The thick sheet of water cascades 101 feet down to a pool, throwing up stunning rainbows of mist. For the best rainbows at the falls, hike the three miles (round-trip) from Red Meadow toward the middle of the day when the sun is high in the sky.

In an effort to limit traffic on the narrow road down into the Monument, a shuttle runs from a spot near the gate down to the trailheads. Ample parking is available, and the shuttles run every half-hour, letting you jump on and off as you wish to hike, have a picnic, or just enjoy the fresh smell of the clean woods.

June Lake Loop

This 15-mile scenic drive takes you out away

from the high-traffic tourist areas of the Eastern Sierra. Along the June Lake Loop (Hwy. 158, accessible from Hwy. 395 south of Lee Vining), you get the full-fledged alpine experience. Naturally, the loop's namesake June Lake has the most recreation along its shores. You can take a hike, go fish, or even plan to stay overnight at one of the campgrounds. Next you'll come to Gull Lake, then Silver Lake—two other popular boating and angling waterways. As you drive north on the loop, stop at least once to admire Reversed Peak, a 9,500-foot Sierra peak. Finally, you'll come to Grant Lake. No resorts cluster here, nor will you find any major trailheads. What you will find are a boat launch and some spectacular alpine trout fishing. Finally, take a break at the Mono Craters Monument before heading back out to Highway 395 toward Lee Vining or Mammoth Mountain.

Mammoth Ski Museum

One of the jewels of Mammoth Lakes, the

Mammoth Ski Museum (100 College Pkwy., 760/934-6592, www.mammothskimuseum .org, Thurs.–Mon. 11 A.M.–6 P.M., $5 adults, $3 children) houses the largest collection of skiing-related art in the world. Here you'll find artistic homage in every medium the human fascination with sliding down snowy mountains on boards. The museum features the permanent Beekley Collection of sculptures, original paintings, vintage posters, and much more. Short films run daily, and each Friday night at 6 P.M. a full-length ski-themed feature film runs in the Pioneer Theater. Visit the gift shop to purchase your own reproduction vintage ski posters, books, and DVDs.

Old Mammoth Road

Like most of the Eastern Sierra region, Mammoth Lakes became of interest to miners in the 19th century after the Gold Rush began—miners got out this far in 1877. Along Old Mammoth Road (Hwy. 203 to Main St., turn left on Old Mammoth Rd.) you'll find a number of old mining sites. At the height of the short-lived boom in Mammoth, about 20 different small mines operated in the area.

You'll see the grave of a miner's wife, a stamp mill's flywheel, and then the meager remains of Mammoth City and the nearby Mammoth Mine. The highlight of this summertime half-day trip is the ruins of the Mammoth Consolidated Mine. You can still see some bits of the camp, housing buildings, the assay office, mill, and mining equipment. The mine shaft also appears, but *do not attempt to get around the security features to head down there!* Old mine shafts are unbelievably dangerous, and should not be explored by anyone for any reason.

SKIING AND SNOWBOARDING

Mammoth Lakes exists primarily to support the winter sports industry. The downhill skiing, snowboarding, and cross-country skiing here attract sports enthusiasts of all ages and ability levels. If you don't own your own equipment, you can rent skis, snowboards, and all the necessary accessories at a dozen different shops in town.

Mammoth Mountain

The premier downhill ski and snowboard mountain is, aptly, Mammoth Mountain (800 Mammoth, ski school 760/934-0685,

YOSEMITE

PHOTO COURTESY OF THE MAMMOTH LAKES VISITORS BUREAU

A bronze mammoth by sculptor Douglas Van Howd stands at the main lodge of Mammoth Mountain.

snow report 760/934-6166, http://mammoth mountain.com, lift hours daily 8:30 A.M.–4 P.M.). Whether you're completely new to downhill thrills or a seasoned expert looking for different terrain, you'll find something great on Mammoth Mountain. More than two-dozen lifts (including three gondolas and nine express quads) take you up the 3,100-foot vertical rise to the 3,500 acres of skiable and boardable terrain (plus three pipes). If you're staying at Eagle Lodge, Canyone Lodge, Mammoth Mountain Inn, or the Village, enjoy the convenience of a lift or gondola right outside your lodging door. All these, plus the Mill Café and McCoy Station halfway up the mountain offer hot drinks, tasty snacks, and a welcome spot to rest during a long day of skiing.

The easiest runs on the mountain cluster mostly around the ski school and the lower area around the Mammoth Mountain Inn, and are recognizable for their cute nursery-school names. If you're an intermediate skier, runs swing down all over the mountain just for you. Build your confidence by taking the Panorama Gondola up to Panorama Lookout at the top of the mountain, then skiing all the way down the east side of the mountain along the intermediate-to-a-bit-harder ridge runs. Advanced skiers favor the bowls and chutes at the front of the mountain, and hardcore experts go west from Panorama Lookout to chase the dragon.

June Mountain

South of Mammoth Lakes, the June Mountain ski area (3819 Hwy. 158, 760/648-7733, www .junemountain.com, lifts 7:30 A.M.–4 P.M., adults $60, youth $54, teens $45, children/ seniors $30) offers more than 2,500 feet of vertical rise on more than 500 skiable acres. This resort caters to beginners and intermediate skiers, and 80 percent of its trails are green or blue. Beginners can even take a lift up to the top of Rainbow Summit and enjoy a long run down the Silverado Trail. However, a number of black and double-black diamond slopes make a trip to June Mountain fun for more advanced skiers and boarders as well. Thrill-

seeking experts and adventurous intermediates head up to the top of June Mountain Summit then plummet down the bowl (hardcore double-blacks) or slide along the ridgeline (blue). Be sure to check your trail map before going up this way unless you're very sure of your abilities. For a cup of hot coffee or chocolate, stop at the June Meadows Chalet at the center of the ski area.

Sierra Meadows

Go just south of Mammoth Lakes to get to the Sierra Meadows (1 Sherwin Creek Rd., 760/934-6161), a cross-country ski area with 20 miles of groomed trails. Sierra Meadows is perfect for beginner cross-country skiers, offering ski rentals, lessons, and beginner terrain that's easy on the legs—and the mind!

Tamarack Cross Country Ski Center

Here's your chance to explore the snow-covered Mammoth Lakes Basin in wintertime. Tamarack (Lake Mary Rd. at Twin Lakes, 760/934-2442, www.tamaracklodge.com/ xcountry, Nov.–Apr. daily 8:30 A.M.–5 P.M.) offers almost 25 miles of groomed cross-country ski tracks geared for all ability levels. For non-skiers, you'll also fined groomed skating lanes, plus a restaurant in which to enjoy a nice cup of hot chocolate and good book while your more outdoorsy friends and family ply the terrain.

Blue Diamond Trails

This trail system starts just behind the Mammoth Lakes visitors center and winds through 25 miles of Mammoth forest land, predictably marked by signs bearing a blue diamond on the trees. Blue Diamond Trails (www.mammothdirect.com) are not groomed, so be prepared to deal with varying snow conditions and unbroken trails. However, there's plenty of relatively flat land here for beginners. The Shady Rest Trails (off Hwy. 203 just before visitors center) might sound like a cemetery, but in fact they are beginners' loops with plenty of shade trees that keep skiers cool through their exertions. The Knolls Trail (Mammoth Scenic

Loop 1.5 miles north of Hwy. 203) makes a good intermediate day out, passing through lovely stands of Jeffery and Lodgepole pines. If you're up for a serious expert trek, try the Earthquake Fault Trail (Minaret Rd., unlabeled parking lot before Mammoth Mountain Main Lodge). Expect steep descents, unused areas, and narrow paths along this approximately 12-hour trail. Beginners beware of the deceptively named Scenic Loop Trail (Mammoth Scenic Loop across from Knolls Trail); this reasonably short trail (about four miles) includes steep descents and some more difficult terrain.

SPORTS AND RECREATION

Even beyond skiing and snowboarding, outdoor activities are a central focus of life in and around Mammoth. People come here from all over to hike, bike, fish, and more.

Hiking

Not surprisingly, hikers find plenty of worthwhile terrain around Mammoth Lakes for both short day walks and longer backpacking adventures. The **Mammoth Mountain Bike Park** (1 Minaret Rd., 800/626-6684, www.mammoth mountain.com/bike_ride, daily 8 A.M.–6 P.M.) includes a number of great hiking trails. For an all-downhill walk, take the Scenic Gondola up to the Panorama Overlook and hike back down to town. Just be sure to get a trail map at the **Mammoth Adventure Center** (1 Minaret Rd., 800/626-6684, www.mammothmountain .com/bike_ride/index.cfm, June.–Sept. daily 8 A.M.–6 P.M.) so you can keep to the hiking areas and avoid being flattened by fast-moving mountain bikers.

Mammoth Lakes also acts as a jumping-off point for adventurers who want to take on the **John Muir Wilderness** (south of Mammoth Lakes to Mount Whitney, http://sierrane-vadawild.gov/wild/john-muir). John Muir pioneered sustainability and preservation in the Sierra Nevadas, and more than half a million acres in the area have been designated national wilderness areas in his honor. Day hikers are welcome and there's plenty to see. Check with the Inyo National Forest service

and the Sierra National Forest for trail maps of the area. But the main attractions to the John Muir (as it's called locally) are the John Muir and Pacific Crest Trails—both hundreds of miles long and sought by backpacking enthusiasts around the world. If you're planning an overnight camping trip in the area—on your own or with a tour or guide company—you must obtain a permit. It's also a good idea to plan backcountry trips well in advance, to make sure you've got everything you need and all the proper permits and information ready at hand.

Biking

Come summertime and melting snow, Mammoth Mountain transforms from a ski resort to a mountain bike mecca. The **Mammoth Mountain Bike Park** (1 Minaret Rd., 800/626-6684, www.mammoth mountain.com/bike_ride, daily 8 A.M.–6 P.M., $10–39) spans much of the same terrain as the ski areas, with almost 90 miles of trails that suit all biking ability levels. The park headquarters sits at the **Mammoth Adventure Center** (1 Minaret Rd., 800/626-6684, www .mammothmountain.com/bike_ride/index. cfm, June.–Sept. daily 8 A.M.–6 P.M.). You can take your bike onto the Scenic Gondola and ride all the way to the top of Mammoth Mountain, then ride all the way down (3,000-plus feet) on the single tracks. Be sure to pick the trails that best suit your fitness and experience level! Several other major lodges offer rider services, including the Village at Mammoth, Juniper Springs, the Panorama Lookout, and Outpost 14. If you value scenery as much as extreme adventure, pack your camera and plan to rest at the various scenic overlooks throughout the trail system.

If you need to rent a bike (and to buy park tickets), go to the Adventure Center or to the **Mammoth Mart at the Village** (6201 Minaret Rd., inside The Village, 760/934-2571, ext. 2078). Both locations offer new high-end bikes for adults and kids. These shops can also help with parts and repairs for bikes you've brought up with you, and sell accessories.

Horseback Riding

Perhaps the most traditional way to explore the Eastern Sierra is on the back of a horse or mule. Early pioneers to the area came on horseback, and you can follow their example from several locations near Mammoth. From the **McGee Creek Pack Station** (760/935-4324, www.mcgeecreekpack station.com, one hour $30) 10 miles south of Mammoth Lakes on Highway 395, you can ride into McGee Canyon, a wilderness area little visited by tourists. Other one-day destinations include Baldwin Canyon and Hilton Lakes. Standard rides range from one hour to all day. But McGee's specialty is multi-day and pack trips that let you really get out beyond the reach of paved roads to camp for a number of days out by one of the many pristine lakes dotting the mountains. If you love the outdoors and really want a vacation as far "away from it all" as you can get, consider a few days' camping in Convict Basin or near Upper Fish Creek in the John Muir Wilderness. The McGee Creek guides will help you pack your gear and guide you through the incredible backcountry of the Eastern Sierra.

Operating out of Bishop, **Rainbow Pack Outfitters** (760/873-8877, www.rainbow packoutfit.com) offers day trips to a number of lovely local destinations, plus a full-day fishing trip with all gear carried by mule. Small children will enjoy an at-the-stables led ride on a pony or horse, while the bigger kids and adults can get out for rides to local meadows and lakes. If you're looking for a longer horseback vacation, check into Rainbow's options for full-service guided trips, hunting and fishing trips, photography and birding treks, and more. Rainbow operates from the John Muir Wilderness near Mammoth and Bishop all the way down to Sequoia and Kings Canyon parks. Pick your ideal destination and pack in!

Snowshoeing

If you prefer walking to all that sliding around on planks, rent or bring your own snowshoes to Mammoth and enjoy a snowy hike through the mountains and meadows. Check the cross-country ski areas first—many have specifically designated snowshoe trails. Or head out to the backcountry and explore Mammoth Lakes Basin or the Sherwin Range. Groomed trails head off from right behind the Mammoth Lakes Welcome Center.

ATVs and Snowmobiles

ATVs, dirt bikes, and snowmobiles are a big no-no at most national parks. Not so at Mammoth! Here you'll find miles of trails set aside for motorized fun. Eighty miles of groomed trails and 75,000 acres of snow-covered meadows and mountainsides await snowmobilers each winter. Much of the same territory is open to ATV and dirt bike traffic in the summer. Get a copy of the *Mammoth Lakes Winter Recreation Guide* for a complete trail and area map to find the best (and legal) places to play.

If you want to rent a vehicle, you can get single- and double-seat snowmobiles and ATVs at **Arctic Cat/Yamaha of Mammoth** (58 Commerce Dr., Mammoth Lakes, 760/934-0347, www.sierraengine.com). Reservations are recommended! Your rental includes instructions on how to operate your vehicle, local trail maps, and helmets for everyone who's going to ride. At **Bishop Motorsports** (156 E. Pine St., Bishop, 888/872-4717, www.harleyrentalsbishop mammoth.com), in addition to snowmobiles and side-by-side ATVs, you can rent Harleys and dirt bikes to take out on the Eastern Sierra roads and trails. If you're on an extended vacation, check out the weekly rental rates.

Golf

If you're in the Mammoth area in summertime, you can enjoy a round of golf at a beautiful course with stunning mountain views. The 18-hole, par 70 **Sierra Star Golf Course** (2001 Sierra Star Pkwy., 760/924-4653, http://mammothmountain.com, $125 weekends, $100 weekdays) is open to the public. Walk this wonderful course for the best views of the surrounding Sierras, or concentrate all your efforts on the game. Amenities include a full-service pro shop, PGA golf pro on-site, and a café with full bar.

Spas

If you want to enjoy some pampering after a hard day of skiing, book a treatment at one of Mammoth Lakes' day spas. The **Bodyworks Mountain Spa** (3399 Main St., 760/924-3161, www.bodyworksmountainspa.com) located upstairs at the Luxury Outlet Mall, offers massage therapy, spa treatments, and facials, plus a wide range of combination packages to maximize your time and money at the spa.

The **InTouch MicroSpa** (3325 Main St., 800/786-4414, www.intouchmicrospa.com) offers a full menu of treatments with a focus on the four elements of earth, air, fire, and water. Using Aveda products exclusively, InTouch caters to spa-goers who care about what's put onto their skin. A number of different styles of facials and aesthetic treatments are available. If you're in town with a group, InTouch offers several spa-party options that get everyone great treatments at discounted rates.

Somewhat incongruously located inside the local Holiday Inn, the **BellaDonna** (3236 Main St., 760/934-3344, www.belladonna mammoth.com) day spa offers a crackling fireplace, serene setting, and massage and aesthetic services. Come for a hot stone massage, a mani-pedi, or a complete makeover with natural mineral-based makeup products. If you're looking for romance, check out the couples side-by-side fireside massage. Yum!

Casino Gambling

If an hour or three at the slots or the blackjack tables sounds like a good way to unwind, go to the **Paiute Palace Casino** (2742 N. Sierra Hwy., Bishop, 888/372-4883, www.paiute palace.com). You can play over 300 slots, plus table blackjack and poker. Look for Texas Hold 'Em tournaments every Wednesday and Sunday. The in-house restaurant is open for breakfast, lunch, and dinner.

ENTERTAINMENT AND EVENTS
Bars and Clubs

What would a ski resort town be without a selection of aprés-ski activities? Mammoth Lakes has a number of bars that open their doors to chilled and thirsty skiers.

For possibly the best (night) time in Mammoth, try the **Clocktower Cellar Pub** (6080 Minaret Rd. at Alpenhof Lodge, 760/934-2725, www.alpenhof-lodge.com, daily until 2 A.M.). This happening nightspot offers 30 luscious brews on tap and served properly, glasses of fine wine cadged from Petra next door, and a casual atmosphere complete with sports on TV, vintage video games, and a pool table. Instead of an obnoxious yuppie tourist pick-up joint, the Clocktower acts as a refuge for locals looking for some after-work relaxation and a pint or two. Expect informal dress and friendly conversation up at the bar, along with the delicious and unusual variety of beers. The location is perfect—in the basement of the Alpenhof just across the street from the Village.

If you prefer a French-style wine bar experience to a noisy British-ish pub, try the vintages at the **Side Door** (100 Canyon Blvd., #229, 760/934-5200, www.sidedoormammoth.com, daily 6 A.M.–midnight). The bad news: Side Door is only open until midnight. The good news: Not only can you enjoy several glasses of California's top wines, you can order up a delicious dinner or dessert crepe to go with your favorite varietal. Expect to pay ski resort prices here, and to be somewhat disappointed in plain sandwiches. But the crepes rate as excellent and the wine list is sometimes called the best in the Village.

Didn't get enough sports during your day at Mammoth? Spend the evening at **Grumpy's** (361 Old Mammoth Rd., 760/934-8587, http:// grumpysmammoth.com, daily 11 A.M.–2 A.M., kitchen closes 10 P.M.). This sports bar has the usual array of TVs showing major sporting events, plus pool tables and an arcade. Grumpy's has a full bar and serves up a full lunch and dinner menu of both Mexican and American specialties. Come for the big-screens, stay for the surprisingly tasty food and drink.

The **Lakanuki Tiki Bar** (6201 Minaret Rd., 760/934-7447, www.lakanuki.com, Mon–Thurs 2 P.M.–2 A.M., Fri–Sun 10 A.M.–2 A.M.,

YOSEMITE

kitchen closes 10 P.M.) does serve food, but it's the nightlife in the tacky tiki bar that packs the place, especially on weekends. Just expect the name to hold true—the vast majority of the clientele at the Lakanuki run to the young, male, snowboarding variety. That makes it tough to pick up any cute chicks—they're drinking elsewhere.

Live Music

For a high-class evening of classical music in the mountains, check out a performance of **Chamber Music Unbound** (760/934-7015, www.chambermusicunbound.org). This nonprofit orchestra performs at several locations in Bishop and Mammoth Lakes, creating unique (often humorous and fun) concerts from familiar and out-of-the-way classical pieces. With titles like Bass-Ic Instinct and Sense and Sensuality, CMU concerts may sound like adult fare, but in fact they are family-oriented shows geared for all ages and genteel musical tastes. At Christmas you might catch a performance of the classic Nutcracker, and in the spring an uplifting vocalist show.

SHOPPING

While it's not a heavy shopping town, the upscale boutiques and galleries, plus a small outlet mall, allow weary outdoors-lovers to take a day off the slopes and engage in some retail therapy.

If you'd like to take in some art while you're in the Mammoth area, several galleries offer an array of photographic art, some for reasonable prices. The **Mountain Light Gallery** (106 S. Main St., Bishop, 760/873-7700, www.mountainlight.com) showcases the wild scenic photography of Galen and Barbara Rowell, world adventurers who died in an accident in 2002. At the gallery, you can view and purchase prints of their scenic photos as well as calendars, note cards, posters, and books. The guest gallery features the work of other landscape photographers. You can even take classes in nature photography and attend other special events.

Another photo gallery in Bishop, the

Vern Clevenger Gallery (905 N. Main St., 888/224-8376, www.verclevenger.com) features only the nature photography of Mr. Clevenger himself. Each of Clevenger's photos is shot on film, then a mixed digital and traditional wet process creates the large-format prints you see in the gallery. What you see is all natural, without digital enhancement to the images or colors. Inexpensive note cards and posters are available for purchase in addition to the lovely framed fine-art prints. Or take a workshop to learn how to create these gorgeous images for yourself.

In downtown Mammoth Lakes, visit the **Mammoth Gallery** (425 Old Mammoth Rd. and Minaret Rd., 888/848-7733, http://mammothgallery.com, daily 10 A.M.–5 P.M.). Here you'll see the work of a number of local photographers and watercolor artists, plus a large collection of vintage ski poster reproductions.

ACCOMMODATIONS

Accommodations at Mammoth run to luxurious ski condos with full kitchens, perfect for spending a week plying the slopes of the local mountains with family or friends. Motels and inns offer comfort as well, often for a little less money and shorter minimum stays.

Under $100

Want to ski the slopes of exclusive Mammoth, but can't afford the hoity-toity condo resorts? Stay at the **Innsbruck Lodge** (Forest Trail btwn. Hwy. 203 and Sierra Blvd., 760/934-3035, www.innsbrucklodge.com, $93–240). Economy rooms offer twin beds, table and chairs, and access to the motel whirlpool tub and lobby with stone fireplace at super-reasonable nightly rates. Other rooms can sleep 2–6, and some include kitchenettes. The quiet North Village location sits on the ski area shuttle route for easy access to the local slopes.

If you're planning to ski June Mountain, stay at the **Boulder Lodge** (2282 Hwy. 158, 800/455-6355, $77). This inexpensive lodge provides an array of options, from simple motel rooms for short stays to multi-bedroom

Austria Hof

apartments and even a five-bedroom lake house for longer trips and larger groups. The Boulder Lodge takes guests back a few decades with its decorating style—the browns, wood paneling, and faux leather furniture recall the 1950s. But the views of June Lake, the indoor pool and spa, and the wonderful outdoor recreation area surrounding the lodge are timeless.

$100-150

The **Sierra Lodge** (3540 Main St., 800/356-5711, www.sierralodge.com, $125–135) boasts reasonably priced all-non-smoking rooms located right on the ski shuttle line, and only a mile and a half from the Juniper Ridge chair lift. This small motel's rates are rock-bottom in the off-season and on weekdays in wintertime. Rooms have either a king or two double beds, a kitchenette with microwave and dishes, and plenty of space for your snow and ski gear. The decor shows simple motel styling in cool, relaxing blues. Breakfast, cable TV, and Wi-Fi access are included with your room.

$150-250

From the outside, the ornate, carved-wood, fringed **Austria Hof** (924 Canyon Blvd., 866/662-6668, www.austriahof.com, $170–195) might be a ski hotel tucked into a crevice of the Alps. But on the inside, you'll find the most stylish American appointments. Peaceful sea-green motel rooms—even those with a king bed and a spa bathtub—can be rented for under $200 per night. If you've got a larger party or a desire to cook your own meals, check out the one- and two-bedroom condo options. Austria Hof's location adjacent to the Canyon Lodge and the Village gondola make it a great winter ski or summer mountain bike base camp. In the evenings, head down to the restaurant and bar for some hearty German food and drink. Or if you prefer, slip into a swimsuit and enjoy the views from the large outdoor spa.

Over $250

It's not cheap, but the **⬛ Juniper Springs Resort** (4000 Meridian Blvd., 800/626-6684, www.mammothmountain.com, $290) has absolutely every luxury amenity you could want to make your ski vacation complete. Condos come in studio, one-bedroom, two-bedroom, three-bedroom, and townhouse sizes, sleeping up to eight people. The interiors boast stunning appointments, from snow-white down comforters to granite-topped kitchen counters to 60-inch flat-screen TVs. Bathrooms include deep soaking tubs, perfect to privately relax aching muscles after a long day on the slopes. The resort also features heated pools year-round and three outdoor heated spas—there's nothing like jumping into a steaming hot tub on a snowy evening, then jumping back out to find the cold perfect and refreshing. The Talon restaurant serves breakfast and lunch, and the Daily Grind offers coffee and take-out snacks. Juniper Springs is located next door to the Eagle Lodge, which serves as one of the Mammoth Mountain base lodges complete with a six-person express chair up to the main ski area. You can rent skis right inside the hotel, and ski back down to Juniper after a day on the slopes. In the summertime, Juniper Springs' proximity to local golfing and the Mammoth Mountain bike park make it a perfect retreat.

The company that owns Juniper Springs also owns the luxury condo complex at **The Village at Mammoth** (1111 Forest Trail, 800/626-6684, www.mammothmountain .com, $360). Check them out if you can't get the condo of your dreams at Juniper.

For a unique condo rental, check out **Mountainback** (Lakeview Blvd,. 800/468-6225, www.mountainbackrentals.com, $290–460, two-night minimum). This complex boasts an array of all two-bedroom units, some of which sleep up to six people. Every individual building has its own outdoor spa, and the complex has a heated pool and a sauna. Every condo is decorated differently (and you might be able to buy and redecorate one if you want to and have enough cash). Check the website for photos to find what you like—big stone everywhere, wood paneling, gentle cream walls, or even red-and-green holiday-themed furniture. Walk to the ski lifts, or enjoy a round of golf or day of fishing in the summertime.

FOOD

Plenty of dining options cluster in Mammoth Lakes. You can get your fast-food cheeseburger and your chain double-latte here, but why would you with so many more interesting independent options just lying around? Fare runs to American food and pizza, with a few ethnic options thrown in for variety.

American

A favorite with locals and repeat visitors, the **Whiskey Creek** (24 Lake Mary Rd., 760/934-2555, daily 5:30 P.M.–2 A.M., $15–30) combines casually elegant California fare in the downstairs dining room with a homey nighttime bar up above. Only half a block from the Village, you can walk in and enjoy an unusual array of entrées, a surprisingly wide selection of wines, and tasty beers. Whisky Creek maintains its own tiny on-site brewery, so some of the beers they serve really are as local as it gets. The crowd, both for dining and for drinking, feels warm and friendly, as do the hearty dishes served to hungry après-skiers. Be sure to make reservations on weekends as it can get crowded here. If you've just come for a drink and a good time, expect live music to heat up the upstairs starting at about 9 P.M., and to keep on playing long past midnight.

California

◖ **Petra's Bistro and Wine Bar** (6080 Minaret Rd., 760/934-3500, dinner Tues.–Sun.) brings a bit of the California wine country all the way out to Mammoth Lakes. This eatery offers a seasonally changing menu that's designed to please the palate and complement the wine list. That wine list is worth a visit itself—an eclectic mix of vintages highlights the best of California, while giving a nod to European and South American wines. Wine-lovers will recognize many names, but still might find something new on the unusual list. The by-the-glass offerings change each night, and your server will happily cork your half-finished bottle to take home for tomorrow. Two dining rooms and a wine bar divide up the seating nicely, and the atmosphere succeeds in feeling romantic without being cave-dark. Petra's stays open all year, so if you're visiting in the off-season you'll get a pleasantly uncrowded treat. Reservations are a good idea during high season.

A popular gourmet establishment, **Skadi** (587 Old Mammoth Rd., Ste. B, 760/934-3902, http://restaurantskadi.com) describes their menu as containing "alpine cuisine." In truth, this chef-owned restaurant boasts a menu filled with California-style innovation using mountain-inspired ingredients to their best advantage. (You'll see a lot of venison!) Everything on the list looks tasty, but if you're not ready for a heavy entrée, consider ordering a couple of items from the long list of appetizers for a "small plates" experience. Oh, and don't skip dessert! Whatever you choose, the European-heavy wine list will have something perfect to pair with it. If you're in town in the ski season, make reservations in advance, especially on weekends.

Mexican

Even Californians who eat Mexican food on a regular basis tend to agree on the quality of the fare at **Roberto's Mexican Café** (271 Old Mammoth Rd., 760/934-3667). This casual spot serves classic California-Mexican food (*chiles rellenos,* enchiladas, burritos, and so on) in great quantities (check out the huge three-combo platter) perfect for skiers and boarders famished after a long day on the slopes. For a quiet meal, stay downstairs in the main dining room. To join in with a lively younger crowd, head upstairs to the bar, which has tables and serves the full restaurant menu. Wherever you sit, even the stoutest of drinkers should beware Roberto's lethal margaritas.

INFORMATION AND SERVICES
Tourist Information

The town of Mammoth Lakes has an awesome **Visitors Bureau** (2520 Main St., 760/934-2712, www.visitmammoth.com) that can help you with everything from condo rentals and restaurant reservations before you arrive, to the latest bar openings and advice about best seasonal recreation options. These folks are well worth a stop early in your visit.

Media and Communications

Mammoth Lakes does indeed publish its own newspaper, the *Mammoth Times* (www .mammothtimes.com). This weekly paper serves the whole of the Eastern Sierra region. Check for local events and good nightspots, and visit the website for up-to-date weather and road conditions.

Despite its tiny size, the town of Mammoth Lakes boasts a cosmopolitan atmosphere that includes plenty of Internet access. Many of the condos and hotel rooms have some species of Internet access, and you're likely to find a Starbucks with Wi-Fi somewhere downtown.

Banks and Post Offices

Plenty of ATMs crowd into Mammoth Lakes at gas stations, mini-marts, and even bank branches. Check the Village, Main Street, and Minaret Road for the most likely places to find banks and cash machines in town.

The **Mammoth Lakes post office** (760/934-2205) sits at 3330 Main Street, a.k.a. CA-203.

Gas and Automotive Services

Mammoth Lakes is a great place to gas up before hitting the more wild parts of the Eastern Sierra. Gas stations cluster right at the eastern edge of town, where CA-203 becomes Main Street, and more gas can be found throughout the downtown area. Just be prepared to pay a premium. This is a resort town, and they know how far away the next gas station is!

Many gas stations, plus big-box stores and even pharmacies and supermarkets sell tire chains in the wintertime.

Medical Services

Need medical service beyond that offered at the ski resorts? You can get it at **Mammoth Hospital** (85 Sierra Park Rd., 760/934-3311, mammothhospital.com), which has a 24-hour emergency room.

GETTING THERE AND AROUND
Air

The nearest airport to Mammoth is the **Mammoth Yosemite Airport** (MMH, 437 Old Mammoth Rd., 760/934-8989, www .ci.mammoth-lakes.ca.us/airport/awos.htm). Extensively remodeled in 2008, this airport offers limited, expensive commercial service in and out of the Eastern Sierras, plus a single rental-car outlet. For a less expensive spot to fly into, try the Reno airport and drive in from there.

Car

California's Highway 395 acts as the main access road to the Mammoth Lakes area. To get to Mammoth Lakes proper, from Highway 395 north or south, turn onto State Highway 203, which will take you right into town.

Mammoth Lakes (and most of the rest of the Eastern Sierra) isn't near any of California's major hot spots. Expect a six-hour drive from Los Angeles and (at best!) a seven-hour drive from San Francisco if the traffic and weather cooperate. If you fly into Reno, the drive out to Mammoth takes about three hours.

In the wintertime, be aware that it snows in Mammoth more than it does in almost any other place in California. Carry chains! Even if the weather is predicted to be clear for your visit, having chains can prevent a world of hurt and turning back in sudden storms. The longer you plan to stay, the better you should stock your car with items such as ice scrapers, blankets, water, food, and a full tank of gas whenever possible. For the latest traffic information, including chain control areas and weather conditions, call CalTrans at 800/427-7623.

Parking in Mammoth Lakes in the off-season is a breeze. In the winter, it can get a bit more complicated, as constant snow removal means that parking on the street is illegal throughout town. Most of the major resorts and hotels offer heated parking structures, and many of the restaurants, bars, and ski resorts have plenty of parking in their outdoor lots. If you're concerned about parking, call ahead to your resort and restaurants to get the lowdown on how best to get there and where to leave your car.

Shuttles and Buses

Devil's Postpile National Monument (760/924-5500, www.nps.gov/depo, $7) runs a shuttle into the park that's mandatory for all visitors during high season (vehicles with handicap placards excepted). The shuttle runs every 20–30 minutes between Mammoth Mountain Ski Area and Reds Meadow Valley 7 A.M.–7 P.M. mid-June–mid-September.

A daily **Mountain Express Shuttle** (760/924-3184, adults $5.50, reservations recommended) runs from the Mammoth Lakes McDonald's to the June Lake ski area, arriving at 9 A.M. The return shuttle leaves June Lake at 3:30 P.M.

Sequoia and Kings Canyon National Parks

The trees are the stars of the show at Sequoia and Kings Canyon National Parks (www.nps .gov/seki). Groves of giant sequoias, including the largest known tree on earth, soar out of the fertile Sierra soil. But in these parks you'll also find rugged granite formations (including Kings Canyon—a deeper gulch than the Grand Canyon), marble caverns, rushing rivers, and an astounding variety of ecosystems, from chaparral to alpine meadow.

SIGHTS
General Grant Grove

One of the largest of these parks' giant sequoia groves, the General Grant Grove (one mile northwest of the Kings Canyon Visitor Center) is home to dozens of monumental trees. The largest of these is the General Grant Tree, the third-largest tree on earth, an American National Shrine, and "America's Christmas Tree." Another feature of this area, the Fallen Monarch was once

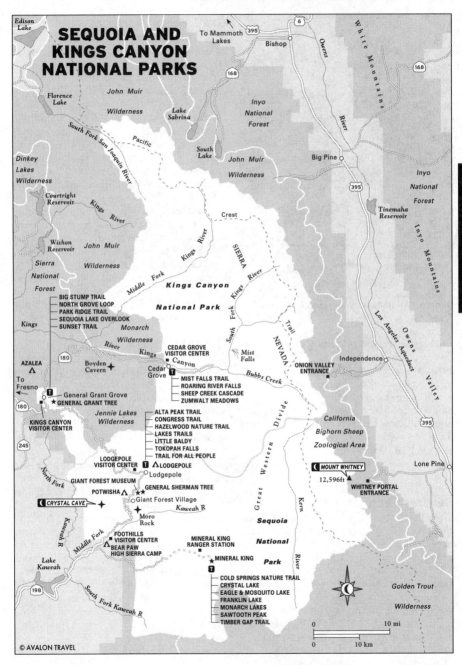

© AVALON TRAVEL

General Grant Tree, "America's Christmas Tree"

Giant Forest Museum

The Giant Forest Museum (559/565-4480, 16 miles from the Hwy. 198 entrance) perches on the side of the Generals Highway. Inside this fun interactive museum, you'll learn everything you ever wanted or needed to know about giant sequoia trees, which grow only here in the Sierra Nevada range. Kids and adults alike love the touchable, spinnable exhibits that provide context to the stated sizes of the trees. This newer museum goes into great detail about the importance of fire in the life of a giant sequoia (and other plants and trees that grow in the same areas). Ironically, a commitment to stamping out *all* forest fires, even those caused naturally by lightning strikes, severely endangered the giant sequoias, which rely on fire to create the right habitat for their growth and reproduction. You'll also learn about how the park used to look, and why many of the buildings have been removed to make way for more trees. This is a great stop for families whose kids need a rest from hiking and long intervals in the car.

an immense tree but now acts as a tunnel along the trail, with enough head room for almost the tallest of visitors to get through without ducking. The walk among the sequoias at all stages of development is easy, with a well-built flat half-mile trail (much of this area is wheelchair accessible). But consider purchasing a trail guide at the nearby visitors center, because the circuitous trail can be difficult to follow and you may find yourself lost in the beautiful forest trying to find its star attraction.

General Sherman Tree

There can be only one. The General Sherman Tree (Wolverton Rd. off Generals Hwy.) is the largest tree known on the planet. At just under 275 feet, it is not the tallest tree, nor at 2,200 years old is it the oldest, but by sheer volume of wood it is the biggest. If you love statistics, pick up a sheet at any of the visitors centers that lists the worlds' 30 largest giant sequoias. Take the trail down the hill to visit the tree, then past it to the shuttle stop where you can catch a shuttle back up the hill to your car.

◖ Crystal Cave

You'll find no trees in the Crystal Cave (Generals Hwy., three miles south of the General Sherman Tree). Instead, you'll find immense underground rooms filled with incredible natural calcite formations and shining polished marble. This is the underside of the parks—perhaps the most impressive (and one of only two publicly accessible) of the over 250 marble caverns within the park and national forest boundaries. The regular tour lasts 45 minutes and takes visitors through walkable, well-lit tunnels and into grand chambers filled with curtains, stalactites, and other weird and beautiful calcite creations. A longer two-hour tour takes you deeper into the caverns, and gives you a much more detailed lesson on the cave's history and geology. Best of all, serious spelunkers can sign up for the Wild Cave Tour, a four- to six-hour crawl off the lit tourist trails in Crystal Cave. With a limit of six people per party, you'll get the most serious caving experience available anywhere in Sequoia and Kings Canyon National Parks.

You can't buy a ticket for a tour at the

© LIZ HAMILL SCOTT

Sequoia and Kings Canyon

entrance to Crystal Cave. You'll need to stop at either the Foothills or the Lodgepole visitors center to purchase your tickets. Then proceed on to the cave parking lot, which can take over an hour from either visitor center. No trailers or RVs over 22 feet are allowed on the road. Be aware that even in the fall, tours fill up quickly so if possible get tickets early in the morning or even a day in advance.

Mineral King

Ironically, the onetime boom town of Mineral King (25 miles off Hwy. 198) never had a successful mining industry nearby. Silver was discovered here and mining began in 1873, but not many minerals moved out of the mountain. Instead, the road built in 1879 attracted loggers and the hydroelectric industry, and the town managed to flourish for a while. Today, visitors drive up the long, winding road to enjoy the resurgence of nature in the area at the expense of human construction. Mineral King Valley draws both geology and botany buffs with its unique glacier-carved array of rocks and minerals, some overgrown with a variety of native plants. The Atwell Mill that once cut first-growth sequoia timber has been reduced to a few relics—a steam engine, a wheel, miscellaneous junk—while all around young giant sequoias reclaim their territory. High above the former town, Sawtooth Peak, at more than 12,000 feet, looms large and reminds many visitors and scientists of similar mountains in the Rockies. The peak is perfect for intrepid day hikers, and also allows multi-day treks with a backcountry permit.

Trying to drive your RV or trailer up Mineral King Road is hazardous to you, your vehicle, and other motorists. Also, marmots frequent the Mineral King area, and these furry critters won't seem quite so cute after you discover they've chewed through your radiator hoses! Check with the ranger station for current activity, and notify the rangers if your car has been disabled.

◖ Mount Whitney

It's not just the tallest mountain in California. At 14,505 feet, Mount Whitney (www.nps.gov/seki/planyourvisit/whitney.htm) boasts the highest altitude of any peak in the 48 contiguous United States. Yes, it beats out all the mighty Rocky Mountains! You can see and photograph the impressive peak from several points along the Generals Highway in Sequoia and Kings Canyon. However, it's well away from the main part of the parks, sitting near the town of Lone Pine to the southeast. Plan a long drive to get there from either park entrance.

Amazingly, you can climb all the way to the top of Mount Whitney and back in one day, if you're in good shape and prepared properly for the journey. However, you can't just park at the trailhead and head out during high season (May–Nov.). To preserve the natural beauty of the fragile mountain ecosystem, only 100 day-hikers and 60 backpackers are permitted to hit the main trail each day, and you'll find some severe restrictions on how you must behave. Whitney Portal (13 miles west of Lone Pine) provides the most direct access along a 10.7-mile trail.

If you want to make the climb (or even day-hike), apply for a permit in advance and check reservations (Wilderness Permit Office, 760/873-2483, www.fs.fed.us/r5/inyo/recreation/wild/whitneyavail.shtml, daily 8 A.M.–4:30 P.M.). Also check the website for information about how to prepare for a Mount Whitney hike. Mount Whitney also marks the southern end of the John Muir Trail. Whether you begin here or end here, you'll find the mountain a worthwhile marker on this epic foot journey through California.

Boyden Cavern

Tucked back in the wilds of the Sequoia National Forest, between Sequoia and Kings Canyon Parks, Boyden Cavern (74101 E. Kings Canyon Rd., 559/338-0959, www.caverntours.com/boydenrt.htm, tours daily mid-Apr.–mid-Nov., $20 park fee plus tour cost) gives visitors an up-close and personal cave experience. Inside Boyden, "please try not to touch the formations" takes on a new meaning—that is, turn sideways to avoid the walls and duck to keep from hitting your head on stalactites

that are many thousands of yeards old. This modest-sized cavern network contains plenty of draperies, pancakes, stalactites, and other calcite structures. You can stare right at them, up into them, and in some cases walk all the way around them.

SPORTS AND RECREATION
Hiking

Sequoia and Kings Canyon attract hikers all year long-especially those looking for a wild Sierra experience without the overcrowding that's so often prevalent at Yosemite. Many areas of the parks offer lovely day hikes, or you can get a backcountry permit for a backpacking trek through this large, gorgeous area, much of which is only accessible on foot.

GENERAL GRANT GROVE

This popular stop just north of the northern Kings Canyon park entrance offers a variety of short, flat trails that are perfect for day visitors. After visiting the General Grant Tree, take the **North Grove Loop** half a mile along an old park road through the grove. You might find yourself on the North Grove Loop even if you didn't intend to; it's not particularly well differentiated from the General Grant Tree Trail and it takes in much of the same area.

Outside the grove, take the **Big Stump Trail** (near the Big Stump park entrance) one mile round-trip through a grove that was heavily logged in the late 19th century, but is now reclaiming its true nature as a sequoia grove. Or enjoy the vistas from the **Park Ridge Trail** (Panoramic Point Rd. parking area, closed in winter). If you pick a clear day, you can see all the way out to the Coast Range of mountains in the San Francisco Bay Area from this trail! While there's little elevation change on this almost five-mile walk, consider the altitude of the area before deciding that this trail and the fire-road route back will be an easy trip. For a different view on the life and death of the giant sequoias, and humanity's intervention in this area, hike the **Sequoia Lake Overlook/Dead Giant Loop** (lower end of General Grant Tree parking area). The two-mile trail takes you to the Dead Giant, a first-growth giant sequoia that was mostly likely killed by loggers trying (and failing) to cut it for lumber. Sequoia Lake is actually an old mill pond from the logging days.

For a longer, more demanding day hike, check out the **Sunset Trail** (Grant Grove Visitor Center). You'll climb about 1,400 feet over this six-mile (round-trip) trail, which takes you past Viola Falls and through the magnificent mixed forests.

MINERAL KING

A good place to start walking in Mineral King is the **Cold Springs Nature Trail.** This easy, one-mile interpretive walk describes and displays the natural wonders and the formation of the valley.

A bit more strenuous, the **Timber Gap Trail** follows an old mining road through a forest of red fir trees. You'll see pretty views out to Alta Peak and the middle fork of the Kaweah River. The short version of this trail runs four miles round-trip. Note the altitude: You'll start at over 7,500 feet. For a longer hike, take the fork to **Monarch Lakes.** This trek runs about 8.5 miles round-trip, but it's mostly flat and easy walking. Consider bringing a picnic to enjoy beside the lakes. For hikers in great shape looking for the most tremendous views of the southern Sierra Nevada range, keep on going past the lakes up to the top of **Sawtooth Peak.** This trail isn't for the faint of breath or shaky of leg. It climbs 1,200 feet in just over a mile of loose, difficult ground. But once you're at the top, you'll get a fine chance to rest as you photograph the majestic peaks all around you.

Many other hikes begin in Mineral King Valley. You can visit a number of charming alpine lakes if you're up for a hike of 7–11 miles. Plan to take food and water and spend all day on hikes out to **Eagle and Mosquito Lakes** or **Crystal Lake.** You can also get to **Franklin Lake** and back in a day, though the pristine beauty of the water and fascinating geology of the area often draw backpackers on their way to Mount Whitney over several days.

LODGEPOLE

For a charming interpretive walk at the Lodgepole Village area, head down the **Hazelwood Nature Trail** (Giant Forest Lodge). Signs along this flat one-mile stroll tell the history of humans' relationship with the giant sequoia trees—good and bad, beneficial and destructive. This walk works well for families with school-aged kids. In the same vicinity, you can putter along the quarter-mile **Trail For All People.** This interpretive nature walk's pride comes in spring, when the wildflowers bloom. A bit longer but perhaps the most representative of life in Sequoia National Park, the **Congress Trail** starts at the General Sherman Tree. Grab a pamphlet with map at the Sherman Tree to get the best experience on this trail, which includes many of the park's most famous named giant sequoias. This two-mile round-trip trail is paved, making it wheelchair accessible and a non-strenuous walk even for folks who usually aren't big hikers.

How can you resist a hike to a granite formation called **Little Baldy** (11 miles north of General Grant Grove)? This moderate climb takes you up about 700 feet to the top of the cutely named granite dome. Look down from the peak, which tops out at over 8,000 feet, into the Giant Forest and snap a few photos. Or if you prefer water to stone, head for **Tokopah Falls** (Lodgepole Campground). Early summer, when the flow is at its peak, is the best time to trek out the almost two miles along the Marble Fork of the Kaweah River to this fantastic 1,200-foot waterfall.

Hardcore hikers willing to brave steep climbs at high altitudes can either take day hikes or obtain overnight backcountry passes for the region's major trails. The **Lakes Trails** (Wolverton picnic area) vary in length, but you're definitely going to have to climb a ways up to the glacial lake areas. From the trail, you'll be able to visit Heather Lake, Emerald Lake, and Pear Lake. The minimum distance round-trip for a day hike to Heather Lake is eight miles. Heights-lovers choose the **Alta Peak Trail,** which ascends all the way up to the 11,204-foot summit of Alta Peak. Pick a

© LIZ HAMILL SCOTT

Sequoia's namesake stars

clear day for this grueling 14-mile hike and you'll get a view of Mount Whitney across the Great Western Divide.

CEDAR GROVE

Even if you hate hiking, you'll want to get out of the car and stroll the negligible distance (less than 0.25 mile) from the parking area three miles east of Cedar Grove Village to the **Roaring River Falls.** The whole tiny trail sits under a canopy of trees, making it cool even in the hottest parts of summer, and just looking at the falls feels refreshing after driving the Generals Highway. Another easy meander comes only a mile from Road's End (the northeast terminus of Generals Highway). **Zumwalt Meadows** offers a flat one-mile loop around the meadow of the same name, then a shady walk through a grove of heavenly smelling incense cedar and pine trees along the Kings River.

Moderate hikes abound in this area. A good place to bring a picnic is **Sheep Creek Cascade.** This hike takes about an hour and a half, ascends 600 feet, and runs about two

miles total. You end up in a picturesque shaded glen that's perfect for taking a load off your feet and enjoying the serene surroundings. The **Mists Falls Trail** (Road's End) is a popular jumping-off point for backpackers destined for the Kings Canyon backcountry. However, you can go eight miles out and back to Mists Falls in about five hours. Plan for dust and heat on the first couple of miles of the trail, then steep switchbacks that take you up 1,500 feet to the falls. If you're passing through on your way to the John Muir Trail for a longer trek, keep going past the falls, up to Paradise Valley, then to the trail crossing at Upper Woods Creek.

Climbing

It shouldn't surprise anyone to learn that **Mount Whitney** is a wonderful place to rock climb. You can climb up the steep East Face of the mountain or head up the Needles. These climbs are not beginners' journeys, but the East Face isn't the hardest climb ever either. First climbed by John Muir himself in 1931, most of the East Face rates at a Class 3, with the worst bits rated 5.4. The Needles are famed among big-wall climbers who attack the Sierras each year. See the *Mount Whitney* section for permit information and regulations.

Horseback Riding

A number of horse-accessible trails meander through Sequoia and Kings Canyon. Rent a horse for a day ride from the pack stations at **Cedar Grove** (559/565-3463 summer, 559/337-2314 off-season) and **Grant Grove** (559/335-9292 summer, 559/337-2314 off-season). If you're new to horses, pick a gentle one-hour ride. For more hardy or experienced riders, both pack stations offer half-day and full-day rides.

If you're looking for a multi-day horseback adventure, you can find that too at Sequoia and Kings Canyon. Call either of the pack stations to arrange a guided backcountry pack trip.

Fishing

Fishing is allowed in any of the lakes inside Sequoia and Kings Canyon. You can purchase a fishing license and tackle at the markets at the Grant Grove, Cedar Grove, and Lodgepole visitors centers. The visitor centers can also advise about season opening and closing dates. Anglers are permitted up to five trout per day. The lakes and the Kaweah drainage hold rainbows, eastern brook, German brown, and golden trout.

ACCOMMODATIONS
Camping
The park offers 13 campgrounds, three of which are open year-round (Lodgepole, Azalea, and Potwisha). Campgrounds are first-come, first-served, except for Lodgepole (summer visits only). A list and map of all campgrounds is available at www.nps.gov/seki/planyourvisit/campgrounds.htm.

Lodgepole (summer reservations 877/444-6777, www.recreation.gov, $18–20) is located along the Kaweah River and is 21 miles from the Sequoia entrance. In summer, there are 214 sites for tents and RVs, flush toilets, showers, laundry, and bear-proof containers. Off-season, there are 25 walk-in tent sites (first-come, first-served).

Azalea (Grant Grove, 110 sites, $18) is located 3.5 miles from the Kings Canyon park entrance and within a half-mile of the visitor center. **Potwisha** (42 sites, $18) is also on the Kaweah River, about four miles from the Sequoia entrance. Amenities include flush toilets, RV disposal, and bear-proof containers.

More adventurous campers should check out the High Sierra Camps. Start at Crescent Meadow, about 10 miles south of Wuksachi on Generals Highway, to get to the **Bearpaw High Sierra Camp** (866/807-3598, www.visitsequoia.com, June–Sept.), an 11.5-mile hike into the gorgeous Sequoia back country. This camp takes a leaf from Yosemite's book with its accommodations and amenities. This camp offers six tent cabins that sleep two people apiece, and come complete with bedding, towels, and sleeping pads. You can even fit a third person on the floor of your cabin, if that person brings bedding and a towel for herself. A bath house offers flush toilets and hot showers

(heaven!), and each stay comes with a full dinner and full breakfast, served family-style. You can even buy a box lunch to take with you on your next day's journey.

Under $100
Centrally located in the Grant Grove Village, the **Grant Grove Cabins** (866/522-6966, www.sequoia-kingscanyon.com, $65–75/tent cabins) offer a wide array of lodging styles for a variety of prices. Many of these cabins have been around awhile—some since the early days of what was then the General Grant National Park. The economy option here are the tent cabins, which are short on amenities, with no electricity or heat and with shared, central bathrooms. From May through October, a number of Camp, Rustic, and Oversized cabins offer solid walls ($77–140), a small propane heater plus an outdoor wood-burning stove, electricity, and daily maid service. When you make reservations, ask about larger cabins if you've got a bigger group or family. It can start snowing in Sequoia and Kings Canyon as early as mid-September. If you're visiting in the spring or the fall, consider whether you're willing to chance an unheated or minimally heated cabin should a storm come up in the park. Open all year are the historic cabins with private baths. Most are duplexes, one log cabin is a single that sleeps two. These cabins have heating, historic Mission-style decor, and amenities such as coffee makers.

$150-250
Built in 1999, the **Wuksachi Lodge** (Hwy. 198 just west of Lodgepole, 866/786-3197, www.visitsequoia.com, $215–285, year-round) offers the most luxurious accommodations available inside the parks. With 102 rooms of various sizes, the Wuksachi Lodge offers ample luxury housing for tree-lovers who just can't give up their creature comforts. Guest rooms boast "woodsy-motel" decor, with colorful Native American print bedspreads and slightly more interesting Mission-style wooden furniture. Each room has a private bath, a TV, a phone, a coffee maker, ski racks, and daily maid service.

© LIZ HAMILL SCOTT

Clear water runs through Sequoia National Park.

The Wuksachi's superior rooms offer space and comfort, particularly for families who cannot imagine a vacation without digital entertainment readily available. An on-site restaurant (the best in the parks), a Native American thematic gift shop, and close access to the Lodgepole visitors complex round out the attractions of this popular lodge.

The shining new **John Muir Lodge** (Grant Grove Village, 866/522-6966, www.sequoia-kingscanyon.com, $150–200, year-round) brings together the concepts of a comfortable motel and a classic woodsy lodge. Expect big timber poles combining form and function in the huge common room. This space acts as a living room or lounge, with a fireplace, wireless Internet access, tables, sofas, and a number of board games. Guest rooms are simply decorated in an alpine theme, complete with comfortable beds, clean bathrooms, and charming views out into the forest. Since you're up at the edge of General Grant Village, you'll find plenty of nearby food and services, including the Village restaurant, mini-mart, souvenir shop, and the Grant Grove visitors center.

The lodge is convenient to hiking, and to the Generals Highway through the park.

FOOD
Restaurants

The national parks have their visitors good and trapped when it comes to dining options. Guests who want a wide range of options should bring in their own food. One option is to bring a cooler and stop at a supermarket before you enter the park.

One of the Sequoia restaurants sits at the Grant Grove complex, servicing both the John Muir Lodge and the surrounding tent cabins. **Grant Grove Restaurant** (Hwy. 180 at Generals Hwy., 559/335-5500, Sun.–Thurs. 8 A.M.–2 P.M., 5–7 P.M., Fri.–Sat. 8 A.M.–2 P.M., 5–8 P.M.) serves three meals each day, and is closed in between. This basic dining room offers standard American fare at pretty high resort prices. Though the food is nothing special at lunch or dinner, you can get a palatable meal and a glass of wine. Breakfast, on the other hand, is a monument to the value of cereal bars, apples, and OJ. Morning service at the Grant Grove

Restaurant is weak to disastrous (expect to wait 20–30 minutes for a table in a half-empty dining room), the coffee has both mediocre taste and strength, and the food is simply appalling. If you have *any* other breakfast option, go with it.

The closest thing to an upscale restaurant in Sequoia and Kings Canyon is the **Wuksachi Lodge Restaurant** (off Generals Hwy. west of Lodgepole, open daily year-round for breakfast, lunch, and dinner, $9–24). The elegant dining room has white cloths on the tables and sweeping forest views outside the picture windows. The Wuksachi Restaurant offers three meals per day to service the lodge's overnight guests. But dinner stars as *the* meal of the day, boasting fancier preparations and California-style ingredients. Make a reservation if you plan to dine at the Wuksachi on a summer weekend.

On the other end of the dining spectrum, but no less fun, you'll find the **Kings Canyon Lodge Restaurant** (Hwy. 180 approx 20 miles east of Grant Grove Village). Warning: If taxidermy puts you off your food, do not eat here! Stuffed heads of deer, elk, and other animals decorate the walls, and every other inch of space in the long narrow dining room/lobby is covered with Western-themed knickknacks, geegaws, and tchotchkes. Some of these might even be antiques. Ancient refrigerators and freezers hold cold soft drinks, beer, and ice cream, and the classic diner food is made to order in the least pretentious open kitchen anywhere in the state of California. The restaurant remains open through the long, hot afternoon, making the Kings Canyon Lodge a welcome rest stop for kids needing ice cream and to run around, and adults who prefer to eat late (or have no other choice).

Markets

You'll find minimally stocked mini-marts at both the **Grant Grove Village** (Hwy. 180 at Generals Hwy., Sun.–Thurs. 9 A.M.–7 P.M., Fri.–Sat. 9 A.M.–8 P.M.) and the **Lodgepole Market** (Generals Hwy. at Lodgepole, daily late May–fall 8 A.M.–8 P.M., fall–spring 9 A.M.–6 P.M.). These sell a few staples, soda, beer, s'mores makings, and some packaged food suitable for reheating over a campfire.

INFORMATION AND SERVICES
Tourist Information

Sequoia and Kings Canyon National Parks boast several visitors centers and rangers stations. When you enter the park, you'll be given both the glossy pamphlet and the up-to-date National Park Guide for Sequoia and Kings Canyon. These will provide you with all the in-park information you need to have a great time and keep up on any activities and events.

In Sequoia, the **Foothills Visitor Center** (559/565-3135, daily) is located on Generals Highway, one mile from the park entrance. Crystal Cave tour tickets are sold here until 3:45 P.M. and wilderness permits are issued here as well. **Lodgepole Visitor Center** (Lodgepole Rd., 559/565-4436, spring–fall), off Generals Highway, is 21 miles from the Sequoia entrance. Crystal Cave tour tickets are sold until 3:30 P.M. and wilderness permits are issued here. The **Mineral King Ranger Station** (Mineral King Rd., 559/565-3768, May–Sept.) is located up a narrow road and offers basic seasonal services.

In Kings Canyon, there is the **Kings Canyon Visitor Center** (Grant Grove, 559/565-4307, Apr.–Oct. daily 8 A.M.–5 P.M., Nov.–Mar. daily 9 A.M.–4:30 P.M.) three miles east of the Highway 180 entrance and **Cedar Grove Visitor Center** (559/565-3793, mid Apr–mid–Nov.) in Cedar Grove Village.

Media and Communications

You're a long way from civilization when you visit Sequoia and Kings Canyon National Parks. Don't expect flawless coverage from your cell phone. If you're lucky you might find some signal; if you're unlucky, you're stuck with land lines at the visitors centers and lodgings for the duration of your stay. Likewise with Internet service. The more cosmopolitan lodges inside the park offer some Wi-Fi in common areas, but that's about the extent of Internet service here. So consider forgetting the laptop and the PDA and unplugging for a few days so you can get to understand the sights and sounds of the woods all around you.

YOSEMITE

Banks and Post Offices

No banks lie inside the park, but you can find ATMs at the major visitors complexes at Grant Grove, Lodgepole, and Cedar Grove (summer only).

Though you can no longer post a letter from the old log cabin post office, you can make use of the **Park Post Office at Lodgepole** (Lodgepole Visitor Center, Mon.–Fri. 8 A.M.–1 P.M., 2–4 P.M.). Address any mail to General Delivery, Sequoia National Park, 93262.

Medical Services

No medical services beyond the first aid provided by rangers are available in Sequoia and Kings Canyon. In a medical emergency, dial 911 from your cell phone, your lodgings, or a call box if possible. The nearest hospitals sit out in Fresno and Visalia.

GETTING THERE AND AROUND
Car

Visitors can enter Sequoia at the Ash Mountain entrance on Highway 198 or at Big Stump in Kings Canyon on Highway 180. There are no road entrances on the east side of either park.

The closest major highway to the park is Highway 99. Turn east onto CA-180 from Fresno to get to the north entrance and onto CA-198 from Visalia in the south. The main road running through the two parks is called **The Generals Highway.** It connects CA-180 (Kings Canyon Highway) in the north to CA-198 in the southwest.

Drive carefully in Sequoia and Kings Canyon. They might call it a "highway," but in truth the Generals Highway is a steep, narrow, twisting mountain road that can be treacherous in bad weather and when driven too fast by unfamiliar and inexperienced motorists. Maximum RV length is 22 feet on Generals Highway and Crystal Cave Road (no trailers permitted on the latter). RVs and trailers are not permitted on Mineral King Road or Moro Rock/Crescent Meadow Road.

Parking lots grace most major attractions, but these can fill up quickly in the summer. Some parking is permitted along the roadsides, but *please* don't park your hot car on dry grass—you can set the park (and your car) on fire this way.

Several of the park's roads close in the winter, though the Generals Highway remains open. The Mineral King Road, Crystal Cave Road, and Panoramic Point Roads close from about the beginning of November to the end of May each year. Check the website or call 559/565-3341 for current road information.

Drive times from either San Francisco or Los Angeles can easily run 5–7 hours, depending on traffic and weather conditions.

When you approach the parks, you'll be told by everybody and their little dog Spot that there's no gas anywhere in Sequoia or Kings Canyon National Parks. And technically, that's true. The Kings Canyon Lodge gas station sits on national forest land rather than inside the park borders proper. And many visitors are dubious when they see the genuine antique gravity gas pumps sitting outside the funky old lodge. But those pumps work, and while you can't fill up your SUV, you can get enough gas here to at least get you out of the park and to one of the border towns.

Two other stations sit in the national forest at Hume Lake (Hwy. 180, 11 miles north of Grant Grove) and Stony Creek (Generals Hwy., btwn. Lodgepole and Grant Grove).

Shuttles

Sequoia National Park provides free shuttle service (559/565-3341, www.nps.gov/seki/plan yourvisit/publictransportation.htm) within the park May 21–September 1. The "green" route connects Giant Forest with the Lodgepole Visitor Center, the General Sherman Tree, and the Giant Forest Museum. The "gray" route connects the Giant Forest Museum to Moro Rock and Crescent Meadow.

The **Sequoia Shuttle** (877/287-4453, www. sequoiashuttle.com, $15) connects Visalia to the Giant Forest Museum.

CENTRAL COAST

Here begins the California coast that movies and literature have made legendary. Soaring cliffs drop straight down into the sea in some areas, making the white sand beaches that occasionally appear beneath and beyond them all the more inviting. From north to south, the Pacific Ocean changes from slate gray to a gentler blue. Scents of salt and kelp waft up the beaches, and the endless crash of the breakers against the shore is a constant lullaby in the coastal towns.

The seacoast city of Santa Cruz, with its ultra-liberal culture, redwood-clad university, and general sense of funky fun, prides itself on keeping things weird. The beach and Boardwalk are prime attractions for surfing and enjoying the sun.

Gorgeous Monterey Bay is famous for its sealife. Sea otters dive and play at the world-renowned aquarium while sea lions beach themselves for sunning pleasure on offshore rocks. The historic Cannery Row was immortalized by Steinbeck in his novel of the same name, but the now touristy wharf area bears only a superficial resemblance to its fishing past.

One of the most exclusive enclaves of the wealthy in all of California, nearby Carmel rivals Malibu for its charming ocean views, well-traveled beaches and parks, and, most of all, for its unbelievably expensive real estate. (Clint Eastwood was once mayor here.) The legendary Pebble Beach golf course and resort sits just north of downtown.

South of Carmel, Highway 1 begins its scenic tour down Big Sur. The Big Sur coast might be the single most beautiful part of

© MONTEREY COUNTY CONVENTION AND VISITORS BUREAU

HIGHLIGHTS

◖ **Santa Cruz Beach Boardwalk:** This is the best traditional beach boardwalk in the state (page 433).

◖ **Monterey Bay Aquarium:** This mammoth aquarium was the first of its kind in the United States and still astonishes with a vast array of sea life and exhibits (page 447).

◖ **17-Mile Drive:** This gorgeous scenic drive is worth the toll for an introduction to the region's coastal beauty (page 455).

◖ **Carmel Mission:** Father Junipero Serra's favorite California mission is still a working parish, with an informative museum and stunning gilded altar (page 457).

◖ **Big Sur Coast Highway:** This twisty, coastal drive is iconic Big Sur, with jutting cliffs, crashing surf, and epics views all the way (page 464).

◖ **Pfeiffer Big Sur State Park:** Whether you're camping at the park or not, it's worth your time to hike through the stunning redwoods of Pfeiffer Big Sur (page 467).

◖ **Hearst Castle:** No visit to the Central Coast is complete without a tour of Hearst Castle, the grand mansion on a hill conceived and built by publishing magnate William Randolph Hearst (page 478).

◖ **Santa Barbara Museum of Natural History:** The museum's large galleries house

exhibits highlighting the natural history and inhabitants of the area. Take a stroll along the nature trail or peruse the accompanying planetarium (page 487).

LOOK FOR ◖ TO FIND RECOMMENDED SIGHTS, ACTIVITIES, DINING, AND LODGING.

California. The rugged cliffs and protected forests have little development to mar their natural charms. Travelers called to the wilderness will feel right at home in Big Sur. It's a sin to remain in your car, however, when an such an embarrassment of natural riches await. Waterfalls and redwoods beckon hikers and campers while cliffside resorts pamper guests.

Seaside Cambria makes a good base from which to visit much of the Central Coast, including Paso Robles and San Simeon, home to the grand Hearst Castle, an homage to excess.

The coast becomes less rugged here, though no less beautiful.

Beach lovers will flock to temperate Santa Barbara farther south, where the relaxed yet cultured pace reflects its mission and university influences, as well as its affluence. Wine is a growth industry here as well—look for the Central Coast to become the next great California wine region.

PLANNING YOUR TIME

The Central Coast is a favorite of many California residents for romantic weekend getaways. If you're coming to this part of the state for a weekend, pick an area and explore it in depth. Don't try to get everywhere in only two days—this is a big region and driving from one spot to another can take hours.

For a relaxed weekend without much travel, focus your trip on Santa Cruz, Carmel, Big Sur, Cambria, or Santa Barbara. If you're up for more adventure, add a day of wine tasting in Paso Robles to your Cambria trip, or head over to the Monterey Bay Aquarium from Carmel one morning.

If you've got a whole week, start in either Santa Cruz or Santa Barbara and work your way down or up the coast on Highway 1, with side trips into the Carmel Valley and Paso Robles. Alternately, it's easy to spend a whole week chilling out and becoming one with nature in Big Sur.

Santa Cruz

There's no place like Santa Cruz. Not even elsewhere in the wacky Bay Area can you find another town that has embraced the radical fringe of the nation and made it into a municipal-cultural statement quite like this. In Santa Cruz, you'll find surfers on the waves, nudists on the beaches, tree-huggers in the redwood forests, tattooed and pierced punks on the main drag, and families walking the dog along West Cliff Drive. Oh, and by the way, that purple-haired woman with the tongue stud might well be a dedicated volunteer at her local PTA. With the kind of irony only Santa Cruz (a town that has openly decriminalized marijuana) can produce, a massive illegal fireworks storm erupts over the beaches in patriotic celebration each Fourth of July.

Most visitors come to Santa Cruz to hit the Boardwalk and the beaches. Locals and UCSC students tend to hang at the Pacific Garden Mall and stroll on West Cliff. The east side of town can get dicey, especially a few blocks from the Boardwalk, while the Westside tends more towards families with children. The food of Santa Cruz qualifies as a hidden treasure, with myriad ethnicities represented.

The Santa Cruz area includes several tiny towns that aren't inside Santa Cruz proper, but blend into each other with the feeling of beach-town suburbs. Aptos, Capitola, and Soquel all lie to the south of Santa Cruz along the coast. Each has its own small shopping districts, restaurants, and lodgings. They've also got charming beaches all their own, which can be as foggy, as crowded, or as nice to visit as their northern neighbors.

SIGHTS
◖ Santa Cruz Beach Boardwalk
The Santa Cruz Beach Boardwalk (400 Beach St., 831/423-5590, www.beachboardwalk.com, daily 11 A.M.–close, parking $10), or just "the Boardwalk" as it's called by the locals, has a rare appeal that beckons to young children, too-cool teenagers, and adults of all ages.

The amusement park rambles along each side of the south end of the Boardwalk; entry is free, but you must buy either per-ride tickets or an unlimited ride wristband. The Great Dipper boasts a history as the oldest wooden roller coaster in the state, still giving riders a thrill after all this time. The spinner and the Zipper tend to be more fun for kids (or at least folks with hardy inner ears). In summertime, a log ride cools down guests hot from hours of tromping around. The Boardwalk also offers several toddler and little-kid rides.

At the other end of the Boardwalk, avid gamesters choose between the lure of prizes from the traditional midway games and the large arcade. Throw baseballs at things, try your arm at skeeball, or take a pass at classic or newer video game. The traditional carousel actually has a brass ring you (or your children) can try to grab.

After you've worn yourself out playing games and riding rides, you can take the stairs down to the broad, sandy beach below the

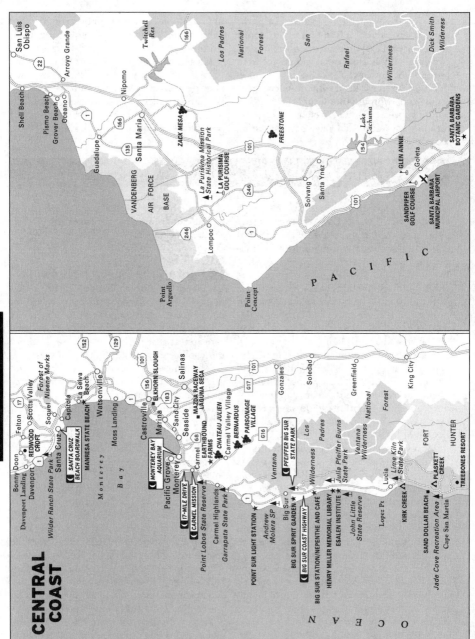

CENTRAL COAST

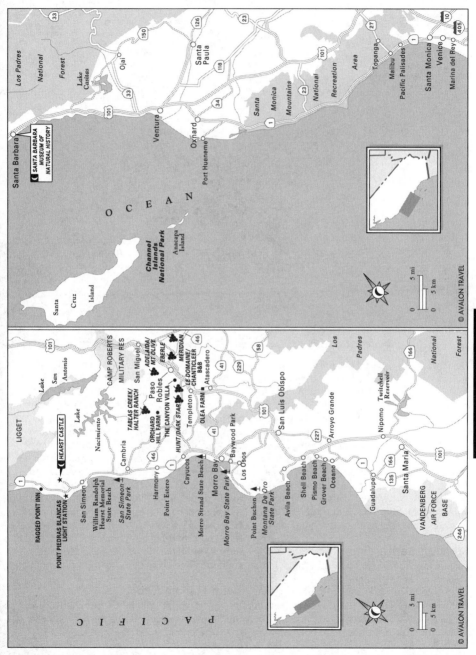

CENTRAL COAST

© AVALON TRAVEL

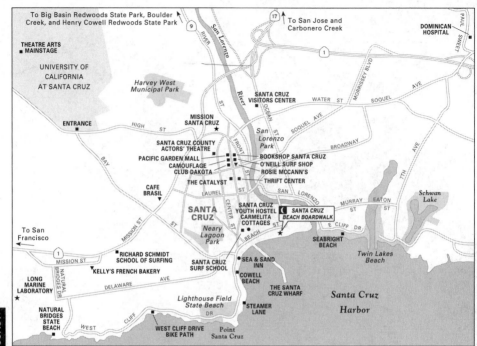

Boardwalk. It's a great place to flop down and sun yourself, or brave a dip in the cool Pacific surf. Granted, it gets a bit crowded in the summertime. But you've got all the services you could ever want right there at the Boardwalk, plus the sand and the water (and the occasional strand of kelp). What could be more perfect?

Looking for something tasty to munch on or a drink to cool you off? You can definitely find it at the Boardwalk. An old-fashioned candy shop sells sweets to the sweet, while the snack stands offer corn dogs, burgers, fries, lemonade, and other generally unhealthy traditional carnival food.

Mission Santa Cruz

Believe it or not, weird and funky Santa Cruz started out as a Mission town. Mission Santa Cruz (126 High St., 831/426-5686, Tues.–Sat. 10 A.M.–4 P.M., Sun. 10 A.M.–2 P.M.) was one of the later California missions, dedicated in 1791. Today, the attractive white of the building with its classic red-tiled roof welcomes parishioners to

the active Holy Cross church and fourth-grade students from around the Bay Area to the historic museum areas of the old mission. In fact, the buildings you can visit today, like many others in the mission chain, is not the original complex built by the Spanish fathers in the 18th century. Indeed, none of the first mission and only one wall from the second mission remains on the site today—the rest was destroyed in an earthquake. The church you'll tour today is the fourth one, built in 1889. After you finish your tour of the complex and grounds, be sure to stop in at the Galeria, which houses the mission gift shop and a stunning collection of religious vestments—something you won't see in many other California missions.

Long Marine Lab

If you love the sea and all the critters that live in it, be sure to come take a tour of the Long Marine Laboratory (Delaware Ave., 831/459-3800, www2.ucsc.edu/seymourcenter, Tues.–Sat.

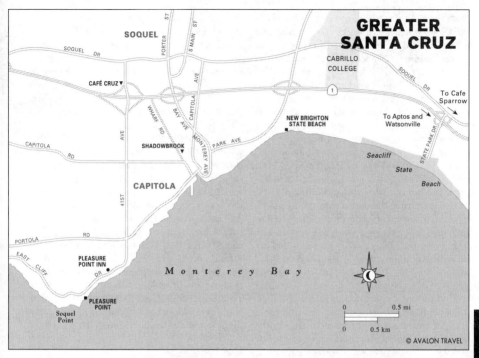

GREATER SANTA CRUZ

SOQUEL

CABRILLO COLLEGE

CAFÉ CRUZ ▾

To Cafe Sparrow

NEW BRIGHTON STATE BEACH

To Aptos and Watsonville

SHADOWBROOK

Seacliff

State

Beach

CAPITOLA

PORTOLA RD

EAST CLIFF

PLEASURE POINT INN

M o n t e r e y   B a y

PLEASURE POINT

Soquel Point

0   0.5 mi
0   0.5 km

© AVALON TRAVEL

10 A.M.–5 P.M., Sun. noon–5 P.M., adults $6, children $4). The large, attractive gray building complex at the end of Delaware Avenue sits right on the edge of the cliff overlooking the ocean—convenient for the research done primarily by students and faculty of UCSC. Your visit will be to the **Seymour Marine Discovery Center**—the part of the lab that's open to the public. You'll be greeted outside the door by a full blue whale skeleton that's lit up at night. Inside, instead of a standard aquarium setup, you'll find a marine laboratory similar to those used by the scientists elsewhere in the complex. Expect to see pipes and machinery around the tanks, which are designed to display their residents rather than to mimic habitats. Kids particularly love the touch tanks, while curious adults enjoy checking out the seasonal tank that contains the wildlife that's swimming around outside in the bay *right now.*

If you've never been to Long/Seymour before, the best way to introduce yourself to the lab is to take a tour. Tours run at 1 P.M., 2 P.M.,

and 3 P.M. each day; sign up an hour in advance to be sure of getting a slot.

UC Santa Cruz

The University of California at Santa Cruz (Bay St., 831/459-0111, www.ucsc.edu) might be the single most beautiful college campus in the country. Set up in the hills above downtown Santa Cruz, the classrooms and dorms sit underneath groves of coast redwood trees, amongst tangles of ferns and vines and cute woodland creatures. Call 831/459-4118 for a tour of the campus (groups of six or more, reservations required). Or just find a parking lot and wander out into the woods like the students do, looking for a perfect circle of trees to sit and meditate within.

ENTERTAINMENT AND EVENTS
Bars and Clubs

Down on the Mall, you can stroll upstairs to

Rosie McCann's (1220 Pacific Ave., 831/426-9930, www.rosiemccanns.com) for a pint and a bite. This dark-paneled, Irish-style saloon serves Guinness, Black and Tans, Snake Bites, and several tasty draft beers. You can also get a hefty meal at Rosie's, whose menu runs to sausage, mashed potatoes, and other weighty pub foods. A largely local crowd hangs out here, and you'll find the bar crowded and noisy, but the vibe friendly and entertaining.

For club-goers of the gayer persuasion, there's **Club Dakota** (1209 Pacific Ave., 831/454-9030). This local favorite tends toward the less crowded and more friendly end of the spectrum; the dance club might not be packed, but the bartenders are more likely to be happy when they get you your drinks. The only times the Dakota really gets crowded are on Saturday nights after 11 P.M., and on Pride and Party nights. If you come in before 10 P.M., you won't be charged a cover and you're likely to find plenty of space out on the dance floor. This being Santa Cruz, you might find more straight women than gay men dancing in the Dakota—it's known as a safe haven where few slimy guys hit on women. If you're a guy…well, the bouncers do a good job of keeping things fun rather than creepy here. Thursday nights equal cheap drinks, so come early to imbibe your fill.

Live Music

The Catalyst (1011 Pacific Ave., advance tickets 866/384-3060, door tickets 831/423-1338, www.catalystclub.com, $12–35), right downtown on the Mall, is *the* Santa Cruz nightclub. This live rock venue hosts all sorts of big-name national acts, most of whom now play clubs rather than stadiums. The Catalyst is completely democratic in its booking—you might see Ted Nugent one week, the Indigo Girls the next, and a ska band the week after that. In between, the Catalyst hosts DJ dance nights, teen nights, and other fun events. Be sure to check the calendar when you buy tickets—some shows are 21 and over only. (Mmm… music, dancing, and a full bar!) The main concert hall is a standing-room-only space, while

the balconies offer seating. The bar sits downstairs adjacent to the concert space. The vibe at the Catalyst tends to be low-key, but it depends on the night and the event. Some of the more retro acts definitely draw an older crowd, while the techno-DJ dance parties cater to the UCSC set. You can buy tickets online or by phone; purchasing in advance is recommended, especially for national acts.

The **Crow's Nest** (2218 East Cliff Dr., 831/476-4560, www.crowsnest-santacruz.com) functions as a venue for all kinds of live musical acts. You might see a contemporary reggae-rock group one night and a Latin dance band the next. Lots of funk bands play the Nest—it's just appropriate to the Santa Cruz ethos. A few tribute bands, usually to hippie 1960s and '70s legends like Jimi Hendrix and Santana, perform on occasion as well. Most shows are free, but if there's a really popular act you might be charged $5 at the door. Check the website for a performance calendar, but it's a good bet that you'll get live musical entertainment here every night from Wednesday through Saturday.

Comedy

For a good laugh in Santa Cruz, the **Crow's Nest** (2218 East Cliff Dr., 831/476-4560, www.crowsnest-santacruz.com, comedy Sun. 9 P.M., $7) also hosts a weekly stand-up comedy show. Because the show runs on Sunday nights, the Crow's Nest takes advantage of the opportunity to hire big-name comics who have been in San Francisco or San Jose for weekend engagements. This lets folks see headliners in a more casual setting for a fraction of the cost of the big-city clubs. The Crow's Nest, with its great views out over the Pacific, also has a full bar and restaurant. You can enjoy drinks and dinner while you get your giggle on.

Theater

Santa Cruz is home to several community theaters and an outdoor summer Shakespeare festival that draws theatergoers from around the Bay Area.

The **Santa Cruz County Actors' Theatre** (1001 Center St., 831/425-7529, www.actorssc

.org) acts as Santa Cruz's permanent local theater company. The Actors' Theatre does it all: performs a subscription season, holds theater arts workshops, sponsors playwriting contests for kids and adults, and stages improv shows. All shows at this low-cost theater are contemporary works, including the full production series plays. But the most exciting (though not necessarily the highest quality) shows you can see here are the new works festivals featuring completely new plays, mostly by local authors, which have won Actors' Theatre contests. If one of these, especially the "Eight Tens at Eight," appears during your stay, consider getting tickets so you can see something completely different.

If you prefer historic theater to modern, UCSC puts on an annual summer Shakespeare festival: **Shakespeare Santa Cruz** (831/459-2121, http://shakespearesantacruz.org, adults $32–44, seniors/students $29, children $18). This six-week festival usually runs in the second half of July and through August. Venues both sit on the UCSC campus, one indoor at the Theatre Arts Mainstage (1156 High St.) and the other out in the redwood forests in the Festival Glen (Meyer Dr.). Each year the festival puts up at least two Shakespeare plays— 2008 selections included *Romeo and Juliet* and *All's Well That Ends Well*—plus at least one other production (often a more contemporary play). At the outdoor glen, audience members are encouraged to bring their own picnics. This can make for the perfect romantic date, or a fun outing for the whole family.

SHOPPING

There's no shopping area in California quite like the **Pacific Garden Mall** (Pacific Ave., 831/429-8433). Hanging out "on the Mall," as the locals call it, is a pastime for many teens and adults from Santa Cruz and beyond. The Mall runs on Pacific Avenue and its offshoots, and is usually open to (very slow) auto traffic. Park in one of the structures a block or two off the Mall proper and walk from there. At the north end, shoppers peruse antiques, boutique clothing, and kitchenware. Down at the seedier south end of the mall, visitors can get shining

new body jewelry, a great new tattoo, or a silicone sex toy. In the middle (and to a lesser degree throughout the Mall), you can grab a bite to eat, a cappuccino, or a cocktail in one of the many independent eateries. You'll find only a select few chain stores on the Mall, and those are uniformly reviled by the fiercely anti-mega-corporation residents of Santa Cruz. The Borders across the street from the **Book Shop Santa Cruz** (1520 Pacific Ave., 831/423-0900, www.bookshopsantacruz.com, Sun.–Thurs. 9 A.M.–10 P.M., Fri.–Sat. until 11 P.M.) takes shockingly little business away from its local independent rival.

Sure, you will find an **O'Neill Surf Shop** (110 Cooper St., 831/469-4377) on the Mall, but surf shops are a staple of Santa Cruz. This one specializes in surfboards, wetsuits, and brand-name clothing. If your trip to California has gotten you hooked on riding the waves, and you just have to invest in your own equipment, O'Neill can be a good place to start. (If you're an expert who prefers custom work, you already know that pre-fab chain stuff isn't for you.) You can also buy a T-shirt or some sweats here—handy if you didn't pack quite right for Central Coast summer fog.

If you're wanting to buy clothes in Santa Cruz, chances are you're looking for a secondhand store. This town has plenty of 'em. One of the largest of these sits only a block off Pacific Avenue—the aptly if redundantly named **Thrift Center Thrift Store** (504 Front St., 831/429-6975). This big, somewhat dirty retail space offers a wide array of cheap secondhand clothes. You'll need to hunt a bit to find that one perfect vintage item that's just too perfect, but isn't that the fun of thrift shopping?

Down toward the great divide between the "good side" and the "less good side" of the Mall you can price some more adult merchandise. **Camouflage** (1329 Pacific Ave., 888/309-2266, http://experiencethefantasy. com, Mon.–Thurs. 10 A.M.–8 P.M., Fri.–Sat. 10 A.M.–10 P.M., Sun. 11 A.M.–7 P.M.) is an independent, women-operated and women-friendly adult store. The first room contains mostly lingerie and less-shocking items. Dare to walk through the narrow black-curtained passage, and you'll find the *other* room, which is filled with grown-up toys designed to please women of every taste and proclivity. (A few cool gizmos and gadgets can make things fun for the men as well.) As many ladies as men shop here, and can feel comfortable doing so.

SPORTS AND RECREATION
Beaches

At the tip of the West Side, **Natural Bridges State Park** (West Cliff Dr., 831/423-4609, www.parks.ca.gov, daily 8 A.M.–sunset) offers nearly every kind of beach recreation possible. The sand strip doesn't stretch wide, but falls back deep, crossed by a creek that feeds out into the sea. An inconsistent break makes surfing at Natural Bridges fun on occasion, while the near-constant winds that sweep the sands bring out windsurfers nearly every weekend. Hardy sun-worshippers brave the breezes, bringing out their beach blankets, umbrellas, and sunscreen on rare sunny days (usually in late spring and fall). Back from the beach, a wooded picnic area has tables and grills for small and larger parties. Even farther back, the visitors center can provide great stories about the various national wonders of this surprisingly diverse state park. Rangers offer guided tours of the tidepools that range out to the west side of the beach. You can access these by a somewhat scrambling short hike (0.25–0.5 mile) on the rocks cliffs. These odd little holes filled with sea life aren't like most tidepools—many are nearly perfect round depressions in the sandstone cliffs worn away by harder stones as the tides move tirelessly back and forth. Just don't touch the residents of these pools, since human hands can hurt delicate tidepool creatures.

At **Cowell Beach** (350 West Cliff Dr.), it's all about the surfing. This West Side beach sits right at a crook in the coastline, which joins with underwater features to create a reliable small break that lures new surfers by the dozens. (See *Surfing* section for more information about surfing Cowell.)

At the south end of Santa Cruz, down by the harbor, beachgoers flock to **Seabright Beach** (East Cliff Dr. at Seabright Ave., 831/685-6500, www.santacruzstateparks.org, daily 6 A.M.–10 P.M., free) all summer long. This miles-long stretch of sand, protected by the cliffs from the worst of the winds, is a favorite retreat for sunbathers and loungers. While there's little in the way of snack bars, permanent volleyball courts, or facilities, you can still have a great time at Seabright. There's lots of soft sand to lie in, plenty of room to play football or set up your own volleyball net, and, of course, easy access to the chilly Pacific Ocean. There's no surfing here—Seabright has a shore break that delights skim-boarders, but makes wave riding impossible.

Each Fourth of July, the Santa Cruz police force cordons off the area surrounding Seabright Beach. No one can park nearby or even walk in after a certain point in the afternoon (which seems to change annually). But if you show up early to cart in yourself and all your stuff down onto the sand, you can participate in the unbelievable fireworks extravaganza that starts almost as soon as the sun goes down. Though it's technically illegal, people still create professional-grade pyrotechnical productions and launch them from Seabright. The effect quickly becomes overwhelming, but for those who can handle, the night is truly magical.

Down in Capitola, one of the favorite sandy spots is **New Brighton State Beach** (1500 Park Ave., Capitola, 831/464-6330, www.parks.ca.gov). This forest-backed beach has everything: a strip of sand that's perfect for lounging and cold-water swimming, a forest-shaded campground for both tent and RV campers, hiking trails, and ranger-led nature programs. If you plan to camp, call in advance to make reservations at this popular state park, or just come for the day and set up your spot out on the sand. New Brighton can get crowded on rare sunny summer days, but it's nothing like the wall-to-wall people of the popular Southern California beaches.

Surfing

The coastline of Santa Cruz has more than its share of great surf breaks. The water is cold, demanding full wetsuits year-round, and the shoreline is rough and rocky—nothing at all like the flat sandy beaches of SoCal. But that doesn't deter the hordes of locals who ply the waves every day they can. The surfing culture pervades the town—if you walk the cliff, you'll likely pass the *To Honor Surfing* sculpture. Santa Cruz loves this statue, and it's often dressed up and always gets a costume for Halloween.

If you're a beginner, the best place to start surfing Santa Cruz is **Cowell's** (stairs at West Cliff and Cowell Beach). The waves are low and long, making for fun longboard rides perfect for surfers just getting their balance. Because the Cowell's break is acknowledged as the newbie spot, the often sizeable crowd tends to be polite to newcomers and tourists.

For more advanced surfers looking for smaller crowds in the water, **Manresa State Beach** (San Andreas Rd., Aptos, www.parks.ca.gov) offers fun rides under the right conditions. Manresa is several minutes' drive south toward Aptos. You'll usually find a good beach break, and the waves can get big when there's a north swell.

Visitors who know their surfing lore will want to surf the more famous spots along the Santa Cruz shore. **Pleasure Point** (btwn. 32nd Ave. and 41st Ave., Soquel) encompasses a number of different breaks. You may have heard of The Hook (steps at 41st Ave.), a well-known experienced longboarder's paradise. But don't mistake The Hook for a beginner's break; the locals feel protective of the waves here and aren't always friendly towards inexperienced tourists. The break at 36th and East Cliff (steps at 36th Ave.) can be a better place to go on weekdays—on the weekends, the intense crowding makes catching your own wave a challenge. Up at 30th and East Cliff (steps at 36th Ave), you'll find challenging sets and hot-dogging shortboarders.

The most famous break in all of Santa Cruz can also be the most hostile to newcomers. **Steamer Lane** (West Cliff btwn. Cowell's and the Lighthouse) has both a fiercely protective crew of locals and a dangerous break

that actually kills someone about every other year. But if you're into adrenaline and there's a swell coming in, you'll be hard pressed to find a more exciting ride on the Central Coast, or indeed in most of California.

Yes, you can learn to surf in Santa Cruz despite the distinct local flavor at some of the breaks. Check out either the **Santa Cruz Surf School** (322 Pacific Ave., 831/426-7072, www.santacruzsurfschool.com) or the **Richard Schmidt School of Surfing** (849 Almar Ave., 831/423-0928, www.richardschmidt.com) to sign up for lessons. Who knows, maybe one day the locals will mistake you for one of their own!

Windsurfing and Parasurfing

If you prefer to let the wind help you catch the waves, you probably already know that Santa Cruz has some prize windsurfing and parasurfing locales. Beginning windsurfers vie with longboarders for space at **Cowell's,** which sits right next to the City Wharf (stairs at West Cliff and Cowell Beach). For a bigger breeze, head up West Cliff to **Natural Bridges State Park** (West Cliff Dr., www.parks.ca.gov, $6 parking). Natural Bridges offers the best spot to set up, plus restroom facilities and ample parking. Serious sailors head farther north to **Davenport Landing** (Hwy. 1, 20 miles north of Santa Cruz). You'll be able to discern that you've found the right rugged and windswept stretch of coast by the endless crowd of sailors and parasurfers out on the waves. Parking can be a bit haphazard here, but even if you're just stopping by to watch, it can be worth your time since the sight of these athletes using both wind and waves to create ultra-fast rides is nothing short of amazing.

If you want to try your luck at windsurfing for the first time, contact **Club Ed** (831/464-0177, www.club-ed.com) to set up a lesson. They operate in the gentle breezes and small swells at Cowell's, and make it easy for first-timers to gain confidence and have a great time.

Hiking and Biking

To walk or bike where the locals do, just head

out to **West Cliff Drive.** This winding street with a full-fledged sidewalk-trail running its length on the ocean side is the town's favorite walking, dog-walking, jogging, skating, scootering, and biking route. You can start at Natural Bridges (the west end of West Cliff) and go for miles. The *To Honor Surfing* statue lies several miles down the road, as do plenty of fabulous views. Bring your camera if you're strolling West Cliff on a clear day—you won't be able to resist taking photos of the sea, cliffs, and sunset. Just be sure to watch for your fellow path-users. What with the bicyclists and skaters and such, it can get a bit treacherous if you don't watch where you're going.

ACCOMMODATIONS
Under $100

Staying at a hostel in Santa Cruz just feels right. And the **Santa Cruz Youth Hostel Carmelita Cottages** (321 Main St., 831/423-8304, www.hi-santacruz.org, $25 dorm, $55 private room, $150 cottage) offers a great local atmosphere. Like most historic Santa Cruz edifices, it doesn't look like much from the outside. And certainly the interior doesn't have the newest furniture and paint. But it's clean, cheap, friendly, and close to the beach. You'll find a spot to store your surfboard or bike for free, and car parking is $1 per day. The big homelike kitchen is open for guest use, and might even be hiding some extra free food in its cupboards. Expect all the usual hostel-style amenities, a nice garden out back, free linens, laundry facilities, and a free Internet kiosk.

$100-150

The four-room **Adobe on Green Street** (103 Green St., 831/469-9866, www.adobeongreen .com, $132–242) offers lovely bed-and-breakfast accommodations close to the heart of downtown Santa Cruz. The location, within walking distance of the Pacific Garden Mall, lets you soak in the unique local atmosphere to your heart's content. A unifying decorative scheme runs through all four guest rooms—a dark and minimalist Spanish

Mission style befitting Santa Cruz's history as a mission town. Each room has a queen bed, a private bathroom (most with tubs), a small TV with DVD player, and lots of other amenities that can make you comfortable even over a long stay. An expanded continental spread is set out in the dining room each morning 8–11 A.M. Expect yummy local pastries, organic and soy yogurts, and multicolored eggs laid by a neighbor's flock of chickens. In keeping with the Santa Cruz ethos, the Adobe runs on solar power.

$150-250

For a room overlooking the ocean, stay at the **C Sea & Sand Inn** (201 West Cliff Dr., 831/427-3400, www.santacruzmotels.com/sea_and_sand.html, $189–229). In an unbeatable location on the ocean side of West Cliff at Bay Street, you'll be close enough to downtown and the Boardwalk to enjoy the action of Santa Cruz. But you'll also have a touch more quiet in a neighborhood that's starting to tend toward the residential. Every room in the house comes with an ocean view (hence the high price for what's really a pretty basic motel room), and suites with hot tubs and private patios make for a wonderful seaside vacation. Rooms and suites do have nicer than average decor with pretty furniture, private baths, and free Internet access.

Some travelers prefer to stay in the woods rather than downtown or out by the busy Boardwalk. **Redwood Croft Bed & Breakfast** (275 Northwest Dr., Bonny Doon, 831/458-1939, www.redwoodcroft.com, $145–230) is a funky two-room B&B, set back in the recently charred ruins of the forest to the northwest of Santa Cruz, formerly a beautiful redwood forest. The inn itself takes the woodsy theme indoors, using natural wood in the walls and furniture to create a serene retreat-house feeling. Each of the two guest rooms bursts with beautiful appointments, lovely stone bathrooms, and views out into the recovering woods.

Over $250

Despite its bohemian reputation, there's plenty of

money flowing through Santa Cruz. For plush accommodations, consider staying at the **Pleasure Point Inn** (23665 E. Cliff Dr., 831/475-4657, www.pleasurepointinn.com, $275–325). This small, exclusive inn boasts a rooftop deck with a hot tub, an expansive common living room with views out over the ocean, and four luxurious guest rooms. Each room has wood floors, a gas fireplace, a private deck or patio, a private bathroom, and all sorts of posh amenities. Expect to find a TV, phone, and Internet access in your room. A continental breakfast is laid out each morning, giving you just the right start to the day. All rooms also boast views out over the ocean—the inn does indeed sit on *that* Pleasure Point, so you can sit and watch the surfers as you drink your morning coffee. Or if you prefer to be a part of the action, ask about setting up surfing lessons through the inn and Club Ed when you reserve your room.

FOOD
American
At **Cafe Cruz** (2621 41st Ave., Soquel, 831/476-3801, www.cafecruz.com, Mon.–Sat. 11:30 A.M.–2:30 P.M., daily 5:30 P.M.–close, $16–30), the menu runs toward homey American favorites done up with a California twist (ribs, rotisserie chicken, bowls of pasta, and crunchy fresh salads). Cafe Cruz purchases the freshest local produce, meats, seafood, and even drinks they can find. You can munch locally caught fish with goat cheese from Half Moon Bay and an organic soda from Monterey. The attractive white-tablecloth dining room welcomes casual and elegant diners alike, and if you choose wisely you can get an upscale meal for medium-scale prices.

Asian
When locals who love their sushi get that craving for raw fish, they head for **Shogun Sushi** (1123 Pacific Ave., 831/469-4477, Mon.–Wed. 5–9 P.M., Thurs.–Fri. 5–10 P.M., Sat. 3–10 P.M.). Right on the Pacific Garden Mall, Shogun serves big fresh slabs of nigiri and an interesting collection of maki (rolls). The fish served here is some of the freshest you'll find in this seacoast city. Their meats and other dishes also please diners with fresh ingredients and tasty preparations. While service can be spotty, usually it's efficient—you'll get your order quickly and it will be right on. If you're not used to sushi prices, you may find Shogun expensive, but if you're a connoisseur you'll feel that they're quite reasonable. Do be aware that there's often a wait for a table in the evenings, especially on weekends.

California
The Santa Cruz region boasts one serious upscale eatery. The **Shadowbrook** (1750 Wharf Rd., Capitola, 800/975-1511, www.shadowbrook-capitola.com, Mon.–Fri. 5–8:45 P.M., Sat. 4:30–9:30 P.M., Sun. 4:30–8:45 P.M., $25) has long been worth driving over the hill for. The cliffside location, complete with the namesake brook flowing through the dining room, has perhaps the most impressive views and atmosphere of any restaurant in the area. The Shadowbrook makes for a perfect spot to stage the ultimate romantic date, complete with roses, candlelight, and fine chocolate desserts.

French
In Aptos, **Cafe Sparrow** (8042 Soquel Dr., Aptos, 831/688-6238, www.cafesparrow.com, Mon.–Sat. 11:30 A.M.–2 P.M., Sun. 9:30 A.M.–2 P.M., daily 5:30 P.M.–close, $20) serves country French cuisine that's consistently tasty. Whatever you order, it will be fantastic. The seafood is noteworthy (especially the Friday night bouillabaisse), as are the steaks. Cafe Sparrow's kitchen prepares all the dishes with fresh ingredients, and the chef (who can sometimes be seen out in the dining room checking on customer satisfaction with the food) thinks up innovative preparations and creates tasty sauces. He's also willing to accommodate special requests and dietary restrictions with good cheer. The best deal for your money is the daily-changing prix-fixe menu. For dessert, treat yourself to the profiteroles, which can be created with either ice cream or pastry cream.

South American

Cafe Brasil (1410 Mission St., 831/429-1855, www.cafebrasil.us, daily 8:00 A.M.–3:00 P.M., $10–20) serves up the Brazilian fare its name promises. Painted jungle green with bright yellow and blue trim, you can't miss this totally Santa Cruz breakfast and lunch joint. In the morning, the fare runs to omelets and ethnic specialties, while lunch includes pressed sandwiches, meat and tofu dishes, and Brazilian house specials. A juice bar provides rich but healthy meal accompaniments that can also act as light meals on their own. To try something different, get an acia bowl—acia is a South American fruit—or an Amazon cherry juice and OJ blend.

Coffee and Bakeries

For a casual sandwich or pastry, head for **Kelly's French Bakery** (402 Ingalls St., 831/423-9059, www.kellysfrenchbakery.com, Mon.–Thurs. 7–11 A.M. and 11:30 A.M.–7 P.M., Fri. 7–11 A.M. and 11:30 A.M.–8 P.M., Sat.–Sun. 7 A.M.–11:30 A.M. and noon–7 P.M., $10). This popular bakery makes its home in an old industrial warehouse-style space, and its domed shape constructed out of corrugated metal looks like anything but a restaurant. It's got both indoor and outdoor seating, and serves full breakfasts and luncheon sandwiches. You can order to stay in or to go, and pick up a breakfast or sweet pastry, some bread, or a cake while you're there.

INFORMATION AND SERVICES
Tourist Information

While it can be fun to explore Santa Cruz just by using your innate sense of direction and the bizarre, those who want a bit more structure on their travels can hit the **Santa Cruz Visitors Center** (1211 Ocean Ave., 800/833-3494, www.santacruzca.org) for maps, advice, and information.

Media and Communications

Santa Cruz publishes its own daily newspaper, the *Santa Cruz Sentinel* (www.santacruzsentinel.com). You'll get your daily dose of national wire service news and current events, local news, plus some good stuff for visitors. The *Sentinel* has a Food section, a Sunday Travel section, and plenty of up-to-date entertainment information.

You can get your mail on at the **post office** near the Mall on 850 Front Street (831/426-0144).

Santa Cruz is like totally wired, man. You'll definitely be able to access the Internet in a variety of cafés and hotels. There are Starbucks locations here, and the many indie cafés often compete with their own (sometimes free) Wi-Fi.

Santa Cruz has plenty of banks and ATMs (including some ATMs on the arcade at the Boardwalk). Bank branches congregate downtown near the Pacific Garden Mall. The West Side is mostly residential, so you'll find a few ATMs in supermarkets and gas stations, but little else.

Medical Services

Despite its rep as a funky bohemian beach town, Santa Cruz's dense population dictates that it have at least one full-fledged hospital of its own. You can get medical treatment and care at **Dominican Hospital** (1555 Soquel Ave., 831/426-7700, www.dominicanhospital.org).

GETTING THERE AND AROUND
Car

If you're driving to Santa Cruz from Silicon Valley, you've got two choices of roads. Most drivers take fast, dangerous Highway 17. This narrow road doesn't have any switchbacks and is the main truck route "over the hill." Most locals take this 50-mile-per hour corridor fast—probably faster than they should. Each year, several people die in accidents on Highway 17, and I once crashed my vehicle into an overturned pickup truck on Big Moody curve. So if you're new to the road, keep to the right and take it slow, no matter what the traffic to the left of you is doing. Check traffic reports before you head out; Highway 17 is known to be one of the worst commuting roads in all of the

Bay Area, and the weekend beach traffic in the summer jams up fast in both directions too.

For a more leisurely drive, you can opt for two-lane Highway 9. The tight curves and endless switchbacks will keep you at a reasonable speed; use the turnouts to let the locals past, please. On Highway 9, your biggest obstacles tend to be groups of bicyclists and motorcyclists, both of whom adore the slopes and curves of this technical driving road. The good news is that you'll get an up-close-and-personal view of the gorgeously forested Santa Cruz Mountains, complete with views of the valley to the north and ocean vistas to the south.

Parking

Visitors planning to drive or bike around Santa Cruz should get themselves a good map, either before they arrive or at the visitors center in town. Navigating the winding, occasionally broken-up streets of this oddly shaped town isn't for the faint of heart. Highway 1, which becomes Mission Street on the West Side, acts as the main artery through Santa Cruz and down to Capitola, Soquel, Aptos, and coastal points farther south. You'll find that Highway 1 at the interchange to Highway 17, and sometimes several miles to the south, is a parking lot most of the time. No, you probably haven't come upon a major accident or a special event. It's just like that all the time, and will be until the construction widening the highway to deal with the heavy traffic is complete.

Parking in Santa Cruz can be its own special sort of horror. Downtown, head straight for the parking structures one block away from Pacific Avenue on either side. They're much easier to deal with than trying to find street parking. The same goes for the beach and Boardwalk areas. At the Boardwalk, just pay the fee to park in the big parking lot adjacent to the attractions. You'll save an hour and a possible car break-in or theft trying to find street parking in the sketchy neighborhoods that surround the Boardwalk.

Bus

In town, the buses are run by the **Santa Cruz METRO** (831/425-8600 www.scmtd.com, adults $1.50/single ride, passes available). With 42 routes running in Santa Cruz County, you can probably find a way to get nearly anywhere you'd want to go on the METRO.

Monterey

Monterey is the "big city" on the well-populated southern tip of the wide-mouthed Monterey Bay. The outlying agricultural towns of Sand City and Marina lie to the northeast (closer to the Bay Area), while sleepy residential Pacific Grove lies to the northeast closer to the big golf courses of Pebble Beach.

Neighboring Carmel-by-the-Sea caters to the wealthy, the artsy, and golf afficianados, while Monterey has a long history as a working class town. Originally inhabited by Native Americans, who fished the bay, Monterey became a fishing hub for the European settlers in the 19th century as well. (Author John Steinbeck immortalized the unglamorous fish-canning industry here in his novel *Cannery* *Row*.) It wasn't until the 20th century that the city began to lean toward gentrification—the bay just off the shore became a wildlife preserve, the Monterey Bay Aquarium opened, and the tourist trade became a mainstay of the local economy. Today, Cannery Row resembles a giant shopping mall and the Aquarium is constantly packed with visitors.

SIGHTS
Cannery Row

Welcome to Monterey's own version of Tourist Hell. Cannery Row (Cannery Row, www.canneryrow.com), sitting right on the water, did once look and feel as John Steinbeck described it in his famed novel of the same name. In days

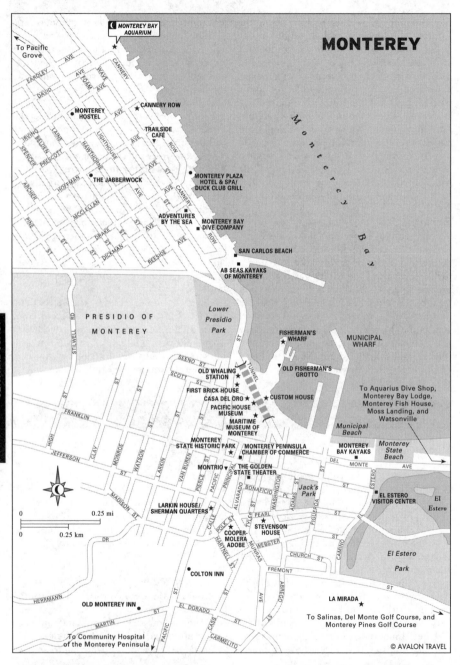

MONTEREY

To Pacific Grove

Monterey Bay Aquarium

CANNERY ROW

MONTEREY HOSTEL

TRAILSIDE CAFÉ

THE JABBERWOCK

MONTEREY PLAZA HOTEL & SPA/ DUCK CLUB GRILL

ADVENTURES BY THE SEA

MONTEREY BAY DIVE COMPANY

SAN CARLOS BEACH

AB SEAS KAYAKS OF MONTEREY

Monterey Bay

PRESIDIO OF MONTEREY

Lower Presidio Park

FISHERMAN'S WHARF

MUNICIPAL WHARF

SEENO ST

SCOTT

OLD WHALING STATION

OLD FISHERMAN'S GROTTO

To Aquarius Dive Shop, Monterey Bay Lodge, Monterey Fish House, Moss Landing, and Watsonville

FIRST BRICK HOUSE

CASA DEL ORO

CUSTOM HOUSE

PACIFIC HOUSE MUSEUM

MARITIME MUSEUM OF MONTEREY

Municipal Beach

FRANKLIN

MONTEREY STATE HISTORIC PARK

MONTEREY PENINSULA CHAMBER OF COMMERCE

MONTEREY BAY KAYAKS

Monterey State Beach

JEFFERSON

MONTRIO

THE GOLDEN STATE THEATER

DEL MONTE AVE

EL ESTERO VISITOR CENTER

El Estero

Jack's Park

0   0.25 mi

0   0.25 km

LARKIN HOUSE/ SHERMAN QUARTERS

COOPER-MOLERA ADOBE

STEVENSON HOUSE

El Estero Park

COLTON INN

HERRMANN

OLD MONTEREY INN

LA MIRADA

To Salinas, Del Monte Golf Course, and Monterey Pines Golf Course

To Community Hospital of the Monterey Peninsula

© AVALON TRAVEL

gone by, it was easy for fishing boats to dock and offload their catches straight into the huge warehouse-like cannery buildings. Low-wage workers processed the fish and put it into cans, ready to ship across the country and around the world.

Today, what was once a workingman's wharf is now a conclave of high-end apartments, boutique hotels, big seafood restaurants, and cheesy souvenir stores. It's anchored at one end by the aquarium and runs for several blocks, which include a beach, then leads into the wharf area. All that's left of the historic Cannery Row are some of the exteriors of the buildings. Inside, history has given way to a wax museum, a Thomas Kincaide gallery, and kitsch by the yard. Kids have fun running from shop to shop, but adults may grow tired of the chain stores and tacky souvenir stalls after a while.

◖ Monterey Bay Aquarium

The first aquarium of its kind in the country, the Monterey Bay Aquarium (886 Cannery Row, 831/648-4800, www.mbayaq.org, daily 10 A.M.–6 P.M., adults $24.95, children $15.95) is still unique in many ways. From the very beginning, the aquarium's mission has been conservation, and they're not shy about it. They have taken custodianship of the Pacific coastline and waters in Monterey County down to Big Sur, and take an active role in the saving and conservation of at-risk wildlife in the area. Many of the animals in the aquarium's tanks were rescued, and those that survive may eventually be returned to the wild. All the exhibits you'll see in this mammoth complex contain only local sea life. If you fear that the tight focus might make the tanks dull, you needn't worry. The exhibits and shows put on by the residents of Monterey Bay delight children and adults alike.

The aquarium displays a dazzling array of species. When you come to visit, a good first step is to look up the feeding schedules for the tanks you're most interested in. The critters always put on the best show at feeding time, and it's smart to show up several minutes in advance of feeding to get a good spot near the glass.

The living, breathing **Kelp Forest** is just like the kelp beds outside the Bay proper—except this one is 28 feet tall. Try to time your visit for either the 11:30 A.M. or 4 P.M. feeding time, when the fish in the tank put on quite a show.

The deep-water tank in the **Outer Bay**

CENTRAL COAST

© LIZ HAMILL SCOTT

Kelp Forest at the Monterey Bay Aquarium

STEINBECK

John Ernst Steinbeck was born in Salinas, California in 1902 and grew up in its tiny, isolated agricultural community. He somehow managed to escape life as a farmer, a sardine fisherman, or a fish canner, and ended up living the glamorous life of a writer for his too-short 66 years.

Steinbeck's experiences in the Salinas Valley farming community and in the fishing town of Monterey informed many of his novels. The best known of these is *Cannery Row*, but *Tortilla Flat* is also set in working-class Monterey (though no one knows exactly where the fictional "Tortilla Flat" neighborhood was supposed to be). The Pulitzer Prize-winning novel *The Grapes of Wrath* takes more of its inspiration from the Salinas Valley. Steinbeck used the Valley as a model for farming in the Dust Bowl – the wretched, impoverished era that was the Great Depression.

In fact, Steinbeck was fascinated by the plight of working men and women; his novels and stories generally depict ordinary folks going through tough and terrible times. Steinbeck lived and worked through the Great Depression – thus it's not surprising that many of his stories do *not* feature happy Hollywood endings. Steinbeck was a realist in almost all of his novels, portraying the good, the bad, and the ugly of human life and society. His work gained almost immediate respect – in addition to his Pulitzer, Steinbeck also won the Nobel Prize for Literature in 1962. Almost every American high school student from the 1950s onward has read at least one of Steinbeck's novels or short stories; his body of work forms part of the enduring American literary canon.

As California's most illustrious literary son in the 20th century, Salinas became equally famous for spawning the author and inspiring his work. You'll find a variety of Steinbeck maps online (www.mtycounty.com/pgs-mty-stnbeck/mty-steinbeck.html) that offer self-guided tours of the regions made famous by his various novels. Poor Steinbeck's name is taken in vain all over now-commercial Cannery Row – even the cheesy Wax Museum tries to draw customers in by claiming kinship with the legendary author. More serious scholars of Steinbeck prefer the **National Steinbeck Center** (1 Main St., 831/796-3833, www.steinbeck.org, Salinas, daily 10 A.M.-5 P.M., $10.95) and the **Steinbeck House** (132 Central Ave., Salinas, 831/424-2735, www.steinbeckhouse.com, summer tours 1-3 P.M.), both in the still-agricultural town of Salinas. And if the museums aren't enough, plan to be in Monterey County in early August for the annual **Steinbeck Festival** (www.steinbeck.org), a big shindig put on by the Steinbeck Center in order to celebrate the great man's life and works in fine style.

exhibit area always draws a crowd. Inside its depths, a monster bluefin tuna that's been an aquarium resident for many years rules the roost. Even the fierce hammerhead sharks and odd-looking enormous sunfish steer clear of the tuna and its brethren.

The **Wild About Otters** exhibit gives visitors an up-close and personal view of rescued otters. The adorable, furry marine mammals come right up to the glass to interact with curious children and enchanted adults. You can watch aquarists feed and train the otters daily at 10:30 A.M., 1:30 P.M., and 3:30 P.M.

In addition to the many exhibits, be sure to check out the life and times of local tidepools, surflines, and even the ecosystems that surround the pillars, cement blocks, chains, and trash of the Monterey piers.

It's easy to spend all day at the aquarium. If you get hungry, try for a table at the full-service restaurant and bar, complete with white tablecloths and a view of the bay. A self-service café offers sandwiches, salads, and ethnic dishes. You'll hardly be able to escape the souvenirs as a different gift shop sits in a corner of almost every exhibit hall.

If you possibly can, plan your visit to the Monterey Bay Aquarium on a weekday rather than a weekend. The aquarium is a wildly popular weekend destination. Especially in the summer, the crowds can be forbidding. Weekdays can be less crushing (though you'll run into school groups during much of the year), and the off-season is almost always a better time to visit. The aquarium has facilities for wheelchair access to almost all exhibits.

Monterey State Historic Park

Monterey State Historic Park (20 Custom House Plaza, 831/649-7118, www.parks.ca.gov, daily 10 A.M.–5 P.M., free), usually called Old Monterey by locals, pays homage to the long and colorful history of the city of Monterey. This busy port town acted as the capital of California when it was under Spanish rule, and then later when the area became part of United States territory. Today, this park provides a peek into Monterey as it was in the middle of the 19th century—a busy place filled with dock workers, fishermen, bureaucrats, and soldiers. And yet it blends into the modern town of Monterey as well, and modern stores, galleries, and restaurants sit next to 150-year-old adobe structures. Free guided tours of several of the museums and adobes are offered most days; a walking tour of Old Monterey takes place at 10:30 A.M. on Monday–Wednesday and on Friday.

It's tough to see everything in just one visit to Old Monterey. If you only get to one spot on your first trip, make it the **Custom House** (Sat.–Thurs. 10 A.M.–4 P.M., Fri. 10:30 A.M.–4 P.M.). It's California State Historic Landmark Number 1, and the oldest bureaucratic building known to still stand in the state. You can spend some time wandering the adobe building, checking out the artifacts on display, or even just looking out the upstairs window towards the sea. Also on the plaza is the **Pacific House Museum** (Fri.–Wed. 10 A.M.–4 P.M., Thurs. 10:30 A.M.–4 P.M.) with exhibits of Native American artifacts.

There are 10 other buildings that comprise the park; most were built with adobe and/or brick between 1834 and 1847. These include: the **Casa del Oro;** the **Cooper-Molera**

Adobe (525 Polk St., guided tours Fri.–Wed. 3 P.M.); the **First Brick House;** the **Larkin House** (510 Calle Principal, guided tours Tues.–Wed. 11:30 A.M. and Sat.–Sun. noon); the **Old Whaling Station;** the **Pacific House;** the **Sherman Quarters;** and the **Stevenson House** (530 Houston St., guided tours Mon. and Fri. 2 P.M. and Sat.–Sun. 10:30 A.M.), the former residence of Robert Louis Stevenson.

Famous artists, writers, and military men have stayed in some of these spots, most of which have long histories playing several different roles. Look down as you walk to see if you're stepping on antique whalebone sidewalks. And be sure to take a few minutes to admire the many beautiful gardens surrounding the adobes, which are lovingly maintained by local groups.

Maritime Museum of Monterey

Part of Old Monterey, the Stanton Center includes the Maritime Museum of Monterey (5 Custom House Plaza, 831/372-2608, www.montereyhistory.org, Tues.–Sun. 10 A.M.–5 P.M.). The large modern facilities provide plenty of space for the art and historical artifacts collected over the decades, most of which pertain directly to the area's history, maritime or otherwise. In the Maritime Museum, explore the history of the native Rumisen and Ohlone people, going through the Spanish exploration and conquistador era, and on in to the American military and fishing presence on the Central Coast. The original Fresnel lens from the Point Sur light station sits in here, as does an array of sardine fishing equipment.

ENTERTAINMENT AND EVENTS
Live Music

Classical music aficionados will appreciate the dulcet tones of the musicians who perform for **Chamber Music Monterey Bay** (831/625-2212, www.chambermusicmonterey bay.org). This society brings talented ensembles and soloists in from around the world to perform on the lovely Central Coast. One night you might find a local string quartet, and on another night you'll get to see and hear a chamber ensemble. (String quartets definitely rule the small stage and intimate theater.) Far from banning young music fans from the **Sunset Cultural Center** (San Carlos St. btwn. 8th and 10th Sts., Carmel), Chamber Music Monterey Bay reserves up-front seats at all its shows for children and their adult companions.

One of the coolest small-rock venues in California is the **The Golden State Theater** (417 Alvarado St., 831/372-3800, www.golden statetheatre.com) in Monterey. This beautiful theater is done up in 1920s era Arabian Nights–style Middle Eastern revival. It's easy to get to, sitting right downtown near the big Hyatt hotel. Get there early so you can spend some time admiring the decor before the lights lower and the show starts. The Golden State hosts acts that often play larger venues, which means that show goers get a reasonably intimate experience in which they can actually *see* their favorite performers. A few performances in 2008 included Los Lonely Boys, the Doobie Brothers, comedienne Paula Poundstone, and a special engagement of the Sally Struthers musical *Nunsense.*

Festivals and Events

The Monterey region hosts numerous festivals and special events each year. Whether your pleasure is fine food or funky music, you'll probably be able to plan a trip around some sort of multi-day festival with dozens of events and performances scheduled during Monterey's busy year.

In keeping with the Central Coast's obsession with food and wine, the annual **Monterey Wine Festival** (800/422-0251, www.montereywine .com, mid-Oct.) celebrates wine with a generous helping of food on the side. A number of tasting events mark this weekish-long festival, including a major day event at the fairgrounds and possibly a swanky nighttime soiree at the Monterey Bay Aquarium. You can also expect a few private events and parties at participating wineries and restaurants. Check the website for this year's venues, ticket prices, and event dates and times. This festival offers the perfect opportunity to introduce yourself to Monterey and Carmel wineries, many of which have not yet hit the "big time" in major wine magazines. The Wine Festival is just one of many similar events held each year in the region, so if you can't make it you'll have plenty of other opportunities to enjoy all the best edibles and drinkables the Central Coast has to offer.

One of the biggest music festivals in California is the **Monterey Jazz Festival** (2000 Fairground Rd., Monterey, 831/373-3366, www.montereyjazzfestival.org). As the site of the longest-running jazz festival on earth, Monterey attracts the top performers from around the world. Held each September—a month that offers the best chance for beautiful weather on the Monterey Bay—this long weekend of amazing music can leave you happy for the whole year. The event is held at the Monterey County Fairgrounds, which lets visitors enjoy all the different concerts without having to drive from venue to venue. Nine stages put up acts day and night, making it easy to either find your favorite stage and settle in for a long stay and multiple musicians, or wander the length and breadth of the fairgrounds to sample the acts at each unique venue. Camping is not permitted at the fairgrounds, but you can camp nearby, or get a room in one of the Monterey lodgings that partner with the festival to provide reasonably priced lodgings for attendees.

SPORTS AND RECREATION

The Monterey Bay is the premier Northern California locale for a number of water sports, especially scuba diving.

Scuba

Any native Northern Californian knows that there's only one really great place in the region to get certified in scuba diving—the Monterey Bay. Even if you go to a dive school up in the Bay Area, they'll take you down to Monterey for your open-water dive. Accordingly, dozens of dive schools cluster in and around the town of Monterey (check Carmel and Santa Cruz as well, if you prefer).

The **Monterey Bay Dive Company** (225 Cannery Row, 831/656-0454, www.mbdcscuba

.com) sits right in the midst of Cannery Row, where all visitors to Monterey eventually end up. You can take dive classes year-round, get certified, rent equipment, fill your own tanks, and even take a quick dive right off San Carlos Beach just behind the dive shop. Monterey Bay Dive Company also maintains its own dive boat, offering both boat and shore guided dive tours of the famous Monterey Bay undersea world.

Another of your many dive shop options is the **Aquarius Dive Shop** (2040 Del Monte Ave., 831/375-1933, www.aquariusdivers .com). Aquarius offers everything you need to go diving out in Monterey Bay, including air and nitrox fills, equipment rental, certification courses, and help booking a trip on a local dive boat. Aquarius works with four boats to create great trips for divers of all interests and ability levels. Call or check the website for current local dive conditions as well.

Kayaking

With all the focus on sustainable tourism in Monterey, coupled with the lovely recreation area formed by Monterey Bay, it's no wonder that sea kayaking is popular here. Whether you want to try paddling your first kayak, or you're an expert who hasn't brought your own gear out to California, you'll find a local outfit ready and willing to hook you up.

Adventures by the Sea (299 Cannery Row, 831/372-1807, www.adventuresbythesea .com, 9 A.M.–sunset, tours $50/person, rentals $30/day) rents kayaks for whole days to let you choose your own route in and around the magnificent Monterey Bay kelp forest. If you're not confident enough to go off on your own, Adventures offers tours from Cannery Row. Your guide can tell you all about the wildlife you're seeing: harbor seals, sea otters, pelicans, seagulls, and maybe even a whale in the wintertime! The tour lasts about 2.5 hours, cost $50 per person, and the available tandem sit-on-top kayaks make it a great experience for school-age children. Adventures by the Sea also runs a tour of Stillwater Cove at Pebble Beach. Reservations are recommended for all tours, but during the summer the Cannery Row tour leaves regularly

at 10 A.M. and 2 P.M., so you can stop by on a whim and see if there's a spot available.

Monterey Bay Kayaks (693 Del Monte Ave., 831/373-5357, www.montereybay kayaks.com, tours $50–60/person) specializes in tours of both central Monterey and up north in Elkhorn Slough. You can choose between open-deck and closed-deck tour groups, beginning tours perfect for kids, romantic sunset or full moon paddles, or even long paddles designed for more experienced sea kayakers. Most tours cost $50–60 per person; check the website for specific tour prices, times, and reservation information. If you prefer to rent a kayak and explore the bay or slough on your own, Monterey Bay Kayaks can help you out there too. If you really get into it, you can also sign up for closed-deck sea kayaking classes to learn about safety, rescue techniques, tides, currents, and paddling techniques.

A third company, **AB Seas Kayaks of Monterey** (32 Cannery Row, #5, 831/647-0147, www.montereykayak.com, tours $60/person, rentals $30/day), also has plenty of sit-on-top sea kayaks for rent—choose a single or double kayak as you need. Or take a tour of Monterey Bay with an experienced guide.

Fishing and Whale-Watching

Whales pass quite near the shores of Monterey year-round. While you can sometimes even see them from the beaches, any number of boats can take you out for a closer look at the great beasts as they travel along their own special routes north and south. The area hosts many humpbacks, blue whales, and gray whales, plus the occasional killer whale, Minke whale, fin whale, and pod of dolphins. Bring your own binoculars for a better view, but the experienced boat captains will do all they can to get you as close as possible to the whales and dolphins. Most tours last 2–3 hours and leave from Fisherman's Wharf, which is easy to get to and has ample parking. If you prefer not to rise with the sun, pick a tour that leaves in the afternoon.

Monterey Bay Whale Watch (84 Fisherman's Wharf, 831/375-4658, www.montereybay whalewatch.com) leaves right from an easy-to-find red building on Fisherman's Wharf and runs tours in every season. (Call or check the website for schedules.) You must make a reservation in advance, even for regularly scheduled tours. Afternoon tours are available. **Monterey Whale Watching** (96 Fisherman's Wharf, 800/979-3370, www.baywatchcruises .com) prides itself on its knowledgeable guides/ marine biologists and its comfortable, spacious cruising vessels. The *Princess Monterey* offers morning and afternoon tours, and you can buy tickets online or by phone.

If you'd rather catch fish than watch mammals, **Randy's Fishing Trips** (800/979-3370, www.randysfishingtrips.com) can take you out for salmon, halibut, albacore, mackerel, rock cod, flatfish, and even squid and Dungeness crab in season. They can also take you out for a whale-watching trip if that's your preference. Trips begin early in the morning and can last for several hours. You can bring your own food—catering is not provided—including a small cooler for your drinks. If you don't have a California fishing license, you can purchase a one-day license at the shop before your trip. While you can try to walk up to the bright teal-painted shop at Fisherman's Wharf, it's best to get tickets for your trip in advance; either call or buy online from Randy's website.

Chris's Fishing Trips (48 Fisherman's Wharf, 831/372-0577, www.chrissfishing.com, $55–90/per person) offers both scheduled trips and boats for charter. If you want to go solo, get on one of the daily salmon or cod trips, which include bait and ice; tackle, a one-day license, and fish cleaning are extras.

Bird-Watching

Some of the best birding in the state can be had at **Elkhorn Slough** (1700 Elkhorn Rd., Watsonville, 831/728-2822, www.elkhorn slough.org, Wed.–Sun. 9 A.M.–5 P.M., free), a few miles north of Monterey proper in Moss Landing. This large waterway/wetland area is incongruously marked by the mammoth smokestacks of the Moss Landing power plant. While you can access the wetlands and bird habitats from Highway 1 in Moss Landing, to get to the visitors center you must drive several miles into the agricultural backcountry. But once you're there, knowledgeable and dedicated rangers can provide you with all the information you need to spot your favorite birds, plus find a few you've never seen before.

Golf

Yes, you can play golf in middle-class Monterey! And it's often much cheaper to play here than to head for the hallowed courses of Carmel.

The public **Monterey Pines Golf Course** (1250 Garden Rd., 831/656-2167, $25–38, cart $20) offers 18 holes for a comparatively tiny green fee. It's a short par-69 course that's got four levels of tee to make the game fun for players of all levels. Monterey Pines was originally built as a private Navy course for the pleasure of the officers at the major naval installation north of town. Today, it is open to all who want to play. Call ahead for tee times.

A bit more pricy but still not Poppy Hills or Pebble Beach, **Del Monte Golf Course** (1300 Sylvan Rd., 831/373-2700, www.pebblebeach .com, $34–95, cart $20) is part of that legendary set of courses. This historic 18-hole, par-72 course, along with two other courses, still plays host to the Pebble Beach Invitational each year. You won't get the ocean views of Pebble Beach, but you will be treated to lovely green mountains surrounding the course as you play through. The property includes a full-service pro shop and the Del Monte Bar & Grill. You can check available tee times online, then call 800/877-0597 to book your preferred time.

Motor Sports

If you're feeling the need for speed, you can get lots of it at the **Mazda Raceway Laguna Seca** (1021 Monterey-Salinas Hwy., 831/242-8201, www.laguna-seca.com), one of the country's premier road-racing venues. Here you can see historic auto races, superbikes, speed festivals, and an array of Grand Prix events. The major racing season runs May–October of most years. In addition to the big events, Laguna Seca hosts innumerable auto clubs and small sports car and stock car races. If you've always wanted to learn to drive or ride racecar-style, check the schedule to see if one of the track classes is happening during your visit. These often happen in the middle of the week, and are a near daily event in the off-season.

Be sure to check the website for parking directions specific to the event you plan to attend—this is a big facility. You can camp here, and certainly you'll find plenty of concessions during big races.

ACCOMMODATIONS
Under $100

The **Monterey Hostel** (778 Hawthorne St., 831/649-0375, http://montereyhostel.com, $28/bunk, $62/private room) offers inexpensive accommodations within walking distance of the major attractions of Monterey. Frankly, when it comes to rooms and amenities, this isn't the best hostel in California. You must pay extra to rent a locker, there's no laundry facility on-site, and the dorm rooms can be pretty crowded. On the other hand, the hostel puts on a free pancake breakfast every morning, linens are included with your bed, and there are comfy, casual common spaces with couches and musical instruments. And then there's that location.… You can walk to the aquarium and Cannery Row, stroll the Monterey Bay Coastal Trail, or drive over to Carmel to see a different set of sights.

$100-150

A cute, small, budget motel, the **Monterey Bay Lodge** (55 Camino Aguajito, 831/372-8057, www.montereybaylodge.com, $134) brings a bit of the Côte d'Azur to the equally beautiful coastal town of Monterey. With small rooms decorated in classic yellows and blues, a sparkling pool with a fountain in the shallow end, and an on-site restaurant serving breakfast and lunch, the Lodge makes a perfect base for budget-minded families traveling in the Monterey region.

$150-250

The **Colton Inn** (707 Pacific St, 831/649-6500, www.coltoninn.com, $165) offers a touch of class above that of a standard beach-town motel. Located in the midst of downtown Monterey, the queen and king bedrooms boast attractive fabrics, designer bathrooms, and pretty appointments. While you'll find restaurants and historic adobe buildings adjacent to the Colton, expect to drive or take public transit to Cannery Row and the Aquarium.

Be sure to call in advance to get a room at ◖ **The Jabberwock** (598 Laine St, 831/372-4777, www.jabberwockinn.com, $215), a favorite with frequent visitors to Monterey. This Alice in Wonderland—themed B&B is both whimsical and elegant; expect to find a copy of the namesake novel in your tastefully appointed guest room. Be sure to take the owners up on their daily wine and cheese reception in the afternoon-they are gold mines of information about the area, and will be happy to recommend restaurants and activities for all tastes. Though located up a steep hill, the Jabberwock is within walking distance of Cannery Row and all its adjacent attractions (it's worth the extra exercise to avoid the cost or hassle of parking in the tourist lots).

Over $250

Monterey visitors looking for elegant accommodations love the **Old Monterey Inn** (500 Martin St., 831/375-8284, www.oldmonterey inn.com, $275–400). The lovely old edifice stands in the midst of mature gardens that blossom all spring and summer, showing their sedate green side in autumn and winter. Inside the inn, the garden motif echoes in the upscale bed linens and window treatments, which compliment the pretty furnishings and cozy fireplaces. Spa bathtubs pamper guests. Additional amenities include a full breakfast (often served in the garden) and a menu of spa treatments that can be enjoyed downstairs in the serene treatment room.

Want to stay right on Cannery Row in a room overlooking the bay? You'll pay handsomely—but it's worth it—at the **Monterey Plaza Hotel & Spa** (400 Cannery Row, 831/646-1700, www.montereyplazahotel.com, $388). This on-the-water luxury hotel has it all: two restaurants, a spa, a private beach, room service, and upscale guest room goodies. Rooms range from "budget" garden and Row-facing accommodations to ocean-view rooms with private balconies and huge suites that mimic a posh private apartment. Bring your credit card and enjoy!

FOOD

The organic and sustainable food movements have caught hold on the Central Coast. The Monterey Bay Seafood Watch program (www.montereybayaquarium.org) is the definitive resource for sustainable seafood, while the Salinas Valley inland hosts a number of organic farms.

American

For coffee, espresso, and homebaked beignets, head to the **Trailside Café** (550 Wave St, 831/649-8600, www.trailsidecafe.com, daily 8 A.M.–4 P.M., $10–15). This Cannery Row restaurant offers breakfast, lunch, and dinner on a heated patio overlooking the bay.

For more views and exemplary American cuisine, stop by the **Duck Club Grill** (400 Cannery Row, 831/646-1706, www.montereyplazahotel.com, daily 6:30–11 A.M. and 5:30–9:30 P.M., $30) in the Monterey Plaza Hotel. Steaks, lamb chops, and the namesake duck are what's on order here and the extensive wine list offers many complements. **Montrio** (414 Calle Principal, 831/648-8880, www.montrio.com, $15–20) is another entry in elegantly casual Monterey dining. The crab cakes are legendary.

Seafood

The **Old Fisherman's Grotto** (39 Fisherman's Wharf, 831/375-4604, daily 11 A.M.–10 P.M., $) is a relaible wharf staple for both seafood and views over Monterey Bay. The menu focuses on fresh seafood and Italian standards and the restaurant includes a full bar. If you're craving fresh seafood but want to esacpe the touristy wharf, head to the **Monterey Fish House** (2114 Del Monte Ave., 831/373-4647, daily 11:30 A.M.–2:30 P.M. and 5–9:30 P.M., $15–25) where the local go for cioppino and grilled oysters. The tiny dining room ensures its social atmosphere.

Markets

The **Monterey Bay Farmers Market** (980 Fremont St., www.montereybayfarmers.org, Thurs. 2:30–6:30 P.M.) showcases almost 50 farmers and vendors selling fresh produce, flowers, plants every Thursday afternoon.

INFORMATION AND SERVICES

In Monterey, the **El Estero Visitors Center** (401 Camino El Estero, www.montereyinfo.org) is the local outlet of the Montery Country Convention & Visitors Bureau. The **Monterey Peninsula Chamber of Commerce** (380 Alvarado St., 831/648-5360) can also provide helpful information.

The local newspaper is the **Monterey County Herald** (www.montereyherald.com). Monterey has two convenient **post offices:** one at 565 Hartnell St. and another at 686 Lighthouse Ave.

For medical needs, the **Community Hospital of the Monterey Peninsula** (CHOMP, 23625 Holman Hwy., 831/624-5311) provides emergency services to the area.

GETTING THERE AND AROUND

Most visitors drive into Monterey via the scenic Highway 1. Inland, U.S. 101 allows access into Salinas from the north and south. From Salinas, Highway 68 travels west into Monterey.

For a more leisurely ride, **Amtrak's** Coast Starlight train (Station Pl. and Railroad Ave., Salinas, daily 8 A.M.–10 P.M.) travels through Salinas daily. For Amtrak travelers, there is free bus service to downtown Monterey (30 min.); for everyone else, the **Greyhound** bus station (19 W. Gabilan, Salinas, 831/424-4418, www.greyhound.com, daily 5 A.M.–11:30 P.M.) offers service into Monterey.

Once in Monterey, take advantage of the free **WAVE** bus (9 A.M.–7:30 P.M.) which loops between downtown Monterey and the Aquarium.

Carmel

Carmel's landscape is divided into two distinct parts. The adorable village of Carmel-by-the-Sea perches on the cliffs above the Pacific, surrounded to the north and the south by golf courses and beach parks. Carmel-by-the-Sea boasts the highest number of art galleries per capita in the United States. When most Californians talk about Carmel, they mean Carmel-by-the-Sea. The streets are perfect for strolling, and if ever there was a town that feels comfortable and safe for a woman traveling alone, it's Carmel.

Inland, the far less-traveled Carmel Valley has its share of huge estates owned by some of the wealthiest folks in the state. The narrow valley, surrounded by verdant hillsides, has recently discovered its footing as a niche wine region. Visitors can also play a few holes at the inevitable golf courses and check out the tiny hamlets that line the lone main road through the valley.

Both Carmel by-the-Sea and Carmel Valley residents love dogs. Your pooch is welcome at many establishments, and a number of stores and restaurants offer doggie treats and keep fresh water outside for the canine set.

SIGHTS
◖ 17-Mile Drive

If you're a first-time visitor to the Carmel and Monterey area, 17-Mile Drive ($9/vehicle) can introduce you to some of the most beautiful and representative land and seascapes on the Central Coast. But don't get too excited yet—long ago, the locally all-powerful Pebble Beach Corporation realized what a precious commodity they held in this road, and began charging a toll. The good news is that when you pay your fee at the gatehouse, you'll get a map of the drive that describes the parks and sights that you will pass as you make your way along the winding coastal road. These include the much-photographed Lone Cypress, the beaches of Spanish Bay, and Pebble Beach's golf course,

© LIZ HAMILL SCOTT

the view along 17-Mile Drive

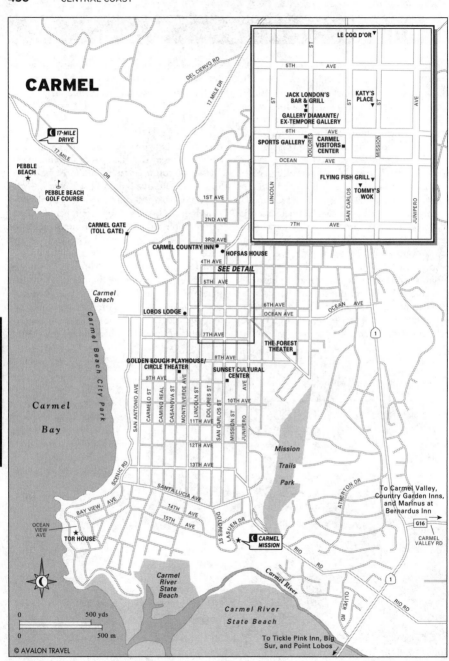

CENTRAL COAST

CARMEL

17-MILE DRIVE

PEBBLE BEACH

PEBBLE BEACH GOLF COURSE

DEL CIERVO RD

17 MILE DR

17 MILE DR

1ST AVE

CARMEL GATE (TOLL GATE)

2ND AVE

3RD AVE

CARMEL COUNTRY INN

HOFSAS HOUSE

4TH AVE

SEE DETAIL

5TH AVE

Carmel Beach

6TH AVE

LOBOS LODGE

OCEAN AVE

7TH AVE

THE FOREST THEATER

8TH AVE

Carmel Bay

GOLDEN BOUGH PLAYHOUSE/ CIRCLE THEATER

SUNSET CULTURAL CENTER

9TH AVE

SAN ANTONIO AVE

CARMELO ST

CAMINO REAL

CASANOVA ST

MONTE VERDE AVE

LINCOLN ST

DOLORES ST

SAN CARLOS ST

MISSION ST

JUNIPERO

OCEAN AVE

10TH AVE

Carmel Beach City Park

11TH AVE

12TH AVE

13TH AVE

Mission Trails Park

SCENIC RD

SANTA LUCIA AVE

BAY VIEW AVE

14TH AVE

15TH AVE

DOLORES ST

LAS UEN DR

ATHERTON DR

To Carmel Valley, Country Garden Inns, and Marinus at Berhardus Inn

OCEAN VIEW AVE

TOR HOUSE

CARMEL MISSION

RIO RD

G16

CARMEL VALLEY RD

Carmel River State Beach

Carmel River

1

OLIVER RD

RIO RD

Carmel River State Beach

To Tickle Pink Inn, Big Sur, and Point Lobos

0   500 yds
0   500 m

© AVALON TRAVEL

Detail:

LE COQ D'OR

5TH AVE

JACK LONDON'S BAR & GRILL

KATY'S PLACE

ST

ST

ST

AVE

GALLERY DIAMANTE/ EX-TEMPORE GALLERY

6TH AVE

SPORTS GALLERY

CARMEL VISITORS CENTER

MISSION

DOLORES

OCEAN AVE

LINCOLN

FLYING FISH GRILL

TOMMY'S WOK

SAN CARLOS

JUNIPERO

7TH AVE

resort, and housing complex. There are plenty of turnouts where you can stop to take photos of the stunning ocean and the iconic cypress trees. You can picnic at many of the formal beaches, most of which have basic restroom facilities and ample parking lots. The only food and gas to be had are at the Inn at Spanish Bay and the Lodge at Pebble Beach. If you're in a great hurry, you can get from one end of the 17-Mile Drive to the other in 20 minutes—but that would defeat the main purpose of taking 17-Mile Drive, which is to go slowly and stop often to enjoy the beauty of the area.

◖ Carmel Mission

The Carmel Mission (3080 Rio Rd., 831/624-1271, www.carmelmission.org, Mon.–Sat. 9:30 A.M.–5 P.M., Sun. 10:30 A.M.–5 P.M., adults $5, children $1), formally called the San Carlos Borromeo de Carmelo Mission, was Father Junipero Serra's personal favorite among his California mission churches. He lived, worked, and eventually died here, and visitors today can see a replica of his cell. A working Catholic parish remains part of the complex, so please be respectful when taking the self-guided tour. The rambling buildings and courtyard gardens show some wear, but enough restoration work has gone into the church and living quarters to make them attractive and eminently visitable. The Carmel Mission has a small memorial museum in a building off the second courtyard, but don't make the mistake of thinking that this small and outdated space is the only historical display. In fact, the "museum" runs through many of the buildings, showing a small slice of the lives of the 18th- and 19th-century friars. The highlight of the complex is the church with its gilded altar front, its shrine to the Virgin Mary, the grave of Father Serra, and ancillary chapel dedicated to the memory of Father Serra. Round out your visit by walking out into the gardens to admire the flowers and fountains and to read the grave markers in the small cemetery.

Tor House

Local poet Robinson Jeffers built this rugged-looking castle on the Carmel coast in 1919. He named it Tor House (26304 Ocean View

CENTRAL COAST

© LIZ HAMILL SCOTT

Carmel Mission

Ave., 831/624-1813, www.torhouse.org, tours Fri.–Sat. 10 A.M.–3 P.M., $7), after its rocky setting, and added the majestic Hawk Tower a year later. The granite stone structure exists today as an example of the Carmel ethos that Jeffers embodied and as a monument to his work and poetry.

Earthbound Farms

One of the largest purveyors of organic produce in the United States, Earthbound Farms (7250 Carmel Valley Rd., 831/625-6219, www.ebfarm.com, Mon.–Sat. 8 A.M.–6 P.M., Sun. 10 A.M.–5 P.M.) offers visitors easy access to its smallish facility in the Carmel Valley. Drive up to the farm stand and browse a variety of organic fruits, veggies, and flowers. Outdoors, you can ramble into the fields, checking out the chamomile labyrinth and the kids' garden (yes, your kids can look *and* touch). Select and harvest your own fresh herbs from the cut-your-own garden, or leave the cooking to the experts and purchase delicious prepared organic dishes at the farm stand. If you're interested in a more in-depth guided tour of the farm, check the website for a schedule of walks, which will take you, a group, and an expert guide—perhaps a chef or local famous foodie—out into the fields for a look at what's growing and how to use it.

Pebble Beach

While the legends of Pebble Beach (Palmero Way, www.pebblebeach.com) surround its championship golf course, there's a lot more to it than just greens and sand traps. A gated community surrounding the course and spreading back towards the trees encompasses some of the most expensive homes in California. From 17-Mile Drive, turn off onto the lengthy driveway to visit the ultra high-end resort. Any visitor can park and walk into the main lobby of the hotel area. Most tourists walk right through and out onto the immense multi-level patio area to take in the priceless and oft-photographed views. Whether you stay on the flagstones and enjoy a drink from the lobby bar or take a walk out onto the wide lawns, your eyes will be caught by the dramatic cliffs plummeting down to the small blue-gray bay. The golf

Pebble Beach

course draws right up to the lawns, allowing even the poorly heeled to check out a couple of the hallowed greens and fairways dotted with cypress trees. The lodge itself is worth touring, too; you can take footpaths to see the outsides of the posh accommodations, walk in to the lobby of the exclusive spa, and peer at the tables of the gourmet dining room.

WINERIES

Its tiny size necessarily limits the number of vineyards and wineries that can set up shop in the Carmel Valley. But this small, charming wine region makes for a perfect wine-tasting day trip from Carmel, Monterey, or even Big Sur. Small crowds, light traffic, and meaningful tasting experiences categorize this area, which still has many family-owned wineries. You'll get personal attention and delicious wines, all in a gorgeous green setting.

The **Bernardus Winery** (5 W. Carmel Valley Rd., 800/223-2533, www.bernardus.com/winery, daily 11 A.M.–5 P.M., $5–10) sits on a vineyard estate that also hosts a connected luxurious lodge and gourmet restaurant. Bernardus creates a small list of wines. The grapes growing all around you go into the pride of the winery: the Bordeaux-style blended red Marinus Vineyard wine. Other varietals (Chardonnay, Pinot Noir, and Sauvignon Blanc) come from cool coastal vineyards. If you're interested and lucky, you might also get to sip some small-batch vintages of single-vineyard wines that are available only in the tasting room.

The biggest name in the Carmel Valley is **Chateau Julien** (8940 Carmel Valley Rd., 831/624-2600, www.chateaujulien.com, Mon.–Fri. 8 A.M.–5 P.M., Sat.–Sun. 11 A.M.–5 P.M.). The European-styled white estate building with the round turret is visible from the road. The light, airy tasting room is crowded with barrels, wine cases, souvenirs, and tasting glasses. When you enter, you'll be offered sips from the wide selection of Chardonnays, Cabernets, Syrahs, Merlots, and more. If you're lucky, you might find yourself tasting a rare Reserve blended red or a 10-year-old port. For a treat, call ahead and reserve a spot on the

twice-daily complimentary vineyard and winery tours. These tours conclude with a special tasting outside on the flagstone patio when weather permits.

On the other end of the spectrum, tiny **Parsonage Village Vineyard** (19 E. Carmel Valley Rd., 831/659-7322, www.parsonagewine.com, Fri.–Mon. 11 A.M.–5 P.M., $5) often doesn't make it onto Carmel Valley wine maps—which is a shame, because some of the best Syrah coming out of California (arguably) comes from this unpretentious little winery with only a nine-acre estate vineyard to work with. The tasting room sits in a tiny strip of shops, the space glowing with light that bounces off the copper of the bar. On the walls, you'll find an array of quilts made by Mary Ellen Parsons herself. At the bar, you'll taste wonderful Syrahs, hearty Cabernet Sauvignons, and surprisingly deep and complex blends—the Snosrap (that's Parsons spelled backwards) table wine is inexpensive for the region and incredibly tasty. If you find a vintage you love at Parsonage, buy it then and there since they sell out of many of their wines every year.

ENTERTAINMENT AND EVENTS

The events and entertainment in Carmel tend to center around either art or food. This town loves its haute culture, so you won't find too many sports bars or generic movie theaters here. Instead, enjoy classical music, a wealth of live theater, and a glass of wine in the mild evenings.

Bars and Clubs

The population of Carmel tends toward wealthy seniors. Hence, the nightlife isn't too hopping here, and live music in bars in Carmel was illegal until 2006—seriously. Most of the drinking tends toward restaurants and the occasional hotel lounge. If you're looking for an evening out within Carmel city limits, try a night at the theater.

If you simply must go out for a drink, try **Jack London's Bar & Grill** (Dolores St. and Fifth Ave., 831/624-2336, www.jacklondons

.com). All dark wood, fancy ceiling, and quiet elegance, it's no surprise that Jack London's has a full menu of fancier-than- average bar food and a wine list that would do a high-end restaurant proud. But it's also got big-screen TVs tuned to the games of the day and live blues each Friday. If you've brought your favorite canine companion, you'll find a welcoming seat outside on the patio, where the full menu is served.

Theater

Despite its small size, Carmel has nearly a dozen live theater groups. In a town that defines itself by its love of art, theater arts don't get left out. Don't hesitate to ask the locals what's playing where when you're in town.

The **Pacific Repertory Theater** (831/622-0100, www.pacrep.org, adults $16–38, students $10–20, children $7) is the only professional theater company on the Monterey-Carmel Peninsula. Its shows go up all over the region, most often in the **Golden Bough Playhouse** (Monte Verde St. and Eighth Ave.) the company's home theater. Other regular venues include the **The Forest Theater** (Mountain View St. and Santa Rita St.), and the **Circle Theater** (Casanova St. btwn. Eighth and Ninth Aves.) within the Golden Bough complex. Also look for their plays in the Monterey State Historic Park and in Pebble Beach. The company puts up dramas, comedies, and musicals both new and classic. You might see a work of Shakespeare or John Patrick Shanley's *Doubt,* enjoy your favorite songs from *The Fantasticks,* or sing along to the newer tunes of *High School Musical.* Check the website for upcoming shows, and buy tickets online or over the phone to guarantee you'll get seats while you're in town.

Each fall, PacRep puts up the **Carmel Shakespeare Festival** (www.pacrep.org), a short showing of Shakespeare that's good enough to draw the notice of Bay Area theater snobs. Check the website for information on this year's shows and the venues.

Festivals and Events

In a town famed for art galleries, one of the biggest events of the year is the **Carmel Art Festival** (Mission St., Carmel-by-the-Sea, www.carmelartfestival.org, May). This four-day event celebrates visual arts in all media with shows by internationally acclaimed artists at galleries, parks, and other venues all across town. This wonderful festival also sponsors here-and-now contests, including the prestigious Plein Air (outdoor painting). Visitors get a rare opportunity to witness the artists outdoors, engaging in their creative process as they use the Carmel scenery for inspiration. Round out your festival experience by bidding on paintings at the end-of-event auction. You can get a genuine bargain on original artwork while supporting both the artists and the Festival. Perhaps best of all, the Carmel Art Festival is a great place to bring your family—a wealth of children's activities help even the youngest festival goers become budding artists.

For a more classical experience, one of the most prestigious festivals in Northern California is the **Carmel Bach Festival** (www .bachfestival.org). For three weeks each July and August, Carmel-by-the-Sea and its surrounding towns host dozens of classical concerts. Naturally the works of J. S. Bach are featured, but you can also hear renditions of Mozart, Vivaldi, Handel, and other heavyweights of Bach's era. Choose between big concerts in major venues or intimate performances in smaller spaces with only a small audience between you and the beautiful music. Concerts and recitals take place literally every day of the week—budget-conscious music lovers can just as easily enjoy the Festival in the middle of the week as on the weekends.

SHOPPING

Downtown Carmel-by-the-Sea is a great place to get out of your car and stroll the streets, peering in the windows of the boutiques and countless galleries.

Carmel boasts more art galleries per capita than any other town in the United States. Accordingly, shopping in the downtown pedestrian area means "checking out the galleries." **Gallery Diamante** (Dolores St. betw. 5th

and 6th, 831/624-0852, www.gallerydiamante
.com) represents a typical Carmel Gallery, with
a large collection of landscape paintings by different artists and interesting sculptures scattered about. The most popular modern styles
in painting, sculpture, and even art glass and
jewelry are on display. Jewelry here can be reasonably priced, but expect to spend a more for
an original painting.

Bucking the current trends in Carmel art
is Boban Bursac, sole owner of the tiny **EX-
tempore Gallery** (Dolores St. betw. 5th and
6th, 831/626-1298, bobanart@yahoo.com).
Burasac's amazing large-format paintings evoke
feelings in even the most casual passerby; lucky
visitors might even get to chat with the artist.
Sadly, these works of art do not come cheap,
understandable given their size and the skill
and devotion with which they are painted.

For something altogether different and
perhaps less intimidating, there's the **Sports
Gallery** (Dolores St. betw. Ocean and 6th,
831/624-6026, www.sportsgalleryweb.com).
In this more casual and down-to-earth space is
memorabilia, signed photos, and even paintings
of your favorite sports heroes and legends, many
at reasonable prices. This is a great spot to look
for gifts for that sports fanatic back home.

SPORTS AND RECREATION
Beach
At the west end of Ocean Avenue, you'll find
the (occasionally) sparkling white sands of
Carmel Beach (Ocean Ave., 831/624-4909,
daily 6 A.M.–10 P.M.). This lovely stretch of
south-facing sand offers free running for canine guests, bonfires south of 10th Avenue, and
all the surfing, wading, and sunbathing (when
there's sun) you can handle. Enjoy the beautiful local cypress trees and consider bringing a
kite to fly on this often windy beach.

Biking
17-Mile Drive also makes a great bike route.
Cyclists can follow this road and enjoy the
smells and sounds of the spectacular scenery
in a way that car drivers just can't. Expect fairly
flat terrain with lots of twists and turns, and a
ride that runs…about 17 miles. Foggy conditions can make this ride a bit slick in the summer, but spring and fall weather are perfect for
pedaling here.

Golf
There's no place for golfing in all of California
like Carmel-by-the-Sea. You can play courses
trodden by the likes of Tiger Woods and Jack
Nicholson, pause a moment before you putt to
take in the sight of the stunning Pacific Ocean,
and pay $300 or more for a single round of golf.
Golf has been a major pastime here since the
late 19th century, and today avid golfers come
from around the world to tee off in Carmel.

One of the Pebble Beach Resort courses,
Spyglass Hill (1700 17-Mile Dr., Pebble
Beach, 800/654-9300, www.pebblebeach
.com, 18-hole Par 72) gets its moniker from
the Robert Louis Stevenson Novel *Treasure
Island*. But don't be fooled—the holes on this
beautiful course may be named for children's
characters, but that doesn't mean they're easy.
Spyglass Hill boasts some of the most challenging play even in the golf course-laden Carmel
region. Expect a few bogeys if you choose to
play here, and tee off from the Championship
level at your own (ego's) risk.

Another favorite with the Pebble Beach golf
crowd is the famed **Poppy Hills Golf Course**
(3200 Lopez Rd, Pebble Beach, 831/622-8239,
www.poppyhillsgolf.com, 18-hole Par 72).
Though it's not managed by the same company,
Poppy Hills shares amenities with Pebble Beach
golf courses; you can expect the same level of
care and devotion to the maintenance of the
course and your experience as a player there.
If you're looking to improve your game, check
out their program that runs two days and gets
you out onto both Poppy and Spyglass Hill for
a great chance to really pick up some new skills
(and a few incidentally gorgeous views).

Hiking
South of Carmel-by-the-Sea, is **Point Lobos
State Reserve** (62 Hwy. 1, 831/624-4909,
http://pt-lobos.parks.state.ca.us, daily 8 A.M.–
sunset, $10). Known as one of the most

CENTRAL COAST

beautiful parks in the state park system, Point Lobos offers hiking through forestland and along the beach, scuba diving (831/624-8413) off the shore, picnicking, and nature study. Take a walk through unique ecosystems and observe the indigenous wildlife while strolling through the rugged landscape. Be aware that from July through September fog often dims the summer sun at Point Lobos, even mid-day. Spring and fall are the best times to visit, weather-wise.

ACCOMMODATIONS
$100-150
Lobos Lodge (Monte Verde and Ocean Aves., 831/624-3874, www.loboslodge.com, $147) sits right in the midst of downtown Carmel-by-the-Sea, making it a perfect spot from which to dine, shop, and admire the endless array of art in the upscale town. Each of the 30 rooms and suites offers a gas fireplace, a sofa and table, a bed in an alcove, and enough space to stroll about and enjoy the quiet romantic setting. Do be aware that Lobos Lodge bills itself as an adult retreat. While families with children can stay here, expect to pay extra for more than two guests in your room, and there is little in the way of child-friendly amenities.

$150-250
The name and exterior of the **Hofsas House** (San Carlos St. and 3rd Ave., 831/624-2745, www.hofsashouse.com, $150) evokes a quaint inn set in the Netherlands countryside. Yet the Hofsas House actually sits in a quiet semi-residential neighborhood within easy walking distance of downtown Carmel-by-the-Sea. Rooms in the rambling multi-story structure are surprisingly spacious, with nice furniture and linens that show just a touch of wear, and adequate bathrooms. If you can, get an ocean-view room with a patio or balcony, buy a bottle of wine, and spend some time sitting outside looking over the town of Carmel out toward the serene (from a distance) Pacific waters.

For folks who come to Carmel to taste wine, hike in the woods, and enjoy the less expensive golf courses, **Country Garden Inns** (102 W. Carmel Valley Rd., Carmel Valley, 831/659-5361, www.countrygardeninns.com, $170) offers a perfect spot to rest and relax. Actually composed of two inns, the Acacia and the Hidden Valley, Country Garden's small B&Bs offer violet and taupe French Country—style charm in the guest rooms, as well as a pool, a self-serve breakfast bar, and strolling gardens outdoors. Rooms run from romantic king-bed studios up to big family suites and most sleep at least four people (with daybeds in the window nooks).

Over $250
Travelers with dogs and cats are welcome at the pet-friendly **Carmel Country Inn** (Dolores and 3rd Aves., 831/625-3263, www.carmelcountry inn.com, $245). The Inn does not, however, welcome children under six years old-it's a romantic hideaway, not a family motel. Rooms and suites boast comfortable furnishings that feel more like a friend's home than a generic hotel—you may find a fireplace, a reading nook, or even a Jacuzzi tub inside.

Despite its ghastly name, the cliff top **Tickle Pink Inn** (155 Highland Dr., 831/624-1244, www.ticklepinkinn.com, $314) offers tasteful luxury. Each room has a view of the ocean, an array of high-end furniture and linens, and all the top-end amenities you'd expect from a distinctive Carmel hostelry. For a special treat, shell out for the spa bath suite and watch the ocean while you soak in the tub with your sweetie.

FOOD
Breakfast
Need breakfast? Get it at **Katy's Place** (Mission and 6th Aves., 831/624-0199, www.katysplace carmel.com, daily 7 A.M.–2 P.M., $10–20), a self-described "Carmel Tradition" that can get quite crowded on weekend mornings. You can get your favorite breakfast all day, whether you love heavy eggs Benedict or light Belgian waffles…well, as long as they're open.

Asian
For a more authentic hole-in-the-wall locals' dining experience, seek out **Tommy's Wok**

(Mission St. and Ocean Ave., 831/624-8518, Tues.–Sun. 11:30 A.M.–2:30 P.M. and 4:30–9:30 P.M., $10–20). All the veggies are fresh and organic, and the dishes taste reliably good whether you dine in or order takeout to enjoy elsewhere.

California

For a taste of wine country cuisine in the Carmel Valley, reserve a table at **Marinus at Bernardus Lodge** (415 W. Carmel Valley Rd., Carmel Valley, 831/658-3550, www .bernardus.com, daily 6–10 P.M., $40–70). The exquisite California cuisine features the produce, fish, and meat of local producers, and has been served to the likes of Julia Child and Leonardo diCaprio. Choose a three-, four-, or five-course meal, or go for broke and get the chef's tasting menu.

French

Let go of any prejudices against "fancy French restaurants" and try a country-style meal in the unprepossessing dining room of **Le Coq D'Or** (Mission and 4th Sts., 831/626-9319, www .lecoqdor.com, daily 5–10 P.M., $35). Order a classic French beef stew or a German schnitzel, and perhaps share a juicy morsel with your canine companion, who is always welcome to dine with you out on the heated porch.

Mediterranean

For cute ambiance, you can't beat the flower gardens and traditional cottage of **PortaBella** (Ocean Ave. and Monte Verde, 831/624-4395, www.carmelsbest.com, daily 11:30 A.M.– 11 P.M., $20–40). This upscale-meets-kitsch restaurant serves Mediterranean inspired cuisine with a distinct local flair.

Seafood

The **Flying Fish Grill** (Mission St. betw. Ocean and 7th Aves., 831/625-1962, Sun.– Thurs. 5–9 P.M., Fri.–Sat. 5–9:30 P.M., $30–40) serves Japanese-style seafood with a California twist in the Carmel Plaza open-air shopping mall. While the food isn't universally revered, the service at the Flying Fish and the presentation of the plates makes a visit worth the time and expense.

INFORMATION AND SERVICES

You'll find the **Carmel Visitors Center** (San Carlos betw. 5th and 6th, 831/624-2522, www. carmelcalifornia.org, daily 10 A.M.–5 P.M.) right in the midst of downtown Carmel-by-the-Sea.

For more information about the town and current events, pick up a copy of the weekly *Carmel Pine Cone* (www.pineconearchive. com), the local newspaper.

The nearest major medical center to Carmel-by-the-Sea and the Carmel Valley is in nearby Monterey. For minor issues, head for the **Community Hospital of Monterey** (23625 Holman Hwy, Monterey, 831/622-2746, www .chomp.org).

GETTING THERE AND AROUND

If you've made it to Monterey by car, getting to Carmel is a piece of cake. The quick and free way to get to Carmel from the north or the south is via Highway 1. From Highway 1, take Ocean Avenue into the middle of downtown Carmel. A more expensive but more beautiful route is the 17-Mile Drive (see *Sights*).

To get to the Carmel Valley, take Highway 1 to Carmel Valley Road, which is a major intersection with a stop light. Signs point the way to Carmel Valley.

As you read the addresses in Carmel-by-the-Sea and begin to explore the neighborhoods, you'll realize something interesting. There are no street addresses. (Some years ago Carmel residents voted not to enact door-to-door mail delivery, thus there is no need for numeric addresses on buildings.) So you'll need to pay close attention to the street names and the block you're on. Just to make things even more fun, street signs can be difficult to see in the mature foliage and a dearth of streetlights can make them nearly impossible to find at night. If you can, show up during the day to get the lay of the land before trying to navigate after dark.

Big Sur

Big Sur beckons to many types of visitors. Nature-lovers come to camp and hike the pristine wilderness areas, to don thick wetsuits and surf the oft-deserted beaches, and even to hunt for jade in rocky coves. Some of these folks come to stay and find themselves at the amazing retreats hosted by the Esalen Institute.

On the other hand, some of the wealthiest people from California and beyond visit Big Sur to luxuriate at unbelievably posh hotels and spas with dazzling views of the ocean, flower-strewn meadows, art galleries, and fabulous cuisine.

Whether you prefer a low-cost camping trip or a pampered look into how the other 0.01 percent live, Big Sur offers its beauty and charm to all comers. Part of that charm is Big Sur's determination to remain peacefully apart from the Information Age—yes, this means that your cell phone won't work in many parts of Big Sur. Horrors!

Note: The term "Big Sur" can be confusing to non-locals. It's both a town and the semi-official name of the coastal region that runs south of Carmel and north of San Simeon delineated by Highway 1.

SIGHTS
◖ Big Sur Coast Highway

Even if you're not up to tackling the endless hiking trails and deep wilderness backcountry of Big Sur, you can still get a good sense of the glory of this region just by driving through it. The Big Sur Coast Highway, a 90-mile stretch of Highway 1, runs along jagged cliffs and rocky beaches, through dense redwood forest, over historic bridges, and past innumerable parks. Construction on this stretch of road was completed in the 1930s, connecting Cambria to Carmel. You can start out at either of these towns and spend a whole day making your way to the other end of the road. The road has plenty of wide turnouts set into picturesque cliffs to make it easy to stop to admire the glittering ocean and stunning wooded

Big Sur's famous coastline

cliffs running right out to the water. Be sure to bring a camera on your trip along Highway 1-you'll find yourself wanting to take photos every mile for hours on end.

Bixby Bridge

You'll probably recognize the Bixby Bridge when you come upon it on Highway 1 in Big Sur. The picturesque cement open-spandrel arched bridge is one of the most photographed bridges in the nation, and it's been used in countless car commercials over the years. The bridge was built in the early 1930s as part of the massive Government Works project that completed Highway 1 through the Big Sur area to connect the road from the north end of California to the south. Today, you can pull out either to the north or to the south of the bridge to take photos or just look out at the attractive span and Bixby Creek flowing into the Pacific far below.

Are there two Bixby Bridges? Nope, but the Rocky Creek Bridge (north of Bixby Bridge on Hwy. 1) is similar in design, if not quite as grand and picturesque.

Big Sur Station

If you haven't yet stopped at one of the larger state parks in the area and hit the visitors center, pull in at Big Sur Station (Hwy. 1 south of Pfeiffer Big Sur, 831/667-2315, daily 8 A.M.–4:30 P.M.). The ranger station offers maps and brochures for all the major parks and trails of Big Sur, plus a minimal bookshop. Frankly, the visitor center and attendant services at Pfeiffer Big Sur State Park have the same or superior information to that available at Big Sur Station, so if you're planning to hit that park, skip this stop. However, several of the lesser parks and beaches (Limekiln, Garrapata, Sand Dollar) have no visitors services, so Big Sur Station serves a good purpose for visitors who plan to go only to those less-traveled spots. You can also get a free backcountry permit for the Ventana Wilderness here.

Henry Miller Memorial Library

A number of authors have done time in Big Sur, soaking in the remote wilderness and sea air to gather inspiration for their work. Henry Miller lived and wrote in Big Sur for 18 years, and one of his works is titled for the area. Today the Henry Miller Memorial Library (Hwy. 1, 0.25 mile north of Deetjens, 831/667-2574, www .henrymiller.org, Wed.–Mon. 11 A.M.–6 P.M.) celebrates the life and work of Miller and his brethren in this quirky community center/ museum/coffee shop/gathering place. The library is easy to find as you drive either north or south on Highway 1—look for the hand-painted sign and funky fence decorations. What you won't find is a typical lending library, bookshop, or slicked-up museum. Instead, you'll wander the lovely sun-dappled meadow soaking in the essence of Miller's life here, come inside and talk to the docents about the racy novels Miller wrote, and maybe sit back with a cup of coffee to meditate on life and art and isolated gorgeous scenery. The library offers a glimpse into the "real" world of Big Sur as a spread-out artists' colony that has inspired countless works by hundreds of people.

Point Sur Light Station

Sitting lonely and isolated out on its cliff, the Point Sur Light Station (Hwy. 1, 0.25 mile north of Point Sur Naval Facility, 831/625-4419, tours year-round Sat.–Sun. 10 A.M. and 2 P.M., plus Apr.–Oct. Wed. 10 A.M. and 2 P.M., July–Aug. Thurs. 10 A.M., adults $8, children $4) keeps watch over ships navigating near the rocky waters of Big Sur. It's the only complete 19th-century light station in California that you can visit, and even here access is severely limited. First lit in 1889, this now fully automated light station still provides navigational aid to ships off the coast; families stopped living and working in the tiny stone-built compound in 1974. But is the lighthouse truly uninhabited? Take one of the moonlight tours (call for information) to learn about the haunted history of the light station buildings.

You can't make a reservation for a Point Sur tour, so you should just show up and park your car off Highway 1 on the west side by the farm gate. Your guide will meet you there and lead you up the paved road 0.5 mile to the light station. Once there, you'll climb the stairs up to the light, explore the restored keepers' homes and service buildings, and walk out to the cliff edge. Expect to see a great variety of wildlife, from brilliant wildflowers in the spring to gray whales in the winter to flocks of pelicans flying in formation at any time of year. Be sure to dress in layers; it can be sunny and hot or foggy and cold, winter or summertime, and sometimes both on the same tour! Tours last three hours and require more than a mile of walking, with a bit of slope and more than 100 stairs.

The farm gate is locked and there's no access to the light station without a tour group. Tour schedules can vary from year to year and season to season; it's a good idea to call ahead before showing up. If you need special assistance for your tour or have questions about accessibility, call 831/667-0528 as far in advance as possible of your visit to make arrangements. No strollers, food, pets, or smoking are allowed on light station property.

Big Sur Spirit Garden

A favorite among local art-lovers, the Big Sur Spirit Garden (Hwy. 1, Loma Vista, 831/667-1300, www.bigsurspiritgarden.com, daily 9 A.M.–6 P.M.) changes a little almost every day. The "garden" part includes a variety of exotic plants, while the "spirit" part devotes itself to modern and postmodern Fair Trade art from as nearby as a few miles and as far away as India. The artwork tends toward brightly colored small sculptures done in a childlike, exuberant style. The Spirit Garden offers educational programs, community celebrations, musical events, and more. Call ahead for information on upcoming events.

HIKING

The main reason to come to Big Sur is to hike its beaches and forests. As you cruise Highway 1, the parks line up for you.

Garrapata State Park

A narrow two-mile long band of pretty light sand creates the beach at Garrapata State Park (Hwy. 1, gate 18 or 19, 831/624-4909, www.parks.ca.gov), north of the Point Sur Light Station. Stroll along the beach, scramble up the cliffs for a better view of the ocean, or check out the seals, sea otters, and sea lions near Soberanes Point. In the wintertime, grab a pair of binoculars to look for migrating gray whales passing quite close to shore here. The **Soberanes Canyon Trail** to the east of the highway is one of the more challenging and fun hikes to tackle at Garrapata.

Expect little in the way of facilities here—you'll park in a wide spot on Highway 1, and if you're lucky you might find a pit toilet open for use.

Andrew Molera State Park

The first "Big Sur" park you'll encounter is Andrew Molera State Park (Hwy. 1, 22 miles south of Carmel, 831/667-2315, www.parks.ca.gov, day use $8). Once home to small camps of Esselen Native Americans, then a Spanish land grant, this chunk of Big Sur eventually became the Molera ranch. The land was used to grow crops and ranch animals, and as a hunting and fishing retreat for family and friends. In 1965, Frances sold the land to the Nature Conservancy, and when she died three years later the ranch was sold to the California State Park system as per her will. Today, the **Molera Ranch House Museum** (831/620-0541, bshs@mbay.net, Sat.–Sun. 11 A.M.–3 P.M.) displays stories of the life and times of Big Sur's human pioneers and artists as well as the wildlife and plants of the region. Take the road toward the horse tours to get to the ranch house.

The park has numerous hiking trails that run down to the beach and up into the forest along the river—many are open to biking and horseback riding as well. Most of the park trails lie to the west of the highway. The beach is a one-mile walk down the easy, multi-use **Trail Camp Beach Trail.** From there, climb on out on the **Headlands Trail,** a 0.25-mile loop, for a beautiful view from the headlands. If you prefer to get a better look at the Big Sur River, take the flat, moderate **Bobcat Trail** (5.5 miles round-trip) and perhaps a few of its ancillary loops. You'll walk right along the riverbanks, enjoying the local microhabitats. Just be sure to look out for bicycles and the occasional horse and rider. For an even longer and more difficult trek up the mountains and down to the beach, take the eight-mile **Ridge Bluff Loop.** You'll start at the parking lot on the Creamery Meadow Beach Trail, then make a left onto the long and fairly steep Ridge Trail to get a sense of the local ecosystem. Then turn left again onto the Panorama Trail, which runs down to the coastal scrublands, and finally out to the Bluffs Trail, which takes you back to Creamery Meadow.

At the park entrance, you'll find bathrooms but no drinkable water and no food concessions. If you're camping here, be sure to bring plenty of your own water for washing dishes as well as drinking. If you're hiking for the day, pack in bottled water and snacks.

🄲 Pfeiffer Big Sur State Park

The biggest, most developed park in Big Sur is Pfeiffer Big Sur State Park (47225 Hwy. 1, 831/667-2315, www.parks.ca.gov, day use $8). It's got the Big Sur Lodge, a restaurant and café, a shop, an amphitheater, a somewhat incongruous softball field, plenty of hiking-only trails, and lovely redwood-shaded campsites. This park isn't situated by the beach; it's up in the coastal redwoods forest, with a network of roads that can be driven or biked up into the trees and along the Big Sur River.

Pfeiffer Big Sur has the tiny **Ernest Ewoldsen Memorial Nature Center,** which features stuffed examples of local wildlife. It's open seasonally; call the park for days and hours. Another historic exhibit is the **Homestead Cabin,** once the home of part of the Pfeiffer family—the first European immigrants to settle in Big Sur. Day-trippers and overnight visitors can take a stroll through the cabins of the Big Sur Lodge, built by the Civilian Conservation Corps during the Great Depression.

No bikes or horses are allowed on trails in this park, which makes it quite peaceful for hikers. For a starter walk, take the easy, 0.7-mile **Nature Trail** in a loop from Day Use Parking Lot 2. Grab a brochure at the lodge to learn about the park's plant life as you walk the trail. For a longer

McWay Falls

stroll, head out on the popular **Pfeiffer Falls Trail,** 1.5 miles round-trip. You'll find stairs on the steep sections and footbridges across the creek, then a lovely platform at the base of the 60-foot waterfall where you can rest and relax midway through your hike. For a longer, more difficult, and interesting hike deeper into the Big Sur wilderness, start at the Homestead Cabin and head to the **Mount Manuel Trail** (10 miles round trip, difficult). From the Y-intersection with the Oak Grove Trail, it's four miles of sturdy hiking to Mount Manuel, one of the most spectacular peaks in the area.

Need to cool off after hiking? Scramble out to the entirely undeveloped Big Sur River Gorge, where the river slows and creates pools that are great for swimming. Relax and enjoy the water, but don't try to dive here.

This is one of the few Big Sur parks to offer a full array of services. Before you head out into the woods, stop at the Big Sur Lodge restaurant and store complex to get a meal and some water, and to load up on snacks and sweatshirts. Between the towering trees and the summer fogs, it can get quite chilly and somewhat damp on the trails.

Julia Pfeiffer Burns State Park

One of the best-known and easiest hikes in all of the Big Sur region sits in Julia Pfeiffer Burns State Park (Hwy. 1, 12 miles south of Pfeiffer Big Sur State Park, 831/667-2315, www .parks.ca.gov). The **Overlook Trail** runs only two-thirds of a mile round-trip, along a level wheelchair-friendly boardwalk. Stroll under Highway 1, past the Pelton wheel house, and out to the observation deck and the stunning view of **McWay Falls.** The medium-sized waterfall cascades year-round off a cliff and onto the beach of a remote cove, where the water wets the sand and trickles out into the sea. The water of the cove gleams bright cerulean blue against the just-off-white sand of the beach—it looks more like the South Pacific than Northern California. Anyone with an ounce of love for the ocean will want to build a hut right there beside the waterfall. But you can't—in fact, the reason you'll look down on a pristine and empty stretch of sand is that there's no way down to the cove that's even remotely safe.

The tiny Pelton wheel exhibit off the Overlook Trail isn't much unless you're a huge fan of hydraulic engineering history. It does have an interpretive exhibit (including the old Pelton wheel itself) describing what a Pelton wheel is and what it does. No other museums make their homes here, though there's a small visitors center adjacent to the parking lot.

If you're up for a longer hike after taking in the falls, go back the other way to pick up the **Ewoldsen Trail** (4.5 miles round-trip, moderate–difficult). This trek takes you through McWay Canyon, and you'll see the creek and surrounding lush greenery as you walk. Then you'll loop away from the water and climb up into the hills. Be sure to bring water, as this hike can take several hours.

If you want to spend all day at Julia Pfeiffer Burns State Park, drive north from the park entrance to the Partington Cove pullout and park along the side of the highway. On the east side of the highway, start out along the **Tanbark Trail** (6.4 miles round-trip, difficult). You'll head through redwood groves and up steep switchbacks to the top of the coastal ridge. Be sure to bring your camera to record the stunning views before you head back down the fire road to your car.

Jade Cove Recreation Area

Jade Cove Recreation Area (Hwy. 1, two miles south of Sand Dollar Beach) is easy to pass as you barrel down Highway 1 towards San Simeon. A road sign marks the area, but there's not much in the way of a formal parking lot or anything else to denote the treasures of this jagged, rough part of the Big Sur coastline. Park in the dirt/gravel strip off the road and head past the fence and into the park. It's fun to read the unusual signs along the narrow, beaten path that seems to lead to the edge of a cliff. The signs explain that you cannot bring in mining equipment, or take away rocks or minerals obtained from behind the high-tide line. If you're into aerial sports, you can hang-glide off the cliffs here.

Once you get to the edge of the cliff, the short trail gets rough. It's only 0.25 mile, but it's almost straight down a rocky, slippery cliff. Don't try to climb down if you're not in reasonable physical condition, and even if you are, don't be afraid to use your hands to steady yourself. At the bottom, you'll find huge boulders and smaller rocks and very little sand. You may also see a small herd of locals dressed in wetsuits and scuba gear. But most of all, you'll find the most amazing minerals in the boulders and rocks. Reach out and touch a multi-ton boulder shot through with jade. Search the smaller rocks beneath your feet for chunks of sea-polished jade. If you're a hard-core rock nut, you can join the locals in scuba diving for jewelry-quality jade. As long as you find it in the water or below the high-tide line, it's legal for you to take whatever you find here.

Jade Cove has no water, no restrooms, no visitors center, and no services of any kind.

SPORTS AND RECREATION
Horseback Riding

You can take a guided horseback ride into the forests or out onto the beaches of Andrew Molera State Park with **Molera Horseback Tours** (831/625-5486, http://molerahorsebacktours.

com, $25–60). Tours of 1–2.5 hours depart each day starting at 9 A.M.—call ahead to guarantee your spot, or take a chance and just show up at the stables 15 minutes ahead of the ride you want to take. If you prefer, call to book a private guided ride for yourself and your party. Each ride takes you from the modest corral area along multi-use trails through forests or meadows, or along the Big Sur River, and down to Molera Beach. You'll guide your horse along the solid sands as you admire the beauty of the wild Pacific Ocean.

Molera Horseback Tours are suitable for children over six and riders of all ability levels; you'll be matched to the right horse for you. All rides go down to the beach. Tours can be seasonal, so call ahead if you want to ride in the fall or winter. Guides share their knowledge of the Big Sur region and wildlife, and welcome questions about the plants you're seeing as you walk your horse down the trail. Early-morning and sunset rides tend to be the prettiest and most popular.

Backpacking
If you long for the lonely peace of backcountry camping, the **Ventana Wilderness** (www .ventanawild.org) area is ideal for you. This area comprises the peaks of the Santa Lucia Mountains and the dense growth of the northern reaches of the Los Padres National Forest. You'll find many trails beyond the popular day hikes of the state parks, especially as Big Sur stretches down to the south. Check the website to find reports on the conditions of the trails you've decided to tackle in advance, and stop in at Big Sur Station or the ranger station at Pfeiffer Big Sur State Park to get the latest news on the backcountry areas.

Fishing
No harbors offer deep-sea charters around Big Sur, but if your idea of the perfect outdoor vacation must include a rod and reel, you can choose between shore and river fishing. Steelhead run up the Big Sur River to spawn each year, and a limited fishing season follows them up the river into **Pfeiffer Big Sur State Park** and other accessible areas. Check with

Fernwood Resort (831/667-2422, www.fern woodbigsur.com) and the other lodges around Highway 1 for the best spots this season.

The numerous creeks that feed into and out of the Big Sur River also play home to their fair share of fish. Cast for trout in the creeks of Pfeiffer Big Sur and other clear-water streams in the area. The California Department of Fish and Game (www.dfg.ca.gov) can give you specific locations for legal fishing, season information, and rules and regulations.

If you prefer the fish from the ocean, you can cast off several of the beaches for the rock fish that scurry about in the near-shore reefs. **Garrapata State Beach** has a good fishing area, as do the beaches at **Sand Dollar.**

Scuba Diving
There's not much for beginner divers in Big Sur, but if you've got some underwater experience, you'll want to bring your gear when you visit this region. Expect cold water. Temperatures range in the mid 50s in the shallows, dipping into the 40s as you dive deeper down. Visibility is 20–30 feet, though rough conditions can diminish this significantly; the best season for clear water is September through November.

The biggest and most interesting dive locale here is the **Julia Pfeiffer Burns State Park** (Hwy. 1, 12 miles south of Pfeiffer Big Sur, 831/667-2315, www.parks.ca.gov, daily sunrise–sunset). You'll need to acquire a special permit at Big Sur Station and prove your experience to dive at this protected underwater park. The park, along with the rest of the coast of Big Sur, is part of the Monterey Bay National Marine Sanctuary. You enter the water from the shore, which gives you the chance to check out all the ecosystems, beginning with the busy life of the beach sands and heading out to the rocky reefs, then into the lush green kelp forests.

Divers at access-hostile **Jade Cove** (Hwy. 1, two miles south of Sand Dollar Beach) aren't usually interested in cute, colorful nudibranchs or even majestic gray whales. Jade Cove divers come to stalk the wily jade pebbles and rocks that cluster in this special spot.

The semi-precious stone striates the coastline right here, and storms tear clumps of jade out of the cliffs and into the sea. Much of it settles just off the shore of the tiny cove, and divers hope to find jewelry-quality stones to sell for a huge profit.

If you're looking for a guided scuba dive of the Big Sur region, contact **Adventure Sports Unlimited** (303 Potrero St., #15, Santa Cruz, 831/458-3648, www.asudoit.com).

Bird-Watching

Many visitors come to Big Sur just to see the birdies. The Big Sur coast is home to innumerable species, from the tiniest bush tits up to grand pelicans and beyond. The most famous avian residents of this area are no doubt the rare and endangered California condors. Once upon a time, condors were all but extinct, with only a few left alive in captivity and conservationists struggling to help them breed. Today, more than 30 birds soar above the trails and beaches of Big Sur. You might even see one swooping down low over your car as you drive down Highway 1! (You'll know it if one does this—a condor's wingspan can exceed nine feet.) Check with the park rangers for the best times and places to see condors during your visit.

The **Ventana Wilderness Society** (www.ventanaws.org) watches over many of the endangered and protected avian species in Big Sur. As part of their mission to raise awareness of the condors and many other birds, the VWS offers bird-watching expeditions; these can be simple two-hour tours or overnight wilderness camping trips, depending on your level of interest. Check their website for schedules and prices.

One of the hot spots of VWS conservation efforts and tours is Andrew Molera State Park. You can head out on your own to take a look around for some of the most interesting species in the Big Sur area. But wherever you choose to hike, be it beach or forest, you're likely to see a variety of feathered friends fluttering about.

Spas

The **Allegria Spa at Ventana** (831/667-4222, www.ventanainn.com/spa.asp, daily 9 A.M.–7 P.M.,

Japanese baths at the Allegria Spa, Ventana

© LIZ HAMILL SCOTT

until 8 P.M. in summer, $120/50-minute massage) offers a large menu of spa treatments to both hotel guests and visitors. You'll love the serene atmosphere of the treatment and waiting areas. Greenery and weathered wood create a unique space that help to put you in a tranquil state of mind, ready for your body to follow your mind into a state of relaxation. Indulge in a soothing massage, purifying body treatment, or rejuvenating or beautifying facial. Take your spa experience a step further in true Big Sur fashion with a reiki or craniosacral treatment. Or go for a private New Age reading, a personal yoga or meditation session, or a private guided hike. If you're a hotel guest, you can choose to have your spa treatment in the comfort of your own room or out on your private deck.

Just across the highway from the Ventana, the **Post Ranch Inn and Spa** (Hwy. 1, 831/667-2200,, $135/hour massage) is another ultra-high-end resort spa. Massage, body, and facial work focuses on organics and gem and crystal therapies. You can also indulge in private sessions, including Shamanic meetings

ESALEN:
AN ADVANCED CALIFORNIA EXPERIENCE

The Esalen Institute is known throughout California as the home of California massage technique, a forerunner and cutting-edge player in ecological living, and a space to retreat from the world and build a new and better sense of self. Visitors journey from all over the state and beyond to sink into the haven that's sometimes called "The New Age Harvard."

One of the biggest draws of the Institute sits down a rocky path right on the edge of the cliffs overlooking the ocean. The bath house includes a motley collection of mineral-fed hot tubs looking out over the ocean – you can choose the Quiet Side or the Silent Side to sink into the water and contemplate the Pacific Ocean's limitless expanse, meditate on a perfect sunset or arrangement of stars, or (on the Quiet Side) get to know your fellow bathers.

Who will be naked. Regardless of gender, marital status, or the presence of others.

Esalen's bath house area is "clothing optional," its philosophy puts the essence of nature above the sovereignty of humanity, and it encourages openness and sharing among its guests – to the point of chatting nude with total strangers in a smallish hot tub. You'll also find a distinct lack of attendants to help you find your way around. Once you've parked and been given directions, it's up to you to find your way down to the cliffs. You'll have to find your own towel, ferret out a cubby for your clothes in the changing rooms, grab a shower, then wander out to find your favorite of the hot tubs. Be sure you go all the way outside

past the individual clawfoot tubs to the glorious shallow cement tubs that sit right out on the edge of the cliff with the surf crashing just below.

In addition to the nudity and new-age culture of Esalen, you'll learn that this isn't a day spa. You'll need to make an appointment for a massage (at $150 a pop), which grants you access to the hot tubs for an hour before and an hour after your 75-minute treatment session. If you just want to sit in the mineral water, you'll need to stay up late. Very late. Inexpensive ($20) open access to the Esalen tubs begins on a first-come, first-serve basis at 1 A.M. and ends at 3 A.M. Many locals consider the sleep deprivation well worth it to get the chance to enjoy the healing mineral waters and the stunning astronomical shows.

If you're not comfortable with your own nudity or that of others, you don't approve of meditation or non-Christian spiritual philosophy, or you find it impossible to lower your voice or stop talking for more than 10 minutes, Esalen is not for you. If you've never done anything like this before, think hard about how you'll really feel once you're in the changing area with its open cubbies and naked hippies wandering about.

But if this description of a California experience sounds just fabulous to you, make your reservations now! The Esalen Institute (55000 Hwy. 1, 831/667-3000, fax 831/667-2724, www. esalen.org) accepts reservations by fax, mail, and phone if necessary. Go to the website for more information.

that focus on indigenous techniques that are said to enhance your life.

ENTERTAIMENT AND EVENTS

The primary entertainment in Big Sur takes place out of doors. Listen to the symphony of the surf against the cliffs, admire the sculpture of 1,000-year-old coast redwoods, and pick up jewelry in the raw right off the beaches. But if you need a bit more, a few events and

entertainment options appear in quiet, nature-loving Big Sur.

Live Music

It probably won't surprise you to learn that Big Sur is not a hotbed of cutting-edge clubs and bars. Most folks who come here spend their days outside, hiking or doing some other vigorous activity. They drop into bed early, exhausted and needing the rest to get back out into the wilderness again the next day. But if you just can't bear to hit the sack before 10 P.M., you can find some fun at the **Fernwood Tavern** (Hwy. 1, 831/667-2422, Sun.–Thurs. noon–midnight, Fri.–Sat. noon–1 A.M.). Live music acts entertain locals and visitors alike, and you might hear country, folk, or even indie rock from the small stage. Most live music happens on weekends, especially Saturday nights, starting at 9 P.M. Even without the music, the tavern can get lively in the evenings (it's good to be the only game in town), with locals drinking from the full bar, eating, and holding parties in the meandering dim rooms.

Festivals and Events

Each year, the Pacific Valley School hosts the fundraising **Big Sur Jade Festival** (www.big surjadeco.com/festival.html, Oct.). Come out to see the artists, craftspeople, jewelry makers, and rock hunters displaying their wares in the early fall. The school is located across Highway 1 from Sand Dollar Beach. Munch snacks as your feet tap to the live music playing as part of the festival. Check the website for the exact dates and information about this year's festival.

CAMPING

Many visitors to Big Sur want to experience the unspoiled beauty of the landscape daily. To accommodate true outdoors lovers, many of the parks and lodges in the area have overnight campgrounds. You'll find all types of camping here, from full-service, RV-accessible areas to environmental tent campsites to wilderness backpacking. You can camp in a state park, or out behind one of the small resort motels near a restaurant and a store and possibly the cool refreshing Big Sur River. Pick the option that best suits you and your family's needs.

Andrew Molera State Park

Andrew Molera State Park (Hwy. 1, 22 miles south of Carmel, 831/667-2315, www.parks .ca.gov, $10/night) offers 24 walk-in, tent-only campsites located 0.25–0.5 mile from the parking lot via a level, well-maintained trail. You'll

pitch your tent in a pretty meadow near the Big Sur River, in a site that includes a picnic table and a fire ring. No reservations are taken, so come early in summertime to get one of the prime spots under a tree. While you're camping, look out for bobcats, foxes, deer, raccoons (stow your food securely!), and any number of birds.

As of 2007, no potable water was available at Andrew Molera. Toilets sit a short walk from the camping area, but you cannot shower here.

Fernwood Resort

The Fernwood Resort (Hwy. 1, 831/667-2422, www.fernwoodbigsur.com) maintains a large campground area on both sides of the Big Sur River. You can choose between pitching your own tent, pulling in in an RV, or renting a tent cabin. The resort has easy access to the river, where you can swim, inner tube, and hike. You'll also have access to the restaurant, store, and tavern.

Tent cabins offer small canvas-constructed spaces with room for four in a double and two twins. You can pull your car right up to the back of your cabin. Bring your own linens or sleeping bags, pillows, and towels to make up the inside of your tent cabin. Hot showers and bathrooms are a short walk away. Tent campsites are scattered in great places—tucked in down by the river under vast shady redwood trees. You can even park your RV under a tree, then hook it up to water and electricity.

Pfeiffer Big Sur State Park

The biggest and most developed campground in Big Sur sits at Pfeiffer Big Sur State Park (Hwy. 1, 800/444-7275, www.parks.ca.gov, $20). With 212 individual sites, each of which can take two vehicles and eight people or an RV (32 feet or shorter, trailers 27 feet max, dump station on-site), there's enough room for almost everybody here. During the summer, a grocery store and laundry facilities operate within the campground for those who don't want to hike down to the lodge, and plenty of flush toilets and hot showers are scattered throughout the campground. In the evenings, walk down to the Campfire Center for entertaining and educational programs. If you prefer a quieter and less asphalt-oriented camping experience, check out the hike-in and bike-in campgrounds that make up part of the Pfeiffer Big Sur complex.

Pfeiffer Big Sur fills up fast in the summertime, especially on weekends. Advance reservations (800/444-7275, www.reserveamerica.com) are highly recommended. Note that some campground sites were scheduled to be under construction until December 2009.

Limekiln State Park
The small but pretty campground at Limekiln State Park (Hwy. 1 two miles south of Lucia, 831/667-2403, www.parks.ca.gov, summer only, $18) offers 33 campsites with hot showers and flush toilets out along an attractive creek that runs toward the nearby ocean. RVs and trailers can stay here (call for maximum length restrictions), though hookups and dump stations aren't available. In the summertime, the park recommends making reservations early. In the winter, no reservations are available and many sites are closed. Call for more information if you want to camp here in the off-season.

Treebones Resort
For the ultimate high-end California green lodging-cum-camping experience, book a yurt (a circular structure made with a wood frame covered by cloth) at the Treebones Resort (71895 Hwy. 1, 877/424-4787, www.treebonesresort.com). The resort got its name from the locals' description of this scrap of land, which was once a wood recycling plant with sun-bleached logs lying about—"tree bones." Yurts ($155–280) at Treebones tend to be spacious and charming, with polished wood floors, queen beds, seating areas, and outdoor decks for lounging. There are also five walk-in campsites ($65 for two people). In the central lodge, you'll find nice hot showers and usually clean restroom facilities. Treebones offers a somewhat pricey casual dinner each night, and

basic linens. If you like extra pillows and towels, you'll have to bring your own. Check the website for a list of items to bring and the FAQ about the resort facilities to make your stay more fun. While children are allowed in four of the yurts, Treebones recommends leaving behind kids under 12 years old—without any TVs, phones, or digital entertainment, little ones often get bored and unpleasantly loud.

ACCOMMODATIONS
Under $100
When locals speak of Deetjens, they could be referring to the inn, the restaurant, or the family that created both. But they all do speak of Deetjens, which operates as a non-profit organization dedicated to offering visitors to the Big Sur region great hospitality for reasonable rates. To stay at **Deetjens Big Sur Inn** (48865 Hwy. 1, 831/667-2377, www.deetjens.com, $80–200) is to become a small part of Big Sur's history and culture. It doesn't look like a spot where legions of famous writers, artists, and Hollywood stars have laid their precious heads, but Deetjens can indeed boast a guest register that many hostelries in Beverly Hills would kill for. And yet, the motley collection of buildings also welcomed transient artists, San Francisco bohemians, and the occasional criminal looking for a spot to sleep as they traversed the coast on bicycles or even on foot.

Your guest room will be unique, still decorated with the art and collectibles chosen and arranged by Grandpa Deetjen many moons ago. The inn prides itself on its rustic historic construction—expect thin weathered walls, funky cabin construction, no outdoor locks on the doors, and an altogether unique experience. Many rooms have shared baths, but you can request a room with private bath when you make reservations. Deetjens prefers to offer a serene environment, and to that end does not permit children under 12 unless you rent both rooms of a two-room building. Deetjens has no TVs or stereos, no phones in guest rooms, and no cell phone service. Two pay phones are available for emergencies, but other than that you're truly cut off from the outside world.

CENTRAL COAST

Decide for yourself whether this sounds terrifying or wonderful.

$100-150

Along Highway 1 in the town of Big Sur, you'll find a couple of small motels. One of the more popular of these is the **Fernwood Resort** (Hwy. 1, 831/667-2422, www.fernwoodbigsur .com, $110). The low sprawl of buildings includes a 12-room motel, a small grocery-cum-convenience store, a restaurant, and a tavern that passes for the local nighttime hot-spot. Farther down the small road, you'll find the campgrounds, which include a number of tent cabins as well as tent and RV sites. If all this a "resort" makes, so be it. Your motel room will be a modest space in a blocky, one-level building off to the side of the main store and restaurant buildings. Not too much sunlight gets into the guest rooms, but the decor is light-colored and reasonably attractive. Rooms have queen beds and attached private bathrooms, but no TVs. If you tend to get chilly in the winter (or the summer fog), ask for a room with a gas stove. One room has a two-person hot tub sitting just outside on the back deck. In the summertime, book in advance to be sure of getting a room, especially on weekends.

Another lodge-style motel set in the redwood forest, the **Big Sur River Inn** (Hwy. 1 at Pheneger Creek, 800/548-3610, www .bigsurriverinn.com, $125–150) sits in one of the "populated" parts of Big Sur. First opened in the 1930s by a member of the legendary Pfeiffer family, the inn has been in continuous operation ever since. Today, it boasts 20 motel rooms, a restaurant, and a gift shop. Guest rooms are small but comfortable, with a juxtaposition of chain-motel comforters and curtains with rustic lodge-style wooden interior paneling. Budget-conscious rooms have one queen bed. Families and small groups can choose between standard rooms with two queen beds and two-room suites with multiple beds and attractive back decks that look out over the Big Sur River. All guests can enjoy the attractively landscaped outdoor pool with its surrounding lawn leading down to the river.

The attached restaurant offers three meals a day. Be sure to make reservations in advance for summertime weekends!

$150-250

If you want to stay inside one of the parks but tents just aren't your style, book a cabin at the **Big Sur Lodge** (47225 Hwy. 1, 800/424-4787, www.bigsurlodge.com, $199–289) in Pfeiffer Big Sur State Park. The lodge was built in the 1930s as a Government Works project to create jobs for people suffering in the Great Depression—by then Big Sur's astounding beauty and peace had been recognized by both federal and state governments, and much of the land was protected as parks for the enjoyment of the populace. Though the amenities have been updated, the cabins of Big Sur Lodge still evoke the classic woodsy vacation cabin. Set in the redwood forest along an array of paths and small roads, the cabins feature patchwork quilts, rustic furniture, understated decor, and simple but clean bathrooms. Many cabins have lots of beds—perfect for larger families or groups of adults traveling together. The largest cabins have fireplaces and kitchens. You can stock your kitchen at the on-site grocery store, or just get a meal at the lodge's restaurant or café.

The lodge has a swimming pool for those rare sunny summer days in the Big Sur forest. But the real attraction is its right-outside-your-door access to the Pfeiffer Big Sur trails. You can just leave your car outside your room and hike the day away inside the park. Or take a short drive to one of the other state parks and enjoy their charms for free with proof of occupancy at Big Sur Lodge.

Despite the forbidding name, **Ragged Point Inn** (19019 Hwy. 1, 805/927-4502, http:// raggedpointinn.net, $200–300) takes advantage of its location to create an anything-but-ragged hotel experience for its guests. If you've come to Big Sur to bask in the grandeur of the Pacific Ocean, this is your hotel. The Ragged Point Inn perches on one of Big Sur's famous cliffs, offering stellar views from the purpose-built glass walls and private balconies or patios of almost every room in the house. Budget-friendly rooms still have plenty of space, a comfy king or two double beds, and those unreal ocean views. If you've got a bit more cash to burn, go for a luxury room, with optimal views, soaring interior spaces, plush amenities, and romantic two-person spa bathtubs. Outside your room, enjoy a meal in the full-service restaurant or get picnic supplies from the snack bar or the mini-mart, fill up for a day trip at the on-site gas station, or peruse the works of local artists in the gift shop or jewelry gallery. A special treat is the hotel's own hiking trail, which makes a 400-foot drop past a waterfall to Ragged Point's private beach.

Over $250

If money is no object, you cannot possibly beat the lodgings at ◖ **Ventana** (48123 Hwy. 1, 800/628-6500, www.ventanainn.com, $385), a place where the panoramic ocean views begin in the parking lot. This might well be the best hotel in all of California. Picture home-baked pastries, fresh yogurt, in-season fruit, and organic coffee delivered to your room in the morning, then enjoying that sumptuous breakfast outdoors on your own private patio overlooking a wildflower-strewn meadow that sweeps out toward the blue-gray waters of the ocean. And that's just the beginning of an unbelievable day at the Ventana. Next, don your plush spa robe and rubber slippers (all you are required to wear on the grounds of the hotel and spa) and head for the Japanese bathhouse. Choose from two bath houses, one at each end of the property. Both are clothing-optional and gender segregated, and the upper house has glass and open-air windows that let you look out to the ocean. Two swimming pools offer a cooler hydro-respite from your busy life; the lower pool is clothing-optional, and the upper pool perches on a high spot for enthralling views. Almost every other amenity imaginable, including daily complimentary yoga classes, can be yours for the asking.

The guest rooms range from the "modest" standard rooms with king beds, tasteful exposed cedar walls and ceilings, and attractive green and earth tone appointments, all the way up through generous and gorgeous suites to full-sized multi-bedroom houses. If you have a stupid amount of money available, the Vista Suites boast the most beauteous hotel accommodations imaginable. You'll reach your room by walking along the paved paths crowded by lush landscaping, primarily California native plants that complement the wild lands of the trails behind the main hotel buildings. You can also take an evening stroll down to the Cielo dining room—the only spot on the property where you need to wear more than your robe and flip-flops. If you're headed to the Allegria Spa for a treatment, you can go comfy and casual.

Post Ranch (47900 Hwy. 1, 800/527-2200, www.postranchinn.com, $550–2,185) is another exclusive luxury resort perched on the cliffs of Big Sur. Spa, yoga, and a unique yet rustic atmosphere are just a few of its perks.

FOOD

As you traverse the famed Highway 1 through Big Sur, you'll quickly realize that a ready meal isn't something to take for granted here. You'll see no McDonald's, Starbucks, 7-11s, or Safeways lining the road here. While you can find groceries, they tend to appear in small markets attached to motels. The motels and resorts usually have restaurants attached as well, but they're all-meals all-day or 24-hour kinds of places. Plan in advance to make it to meals during standard hours, and expect to have dinner fairly early. Pick up staple supplies before you enter the area if you don't plan to leave again for a few days to avoid paying premiums at the mini-marts.

Casual Dining

Serving three meals each day to lodge guests and passersby, the **Big Sur Lodge Café and Restaurant** (47225 Hwy. 1, 800/242-4787, www.bigsurlodge.com, daily 7 A.M.–9 P.M., $23) has a dining room as well as a cute espresso and ice cream bar out front. The dining room dishes up a full menu of American classic for every meal, while you can grab a quick sandwich to go from the espresso bar.

The **Redwood Grill** (Hwy. 1, 831/667-2129,

www.fernwoodbigsur.com, daily 11:30 A.M.–9 P.M., $20) at Fernwood Resort looks and feels like a grill in the woods ought to. Even in the middle of the afternoon, the aging, wood-paneled interior is dimly lit and strewn with slightly saggy couches and casual tables and chairs. Walk up to the counter to order somewhat overpriced burgers and sandwiches, then on to the bar to grab a soda or a beer.

The northernmost restaurant on the Big Sur coast, **Rocky Point Restaurant** (36700 Hwy. 1, 831/624-2933, www.rocky-point.com, daily 9 A.M.–3 P.M. and 5 P.M.–close, $35) offers decent food and great views to Highway 1 travelers. Enjoy the smell of mesquite from the grill as you wait for your steak or fish to bring that scent right to your nose. Though meat-eaters will find all the good solid dishes they want for breakfast, lunch, and dinner, vegetarian options are limited.

The **Big Sur Bakery** (47540 Hwy. 1, 831/667-0520, www.bigsurbakery.com, Tues.–Sat. 5:30 P.M.–close, Sat.–Sun. 10:30 A.M.–2:45 P.M.) might sound like a casual, walk-up eating establishment, and the bakery part of it is. You can stop in from 8 A.M. every day to grab a fresh-baked scone, a homemade jelly donut, or a flaky croissant sandwich for lunch later on. But on the dining room side, an elegant surprise awaits diners who've spent the day hiking the redwoods and strolling the beaches. Be sure to make reservations or you're unlikely to get a table, and you'd miss out on the amazing clam chowder (with whole clams in their shells) and other unique California takes on classic American cuisine.

According to Big Sur locals, the best breakfast in the area can be had at **Deetjens** (48865 Hwy. 1, 831/667-2377, www.deetjens.com, breakfast and dinner daily, $10–28). The funky dining room with its mismatched tables, dark wooden chairs, and cluttered wall decor belies the high quality of the cuisine served here. Enjoy delectable dishes created from the freshest local ingredients for breakfast and then again at dinnertime.

Fine Dining

You don't need to be a guest at the gorgeous Ventana to enjoy a fine gourmet dinner at **The Restaurant at Ventana** (Hwy. 1, 831/667-4242, www.ventana inn.com, daily noon–3:30 P.M., 6–9 P.M., $28–38). The spacious dining room boasts a warm wood fire, an open kitchen, and comfortable banquettes with plenty of throw pillows to lounge against as you peruse the menu. If you're visiting for lunch or an early supper on a sunny day, be sure to request a table outside so you can enjoy the stunning views with your meal. The inside dining room has great views from the bay windows too, along with pristine white tablecloths and pretty light wooden furniture. Even with such a setting as Cielo has, the real star at this restaurant is the cuisine. The chef offers a daily-changing spread of haute California cuisine dishes, many of which feature organic or homegrown produce and local meats. To go with the seascape theme, Cielo's menu is heavy on sustainable seafood offerings. Be sure to tell your server if you're a vegetarian or have other dietary limitations—the chefs can whip up something special just for you. The best value at Cielo is the prix fixe menu, from which you can choose several courses. If you can possibly afford it, get the wine pairing with each course, and be sure to save room for dessert.

When you dine at **Nepenthe** (48510 Hwy. 1, 831/667-2345, www.nepenthebigsur.com, daily 11:30 A.M.–10 P.M., $30), be sure to ask for a table outdoors on even the partly sunny days. That way you get to enjoy both your Ambrosiaburger and the phenomenal cliff-top views. Open for lunch and dinner, the restaurant offers a short but tasty menu of meats, fish, and plenty of vegetarian dishes.

Outside, the seasonal **Café Kevah** at Nepenthe (breakfast and lunch Mar.–Jan., $10–12) patio offers a similar sampling at slightly lower prices. Just remember to keep munching on your Benedict or sandwich as you drape your arms over the wrought-iron railing and stare out into the mesmerizing blue-gray of the Pacific below and beyond you.

The **Sierra Mar** (47900 Hwy. 1, 831/667-2800, www.postranchinn.com, daily

8–10:30 A.M., noon–3 P.M., and 3–9 P.M., $100) restaurant at the Post Ranch Inn offers a decadent four-course prix fixe dinner menu in a stunning ocean-view setting. Lunch and snacks are served all through the afternoon to casual travelers, but expect to put on the ritz for a formal, white-tablecloth dining experience at this over-the-top-of-upscale restaurant.

Markets

With no supermarkets or chain mini-marts in all of the Big Sur region, the local markets do a booming business. You can stock up on staples such as bread, lunch meat, eggs, milk, marshmallows, and graham crackers at various local stores. In town, the all-encompassing **Fernwood Resort** (Hwy. 1, 831/667-2422, www.fernwoodbigsur.com) has a market. You'll also find a seasonal market in the campground at Pfeiffer Big Sur State Park.

INFORMATION AND SERVICES

The two most comprehensive visitors centers in Big Sur lie within **Pfeiffer Big Sur State Park** (47225 Hwy. 1, 831/667-2315, www.parks.ca.gov) and **Julia Pfeiffer Burns State Park** (Hwy. 1, 12 miles south of Pfeiffer Big Sur, 831/667-2315, www.parks.ca.gov). At Pfeiffer Big Sur, you'll find the visitors center grouped in with the Big Sur Lodge Restaurant, the hotel check-in, and a small store. A tiny nature museum lies a quarter mile or so up the park's main road. This visitors center is a good spot to get maps and information for hiking here and at other Big Sur parks that don't have manned visitors centers. This large park also offers laundry facilities, some basic staples at the store, and food all day long at the restaurant and attached espresso bar.

Farther south at Julia Pfeiffer Burns, the visitors center is easily accessible from the main parking lot. Again, rangers can advise you about hiking and activities both in their park and at other parks in the region. You'll find fewer services here than at Pfeiffer Big Sur—if you need to shop, do laundry, or gas up, head north.

Be aware that your cell phone may not work in all of Big Sur, especially out in the undeveloped reaches of forest and on Highway 1 away from the town of Big Sur and the Post Ranch. Call boxes are set at regular intervals along the highway.

For health matters, the **Big Sur Health Center** (46896 Hwy. 1, Big Sur, 831/667-2580, Mon.–Fri. 10 A.M.–5 P.M.) can take care of minor medical needs, and provides an ambulance service and limited emergency care. The nearest full-service hospital is the **Community Hospital of the Monterey Peninsula** (23625 Holman Hwy., Monterey, 831/624-5311).

GETTING THERE AND AROUND

"Highway 1" sounds like a major freeway to many visitors, and down south it does get big and flat and straight. But along Big Sur, Highway 1 is a narrow, twisting, cliff-carved track that's breathtaking both because of its beauty and because of its dangers. Once you get five miles or so south of Carmel, expect to slow down—in some spots north of the town of Big Sur you'll be driving no more than 20 miles per hour around hairpin turns carved into vertical cliffs. If you're coming up from the south, Highway 1 is fairly wide and friendly up from Cambria, only narrowing into its more hazardous form as the cliffs get higher and the woods thicker. Be aware that fog often comes in on the Big Sur coast at sunset, making the drive even more hazardous (and much less attractive). If you must drive at night, take it slow!

Plan to spend several hours driving from Carmel to Cambria, partly to negotiate the difficult road and partly to make use of the many convenient turnouts to take photos of the unending spectacular scenery. Most of the major parks in the Big Sur region spring right off Highway 1, making it easy to spend a couple of days meandering along the road, stopping at Julia Pfeiffer or Andrew Molera to hike for a few hours or have a picnic on the beach.

Cambria and San Simeon

The small beach town of Cambria becomes surprisingly spacious when you start exploring it. Plenty of visitors come here to ply Moonstone Beach, peruse the charming downtown area, and just drink in the laid-back, art-town feel. But Cambria owes much of its prosperity to the immense tourist trap on the hill that is Hearst Castle. Located about seven miles north in San Simeon, Hearst Castle, quite frankly, *is* San Simeon; the town grew up around it to support the overwhelming needs of its megalomaniacal owner and never-ending construction.

SIGHTS

When it comes to this area, there is only one true sight. But once you're through with the castle tours, a few attractions in the lower elevations beckon as well. Nearby Cambria began and to a certain extent still is an artists colony; the windswept hills and sparkling ocean provide plenty of inspiration for painters, writers, sculptors, glassblowers, and more.

【 Hearst Castle

There's nothing else in California quite like Hearst Castle (Hwy. 1 and Hearst Castle Rd., 800/444-4445, www.hearstcastle.com, tours daily 8:20 A.M.–3:20 P.M., $24). Newspaper magnate William Randolph Hearst conceived of the idea of a grand mansion in the Mediterranean style, on the land his parents bought along the central California coast. His memories of camping on the hills above the Pacific led him to choose the spot on which the castle now stands. He hired Julia Morgan, the first female civil engineering graduate from UC Berkeley, to design and build the house for him. She did a brilliant job with every detail, despite the ever-changing wishes of her employer. By way of decoration, Hearst assisted in the relocation of hundreds of European medieval and Renaissance antiquities, from tiny tchotchkes to whole gilded ceilings. William Randolph also adored exotic animals, and created one of the largest private zoos in the nation on his thousands of Central Coast acres. Though most of the zoo is gone now, you can still see the occasional zebra grazing peacefully along Highway 1 to the south of the castle, acting as heralds to the exotic nature of Hearst Castle ahead.

The visitors center is a lavish affair with a gift shop, restaurant, café, ticket booth, and movie theater. Here you can see the much-touted film *Hearst Castle—Building the Dream,* which will give you an overview of the construction and history of the marvelous edifice, and of William Randolph Hearst's empire. After buying your ticket, board the shuttle that takes you up the hill to your tour. (No private cars are allowed on the roads up to the castle proper.) There are five tours to choose from, each focusing on different spaces and aspects of the castle. Tour 1 is recommended for first-time visitors, and you're welcome to sign up for several tours over the course of one day. Tour 5 is a seasonal evening tour with volunteers

Hearst Castle

dressed in 1930s fashion welcoming guests as if to one of Hearst's legendary parties.

Expect to walk for at least an hour on whichever tour you choose, and to climb up and down many stairs. Even the most jaded traveler can't help but be amazed by the beauty and opulence that drips from every room in the house. Lovers of European art and antiques will want to stay forever. The two swimming pools—one indoor and one outdoor—shine with grandeur, all marble, glass tile, and mixed antique and custom-created statuary and fixtures.

The park recommends that visitors buy tour tickets at least a few days in advance, and even further ahead for Tour 5 and on summer weekends. For visitors with limited mobility, a special wheelchair-accessible tour is available. Strollers are not permitted. The restrooms and food concessions all cluster in the visitors center—but no food, drink, or chewing gum is allowed on any tour.

Historic San Simeon

The tiny town of San Simeon existed primarily to support the construction efforts up the hill at Hearst Castle. The town dock provided a place for ships to unload tons of marble, piles of antiques, and dozens of workers. The general store and post office acted as a central gathering place for the community, and you can still walk up the weathered wooden steps and make a purchase here. Around the corner at the building's other door, you can buy a book of stamps or mail a letter at the tiny but operational post office.

The **William Randolph Hearst Memorial State Beach** (750 Hearst Castle Rd., San Simeon, 805/927-2020, www.parks.ca.gov, daily dawn–dusk) sits in San Simeon's cute little cove and encompasses the remaining structure of the old pier. You can lie on the beach or have a picnic up on the lawn above the sand.

Nitt Witt Ridge

While William Randolph Hearst built one of the most expensive homes ever seen in California, local eccentric Arthur Harold Beal (a.k.a. Captain Nit Wit or Der Tinkerpaw) got busy building the cheapest "castle" he could.

Nitt Witt Ridge (881 Hillcrest Dr., 805/927-2690, tours free by appointment only) is the result of five decades of scavenging trash and using it as building supplies to create a multi-story home like no other on the coast. Today, you can make an appointment with owners Michael and Stacey O'Malley to take a tour of the property. (Please don't just drop in.) It's weird, it's funky, and it's fun—an oddly iconic experience of the Central Coast.

Cambria Cemetery

"Artsy" isn't a word that's usually associated with graveyards, but in Cambria it fits. The Cambria Cemetery (6005 Bridge St., 805/927-5158, www.cambriacemetery.com) reflects the artistic bent of the town's residents in its tombstone decor. Unlike many cemeteries, at Cambria the family and friends of the deceased are allowed to place all manner of personal objects at their loved ones' graves. You'll see painted tombstones, beautiful panes of stained glass, unusual wind chimes, and many other unique expressions of love, devotion, and art as you wander the 12 wooded acres.

ACCOMMODATIONS
$100-150

A favorite even among the many inns of Cambria, the **Olallieberry Inn** (2476 Main St., Cambria, 888/927-3222, www.olallieberry.com, $145) sits in a charming 19th-century Greek Revival home and adjacent cottage. Each of the nine rooms features its own quaint Victorian-inspired decor with comfortable beds and attractive appointments. A full daily breakfast (complete with olallieberry jam) rounds out the comfortable personal experience.

Her Castle Homestay Bed and Breakfast Inn (1978 Londonderry Ln., Cambria, 805/924-1719, www.HerCastle.cc, $127–170) is a bit different from your average B&B, with only two rooms available and lots of personal attention from the owners. When you make your reservations, you can ask about a half-day wine tour, dinner reservations, or even lunch and dinner provided by the inn. The Her Castle can be the perfect hideaway for two couples traveling together who desire the privacy of "their own house."

$150-250

Many of the accommodations of Cambria sit along the small town's very own Hotel Row, a.k.a. Moonstone Beach Drive. One of these is the **Moonstone Landing** (6240 Moonstone Beach Dr., Cambria, 805/927-0012, www .moonstonelanding.com, $155), which provides inexpensive partial-view rooms with the decor and amenities of a mid-tier chain motel, as well as oceanfront luxury rooms featuring travertine marble bathrooms.

A charming log cabin structure shelters the eight rooms of the **J. Patrick House Bed and Breakfast** (2990 Burton Dr., Cambria, 805/927-3812, www.jpatrickhouse.com, $175). Each room has modern-country kitschy decor, a private bath, and plenty of amenities. They're dedicated to feeding you at the J. Patrick, with a big breakfast in the morning, hor d'oevres in the afternoon, and chocolate chip cookies at bedtime.

The Burton Inn (4022 Burton Dr., Cambria, 805/927-5125, www.burtoninn.com, $225) offers modernity in an attractive setting. Even the standard guest rooms offer tons of space, and the family suites have multiple bedrooms that promote both togetherness and privacy.

One of the cuter and more interesting lodgings on Moonstone Beach Drive, **Moonstone Cottages** (6580 Moonstone Beach Dr., Cambria, 805/927-1366, http://moonstone-cottages.com, $234) offers peace and luxury along with proximity to the sea. Expect your cottage to include a fireplace, a marble bathroom with a whirlpol tub, a flat-screen TV with a DVD player, Internet access, and a view of the ocean.

For a great selection of anything from economical standard rooms up to sizeable cabins, pick the **Cambria Pines Lodge** (2905 Burton Dr., 800/445-6868, www.cambria pineslodge.com, $150–400). All rooms have plenty of creature comforts, including TVs, private bathrooms, kitchenettes, and, in some cases, fireplaces.

FOOD

The Sow's Ear (2248 Main St., Cambria, 805/927-4865, www.thesowsear.com, daily 5–9 P.M., $10–30) does its best to create the proverbial "silk purse" dining experience with its upscale comfort foods and romantically dim atmosphere. Some diners feel that the prices for items such as lobster pot-pie and chicken and dumplings can run a bit high, but if you're longing for a taste of old-fashioned Americana, you can get it here.

If the smell of the salt air on Moonstone Beach leaves you longing for a seafood dinner, head for the **Sea Chest Oyster Bar** (6216 Moonstone Beach Dr., Cambria, 805/927-4514, daily 5:30–9 P.M., $20–30, cash only). No reservations are accepted, so expect a long line out the door at opening time, and prepare to get there early (or wait a long while) for one of the window-side tables. The seafood here tends to be fresh, with a good selection of raw oysters, and touristfriendly.

Perhaps the most famous, if slightly overrated, restaurant in Cambria is the **Black Cat Bistro** (1602 Main St., Cambria, 805/927-1600, www .blackcatbistro.com, Thurs.–Mon. 5 P.M.–close, $20–40). An interesting California-French menu contains both small and large plates, each with a suggested wine pairing. Despite its fancy food, the Black Cat prides itself on its casual resort-town atmosphere.

Part of an expansive but still totally local family business, **Linn's Restaurant** (2277 Main St., Cambria, 805/927-0371, www.linnsfruitbin.com/restaurant, daily 8 A.M.–9 P.M., $10) serves tasty, unpretentious American favorites in a casual, family-friendly atmosphere. If you love the olallieberry pie with your meal, you can purchase a ready-to-bake pie, jam, or even vinegar at the Linn's café, gourmet shop, or their original farm stand while you're in Cambria.

In ubiquitously high-priced Cambria, one of the best food bargains in town is **Wild Ginger** (2380 Main St., Cambria, 805/927-1001, www.wildgingercambria.com, Fri.–Wed. 11 A.M.–2:30 P.M., 5–9 P.M., $15). This tiny pan-Asian café serves delicious, fresh food at its few tables, and carries an array of take-out fare displayed in a glass case crammed into the back of the dining room. Come early for the best selection of dishes.

INFORMATION AND SERVICES

The town of Cambria does not boast a bricks-and-mortar visitors center, but you can do research in advance of your stay at http://cambriavisitorsbureau.com. If your primary interest is Hearst Castle, you'll find a huge visitors center at the parking lot below the castle where all tours start. Inside, you can buy and pick up tour tickets, grab a cup of coffee and a meal, and peruse the extensive bookshop, which includes many books about the Hearst family, the castle, and the town of Cambria.

The nearest hospital to Cambria is the **Twin Cities Hospital** (1100 Las Tablas Rd., Templeton, 805/434-3500), well east of the coast town. It sits near U.S. 101, just south of the junction of state Highway 46 and U.S. 101.

GETTING THERE AND AROUND

Most Californians making a weekend getaway to Cambria from either Northern California or Southern California drive there. You can drive the Pacific Coast Highway (Highway 1) right into Cambria—this is the prettiest but not the fastest way to get there. For a quicker route, take U.S. 101 to the Paso Robles area and then turn west onto CA-46, which brings you right to the town of Cambria.

If you prefer to travel by rail, you can take **Amtrak's** Coast Starlight (www.amtrak.com) to either the Paso Robles or the San Luis Obispo (SLO) stations, and make arrangements to rent a car (easiest from SLO) or get alternative transportation out to the coast.

Paso Robles

As an up-and-coming wine-growing region, Paso Robles has become a familiar destination and appellation for state residents and as well as a popular side trip from nearby Cambria. Huge crowds do not descend on Paso every weekend as they do in the more popular wine regions and you can still find room at the tasting bars, engage with knowledgeable tasting room staff, meet the occasional winemaker tending bar, and enjoy a friendly country atmosphere both in town and on the wine roads. For the best tasting experience, visit the Paso region over the weekend—many of the smaller winery tasting rooms are open only Thursday–Monday or even only Friday–Sunday.

WINERIES

The wine industry is growing by leaps and bounds in and all around Paso. The Paso Robles region now boasts more than 200 wineries, over 100 of which have tasting rooms open to the public. For the purposes of this book, the sprawled landscape is divided into four easily navigable parts: Highway 46 West, Highway 46 East (which does not directly connect to Hwy. 46 West), Downtown Paso Robles, and Remote—the area to the north of town on several roads branching away from U.S.101.

Highway 46 West

The densest concentration of wineries cluster along Highway 46 West and the little roads that spring off that main thoroughfare. Many intrepid wine tasters never make it past this short and easy-to-travel stretch, which locals refer to as the Westside.

One of the best of wineries in these parts is **Hunt Cellars** (2875 Oakdale Rd., 805/237-1600, www.huntcellars.com, daily 10:30 A.M.–5:30 P.M., tasting fee $5–10). Friendly and intensely knowledgeable staff members pour some of the best wines in Paso at this mid-sized, informal tasting room. You'll enter a building that looks more like a house than a winery, then choose the regular or reserve tasting. Also be sure to check the chalkboard behind the bar for the day's specialty offerings. All the wines at Hunt are grown in the family-owned Destiny Vineyard. The specialty of the house is Cabernet Sauvignon, and Hunt makes some of the best in California. You'll also get to taste a few Chardonnays, other red varietals, some red blends, and the famed (and expensive) port and dessert wines.

If you favor small wineries that only produce tiny runs of wine, **Dark Star Cellars** (2985 Anderson Rd., 805/237-2389, www.darkstar cellars.com, Fri.–Sun. 10:30 A.M.–5 P.M.) is perfect for you. Be sure to ask at the bar about the "synthetic gravity" that's so important to the slow fermentation process used at Dark Star. You'll taste about five vintages here—all red wines of the Bordeaux tribe. Most visitors think that the best of the lot is the much-lauded Ricordati, a Bordeaux blend that wins international awards year after year. Perhaps the nicest surprise of all comes when you've picked your favorites; prices at Dark Star range up to about $35 a bottle, and many are under $30.

Highway 46 East

It's not as crowded as 46 West, but Highway 46 East has plenty of great wineries. You might even recognize one or two names out in the Eastside.

One of the biggest winemakers to maintain a tasting room in the Paso region is **Meridian** (7000 Hwy. 46 E., 805/226-7133, www .meridianvineyards.com, daily 10 A.M.–5 P.M., tasting fee $5). You've no doubt seen Meridian on many menus and countless supermarket shelves. Meridian makes all the classic California varietal vintages, with bestsellers in Chardonnay and Cabernet Sauvignon. Check out the Limited Release list for, well, a bunch more of the same plus a few slightly less common wines like a Gewurztraminer and a Sangiovese. Meridian's deli and store provide a perfect place to gather up everything you need for the perfect wine picnic.

It might not be the biggest, but **Eberle Winery** (3810 Hwy. 46 E., 3.5 miles east of U.S. 101, 805/238-9607, www.eberlewinery.

com, daily 10 A.M.–5 P.M., until 6 P.M. in summer, free) is one of the pioneers of the Paso wine region. Gary Eberle has been making wine here for more than 25 years, and winning a passel of gold medals over that time. Be sure to get a spot on a cave tour while you're visiting, then head to the light-wood tasting room. Despite the fun statuary and the great caves at Eberle, the star attraction here is the wine. The medium-sized list features mostly hearty, bold red wines such as Cabernet Sauvignon, Barbera, Zinfandel, and a few fabulous blends. A few whites find their way to the bar, such as the Paso favorite Viognier and the lesser-known Roussanne. Taste as many as you possibly can—and you'll be surprised at how many bottles you'll want to walk away with. With most vintages selling for $15–25, you might be able to afford a few extras.

Downtown Paso Robles

Many wineries have set up tasting rooms right in the middle of downtown Paso. It's hard to resist walking into a tasting room that bears the name **Midlife Crisis Winery** (1244 Pine St., Ste. A, 805/237-8730, www.midlifecrisis winery.com, Thurs.–Mon. 10:30 A.M.–6 P.M.). Midlife Crisis is just that according to its owners, two veterans of the Los Angeles media circus who come up to Paso on the weekends to tend to their new pet winery. They got started in 2004, so you'll find mostly young vintages in the large, eclectic tasting room that's built into an historic Paso building. Heck, you might find one of the owner/winemakers in there, pouring, stocking, or just talking with employees and guests. Though the wines here leave plenty of room for improvement, the chatter and gossip are the best in the area. If you just ask a question or two, you'll learn everything you ever wanted to know about the wines and vineyards of the Paso Robles region.

If you're in town to find the best vintages possible, stop in at **Edward Sellers Vineyards & Wines** (1220 Park St., 805/239-8915, www.edward sellers.com, Thurs.–Mon. 11 A.M.–6 P.M.). This one's a favorite of California cork dorks, creating a number of Rhone varietals and some fabulous blends that transcend their French roots and California styles to create something new. If you're a varietal lover, try Edward's Grenaches and Viogniers—less common wines that are picking up popularity with serious wine aficionados in California. The small tasting room with distressed white woodwork and a shining black counter makes room for several tasters at once, so belly on up and ask for a glass! And if you don't know your Cinsault from your Counoise, be sure to ask. The pourers are happy to answer any and all questions pertaining to Edward Sellers wines and vineyards.

What matches more perfectly with a glass of small-lot wine than a chunk of artisanal cheese? At **Orchid Hill Vineyard** (1140 Pine St., 805/237-7525, www.orchidhillwine.com, daily 11:30 A.M.–6 P.M.), you can get both. From Friday through Sunday, a tasting at Orchid Hill includes pairings with fine, flavorful cheeses that catch the attention of many a taster. Visitors also spend some time gaping at the walls, which bear original modern artwork by Jean Pierre de Rothschild. The small list of varietals, which includes Viogniers, Syrah, Sangiovese, and Zinfandel, includes some tasty wines (but they aren't the best in the area).

Remote Wineries

Even if you don't love wine, it's worth the trip up to **Adelaida Cellars** (5805 Adelaida Rd., 800/676-1232, www.adelaida.com, daily 10 A.M.–5 P.M.). You'll get stunning views of Adelaida's mountain vineyards and down to the valley below. Adelaida wines are made with grapes grown on the estate vineyards, and the results can be fabulous. Adelaida takes advantage of its high elevation and difficult soil to raise grapes that produce small lots of top-tier boutique wines. Smoky, rich, angry-tasting Syrahs make up the backbone of Adelaida's list, which also includes Chardonnays, Rousannes, Vin Gris, Zinfandel, Pinot Noir, Cabernet Sauvignon, and a number of different and delicious blends. The winery produces vintages under four labels; the Reserve and Adelaida labels run toward the higher end, while the SLO and Schoolhouse labels provide tasty and affordable table wines suitable for everyday drinking.

A local producer with prestigious founders and backers, **Tablas Creek Vineyard** (9339 Adelaida Rd., 805/237-1231, www.tablascreek .com, daily 10 A.M.–5 P.M.) specializes in Rhone and Chateauneuf-du-Pape varietals and blends. Taste from the longish list of current commercial and winery-only vintages. Tablas Creek takes its winemaking seriously, maintaining its own grapevine nursery, keeping its vineyards organic, and using only its own yeasts created on-site. If such practices interest you, call in advance to get a spot on the daily vineyard and winery tours. End your survey of this showplace with a visit to the dark bar and bright artwork of the tasting room. You'll find many uncommon-for-California blends and varietals here, and the Tablas Creek bar staff can help you expand your palate and your knowledge of wine.

Halter Ranch Vineyard (8910 Adelaida Rd., 805/226-9455, www.halterranch.com, daily 11 A.M.–5 P.M.) sits on a 900-acre ranch property once owned by a pioneer of the Paso Robles area. In 2000, the ranch was bought by a Swiss emigrant who planted almost 250 acres to grapes from the Bordeaux and Rhone varietal families. All the vineyards are farmed using organic and sustainable methods, which combine with the limestone-rich soil and unique climate to help create intensely flavorful wines. The ranch is fronted by a charming white Victorian farmhouse, and tours (call in advance) take you around both this house and the other historic buildings on the property, as well as the two winemaking facility structures. This newish winery has a small list from which to taste and purchase; its flagship vintages are Syrah and Cabernet Sauvignon, but the less expensive Ranch Red and Ranch White blends are also good buys.

Wine Festivals and Events

Consider coming to town during one of the several wine-oriented festivals held in and around Paso Robles each year. The biggest is the **Paso Robles Wine Festival** (www.paso wine.com/events/winefestival.php, $55–125), which happens over the third weekend of May each year. The central event of the festival, the Outdoor Wine Tasting, happens on Saturday in the Paso's downtown city park. More than 80 wineries bring out their wares, making it fabulously easy to find your favorites and learn about some new vintners in the region. In addition to the central tasting, most Paso wineries keep their tasting room doors open, offering tours, special tastings, food pairings, winemakers, and more. A recent addition to the festival, a golf tournament held on the festival weekend brings golfers from all over out for a round in the perfect Central Coast spring weather. Buy your tickets for the wine festival and the golf tournament well in advance; both events always sell out.

At the other side of the year, the **Harvest Wine Tour Weekend** (www.pasowine.com/events/harvest.php) celebrates the changing foliage of the grapevines and the frantic rush to bring in the grapes and start the juices fermenting. Nearly 100 wineries throughout Paso put on events during the third weekend of October. Check with your favorites to learn what's coming this year. You might want to sign up early for a cooking class, or just show up to join in on some messy but fun grape stomping. If you're lucky, you might even get to take a tour of a winemaking facility in full furor, and learn a bit about how your favorite vintages are made. As with the

MORE THAN WINE

The warm Mediterranean valley climate makes a good landscape for growing olives as well as the grape. Several groves of the silvery-green trees produce high-quality fruit that orchard owners press into small batches of artisan olive oil. A number of orchards cluster here, offering fresh local olive oil and an array of cured olives. If you just can't stomach another ounce of wine, clear your palate at one of the open olive tasting rooms.

One of these growers is **Olea Farm** (2985 Templeton Rd., Templeton, 805/610-2258, www.oleafarm.com, Sat.-Sun. 10 A.M.-4:30 P.M.). This orchard and its tasting room are located to the east of downtown Paso Robles. On a visit, you can take a tour of the orchards, then head inside to taste the different types of olive oil made from the Arbequina olive trees grown here. With five or more distinct flavors of oil to choose from, you'll certainly find a favorite to bring home with you. Be sure to say hi to Oak, the orchard dog, when you visit.

Mt. Olive Organic Farm (3445 Adelaida Rd, Paso Robles, 805/237-0147, www.mtoliveco.com, Thurs.-Sun. 10 A.M.-5 P.M., Apr.-Oct. until 7 P.M.) grows far more than just olives. The diverse crops at Mt. Olive range from cherries and apricots to sprouts to vegetables, as well as grass-fed beef and free-range chickens. The storefront sells meat, eggs, and the wide variety of produce grown here, plus an array of products made from the produce – such as jams, fruit leathers, dried fruits, and nuts. If you've been trekking through the Far Out wineries and need a meal, you can also get fresh, hot, organic cuisine here. The small menu might include steak and chicken dishes, spaghetti, pizza, and soup. To drink, try the fresh-squeezed seasonal juices and slushies.

Down in Atascadero, call ahead to schedule a visit to the **Green Acres Lavender Farm** (8865 San Gabriel Rd., Atascadero, 805/466-0837, www.greenacreslavender-farm.com, daily 10 A.M.-6 P.M., by appointment). One thing is certain: You will leave smelling good. This four-plus-acre farm grows 12,000 lavender plants – mostly Grosso and Provencal for their high oil production. At the farm stand or on the website you can purchase an array of natural products made from and with lavender oil. Choose a bottle of pure essential oil to create your own means for scenting your home, soy candles, lavender soaps, lavender sachets, or even a jar of culinary lavender you can use in cooking. The owners and staff will be happy to give you suggestions for using their products, and to expound on the benefits of lavender in your home.

spring Wine Festival, it's a good idea to book your room and make your plans early for the Harvest Tour—the event has become quite popular with wine aficionados across the state and beyond.

Wine Tours

If you prefer not to do your own driving on your wine-tasting excursions (something to consider if everyone in your party enjoys wine), take one of the many available wine tours. **The Wine Wranglers** (866/238-6400, http://thewinewrangler.com, $90–120 depending on pick-up location) offers daily group tours, plus customized individual tours for a higher fee. Experienced guides will take you to some of the biggest and best wineries in the region. Group tour guests ride in the comfort of a small luxury bus; buses pick up tasters from Cambria, San Luis Obispo, Morro Bay, Pismo Beach, Paso Robles itself, and a number of other towns in the county. A picnic lunch in one of the vineyards is included, as are all tasting fees at the wineries you visit. If you know the region, feel free to request a stop at your favorite winery!

If you prefer to tour the vineyards in the privacy of your own rented limo, book a car with **At Your Service Limousine** (805/239-8785, www.tcsn.net/ays, $200–325). This company offers Paso wine tours up to five hours long, with room for up to eight riders for no additional fee. Tasting fees are included with your car.

SIGHTS

It's not the biggest or most diverse, but you'll have fun exploring the **Charles Paddock Zoo** (Lago Ave. at Hwy. 41, Atascadero, 805/461-5080, www.charlespaddockzoo.org, daily 10 A.M.–4 P.M., adults $5, children $4). Plan an hour or two to make a leisurely tour of the fierce tigers, funky prehensile-tailed raccoons, and famous slender-tailed meerkats. You can also visit the aviary to enjoy the twitters and squawks of more than a dozen varieties of common and exotic birds. The Zoo makes a fun destination if you've brought your kids to the largely adult playground that is Paso Robles.

A good spot for younger kids is the **Paso Robles Children's Museum at the Volunteer Firehouse** (623 13th St., Paso Robles, 805/238-7432, www.pasokids.org, Mon., Thurs.–Sat. 11 A.M.–5 P.M., adults $7, children $6). As much a playground as a museum, the space offers themed interactive exhibits with a slight educational bent for toddlers and elementary school-aged children. Kids can draw, paint, climb, jump, play, and learn in one of the few spots in Paso Robles dedicated entirely to the younger set.

The **Paso Robles Pioneer Museum** (2010 Riverside Ave., 805/239-4556, www.pasoroblespioneermuseum.org, Thurs.–Sun. 1–4 P.M.) celebrates the settlement of San Luis Obispo County. Exhibits have a distinctly Western Americana flavor and includes some larger displays of carriages, farm equipment, and even an old one-room schoolhouse.

SPORTS AND RECREATION

Harris Stage Lines (5995 N. River Rd., 805/237-1860, www.harrisstagelines.com) doesn't offer the typical sedate trail rides. Instead of climbing up onto the back of a horse, you'll get into a refurbished historic coach or wagon and go for a ride like they did in the 19th century. Harris has a restored stagecoach, a chuck wagon, and even a couple of Hollywood-built Roman-style chariots. Call in advance to arrange the perfect outing for your party. If you're really into the historic vehicle scene, you can even book a private driving lesson. Riding lessons are also available.

The craze for floating above vineyards in a balloon basket has made it as far as Paso Robles. This wine region sits in a pretty valley that's perfect for a romantic ballooning jaunt. **Let's Go Ballooning!** (4295 Union Rd., 805/458-1530, http://sloballoon.com, $189/person) can take you on a one-hour ride up over the Paso wine country any day of the week. You'll meet early at the Rio Seco Winery and spend 2–3 hours with your pilot, preparing and learning about how to ride safely.

CENTRAL COAST

Several minutes' drive from downtown Paso, the **River Oaks Hot Springs & Spa** (800 Clubhouse Dr., Paso Robles, 805/238-4600, www.river oakshotsprings.com, Sun.–Thurs. 9 A.M.–9 P.M., Fri.–Sat. 9 A.M.–10 P.M., $12–16/hour) sits on country club land over one of the local sulfur-heavy mineral springs. You'll smell the sulfur even as you drive up and walk from the parking lot to the spacious lobby. An attendant will show you the facilities and guide you to your room. A popular and reasonably priced option here is an hour of relaxation and healing in one of the outdoor or indoor-open-air hot tubs. You can use the faucets to set your own perfect temperature, and gaze out into the thick gardens that screen the spas from the adjacent golf course. For a more thoroughly relaxing experience, pick a massage or facial treatment to go with your hot tub (or alone, if you don't care for sulfur water). Check the website for package specials (many of which include wine served in the privacy of your hot tub room) and aesthetic treatment options.

ACCOMMODATIONS

Accommodations around Paso Robles tend toward upscale wine-themed B&Bs. **Le Domaine at Moss Ridge Vineyard** (1855 Twelve Oaks Dr., 805/227-4372, www.ledomainebb.com, $217, no smoking, no children under 16) sits on the Moss Ridge Vineyard, giving guests an up-close and personal view of the vines from each of the three French country style rooms. Serenity, privacy, luscious wine-country food, and luxurious amenities mark your stay at this tiny boutique inn.

The **Orchard Hill Farm Bed & Breakfast** (5415 Fairhills Rd., 805/239-9604, www .orchardhillbb.com, $220) has a more English country feel. The attractive manor house offers luxurious rooms with top-tier amenities, a gourmet breakfast, and attractive grounds for walking and lounging.

Out in the wooded region between Paso and the coast, the **Chanticleer Vineyard Bed and Breakfast** (1250 Paint Horse Pl., 805/226-0600, www.chanticleervineyard bb.com, $217, no smoking, no children) offers

relaxed vacationing and fun pets. Each of the three rooms includes an iPod dock, organic spa toiletries, a fresh seasonal breakfast, and access to the house stock of cute fuzzy animals.

Rounding out the B&B offerings, **The Canyon Villa** (1455 Kiler Canyon Rd., 805/238-3362, www.thecanyonvilla.com, $224) is built in the Mediterranean style that suits this area so well. The decor of the four guest rooms continues the Italianate theme, while the oversized spa tubs, posh linens, and gas fireplace create a feeling of lush comfort.

FOOD

Gaetanos (1646 Spring St., 805/239-1070, Mon.–Sat. 11:30 A.M.–2 P.M. and 5:30 P.M.–close, $10–30) serves traditional Italian fare with friendly flare. Order the handmade pizza and a glass of the house wine (the restaurant's own label), all accompanied by above-average service.

Getting back to the heavily Mexican influence of Paso's agricultural roots, grab a taco or two at **Papi's** (840 13th St., 805/239-3720, daily 11 A.M.–9 P.M., $10). Prices may be a bit higher than some taquerias, in honor of Paso's new tourist status, but the casual atmosphere and tasty enchiladas make up for it.

It's not the fanciest place in town, but the food at ◖ **Panolivo** (1344 Park St, 805/239-3366, www.panolivo.com, Mon.–Thurs. 8–3 P.M., Fri.–Sat. 8–3:30 P.M., Sun. 9 A.M.–3:30 P.M., dinner Fri.–Sat. nights $17–28) might be the tastiest truly traditional French cuisine in town. Panolivo serves breakfast and lunch on the weekdays, adding dinner on the weekends. The casual dining room makes it easy to linger over a croque monsieur and dark coffee, though visitors just passing through can grab a luscious pastry from the display case up front.

At **Artisan** (1401 Park St., 805/237-8084, www.artisanpasorobles.com, daily 11 A.M.–10 P.M., $10–30) old school American cookery gets a California wine country makeover. The white tablecloths and numerous wine glasses hint at the fancy cuisine to come—unusual soups and sandwiches at lunch and high-end entrées at dinner.

PRACTICALITIES

The closest thing to a visitors center is the **Paso Robles Chamber of Commerce** (1225 Park St., 805/238-0506, www.pasorobles chamber.com, Mon.–Fri. 8 A.M.–5 P.M., Sat.–Sun. 10 A.M.–2 P.M.). Pick up a guide to Paso Robles, or specific dining, lodging, and winery information.

For medical attention, the nearest hospital

is **Twin Cities Hospital** (see *Cambria* for more information).

The two best ways to get to Paso Robles are by car and by train. Drivers can take Highway 101 from the north or the south to directly to town. Once in Paso Robles, take Highway 46 east for the main wine road.

On the rails, the **Amtrak** Coast Starlight (www.amtrak.com) stops right in Paso. Avoid driving altogether by taking the train into town, then renting a limo or getting on with a wine tour.

Santa Barbara

It's called the American Riviera, with weather, community, and sun-drenched beaches reminiscent to some of the European coast of the Mediterranean Sea. In truth, Santa Barbara is all California. Culturally, Santa Barbara sits in Southern California but the pace of life slows down just enough to make for a comfortable vacation. Many of the visitors to Santa Barbara do in fact come from elsewhere in California, and the town is known to residents as one of the best "local" beach resorts. In the town proper, you'll find lots of museums, outdoor shopping areas, and great restaurants. Inland a bit, a growing young wine region thrives. Along the soft, flat sandy beaches cluster fabulous four-star beach resorts.

SIGHTS
Santa Barbara Maritime Museum

It's only fitting that the Santa Barbara Maritime Museum (113 Harbor Way, 805/962-8404, www.sbmm.org, Thurs.–Tues. 10 A.M.–5 P.M., until 6 P.M. Memorial Day–Labor Day, adults $7, children/seniors $4, free for military personnel in uniform) sits right on the working harbor. It began as a Government Works Project during the Depression. For more than 50 years, the station was used by the U.S. Navy as a training facility. After being sold back to the city of Santa Barbara in 1995, construction

began on the museum, which opened in 2000. Over a dozen different exhibits show off the history of the California coast's relationship to the high seas. The Munger Theater screens high-definition educational films each day. The Children's Area features hands-on exhibits that make learning about the sea lots of fun for younger visitors. Many other galleries tell the maritime history of California, beginning with the local Chumash Native Americans, running through the whaling and fur-hunting eras, up through the modern oil drilling and commercial fishing industries. You can also learn a bit about sailing and yachting, safety on the Pacific, and how you can help preserve the ocean's environment.

◖ Santa Barbara Museum of Natural History

Continuing the outdoors theme that pervades Santa Barbara, the Santa Barbara Museum of Natural History (2559 Puesta del Sol, 805/682-4711, www.sbnature.org, daily 10 A.M.–5 P.M., adults $10, youth $7, children $6) has exhibits to delight visitors of all ages. Inside, visit the large galleries that display stories of the life and times of insects, mammals, birds, and dinosaurs. Learn a little about the human history of the Santa Barbara area at the Chumash exhibit. Head outdoors to circle the immense skeleton of a blue whale, and to hike the Mission

CENTRAL COAST

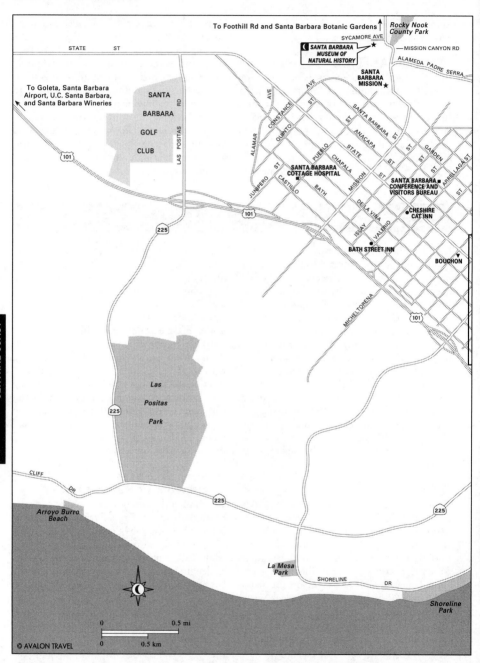

To Foothill Rd and Santa Barbara Botanic Gardens ↑

Rocky Nook County Park

STATE ST

SYCAMORE AVE

☾ SANTA BARBARA MUSEUM OF NATURAL HISTORY ★

— MISSION CANYON RD

ALAMEDA PADRE SERRA

SANTA BARBARA MISSION ★

To Goleta, Santa Barbara Airport, U.C. Santa Barbara, and Santa Barbara Wineries

SANTA BARBARA GOLF CLUB

LAS POSITAS RD

ALAMAR AVE

CONSTANCE AVE

QUINTO ST

AVE

SANTA BARBARA ST

ANACAPA ST

STATE ST

GARDEN ST

ARRELLAGA ST

101

JUNIPERO ST

CASTILLO ST

PUEBLO ST

CHAPALA ST

BATH ST

MISSION ST

SANTA BARBARA COTTAGE HOSPITAL ■

SANTA BARBARA CONFERENCE AND VISITORS BUREAU ■

101

DE LA VINA ST

● CHESHIRE CAT INN

225

ISLAY ST

VALERIO ST

BATH STREET INN

▼ BOUCHON

101

MICHELTORENA

Las Positas Park

225

225

101

225

CLIFF DR

Arroyo Burro Beach

225

La Mesa Park

SHORELINE DR

Shoreline Park

☾

0   0.5 mi

0   0.5 km

© AVALON TRAVEL

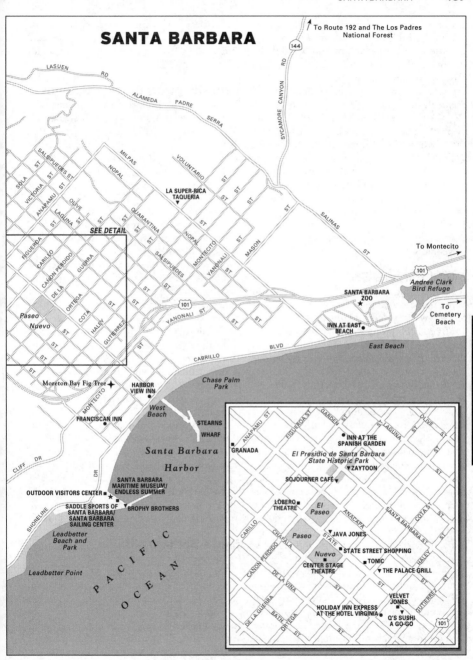

SANTA BARBARA

To Route 192 and The Los Padres National Forest

144

LASUEN RD

SYCAMORE CANYON RD

ALAMEDA PADRE SERRA

MILPAS

NOPAL

VOLUNTARIO

SOLA ST
SALSIPUEDES ST
VICTORIA ST
ANAPAMU ST
OLIVE ST
LAGUNA ST

QUARANTINA

LA SUPER-RICA TAQUERIA ▼

NOPAL

MASON ST

SALINAS ST

MONTECITO
YANONALI

SEE DETAIL

FIGUEROA
CARILLO
CAÑON PERDIDO
DE LA GUERRA
ORTEGA
COTA
HALEY
GUTIERREZ

Paseo Nuevo

101

SALSIPUEDES ST

YANONALI ST

To Montecito

101

SANTA BARBARA ZOO ■

Andrée Clark Bird Refuge

To Cemetery Beach

INN AT EAST BEACH ■

East Beach

CABRILLO BLVD

Chase Palm Park

Moreton Bay Fig Tree ✦

HARBOR VIEW INN ■

West Beach

FRANCISCAN INN ■

MONTECITO

CLIFF DR

Santa Barbara Harbor

STEARNS WHARF

OUTDOOR VISITORS CENTER ■ ★

SANTA BARBARA MARITIME MUSEUM/ ENDLESS SUMMER ▼

SADDLE SPORTS OF SANTA BARBARA/ SANTA BARBARA SAILING CENTER ■

BROPHY BROTHERS ▼

SHORELINE DR

Leadbetter Beach and Park

Leadbetter Point

PACIFIC OCEAN

CENTRAL COAST

Detail inset

ANAPAMU ST
FIGUEROA ST
GARDEN ST
LAGUNA ST
OLIVE ST

INN AT THE SPANISH GARDEN ●

GRANADA ■

El Presidio de Santa Barbara State Historic Park

ZAYTOON ▼

SOJOURNER CAFÉ ▼

CARILLO
CHAPALA
CAÑON PERDIDO
DE LA VINA
DE LA GUERRA
ORTEGA ST
BATH

STATE ST
ANACAPA ST
SANTA BARBARA ST
COTA ST
HALEY
GUTIERREZ ST

LOBERO THEATRE ■

El Paseo

ANACAPA

JAVA JONES ▼

Paseo Nuevo

STATE STREET SHOPPING ■

CENTER STAGE THEATRE

TONIC ▼

THE PALACE GRILL ▼

VELVET JONES ▼

HOLIDAY INN EXPRESS AT THE HOTEL VIRGINIA ●

Q'S SUSHI A GO-GO ●

101

Creek Nature Trail. If you're interested in the nature of worlds other than this one, go into the **Gladwin Planetarium** and wander the Astronomy Center exhibits. The Planetarium hosts daily shows portraying the moon and stars, plus monthly Star Parties and special events throughout the year.

If you're more interested in the Earth's array of sea life, head down to Stearns Wharf and visit the **Ty Warner Sea Center** (211 Stearns Wharf, 805/962-2526, www.sbnature.org/seacenter, daily 10 A.M.–5 P.M.), which is operated by the Museum of Natural History (multi-museum passes at either location, adults $8, youth $7, children $5) Check out the tunnel through the 1,500-gallon surge tank, touch a sea cucumber, examine microscopic sea creatures, and get involved in the science of oceanography.

Santa Barbara Zoo

It's not the biggest zoo in the state, but the Santa Barbara Zoo (500 Ninos Dr., 805/962-5339, www.sbzoo.org, daily 10 A.M.–5 P.M., adults $11, children $8). is a cool little municipal zoo. It shelters its critters in enclosures that resemble those of the San Diego Zoo, including a multi-species habitat that mimics an African savannah with giraffes, tortoises, cranes, and rodents all hanging out together. Granted, the pride of lions next door are corralled away from the giraffes, but you can get close to them and occasionally hear them roar. The Santa Barbara Zoo also takes pride in its local, endangered species—the Channel Island foxes are indigenous to an area only 20 miles from the zoo. The new California condor exhibit shows off one of the rarest birds in the state, still an endangered species. As you slowly stroll along the paths, you'll also see cute lemurs, huge elephants, monkeys, and gibbons. One of the best-named kids' exhibits ever, "Eeeww!" showcases reptiles and wonderful slimy amphibians at children's eye level.

If you need a stroller or wheelchair, you can rent one just inside the zoo. Also close to the gate you'll find the Ridley-Tree House Restaurant, which offers plenty of outside tables and a walk-up arrangement that sells sandwiches and burgers. In season, small carts ply the pathways, selling coffee, popsicles, and more. The gift shop offers cute souvenirs for both kids and adults.

Santa Barbara Botanic Gardens

The year-round perfect weather makes for a perfect spot to grow the gorgeous Santa Barbara Botanic Gardens (1212 Mission Canyon Rd., 805/682-4726, www.santabarbarabotanic garden.org, daily 9 A.M.–5 P.M., until 6 P.M. Mar.–Oct., adults $8, youth $6, children $4). The gardens focus solely on the indigenous plants of California, with plantings from the deserts, chaparral, arroyo, and more. The gardens spread out over many acres, and crosses several hiking trails. Check out the coastal redwood forest, the centerpiece of the park, which remains shaded and cool even when the sun beats down in the heat of summertime. Another proud garden shows off the beauty of native California lilacs. The mission of the gardens encompasses conservation of not only the California wilderness areas, but the water and soil in developed areas as well. Visit the Home Demonstration Garden for an example of beautiful landscaping using California natives that are suited to the climate and conditions, and thus need less irrigation and chemical fertilizers.

Guided tours are offered each day with your admission ticket—join the standard tour or call ahead to arrange a private tour. You can take your own self-guided tour with a map and the advice of the docents. The shop offers books and garden-themed gifts, while the nursery sells native Californian plants. The garden does not include a restaurant or snack bar.

Santa Barbara Mission

Often referred to as "Queen of the Missions," the Santa Barbara Mission (2201 Laguna St., 805/682-4713, http://santabarbaramission.org, daily 9 A.M.–4:30 P.M., tours $5 adults, $4 senior, $1 youth, children 6 and under free) is second to none for its art displays of art and graceful architecture, all of which are complemented by the serene local climate and scenery. Unlike

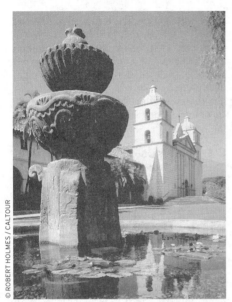

Santa Barbara Mission, Queen of the Missions

many of the California Missions, the church at Santa Barbara remained in service after the secularization of the Mission chain in the 19th century. When you visit, you'll find the collection of buildings, art work, and even the ruins of the water system in better shape than at many other Missions in the state. The self-guided tour through the Mission complex gives visitors a sense of the Mission's story, its church and Native American history, and the lives of the people who lived and worked within it.

WINERIES

Few people outside of the wine world or the state of California realize that Santa Barbara is a budding wine region. The grandfather of Santa Barbara wineries is the **Firestone Winery** (5000 Zaca Station Rd., 805/688-3940, www.firestonewine.com, $10). You'll enter a grand, elegant Napa-style tasting room with a trapezoidal tasting bar and various souvenirs and cases scattered around the room. The tones of the room and the lighting are warm, as are the manners of the staff up at the bar.

Zaca Mesa Winery (6905 Foxen Canyon Rd., Los Olivos, 805/688-9339, www.zacamesa.com, daily 10 A.M.–4 P.M.) is the kind of winery tasters love to discover. A mid-sized producer with a mid-sized facility and tasting room, Zaca quietly makes some of the best Central Coast wines to be found anywhere in the region. The first vineyards on the property were planted in the early 1970s, long before anyone else saw Santa Barbara as a place with potential for great winemaking. The casual tasting room has been tempting customers new and old for almost 30 years. The bar sits at the back of the room, and the procedure to pay your tasting fee is a little convoluted. But once you're at the bar with your glass…oh my. A five-wine tasting can quickly become a 12-wine tasting if you chat up your pourer and express an interest in the vintages. The staff has amazing knowledge of the wines they're pouring, and will enthusiastically tell you the story of each wine, the history of the grapes, and anything else you want to know. Zaca makes many of the Rhone varietals that grow so well in the climate of the Central Coast, such as Viognier, Grenache, Roussanne, and Syrah. Classics lovers will enjoy the Chardonnay, and adventurous types shouldn't skip the Syrahs and the Z Cuvee.

ENTERTAINMENT AND EVENTS

A wealthy town with close ties to cosmopolitan Los Angeles, Santa Barbara offers visitors a wealth of live cultural displays, from a symphony and opera to a near-endless parade of festivals. The students of UCSB add a lively bit of zest to the town's after-dark scene.

Bars and Clubs

The proximity of UCSB to downtown Santa Barbara guarantees a more lively nighttime scene than you'll find elsewhere on the Central Coast. Check with the locals to discover the ever-changing hot spots du jour. Bars cluster on State Street and beyond, and plenty of hip clubs dot the landscape here.

For a uniquely California experience, head for **Q's Sushi a Go Go** (409 State St.,

805/966-9177, www.qsbilliards.com/santa barbara, Mon.–Sat. 4 P.M.–2 A.M.). Shoot a game of pool, get your dance on to local DJs, or sit down to a high-quality sushi dinner. Or do all three in the same night at the same spot! With four bars, a full sushi menu, and a lovely SOS (stands for Sick of Sushi) entrée menu, you can eat and drink the night away at Q's, or fuel up for an energetic session on the dance floor. Q's has three levels to suit a variety of entertainments. At the bar, order any mixed drink you can dream up, or one of the tasty on-tap beers.

Only two blocks up, **Tonic** (634 State St., 805/897-1800, www.tonicsb.com) has a hipster feel, complete with exposed brick walls and a long glass bar. Top-flight DJs spin h a mostly hip hop or house groove, with the occasional mash-up for variety. Check Tonic's Myspace page for a list of upcoming DJs. Two lounges provide a respite from the partiers at the main bar and on the dance floor. To cool down, go outside to the huge outdoor patio, which has its own funky octagonal bar.

If you prefer to dance and drink to live bands, head over to **Velvet Jones** (423 State St., 805/965-8676, www.velvet-jones.com, daily 9 P.M.–2 A.M.). Artists ranging from rapper KRS-One to goth-rock Evanesce to Alien Ant Farm have played Velvet Jones. Thursday through Saturday, bands take the stage for the dancing, yelling crowds. On other nights of the week, you might find karaoke, live comedy, or a DJ spinning. Check the calendar at the website for upcoming events and shows. Even if you're not into the scene, this bar is worth walking into just for the funky giant murals on the walls and the handblown glass ornaments (in a rock club!!) adorning the bar.

Live Music

The **Lobero Theater** (33 E. Canon Perdido St., 805/966-4946, www.lobero.com) plays host to national and international jazz acts, folk and soft rock groups and singers, an annual percussion festival, and more. Everyone from the SFJazz Collective to Ani DiFranco

has performed here. The medium-sized theater has only one level, and it's filled with cushy red velvet seats—perfect for a music-filled night out on the town or a romantic date with your sweetie. Check the website for the shows coming up during your visit. Also be sure to look into the annual film festival. You can buy tickets online, by phone, or at the box office during your stay.

Classical Music

The **Santa Barbara Symphony** (805/898-9626, www.thesymphony.org) aspires to compete with its brethren in Los Angeles and San Francisco. The symphony orchestra puts up seasons that pay homage to the greatest composers the world has ever seen, plus the works of less-known but equally talented artists. Whether you prefer Mozart or Mahler, you can listen to it at the Granada (1214 State St.) concert hall. Every seat has a great view of the stage, and the acoustics were designed with music in mind, making for an overall great symphony experience.

Opera Santa Barbara (www.operasb.com) has put up such classics as *Tosca, Rigoletto,* and *Madama Butterfly.* The festival format OSB has used for the last few years lets you take in two operas in a single weekend, if that's your choice. In fine tradition, OSB enjoys a focus on the classics and little-known works of the Italian masters. Operas are staged at the Lobero Theater (33 E. Canon Perdido St., 805/963-0761, www.lobero.com), a mid-sized space that allows for a more intimate operatic experience than those you find in larger cities.

Dance

At the **Center Stage Theater** (751 Paseo Nuevo, 805/963-0408, www.centerstage theater.org, $22–50 depending on show), look for everything from Pulitzer Prize–winning dramas to traveling nouveau ballet companies. Center Stage focuses on dance, offering more ballet and modern dance performances than it does plays. But the plays, some of which are staged by the Santa Barbara Theater

Company, tend to be some of the newest and best in the country. You won't see much Shakespeare or too many classics—instead you're likely to see *Doubt* or *The Pillowman* or something else that's fresh from Broadway and the Tony Awards.

SHOPPING

If you're looking for a fairly standard shopping expedition in Santa Barbara, go to **State Street.** From end to end, this busy main drag hosts a near-unbelievable array of mall-style stores, plus a few independent boutiques for variety. You'll find lots of lovely women's apparel, plenty of housewares stores, and all the usual stuff you'd expect to find in a major urban shopping center. In truth, there's little that's truly special on State Street—it's a sprawled-out, mid-to-upper tier mall.

SPORTS AND RECREATION

With the year-round balmy weather, it's nearly impossible to resist the temptation to get outside and do something energetic and fun in Santa Barbara. From golf to sea kayaking, you've got plenty of options for recreation here.

Beaches

There's nothing easier than finding a beach in Santa Barbara. Just follow State Street to its end, and you'll be at the coastline. Municipal beaches flank Stearns Wharf on either side—rather uncreatively named **East Beach** (1400 Cabrillo Blvd., www.santabarbaraca.gov, daily sunrise–10 P.M.) and **West Beach** (West Cabrillo Blvd., www.santabarbaraca.gov, daily sunrise–10 P.M.). In fine SoCal tradition, these beaches are broad and flat and sandy, lending themselves to Frisbee and ball games, beach volleyball, and lots of lounging about in the sunshine.

To the north of town, **Arroyo Burro Beach** (Cliff Dr., 805/687-3714, www.sbparks.org, daily 8 A.M.–sunset) is a favorite for dog-owning locals. To the right as you face the water, dogs are allowed off-leash to dash across the packed sand and frolic and fetch out in the gentle surf. Arroyo Burro is rockier than the downtown beaches, making it less friendly to games and sunbathers. But the rocks and shells make for great beachcombing, and you might find a slightly smaller crowd on sunny weekend days. You'll find a snack bar, restrooms, outdoor showers, and a medium-sized pay parking lot for your convenience.

Surfing

It's not one of the legendary California surfing locales, but there are waves to be caught in Santa Barbara, if you don't mind surfing in the shadow of the ever-present oil derricks.

A great spot for newbies to both surfing and the area is **Leadbetter Point** (Cabrillo past Stearns Wharf). The locals are reasonably welcoming, and the small right break makes for easy and fun rides. Another small-wave spot sits right in front of the east edge of **UC Santa Barbara at Isla Vista** (bordered by El Colegio Rd., Ocean Rd., and Camino Majorca). You'll find a big crowd of college students here (UCSB even has a surf team!), but the point break similar to that at Leadbetter is friendly to longboarders and newer surfers. Do watch out for the naturally occurring tar that mars the water and the beach sands.

For a bit more of a challenge, paddle out to the barrels at **Sand Spit** (Santa Barbara harbor). This break only really works in the wintertime when a big western swell comes in, and the water can be unpleasantly dirty. But its location within sight of the Harbor and Stearns Wharf makes it convenient.

If there's such a thing as One True Break in Santa Barbara, it's **Rincon** (U.S. 101 at Bates Rd. on the Ventura County line). If you start at the right spot, you can catch a ride over a mile long here. The sets are reliable and the waves are bigger than most other Santa Barbara breaks. For obvious reasons, locals flock to Rincon so you'll definitely be part of a crowd when you surf here.

Looking for surfing lessons? Check out the **Santa Barbara Surf School** (www.santa barbarasurfschool.com). The instructors have decades of surfing experience and pride themselves on being able to get beginners up and riding in a single lesson.

© LANCE SCOTT

surfers paddling

Kayaking and Sailing

One of the best ways to see the Santa Barbara harbor and bay is under your own power in a kayak. A number of rental and touring companies offer lessons, guided paddles, and good advice for exploring the region. **Paddle Sports of Santa Barbara** (117B Harbor Way, 805/899-4046, www.kayaksb.com, Thurs.–Tues. 10 A.M.–6 P.M., $10–20/hour, tours $50–215) has everything you need to paddle the waters of Santa Barbara and Ventura. You can rent a sit-on-top or closed-deck sea kayak to take your own ride around the harbor or out into the bay. If you want to hit the Channel Islands, you must take a guided tour. Paddle Sports offers all-day trips around Santa Cruz Island, Anacapa Island, and Santa Barbara Island, as well as more sedate two- to four-hour trips around the harbor and down the Santa Barbara waterfront. Most trips are suitable for paddlers of all experience and ability levels, but be sure to tell the staff when you book if you've never been in a kayak before. If that's the case and you prefer to get some experience before you take one of the longer tours, Paddle Sports offers lessons in both sit-on-top and closed-deck kayaking. Whether you choose a lesson or a tour, reservations in advance are recommended, especially for summer weekend days.

The **Santa Barbara Sailing Center** (133 Harbor Way, 805/350-9090, http://sbsail.com, tours $65) offers a full range of kayaking options, from rentals to tours to classes, plus some great trips for more advanced paddlers. The basic excursion takes you to the Mesa Coast via one of the company's yachts, then drops you off onto a single- or double-seat sit-on-top kayak. You might see dolphins, seals, sea lions, or even migrating whales as you paddle along towards your destination: the harbor docks. For something more intense, call the SBSC to arrange a private intermediate or advanced tour.

SBSC also offers sailing excursions aboard the 50-foot *Double Dolphin* sailing catamaran.

Fishing and Whale-Watching

Santa Barbara's prime location on the coast

makes it a great spot for deep-sea fishing and whale-watching. With its proximity to the feeding grounds of the blue and humpback whales, Santa Barbara is one of the best spots to go whale-watching in the state.

If you're looking for a whale-watching expedition or a dinner cruise, check out the **Condor Express** (Harbor Way, 805/882-0088, www.condorcruises.com, adults $50–100, children $30–50). In the summertime, they can take you out to the Channel Islands to see the blue and humpback whales feed; in the winter, the captain sails into the path of migrating gray whales. The boat is a sleek modern speed demon with posh amenities and lots of outdoor deck space that can seat almost 70 people. Whale-watching cruises depart almost daily all year long; call to purchase tickets in advance.

Captain Don's (219 Stearns Wharf, Ste. G, 805/969-5217, www.captdon.com) offers whale-watching and pleasure cruises with a fun pirate theme. Pleasure trips include a quick 30-minute ride around the Santa Barbara Harbor that's geared toward fun for the kids or a 90-minute sunset cocktail cruise that includes rum drinks with your ticket. Whale-watching cruises leave several times each day, heading out to the Channel Islands in the summertime and the Channel itself in winter.

If you want to go fishing, give **WaveWalker Charters** (691 Camino Campana, 805/964-2046, www.wavewalker.com) a call. This private six-passenger charter boat rents for $700 for a three-quarter day—expensive unless you bring five friends along to split the cost! Bait and all tackle are included with the charter, but a fishing license is not. Call for more information about what you can fish for when.

Golf

It might not get the most press of the many golf destinations in California, but with its year-round mild weather and resort atmosphere, Santa Barbara is a great place to play a few holes. There are six public courses within an hour of downtown Santa Barbara—everything from a popular municipal course to championship courses with views of the ocean from the greens.

It's still a golf course, but **Glen Annie** (405 Glen Annie Rd., 805/968-6400, www .glenanniegolf.com, $60–75, carts $6–11) has worked with Audubon International to create wildlife habitats on its land. Who knows what you might see when you're out walking the lush, green, 18-hole, par-72 course? Well, you'll definitely get great views of the town of Santa Barbara, the ocean, and the Channel Islands on this hilly course. The Frog Bar & Grill, the on-site restaurant, draws any number of non-golfers up to Glen Annie for lunch. Set in a castle-like structure, the Frog serves California cuisine dishes that are a far cry from most clubhouse fare. So come for the golf, stay for the unusual and delicious fare.

If you're already interested in exploring Santa Barbara's wine country, consider reserving a tee time at **La Purisima Golf Course** (3455 Hwy. 246, 805/735-8395, $30–80). This golf course, built in 1986, gets high praise for its design and difficulty level—even if you're an expert golfer, "La Piranha" will test your skills. The par 72 course is a 45-minute drive from downtown Santa Barbara, but many locals think it's worth the trip. In addition to the 18 holes, you can access the grass driving range, the short-game practice area, and the pro shop. A number of PGA and LPGA golf pros are on hand to help you improve your game.

The **Sandpiper** (7925 Hollister Ave., 805/968-1541, www.sandpipergolf.com, $60–140, cart $16) boasts some of the most amazing views you'll find in all of Santa Barbara. They're so great because they're right up close, and on several holes your ball is in danger of falling into the world's largest water trap. And hey, there's a great championship rated 74.5, 18-hole, par 72 golf course out there on that picturesque beach too! Take advantage of the pro shop and on-site restaurant, but do be aware of the semi-formal, denim-free dress code Sandpiper enforces. It's not cheap, but a long walk on the beach with a great golf game in the middle of it seems well worth it to an endless stream of golfers who rank Sandpiper as one of their favorite courses.

Spas

Folks who can afford to live in Santa Barbara tend to be able to afford many of the finer things in life, including massages, facials, and luxe skin treatments. You'll find a wide array of day spas and medical spas in town.

Beleza Skin Care Center (219 Gray Ave., 805/966-2373, www.belezaskincare.com) sits in the Studio E Healing Arts center. This high-end spa specializes in the best skin care money can buy, with a focus on anti-aging and acne treatments. Choose from an array of luxurious facials, chemical and herbal peels, microdermabrasion, makeup consultation, and permanent makeup application. You'll walk into the charming spa with its live plants and Eastern decor, check in, and be led back into your treatment room. Most facials and treatments last an hour or more. Beleza also offers a full menu of waxing services.

If you prefer a slightly more natural spa experience, book a treatment at **Le Reve** (21 W. Gutierrez, 805/564-2977, www.le-reve.com). Using biodynamic skin care products and pure essential oils, Le Reve makes good on the advertising billing it as an "aromatherapy spa." Choose from an original array of body treatments, massage, hand and foot pampering, facials, and various aesthetic treatments. If you're up for several hours of relaxation, check out the spa packages that combine facials with massage and body treatments.

Cielo Spa and Boutique (1725 State St., Ste. C, 805/687-8979, www.cielospasb.com) prides itself on its warm, nurturing environment. Step inside and admire the scents and the soft lighting and the natural, new agey decor. Contemplate the colorful live orchids, feel soothed by the flickering candlelight, and get lost in the tranquil atmosphere. The menu of services has an almost Northern Californian flare, with signature Champagne treatments and a focus on organics and natural lotions and potions. Check into the luxury packages that combine massages, facials, and more for a full day in the spa.

ACCOMMODATIONS

If you want a posh beachside room in Santa Barbara, you'd better be prepared to pay for it. All the seaside resorts charge a premium rate. On the other hand, Santa Barbara offers several charming and reasonably priced accommodations near downtown and other attractions.

$100-150

A lovely little boutique hotel in a quiet residential neighborhood near the beach, the **Franciscan Inn** (109 Bath St., 805/963-8845, www.franciscaninn.com, $125–160) looks just like a Spanish Colonial Revival hacienda, with pale adobe-style walls and a traditional red-tiled roof. Guest rooms offer everything from cute, economical, double-bed rooms to luxurious multiple-room suites. The decor tends toward the flowery, with designer wallpaper and comforters. The largest suite sleeps six comfortably; smaller rooms can sleep four if they're friendly. The amenities add to the charm of the place; you can grab a complimentary fresh croissant and a cup of coffee for breakfast, or a warm cookie in the afternoon. Take a swim in the heated pool, check your email with the free Wi-Fi, or even throw in a load of laundry at the on-site coin-op machines. Stearns Wharf and downtown are a short walk away.

The **Bath Street Inn** (1720 Bath St., 805/682-9680, www.bathstreetinn.com, $140–315) specializes in small-town charm and hospitality. It's large for a B&B, with eight rooms in the Queen Anne main house and another four in the more modern summer house. Each room has its own unique color scheme and style. Certainly you'll find some traditional floral Victorian decor, but many of the rooms are done up with elegant stripes rather than cloying blooms. Some rooms have king beds, others queens, and several have two-person whirlpool tubs. Despite the vintage trappings, the Bath Street Inn features modern amenities such as flat-screen TVs and free Wi-Fi. Early each morning, a sumptuous home-cooked breakfast is served downstairs. Choose between sharing your meal with your fellow guests in the dining room, or escaping to the sunny garden patio for a bit of privacy.

If you're in Santa Barbara to soak up the sun on the sandy beaches, book a room at the **Inn at East Beach** (1029 Orilla Del Mar, 805/965-0546, www.innateastbeach.com, $140–400). Unsurprisingly, it's just across the road from East Beach, and a nice walk along the waterfront boardwalk will take you to Stearns Wharf and to downtown. This smallish motor lodge gained notoriety when President Ronald Regan was in office, and his staff stayed at the inn while he spent time at his Santa Barbara ranch. Today, guests find sizeable rooms done up in blue carpets and comforters with pine furniture and a strange plethora of telephones. The inn prides itself on its attractive swimming pool and courtyard area, and you can feel free to bring down a bottle of wine and enjoy the balmy evenings with fellow guests. If you're planning a longer stay, get a kitchen suite so you can cook your own meals and take advantage of the inn's guest laundry facilities.

$150-250

If you're willing to pay a premium rate for your room, the **Cheshire Cat Inn** (36 W. Valerio St., 805/569-1610, www.cheshirecat .com) can provide you with true luxury B&B accommodations. Each room has an *Alice in Wonderland* name, but the decor doesn't really match the theme—instead of whimsical and childish, you'll find Victorian floral elegance. Guest rooms are spread out through two Victorian homes ($199–299), the coach house ($279–379), and two private cottages ($369–399). Some rooms have suite-level space and amenities, including spa tubs and private balconies. Relax in the evening in the spacious octagonal outdoor spa, or order a massage in the privacy of your own room. Each morning, come downstairs and enjoy a light breakfast.

It's a chain now, but the **Holiday Inn Express at the Hotel Virginia** (17 W. Haley St., 805/963-9757, www.hotelvirginia.com, $170–275) has lots of history in Santa Barbara. Sitting right on the corner of the main drag, the Hotel Virginia welcomed guests come to take the waters and enjoy the scenery of Santa Barbara starting in 1925. Ten years ago it was renovated to bring it up to code and to spiff up the older guest rooms. Today it is run by the folks at Holiday Inn Express, but they elected not to eradicate the historic charm and atmosphere of the Virginia. When you walk into the lobby, you'll step onto a red-tiled floor and gaze upon a bright, multihued blue fountain. Upstairs, your room will feature antique-looking furnishings, exuberant floral bedspreads and curtains, and swirly green carpets. The smallish bathrooms feature prized showerheads, and the beds have both cotton and feather pillows to choose from. If you choose to stay in your room for a while, you can make yourself coffee to sip while watching your LCD flat-screen. The restaurants and shops of State Street are steps from the lobby, and the beach isn't too much farther.

Over $250

For a taste of Santa Barbara's posh side, stay at the **Inn at the Spanish Garden** (915 Garden St., 805/564-4700, www.spanishgardeninn .com, $280–575). This small boutique hotel gets it right from the first glimpse; the building in the historic Presidio neighborhood has the characteristic whitewashed adobe exterior with a red-tiled roof, arched doorways, and wooden balconies. Courtyards seem filled with lush greenery and tiled fountains, while the swimming pool promises relief from the heat. Inside, guest rooms and suites whisper luxury with their white linens, earth-toned accents, and rich, dark wooden furniture. Enjoy the benefits of your own gas fireplace, deep soaking bathtub, French press coffee maker, plush bathrobes, and honor bar. The complimentary continental breakfast can be delivered right to your door upon request. Also upon appointment, you can arrange for a massage or facial in the comfort of your room. The Spanish Inn sits only three blocks from State Street, and within walking distance of a number of theaters and historic Santa Barbara attractions.

Are you ready and willing to pay premium prices for a luxury beachfront resort hotel room? If so, check out the **Harbor View Inn** (28 W. Cabrillo Blvd., 805/963-0780, www.harborviewinnsb.com, $352). This stunning Spanish Colonial–style property sits right across the street from the flat white sands of West Beach and steps from Stearns Wharf. Blooming flowers and bright ceramic tiles create beautiful outdoor spaces everywhere on the property. The pool is a focal point of the resort, with long hours and food and beverage service. Inside your lovely guest room, soft lighting and orange-and-red tones create a feeling of warmth. Suites offer palatial spaces and extra amenities. If you want to enjoy a tasty meal without leaving the resort property, choose between room service and the on-site oceanfront restaurant **Eladio's.** Eladio's is best known for its breakfasts, but serves three meals each day and has a good list of wines that's heavy on the local vintages.

FOOD
American
Yes, they do mean *that* 🄲 **The Endless Summer** (113 Harbor Way, 805/564-4666, www.endlesssummerbarcafe.net, daily 11 A.M.–close, $10). When they decided to create a new restaurant out on the pier, the owners went to Bruce Johnson, a Santa Barbara resident and acknowledged creator of the "real" surfing movie genre, and asked him if he would mind having a restaurant named for his most famous film. Bruce thought it was a fine idea, and not only gave the project his blessing, he quickly became a regular in the dining room. Photos of Bruce, other famous surfers, and lots of surfing paraphernalia from the historic to the modern deck the walls of this seaside bar and café. The menu has plenty of salads and sandwiches, includes some intriguing daily specials, and serves from the menu of the Waterfront Grill downstairs. Service is friendly, and the atmosphere tends towards casual local hangout. Many patrons know each other and the staff, and the bar gets crowded as the evening wears on. Live music—sometimes just a talented solo player—provides pleasant background and occasionally a dance track for the more energetic patrons.

Café
Whether you're a vegetarian or not, you'll find something delicious at the **Sojourner Café** (134 E. Canon Perdido St., 805/965-7922, www.sojournercafe.com, Mon.–Sat. 11 A.M.–11 P.M., Sun. 11 A.M.–10 P.M., $20). In fact, a select few dishes include a bit of lean poultry or fish in amongst the veggies. Sojourner features healthful dishes made with ingredients that showcase local organic and sustainable farms. Lots of the cuisine has ethnic flavors, from familiar Mexico to exotic India. Daily specials use ingredients that are fresh and in-season, including some seafood. Then again, Sojourner also serves a classic root beer float and chocolate milkshakes as well as a big selection of house-baked confections to go along with their health food. Sojourner displays the work of local artists on a rotating schedule. If you fall in love with the wall art over your table, inquire with your server about purchasing it.

California
Of the many and varied high-end California cuisine restaurants that crowd Santa Barbara, **Bouchon** (9 W. Victoria St., 805/730-1160, www.bouchonsantabarbara.com, daily 5:30 P.M.–close, $30) might be the best. Though it's no relation to the bistro of the same name in Yountville, Bouchon prides itself on both creative cuisine and top-notch service every night. You'll pay a premium to dine here, but it's worth it for a special night out. Your server will be your guide, helping you make selections from the menu, recommending wine pairings with each course, and answering any questions you might have about the restaurant or the food. California-style dishes are prepared with local and organic ingredients whenever possible, and the menu changes often based on what's available. The wine list is a special treat. It consists almost entirely of local wines—really local—from the Santa Barbara and Paso Robles regions. Servers have favorites and they're generally great. The presentation of the food matches its quality. The dining room features romantic low lighting, smallish tables,

interesting artwork, and an outdoor patio that's perfect for balmy summer nights.

Creole

The Palace Grill (8 E. Cota St., 805/963-5000, www.palacegrill.com, daily 11 A.M.–3 P.M., 5:30–11 P.M., Fri.–Sat. until midnight, $20–40) boasts of being one of Santa Barbara's most popular restaurants and a little piece of old New Orleans in sunny California. The atmosphere gets lively in the evenings, so this isn't the place to come for a quiet meal. Live entertainers delight the crowds several nights each week, and every once in awhile a restaurant-wide sing-along breaks out. The food is pure Louisiana bayou; look for classically prepared etouffes, jambalaya, and gumbo ya-ya. Most of the seafood is flown in fresh daily, the steaks are aged to perfection, and much of the fresh finned fish and meat is served blackened and spiced in Cajun style. Even the appetizers and desserts drip Creole and Cajun flavors. Start off with a house specialty cocktail or a glass of California wine. While you dine, be sure to take a moment to appreciate the particularly fine service that is a staple of the Palace's reputation.

Mexican

Have you ever wanted to know what true, authentic Mexican food might taste like? **La Super-Rica Taqueria** (622 N. Milpas St., 805/963-4940, Thurs.–Tues. 11 A.M.–9 P.M., Fri.–Sat. 11 A.M.–9:30 P.M., $10) can hook you up. Of course, you must be prepared to stand in line with dozens of locals and even commuters up from Los Angeles and the occasional Hollywood celeb who think La Super-Rica's got some of the best down-home Mexican cuisine in all of SoCal. This was Julia Child's favorite taco stand, and it's been reviewed by the *New York Times*.

Folks don't come for the ambiance—expect paper plates, plastic chairs, and shorts and sandals on the diners in a genuine shack of a building. You also need to adjust your concept of Mexican food; if you're looking for a fast-food burrito supreme with chips and salsa, you'll definitely be disappointed. But if you're ready for the real deal, you've found it. The corn tortillas are made fresh each day, the meat is slow cooked and seasoned to perfection, and the house special is a grilled pork-stuffed pasilla chile. Vegetarians can choose from a few delicious meat-free dishes, while carnivores will leave satisfied with their pork-, chicken-, or steak-based entrées.

Middle Eastern

For a Middle Eastern feast, go to **Zaytoon** (209 E. Canon Perdido St., 805/963-1293, www.cafezaytoon.com, Mon.–Sat. 11:30 A.M.–9 P.M., Sun. 4–9 P.M., $10–30). This restaurant and hookah bar appeals to a crowd that wants to enjoy an evening out with a group of friends, to share a hookah around the table, and to ogle talented belly dancers shimmying amongst the tables. While the interior dining room is attractive, with potted palms and gauzy fabric draped from the ceiling, it's not the best place to sit at Zaytoon. Instead, try to get a table out on the garden patio, a large, softly lit space almost completely enveloped by a living green jungle. It is out here that you can order up your own hookah. The menu has most standard Middle Eastern favorites, such as baba ghannouj, hummus, falafel, Greek salad, shawarma, and kebabs of many kinds.

Seafood

It takes something special to make Santa Barbara residents take notice of a seafood restaurant, and **Brophy Brothers** (119 Harbor Way, 805/966-4418, www.brophybros.com, Sun.–Thurs. 11 A.M.–10 P.M. Fri.–Sat. 11 A.M.–11 P.M., $10–30) has it. Look for a small list of fresh fish done up California style with upscale preparations. The delectable menu goes heavy on locally caught seafood. At the clam bar, you can order some fresh raw clams (duh!) or oysters, a bowl of the house clam chowder, or a tasty seafood salad. With a prime location looking out over the masts of the sailboats in the harbor, it's no surprise that Brophy Brothers gets crowded at both lunch and dinnertime, especially on weekends in the summertime.

Coffee

Skip the big chains and head for **Java Jones** (728 State St., 805/962-4721, daily 7 A.M.–11 P.M.), conveniently located in the middle of State Street. This local coffee house has brick walls, cushy couches in the upstairs loft seating area, and local art on the walls. It's also got a better-than-average selection of caffeinated go-juice, including Turkish coffee and Vietnamese coffee. In the morning, locals and visitors alike can order from the limited but tasty breakfast menu. Pastries and salads are available all day and late into the night. Go ahead and bring your laptop (yup, they've got Wi-Fi), grab a chair, and settle in.

INFORMATION AND SERVICES

The **Santa Barbara Conference and Visitors Bureau** (1601 Anacapa St., 805/966-9222, www.santabarbaraca.com) maintains an **Outdoor Visitors Center** (113 Harbor Way, Waterfront Center, 4th Fl., 805/884-1475) for visitors who never want to leave sight of the beach.

As a major metropolitan city, Santa Barbara publishes its own daily newspaper, the *Santa Barbara News Press* (www.newspress.com). Look for it in shops, on newsstands, and in your hotel or inn. Check the *Scene and Life* sections for information about entertainment, events, and attractions.

The major hospital in town is **Santa Barbara Cottage Hospital** (320 W. Pueblo St., 805/682-7111, www.sbch.org), which includes a full-service emergency room.

GETTING THERE AND AROUND

To reach Santa Barbara by air, fly into the **Santa Barbara Municipal Airport** (Moffet Rd., 805/967-7111, www.flysba.com). A number of major commercial airlines fly into Santa Barbara, including United, Alaska/Horizon, Delta, and American Airlines.

A more beautiful and peaceful way to get to Santa Barbara is by train. The **Amtrak** Coast Starlight (www.amtrak.com) runs into town daily. From Los Angeles or San Francisco's east bay, connect to other trains that run into California from points east.

Santa Barbara is located on Highway 101, also known as the Pacific Coast Highway and El Camino Real in this neck of the woods. To head out to the Santa Ynez Valley and other local wine regions, take CA Highway 154 east. If staying in Santa Barbara proper, expect fairly standard city driving, complete with traffic jams during weekday business hours and on beach access roads on the weekends. Parking can be challenging, especial at the beach on sunny summer weekends. Expect to pay a premium for a good-to-mediocre spot, or to walk for several blocks. If possible, take the local public streetcar from the downtown area to the beach and leave your car elsewhere.

Santa Barbara has its own transit authority. The **MTD Santa Barbara** (805/963-336, www.sbmtd.gov) runs both the local bus service ($1.25 regular fare) and the Waterfront Shuttle and Downtown-Waterfront lines ($0.25 regular fare). Have exact change to pay your fare when boarding the bus or shuttle; if transferring buses, ask the driver for a free transfer pass.

BACKGROUND

The Land

GEOGRAPHY

California includes just about every geographical feature imaginable, from alpine lakes to parched and delicate deserts to active volcanoes and sun-swept Pacific beaches. The state is trisected vertically by mountain ranges, with valleys in between, and terminates west at the coast of the Pacific Ocean. Many rivers flow west as the ocean wears away at the land, creating coves, waterfalls, and immense bays.

To the east, the Sierra Nevada mountain range looms above all other geography, with craggy snowcapped peaks, alpine lakes and meadows, and gold-producing foothills. The northern mountains—Shasta and Lassen—are the southern tip of the Cascade Range that stretches far into the Pacific Northwest, all the way through Oregon and into Washington. This youthful volcanic chain is part of the Pacific Ring of Fire, contributing recent eruptions by Mount Lassen and Mount St. Helens. Though it's been a while since Shasta's fires last burbled to the surface, the mountain is classed as dormant, not extinct; if she ever blows again, the effects on the whole of the American West will be staggering.

At the foot of the Sierras sits a giant fertile valley that is the produce capital of the state, and much of the West. Maps and books refer to it as the San Joaquin Valley, but Californians usually call it the Central Valley, and much of the state's massive agriculture industry resides here.

To the south, deserts rule the landscape. California boasts two distinct desert regions: the northern and higher-elevation Mojave Desert, and the southern and low-elevation Colorado Desert (which encompasses Anza-Borrego State Park and the southern half of Joshua Tree National Monument).

The coastal region is bounded by a mountain range, famed in the north for forests filled with enormous coast redwood trees. The northern coastline winds along soaring craggy cliffs overlooking rocky beaches and coves, while the southern coastline tends toward the broad, sandy beaches that California is famous for.

CLIMATE

Though California is known for the mild climate along its southern shores, the state can claim a number of distinct climate zones.

Mark Twain's famous 19th-century quote— "The coldest winter I ever spent was a summer in San Francisco!"—still stands. If you're visiting "the City" in July or August, don't bother bringing shorts—the weather is generally foggy and cool, with temperatures in the 50s and 60s. These cool temperatures persist along the Bay Area coastline as well. But if you head south to Silicon Valley or to the East Bay, expect temperatures to get up to 20–30° warmer and to see sun instead of fog.

Up along the North Coast, the weather stays about the same year-round: chilly, windy, and foggy. Temperatures can get up into the sunny 80s on rare hot summer days, and winter storms can pound the area with rain. These weather patterns turn milder toward coastal Sonoma in the southern Wine Country. Napa's scorching hot valley summers and mild-to-cool winters are perfect for the grapes growing everywhere— and the tourists who come to drink them.

Lake Tahoe, Mount Shasta, Mount Lassen, Yosemite, and the Eastern Sierras all experience harsh, snow-filled winters that can close roads and wreak havoc with travel plans, but present ideal conditions for a multitude of winter sports. The short, hot summers also draw tourists out in droves.

Sacramento and the Central Valley boast high heat in the summers—often over 100°F—and cool but usually clear winters. The surrounding Gold Country, however, often receives snow in winter and can make roads here impassible.

The Central Coast has somewhat warmer temperatures than the Bay Area beaches, but you can still expect average cool temperatures and plenty of fog in the summer, with chill winds and some rain in the winter. The inland Central Coast wine regions mimic the climate patterns of the Wine Country and are more mild.

From the Los Angeles Basin down to San Diego and up the coast to Santa Barbara, temperatures are mild all year long. Expect fog on the beaches during the summer, cool days in the wintertime, and hotter temperatures in the inland valleys and Disneyland. For the best summertime beach weather in the state, head for San Diego.

The central and eastern deserts in the southern end of the state experience typical desert climates. That means mild, comfortable winters perfect for hiking and outdoor sports, but with nighttime temperatures in the 30s and 40s. The deserts' dangerously hot summers can easily reach 110–120°F.

ENVIRONMENTAL ISSUES

Environmental issues are California's political bread-and-butter. Los Angeles is rightly famous for its smog, though the San Francisco Bay Area is rapidly catching up in this unattractive race. If you're sensitive to airborne pollution, take special precautions on days that local air quality officials designate "Spare the Air." These are days, mostly in the summer, when pollution levels are especially high. Stay indoors or, when going out, use public transportation.

Water pollution is also an issue in California;

plenty of sensational news stories crucify the state's drinking water, while others laud it. Most tap water is safe to drink, but swimming in California's plentiful rivers and ocean requires more caution. Sadly, water pollution from dumping into the ocean affects beach goers. Dirt and pollution are common in the waters and on the beaches of Los Angeles and Orange Counties, while fishing is no longer permitted in the San Francisco Bay due to the long-standing pollution problems and high mercury levels in the bay's fish.

There are major restrictions on the types of power boats you can launch at Lake Tahoe, due to protections instituted to keep the azure-blue waters of this huge alpine lake pristine. Similar restrictions can also be found for waterways across the state; check the regulations for any lake or river before planning a boating trip.

The good news is that environmental conservation and protection are taken very seriously in California. Recycling, public transit growth, and water cleanup programs proliferate throughout the state. Even as a short-time visitor, you can help California's efforts to get and stay clean: Use any recycling bins you see on the street; minimize your use of plastic bags; and don't leave litter on the beach or out in wilderness areas—either throw it away or pack it out with you.

FLORA AND FAUNA

California's diverse geography gives rise to dozens of different ecosystems, each of which has its own unique native plants and animals. Botanical gardens, zoos, and wildlife preserves abound throughout the state, giving visitors ample opportunities to smell the flowers, pet the animals, and learn about the complex and varied life that abounds all through the Golden State.

Redwoods

The most famous trees native to California are undoubtedly the redwoods. The **coast redwood** *(Sequoia sempervirens)* grows on the North Coast and down through the Bay Area all the way to Big Sur. Coast redwood trees perch on cliffs overlooking the sea, but most of the best groves are inland, in the mountains. The Redwood National and State Parks do

© LIZ HAMILL SCOTT

redwoods in the sky

the best job of showcasing these grand trees, though any hiker in the Santa Cruz Mountains can reach out and touch soft redwood bark.

The truly immense redwood trees don't grow along the coast—they're much farther inland. The **giant sequoia** *(Sequoiadendron giganteum)* grow in the Sierra Nevada mountains. These redwoods can live for thousands of years and grow to unimaginable heights. The museum at Sequoia-Kings Canyon National Park includes a wonderful interpretive display describing the life cycle of the giant sequoia, including information about the importance of fire to the health and propagation of these trees. Sequoia groves grow aplenty in Yosemite National Park, Calaveras Big Trees, and a few other select spots in the Sierras.

Wildflowers

California's state flower is the **California poppy** *(Eschscholzia californica).* The pretty little orange blossom grows just about everywhere, even on the sides of the busiest highways. Though most California poppies are bright orange, they also appear occasionally in white, cream, and even deeper red-orange.

Reptiles

If you spot California's most infamous native reptile, keep your distance. Several varieties of **rattlesnakes** are indigenous to the state. The Pacific Northwest rattler makes its home in Northern California, while more than half a dozen different rattlesnake varieties live in Southern California, including the Western diamondback and the Mojave rattlesnake.

All rattlesnakes are venomous, though death by snakebite is extremely rare in California. Most parks with known rattlesnakes in residence post signs alerting hikers; your best bet to keep safe is to stay on trails and avoid tromping off into meadows or brush. Pay attention when hiking, especially when negotiating rocks and woodpiles, and never put a foot or a hand down in a spot you can't see first. Wear long pants and heavy hiking boots for protection (from snakes, plus insects, other critters, and unfriendly plants you might encounter).

Butterflies

California isn't the tropics, but its vast population of wildflowers attract an array of gorgeous butterflies. The **Monarch butterfly** has become an emblem of the state. These large orange-and-black butterflies have a migratory pattern that's reminiscent of birds. Each winter, the butterflies fly south from their summertime wanderings to cluster in several groves of eucalyptus trees throughout the temperate coastal zone. As they close up their wings to hibernate for the winter, their crowding and dull outer wing color makes them resemble clumps of dried leaves, thus protecting them from predators. In spring, the butterflies begin to wake up, fluttering lazily in the groves a bit before flying north to seek out milkweed on which to lay their eggs. Santa Cruz and Cambria are two great places to visit the California "butterfly trees."

History and Economy

California boasts a rich history, filled with great stories and fascinating characters. The state's timeline flows from the Native Americans through the first European explorations to the building of the Spanish missions, then the Gold Rush, and on into the millennium.

Today, California takes an active role in the economy and culture of the United States and indeed the world. The Internet began, took off, boomed, busted, and settled into its current iteration as a worldwide communication and commerce web in the Bay Area. Central Valley agriculture remains the state's economic mainstay, while the motion picture industry continues to dominate the Los Angeles landscape.

Movie stars keep getting into politics; actors Ronald Regan and Arnold Schwarzenegger have claimed residence in the Governor's Mansion and Clint Eastwood's credits include a stint as mayor of Carmel-by-the-Sea.

California has had good times and bad, triumphs and shame, but one thing has remained constant—the story of California is never, ever boring.

THE MISSION PERIOD

California's earliest explorers and European colonists were mostly from Spain—hence the proliferation of Spanish-named streets, towns, and even colleges that persist to this day. Monuments to many of these men can be found in various parts of the state.

No single man is credited with as much influence on the early development of California than Father Junipero Serra. The Franciscan monk took an active role in bringing Christianity (and, unfortunately, the corollary syphilis, measles, and smallpox) to native peoples from San Diego all the way up to Sonoma. To that end, the Franciscan order built a string of missions, each of which was meant to be a self-sufficient parish that grew its own food, kept up its own buildings, and took care of its own people. The monks also created a road between the missions—El Camino Real—with the idea that a pilgrim could travel the length of El Camino Real and find a bed at the next mission after only one day's journey. Today, El Camino Real remains a vital part of the state and much of the original path still exists; just look for the mission bells mounted on curved poles posted along the sides of the road. In the Bay Area, El Camino Real isn't a highway—it's a business street running the length of the Peninsula. To the south, El Camino Real and U.S. 101 sometimes merge into one; at other points El Camino rambles away from any main roads.

The missions prospered in the early 1800s, then gradually deteriorated until they were ordered to secularize in the middle of the 19th century. Some took on new uses; others fell into disrepair and outright abandonment. It was only in the 20th century that interest in the history of the missions was rekindled and money was invested into restoring many of the churches and complexes. Today, many (but not all) of the missions have been restored as Catholic parishes, with visitors centers and museum displays of various levels of quality and polish.

THE GOLD RUSH

In 1849, a worker discovered nuggets of gold in the machinery at Sutter's Mill. The news that chunks of gold were just sitting there on the riverbeds for the taking spread like wildfire. The Gold Rush was on. People from the East Coast and all over the world streamed into California by land and by sea, seeking a fortune in gold—or a fortune in serving or selling to the gold-seekers. Thousands of men panned every available stream for nuggets, then water-blasted hillsides away seeking the elusive precious metal. Even then, the wanton destruction caused by the blasting was quickly seen to be a problem. And so the famous hardrock mines of California began construction. Though panning continued (hope springs

Sutter's Mill, the birthplace of California's Gold Rush

eternal, after all), by the 1860s most of the rough men had taken jobs working in the deep, dangerous mines.

With the influx of gold seekers, new cities sprang up almost overnight. The previously small town of San Francisco became the major port of entry for immigrants. Sacramento's river location made it a perfect transportation hub and waypoint between San Francisco and the gold fields. Mining towns like Sonora, Volcano, Placerville, Sutter's Creek, and Nevada City swelled to huge proportions, only to shrink back into obscurity as the mines closed one by one in the 20th century.

As American and European men came to California to seek their fortunes in gold, a few wives and children joined them, but the number of families in the average mining town was small. Yet a few lone women did join in the rush to the gold fields. These ladies took up "the oldest profession," servicing the population of single male miners and laborers in desperate need of (ahem) female companionship.

The other major group of immigrants at this time came to California from a land distant in both distance and culture: China. Thousands of Chinese men came, not to mine, but to labor and serve the white miners. Most were forced to pass through the wretched immigration facilities on Angel Island in the middle of San Francisco Bay—sometimes being essentially imprisoned for months before either being allowed onto the mainland or summarily shipped back to China. San Francisco's Chinatown became a hub for the immigrants, a place where their language was spoken and their culture comprehended. But thousands headed east, becoming low-level laborers in the industry surrounding the mines, or workers on the railroads endlessly spooling out to connect Gold Country to the rest of the state and eventually to the East Coast by way of the Transcontinental Railroad.

THE 1960S

Few places in the country felt the impact of the radical 1960s more than California. In fact, it's arguable that the peace and free love movements began right here, probably on the campus of the infamous and indomitable University of California at Berkeley. Certainly Berkeley helped to shape and grow the culture

to honor the "Ladies of the Evening"

© LIZ HAMILL SCOTT

of hippies, peaceniks, and radical politics. The college campus was the home of the Black Panthers, anti-Vietnam War sit-ins, and numerous protests for all sorts of liberal causes.

If Berkeley was the de facto home of 1960s political movements, then San Francisco was the base of its social and cultural phenomena. Free concerts in Golden Gate Park and the growing fame of the hippie community taking over an area called Haight-Ashbury drew teenagers from across the country. Many found themselves living on Haight Street for months, experimenting with the most popular mind-altering chemicals of the era. The music scene became the stuff of legend and song (sorry). The Grateful Dead—one of the most famous and longest lasting of the 1960s rock bands—hailed from the Bay Area.

ECONOMY

The state of California boasts the eighth-largest economy in the *world*. California's contribution to the United States outpaces even its immense size and population.

Agriculture

Many people guess incorrectly when asked what California's number one economic sector is. It's not high tech. It's not films. It's farming! California's agricultural juggernaut supplies much of the world with crops of almost all kinds, from grapefruit to grass-fed beef.

In warm Southern California, citrus trees rule much of the landscape; you can even find grapefruit groves in the harsh climate of the Anza-Borrego Desert. The Central Valley's flat, fertile fields produce everything from rice to corn to tomatoes. In the summertime, tomato trucks drive routes all around Sacramento to processing plants that create that all-important American staple food: ketchup. The cooler Central Coast region grows sweet strawberries and spiky artichokes in abundance. As the fog gets colder and drippier in Marin, ranchers take advantage of the naturally growing grasses to ranch herds of cattle destined for the growing sustainable-food market. In truth, cattle are ranched all over the state, from the far-north reaches down to the southern deserts.

Today, as awareness grows about the harmful affects of pesticides and petrochemical fertilizers on both the land and consumers, organic farms and ranches are proliferating across California. In addition to the giant factory farms so prevalent in the Central Valley, you'll also see an increasing number of small farms and ranches growing a variety of crops using organic, sustainable, and even biodynamic practices. Most of these farmers sell directly to consumers by way of farmers markets and farm stands—almost every town or county in the state has a weekly farmer's market in the summertime, and many last year-round.

And then there's the wine. It seems like every square inch of free agricultural land in the state now has a grapevine growing on it. The vineyards that were once primarily seen in Napa and Sonoma Counties can now be found on the slopes of the Sierra Foothills, down south in Santa Barbara, and even close to coastside in Mendocino and Carmel. Surprising to some, it's actually the wine industry that's leading the charge beyond mere organic and into biodynamic growing practices, such as using sheep to keep the weeds down in the vineyards and provide natural fertilizer, or harvesting grapes and pruning vines according to the moon's cycles to promote optimum wine quality. (In truth, it makes sense, and serious wine drinkers are willing to pay premium prices for top-quality vintages.)

Industry

The motion picture industry draws the most publicity to California. Though little filming takes place in and around Hollywood today, it's still the home of the major studios and their prominent executives.

In Northern California, Silicon Valley has made a name for itself as the epicenter of the technology industry. Despite the expense of property in the Bay Area, nearly every major high-tech company maintains a presence somewhere near Silicon Valley, as many were founded and are still headquartered there. Major tech legends include Hewlett-Packard in Palo Alto,

Agriculture is California's major economic sector.

Apple Computer in Cupertino, and Intel on the border of Santa Clara and San Jose. Google remains loyal to its hometown of Mountain View, and Microsoft has opened offices throughout Silicon Valley. During the "dot-com boom" of the early 1990s, nearly everyone in the region seemed to somehow be employed by the tech industry, and when the bust came it hit the region like a ton of outdated CRT monitors.

Today, the tech industry still provides hundreds of thousands of top-paying jobs in Silicon Valley and throughout the greater Bay Area and most residents of the region tend towards the tech-savvy.

People and Culture

RELIGION

A wide variety of religions and belief systems have come to characterize California. The state is home to large populations of Catholics, Protestants, Jews, Muslims, Buddhists, and even Wiccan religions and Scientologists. Many urban centers, especially San Francisco and Los Angeles, provide houses of worship or religious centers for practitioners of these and many other faiths.

Many Californians cherish the religious tolerance found here, and the right and ability of all to practice their desired form of worship is widely protected. So expect to see everything from rigorous observance of Lent to traditional Chinese New Year to pagan solstice rituals in the park.

LANGUAGE

As in the rest of the United States, English is the official language in California. However, the state's large immigrant population has resulted in equally large non-English speaking communities. Due to the state's proximity to Mexico, Spanish is the most widely spoken foreign language. Other major spoken and written languages include Chinese, Cantonese, Korean, Vietnamese, Japanese, and various East Indian dialects. Throughout the state, this multilingualism often results in a colorful blend of cultures, creating a multiethnic tapestry of California residents. However, in both Los Angeles and the Bay Area, tightly knit Asian and Hispanic communities sometimes feature little-to-no signs or menus in English, and few proprietors speak standard English. Exploring the culture of California means exploring the backgrounds of those who live here, so be prepared to learn more about the world even as you learn more about the state.

Signs in Chinatown reflect a mix of languages.

ESSENTIALS

Getting There

BY AIR

It's easy to fly in to California, particularly if you're heading for one of the major metropolitan areas. Reaching the more rural or outlying regions of the state is a bit trickier and you'll probably find yourself driving—possibly for hours—from one of the major airports.

San Francisco Bay Area

San Francisco has one major airport surrounded by a few ancillary and less-crowded airports. **San Francisco International Airport** (SFO, www.flysfo.com) isn't in San Francisco proper—it's actually located approximately 13 miles south of the City.

Several public and private transportation options can get you into the City: rental car, taxi, BART, or even CalTrain. As in Los Angeles, if your flight is out of SFO, plan to arrive at the airport up to three hours before your flight leaves. Airport lines, especially on weekends and holidays, are notoriously long.

To avoid the SFO crowds, consider booking a flight into **Oakland International Airport** (1 Airport Dr., Oakland, 510/563-3300, www.flyoakland.com), which services the East Bay

with access to San Francisco across the Bay Bridge, or **San Jose International Airport** (Airport Blvd., San Jose, www.sjc.org), south of San Francisco in the heart of Silicon Valley. These airports are quite a bit smaller than SFO, but service is brisk from many U.S. destinations.

Bay Area Rapid Transit (BART, www .bart.gov) connects directly with SFO's international terminal, providing a simple and relatively fast trip to downtown San Francisco (under an hour). The BART station is an easy walk or free shuttle ride from any point in the airport, and a one-way ticket to any downtown station costs $5.35.

Shuttle vans are also a cost-effective option for door-to-door service, though these include several stops along the way. From the airport to downtown, the average one-way fare is $15–20 per passenger. Shuttle vans congregate on the second level of SFO above the baggage claim area for domestic flights, and on the third level for international flights. Advance reservations guarantee a seat, but they aren't required and don't necessarily speed the process. Some companies to try: Bay Shuttle (415/564-3400, www.bayshuttle.com), Quake City Shuttle (415/255-4899, www.quakecityshuttle.com), and SuperShuttle (800/258-3826, www.supershuttle.com).

For **taxis,** the average fare to downtown is around $40.

BY TRAIN

Several cross-country **Amtrak** (www.amtrak .com) trains rumble into California each day. If you're arriving from another part of the country, the train can be a relaxing way to make the journey to the Golden State; long-distance train routes usually include dining and lounge cars. There are eight train routes that service California: The California Zephyr travels to Chicago, Denver, and Emervyille; the Capitol Corridor services Auburn, Sacramento, Emeryville, Oakland, and San Jose, and a popular route with local commuters; the Coast Starlight travel down the west coast, from Seattle to Portland and ending in Los Angeles; the Pacific Surfliner will get you to the Central Coast and southern California, while the San Joaquins services the Central Valley; the Southwest Chief, Sunset Limited, and Texas Eagle brings travelers from the south and midwest into California.

BY CAR

Many Americans get to visit California by driving here. A number of interstate highways run into the state from points east and north. From the Pacific Northwest, I-5 runs north and south through the state and will get you here quickly. The coastal routes along Highway 1 and Highway 101 are longer, but prettier. I-10 and I-15 allow access from the southeastern regions.

Car Rental

Most major car rental companies are located in one central area at the major airports. To reserve a car in advance, contact **Budget Rent A Car** (800/527-0700), **Dollar Rent A Car** (866/434-2226), **Enterprise** (www.enterprise .com), or **Hertz** (www.hertz.com).

Getting Around

BY AIR

When traversing major cities within the state, flying can be an economical (and faster) option. The **San Francisco International Airport** (SFO, www.flysfo.com), located south of the City provides convenient access to the northern part of the state. Across the bay, the **Oakland Airport** (Hegenberger Rd., Oakland, www.oaklandairport.com) often avoids the fog and inclement weather that socks in SFO.

Los Angeles International Airport (LAX,www.lawa.org) serves the greater Los Angeles, offers a wealth of airline options, and can connect with flights both to San Francisco and Los Angeles. But it can be a hectic and time-consuming maze to navigate. Other options in the area include the **Bob Hope Airport** (2627 N. Hollywod Way, Burbank, 818/840-8840, www.burbankairport.com) and the **Long Beach Airport** (4100 Donald Douglas Dr., 562/570-2600, www.longbeach .gov/airport).

BY TRAIN

Amtrak (www.amtrak.com) trains run several corridors through the state. The California Zephyr, Capitol Corridor, Coast Starlight, and San Joaquins routes offer services to Auburn, Sacramento, Emeryville, Oakland, San Jose, Los Angeles, the Central Coast, and the Central Valley. Train are roomy, comfortable, and offer a dining car for affordable snacks and meals.

BY CAR

California is great for road-tripping. Scenic coastal routes such as Highway 1 and Highway 101 are often destinations in themselves, while inland I-5 is the most direct route north and south through the state. However, traffic jams, accidents, mudslides, fires, and snow can affect highways and interstates at any time. Before heading out on your adventure, check road conditions online at the Calfiornia Department of Transportation (Caltrans, www.dot.ca.gov). Note that mountain passes such as I-80 into Tahoe, I-5 at the Grapevine, and the Shasta and Lassen regions may require snow tires and/ or chains. In rural areas and in the deserts, gas stations may be few and far between.

Visas and Officialdom

PASSPORTS AND VISAS

If you're visiting California from another country, you must present a valid passport upon entry into the United States. You must also hold a return plane or cruise ticket to your country of origin dated less than 90 days from your date of entry (Canada excepted).

If you hold a passport from one of the following countries, you do not need a visa to enter California: Andorra, Australia, Austria, Belgium, Brunei, Denmark, Finland, France, Germany, Iceland, Ireland, Italy, Japan, Liechtenstein, Luxembourg, Monaco, the Netherlands, New Zealand, Norway, Portugal, San Marino, Singapore, Slovenia, Spain, Sweden, Switzerland, and the United Kingdom.

In most other countries, the local U.S. embassy should be able to provide a free tourist visa, often within 24 hours of request. Do plan more time for visa processing if you're requesting travel in the high summer season (June–Aug.).

EMBASSIES

San Francisco and Los Angeles both shelter embassies and consulates from many countries around the globe. If you should lose your passport or find yourself in some other trouble while visiting California, contact your country's offices for assistance. To find an embassy, check www.travel .state.gov for a list of embassies within the state.

CUSTOMS

Before you enter California from another country by sea or by air, you'll be required to fill out a customs form. Check with the U.S. embassy in your country or the Customs Bureau website (www.cbp.gov) for an updated list of items you must declare.

If you require medication administered by injection, you must pack your syringes in a checked bag; syringes are not permitted in carry-ons coming into the United States.

Also pack documentation describing your need for any narcotic medications you've brought with you. Failure to produce documentation for narcotics upon request can result in severe penalties in the United States.

If you're driving into California along I-5 or another major freeway, prepare to stop at Agricultural Inspection stations few miles inside the state line. You don't need to present a passport, a visa, or even a driver's license. Instead, you must be prepared to present all your fruits and vegetables.

California's largest economic segment lies in agriculture, and a number of the major crops grown here are sensitive to pests and diseases. In an effort to prevent known pests from entering the state and endangering the crops, travelers are asked to identify all produce they're carrying in from other states or from Mexico. If you've got produce, especially homegrown or from a farm stand, that might be infected by a known problem pest or disease, expect it to be confiscated on the spot.

You'll also be asked about fruits and veggies on your customs form, which you'll be asked to fill out on the airplane or ship before you reach the United States.

Tips for Travelers

CONDUCT AND CUSTOMS

The legal drinking age in California is 21. Expect to have your ID checked if you look under 30, especially in bars and clubs, but also in restaurants and wineries.

Most California bars and clubs close at 2 A.M.; you'll find the occasional after-hours nightspot in Los Angeles, San Francisco, and Palm Springs.

Cigarette smoking has been all but criminalized throughout the state of California. Don't expect to find a smoking section in any restaurant or an ashtray in the bars. Smoking is illegal in all bars and clubs, but your new favorite watering hole might have an outdoor patio where smokers can huddle. Taking the ban one step further, many hotels, motels, and inns throughout the state are strictly non-smoking, and you'll be subject to fees of several hundred dollars if your room smells of smoke when you leave.

There's no smoking in any public building, and even some of the state parks don't allow cigarettes. There's often good reason for this; fire danger in California is extreme in the summertime, and one carelessly thrown lit butt can cause a genuine catastrophe.

TRAVELING WITH CHILDREN

Many spots in California are ideal destinations for families with children of all ages. In both the San Francisco Bay Area and the Los Angeles region, amusement parks, interactive museums, zoos, parks, beaches, and playgrounds all make for family-friendly fun. Even some of the upscale hotels offer great programs for young people, and many Southern California resorts designate at least one swimming pool as "family" or "loud" to accommodate rambunctious fun and outside voices.

You know your children best, so you can plan a great trip they'll love based on their special interests. Would they prefer Disneyland or the San Diego Zoo? Surf lessons at Huntington Beach or rock climbing school at Joshua Tree? Redwood trees or youth nightclubs?

On the other hand, there are a few spots in the Golden State that beckon more to adults than to children. Frankly, there aren't many family activities in Wine Country. This adult playground is all about alcoholic beverages and high-end dining. Similarly, the North Coast's focus on original art and romantic B&Bs brings out couples looking for weekend getaways rather than families. In fact, before you book a room at a B&B that you expect to share with your kids, check to be sure that the inn can accommodate extra people in their guest rooms and allows guests under 16 years old.

WOMEN TRAVELERS

California's a pretty friendly place for women traveling alone. Most of the major outdoor attractions are incredibly safe, and even many of the urban areas boast pleasant neighborhoods that welcome lone female travelers.

But you'll need to take some basic precautions and pay attention to your surroundings just as you would in any unfamiliar place. Carry your car keys in your hand when walking out to your car. Don't sit in your parked car in a lonely parking lot at night; just get in, turn on the engine, and drive away. When you're walking down a city street, be alert and keep an eye on your surroundings and on anyone who might be following you. In rural areas, don't go tromping into unlit wooded areas or out into grassy fields alone at night without a flashlight; many of California's critters are nocturnal. (Actually, this caution applies to men traveling alone as well. Mountain lions and rattlesnakes don't tend to discriminate.)

Some neighborhoods in the big cities are best avoided by lone women, especially at night. Besides the obvious—the Tenderloin in San Francisco and the Compton, Watts, and Inglewood neighborhoods of Los Angeles—some other streets and neighborhoods can turn distinctly hostile after dark.

SENIOR TRAVELERS

California makes an ideal destination for retired folks looking to relax and have a great time. You'll find senior discounts nearly every place you go, from restaurants to golf courses to major attractions, and even at some hotels, though the minimum age can vary from 50–65. Just ask, and be prepared to produce ID if you look young or are requesting an AARP discount.

For landlubbers, RV parks abound throughout the state, and even many of the state and national parks can accommodate RVs and trailers. The Southern California deserts are particularly popular with snowbirds. Check with the parks you want to visit for size and location restrictions, hookup and dump station information, and RV slot prices.

GAY AND LESBIAN TRAVELERS

California is known for its thriving gay and lesbian communities. In fact, the Golden State is a golden place for gay travel—especially in the bigger cities, and even some of the smaller towns both in the north and the south parts of the state. As with much of the country, the further you venture into more rural and agricultural regions, the less likely you're to experience the liberal acceptance the state is known for.

In Northern California, San Francisco has the biggest and arguably best Gay Pride Festival (www.sfpride.org) in the nation, usually held down Market Street the last weekend in June. All year-round, the Castro District offers fun of all kinds, from theater to clubs to shopping, mostly targeted for gay men but with a few places sprinkled in for lesbians. If the Castro is your primary destination, you can even find a place to stay right in the midst of the action (see *Accommodations* in the *San Francisco Bay Area* chapter).

Both gay men and women flock to Santa Cruz on the coastline, though the quirky town is specially known for its lesbian-friendly culture. A relaxed vibe informs everything from underground clubs to unofficial nude beaches to live-action role playing games in the middle of downtown. Even the lingerie and adult toy shops tend to be female-owned and -operated.

So where do gay and lesbian San Francisco residents go to get away for the weekend? Many flock to Guerneville—an outdoorsy town on the Russian River. Rustic lodges offer cabins down by the river, rafting and kayaking companies offer summertime adventures, and nearby wineries offer and relaxation. The short but colorful Main Street is home to queer-friendly bars and festivals.

Down south, the most gay-friendly town has to be Palm Springs. Gay bars and clubs proliferate here in a relaxed and friendly atmosphere that welcomes men, women, and even straight senior citizens. The White Party and Gay Pride (www.pspride.org, first weekend in November) are huge events that draw tens of thousands of visitors to the desert city. Perhaps best of all, more than a dozen gay resorts cluster in the sun-drenched town, offering swimming pools, hot tubs, and clothing-optional common spaces.

West Hollywood in the Los Angeles Basin has its own upscale gay culture. Just like the rest of L.A.'s clubs, the gay clubs are havens of the see-and-be-seen crowd. The famous Barney's Beanery offers beans and boys, and now has a second location on the Promenade in Santa Monica.

The oh-so-fabulous California vibe has even made it to the interior of the state—Sacramento's newly revitalized Midtown neighborhood offers a more low-key but visible gay evening scene.

Information and Services

When visiting California, you might be tempted to stop in at one of several Golden State Welcome Centers scattered throughout the state. In all honesty, these visitors centers aren't that great. If you're in an area that doesn't have its own visitors venter or tourist bureau, the State Welcome Center might be a useful place to pick up maps and brochures. Check www.visitcwc.com to find a local Welcome Center wherever you're visiting. Otherwise, stick with local, regional, state, and national park visitors centers (see *Internet Resources*), which tend to be staffed by volunteers or rangers who feel a real passion for their locale.

MAPS AND TOURIST INFORMATION

Almost all gas stations and drugstores sell maps both of the locale you're traversing and of the whole state. California State Automobile Association (CSAA, www.csaa.com) offices offer maps to members for free.

Many local and regional visitors centers also offer maps, but you'll need to pay a few dollars for the bigger and better ones. But if all you need is a wine-tasting map in a known wine region, you can probably get one for free (plus a few tasting coupons) at the nearest regional visitors center. Basic national park maps come with your admission fee. State park maps can be free, or can cost a few dollars at the visitors centers.

HEALTH AND SAFETY

Have an emergency anywhere in California? Dial 911. Inside hotels and resorts, check your emergency number as soon as you get into your room. In urban and suburban areas, full-service hospitals and medical centers abound. But in the more remote regions, help can be more than an hour away.

If you're planning a backcountry expedition, follow all rules and guidelines for obtaining wilderness permits and for self-registration at trailheads. These are for your safety, letting the rangers know roughly where you plan to be and when to expect you back. National and state park visitors centers can advise in more detail as to any health or wilderness alerts in the area.

Poison Oak

There is only one major variety of plant in California that can cause an adverse reaction in humans merely upon touching the leaves or stems. That is poison oak, a common shrub that inhabits forests up and down the state. Poison oak has a characteristic three-leaf configuration, with scalloped leaves that are shiny green in the spring and then turn yellow, orange, and red in late summer and fall. In fall the leaves drop, leaving a cluster of innocuous-looking branches. The oil in poison oak is present all year long in both the leaves and branches. Your best protection is to wear long sleeves and long pants when hiking, no matter how hot it is. A product called Tecnu is available at most California drugstores—slather it on *before* you go hiking to protect yourself from poison oak. If your skin comes in contact with poison oak, expect a nasty rash well known for its itchiness and irritation. Poison oak is also extremely contagious, so avoid touching your eyes, face, or other parts of your body to prevent spreading the rash. Calamine lotion can help, and in extreme cases a doctor can administer cortisone to help decrease the inflammation.

MONEY

California businesses accept the U.S. dollar ($). Most businesses also accept major credit cards: Visa, MasterCard, Discover, Diner's Club, and American Express. ATM and check-cards work at many stores and restaurants, and you're likely to find ATMs in most every town of any size.

You can change currency in any international airport in the state. Currency exchange points also crop up in downtown San Francisco and Los Angeles and at some of the major business hotels in the urban areas.

RESOURCES

Internet Resources

It should come as no surprise that California travel leads the way in use of the Internet as a marketing, communications, and sales tool. The overwhelming majority of destinations have their own websites—even tiny towns in the middle of nowhere proudly tout their attractions on the Web.

CALIFORNIA
California Department of Transportation
www.dot.ca.gov/hq/roadinfo/statemap.htm
This website contains state map and highway information.

Visit California
www.visitcalifornia.com
The official tourism site of the state of California.

REGIONAL SITES
Central Coast Regional Tourism
www.centralcoast-tourism.com
A guide to the Central Coast region, including Santa Cruz, Monterey, and Santa Barbara.

NapaValley.com
www.napavalley.com
A Napa Valley tourist website from WineCountry.com.

Sacramento Convention and Visitors Bureau
www.sacramentocvb.org
The official website of the Sacramento Convention and Visitors Bureau.

Shasta and Lassen Regional Tourism
www.shastacascade.org
The California Travel and Tourism Information Network includes information and a downloadable visitors guide to Mt. Shasta, Shasta Lake, Redding, and Lassen.

Visit California Gold Country
www.calgold.org
The website from the Gold Country Visitors Association, with information about Grass Valley, Navada City, Placer Country, Sacramento, and Amador Country.

PARKS AND OUTDOORS
California Outdoor and Recreational Information
www.caoutdoors.com
This recreation-focused website includes links to maps, local newspapers, festivals and events, as well as a wide variety of recreational activities throughout the state.

California State Parks
www.parks.ca.gov
The official website lists hours, accessibility, activities, camping areas, fees, and more information for all parks in the state system.

Lassen Volcanic National Park
www.nps.gov/lavo
The official website for Lassen Volcanic National Park.

Redwood National Park
www.nps.gov/redw
The official website for all Redwood National and State Parks.

Sequoia and Kings Canyon National Parks
www.nps.gov/seki
The official website for Sequoia and Kings Canyon.

State of California
www.ca.gov/tourism/
greatoutdoors.html
Outdoor resources for California state and government organizations. Check for information about fishing and hunting licenses, backcountry permits, boating regulations, and more.

Yosemite National Park
www.nps.gov/yose
The National Park Service website for Yosemite National Park.

Yosemite National Park Vacation and Lodging Information
www.yosemitepark.com
The concessionaire website for Yosemite National Park lodging, dining, and reservations.

Index

List of Maps

www.moon.com

DESTINATIONS | ACTIVITIES | BLOGS | MAPS | BOOKS

MOON.COM is all new, and ready to help plan your next trip! Filled with fresh trip ideas and strategies, author interviews, informative blogs, a detailed map library, and descriptions of all the Moon guidebooks, Moon.com is all you need to get out and explore the world—or even places in your own backyard. As always, when you travel with Moon, expect an experience that is uncommon and truly unique.

MAP SYMBOLS

▨▨▨	Expressway	◖	Highlight	✖	Airfield	⌋	Golf Course
▨▨▨	Primary Road	○	City/Town	✈	Airport	ⓟ	Parking Area
▨▨▨	Secondary Road	◉	State Capital	▲	Mountain	⬟	Archaeological Site
– – – –	Unpaved Road	⊛	National Capital	✦	Unique Natural Feature	⛪	Church
- - - -	Trail	★	Point of Interest				
··········	Ferry	•	Accommodation	⌇	Waterfall	⛽	Gas Station
–·–·–	Railroad	▼	Restaurant/Bar	▲	Park	◌	Glacier
▨▨▨	Pedestrian Walkway	■	Other Location	ⓣ	Trailhead	▨	Mangrove
▥▥▥	Stairs	Λ	Campground	✗	Skiing Area	▨	Reef
						▨	Swamp

CONVERSION TABLES

°C = (°F − 32) / 1.8
°F = (°C x 1.8) + 32
1 inch = 2.54 centimeters (cm)
1 foot = 0.304 meters (m)
1 yard = 0.914 meters
1 mile = 1.6093 kilometers (km)
1 km = 0.6214 miles
1 fathom = 1.8288 m
1 chain = 20.1168 m
1 furlong = 201.168 m
1 acre = 0.4047 hectares
1 sq km = 100 hectares
1 sq mile = 2.59 square km
1 ounce = 28.35 grams
1 pound = 0.4536 kilograms
1 short ton = 0.90718 metric ton
1 short ton = 2,000 pounds
1 long ton = 1.016 metric tons
1 long ton = 2,240 pounds
1 metric ton = 1,000 kilograms
1 quart = 0.94635 liters
1 US gallon = 3.7854 liters
1 Imperial gallon = 4.5459 liters
1 nautical mile = 1.852 km

MOON NORTHERN CALIFORNIA
Avalon Travel
a member of the Perseus Books Group
1700 Fourth Street
Berkeley, CA 94710, USA
www.moon.com

Editor: Sabrina Young
Series Manager: Kathryn Ettinger
Copy Editors: Ellie Behrstock, Amy Scott
Graphics Coordinator: Kathryn Osgood
Production Coordinator: Darren Alessi
Cover Designer: Kathryn Osgood
Cartography Director: Mike Morgenfeld
Map Editor: Albert Angulo
Cartographers: Kat Bennett, Chris Markiewicz, Jon Niemczyk, Brice Ticen
Indexer: Greg Jewett

ISBN: 978-1-59880-252-8
ISSN: 1524-4148

Printing History
1st Edition – 2000
5th Edition – October 2009
5 4 3 2 1

Text © 2009 by Liz Hamill Scott.
Maps © 2009 by Avalon Travel.
All rights reserved.

Printed in Canada by Friesens Corp.

KEEPING CURRENT

If you have a favorite gem you'd like to see included in the next edition, or see anything that needs updating, clarification, or correction, please drop us a line. Send your comments via email to feedback@moon.com, or use the address above.